Y0-BCW-883

WITHDRAWN

| DATE DUE | |
| --- | --- |
| ~~NOV 0 8 1994~~ | |
| | |
| | |
| | |
| | |
| | |
| | |
| | |
| | |
| | |
| | |
| | |
| | |

# FASHION IN HISTORY

# FASHION IN HISTORY

## WESTERN DRESS, PREHISTORIC TO PRESENT

### Second Edition

**Marybelle S. Bigelow**

San Diego State University
San Diego, California

**Burgess Publishing Company**
Minneapolis, Minnesota

Editor: Kay Kushino
Production Editors: Nelda Wright
                   James Montgomery
Production Manager: Morris Lundin
Art Director: Joan Gordon
Layout Artist: Mari Ansari
Compositor: Deborah Koch

Cover Illustration: Marybelle S. Bigelow

Copyright © 1979, 1970 by Burgess Publishing Company
Printed in the United States of America
Library of Congress Catalog Card Number 78-62539
ISBN 0-8087-2800-8

All rights reserved. No part of this book may be reproduced in any form whatsoever, by photograph or mimeograph or by any other means, by broadcast or transmission, by translation into any kind of language, nor by recording electronically or otherwise, without permission in writing from the publisher, except by a reviewer, who may quote brief passages in critical articles and reviews.

J I H G F E D C

*To the two who helped most and kept*
*me going, Olive and Mary*

# Preface

Fashion has three facets: history of costume, costume design, and fashion illustration. Contemporary forms and styles are dependent on and indebted to past costume forms and fancies. The historical record of these forms and styles has been left by master painters and sculptors. Through this legacy, we can develop patterns of past civilizations. These resources often give rise to inventive contemporary adaptations. Since historic costume is one of the significant contributors to modern costume design, the student of fashion design must be aware of these modes of his ancestors.

The young designer gives form to a design concept for a costume in a number of ways—draping, pattern drafting, and drawing or sketching. The last is most readily mastered and clearly bridges the content development of this text. Fashion drawing and illustration report current vogues and record fashions of a specific period. These reports and records are dependent on sensitive and skillful drawing. By combining these three facets of fashion—the history of costume, the procedures of designing, and the qualities of drawing required in creating a reporting record—a comprehensive and unified approach to the total concept of personal adornment develops.

The second edition of *Fashion in History* includes a number of new features. Some of these additions are a chapter on dress of the Mesopotamian era, expanded information on the life-styles of differing periods, and many clear illustrations. Coverage now ranges from Mesopotamia into the mid-1970s, enabling students to see how today's fashions reflect the styles of other times and cultures. Unique additions to the second edition include a pronunciation key and a glossary of terms describing costume, identifying the country of origin, listing chapter locations, and indicating the correct pronunciation of the word.

Careful research into the customs of the past—dress, jewelry, coiffures, and footwear—documents the psychological, sociological, and political trends that influenced the course of fashion. This definitive study of fashion uncovers one of the most fascinating aspects of human history.

M.S.B.

# Acknowledgments

The author wishes to thank the following, whose great help has assisted in abstract and concrete ways in putting together this book: Condé Nast Publications, Inc., for allowing the reproduction of the many illustrations listed specifically in the credits; the many international museums and galleries for their kind help, particularly the Metropolitan Museum of Art, New York City, and Mr. Paul Stone, who is the Costume Institutes Librarian; but most especially Olive Whaley Schmidt, without whose patience, wisdom, encouragement, and help the manuscript never would have been completed; and Dr. Kenneth Oliver Courtney, who set me straight when I got slightly off the track.

Illustrations from VOGUE copyright © 1938 (renewed 1966), 1944 (renewed 1972), 1947, 1948, 1949, 1952, 1969, 1972, 1974 by Condé Nast Publications, Inc.

All illustrations credited to the Metropolitan Museum of Art by its permission for the first edition.

# Contents

# Introduction

## A Survey of the Factors Influencing Clothing Shapes

Tracing the myriad means by which humans have covered their bodies is often bewildering. Most authorities suggest that the need for protection was the foremost motivation for the invention of rudimentary garment forms. Others comment on the basic needs for food, shelter, and clothing. Some even suggest that the use of body coverings can be dated from the time of Adam and Eve's fall from grace in that traumatic, Satan-nudging experience in the legendary Garden of Eden.[1]

More sophisticated approaches, however, research visually the cave paintings of Font de Gaume near les Eyzies, France; and Altamira or Saltadora in Spain (Figure I.1). Many authorities stress overlapping origins.[2, 3] The forms simultaneously evolving in separate geographical locations were determined by climate and available material.

This text will explore the major trends in body coverings from eons past to the most recent present. It is well known that, before recorded history, humans felt the need to protect their bodies. Tracing the means by which this was done—because of mores, manners, or morals—makes a marvelously intricate study. In surveying this involved aspect of humanity, it becomes increasingly apparent that there are inseparable factors which have governed this facet of human life.[2] Body coverings and their forms and fabrics have been in constant flux. Changes took place slowly at first, but changes did and continue to occur. This constancy of change is based on three dominant factors, each with contributing subfactors. The dominant factors include: (1) sociological and political exterior influences; (2) technical advances and production capabilities; and (3) aesthetic and cultural concepts. The subfactors of influence are: (1a) philosophical, economical, psychological; (2a) availability, invention, industrialization; and (3a) line, color, texture, and mass. These influences can cross-couple and interrelate in a number of combinations, e.g., invention and texture, referring to new textures created by the invention of synthetic fibers.

The tangled web of the "why" of clothing becomes increasingly complex. As each successive political power became more sophisticated, the manner of personal

**Figure I.1.** Prehistoric garments for females of the Neolithic era resembled the sleeveless Egyptian **kalasiris.** The ancient artist may or may not have faithfully depicted the neckline which has an asymmetric design. The head may have had a snug-fitting cap with a protective neck cape in back, or the artist may have been interpreting typical hairstyling. (Neolithic cave painting: *The Herd,* detail. Saltadora, Spain.)

adornment adjusted. These adjustments took place because technology advanced, philosophical attitudes altered, and psychological needs adapted to the overall cultural changes.

When the people of the Mousterian period roamed over northern Europe during part of the Würm glacial epoch, they felt the need to retain warmth through some form of body protection. As the ancients of the third millennium B.C. developed a more stable social order in Mesopotamia, garments changed from mere functionality to costumes with frivolous decoration.[3] This evolution from protective garments to decorative clothing was made possible by the influence of technical advances, the second of the conditioning factors.

Human needs and practical solutions for these needs were slow to evolve. Early humans developed methods to make animal skins permanently pliable. Then the means to handstitch these skins into body-conforming costumes were invented. The hand-sewn method of garment making lasted from the invention of the needle over 41,000 years ago until the invention of the sewing machine in 1846. The needles of prehistoric humans, their shaping blades, and their scrapers took an equally long time to evolve into modern tailoring tools. In gradual stages, the shaping blades were replaced by more refined, efficient, and sophisticated tools. One such tool is the electrically powered cutter used by skilled craftsmen of the modern garment industry. With this odd-looking and noisy device, garment patterns can be duplicated in fabric in multiples of hundreds. The cutter accurately cuts through many layers of man-made fiber fabrics on the cutting table, making it possible to reproduce handsome, inexpensive fashions in gross lots. Modern marketing techniques of distribution and sales make these garments available to the mass consumer.

In the beginning, even the rude technical advance of fashioning clay or bronze containers for liquids was a major step in altering the character of garments. Tanning of hides depended on the availability of large vats in which to soak first the tree bark, and then the animal hides. During the centuries in which animal skins were the only raw material, methods were developing to manufacture woven fabrics from animal and vegetable fibers. With advances in navigation and land transport, materials such as linen, ramie cloth, silk, and cotton became available to many people in widely separated areas. Increased production of cotton was given impetus by Eli Whitney's invention of the cotton gin. This was one of many technological advances which took place during the Industrial Revolution. Weaving thread into great lengths of fabric was the result of the eighteenth-century invention of semimechanized looms.

Many centuries elapsed between the invention of hand-loom methods of ancient China and contemporary, technologically sophisticated weaving processes. From the hand loom to the first mechanized methods, weaving technology has progressed to the point where twentieth-century looms can be computer programmed to produce innumerable textures or patterns. Complex chemical formulas and elaborate means of producing synthetic fibers were an achievement of the mid-twentieth century. Science has replaced nature's fibers of linen, silk, and fur with fibers of nylon, orlon, dacron, and polyester, which simulate heavy silks, wools, gossamer transparents for hose, and even synthetic furs. All of these synthetic fibers can be washed in an automatic washer and spun dry in gas or electric dryers. Knitting too, originally a refined handcraft perfected during the reign of Elizabeth I, can now be produced by electronically guided machines or hand gadgets for home use. To some extent both of these devices have replaced the knitting needles of the past. Fabrics and trims, once crafts of home and hearth, have become products of industry. However, not until the late

eighteenth century did this revolution affect garment production.

How different, also, is the modern method of putting together the individual pieces of a garment from that used to make up the first simple body covering. Hand sewing was not replaced by machine sewing in home or factory until the turn of the century. Even today, the great couturiers depend on the hand and quick needle to add the last finishing refinements to these artists' fabric masterpieces. From the bone needle to the rapid stitch of the industrial sewing machine, and the complex zigzag version, is a giant step which took many millennia to accomplish.

The first needles predate historical records. Originally, they were no more than a small eyeless awl. Archaeological digs have uncovered a variety of these garment-making tools made from tusks, thorns, horns, and bones of fish, birds, and animals. The Egyptians used bone or bronze for needles and the Romans had needles made of bronze and iron. Both of these ancient civilizations used needles with eyes. During the fourteenth century in Nürnberg, Germany, a method of producing eyed steel needles was invented. Mary Tudor, Queen of England during the sixteenth century, was supplied eyed needles by a Spaniard whose name is now forgotten. This ingenious gentleman died before passing on his technique of mass-producing such needles. Possibly it was Elias Grouse who rediscovered the technique. In any case, he taught the English the art of needle making. Needle making became one of England's principal industries, and to this day needles are one of the products upon which the English economy depends.

Compared to its twentieth-century counterpart, Elias Howe's 1846 invention of the lockstitch sewing machine is almost as crude as the Neolithic bone needle in contrast to the slender, stainless-steel version of today. Isaac Singer and A. B. Wilson were the refiners of this new mechanical stitching device.

Methods of pattern making and sizing have ranged from crude, tenuous efforts to mathematically calculated production of patterns for mass sales to modern consumers. Patterns for garments first were mass-produced for home use in Germany during the latter half of the nineteenth century. Today, patterns have become personalized to give perfect fit by the use of computer programming.

These advances have not only altered garment-producing techniques but have influenced many countries' economic growth as well. Trade by the Babylonians was based in part on barter for materials, fabrics, and trimmings for clothing. The growth of Venice as a powerful city-state was based on Marco Polo's trading expeditions to the Orient for silken fabrics. Napoleon Bonaparte was forced to counter England's challenge in fabric and fashion production by reinstating the use of elegant, heavy velvets, silks, laces, and gold-braid trims to revive the sagging economies of Lyons and other fabric-producing centers of his empire. The rise of the economy of the new world's colonial South—based on cotton crops to supply English mills—developed because of fashion's demands. The American Civil War resulted, in part, from the conflict between the agrarian, cotton-based economy of the South and the fabric-producing mills of the newly industrialized North.

Fashion has been said to be the seventh largest industry in the United States. Fashion-related industries have employed millions of workers in New York alone, from its thousands of cutters, seamstresses, tailors, and pressers to the employees in glittering offices of high-fashion periodicals, the chic shops and elaborate stores on New York's Fifth Avenue, and the small, unique boutiques on midtown Manhattan's Madison Avenue. Reporters, salespeople, merchandisers, consumer researchers, reporters, photographers, designers, and fashion illustrators augment the vast number of people directly dependent on fashion production.

I am not sure what some researchers or professors feel are the dominant considerations in the study of fashion's history. To me it is not merely the cataloging of garments that changed because of social, political, or technological trends. Fashion and its history are irrefutably related to the art of the period during which specific garments were worn. Great artists of every age have reflected, through their creative manipulation of fabrics and trims, the contemporary aesthetics of their times. Their sensitivity and talent also have adapted to changing aesthetics which continued in constant flux during their productive lifetimes.

Clothes—fashion's body coverings—are the wearable, sculptural art forms which individuals use to identify themselves as creatures of a specific period. In addition, individual selection of styles makes the wearer, in part, a creator. By his or her very selection a person retains individuality and personality. By the same selectiveness an individual maintains group and time identity. By combining personal selection and creativity, the modes and manners of individual life-styles and period styles can be traced.

Interest is increasing in the complexities of the history of fashion. The reflections of social concepts can be recognized as they are subtly or blatantly visualized in the fads and fancies of fashion.[4] Whereas military engagements, or the years of a monarch's reign, can be accurately dated, it is difficult to do so with garment styles. The aesthetically dictated fads and intellectual concepts of various geographical areas have been fused with those of other cultures with which contacts have been made in proportion to the power of one nation over another.

In the past, distances have affected communication, and the time span of influence has varied. Countries whose power zeniths have set political, cultural, and, therefore, fashion trends have waxed and waned. With their ascent and decline in power, their philosophical, sociological, technical, and cultural influences have been felt in varying degrees. The rise of a power requires time for impact, acceptance, and interest in these new and different influences to affect other nations and their people. Due to this delaying action, nationalistic trends have been time spaced. Time is necessary for new concepts to be assimilated even with today's fast-paced, instant communication. In past eras, invasions were met with residual resistance, covert though such resistance may have been.[5] These attitudes combined with slow communication to delay concurrent and instant acceptance of the least of all social changes—fashion.

Factors of economic and sociological import are intertwined with other, more obvious political elements. Philosophical and religious concepts change and, in turn, affect costume styles. Costumes throughout the ages have expressed symbolically the inner philosophical thoughts which directed the behavior of a given epoch. As introspective human attitudes have changed, psychological concepts have been introduced into the garments and decorations of the human body. Wars and revolutions have played a role in determining the speed with which a new fashion was accepted. Strong monarchs and cruel dictators have commanded rejection of some fashions popular in other countries.

Nearly everyone will agree that body coverings were first devised to protect the human form from the elements. To a certain extent they were created as a convenience. As soon as the life-style of a given ethnic society was established, even the most rudimentary body coverings took on different attributes. Very early garments were created and designed to be worn as decoration. The decorative qualities of all clothing forms are directly related to the aesthetics of the culture. If not all the garments, certainly the accessories identified the individuality of the wearer, the person's ethnic grouping, social status, and time period.

Clothing and accessories were worn by living people who moved and breathed, made love and war, sang and cried, danced and played instruments, worked in fields or factories, drove oxen or Rolls Royces, or simply stood about palaces or cocktail parties looking wise and elegant. But they did live and move. Perhaps only those of the meanest stations in life did not select wearing apparel as an aesthetic expression of their time and of themselves.[6] The functional, the rational, and the frivolous are thus combined, interacting and creating reasons for the very style of the fashions to be studied here. No culture since earliest times has been devoid of an aesthetic expression through ritualistic dances and contemporary art forms, whether they were verbal, musical, or visual. Clothing is, then, the means by which individuals can become involved in making aesthetic commitments.

As I delve more deeply into the history of fashion, it becomes apparent to me that many students of this facet of our cultural development divorce art from clothing. Perhaps there is no art in clothing, but decidedly there is *art* in fashion.[7] Fashion's history is not merely a study of recognizing garment forms, relating accessories to them, and establishing the cultures from which they came. Fashion and its history are irrefutably related to the art of the period in which the fashions were created and worn. Personal adornments of whatever form are, in and of themselves, moving, sculptural forms. They have been designed to fit over the moving, nude human figure which is of itself a beautifully structured form made up of supple curves and firm, straight lines. To cover this symmetrically ordered human form, function and application to figure movements must be taken into consideration. Artists past and present have been involved in solving aesthetically the restrictions placed on their creative efforts by the human body.

Fashion has line, shape, texture, and color. Line defines the exterior shape and the interior detailing of a garment. The exterior shape establishes a mass and, in turn, the modish silhouette. Fabric establishes texture and color. Art is created by the designer's selective use of line, shape, color, and texture. Is there any difference? Fashion, the design of clothing forms, is an art. We would not be able to study fashion had it not been for the artists of the past who have left their works to illustrate the remarkable and multitudinous variations which body coverings have taken.

It is my thesis that art is as much a part of fashion as are the political and sociological aspects of a period. This may be a case of which came first—the chicken or the egg, or, more accurately for our purposes, the social structure of a period or the aesthetic concepts of a period. I submit that art is life and living life is made more artful through personal selection of fashions, body coverings, and personal adornments. Males and females have been fascinated by dress throughout eons and have found it one means by which to live more artfully.

The least knowledgeable will separate art and fashion. By so doing they deny the contributions of such greats of the visual creative field as Leonardo da Vinci, Ingres, Watteau, David, Coco Chanel, and Balenciaga, to mention only a few who have been directly involved in influencing fashion trends. During his lifetime, Da Vinci was deeply committed to art and creativity in many ways, often turning his prodigious talent to designing exceptionally elaborate, aesthetically related costumes for pageants and balls. If it were possible to ask, I am sure the great couturiere Chanel would voice a vehement argument in defense of the art in her creatively ingenious fashions. No, the great couturiers, past and present, from Bertin to Saint-Laurent, cannot be denied their aesthetic sensitivity and social awareness as well. In the recent Balenciaga retrospective exhibition in the Metropolitan Museum of Art, New York City, his perception of social change was presented dramatically. It is necessary to accept art in fashion. The art in it makes fashion no less academically respectable, for intellect, wit, wisdom, perception, and sensitive creativity are the basic requirements of the artist.[8]

By means of the illustrations in this text, I have attempted to present fashions of the past and near present as having been worn by people who walked, talked, and died. The exact garments of the ancients do not exist and their visual representations often have been so stylized that the quality of life of the wearers is obscured. The intent of the drawings done from primary sources in this country and abroad is to illustrate the artful life achieved through fashion. To expand these visualizations, reproductions of works of art which illustrate the significant garment forms and fashion trends have been included, as well as photographs of garments from my personal collection. I hope that the illustrations will be of sufficient size and number to present an overall visualization of the major costume styles of a given period. It is hoped that careful reproduction and the accompanying text will bring to life the people of the past by the clothing they wore. The very nature of the study of historic relationships of fashion involves an awareness of lines, forms, colors, and textures which, when combined, identify specific periods. Through these qualities of art, the psychological aspects arising from the philosophical concepts of garment design become evident.

The period in which concealment of the body for moral and philosophical reasons began is obscure. The puritanical emphasis on modesty began not with the Puritans of the seventeenth century but with the ancient Israelites.[9] It was they who, to some degree, influenced the Egyptians to cover their persons with fabrics of opacity rather than those of body-revealing transparency. At times Cretans, Etruscans, Greeks, and Romans went about *in puris naturalibus*. The tribes of northern Europe, when weather warmed during the brief summers, also went about scantily clad or not clad at all. Cave dwellers and people all over the globe were as unashamedly bare as today's inhabitants of New Guinea and the hinterlands of Africa. Modern humans were made conscious of the "evil" of their nude bodies by pontifical edicts and zealous nineteenth-century missionaries. It was the missionaries who made the Hawaiians don the enveloping **muumuu**. However, the Quakers, in the first flush of their conversion to this new sect, often ran through fields or streets stark naked. They practiced nudism because they believed themselves to be so wholly pure that clothing was nonessential. It, too, was their way of rejecting the establishment. Now, in the late twentieth century, nude bathing on public beaches is practiced for much the same reason.

My concepts concerning fashion have taken twenty-four years to evolve. Research has been carried out in the modern centers of fashion design, including New York, Paris, Rome, and London. To gather insights into modern apparel design, I have worked for some time in New York on *Vogue*'s Pattern Book. Additional experience was gained by working in the apparel industry in Los Angeles. While on the Condé Nast staff (publishers of *Vogue* and *Mademoiselle*, etc.), I gathered additional insights into relationships between the individual (either sex) and personal adornment.

A quarter of a century of teaching experience in higher education has assisted me in synthesizing these practical experiences with those inherent in academe's approach to historical research. My experience during these teaching years has made me aware of the contemporary student's demands for relevance in course content and for scholarly excellence among the faculty, particularly in their special discipline. Therefore I have researched the major museums here and in Europe, including The Metropolitan Museum of Art of New York City; City of New York Historical Museum; Brooklyn Museum; The Costume Institute of the Metropolitan Museum of Art; The Frick Museum; The Los Angeles County Museum—Costume Collection; The National Gallery, Washington, D.C.; The National Gallery, London; The British Museum, London; The National Portrait Gallery; The Tate; The Wallace Collection (particularly the armor and sixteenth-century waxes); The Tower of London (armor); and The Victoria and Albert Museum—Costume Gallery and Library.

A treasure trove of actual garments is displayed in many of Europe's palaces, castles, and manor houses. Some of these include Warwick Castle, which houses the famous Holbein painting of Henry VIII; Blair Athol Castle, Scotland; the handsome eighteenth-century Royal Summer Palace on Lake Millard, Sweden; and the Royal Pavilion, Brighton.

English perpendicular Gothic cathedrals contain extraordinarily explicit brasses. Some cathedrals where I have spent many hours studying these funerary memorial plaques include Canterbury, Exeter, Winchester, Salisbury, and St. Giles in Scotland. Sarcophagi of the Renaissance depict costumes of that period on the sculptured effigies of those buried within. These, too, can be found in cathedrals and abbies. Westminster contains many, including those of Elizabeth I and the tender group of "Methilda's Grandchildren." Exeter holds a monument for two young girls of the early nineteenth century. In the close of that same cathedral, a monument for a bishop of Exeter defines in stone his ecclesiastical garments as well as his duck-bill slippers. The Cloisters in Ft. Tryon, Manhattan, contains other visual resources for medieval costuming.

Research was undertaken in libraries connected with major museums; public libraries (New York Public Library); and libraries at the University of California, Los Angeles, and Columbia University. University libraries contain not only books but prints, which are wonderful research resources.

The most exciting of all the hours spent in library research occurred just recently when I was invited to use the Condé Nast Reference Library. Here are housed not only an entire bound collection of *Vogue* from the first edition in 1893 to the present, but, better still, the actual photographs which have appeared in this magazine. This technical advance changed fashion's visual reports from stylized pen-and-ink sketches to accurate, graphic records. In these chic surroundings I was allowed to pore over the entire collection from aging copies of Godey's *Lady's Book, Patterson's Magazine,* and Frank Leslie's *Ladies Gazette* to the contents of some of the huge envelopes storing fashion photographs of the recent past. Equally fruitful were the weeks spent researching in the Costume Institute's Library at the Metropolitan Museum of Art.

I have spent the past twenty years establishing my own collection of garments. To date, this collection includes over 200 examples ranging from pumpkin breeches to twentieth-century frocks. The most prized pieces are an eighteenth-century silk **frac** and a long **justaucorps** of coarse worsted from the same period. While the fabrics are quite worn, both garments are handsewn. Handsomely designed brass buttons which decorated the eighteenth-century coat of George Caldwell, a drummer boy in the Continental Army and one of my ancestors, are also in my collection.

My print collection of nearly fifty fashion plates from famous modish folios of the past is significant for the breadth of its representative examples. My library includes fashion books and catalogs dating from 1878.

Help from many sources has given me the courage to attempt this task again. I sincerely trust that the information presented is a lively reading experience and is visually exciting.

FOOTNOTES
1. Blanche Payne, *History of Costume*, p. 10.
2. Raymond Somers Stites, *The Arts and Man*, pp. 42-45; and Carl Köhler, *A History of Costume*, p. 52.
3. Samuel Noah Kramer, *Cradle of Civilization*, pp. 33-34.
4. Bernard Rudofsky, *The Unfashionable Human Body*, p. 56.
5. Arnold Toynbee, *A Study of History*, p. 89.
6. Köhler, *A History of Costume*, p. 51.
7. Bettina Ballard, *In My Fashion*, pp. 45-46.
8. Diana Vreeland, *The 10s, The 20s, The 30s—Inventive Clothes 1909-1939*, pp. 4, 16.
9. Gen. 3:14-21; also see the *Talmud*.

# Chapter 1

# Origins of Body Coverings and Mesopotamian Garments

## (Prehistory–500 B.C.)

**Figure 1.1.** Prehistoric humans celebrated many activities which were part of their life-style, decorating their heads and bodies with the materials at hand. (Neolithic cave painting: *The War Dance*, detail. Saltadora, Spain.)

The exact date when *Homo sapiens* first felt the need for body protection is obscured by eons past. The earliest of human body coverings must be imagined, for time and the vicissitudes of climate have robbed us of much of this pertinent information. These factors, plus the millennia during which the major human concern was survival, left no time for contemplation and the invention of a verbal means of recording human history.

However, very early *Homo sapiens* devised a method of making pictorial records. From these primitive but vital cave drawings and paintings, the earliest decorative and protective body coverings can be partially conceived (Figure 1.1). Because these visual records report activities explicitly, it can be assumed that basic human concerns centered around the pursuits which were illustrated: hunting, fishing, herding, warfare, and primitive religious rituals. The drawings themselves were part of the rites offered to god spirits to insure success in those activities necessary to survival.[1]

Early humans were hunters and gatherers, killing fish or animals and gathering edible vegetables native to their geographical location. Both of these activities created the need for a rudimentary piece of wearable apparel. The invention of a pouch made it possible to gather more and also served to carry tools of the hunting expeditions. By belting the pouch around the body, an individual could store food and tools, freeing the hands to carry back to the cave whatever creature had been killed. It is possible that the belted pouch was the first functional piece of apparel and was doubtless made from an animal killed during the hunt. The belt may have been made from the animal's tail

or from plaited grasses. These functional pouches, in time, may also have been trimmed with shells or colored stones. Thus, the belted pouch changed from a utilitarian to a decorative item.

Humans very early realized that the animals they hunted not only provided life-sustaining food but materials from which to fabricate crude body coverings (Figure 1.2). Similarly, the vegetation of their ranging and searching areas afforded potential materials from which protective garments might be fashioned. Geographical location and climate determined the kinds of materials available and the kinds of protective coverings needed. It is logical to assume that, in warm climates, early humans did not

**Figure 1.2.** The first skin protection was worn about the shoulders; later, skins were used as a skirt or **kaunakes.** Both cape and skirt were combined when the need arose. Women's garments were the same as men's until better cutting tools were fashioned. (Drawn from description in William J. Miller's *Introduction to Historical Geology,* Fourth Edition, D. Van Nostrand, New York, 1937.)

need garments for warmth, so they wore little, if anything, unless for decorative purposes. If some form of body covering was wanted or needed, doubtless these people fashioned it from grasses, palm leaves, or similar vegetable fibers.

It is known that a tribe native to the North American continent wore a **loincloth** form made of grasses. The section worn between the legs was a narrow basket shape, which was woven so that a lengthy fringe of grass was left at either end. These fringe projections were caught by a belt which was braided from grasses.

The people of the Polynesian area of the Pacific also made body coverings from available grasses and and palm leaves. Inner bark of the mulberry tree was made into **tapa cloth** by first soaking and then beating together layers of this fibrous material. These in turn were stained with dyes of vegetable origin. Feathers of birds were intricately fashioned into enveloping capes and decorative headgear. Colorful plumage of birds was used to add a festive quality to primitive rituals offered to Polynesian gods prior to the hunt.

In colder climates, protection from the elements was first achieved by simply tossing an animal hide over the shoulders. The hide or furry animal skin was a by-product of the hunt-produced food. In time, as the need for more decorative personal adornment became dominant, animals were hunted solely for their skins which were turned into primitive garments. Humans may have ultimately concluded that animals, protected by their fur, could supply the raw material from which to create warm human body protection and decoration.[2] The idea was logical, but the raw material was resistant to the creation of close-fitting garment forms. Paleolithic (40,000 B.C.-8000 B.C.) humans had little else to work with but the simple, chipped tools they had originally invented to secure food and to protect themselves from marauding beasts and human enemies. The first body coverings might well have developed in this Paleolithic period. It was during this period that humans became sophisticated enough to devise hand axes, scrapers, awls (borers), and blades. With the development of the scraper they were able to remove the flesh from the animal skin. With the blade they managed some crude shaping, and with the awl they pierced holes through the animal skins to facilitate rudimentary sewing with rawhide or sinews and bone needles.

Hides, when untreated, lose their plasticity and all but lose their effectiveness as body protection. In time, ancient humans discovered that chewed hide retained its malleability. This method was the same as that used by Eskimo women even in modern times.

Humans had not completely solved their problem, for when skins were drenched with torrents of rain or soaked through by snows melted by body warmth, the skins again became rigid. It took the discovery of tanning to make skins withstand the rigors of climatic conditions. Thorough scraping, followed by alternate beating and soaking, was the method used to make skins pliable before the tanning technique had been discovered, and the chewing process had been discarded. We do not know when humans learned that soaking willow or oak bark in vats of water would saturate the liquid with tannic acid. The person who realized that hides soaked in this diluted tannic-acid solution for a period of time became pliable is also unknown. However, the discovery of one additional step was necessary for the skins to be made permanently soft. This last step—the oiling of the skins—made them a truly adaptable material for making clothes.[3]

The bark of some trees served to tan hides, while other barks served as a material from which crude cloth might be manufactured. It was learned that the bark of the mulberry and the fig could be soaked for long periods in vats of water. While still wet, the bark was stoutly beaten until the fibers of the bits of bark adhered to one another. Generally, this laying down of scraps of bark was repeated until three layers had been firmly beaten into one another.

Flax and cotton appeared as vegetable fibers from which clothing was fashioned only after humans established stable life-styles. A permanent home base was required because the community had to stay in one location long enough for the crop of flax or cotton to mature. In the intervening epochs, humans made pliable clothing materials by saving their own hair. When they had a large enough quantity, this too was alternately soaked, layered, and beaten, producing a basic form of felt material.[4] They also used hair cut from animals to make a feltlike cloth, using the same technique as that used for processing human hair.

As humans discovered a variety of materials from which they could devise clothing, they developed more intricate tools. Among these, in addition to scrapers and blades, were needles, several of which have been found in Paleolithic caves. These needles were created from walrus or mammoth tusks, or reindeer horns, depending on the geographical location of the cave. Eventually the awl was used to bore an eye through which "thread" of sinew or rawhide thong could be passed, and flint was used to polish the needles to a point. With the improvement of tools came an improvement in the fit and function of the sewn garments. These improvements provided more body protection and suggested possibilities for decoration.

Wool became an important fiber from which material could be made during the Neolithic period. While people of this time were basically nomadic, they kept flocks of sheep to provide food and material for making clothing. In the Western Hemisphere, the wool-bearing animals, such as llamas and alpacas, were domesticated to provide wool for clothing. At first, wool was made into felt in much the same manner as human-hair felt.

However, a more stable social order was emerging, and weaving techniques appeared. This cloth-making process, which originated in ancient China, was practiced in most Middle-Eastern civilizations by the Neolithic period and then was introduced into the European areas.[5] Shearing, carding, spinning the fibers into yarn, setting up the loom, and finally weaving the cloth were time consuming. A semipermanent home and considerable time were required for weaving sufficient lengths of fabric to make garments for an entire family. Actual examples from the peat-bog burial grounds in Scandinavia clearly show that great lengths of fabric seldom were woven during the first phases of weaving. Rather, fabric of the required size was pieced together from many smaller rectangular pieces that were then cut and sewn into the desired form.

Climatic conditions also affected decorative aspects of personal adornment. Where the need for warmth did not exist, people collected sea shells or colorful stones, and strung them together on rawhide thongs or lengths of thread made from vegetable fiber to wear for personal adornment.[6] Shells gathered by the California coastal Indians were traded to those living inland in what is now Arizona. The shells became treasured, decorative trinkets. The wearing of jewelry in earliest times soon became symbolic of status. The greater the wealth of the wearer, the more numerous and complex the necklaces became.

Some primitive people combined colorful bird feathers with brightly colored stones. Others used pearls. In some regions humans painted their faces and bodies with a variety of colored clays and used chalks to whiten their bodies. Others made garish gashes on their cheeks and limbs. This was the earliest form of tattooing. In every case, the wearer was creating a personal identity, group identity, or status identity. Hair was braided, twisted, befeathered, or packed with muds and clays. Certain tribes braided strings of stone beads with strands of hair, while others shaved their heads completely or in patterns. The forms of hairdressing might be tribal fad or personal preference.

Fanciful personal adornment appeared as early as the primitive humans' basic needs for housing, clothing, and food were satisfied. A stable society permits imagination and invention to enter the life pattern. Such a society allows for an amount of self-expression, and clothing and personal decoration are the outward signs of the inner need to set oneself apart from one's peers. Perhaps the region between the Tigris and Euphrates rivers, identified as Mesopotamia, was the first such area where the inhabitants enjoyed sufficient stability to consider personal decoration as a form of frivolous self-expression. [7]

For many years this area, where Babylon once existed, was thought to have been the birthplace of Western civilization. However, in 1948, Robert J. Braidwood suggested that the foundations for such an organized society were begun much before the generally accepted date of 3000 B.C. In pursuit of facts to support his theory, he went north to the hilly flanks of the Zagros range. Here, after careful digging and carbon dating, he established rather conclusively that civilization's cradle, Mesopotamia, had its roots in this foothill region. He placed the origins of Mesopotamian culture at 7000 B.C. Not satisfied that the people of Jarmo were the earliest people to thrive on an agriculture and trade economy, he sought more evidence. Other sites were plumbed, including Karim Shahir. Both the multilayered Jarmo site and the single-layered Karim Shahir site yielded evidence of early agricultural societies. In Jarmo, houses with ovens, clay storage bins for grain, and jewelry made from stone and shell indicated that the settlers were thriving there before the arrival of settlers in Sumer.

Still other archaeologists investigated lands adjacent to Mesopotamia and produced evidence of a life-style similarly based on primitive agriculture. Jericho, of Biblical fame, on the northern end of the Dead Sea was an area that produced evidence contradictory to the hilly-flank theory. [8] The valley region, although dry and arid in modern times, yielded grinding stones and other tools, leading to the assumption that grains had been grown there at least a thousand years before the settlements at Jarmo and Karim Shahir. The town site of Jericho was a large one for that time, covering ten acres. The inhabitants were estimated to be 2000 in number. Carbon-14 testing of charcoal and bone from the site proved that Jericho predated Jarmo by a thousand years. It became apparent that urbanization began in this location.

The forces that made humans reject their nomadic life-style of hunting and gathering food were many. Doubtless, women were in some ways responsible. Bearing and raising children was more easily accomplished in an established environment. Success in the early experiments of stationary living produced conditions that led people to adapt to this new form of society. The family and exclusive loyalty to it were superseded by loyalty to the community. Early humans in Jericho and Jarmo, as well as in Karim Shahir, soon discovered that a community working together could achieve greater success than one individual or one family working alone. Family, of course, continued to have a place in this new scheme. As families grew, more crops and larger herds could be raised. A surplus of crops afforded the opportunity to trade for necessities and even for materials from which to produce decorative accessories for personal adornment.

The success of Jarmo, in turn, produced a society of successful people and also malcontented failures. It has been surmised that those who failed in Jarmo's society turned south and settled on the fertile lands near rivers with natural levees. The area known as Sumer was the site chosen at the time of Jarmo's enterprising success, dating back perhaps to 7000 B.C. In the middle of the sixth millennium B.C., when Sumerian dating can be fixed through evidence of predecessors, Hassuna inhabitants and the later inhabitants of Tell Halaf spread their influence from the Zagros foothills northward to the Mediterranean. They bartered grain surpluses, which were their trade items, for obsidian tools, malachite, antimony (eye makeup of these ancients), stone necklaces, or the stones to make necklaces. The trade routes extended from the eastern borders of contemporary Turkey and Iran to the Persian Gulf. From the Persian Gulf, shells were obtained for making necklaces and other adornments.

With the end of the Stone Age, the influence shifted again—Sumer superseded its predecessors. Again the shift came about by the migration of malcontents from the Zagros area. Leaving the lands of their forebears, these people took with them the grain seeds and tools needed to establish a new settlement. This migration from the north, where a city-state form of society had evolved, is set in the fifth millennium B.C. In Mesopotamia, situated between the Tigris and the Euphrates rivers, a similar social order evolved. It is believed that a stable social order had its origins in this region of Asia Minor during the Paleolithic period.

Around 3500 B.C. regional differences appeared. In the north, Assyria, Assur, Nineveh, and Calah (Nimrud) developed into bustling city-states. To the south, the Babylonian Empire began to take form; the city-states of Sumer and Akkad were the centers of this empire. These ancient people flourished on the central plain between the two mighty rivers where the land was fertile. The land was made productive by the invention and installation of a vast system of canals. From these canals, water was drawn off to irrigate pasture lands and individual acres where grain was cultivated for human consumption and fodder for cattle. Through the production of food and livestock, which the kings dominated, Babylonian social order thrived. The Babylonians' influence spread as they expanded their territory by invasion and conquest and continued trade with people of neighboring lands. However, it was their warring nature that led them to destruction. Invasions and conquests particularly characterized the 900-year period between 2800 B.C. and 1950 B.C.

Many authorities suggest that, while animal skins were still the primary material used by the people of Mesopotamia, it was they who first recognized the decorative potential in the **kaunakes** treatment of clipped and shaped fur (Figures 1.4 and 1.6). After the mass of fur was combed and untangled, it was clipped and shaped into patterns, generally with pointed or rectangular segments. The interest in designing a variety of textural effects led to many variations, including a V-shaped trim along the hem. This is similar to a trim motif used by the northern tribes and the people living during the Dark Ages. Elaboration of this original, fanciful, decorative trim reached its zenith during the Renaissance.

However, during Neolithic Mesopotamia, while textural patterns became refined, the basic structure of the

**Figure 1.4.** Garb of the women of Mari often included a large, dome-crowned hat. The cape with **kaunakes** treatment is held on by wrist straps which develop out of the cape's front edge trim. (Redrawn from votive figure of *Female Suppliant*, Mari, 2800 B.C. Louvre, Paris.)

**Figure 1.3.** Clipped **pagne** skirt with **kaunakes** treatment. Note stylization of belt ending in a triangular tuft shape. (Redrawn from bas-relief of Ur-Nanshe, Lagash, third millennium B.C. Louvre, Paris.)

garment remained constant. The male figure in Figure 1.3 wears a wrapped skirt with a rather high waistband, secured about the body by a belt.[9] The belt form seems to be made of a rudimentary woven material. The hem of the skirt has a scalloped effect.

The small votive figure of *The Female Suppliant* in Figure 1.4 wears a tall-crowned hat and what seems to be a full, figure-covering garment beneath a mantle or cape form which has been thrown around the body and drawn over the arms. Whether artistic license or actual detail, the cape form appears to have a binding on the front edges. Further, this charming statuette has been created so that one might conclude that this front trim ended in loops through which the hands passed. Fixed at the wrists, these trim loops might have held the cape closely about the figure. Figures 1.3 through 1.6 illustrate similar wrapped kaunakes garments.

The seated image of a temple superintendent (Figure 1.5) shows tufts of fur that have been shaped and combed into forms resembling a tiered leaf pattern. The profile clearly indicates the bustle silhouette achieved by tucking the bulky fur skirt into a bulky belt which was donned first and knotted in the back.

Figure 1.6 shows a warrior who wears a wrapped skirt of woven fabric and a **rhino,** a fur cloak trimmed, as were the original kaunakes skirts, in tiered spear-point shapes. His boots are the typical upturned-toe foot coverings readily identified as shoe forms of the Near East even in more recent times.

Many votive figures have been unearthed in Nippur. These statuettes of alabaster and gold are stylized examples of clothing worn during the twenty-ninth century B.C. The main body garment was generally a short-sleeved tunic similar to the Egyptian kalasiris or haik, over which was wrapped a scarf very much like the Etruscan chlamydon. On occasion, a cape was worn over one shoulder.

**Figure 1.6.** Cape, or **rhino**, with **kaunakes** treatment, wrapped skirt, and tunic. (Redrawn from bas-relief of *Tribute Bearers Leading Horses*, fragment, Khorsabad, c. 700 B.C. Louvre, Paris.)

**Figure 1.5.** Sumerian **pagne** skirt with **kaunakes** treatment. In this sketch, the bustle profile of the skirt arrangement, tucked into the belt, can be noted. It is fashion authority François Boucher who suggests that this is a pagne skirt. (Redrawn from statue of *Ebikil, Superintendent of Ishtar,* Mari. Louvre, Paris.)

Statuettes of women illustrate that a band trim sewn along the top hem was used in fastening this cape under the bare shoulder. In some figurines, the kaunakes treatment is carefully detailed. Angular lozenge shapes repeated over the wound cape created a stylized leaf motif but were intended, no doubt, to represent the tufted kaunakes cloth. Other statuettes indicate that these outer wraps were smoothly woven fabric. It was the smooth-finish fabric style that was represented with the tape-tie fastening.

Workers' skirt garments were generally knee length. In the series of figures on the *Royal Standard of Ur,* the laborers bearing burdens have a line incised in the center front. This stylized imagery leads to the assumption that these skirts were scant, wrapped around the figure only once and not wound in a spiral (Figure 1.7). The short, vertical lines on the skirt hem suggest that even the poorer classes imitated the kaunakes treatment. These skirts

**Figure 1.7.** An illustration of the simple type of garments worn by laborers. (Redrawn from *Royal Standard of Ur,* Sumerian, third millennium B.C. British Museum, London.)

trims. This decorative element resulted from tying off the warp. Fringe decorated the spirally wound skirt. An apron form was worn over these skirts by priests and on their god-image sculptures. The male figure continued to be covered by a short-sleeved tunic and wrapped skirt. The material of both was intricately patterned in overall repeats of stylized geometric forms and bordered edges. Examples of the skirts of a much later period show that the upper classes wore skirts cut knee length in front and calf or ankle length in back.

Figure 1.8 gives a concise concept of ceremonial robes. This artifact from Nineveh shows a bare-chested deity in a floor-length skirt. The overall repeated circular-pattern fabric of the skirt is bordered and fringed. His beard and his shoulder-length hair are formally trimmed and arranged in pencil curls. His feet are clad in slippers. About his waist is a triple girdle belt that may have been created by rolling up a thin scarf.

The complexity seen in the art forms of this later Mesopotamian period also dominates the costumes of the nobility. Social status can be recognized through the richness of dress. Homes, temples, and pictorial records of this culture, during its late power zenith, all contain the same richness of repeated patterns. Tile trim on temple walls, fabric patterns, horses' manes, and ladies'

were held in place by visible double girdling, different from the skirt seen on the figure of the *Superintendent of Ishtar* (Figure 1.5).

A singer from the same series on the *Royal Standard of Ur* appears to be a female. Her upper torso is nude and is shown in a waist-to-calf-length wrapped skirt with a belt tied in the back. The harpist accompanying her also wears a similar garment. Both skirts have the vertical slashes with a tooth edge at the hem.

The King of Ur is depicted in a sheepskin skirt. The kaunakes treatment is not as stylized or geometric in its representation, suggesting that it is combed animal fur rather than the overall geometric-cut, lozenge shapes in other images.

Warriors from this same standard are depicted wearing wrapped skirts and mantles that cover both shoulders and are fastened over the clavicle with rectangular pins. The mantles are covered with irregularly spaced dots. It is possible that these mantles were made of leopard skins.

With the decline of Sumerian power at the time when Ur was destroyed, Babylonia and Assyria rose in political significance. However, the rich elegance of Sumer still influenced the cultural aspects of the Mesopotamian region. The tufted kaunakes treatment was reduced to fringe

**Figure 1.8.** Kingly fringed wrapped skirt of the Assyrian ruler illustrates the spiral winding style of this male garment. The upper body was clad in a close fitting tunic. (*King Assurbanipal II,* statue, 883–859 B.C. from Nimrud, British Museum, London.)

hairstyles all indicate the aesthetic involvement with textures created by repeated shapes.

Sumptuous dress was characteristic of those persons living in the major cities. The ancient metropolis of Azade boasted many handsome public buildings and parks with beautiful landscaping. Private homes were elegant and often multistoried, and the "walls reached skyward like a mountain," as an ancient chronicler wrote.[10] Houses and cities had protective walls encircling them. Azade, Calah, and Dur-Sharreikin had broad streets laid out in orderly patterns. However, most of the cities of Mesopotamia were merely enlargements of prehistoric villages. The average city was made up of houses crowded within the walls along twisting, narrow streets. Few households, if any, had running water or sewage disposal systems and refuse was dumped into the streets. The habitations occupied by the general populace were dark and dreary, with living quarters arranged around an open court and with few, if any, windows. Grand houses were few in these small, walled cities.

Later, more prosperous urban dwellers constructed two-story townhouses. Steps from the street led to the rooms serving domestic functions and a reception area or inner patio. The upper level served as the living quarters for the family and an inner balcony overlooked the reception patio below. The lower level had tile flooring. Clothing and environment were adapted to the warm climate of the plains and naturally terraced levees on the river's edge.

For all the drawbacks and unpleasantness of the city environment, the residents had city pride and intense loyalty to their homes. The one or two main city thoroughfares were the congregating areas for the populace where families strolled, greeted friends, and attended the busy bazaar. These ancients were a vital lot and enjoyed the bustle of the marketplace as they went from one vending stall to another in the shade of awnings stretched across the street from one building to another. It was in such a market that food supplies were purchased daily. The diet consisted of beans, cheeses, fruits, pork, fish, lamb, and duck.

In each of these small cities, temples dedicated to the city's protective god were erected. Here, attended by priests, the protective gods were housed, clothed, and fed. Pride in these temples and the necessity for their upkeep led to the establishment of the priest class, who were selected from the most learned members of the community. In the evolution of these societies, religious feast days and festivals were adopted, and prayers and hymns were composed to be recited and sung in honor of the city's diety. In time these and other facts were recorded in cuneiform writing, which the Mesopotamians invented. Thus, communication, records, and religious rites were set down for future generations. The many votive figures which supply the visual record of apparel were part of their religious practice. The votive figures were stand-ins for persons who could not be at the temple in person.

The earthly administrator of the god's city was the king, who insured the god's favor by properly conducting the city's business. The king was an elected official selected by the combined votes of a house of elders and a house of men of arms-bearing age. After 2000 B.C. this arrangement was disbanded, and kings were eventually determined by hereditary succession. Individualistic by nature, the early inhabitants of Mesopotamia were devoted to law and justice. The ruler was responsible for the preservation of both. These people evolved the earliest known code of law and ethical practice. However, the code applied only to freemen; slaves had few, if any, human rights. The prosperity of this region depended to a great degree on the labor of the slave class, and economy rested on the success of the farmer, who produced food and grain, and the merchant and trader, who exchanged crop surpluses for commodities which they did not produce.

Inventors of the calendar, the wheel, irrigation systems, and the cuneiform written language, these people indeed can be said to have given birth to civilization. Before their fall from power, they also proved to be remarkable structural engineers. In contrast to the circum-

**Figure 1.9.** Sumerian woman wearing garments typical of an urban housewife. The stylization of the original sculpture shows a tight-fitting tunic form with an off-the-shoulder cape held to the figure with an underarm tape. In the representation of this cape, it can be conjectured that the fabric was doubled, for the incised delineation clearly indicates that there is space between the inner and outer layer. (Redrawn from votive figure, Tell Asmar, third millennium B.C. University of Chicago Oriental Institute.)

stances of the masses, their kings lived in sumptuous splendor. However, the Mesopotamians' pride, vitality, inventiveness, and individual nature contributed to the viable social order under which they lived.

These, then, are the beginnings of fashion with hints at the complexity of the trade which built up to supply the ancients with materials from which to make their apparel. The time span has been compressed, but it must be remembered that concurrent cultural developments were progressing apace. While animal skins were used for clothing by the earliest humans, they also used animal skins and vegetable fibers to provide shelter. As each epoch passed, clothing forms changed with the fortunes of military conquest, and housing forms too were modified. The environment has always greatly influenced the evolution of body-protecting garments. Therefore, political, social, environmental, and aesthetic considerations combined to produce the fashions of humans from the dim, dark, prehistoric past to the period when trade and commerce molded and shaped garments.

# Body Covering from Earliest Times through Mesopotamia (Prehistory–500 B.C.)

## KAUNAKES (8000 B.C.)

The earliest form of body covering for men and women was created from the skins of available animals. In its first stages, around 8000 B.C., the **kaunakes** was merely the rough pelt or hide stripped of its flesh and thrown about the shoulders. As methods for making skins more pliable improved, it was wound about the lower part of the body. The skin was held to the human figure with the tail of the animal used as a belt (Figure 1.2). The tufted tip was the earliest garment decoration. The animal's tail was believed to have magical and protective powers; hence, long after the tail belt was discarded, the practice of wearing a girdle with fringed ends persisted.

The female version of the kaunakes of the third millennium B.C. was worn wound spirally about the figure, covering one shoulder. Later versions of the same form were waist-to-ankle length and were combined with the tunic of a short kalasiris that was secured about the figure with a bulky, padded belt.

During a period of comparative peace around 3000 B.C., a male kaunakes was designed with pleating and fringed edges and worn in much the same spiral manner as the female wound skirt. Fashion authority François Boucher suggests that such fringes were rawhide strips.[11] These early garments were made first of fur and later from available woven fabrics.

## KALASIRIS (5000–2000 B.C.)

While the basic garments were originally wrapped, the more skillful use of needles and shaping tools between 5000 and 2000 B.C. made the more figure-fitting tunic or **kalasiris**—also spelled **kalasyris**—a possibility (Figure 1.9). Constructed very much like the Egyptian counterpart, the kalasiris worn in Asia Minor had elbow-length sleeves. Some authorities refer to these garments as either robes or gowns. Many retained the fringed, looped texture characteristic of the first human garments which were made of animal skins (possibly sheep or goat). The fabric was woven of coarse yarn, and, after 2500 B.C., this fabric was called kaunakes.

Gowns worn by Sumerian women were tiered with rows of tufted yarn that closely resembled the combed, shaped, and cut animal skins. By the sixth century B.C., Greek influence had played its part in altering many garment forms in Asia Minor. While the artists' representations of the people and their wearing apparel suggest that the robes and gowns of both men and women were close fitting, it is believed that this was not the case. Rather, the visual representation was created to clearly indicate the elaborate check and lozenge patterns woven into fabric. It is supposed that the wrist-length sleeves sewn into the robes and gowns were the result of garments having been accepted as suitable attire from a people inhabiting cooler climates. Women wore belts of rolled fabric, adding bulk to the midsection.

## RHINO (3000–600 B.C.)

The cape form of the kaunakes, or, as some authorities call it, the **rhino**, was worn as shoulder protection for many centuries even after woven fabrics had been introduced. It is possible that the Sumerians wore the fur side facing inward and the hide outside. Some authorities report that the skin side was worn inside during the more moderate seasons, and, in extremely cold weather, the reverse was the custom. These cape forms were generally made of goat or sheepskin. Smaller animals appear to have been used by the people of Telloh, for their cape forms appear to have been made of pelts sewn together. Some of the cape forms had arm-covering flaps. Perhaps these were the forerunners of what were later to become sleeves in tunics and kalasiris.

## SHAWL (2800–2500 B.C.)

The other form of full body protection, the **shawl,** was worn in a variety of ways. At first, of course, there was little if any difference in the style of garments worn by the two sexes. A simple rectangle of woven fabric served as a skirt for men and women. As a cape form, it was fastened at the chest and, in some cases, a calf-length cape with a half-cape effect was created by an overfold. When used as a skirt, it could be folded in half to make a calf-length skirt

**Figure 1.10.** A distinct Oriental influence is evident in the Syro-Phoenician costumes of the first millennium B.C. The long-sleeved tunics have skirts with slits in front and back. The basic garments are white with red and blue braid edging the seams and skirt slits. The spirally wrapped shawls which cover the lower figures from waist to calf are similarly decorated. (Tomb painting: *Syrians Bearing Tribute,* detail. Tomb of Sebekhotep, Thebes.)

or left full width and worn as an ankle-length skirt. At first the fabric was wrapped about the human figure and tucked into the girdle (Figure 1.10). This simple belt was knotted in back. When the skirt was tucked over it, a bustle effect was created in profile silhouette.

Shawls, when worn by women, were arranged in several ways. When worn wound about the figure, after the manner of the East Indian sari, it was tossed over the left shoulder, the end trailing behind. In some cases, the rectangular length of material was formed into a roll of material. This roll was then placed about the figure, encircling it at the waist, and one end was tossed over the shoulder after being loosely knotted. More generally, if the remaining sculptural visualizations are to be believed, the shawl form was worn around the shoulders, crossing the back and making a half cape. The ends were allowed to hang free in front.

The shawl was worn in yet another manner by men, arranged in much the same manner as the Egyptian **shenti** (2000 B.C.). The rectangle of fabric was wound about the figure, beginning at the waist. The length was determined by the width of the material. The beginning corner of this wrapped kilt, or skirt, was left to protrude, and the outer end was tied to it over one or the other shoulder. Perhaps the bared-shoulder dress depicted in the Saltadora cave painting (Figure I.1) is an economical representation of such a system of wrapping the figure. Shawl forms of this type are difficult to properly date because, if the cave drawing does represent such a garment, the time period predates historic record.

# Accessories (Prehistory–500 B.C.)

### FOOTWEAR

Although in the predawn of recorded history humans went unshod, several foot-covering styles appeared as the cultural exchange broadened between nations. Most people of Asia Minor, including the Egyptians, went barefooted except when venturing over the hot sands. Then a simple sandal form was used. Bas-reliefs indicate that soldiers of the area that is now Iraq wore boots which reached to the calf and laced over the shin. The toes of these boots were upturned. Some shoes were merely soles held on by a toe-ring that passed over the big toe. Still other styles, determined by close examination of existing wall sculptures, suggest that the bottom of the foot was protected only by a sole that was held in place by the toe-ring, and the calf of the leg was protected by a cross-laced leather sheath.

### JEWELRY

Beads of stone and semiprecious stones, as well as shells, feathers, and animal teeth, were the first forms of personal adornment worn by humans. Later these were fashioned of precious metals from gold mines in the areas bordering the Mediterranean, notably the gold fields between Mesopotamia and Egypt. There are examples of fine jewelry which originated in the northerly reaches of Europe, and jewelry of the period is depicted in the statuary and bas-reliefs of the Near East. Bracelets, necklaces, and arm bands of precious metals set with a variety of semiprecious stones can be recognized.

## BELTS

Belts and girdles were important devices for securing garments about the figure. At first the tails of animals in their original forms were used to girdle the kaunakes. Later, braided vegetable fibers and woven yarns were used. The rolled shawl served as a girdle or belt form also.

# Hairstyles (Prehistory–500 B.C.)

To cover the innumerable hairstyles that were used by people in this vast geographical area during such an

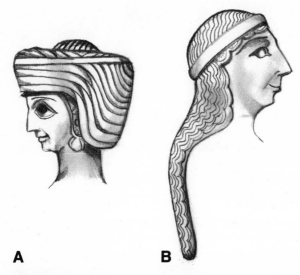

**A**          **B**

**Figure 1.11.** Headwear and hairstyling ranged from elaborate to simple. *A* illustrates one of the intricately pleated linen turbans worn during the third millennium B.C. *B* indicates the hairstyling. The hair is parted in the middle, waved, and left to fall close to the sides of the face. The hair is kept in place by a band of ribbon or linen. (*A* redrawn from statuette in the Iraq Museum, Baghdad. *B* redrawn from statuette in the British Museum, London.)

extensive time span would be impossible. The earliest hairstyling attempts were crude. Feathers and loops of braided hair predominated. In later times, particularly in Sumeria and Persia, men took great care of their hair. Ringlets, closely curled, fringed the face. Beards were given attentive care as well and were shaped and combed into pencil curls. The upper lip, for the most part, was shaven.

Women let their hair fall free during the earliest epochs. Those of Asia Minor affected a variety of styles; the most notable was an arrangement of close curls worn snugly around the head (Figure 1.11). Another coif included a bun of rather large proportions that was supported by a small scarf with a band worn low over the forehead. The higher the social status of the woman of this period, the higher she piled the knot of hair on her head. In certain areas, the custom of married women wearing veils in public began in antiquity. Hat forms were seldom worn, although, as in the case of the sculpture from Mari (Figure 1.4), either a cap or a tall-crowned head covering was depicted.

## FOOTNOTES

1. Raymond Somers Stites, *The Arts and Man*, p. 46.
2. James Laver, *The Concise History of Costume and Fashion*, p. 10.
3. Ibid., pp. 10–12.
4. Ibid.
5. *Funk and Wagnalls New Encyclopedia*, edited by Joseph Laffin Morse, vol. 21, p. 158.
6. James Laver, *Costumes in Antiquity*, p. 37.
7. Katherine M. Lester and Bess Oerke, *Accessories of Dress*, p. 96.
8. Samuel Noah Kramer, *Cradles of Civilization*, pp. 15–16.
9. Laver, *The Concise History of Costume and Fashion*, p. 12.
10. Kramer, *Cradles of Civilization*, p. 11.
11. François Boucher, *20,000 Years of Fashion*, pp. 34–36.

# Chapter 2

# Costumes of Ancient Egypt
## (3700–500 B.C.)

**Figure 2.1 Gala gown,** or perhaps a goffered tunic **(haik),** is worn by the female. Also, the everpresent necklace collar and wig, which is bright blue. The male is wearing a goffered, ankle-length **kilt** and **shendot.** His feet are clad in simple one-thong sandals. (Back of the Throne, Tomb of Tutankhamen, XVIII Dynasty, c. 1500 B.C. Egyptian Museum, Cairo.)

The people who ultimately united to become the great ancient nation of Egypt made their first tentative starts about 10,000 B.C. in the valley of the Nile River. In prehistoric times, the Nile Valley had a mild climate and it was covered with luxuriant vegetation. It was a viable environment which encouraged human inhabitants to settle there. This area was separated from Mesopotamia by Arabia and the Red Sea. Just as the isolated city-states of Jarmo, Karim Shahir, and Jericho developed because they were able to provide for human needs, so it was with the earliest Egyptian settlements.

The gentle climate of the Nile Valley was dependent on weather conditions much farther north. During the glacial phases of the Pleistocene epoch, early Egyptians lived with comparative ease while humans farther north were battling for survival in four successive glacial advances. When the most recent ice flow began to recede, it affected the climate of the Nile Valley, causing it to become more and more arid. The once fertile lands, which had sustained family groups, became desert areas. Only along the river banks and in widely separated oases was vegetation sustained, and to these areas were drawn the family groups which eventually became organized communities. Thus, the weather, and the flora and fauna it supported, determined the development of Egypt's earliest social order—the city-states. In turn, climate determined the earliest survival patterns, set the life-style in housing and clothing, and established the roots of the religion of Egypt.

The Paleolithic or Old Stone Age, typified by the use of chipped tools, faded into a transitional period called the Mesolithic. As humans slowly developed tool-making skills, the Mesolithic evolved into the Neolithic period. It was in this period of the New Stone Age that the first phases of a stable society appeared in the Nile Valley.

Around 4000 B.C. the ancient Egyptians made four major advances which made a stable life-style possible. These advances hinged on the invention of polished stone tools. Most important for establishing an agrarian-based economy were the inventions of the hoe and the plow. With these tools, the Nile Valley inhabitants were able to plant and till their two major grain crops—barley and wheat. These Neolithic people also domesticated animals native to their lands. Pigs, goats, sheep, oxen, and cattle were the first animals to be put to human use. The domestication of oxen made it possible to cultivate more land by using beasts of burden to pull the plows.

People and oxen together worked to irrigate the land and crops, for ancient Egyptians had developed a system of field irrigation. Water was drawn up from the Nile, turning the rich, alluvial soil into arable, food-producing acreage. Successful crop harvests were assured, thereby producing stable food supplies that contributed to the maintenance of permanent communities. An orderly, stable social system allowed time for leisure and contemplation, resulting in new inventions and refinements of older ones.

By 3400 B.C. the Egyptians had invented a pictorial method of written communication. These pictograms were later to become ideograms (one symbol equalling a thought), and finally the hieratic, calligraphic writing used by the priestly class. The Egyptians also invented a calendar. As the ancient Egyptian culture became more sophisticated, methods for metal working, boat building, and producing baked clay vessels were developed.

The ultimate of sophistication was architectural engineering. The mammoth structures which they built testify to the land area under Egyptian domination. In the delta region are the pyramids of Khafre and Khufu, and the Great Sphinx. Located in what was once the southernmost region of the ancient Egyptian Empire, near Abu Simbel, are the temples of Ramses II and Queen Nofretari.[1] Scattered between these two distant geographical locales are thirteen other temples and colossi.

In the early social order, family groups formed small communities. These in turn became city-states. Larger populations presented the need for laws and a ruler. Ultimately, the city-states were consolidated into two kingdoms, referred to as Upper Egypt and Lower Egypt.[2]

Each of the kings had a very definite identifying crown called a **pschent.** The pschent of Upper Egypt was white, conical, and topped by a knob. That of Lower Egypt was red and cylindrical, with a scoop shape projecting upward at the back.

Most authorities assert that the unification of Upper and Lower Egypt occurred during the third millennium B.C. The king credited with the consolidation is as widely disputed as is the dating of unification. Some authorities list the king as Menes and establish the date of unification at 3100 B.C. Others suggest that the two kingdoms were united during the year 2900 B.C. under the leadership of Narmer.

The complex political system that developed thereafter was dominated by a supreme ruler or pharaoh, who had complete control of all land, power to establish a nobility, and total direction of the masses. After unification, these early powerful pharaohs and their appointed nobility established a feudalistic form of government. The power structure of this system was, ironically, pyramidal. At the apex was the pharaoh, who was considered an omnipotent, all-seeing god and king. At the base of this social structure were the peasants, slaves, and unskilled laborers.

The pharaoh was assisted by the most select of nobles, one of whom was designated as the vizier. These men only represented the pharaoh. All decisions were made by the pharaoh, for as god-king, he was responsible for the rise and fall of the Nile, the success of crops, the success of the economy, and the success of the military. The pharaoh was law, both originator and administrator of justice.

The Egyptian elite were members of the aristocracy by virtue of royal favor. They were the leisure class, small in number and perpetuated by inheritance. The affluence of a noble family depended on the success of the annual crop yield and, in turn, the revenue from taxes. The nobility were waited upon and entertained by slaves, many of whom were Nubians from the headwaters of the Nile, or Asians taken as prisoners during wars or bought in the slave market.

Great and frequent feasts were an integral part of the aristocracy's life-style. They ate such delicacies as pigeon, ox, and duck, accompanied by vast quantities of beer and wine. Among other taste treats at such feasts were almost forty different varieties of breads and sweet cakes. Such sumptuous banquets often grew raucous, and, as one in attendance is credited with saying, "Look at you beside a pretty girl, drenched in perfume . . . beating your stomach, reeling and rolling about on the ground."[3]

In addition to the culinary extravaganzas of these banquets, there were planned entertainments. Some were morbid in concept, but most were joyful. Dwarfs, dancers, storytellers, and wrestlers were among the entertainers. The dancers performed wild acrobatic numbers or sensuous, erotic ones. Egyptian dancers were agile and had mastered cartwheels, splits, somersaults, backbends, and pirouettes. Ancient Egyptians also enjoyed instrumental and choral music.

The development of a stratified class structure with the pharaohs designated as god-kings led to the clarification of religious beliefs. Early in the period of stabilizing their society, Egyptians credited nature with providing them with the conditions necessary for survival. They recognized that warmth from the sun caused grain to ripen and that the rise and fall of the Nile provided rich land in which to grow crops and the water with which to irrigate them. This awareness provided the basic concepts of Egyptian religion. Worship of the sun and the Nile was part of daily life. The sun and the river gods were closely associated with the belief in an afterlife, and they became incarnate gods. The sun god was called Re, Ra, or Amen Re, and sailed through the sky each day from east to west. The religion of Re was worldly; he was thought to be a dynamic, masculine diety.

In contrast to the sun god, the Osirian aspect of Egyptian religion was based on the creative power of the river which had dominion over the afterlife. The river was thought to be the resurrected Osiris, consort of the goddess Isis. The consort of Isis became known as the god of death and the king of the Dark Nile, the river of the world after death. The rebirth of Osiris was symbolized by the rising each year of the river. The Egyptians identified with the Osirian annual life cycle, believing that after death, rebirth to a new life was possible.

Ka was the name given to the human soul. Ba was the physical vitality that fled the body at death. It was for the Ka that tombs were filled with food and the accoutrements of the life to which Ba had become so accustomed. An Egyptian's earthly behavior was judged by Osiris, god of the underworld. If the judgment were favorable, the Ka was awarded renewed life for eternity. Extinction, or a second death, resulted if the behavior of the deceased were found wanting.

From the Egyptian nature-oriented religion evolved a number of anthropomorphic gods. Included in religious observances was the worship of the animal gods. The lion was given homage and admired because of its ferocity, the crocodile for its strength, and the cow for its tenderness toward her offspring. The cat became the god of love. Many ceremonial headdresses incorporated creatures as dominant design motifs. One such was Horus, a falcon, who was the god of the sky. The Egyptian anthropomorphic gods were assigned duties or given mystical and magical powers. Many of the Egyptian gods were part human, part animal. For example, Sekhmet, part woman and part lion, was the goddess of war. Superstition and nature were not the only concepts inherent in Egyptian religion, for they also worshiped Thoth, god of learning and wisdom. Many of the symbols of the gods were incorporated into the costumes of the royalty.

Because of their religion, the Egyptians were fascinated with and gave constant attention to preparations for the afterlife. They were once thought to be a morbid people. This was not the case, for, in addition to banquets and festivals, the upper class enjoyed hunting crocodiles, hippopotamuses, and birds. They also enjoyed boating leisurely down the Nile. They spent many hours in grooming. The manner in which they stocked their tombs is evidence that they enjoyed life and were expecting to do so in the underworld. Methods of preparing for the afterlife and means of earthly enjoyment varied according to the affluence of the individual or family.

Equally varied in size and decor were the shelter structures. Common materials were used, primarily mud-and-wattle brick and palm-trunk beams for the lower classes and lesser nobilities, and cut sandstone for palaces or residences of prominent people. Egyptian houses for all but the poorest, had two stories. Two stairways, one on each side of the house, led to the upper level, and in some of the dwellings an additional stairway led to the roof.

The houses of the merchant class were constructed of mud-and-wattle brick with palm-trunk supports and generally included shops on the street level, with the sleeping quarters on the second level. The top floor was an open gallery and was used as the living space. The higher-class homes had plastered walls and floors. Interior and exterior walls were painted with colored borders; the wealthiest Egyptians covered the interior walls with murals.[4]

At first, furniture was basic, with mats serving as both floor coverings and sleeping facilities in lesser homes. Native grasses, which grew in great abundance along the river banks, supplied the material from which the mats were made. The same fibers were used as seats for the simple cross-legged folding stools. Often the mats were stained with vegetable dyes in decorative patterns. In upper-class homes, the interior walls and the floors were decorated with these colorful mats.

Grand houses of the aristocracy were set in the center of a walled compound. At one end of the garden area, opposite the entrance, stood the family chapel. A pool surrounded by trees was another feature of this garden space. At the opposite end of the compound were areas used for grain storage, servants' quarters, food storage, and cooking. A stockade for cattle, stalls, a paddock, a tack room, and a workshop for horses comprised the other outbuildings of the compound.

The main house had sleeping and living quarters. The entrance led into the loggia and on into a large, impressive central or main hall, where the festive banquets were held. Just off the main hall were the quarters of the harem. At the main gate stood the caretaker's cottage.

The whole orderly operation of these sumptuous homes was run by the noble's stewards, who received their orders from the noble's wife. Even in the lowliest of houses, the wife was the director of the home. Egyptian fatherly advice has been quoted as, "You should not supervise your wife in her house."[5]

The furnishings for the homes of the elite were as elegant as the structures. Beds and chair legs were graceful and finished with stylized details of ox hooves or lion's feet. Beds had inch-wide thong strips serving as springs. Stools, similar to campstools in construction, had simple, straight lines contrasted with gentle curves. Animal hides were used for the seats. Large braziers on tall tripod stands burned oil to provide illumination. Inlaid chests for storage of linen, cosmetics, and jewelry were handsome in their simplicity.

Egyptian males from the lowliest man up to the pharaoh participated in warfare. When the national security was in danger, ancient Egypt mobilized for total war. Pharaohs, courtly youths, and fieldhands served on the front. Their weapons included maces, spears, daggers, and bronze-tipped arrows. The foot soldiers fought fiercely amid chariots that charged into the fray. Chariot drivers were generally an elite class selected from wealthy families. Often the charioteer supplied his own conveyance, which he proudly displayed at home after the battle.

Gallant on the field of battle, fun loving at home, and dedicated to their religious beliefs, Egyptians evolved a unique aesthetic. A love of nature was incorporated into dwellings, furnishings, burying places, and costumes. Decorative motifs depicted stylizations of natural forms. The radial necklaces and goffered gowns reflected their reverence of the sun god Re.

Angularity and a strong verticality were the basic aesthetic considerations of ancient Egyptian art and architecture. In combination with these thematic design systems were geometric curvilinear forms. These curvilinear forms were stylizations of shapes found in nature. The two predominant design motifs were the lotus and papyrus decorative embellishments that were reproduced on walls and columns. The human images in wall paintings were arranged in a row composition that reflected the mighty Nile's reed-covered banks.

As did all emerging peoples, the Egyptians first used animal skins—or the **kaunakes**—as basic clothing. This body covering eventually became part of the ritualistic garb of priests. Because of the Egyptian stylization of the images of people, many historians have determined that the clothing of the Egyptians was form fitting and snug. To be sure, most of their garments were not as draped and flowing as were those of the ancient Greeks. However, because of the elasticity of the fabrics used, body movements were neither hampered nor curtailed.[6] Figure silhouettes were in keeping with the basic aesthetic sensitivity of these ancients.

The most widely used garments of these people were basic forms that were worn by both sexes. Both men and women often wore nothing on the upper torso. The **loincloth,** wound about the body in a variety of ways, was

**Figure 2.3.** Male figure wears a loose, rectangular cape; **kilt** with **shendot** decoration; and **pano,** the ankle-length, transparent overskirt. Female figure is clad in a snug-fitting **kalasiris** made from patterned fabric. Her wig is elaborately coiffed. (Painted relief: *Seti I and the Goddess Hathor,* XIX Dynasty. Louvre, Paris.)

**Figure 2.2.** The apparel visible on the male figure consists of a goffered, rectangular cape and **shendot.** The female is dressed in a close-fitting **kalasiris,** trimmed with a circular collar necklace. *(Chief Royal Secretary, Yuni, Son of the Chief Physician, and His Wife, the Chantress of Amen-Re,* XIX Dynasty. Metropolitan Museum of Art, New York City.)

the basic garment common to both sexes (Figures 2.8 and 2.9). There were, however, sexual differentiations as the culture grew in complexity and sophistication. In general, female garments were longer and worn high on the rib cage. The age and rank of the individual were also indicated by the garment's length.

The Egyptians, because of their reverence for nature, chose to wear figure-revealing garments. Thus, they wore either a snugly fitted tunic form called a **haik,** a **kalasiris,** or **kalasyris** (Figure 2.2), a transparent **gala gown,** or nothing more than a *cache-sexe,* a hip-encircling belt. The cache-sexe was often made of gold thread worked with lapis lazuli beads as decoration. Though the climate was warm, the Egyptians often covered their bodies with many layers of transparent garments. The **skent** (Figure 2.13) and **pano** (Figure 2.3) were two such body coverings. The skent, a transparent wraparound skirt worn over an opaque loincloth, was usually thigh length, and was worn by people of high status. The pano was a long, transparent overskirt reaching from the bust to the ankles. Personages of high rank wore their garments girdled with decorative belts, many of which had long, hanging ends that were fringed and multicolored. The long, hanging ends were left to fall either down in front or in the back.

Greatly enamored by goffering, or pleating, the Egyptians organized the pleats to radiate from a focal point in the front of the garment (Figures 2.1 and 2.2). Pleating was made semipermanent by drenching the fabric in vegetable starch. The lengths of wet, starched fabric were laid out, arranged in pleats of the desired width, and pressed. Hot stones were used to press in the pleats. These stones were laid on the pleated fabric and allowed to stay until the material was thoroughly dry.

The Egyptian fashion silhouette was dominated by the head and shoulders. This focal point was created by the use of wigs and large, radiating necklaces. Thus, the figure presented a statuesque appearance, and its dominant form related to the columns in Egyptian architecture in which the capital spread outward to support the roof beams. Wigs became increasingly large, and the arrangement of the hair in rows of pencil curls carried out the repeated motifs dominant in the pictorial arts, such as the rows of figures, columns, and reeds.

Wigs were not only decorative but were worn as a practical protection against the hot, bright sun.[7] The practice of shaving the head for the sake of cleanliness demanded that some form of head covering be worn.

**Figure 2.5.** Goffered **gala skirt** with balloon-style wig. (Redrawn from standing statue of *Mitry, Privy Council and Priest of ma'et,* V Dynasty. Brooklyn Museum.)

Wigs, the **klaft** (a kerchief head covering), or the more elaborate royal **Nemes headdress** (Figure 2.6), were the fashions that the Egyptians developed. Wig design and hair arrangement changed over the centuries. Styles ranging from the simple balloon-wig forms to the complex pencil-braid arrangements covered with "veils of gold" (Figures 2.4 and 2.5) assist in dating the costumes and aid in determining the dynasties during which they were worn.

The same is true of the garments worn. The simpler wraparound skirt forms or kilts were the earliest costume shapes. The gala gown, with its elaborately goffered sleeve area and frontal panel, colorfully decorated girdles, and massive collar necklaces occurred late in the New Kingdom.

The variety of garments that were created from simple rectangles of fabric was multitudinous. The **kilt,** a type of loincloth, was such a wrapped garment. To make it more festive, it was sometimes goffered (Figure 2.5). The front

**Figure 2.4.** Headdress of a lady of the Egyptian court, c. 1700 B.C. It was made of delicate, linked, golden discs, each chased in a radiating pattern. *(Headdress of a Lady of the Court,* XVII Dynasty, Wadi Garbamat, Thebes. Metropolitan Museum of Art, New York City.)

**Figure 2.6.** Male figure wears a goffered **kilt** with **shendot** and jewel-encrusted girdle, and a **Nemes headdress,** the royal adaptation of the **klaft.** (Redrawn from seated statue, with modifications, of *King Sesostris,* XII Dynasty, 2000–1788 B.C. Brooklyn Museum.)

overflap was cut in a curved shape and the frontal decorative appendage, the **shendot,** added a richer, more elegant, personal, and rank-identifying note (Figure 2.6). Transparent capes and gala gowns were also created from a simple rectangle. With needles of bronze, thorn, or bone, Egyptian tailors and seamstresses created the sleeveless kalasiris from a simple rectangle, sewing up the side seams, leaving armholes, and cutting the neckline out of the center.

An example of this type of garment is in the Costume Institute of the Metropolitan Museum of Art in New York. It appears to have been amply cut of now-yellowed linen. This actual garment gives further substantiation to the supposition that the kalasiris was not always skimpily cut.

To counter this concept, however, is the wall painting from the Tomb of Rekhmire at Thebes from the New

Kingdom. In this example, a servant is depicted in an ankle-length haik, or a kalasiris with the elbow-length sleeves snugly fitted to the upper arm (Figure 2.7). The standing figure is wearing a cache-sexe beneath her tunic which is, apparently, made of transparent cloth. The uniquely coiffed image wears a ponytail falling from the crown and a fringe of pencil braids falling from just behind the ears to well forward on the forehead.

There is a variety of garment forms in a wall painting from the Tomb of Djeserkara, also from the period of the New Kingdom. In the group of female musicians, the harpist wears an ankle-length loincloth over which is worn a pano; the upper figure is covered by a goffered shenti which ends just below the buttocks; two figures wear only the cache-sexe; the musician performing on the double flute is clad in an ungirdled, transparent kalasiris; and the girl playing the lyre wears the single-strap procardium.

*Danseuse Acrobatique* (Figure 2.8), a fragment in the Turin Museum, illustrates the agility of the Egyptians. The figure wears a kilt or female loincloth which is drawn around the back of the figure and tied in front. The section

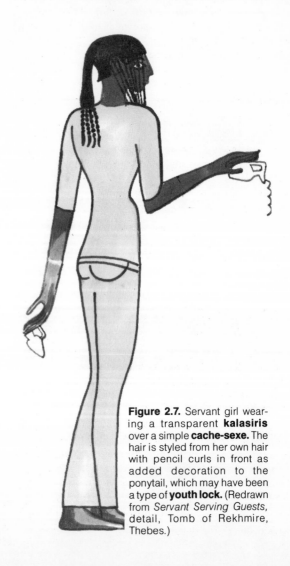

**Figure 2.7.** Servant girl wearing a transparent **kalasiris** over a simple **cache-sexe.** The hair is styled from her own hair with pencil curls in front as added decoration to the ponytail, which may have been a type of **youth lock.** (Redrawn from *Servant Serving Guests,* detail, Tomb of Rekhmire, Thebes.)

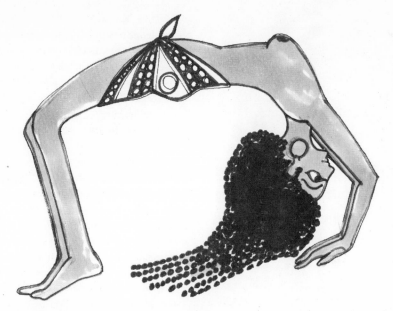

**Figure 2.8.** Female loincloth of the New Kingdom (1580–1085 B.C.) made from a simple rectangle of patterned fabric. (Redrawn from *Danseuse Acrobatique.* Turin Museum, Italy.)

covering the back reaches from mid-thigh to above the normal waist. The front is drawn down well below the navel and above the pubic region in front. In addition to the kilt, which had a pattern much like that of a modern-day bandana handkerchief, this lithe dancer wears huge hoop earrings.

A rare example of male apparel of the Eighteenth Dynasty illustrates a Nubian soldier in a short kilt with an animal tail at the waist and another tied about the knee and calf of the leg.[8] A mesh section of diamond pattern covers the back of the figure from waist to calf and was possibly made of cut leather (Figure 2.9).

Color was important to Egyptian dress. From wigs of deep, nearly iridescent blue to multicolored collar necklaces, color played an important role in the overall adornment of the body. The color accents were generally centered in the neck and head area, but colorfully patterned fabrics were also used in the kalasiris and the single- or double-strapped **procardium** (Figure 2.10). Colors of belts, shendots, and some of the gods' crown forms also included deep turquoises, greens, and earth reds. Only the pschent of Lower Egypt, the northern Nile area, was red. However, bright red was believed to be the color of violence and was not used in daily apparel. Gold thread and feathers were additional decorative devices used on royal apparel. Goffering was more generally reserved for the nobility, and the slave and laboring classes wore simpler forms of apparel.

Color and pattern were so greatly admired by the ancient Egyptians that in their earliest phase they selected skins which were patterned, such as leopard skins. The leopard-skin garment of Egypt was retained as

**Figure 2.9.** Simple loincloth with slashed-back overskirt, possibly of leather, with an animal-tail trim. (Redrawn from wall painting of *Nubian Standard Bearer,* detail, Tomb of Tjanuy, XVIII Dynasty, 1420–1411 B.C., Thebes.)

**Figure 2.10.** Credited with being either Semitic or Asiatic, this detail from a wall painting shows three women in patterned **kalasiris,** or tunics. The hairstyling is quite Egyptian in arrangement. This illustration shows the infusion of costume styles resulting from trade between ancient nations. *(Family Arriving in Egypt,* detail, Tomb of Khnumhotep, Beni Hasan, XII Dynasty, c. 1900 B.C. Bibliothèque Nationale, Paris.)

a part of ceremonial and ritualistic apparel. Appliqué decorations and embroidered designs were also used to introduce color into garments of later periods. Embroidered costumes featured repeating patterns of either geometric figures or stylized feather shapes.

Ancient Egyptians of high rank and affluence strove to wear the newest innovations of dress. As the Egyptians mingled with the people of the Mediterranean and their land neighbors, new fashions were introduced. When persons of high social status discarded older styles, people with lesser social standing adopted the older styles. Officials of lesser importance can usually be recognized by their long, full kilts. This kilt had previously identified royalty. Priests of the Old Kingdom had no distinguishing habits and wore the dress of royalty. Soldiers wore no uniform costume but their professional occupation was identified by headbands with ribbons hanging down the back. Although Egyptian soldiers had no metal helmets, a leather headdress was adopted during

the New Kingdom (Figure 2.11). Oddly, non-Egyptian mercenaries wore horned helmets much like those worn by the Vikings from northern Europe. Commoners wore simple garments of coarse linen in contrast to the delicate linen lawn used for the costumes of the nobility. Laborers wore nothing or a loincloth with a segment of fabric falling down in front.

These ancients, especially those with leisure time, devoted many hours to grooming themselves.[9] Oils and perfumes were used to freshen the body. Great care was taken with hair and wigs. Makeup was important, especially for outlining the eyes. Because of the importance of the dance, the pencil curls were weighted in such a manner as to exaggerate the rhythms established by the body's movements. Although the somewhat stiff, stylized figures portrayed by ancient Egyptian artists might lead one to believe otherwise, grace of movement was part of the entire spectrum of dress. Dignity and grace combined and were emphasized by the color and line design of Egyptian garb.

**Figure 2.11.** Simple wraparound **kilt,** circular collar, and leather helmet typical of the type worn during the New Kingdom. (Redrawn from bas-relief in Sebekhotep's Tomb, XVII Dynasty, Thebes.)

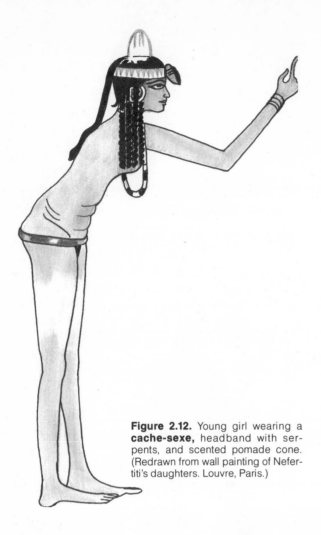

**Figure 2.12.** Young girl wearing a **cache-sexe,** headband with serpents, and scented pomade cone. (Redrawn from wall painting of Nefertiti's daughters. Louvre, Paris.)

# Basic Garments of Ancient Egypt (3700–500 B.C.)

### CACHE-SEXE

The *cache-sexe* was a simple belt worn by females as the only body adornment (Figure 2.12). It was generally worn by young girls, dancers, and slaves, and, when worn by young girls and dancers, was elegantly made of golden threads and embellished with beads, often made of lapis lazuli.

### SKENT

The **skent** (Figure 2.13) was a thigh-length wraparound skirt for men. It was fashioned of transparent linen lawn and revealed the kilt or loincloth worn beneath it.

### PANO

The **pano** worn by both sexes was also a transparent overskirt. It differed from the skent in that it was long, and the hemline reached to the ankle or just above.

### LOINCLOTH

Statues of kingly figures are shown wearing a **shaped loincloth** with rounded or curved front segments pleated or goffered to add to the elegance and prestige of the pharaoh (Figure 2.14). In some instances, the segment passing between the legs may have been lengthened and

**Figure 2.13.** Servants wearing **haik** (sleeved tunic), thigh-length **kilt,** and transparent overskirt, or **skent.** *(Servants from House of Sebekhotep,* XVII *Dynasty. Louvre, Paris.)*

**Figure 2.14.** Shaped loincloth with modified **shendot.** (*Prince Tha-Hap-Breccia,* Memphis. Metropolitan Museum of Art, New York City.)

figure, beginning at the left front, across the back, and then to the center front (Figures 2.3, 2.6, and 2.11). The kilt was held in place by a belt that was tied or knotted in front. This wound and belted garment was usually thigh length. Egyptian men also wore a shaped loincloth. This was a T-form worn between the legs, with the horizontal section covering the back of the figure as well as the front just below the waist. It was tied in front by tapes which held in place the section that was passed between the legs.

Kilts of the New Kingdom were often worn in pairs. The longer, slimmer of the two was put about the figure first; over this was worn a more decorative one, goffered in front, pulled up to reveal the more snugly fitting kilt beneath. These were often handsomely girdled, and were worn with a shendot, an outgrowth of the phallic sheath, encrusted with decorative plaques.

left to hang to the knees. Men often wore the shaped loincloths over the loinskirt or kilt. This was particularly a fashion of the New Kingdom.

The **loincloth** was the basic garment of men and women (Figures 2.8 and 2.9). Simple in concept, this mid-body covering was made by wrapping a length of fabric about the figure just below the waist and tying it in front. The ends were left to hang loosely and covered the genitals of males and the pubic hair of females. Other arrangements included passing a length of fabric between the legs and securing it to the figure with a belt. These earliest body coverings scarcely concealed the figure. They certainly afforded minimal protection and had few decorative attributes. A more decorative style of female loincloth, made of patterned and colorful fabrics, was little more than an adornment. It covered the buttocks and was knotted in front below the navel and well above the pelvis, around mid-abdomen.

A later version (3400-525 B.C.) of the loincloth was the **kilt** (Figure 2.15). A basic garment of both men and women in Egypt, it too was a simple length of fabric, rectangular in shape, taken directly from the loom on which it was woven. The original manner of donning this one-piece body covering was to wrap the fabric around the

**Figure 2.15.** Servant wearing wrapped **kilt.** (Redrawn from *Funeral Procession,* Tomb of Ramose, XVIII Dynasty, Thebes.)

The **shenti,** a version of the loincloth, was put around the figure in the same manner as the style described above, with the exception that the first left corner protruded above the waist. The fabric was then wound one and three-fourths times around the figure, ending in the back. The outer end was brought over the left shoulder and tied to the first or protruding end. This style was belted with a long sash that was tied in back, the ends trailing to the level of the ankles. A decorative series of woven tassels was suspended from the front of the sash belt. The shenti was a simpler fabric arrangement without the shoulder strap but with a pleated or goffered front panel; the length of the shenti and kilt varied throughout the centuries. During the Old Kingdom, the general wearing length covered the figure from waist to mid-thigh, but later the hemline gradually dropped in the male style, falling first to the calf and then to the ankle. Men wore the longer versions of kilts, belted at the waist with long decorative sashes.

The female wearing fashion of this basic garment was the same as that of the male, but the garment covered the figure from just under the bust and extended to just above the ankle bone. Women wore elaborate and decorative belts just under the breasts. These accessories, tied in front, extended to the hem.

## PROCARDIUM (2000 B.C.)

The **procardium** (2000 B.C.) was also a wrapped garment that was worn by men and women. The rectangular length of material was wound around the body in the same manner as the loincloth; however, one shoulder strap—often decorative—was added. In the female version, this strap was attached to the upper edge of the bust-to-ankle procardium at a point between the breasts. The waist-to-calf or waist-to-ankle length male procardium positioned the shoulder strap off center and secured it in back on the opposite side.

Later versions were made with two straps which were very decorative (Figure 2.16). These V-shaped straps were fastened in the center of the upper edge of this garment which revealed the breasts. The double straps of the procardium were sometimes tied together at the back of the neck. There are examples which show that at times the double braces covered the bust.

As this garment was refined in styling, both men and women wore the bust-to-ankle variation. It was worn with or without a belt. If belted, the belt was worn just below the bust. The design of the procardium belt varied, but one style consisted of a long band about five inches wide. This was tied in front, and the trailing ends reached to the hem. The front tabs were often decorated with small, metal shapes and semiprecious stones. These belts added elegance to an otherwise basic body covering.

## KALASIRIS (1000 B.C.)

The **kalasiris** of 1000 B.C. was a simple garment for men and women made from a rectangular length of material (Figure 2.17). The piece of fabric used in making this tunic was twice the height of the wearer from shoulder to ankle. It was folded in half with a slit cut on the fold to create the neckline. The side seams of the sleeveless kalasiris were sewn together, tapering from hem to armhole. The version with sleeves had straight side seams, a slit or round neckline, and elbow-length sleeves. They were often wider or flared at the open end. The latter style was worn with a belt or girdle tied at the normal waistline. Depicted as a close-fitting garment by the artists of the

**Figure 2.16.** Double-strap **procardium,** circular collar, and elaborate crown. Note complex girdling and diamond-shape pattern in straps, all but hidden by the left arm. (Redrawn from wall painting, Tomb of Amanklapodef, detail, XX Dynasty, 1198–1167 B.C., Thebes. Metropolitan Museum of Art, New York City.)

**Figure 2.17.** A simple, close-fitting **kalasiris** of the V Dynasty and the pyramidal wig form typical of earlier styles. (*Wife of the Official, Mitry; A Priestess of Hathor*, Tomb of Sakkara, c. 2500 B.C. Metropolitan Museum of Art, New York City.)

period, the kalasiris was actually amply cut, allowing for ease of movement.

## GALA GOWN (800–600 B.C.)

Simple in construction, the **gala gown** (800–600 B.C.) was a garment worn for festive occasions by men and women (Figure 2.18). The gown was made of very fine linen that was often heavily starched. The rectangular length of fabric was twice the height of the wearer, and the width was that of the wearer's outstretched arms. The fabric was folded in half and covered the figure front and back and from shoulder to ankle. A small, round hole was cut on the fold to form the neckline. This versatile garment was revealing, and often worn as the only body covering, either loose or belted.

Because of the sheer quality of the fabric and the heavy starching, elaborate pleated effects were possible. The pleats were concentrated in the center front, created by creasing the front section in vertical accordion folds and by bringing the back forward and pleating the front edges in the same manner. A slight side drape was thus created over the hips, and pleated sleeves were formed when the gala gown was tightly girdled. The center pleat-

ing radiated upward over the arms, adding breadth to the shoulder line.

This festival garment of royalty was decorated with large, jeweled collars and elaborately designed belts and shendots. Egyptian women often wore massive, circular collars about their necks and decorative braided belts about their waists beneath the gown. On occasion, men wore loose gala gowns over kilts, but generally men wore them as the only body covering.

## GALA SKIRT (2000 B.C.)

The **gala skirt** (2000 B.C.) was a wraparound garment which men wore in much the same manner as the loincloth (Figure 2.19). It was wound around the figure one and one-half times and was held in place by a girdle. The gala skirt varied in length from waist to mid-thigh or waist to mid-calf. The curved front panel, often goffered, was the distinguishing design detail of this male skirt.

If the skirt had a smooth front panel, the large, truncated, triangular projection, the **shendot,** was worn

**Figure 2.18.** Queen Nofretari (left) wears a **gala gown** with goffered sleeve treatment, colored necklace, and handsomely patterned woven girdle. The right-hand figure is dressed in a double-strap **procardium** made of patterned fabric. (Wall painting: Tomb of Nofretari, Valley of the Queens, Thebes, 1292–1225 B.C. Metropolitan Museum of Art, New York City.)

**Figure 2.19.** Goffered **gala skirt** with **klaft** head covering. (*Mitry, Privy Council and Priest of Ma'et,* Tomb of Sakkara, 2500 B.C. Metropolitan Museum of Art, New York City.)

that revealed the nude figure beneath the tight-fitting blouse section and through the deep skirt slit. Frequently, tunics and kalasiris, which were very similar in cut, were made from patterned fabrics (Figure 2.10). Several important queens, including Nefertiti, preferred transparent fashions, and the tunic was said to be this magnificent queen's favorite style.

In the Egyptian culture, interest in the nude figure was a dominant factor in all clothing design. Nobles and servants often went without clothes, and for court dances, they seldom wore more than decorative belts which enhanced their supple bodies and the movements of the dances they performed.

The male tunic, or haik, was a more utilitarian upper-body cover (Figure 2.13). The male version was

as a decorative device. This decoration took many different forms (Figure 2.20). It was either flat and encrusted with jewels and metal shapes, or a stiff three-dimensional projection that was usually goffered or pleated with vertical accordion pleats radiating from the center to the wide hemline. This style might have been created by gathering the skirt in the front, creasing it into pleats, and securing it with a belt. The flat, triangular versions varied in size and shape from long, thin, ankle-length tabs to wide forms that extended to the knees. These styles were attached to belts, which encircled the figure at the waist (Figure 2.6).

The shendot was introduced as a decorative male accessory sometime after 2500 B.C. When the gala skirt was worn without the shendot, it was girdled with a variety of belts which were frequently elaborately patterned and trimmed with fringe. The gala skirt, like the gala gown, was a royal garment.

## HAIK

The **tunic**, or **haik**, worn by Egyptian women was a slender garment with deep bat-wing sleeves and a long center slit from waist to hem. The finest linen was used for women's clothing which was designed to expose the body. The tunic was such a garment, made of transparent fabric

**Figure 2.20.** Calf-length **kilt** of the V Dynasty with rigid, hem-length **shendot.** Note **postiche** held to the face with cords looped around the ears. (Redrawn from statue of Methethy, slightly modified, 2420 B.C. Brooklyn Museum.)

more often shoulder to hipbone in length and was worn tucked into the kilt or loincloth or left to hang free.

## CAPES

While wraps worn for warmth were not necessary in the warm climate of Egypt, thin outer garments or capes were often used by both sexes. Two basic styles persisted for many centuries The earliest cape form was rectangular (Figures 2.2 and 2.3). It was made from a length of fabric slightly longer than twice the height of the wearer and about thirty inches wide. It was placed across the back, brought forward over the shoulders, and arranged over the upper arms. The rectangular cape was fastened in the front with a pin or clasp positioned either at the level of the breast bone or just above the waistline. This cape was never belted, and the ends hung loosely to the ground.

The oval style was made of sheer fabric cut in the form of a circle or an oval. The diameter was equal to the width of the wearer's outstretched arms. A round or elliptical hole was cut in the center for the neck opening. If the neckline was small, a slit was made in the back. It is possible that in some variations of the oval cape the slit extended from the neckline to the hem. A pin was used at the back of the neckline to hold this wrap snugly about the throat.

Tanned animal skins, usually leopard, were worn by warriors. Leopard skins were also part of a priest's liturgical regalia. The furs or skins were never cut or sewn together but were left in the original shape of the animal. The skins of the legs were loosely knotted at the chest with the main body of the animal covering the back, the shoulders, and the upper arms.

# Accessories (3700–500 B.C.)

## HEADWEAR

Headgear, symbolic of royal rank, and crowns in a variety of shapes were worn throughout the many periods of ancient Egypt. The tall, flared cylinder; the tall crown with a knob on top; the high, round tube; and the falcon crown are only a few of the many crowns worn by the kings and queens of Egypt.

The characteristic Egyptian head covering, the kerchief, or **klaft,** was made of stiff, heavy fabric, often shot with gold thread when worn by nobility (Figure 2.19). It was worn low over the forehead, fastened in back, with the side pieces arranged in a pyramidal form that reached to the shoulders. The **Nemes headdress,** a klaft variation worn by royalty, had two elongated tabs that fell in front of the shoulders and covered the chest (Figure 2.6). The simpler form of klaft was generally worn by men and women of less important status.

More decorative, and perhaps in the **golden-veils** classification of jewelry, were the golden-disc and golden-chain wig coverings (Figure 2.4). The discs, often delicately chased, measured about five-eighths of an inch in diameter and were attached to each other with small gold links. Such elaborate golden veils were made in a number of intricate patterns. Some were designed to cover the crown of the head, while others were suspended from a band that encircled the forehead.

The crowns and head-covering devices, as well as the wigs, often were held in position with long hairpins made of thorn, bone, bronze, and gold, that were designed with large, decoratively carved heads.

## FOOTWEAR

Foot coverings were not an important Egyptian accessory. Simple sandals made of woven palm leaves or papyrus with a single, plaited-fiber thong were worn out-of-doors. The thong slipped between the first and second toes and attached to the sole at either side. A sturdy leather sandal with a closed heel and several thong straps arranged over the toes and instep developed during the later period. The sole of this style was made of woven papyrus. Delicate golden duplicates of the single-thong sandal, the funeral sandal, were placed on the feet of mummies.

## JEWELRY

Massive jewelry was an important element of Egyptian costume (Figures 2.1 and 2.21). Beaded collars were fashioned of semiprecious stones, glass, pottery, and hollow gold beads. Beads ornamented this familiar Egyptian accessory in rows; often each row varied in size, shape, and type of bead. Generally, it went about the neck and tied with thin cords in back, forming a circular collar that covered the shoulders and chest.

The Egyptian jewelers and goldsmiths were not slaves to precise duplication of repeated gems and motifs. The variations which occurred between strands of similarly shaped and colored beads in a collar necklace added to the total vitality of the piece. The repetitious, encircling, joined rows of beads were given visual excitement because of these subtle variations. The importance of color in all Egyptian jewelry cannot be assessed in black and white reproductions, but the subtle variations are evident. It is interesting to note that the exacting aesthetic formulas for painting and sculpture were not imposed upon jewelry craftsmen. The myriad styles and intricate patterns of the face-framing collars are evidence of these jewelers' creative ingenuity.

Signet rings were important finger accessories for they were used as official signatures on documents. The engraved stone set of a ring pivoted on the shank, and often each side was decorated with an intaglio image, such as a scarab on one side and a signature hieroglyphic on the other. Other simple band rings, sometimes made of twisted wires of gold, were also worn.

Wide, gold bracelets, made in two parts, were hinged on one side and fastened on the other with an invisible clasp. Egyptians used a number of decorative techniques, including designs created by an enamellike surface. Large segmented bracelets were also hinged together and fastened with hidden latches. This style was set with small sphinx or lion motifs carved from alabaster or other colorful stones.

Single-strand necklaces were made of pottery beads of many shapes—hollow, round, gold beads, and beads of "stone that melts" (glass). Flat gold segments made in the shapes of highly stylized plants, animals, and insects provided other forms of neckwear. The fly design appeared repeatedly as one of the motifs for necklaces and bracelets. Each segment was a copy of the first but not an exact duplicate, and such design variations gave these pieces an interesting and vital quality.

Long, dangling earrings made of gold or "white metal" (silver) formed large, elegant pieces of jewelry that added interest to the emphasis areas of head and shoulders. Large, gold loops, pottery beads arranged in alternating colors and shapes, and a basic pendant style became characteristic earring forms.

## HANDHELD ACCESSORIES

The large feather fan, or umbrella fan, was a symbol of importance. In its manufacture, feathers arranged in a half circle were fitted into a decorative holder that was attached to a long handle. Others were made in the shapes of large leaves and mounted on golden staffs. This type, carried by a slave, served several purposes: for protection from the sun, for creating slight breezes, for adding pomp to festivals, and for driving away insects. Indoors, groups of slaves—each slave with a fan moving gently—kept the air circulating. Individuals used single feather fans, also mounted on long handles. Both types were made of multicolored feathers set in handles decorated with stylized plant or animal-head forms.

The attention given to grooming made the mirror an important personal accessory. The Egyptian mirror was made in a variety of shapes but was usually one of three: oval, pear, or round. Copper or mixed metals polished to a high luster supplied the reflective section, set into a handle which was eight or ten inches long. Handles were made of ivory, wood, or faience, and were beautifully decorated with carved images of birds, flowers, and animals. All Egyptian women, even women slaves, possessed mirrors.

## COSMETICS

The Egyptian toilette included numerous cosmetics. Oils and perfumes were used extensively. During one period, a scented cake of congealed fat was customarily placed on top of the hair (Figure 2.12). As the fat melted, the oils trickled down the face and body, giving off a sweet or spicy aroma. Dyes were used on wigs and hair, as well as on eyebrows and lashes. Lip rouge and eyeliner also greatly enhanced the beauty of these appearance-conscious people.

## BEARDS

Although the custom of being clean shaven at all times prevailed, except when in mourning, pharoahs and queens affected false beards. These were primarily ceremonial accessories that symbolized masculine authority. Made of hair, the beards were of a rectangular shape about 4 inches long and 2 inches wide. Two thin cords with loop ends that were slipped over the ears held each beard in place at the tip of the chin. This false beard was known as a **postiche** (Figure 2.20).

## GARMENT DETAILING

Immigrants introduced bone and bronze buttons into ancient Egypt some time between 2500 B.C. and 1200 B.C. The buttons were used as decorations rather than as fastening devices.

Elaborate embroidery typified Egyptian costumes. One style, worked with a needle, combined linen thread and tufted woolen loops. The motifs often were derived from religious origins and included lotus, papyrus, and geometric patterns. In many cases, the entire kalasiris was embroidered. Gold and silver beaten out with a hammer and cut into thin strips were used as embroidery thread in combination with the more common dyed linen thread. There are indications that this silver and gold thread was worked into a "network of gold," which quite possibly constituted the earliest known form of lace. However, this golden network was not made with the refined pattern usually associated with the lace which was created as a uniformly designed trim in about the sixteenth century A.D.

Fringe, as a garment decoration, resulted from tying off the extra lengths of warp thread of the material. Tassels evolved from this same practice and developed into more complex forms by braiding, twisting, and tying the ends. Fringe and tassels were shot with gold thread when gold thread was used in weaving the basic length of garment fabric. Fringe is mentioned in an antique record listing gifts brought to a pharaoh of the Eighteenth Dynasty. Ribbons were decorative woven bands. They were sewn on just above the fringe to prevent raveling of the fabric. Braid, woven or plaited from bits of handsome fabric, formed belts, girdles, and head, neck, and arm ornaments.

All colors were used except red, which was considered the color of violence. During the later dynasties, white was the color used for the major garment, accented by green, yellow, blue, and magenta.

# Hairstyles (3000–500 B.C.)

Hair and wigs were an important part of the total Egyptian costume. Great care was taken in arranging wigs and real hair. Throughout most of the periods, shaved heads remained the sign of nobility and were always covered. This practice was dictated by the attention these people gave to cleanliness.

In place of their natural hair, ancient Egyptians wore wigs made of human hair, wool, flax, palm fiber, felt, and other materials (Figure 2.21). Wigs were usually black; however, deep blue and gilded wigs were worn also. The wig was constructed over a close-fitting skullcap made of fiber netting. The method used in attaching the natural hair or other materials to the net cap created a large wig with the hair standing out from the skull. This kind of construction formed insulation and protected the wearer's head from the hot rays of the sun. The wigs were intricately arranged and very decorative. Wig styles ranged from simple, closely cropped, head-hugging designs during the Old Kingdom to complicated styles of later periods. Early wigs had curls arranged in rows from the crown of the head to just below the ears. The larger

**Figure 2.22.** Wig styling of the late period when the hair fell down in back and had two face-framing tabs in front. This is a portrait of Cleopatra who is wearing one of the many official crowns which combined the falcon and sun-disc symbol. *(Portrait of Cleopatra,* bas-relief, Temple of Denderah, Ptolemaic period. Courtesy of the Egypt Exploration Society.)

**Figure 2.21.** A style of pencil-curl wig and a necklace collar. (Statue: *Prince Rahotep and His Wife Nofret,* detail. Egyptian Museum, Cairo.)

versions were made of human hair with lamb's wool added to create the desired full, bouffant style that fell straight from the crown to the shoulders. Wig styles favored by men were imitated by women during the early centuries. Generally, the closely cropped style worn over a completely bald head was preferred by both. Later, women reversed this preference, wearing wigs of great bulk over their natural hair. Their own hair was allowed to show beneath the wig.

**Gala wigs** (1000 B.C.) of festive design with golden decorations and colorful braid or bead trimmings were worn much as hats are today (Figure 2.22). By this time the fetish for cleanliness had been abandoned. A "crown cap" of golden pendant discs, linked closely together, was often worn over the wig, all but obscuring the hair. Gold circlettes and colorful braid headbands were worn low on the forehead. The famous bust of Nefertiti indicates that at

**Figure 2.23.** Nefertiti wearing royal headdress without a wig. (Netertiti bust, copy of original. Los Angeles County Museum of Art.)

crown of the head. The hair that was left was then braided and allowed to fall down the back or over one shoulder. Young boys had their heads shaved except for the **youth lock**, a small curl originating in front of one ear.

In time, the short, round adult wig fashions were discarded, and, during the Middle Kingdom, shoulder-length, braided wigs were worn. As wig forms continued to change, they lengthened, and, by the Eighteenth Dynasty, the hair in back was long enough to cover the shoulder blades. The hair in front was shorter and pulled forward to frame the face. The dominant fashion for centuries was the **balloon-shaped wig** (Figure 2.5). This wig style was made up of many tiny braids or pencil-thin curls.

Creams, dyes, oils, and fixatives were used to care for the hair and wig. Intricately made crowns and hat forms, symbolically indicating rank, were worn over the wigs.

The slaves and servants of Egypt were not allowed to wear wigs or to shave their heads; however they fashioned their own hair in elaborate styles that mimicked the wigs of the nobility. Mud and clay were used by the lower classes to set their hair into large, bouffant shapes. Black felt caps, shaped like the wigs of royalty, were also worn by slaves. Warriors wore heavy fiber wigs as head protection, for Egyptians never devised helmets of metal.

times she wore her crown without a wig (Figure 2.23). She was noted, however, for her large, deep blue wigs.

During one period, beginning about 1400 B.C., a shaved, artificially elongated head was the fashion. The distortion of the head was achieved by wearing a padded form at the nape of the neck. This strange vogue was originated by the daughters of Nefertiti, whose heads had been deformed at birth and whose appearance was copied by the women of the court.

Early hair and wig styles were short, with small curls arranged in horizontal rows. Wigs were worn by adults, while children's hair was cut, shaved, and styled in a number of unique coifs. Young girls' heads were often shaved except for two locks in front of each ear. These were either curled into long corkscrew curls or braided. During other periods, the head was shaved except for the

FOOTNOTES

1. Helen Gardner, *Art Through the Ages*, p. 24.
2. Lionel Casson, *Ancient Egypt*, p. 12.
3. Ibid., p. 111.
4. Raymond Somers Stites, *The Arts and Men*, p. 97.
5. Casson, *Ancient Egypt*, p. 104.
6. Louise Pickney Sooy, *Syllabus on Costume*, p. 4; and François Boucher, *20,000 Years of Fashion*, p. 94.
7. Ludmila Kybalová; Olga Herbenová; and Milena Lamarová; *The Pictorial Encyclopedia of Fashion*, p. 40.
8. Ahmad Badawi, *Le Costume Dans L'Egypt Ancienne*, p. 8
9. Kybalová, Herbenová, and Lamarová, *Encyclopedia of Fashion*, p. 40.

# Chapter 3
# Dress of Crete
## (3000–1400 B.C.)

Behind the cultural development of Greece lay the influences of several prehistoric peoples and early civilizations. One of the more dominant of these civilizations was the Minoan. This civilization was stabilized on the Isle of Crete, a geographical island bridge between Asia Minor and the Grecian peninsula, the southernmost region of Europe. Between this landmass and that of Turkey are numerous small islands in the Aegean, of which Crete is the largest.

On this scattering of islands, three different social orders evolved during the second and third millennia B.C. Archaeologists have named these the Aegean cultures and have categorized them as the Cretan or Minoan culture; the Cycladic culture, occupying the chain of islands north of Crete; and the Hellenic culture, located on the mainland of Greece. Each of these Aegean cultures had three developmental phases. The three phases of the Minoan civilization coincide chronologically with the three major phases of the ancient Egyptian social and political structure.

Very little was known about the Minoan civilization until excavations were begun in the late nineteenth century. Much of the information available prior to 1870 was supposition gleaned from Homer's *Iliad*. Even the name Minoan was derived from the legendary King Minos of Crete.[1] Two scholars, Heinrich Schliemann (in 1870) and Sir Arthur Evans (in 1900) were the first to undertake the task of sifting for finds at the excavation sites. They tested lore against the artifacts recovered during several digs. Eventually they arrived at a factual base by which the ancient Cretans might be understood.

Information relating to the origins of the Cretans and the nature of their social order is obscure, although their identifiable culture spanned the period between the third and first millennia B.C. There are indications that the Minoan culture developed contemporaneously with that of ancient Egypt and that the two other Aegean cultures predate these societies by several centuries. The Cycladic island culture (7000–2000 B.C.) has been determined as the most immediate civilization preceding that of the Minoan in the Aegean. The Cretans assimilated much from their neighbors through trade with the kingdoms of North Africa and, Asia Minor and the civilizations bordering the Aegean. Whether the impetus for the growth of the

**Figure 3.1.** This skirt style is believed to have been a bifurcated style worn with the usual bare-breasted bodice. (Redrawn from wall painting, Tiryns, c. 1400 B.C. National Museum, Athens.)

Minoan civilization came from these outside sources or whether it was inspired by the society's natural vital character has not been determined.

It is believed that the population of Crete was composed primarily of the Grimaldi-Negroid people from southern Europe and the Celto-Germanic races.[2] Indeed, the population was made up of many diverse migrating peoples including Dorians, Achaeans, Cydonians, and Pelasgians.

The Minoan civilization at its zenith embraced the island of Crete and mainland areas including Mycenae, Tiryns, and Troy. It was the most curious of the civilizations centered in the Aegean. While Crete had the richest culture of these sea-bound civilizations, there were several periods when the Minoan social order and life-style all but disappeared. Because of these recurring periods of obliteration, Minoan culture did not have a steady evolutionary development. It has been assumed that the three known destructions were caused by external forces, perhaps by a cataclysmic natural force such as a violent earthquake. Because of the violent erasures of its cultural advances, the Early Minoan period (2800–2000 B.C.) made slow strides toward establishing a social and political structure more sophisticated than a basic Neolithic system. The social order centered about village life. Trade routes were established, and commerce between Egypt and Crete may have been one of the growth-motivating factors for the Minoan civilization. By 2700 B.C. and throughout the second millennium, there occurred important strides toward the culture's ultimate sophistication.

During this period, the Minoans developed a workable writing system. The earliest writing was a hieroglyphic form called Minoan script. Around 1750 B.C. it was supplanted by Linear A, a more stylized stroke form, which remained in use for about three centuries until it was supplanted by Linear B. Linear A has yet to be deciphered. Linear B was deciphered in 1952 when it was discovered to be an early variation of archaic Greek. Linear B was a cumbersome writing form confined primarily to keeping inventories, receipts, and accounts. It was of little use in recording the social and political structure of Crete.

Contemporary archaeologists have established the period of stable society on Crete between 3400 B.C. and 1100 B.C. At the height of the Minoan civilization there were ninety urban settlements on the mountainous island of Crete, which lies 250 miles off the coast of North Africa. The landmass of Crete is in excess of 3000 square miles with the greatest length east to west at 160 miles. At the widest point, the isle is thirty-five miles, at its narrowest, a mere six. The Levka Ori mountain range has peaks which reach altitudes of over 7500 feet. The coastline on the northern side of the island has many accessible and protected bays. The southern coast, however, is steep and craggy and offers a natural fortification.

Despite the island's mountains and caves, the tillable lands were then very fertile and the Minoans were able to establish an agriculturally based economy, using the surplus agricultural products for trade with their neighbors. Agricultural products, beautifully handcrafted pottery, and silversmithed goods packed in amphoras were loaded onto Minoan sailing vessels to ply the Mediterranean and Aegean seas.[3]

The people that made up the Minoan civilization naturally made their original migrations by sea. Seafaring was a logical means of maintaining commercial ties with the known world. Their initial arrival seems to have been planned, and they had thoughtfully brought with them the essentials for their life-style. Some of these essentials included livestock (pigs, sheep, cattle), seeds, and tools. There is evidence that they cultivated barley, Eurasian wheat, peas, beans, and olive trees. By 2000 B.C. a giant thalassocracy was established—a thriving social and economic system based on seafaring trade of these products. The trade routes of this sea empire extended westward to the French port known today as Marseilles and in the Aegean to Rhodes, Cyprus, and Thebes on the Greek mainland.

The greatest Minoan palaces known in modern times were erected at Knossos, Mallia, and Phaistos, site of the summer palace in the south. Each of these was destroyed and then rebuilt three times at approximate 100-year intervals. The interiors of the gigantic structures were elegantly appointed, and the room arrangements were mazelike. Broad stairways, lightwells, and large, though low-ceilinged, apartment living spaces opened into courtyards. Plumbing was developed to an efficient level, and hot and cold water flowed from gold or silver taps. Sewage was carried off efficiently. Cellars of great size were used to store grain, olive oil, and wine in ceramic vessels as tall as a human. The living-area walls were decorated with scenes of feasts, festivals, and daily activities; these scenes are the only record of the life-style of the Minoan civilization.

The Minoans depicted in the wall paintings seem to have had a vigorous and fun-loving character. Their energetic and graceful ritualistic performances to honor the sacred bulls display their lithe physiques (Figure 3.2). Their narrow, cinched waists accentuated broad shoulders and slim, long legs. Male and female youths shown somersaulting over the backs of bulls clearly illustrate that both sexes participated in athletic activities.[4] Young females are depicted with fair, white skin, while male youths are always bronzed, presumably a result of the clear sun's rays. There is a debonair quality about the performers in this rite, and movements of precision and grace were qualities admired by the Minoans.

Perhaps equally characteristic of the Minoans is an interest in complexity. This assumption is based on the mazelike quality of their palace living spaces, the intricacy of the female skirt design, and the involved designs on silver cups. Rhythmic organizational arrangements dominated the linear patterns of Minoan art. The decorative motifs employed by Minoan artisans were based on the human figure, plantlife, and the sea.

Not every Minoan inhabitant enjoyed the grandeur of a palace environment. While the palace of Knossos was the city's center, with broad boulevards leading to it, the commoners lived in helterskelter hovels surrounding it. Wattle-and-daub huts served as housing for the peasants. The upper classes resided nearby in great homes with luxurious appointments, central heating systems, and bathrooms with silver and gold basins and bathtubs. Utilitarian objects were highly refined and included gold and silver cups with repoussé decorations, pottery vessels of eggshell thinness, and gaming boards of ivory, gold, and silver, elaborately inlaid and engraved. Comfort and luxury were of major concern to wealthy Minoans.

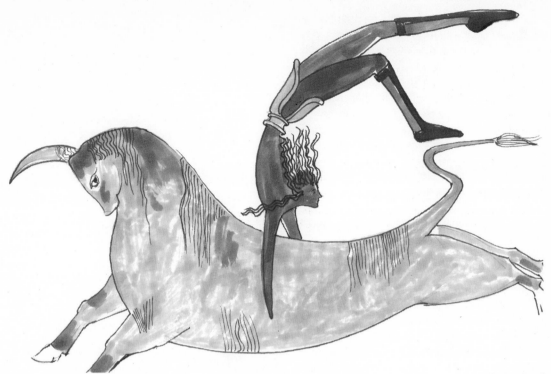

**Figure 3.2.** Clad only in **phallustaches,** young men and women of Crete performed skillfully on and over the backs of bulls. *(The Toreador Fresco,* 1500 B.C. Archaeological Museum, Candia, Crete.)

Cretans did not fortify their palaces or cities, and weapons were not used until the height of the thalassocratic political structure. The Cretans were neither invaders nor conquerors; they were traders, planters, and artisans who were seemingly self-sufficient and content with the landmass on which they had settled. Crete was able to support their demands for the luxurious life.

The manner in which Cretans clad themselves reinforces the assumption that they had a great capacity to enjoy the sun-drenched isle on which they lived. They reveled in the forms, shapes, and actions of the human body and they chose costumes which revealed and enhanced the body's natural form. The crown of the female head with its almost whimsical rampant curls, the face-framing "snake curls," the revealed upper torso, and the unshod feet all emphasize delight in the female figure. Male figures, completely nude or in patterned **pagne** also reinforce this emphasis. The bare bosoms depicted in goddess statuettes hint at the interest in sensuality. Many of the goddesses were images dedicated to fertility. The pagne, a phallic sheath worn by males, further emphasized an erotic quality perhaps inherent in Minoan religion.[5]

The Cretan women were as zestful as their garb indicates. Included in all of the activities of this civilization, they attended the hunts and sports events as either observers or participants. The clever Minoan seamstress fashioned exotic blouse and skirt styles more complex than the female apparel of their contemporary civilizations. Cretan women were said to be the "best dressed of the known world." To earn this appellation, the ladies of Crete took great care with their toilette as well as with their clothing. Because of this clothes consciousness, styles changed frequently.

Blouses and skirts were altered in design but the skirts changed more radically and with greater frequency. Originally bell shaped and snugly fitted over the hips, the skirt was altered through the years until, in the Late Minoan period, it was intricately tiered and ruffled. Some authorities suggest that a hoop skirt made of reeds was worn as an undergarment to maintain the desired fullness.[6] Swags of ribbons and garlands of flowers were often used to embellish the skirts. The most elaborate and costly decorative treatment was composed of golden plaques sewn all over the skirt. These hinged plaques were created in many fanciful forms, including butterflies, cuttlefish, and palm leaves.

There is also some indication that Minoan females wore bifurcated skirts closely resembling the lounging pajamas of the 1920s or the bell-bottom pants of the 1970s. This is an assumption based on wall paintings such as the one shown in Figure 3.1. It is quite possible that a bifurcated skirt was being illustrated because there is a decided double curve at the hem, and the patch-quilt pattern below the pelvis may have been intended to suggest pant legs. This assumption cannot be proven, of course, for no actual garments of this civilization have survived. Because of the stylized imagery so characteristic of the art of this culture, it is impossible to determine the exact form.

The silhouettes of the Minoan full-skirt forms accentuated the minute, cinched waists. It has also been suggested that Cretan women were the first females to wear figure-controlling corsets, which are believed to have been constructed with bronze stays arranged vertically at intervals. Attention was focused on the waist by wearing decorative leather or metal cinch belts which were bejeweled and encrusted with precious metal rosettes— further evidence of Minoan elegance. Other jeweled accessories included dangling earrings and ropes of pearls worn around the neck or entwined in intricately coiffed hair.

While the skirt forms were often modified, the basic bare-bosomed bodice pattern was retained throughout the Cretan period. During the Middle Minoan period (2100 B.C.), the bodice was styled with a tall, standing collar. The collar was discarded by 1500 B.C., and sleeves, which had always remained elbow length, became the focal point. They were snug at first and evolved into a puffed form. Some frescoes and statuette images suggest that the puffed sleeve form was tied to the bodice front and back.

Minoan men were equally intrigued with the potential of clothing as body decoration. In the earliest period, Minoan styles for men were similar to those of other Paleolithic and Neolithic males. The basic male garments—loincloth, pagne, and **phallustache**—were worn from the waist to below the buttocks. A type of short trouser was also worn, but this is believed to be a later garment form introduced after many years of association with Near Eastern people. In the wall painting, *The Prince in Fleur-de-lis Crown* (Figure 3.3), the prince seems to be wearing such a garment. This author has concluded that these shorts were fashioned by tucking a rectangle of fabric under the cinch belt, passing it between the legs, and securing it on the opposite side of the figure in the same manner. Of course, this is conjecture but it is a conclusion arrived at after close scrutiny of images in the remaining wall paintings.

In many festival garments, trim for male garb was devised of chains of pearls, ribbon strips, and nets of leather. Men also wore handsome leather or metal cinch belts over the pagne, which was fashioned of leather, wool, or linen. Many of these garments resembled a double apron with points front and back. The point in the back had an attached tassel which may have been an element retained from the animal-tail-secured kaunakes of prehistoric times. Perhaps the animal-skin belt affected by some wearers was a remnant of the same fetish about the magical powers of animals' tails.

Neither men nor women wore shoes of any form indoors. However, they did wear a wide variety of foot

**Figure 3.3.** The garment worn by this prince is the sheath loincloth, or **phallustache.** The back of the figure is covered with a curved apron form. The right leg is draped with what appears to be part of the underloincloth, suggesting a pant leg. (Redrawn from wall painting of *The Prince in Fleur-de-lis Crown*, c. 1550–1450 B.C. Palace of Knossos, Crete.)

coverings when going outside. These included calf-high boots of white, buff, or red leather, and decorative sandals sometimes covered with gaily colored beads. Ankle-high, foot-concealing, soft leather shoes, often with high heels, were the favorite female footwear for shopping expeditions.

Men and women bathed daily, applied scented oils, and enjoyed daily massages. The ritual tumblers' bodies glistened as they performed because of oil rubs. Skin care and hair care occupied many hours of the day for the leisure classes. It can be assumed that eye and eyebrow makeup was used extensively. Note the differing angles of commerce between the Aegean trading communities. Examples of the intricacy of the dyeing processes can be found on existing artifacts. A record of a color process exists on a shrine drawing discovered at Knossos. The motifs used on the printed fabrics included purple crocuses, red and yellow boughs, swallows, and other nature forms. Intricately stitched and elaborately embellished, Cretan costumes made Minoan women the fashion figures of the ancient world.

According to carbon-dated remains, Minoan civilization vanished between 1500 B.C. and 1300 B.C. Their art, never grandiose, is the only available record of these people. It is strange that they erected so few monuments to themselves, because they were highly skilled structural and architectural engineers. They contributed to and borrowed from the contemporary civilizations geographically adjacent to them. They evolved a highly refined culture in a rather short span of time. A proud people, intensely interested in nature, they were bound by a strange religious cult. They lived and thrived in a mild climate, then their civilization vanished. When, by natural calamity or cataclysmic war, the Minoans were forced to forsake their island, they fled to many lands, including mainland Greece. It was to this next great civilization that they contributed most directly.

**Figure 3.4.** Two noble ladies riding in a horse-drawn chariot to games or the hunt. They wear the Mycenaean-Greek version of a sleeved gown. (Wall painting, Tiryns, thirteenth century B.C. National Archaeological Museum, Athens.)

the brows of the noble women in Figure 3.4. The brows may have been plucked and cosmetically extended so that they reached almost to the hairline. Eyeliner may also have been employed, as evidenced by the large and pronounced eyes in almost all the surviving images.

Technical advances made highly refined body embellishments possible. Minoan needles must have been skillfully fashioned. The art of weaving and techniques for manufacturing dyes were important technical advancements which contributed to the sophistication of Cretan fashion. The first woven textiles were made from wool. Spindle weights have been found that indicate that these people had known the rudimentary techniques of spinning and weaving since the Neolithic period. As the climate altered and skill in agriculture increased, flax was cultivated and used to weave linen for clothing. Spinning and weaving were home industries, and the art of these crafts was highly regarded, for even the queen's apartments at Knossos were identified by a distaff placed over the entry. As this ancient civilization progressed, the woven fabrics often were heavily embroidered.

While weaving was a home activity, the dyeing of fabrics was not. The dyes used were of vegetable or shellfish origin. Trade in dye materials was a major item of

# Basic Garments of Crete (2000–1100 B.C.)

## LOINCLOTH OR SHENTI (1700–1550 B.C.)

Between 1700 B.C. and 1500 B.C., Cretan men wore four basic styles of **pagne**, loincloth, or **shenti.** The simplest was a thigh-length skirt or **phallustache** (Figure 3.5), worn in much the same manner as the Egyptian version of this garment. As a rule, it covered the figure from waist to mid-thigh. Another basic style was the **wraparound skirt,** which generally was ankle length. More complex designs included the short skirt with frontal sheath, and the apron loincloth.

The **short skirt** consisted of a back panel that barely covered the buttocks and a rigidly constructed leather form for the protection of the male organs (Figure 3.3). The panel had curved edges that came forward, just covering the loins.

The **apron loincloth** style was made of a triangular piece of fabric with the point worn in the front. The point was often greatly exaggerated and turned upward, held up by some type of stiffening to create a taillike appendage if it was worn in the rear. Double-apron loincloths were fashioned with points front and back. Multiskirt arrangements of this same style created a tiered skirt variation of this basic male garment.

**Figure 3.5.** Male apron **phallustache** and cinch belt of the Late Minoan period. (Redrawn from wall painting, Palace of Knossos, Crete.)

Polychrome loincloths were introduced about the fifteenth century B.C. Some styles, both elegant and costly, were decorated with fringe. It is believed that materials such as heavy woolen fabric, fine linen, and leather were used in making these male garments. The design of the loincloth depended on the plastic qualities of the materials used.

To emphasize the small waists so characteristic of all Cretans, **cinch belts** of leather or metal were worn with the loincloths (Figure 3.5).[7] The metal belts had rolled edges and were studded with copper, silver, or gold rosettes. Spiral and stylized floral patterns also were used as decorative devices. These belts were often soldered around the waists of children at the ages of six or seven to ensure that as adults they would have the desired waist girth of not more than twelve inches. This practice was begun about 1700 B.C. and lasted until 1550 B.C. The narrowness of the waist made the shoulder and chest areas of the figure seem more robust by comparison.

The apron or **double-apron loincloth** was preferred by early Minoan women when they engaged in athletic events and was not the usual everyday female costume (Figure 3.6). It was made of patterned fabrics with geometrically ordered borders and fringe trim and was worn with the decorative metal belt. Males also wore the double-apron loincloth (Figure 3.7), but each section of it was generally more triangular than the pieces used for women's garments.

**Figure 3.6.** Bare-bosomed females wearing single and double-apron **phallustaches** (or loincloths) of the Late Minoan period (1450–1373 B.C.). (Redrawn from wall painting of *Procession of Cretan Women*, Palace of Knossos, Crete.)

with the shorts. The simple chiton was worn hanging free or tucked into the cinch belt.

## SKIRT (2000 B.C.)

Around 2000 B.C. women wore bell or tiered skirts as illustrated in Figures 3.8 and 3.9. In earliest times, the tiered effect may have been created by wearing several skirts of varying lengths with one on top of the other. During later periods, the skirt assumed a conical shape as a result of the rather complex method used in creating the garment. This Cretan skirt style indicates that sewing and dressmaking techniques were highly refined.

The bell skirt was made of long bands of fabric, gathered on one edge to make a ruffle, or **volant,** which were sewn onto a simple skirt in tiers. The flounces creating the tiers were sometimes of equal size and sometimes of graduated size with the smallest at the waist. Each row of volants was separated by elaborate ornamentation. At one time in Cretan fashion, the skirt fitted the figure snugly from waist to hips, where flounced ruffles were attached to cascade to the floor in ever-widening circles about the legs. Later bell-skirt styles were designed with pleated rather than gathered volants. This costume was in existence for many centuries, appearing on women depicted in seals dated as early as 2400 B.C. This first visual record showed the multilayer style.

There is no complete record of the Minoan people, and it is not known whether Cretan women wore the first

**Figure 3.7.** Late Minoan male wears a double-apron loincloth with **diphtera.** (Redrawn from wall painting, Archaeological Museum, Harakleion, Crete.)

## SHORTS

A form of extremely brief pants or shorts for men was introduced very late in the Minoan period. The general acceptance of this garment form is questionable, for they were referred to in ancient records as "garments of demons" or as "garments of foreigners."[8]

## TUNIC

The males of Crete wore snug-fitting tunics with the brief shorts. The simple tunic form was made by folding a length of fabric in half and sewing up the side seams. A modest space was left just below the fold on either side seam for an armhole. A slit or round hole cut on the fold acted as a neck opening. A basic **chiton,** made by pinning two rectangular pieces of material together on the shoulders, was an alternate upper body covering worn

**Figure 3.8.** These figures illustrate the basic silhouette of the Cretan female costume. The figure on the left wears a hoop-supported skirt; the breadth is greater across than through. The figure on the right wears a bodice and a skirt known as the bell shape. (Diagrammatic sketch: Minoan votive figures. Archaeological Museum, Herakleion, Crete.)

made of a series of hinged metal plates, each about two inches wide by three inches long.

The fabrics used for bell and tiered skirts were linen or wool, depending on the season of the year. Wool was the earliest fabric used, regardless of the climate. After textile trade developed it is possible that the finely pleated volants were made of linen. Unfortunately, no actual remnants of the materials used by these people exist because of the destructive effects of the hot, dry climate of the region.

Small snake-goddess figurines of the period indicate that the colors of the skirts ranged from white through beige to deep, rich browns. Blues and reds were chosen as accent colors, and there is some evidence that more brilliant shades of yellow, red orange, and bright purple were used. Often the skirt tiers were made of fabric in

**Figure 3.9.** This drawing of a polychrome terra-cotta figure illustrates the typical bodice, cinch belt, and tiered skirt of the Late Minoan period. The skirt section is made of gathered rows of multicolored pieces of fabric, over which is worn an apron form. (Redrawn from *Serpent Goddess,* c. 1600 B.C., Knossos. Archaeological Museum, Herakleion, Crete.)

hoop skirts to extend the tiered and the bell skirts in the desired shape. All visual records indicate that the tiered and bell skirts were very stiff and rigid. If there were hoops under the skirts, they could have been made of bone and braid or other available materials, such as reeds (Figure 3.10). A series of underaprons of graduated size could also have served as a functional skirt support. Starches, known and used by the Egyptians to set the horizontal and radiating pleats of their kilts, gala skirts, and gala gowns, may also have been used to hold the tiered skirt in the bell or conical shapes. By 1700 B.C. the female skirt became much slimmer and was tightly fitted over the hips and thighs.

The skirt was usually belted or double girdled with a braid-trimmed tab sash. The double girdle was arranged by placing the sash about the waist, crossing it in the back and bringing it to the front, where it was tied. The metal belt, with its rolled edges, was also worn with the skirt. If neither belt nor sash was used, a corset was worn that was

**Figure 3.10.** Cretan bell skirt with padded reed supports, drawn from a description written by François Boucher, director of the French Center for Costume Studies and the honorary curator of Musée Carnavalet, Paris. The illustration also shows the bare-bosom bodice worn over a gossamer undershift.

alternating colors and arranged to form a checkerboard-patterned skirt.

The decorative bands between each flounce were made of braid. The design motifs for this trim included geometric forms, leaf shapes, trellis patterns, and stylized wave borders. Oval and lozenge shapes were popular decorative elements of the Late Cretan period.

## BLOUSE (2000 B.C.)

Around 2000 B.C. women wore snug-fitting blouses with the skirts. The breast-exposing, plunging necklines may well have been sophisticated adaptations of the forms created when untanned hides were worn to cover the upper body. Usually the neckline was trimmed with a band. The body of the garment was laced together in center front at the waist. Cretan blouses were made with

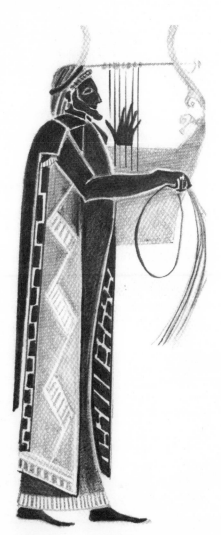

**Figure 3.11.** Late Minoan male garments, including a floor-length gown with short sleeves and a wrap called the **diphtera,** a forerunner of the Greek himation. (Redrawn from vase painting, Late Minoan. Vatican Museum.)

three different types of sleeves: tight sleeves, cap sleeves, and puffed sleeves. The puffed sleeves were held by braids or ribbons crisscrossed in back.

The shifts or undergarments worn by women were made of transparent fabric with a round or oval neckline. All women, except priestesses, wore this garment which, though transparent, did fill in the front of the blouse, functioning as part of its overall design.

In the late Minoan period the blouse was designed with a high, standing collar which framed the back of the head. Two styles of the blouse dominated throughout the period. One was designed with side panels that curved snugly under the bust with a triangular shape beneath the lacings separating the breasts. The other style had sides curving counter to the bustline and the two blouse halves were separated by about three inches between the lacings.

## CLOAK (2000–1000 B.C.)

A simple though ample rectangle of woolen cloth, often trimmed with fringe, formed the protective cloak worn by the Cretan people between 2000 B.C. and 1000 B.C. Both sexes used this very simple style of outer garment exclusively for traveling in their high-speed chariots. For other occasions, a brief cape or **diphtera** was worn as a light wrap (Figure 3.11). The diphtera was first made of animal skins but later was fashioned of heavy woolen material and still later of linen. The vase drawings and wall paintings of the period illustrate that a shawl form of rather stiff fabric was worn also. This shawl may easily have been the diphtera. It was worn wrapped quite high behind the head, drawn over the shoulders, and held in the center front by one hand. This shawl form did not extend below the elbows.

## BOLERO JACKET

A small bolero jacket with short, curved cuffs on the sleeves was a decorative as well as a functional light wrap for women. It was designed in the same manner as the female blouse, snug fitting and with a plunging neckline. It was made of the same fabrics (linen or wool) as other Cretan apparel in bright colors, including yellow, red, blue, and purple, and trimmed with braid or with embroidered bands, using traditional design motifs of the culture.

## GOWN

The one-piece gown, used primarily for ceremonial purposes, was worn at festivals by men and women. Dating this garment is difficult, but, judging from the simplicity of design, it was a remnant of an earlier period and was elevated to ceremonial status in deference to its antiquity. This gown was a simple, sleeved tunic which clung to the figure rather snugly, with a slight flare at the hem (Figure 3.12). Bands of contrasting colors—reds, deep blues, ochres, and blue greens—were used to trim

**Figure 3.12.** Young man wears a simple long tunic, which was used for warmth. More decorative, transparent garments of this styling were worn by men and women over loincloths or **phallustaches.** (Redrawn from sarcophagus painting, Gagia Triade, Late Minoan. Archaeological Museum, Herakleion, Crete.)

the edges of the neckline and sleeves. The decorative bands about the neck extended down the center front to the hem.

## CASSOCK

The cassock was a ceremonial outer garment worn by men, which also protected the wearer from the elements. It had large hinged segments similar to those used in the construction of the **cuirass,** the protective battle apparel. These hinged segments were arranged to give maximum coverage to the arms, and it can be assumed that the cassock was used principally during military victory spectaculars.

# Accessories (2000–1100 B.C.)

## HEADWEAR

Historians believe that the hat was introduced into Europe by the Cretans. Head coverings took many exotic shapes, such as towering truncated cones with tiered effects, turbans, tricorns, and styles with tall, pointed crowns. Decorative trims were equally imaginative and elaborate; rosettes and curled plumes combined with ribbon streamers to add gay touches to Cretan headwear.

## FOOTWEAR

Although Cretan women were not housebound, in wall paintings they were depicted with extremely fair complexions, indicating little exposure to the sun's rays. It has been assumed that, while much of the time was spent indoors, slippers or shoe forms were not worn inside dwellings. This assumption is based on the contrasting condition of the remains of interior and exterior stairways. Exterior stairs were deeply grooved, while interior ones showed little or no wear. Slippers, shoes with heels, and high boots were worn by women when they ventured outdoors. These forms of footwear were functional rather than decorative, but there were several shoe styles, some with heels.[9] Small, ankle-high boots rather like those worn in the nineteenth century A.D. were also worn. Sandals, which men and women apparently wore for party occasions, were intricately cross-laced and decorated with beads.

Men, who spent more time outdoors than women, preferred heavy half boots because of the rugged Cretan terrain. The closed, calf-high boots were tied about the lower leg with thongs. Men also wore another boot style. Those worn while tumbling over bulls' backs were knee-high and buff, white, or red in color. A leather strap covered the shin and a strap encircled the leg just below the knee (Figure 3.2). According to visual records, the foot was completely covered. Men wore sandals when going about the streets of the city. These were made with a leather sole and were cross-laced up the lower leg with thongs. Leather of red, white, and natural color was the basic boot material. Men also went barefoot indoors.

## JEWELRY

For some time, historians believed the Cretan society to have been a rather poor society. The remains of the civilization were so scant that an accurate picture of the true economic condition or social order was difficult to piece together. However, recent archaeological finds indicate that the Cretan culture was rich and possessed the techniques of fine jewelry making and highly refined metalcraft.[10]

On the small figurines in existence, it is difficult to determine the exact forms of the accessories. It has been recently ascertained that Cretan jewelry was elaborate and elegant. Heavy, carved bracelets were worn by men and women. Necklaces were worn by noble and commoner alike. Commoners wore simple necklaces made from stone beads strung on flax thread. Agate, rock crystal, pearls, carnelian, amethyst, and blue steatite were the favored stones used for the necklaces of wealthy and royal Cretans. Paste beads, imitative of lapis lazuli, were also used in creating decorative neckwear. Round beads made from a variety of stones were used alternately with pendants which took the forms of birds, animals, and small stylized human figures.

Earrings were often a combination of pearl beads and pendants fashioned from forms similar to those used in neckwear. Twisted gold-wire earrings were also worn.

Copper and gold hairpins with floral, spiral, and semiprecious-stone heads were beautifully crafted hair ornaments. Diadems of gold were constructed of hinged segments designed in the shape of leaves. Simple golden headbands, worn encircling the forehead, were also used as a type of head and hair decoration.

# Hairstyles (2000–1100 B.C.)

Hairstyles for women of the early Cretan period were simple. Long curls fell from the crown of the head, cascading over the shoulders and reaching to the waist or below. Simple bands were worn as decorations and functioned to hold the hair away from the eyes and face. Later coif arrangements were influenced by the Syrian style, which included drawing the hair back off the forehead and gathering it into a towering pug on the back of the head with two rather lank curls allowed to fall in front of the ears, framing the face.

Another hair arrangement consisted of parting the hair in the center, drawing it in waves low over the forehead, and securing it at the nape of the neck. The hair in back was shoulder length and arranged in small pencil curls or in a series of small braids.

Pointed or conical hair fashions were held in place by headbands, in which three flowers were often worn at the center of the forehead. Garlands of flowers and bright-colored ribbons were also entwined in the free-hanging locks as decorative elements.

Men wore their hair long, smoothed back from the brow, and falling free about the shoulders. Curls were sometimes piled into a peak at the crown of the head. Another fashion for men included drawing the hair to the nape of the neck and forming a club-shaped pigtail in back.

## FOOTNOTES

1. *Funk and Wagnalls New Encyclopedia*, edited by Joseph Laffin Morse, vol. 7, pp. 136–37.
2. Raymond Somers Stites, *The Arts and Man*, p. 147.
3. Helen Gardner, *Art Through the Ages*, p. 116.
4. François Boucher, *20,000 Years of Fashion*, p. 77.
5. Bernard Rudofsky, *The Unfashionable Human Body*, p. 56.
6. Boucher, *20,000 Years of Fashion*, p. 82.
7. Ludmila Kybalová; Olga Herbenová; and Milena Lamarová; *The Pictorial Encyclopedia of Fashion*, p. 51.
8. Boucher, *20,000 Years of Fashion*, p. 86.
9. Katherine Lester and Bess Oerke, *Accessories of Dress*, p. 106.
10. *Horizon* Quarterly, Spring 1967, p. 10.

# Chapter 4
# Garb of the Greeks
## (1500–150 B.C.)

During the period when the Dorians invaded the Greek peninsula and Crete, there were power struggles in many parts of the known world. The birth of the splendid civilization of Greece was conceived prior to 1100 B.C. with the arrival in mainland Greece of the Ionian people from the western Adriatic. Shortly after their immigration, they were joined by Aeolians from Asia Minor. These two nomadic tribes, with the more militant Indo-Europeans who had invaded Greece earlier, and the Dorians composed the earliest inhabitants of Greece. These disparate ethnic groups were the people who initiated the tentative starts in the development of the great Greek civilization. Their migrations occurred while the Mycenaean civilization was flourishing.

The Mycenaeans were at their power zenith between 1600 B.C. and 1200 B.C.[1] Their civilized, sophisticated social order succeeded that of the Minoans. The famous Mycenaean king, Agamemnon, led the ancient Greeks (Achaeans) into the Trojan War, which lasted for ten years. Indeed, it was Mycenae's propensity for war which ultimately led to its downfall. The Mycenaeans had inherited from the peaceful Minoans a written language, structural engineering techniques, aesthetic concepts, and craft skills. Unlike the people of Crete, they left many records using the Linear B system of writing.[2]

The Mycenaean society was highly organized. The political officials were led by a king to whom the military, administrative officers, charioteers, and mayors were directly responsible. Each was beholden to the next higher authoritative personage. This tightly structured system was weakened by Mycenaean conquests of many parts of the known world. Having spread their power so thinly over so vast an area, they were vulnerable when the restless Dorians departed from their tiny peninsula, first to invade Crete and then to overtake the Mycenaeans.

The Dorians obliterated the Mycenaean culture. Cities were laid to ruin, written languages were forgotten, and the conquered people were reduced to wandering searchers, struggling to survive. In the rubble of the devastated city palaces, the Dorian conquerors lived as squatters. They did not rebuild the splendid fortified

**Figure 4.1.** This female **chiton** has an overfold dropping to mid-thigh. First, the fabric was wet, then twisted and left to dry to create a pleated effect. A himation is tossed casually over the left shoulder. *(Young Girl from Antium,* c. 240 B.C. Museo Della Terme, Rome.)

edifices. Instead, the Dorians were preoccupied with developing their own sphere of political and military influence. This 450-year period has been called the Dark Age of Greece.[3]

One finds it difficult to relate these happenings to the origins of the Greek culture, on which was built one of the most philosophically, aesthetically, and intellectually refined democracies of ancient times. After the Mycenaean fall, the earliest governmental form was that of the city-state. At first these separate social units were organized from the Mycenaean cities, surrounding villages, and even family farms. As time passed, and as order was established by military power, city boundaries were defined. Hamlets and farms united with the cities around which they were gathered to form city-states with precise governmental structures.

The ruling authority, serving by divine right, was a hereditary king. Unlike the pharaohs of Egypt or rulers of other civilizations of Asia Minor, no Greek king during this early phase proclaimed himself descended from the gods. The earliest Greek kings did not proclaim their absolute authority, nor did they demand absolute obedience.

From this attitude, a sense of civic pride and a Greek cultural unity developed. Though the language, clothing, and clothing decoration of each city-state had provincial differences, there also developed a respect for the knowledge and the skills mastered by neighboring city-states. Through exchange and assimilation of the skills mastered by adjacent cities, a cultural unity was formed which was expressed in the art of ancient Greece. Regional differences in Hellenic pottery, for example, were slight. These early Hellenes, as the Greeks called themselves, emerged from their own Dark Age to lay the foundation on which was built a civilization based on political freedom for its citizens. With political freedom, art, philosophy, and intellectual curiosity flourished.

Great statesmen, generals, philosophers, artists, architects, and dramatists influenced the cultural developments of the ancient Greek world. The genius of men like Aristotle, Plato, Alexander the Great, Phidias, Sophocles, and Euripides mark the Greek culture as the origin of modern Western civilization.

The history of Greece was dominated by the reactions of the city-states to the Dorian invasion. Sparta was the site where the Dorians chose to settle. Athens, withstanding the Dorians for a time, welcomed the Mycenaeans and other fugitives from Dorian invasions. The settlement of Sparta and Athens by people of such differing character affected the entire life-style of ancient Greece. The Dorians in Sparta and the Mycenaean immigrants in Athens were vigorous people—warlike, proud, and adventurous. However, the Dorians did not develop an aestheticism, invent a written communication, or become proficient builders before or after they settled in Sparta. In contrast, the Mycenaeans had had several centuries in which to develop the basic skills required to build a sophisticated, organized society.

Ultimately, some amount of cultural homogeneity did result from the Dorian-Mycenaean mixture. The many deep-port bays and the chain of Aegean islands were drawn into a loosely cohesive political unit. The economy was established on agricultural production and was augmented by fishing and handcrafts which ranged from skillfully executed ceramics to artfully fashioned personal adornments of precious metals.

As the culture of this region stabilized after the destructive Dorian invasions, the spirit of earlier inhabitants began to formulate the foundations of the Golden Age. Philosophical concepts of the ancient Greeks greatly influenced the shaping of the political structure. The Greeks' strong belief in the importance of the individual was the motivating factor in the formulation of the first historical experiment in a democratic form of government. Their belief in the individual was based also upon religion. Thus, because they strove to mirror the perfection which was embodied in their anthropomorphic gods, they sought to achieve perfection in themselves, their governmental structure, and their art.

The Greek political structure progressed from rule by tribal chiefs to a democracy through several stages. Tribal chiefs of the small Hellenic city-states became kings of the areas they annexed through conquest. Slowly the power of these monarchies was usurped by the aristocracy. Noble families gained power through land acquisition. The 150-year period between 800 B.C. and 650 B.C. was dominated by the nobles.

In turn, the nobility was overthrown by commoners who had taken advantage of their own improved economic status. Such usurpers were called *tyrants*—a Greek word meaning king in all but name—because they had gained power illegally. The ability of the tyrants to assume power came from several sources. The introduction in the eighth century B.C. of the use of currency made it possible for landless commoners in trade to amass large fortunes. Using the power of money and the discontent of the masses, the landless wealthy took over the power structure of several Greek city-states. During this period, only Spartan aristocrats, with the aid of the military, were able to maintain control over their political establishment. The rule of the tyrants lasted from 650 B.C. to 500 B.C. The power that they had gained illegally was used, in most instances, wisely, and the rulers were popular and discerning.

Athens was governed by hereditary kings until 638 B.C. Then the Euratredae of Athens, a council of nobles, assumed power until 594 B.C. when the harsh and restrictive Draconian Code was revised by Solon, an Athenian statesman and lawgiver, to give citizenship to the commoners. Following this revision, which laid the constitutional foundations of Athenian democracy, the tyrants came into power in Athens. Democracy was established under the tyrant Pisistratus and was finalized into a strong political system during the year 502 B.C. During the period that followed, Athens flourished aesthetically, culturally, and economically.

Common cultural pursuits and a religion which grew out of mythological beliefs united the ancient Greeks. This intricate religion, common to all of these peninsular and neighboring island people, demanded rigid rites and observances. Religion also may have been an important factor in the unification of lesser city-states with either of the two dominant city-states, Sparta and Athens.

The land of the ancient Greeks had a diverse topography. Its climate was free from extremes of heat and cold; the sun in the bright sky intensified the forms of nature.

Perhaps it was the intensification of nature which gave rise to Greek religion. Whatever motivated the development of the Greek religion, its effects contributed to all that the ancient Greeks achieved.[4] Perhaps their pursuit of truth and perfection would not have been such a powerful force if they had evolved a rigid theology. The high refinement of philosophical thought, art, and medicine was the result of the Greeks' strong belief in the power of their many gods. These gods were thought to be more beautiful than humans with power to lift the Greek believer above any adversity. The Greeks offered hymns and prayers to specific gods to perform their magical works. Many shrines were erected to these gods where offerings and sacrifices were made as prayers were said. The greatest temple on Mt. Olympus had two areas, one for private devotions at the feet of the gold-plated Athena, and the other for public ceremonies.

All of the people of ancient Greece participated in four great festivals called the Olympian, Isthmian, Pythian, and Nemean games, which were always held out-of-doors. So important were the Olympian games that the Greeks reckoned their history by the occurrence of this once-in-four-years event.

So loosely organized was the ancient Greek theology that beliefs of death and a life after death were not clearly defined. Mythological heroes differed from the gods to whom the Greeks prayed. The myths of Greece and their heroes, including Zeus, Heracles, Europa, Jason, and the warrior Achilles, are known to many.

In the hospitable environment of the Greek peninsula, families were established, grew, prospered, and multiplied. The people's concepts of themselves were dictated by religious beliefs and determined their life-styles. Their anthropomorphic gods embodied grace, nobility, and grandeur which the ancient Greeks sought to emulate, ever striving for perfection.

Perfection of intellectual achievement and grace of movement were paramount concepts which were basic to Grecian life-style. Perfection was so highly prized that a child born either weak or deformed was set out in a public place to die. The fate of a newborn was determined by the father. So important was graceful movement to the Greeks that the boys of Athens and the boys and girls of Sparta were given training in the gymnasiums. It is no wonder that the garb of the Greeks was flowing and draped, accenting the grace of their trained bodies.

To prepare boys for the man's world that was the life-style of ancient Greece, they were also educated in the fundamentals of philosophical thought, reading, mathematics, poetry, and music.[5] The earliest training of Greek children began in the home. Mothers, fathers, and nurses vied to make children perfect. At the age of seven, boys of all families began their formal training. Though the state required that all sons of freemen attend school until they were eighteen, the state did not provide schoolhouses. Nor were teachers paid a regular sum. Taught by teachers who were underpaid, or not paid at all, the boys of ancient Greece were the best educated youth of antiquity.

When the boys went off to school, little girls were given what formal training they were to have at home. They were taught the basics of arithmetic, singing, lute playing, and dancing by their mothers. From a very young age, girls learned that Greek females were to be seen and not heard. Women had house- and home-centered responsibilities. Young girls of Greece learned to keep household accounts using their scant knowledge of mathematics. Daughters were taught to make bread and to prepare family meals using cheese, fish, leeks, grapes, and other fruits.

Both slaves and freemen worked, for an edict of the solons, or lawmakers, pronounced that complete education was a combination of intellectual learning and proficiency in a trade. This was not considered demeaning, for work was honorable. Skilled artisans gloried in the appellation, "lord of the hand," and worked diligently to produce items for trade. Artisans were so highly regarded that they were made members of the assembly.

The agora, or marketplace, such as the plaza of Athens, was the center of daily life; it was a place of hustle and bustle, redolent of fish and perfume. The nearby arsenal was the largest of the city's factories, employing 120 slaves.

Greek trade routes extended from the Cornish coast of England to Ireland, to the Crimea, and to all the neighboring countries of the Mediterranean. The ancient Greeks engaged in sea trade only during the summer months.

The lives of wealthy adult males were centered around the agora. Here they met daily to discuss business, politics, and philosophy, and to exercise in the gymnasium. After a three-day work week, Greek men attended festive banquets. Entertainment at these feasts consisted of dancing girls, acrobats, musicians, and, of course, conversation.

Women did not participate in these festivities. However, they were responsible for the preparation of the feasts. Greek females were dominated by males from adolescence. Their fathers chose the men who would become their husbands. The elaborate wedding ceremony began at the bride's house and ended at the groom's home. Here he carried his bride over the threshold, symbolizing that now she was his possession. After marriage, the life of the female was segregated. She saw that the household ran smoothly, that there was ample production of fabric for the family's clothing needs, and that her husband's guests were properly fed and entertained.

While the banqueting males reveled below, she retired to her apartments on the second floor. Here she bathed, afterward scenting her body with sweet-smelling oils, and continued with the rest of her toilette. Because males and females strove for perfection and beauty, a Greek woman took great pains to make her visual image more lovely.[6] Hair was carefully groomed and complexions were made startlingly white by the use of white lead. Alkanet root was used to color the cheeks red.

Although separated socially from males because of the mores of the period, home life was loving. On evenings when there were no guests, husband and wife shared each other's companionship. They dined together and engaged in animated conversation.

Ancient Greek artists created poetry, sculpture, plays, and paintings honoring gods and heroes. In so doing, their attention to perfection has come down through the ages as the zenith of creativity. Every fold of a deplos as it covered the sculpted figure and every drape of a chiton on a marble image were placed in the most perfect relationship.

**Figure 4.2.** Women of wealth and position during the Classical period of Greece wore **chitons** of increased size and length (right). The figure on the left is shown in trailing **chiton, himation,** and **tholia** with the hair supported by a **sphendon.**

The use of the "golden mean" was the epitome of Greek aesthetic concepts. It reflected their religiously motivated concept, that of striving for the mean, or happy medium. While seeking perfection in art, games, poetry, drama, and philosophy, they were aware of mortal limitations. Though they strove to attain Aristotle's admonition, "We must be as immortal as far as we can," they set themselves reasonable goals. They did nothing to excess, but rather attempted to set an ideal. This became the mean—not less than was possible, not more than was possible. In attempting to achieve the mean, these vigorous, energetic people achieved, in thought and in the arts, a high level of perfection.

The clothes which they wore reinforced this sense of refinement and perfection. Each garment in their wardrobe, remarkably contrived from a simple length of fabric, flattered the human form which they revered. Draped, swathed, or nude, the human figure was an imperfect mirror form of their anthropomorphic gods.

The earliest sculptural records from the Greek Archaic period are, however, much more rigid than those of the better-known Classical period. The Archaic garments of females seem skimpy (Figure 4.7). The wrap is typical of the shawl worn by females of Mesopotamia during the same period. The slimness of the gown, perhaps a derivative of the kalasiris, and the rigidity of posture has an Egyptian geometricity. In comparing the sculptures from the Archaic period with those from Egypt, the relation to earlier Mesopotamian garments is apparent. The Greek clothing styles perhaps were influenced by the Persians. A figurine of a Greek maiden, dating from the sixth century B.C. in the Vathy Museum, Samos, has hair dressed after the style of the Egyptians.

The sculptures of the Classical period illustrate more clearly the ancient Greeks and the manner in which they clad themselves. Males are usually depicted casually draped in a single garment, the **himation.** Some funerary stelae show warriors wearing an **exomis** pushed off the sword-wielding shoulder, others are draped with dignity in the himation. Men and women of this Classical period adopted this practice of pushing the work arm free from the costume's encumbrance.

In the sculpture of *Hestias, Diones, Aphrodite* (437-432 B.C.), the headless figures are clad in softly draped **chitons.** The fibulae pinnings in sleeves are quite distinct. The fibulae depicted on the figure representing Diones are long and slightly curved, while those securing Aphrodite's garb are small and round. The arrangement of the folds was casually organized in such a manner as to reveal the virtues of the female physique.

The freedom men enjoyed was given an outward sign in the lack of apparel they chose to wear. In contrast, while the female form was revealed beneath the chiton, these garments were cumbersome, long, and often overdraped and triple girdled (Figures 4.1 and 4.2). Thus the entire Greek life-style, based on religion, was reflected, not only in art and daily activities, but in clothing as well.

# Basic Garments of Ancient Greece (1500–150 B.C.)

## EXOMIS (1500–150 B.C.)

The most basic garment more commonly worn by slaves than by freemen after 750 B.C. was the **exomis** (Figure 4.3). As the only body covering, it was formed by

**Figure 4.3.** Two male **exomis,** one made from two pieces of fabric pinned on the shoulders and girdled, the other a single length pinned on the shoulder and left ungirdled.

**Figure 4.4.** Infant boy in short, draped **exomis.** (Redrawn from *Seated Temple Boy,* statue. Metropolitan Museum of Art, New York City.)

pinning two rectangular lengths of wool or linen at each shoulder with a fibula and belting it at the waist. The side and shoulder seams may or may not have been sewn together. Belting or girdling was also optional and used at the discretion of the wearer. The exomis was a simple tunic, usually without sleeves, that covered the wearer from shoulder to thigh. Greek infants often wore this simple body covering in a waist-length version.[7] In Figure 4.4, the child is shown wearing such a garment, which appears to have been gathered up the center front. Obviously the child was of the wealthy class to have had a garment styled with this decorative embellishment.

## CHITON (1500–150 B.C.)

The **chiton,** the most characteristic Greek garment worn by men and women from 1500 B.C. to 150 B.C., was an elaborate version of the exomis with sex-defining variations (Figure 4.5). The earliest chitons worn by Mycenaeans and Archaeans were not draped, but were slender garments. In Figures 4.6 and 4.7, the chitons appear to have an overfold, or **apotygma,** falling over a single-strand girdle.

In the early evolutionary phase of the chiton's development, this garment was made of a rectangular length of woolen fabric. Linen from Egypt or Sicily was used later. The earliest garments made in this fashion extended from shoulder to thigh. The length of the chiton was determined by the width of the loom, and the width of the chiton was determined by the length of the warp on the loom. The rectangle of material was folded in half, and the fold

became one side seam. The top selvage became the shoulder seam and the bottom, the hem. The shoulder seam was not sewn but was pinned with fibulae on each shoulder (Figures 4.2 and 4.6). The pin, or **fibula,** at first was a simple, bent metal wire with a twist at the closed end, creating a crude spring, and a point and flattened latch on the open end.

Just as the capitals of Greek columns became more elaborate, so did the main Greek garment. While the different Greek capitals are labeled Doric, Ionic, and Corinthian, chitons are categorized as **Archaic, Doric, Ionic,** and **Classical.**

The **Archaic chitons** were slender, often only thigh length, equal in width to the breadth of the wearer, and the girdling was simple.

**Figure 4.5.** A female **chiton** worn over only one shoulder and double girdled about the waist. *(Wounded Amazon,* Roman copy of Greek work, 440–430 B.C. Metropolitan Museum of Art, New York City.)

**Figure 4.6.** Illustration of **chiton** with shoulder treatment secured by **fibulae** (under lock of hair), **apotygma,** and concealed girdling. *(Peace and Wealth,* 370 B.C. Munich Antikensomnelung.)

The **Doric chiton,** or **Dorian** as the female version was called, was somewhat fuller and double or triple girdled (Figure 4.8). The slight fullness of the Doric chiton was carefully arranged and the women's girdling was generally more elaborate than that used by men. The method of wrapping the long cord or ribbon belting about the figure left several inches between each winding. After the girdle was secured, the fabric forming the chiton was drawn up, allowing it to blouse over the girdling. Figure 4.1 shows a double girdling of the chiton, although the girdling is partially obscured by the casually draped, slender scarf, or **pharos.** The first ribbon belting is placed just under the bust, the second is obviously wound around the normal waist. Figure 4.9, *Mourning Girl,* illustrates a Doric chiton girdled above the normal waist with the cord belting drawn up under the arms and crossed in back.

The chiton was either patterned in vertical stripes or was vertically pleated. The prewear pleating was possibly arranged and set in much the same manner as the Egyptians prepleated or goffered their apparel. Some authorities have speculated that the pleats were first arranged by hand, then twisted and tied at either end and left for several hours. Pleating was possible after the introduction of linen from Egypt.

**Figure 4.7. Archaic chiton** (540–530 B.C.) showing the more scant version of this female garment. Determining the nature of the overfold draping about the left arm is difficult, for the arm is missing in the original sculpture. (Redrawn from *Peplos Kore.* Acropolis Museum, Athens.)

**Figure 4.8.** Young girl's simple **chiton,** or **Dorian,** illustrating the open side of the garment. (Grave relief: *Girl with Pigeons,* Paros, c. 455–450 B.C. Metropolitan Museum of Art, New York City.)

The male Doric chiton was ankle length or thigh length. The longer version was worn by more elderly men, and by young and old for festivals, banquets, weddings, and other important occasions. The Ionic and Classical chitons for both sexes were draped from wider pieces of fabric, resulting in excessively full variations of the earlier styles.

The Dorian lost favor in Athens, yielding to the Ionian costume. According to Herodotus, the Athenian women had worn the **Homeric peplos,** but were forced to accept the Ionic chiton because of a disaster in Aegina in 558 B.C. In that year there was a military defeat and the sole survivor was murdered by Athenian women using their fibulae. The old Homeric peplos, with one open side seam, was altered to create the **Ionic chiton** by sewing up the open side and increasing the size. Thus, the female chiton of this period was extremely bulky and restricted movement to some extent. In total width the Ionic chiton

measured three yards. Boucher describes these chitons as gowns and admonishes researchers not to confuse them with tunics.

Ionic chitons were worn with or without an overfold, or apotygma (Figures 4.6 and 4.7). When hanging free, the overfold was easily drawn over the head for protection against a sudden shower or for a veil if the lady wished to remain incognito. The manner of draping the Ionic chiton remained the same; however, the width of the fabric was twice that of the wearer's outstretched arms. Figure 4.6 clearly demonstrates one of the draping systems used with girdling when the apotygma was allowed to hang free. When the apotygma was bound, it created a peplum effect, known as one variation of the **peplos.** The section beneath the apotygma, that between the topmost girdling and the shoulders, was known as the **kolpos.**

With the increased width used in the Ionic and Classical chitons, many fibulae were used to create sleeves from the excess material. Figure 4.10 graphically illustrates this innovation in the female chiton. The

**Figure 4.9.** Illustration shows the arrangement of crossed-back, under-arm, and waist girdling for the female floor-length **chiton.** The sleeves of this garment appear to be inset, quite unusual in Greek wearing apparel. (Redrawn from *Mourning Girl,* c. fourth century B.C. Berlin Museum.)

**Figure 4.10.** Pinned sleeves of female **chiton** appear on the figure on left; figure on right apparently wears a long-sleeved **undertunic** and **peplos.** Note that the outer garments are of patterned fabric. (Black ceramic plate decoration, detail. Hermitage Museum, Leningrad.)

**Figure 4.11.** Grecian woman's about-the-home garments, including the **supertunic** and **diplax.** *(Diana,* detail, Praxiteles, fourth century B.C. Louvre, Paris.)

fibulae were spaced several inches apart to create a draped, dolman-sleeve effect.

## SUPERTUNIC (1000–146 B.C.)

When the mild climate occasionally turned chilly, females added a **supertunic** to their costume. The supertunic was worn over the chiton and was a smocklike garment with a deep, oval neckline. It, too, was girdled, and the gathers artfully arranged. The calf-length supertunic shown in Figure 4.11 seems to be the major garment worn. However, a concealed, thigh-length chiton may very well have been worn underneath.

The short, off-the-shoulder cape fastened on the right side is a **diplax**, sometimes called a **chloene.** Like the supertunic, it was a utilitarian garment worn primarily for warmth. The decorative form of this same garment was introduced during the Late Grecian era and has been labeled the peplos by some authorities. It too was worn under one arm and tied or fastened with a fibula on the other. Unlike the utilitarian diplax, the peplos was bound on the top edge with a decorative embroidered edging. Often this edging extended beyond the main portion of the peplos fabric, which was gathered and sewn to the decorative band. The extensions served as ties by which the garment was secured to the person.

## PEPLOS (540–146 B.C.)

The **peplos** was worn in various lengths—some were hip length, some were floor length. Often made of patterned or embroidered material, the peplos was decorative and functional because it added some warmth, but it was not as cumbersome or figure-swathing as the himation. The little girl shown in Figure 4.12 wears a late version of the peplos in a unique fashion. Beneath the peplos, which has three visible round-headed fibulae in back, the child wears a sleeveless exomis.

Figure 4.10, also a detail from a vase painting, shows two figures. The seated figure wears only a chiton; however, the standing figure wears several layers of clothing. There are three garments visible: a dot-patterned, floor-length peplos, a sleeved supertunic and, beneath that, a sleeved **undertunic.** The sleeves of the undertunic are gathered to a tiny band cuff at the wrist, and, judging from its appearance in Figure 4.10, the undertunic was made from very fine linen.

While the term *tunic* is not a Greek word, in the case of supertunic and undertunic, it serves to differentiate these additional garments from the exomis and the chiton. The tunics had sewn side seams and sleeves, which were generally cut in one with the main body of the garment.

Bronze-eyed needles were used by the Greeks, making the sewing of seams and the creation of decorative embroidery possible. Sewing with needles permitted variety in garment forms, and embroidery added decoration and individualism. Since most basic garments were neu-

**Figure 4.12.** Back view of a young girl's garment, perhaps a **peplos,** showing the draping that may have been pinned in position with **fibulae.** *(Statue of Girl,* 230 B.C. Palazzo Graziola, Rome.)

proud of their masculine physiques, wore himations loosely draped from the waist down or tossed over one shoulder. The manner of tossing this wrap over the shoulder or winding it firmly about the body displayed the individuality of the wearer because the himation was worn in such a wide variety of ways by men and women. Generally, a man first tucked the himation under the left arm and brought it across the front. Then it was drawn over the back, across the front once again, and up over the left shoulder. The free end was left hanging free, or was wound about the left arm.

While the male wearing style of the himation generally left the upper body bare, women wore this wrap for warmth in such a way as to conceal the figure. Figures 4.13 and 4.14 show two of the variations practiced by Greek women who also used distinctive styles. Generally, Grecian ladies wore the himation as an all-encompassing

tral in tone, colorful embroidery added zest to the otherwise colorless garments.

Late in the culture of Greece, colored lengths of fabric of a single hue served as the material from which chitons, himations, and deplos were fashioned. Pliny credited the painter Polygnotus with introducing "flower colors" into female dress. Figure 4.18 is a drawing of a polychrome figurine wearing a deplos. In the original, the chiton is pale blue, the deplos is blue edged with a wide gold band, and the tholia is earth red and gray. A similar polychrome terra-cotta figurine in the Metropolitan Museum of Art is designed with garments tinted pale pink with floral greenery in delicate tones of green.[8]

## HIMATION (1100–146 B.C.)

The **himation,** a flowing or figure-swathing outer wrap, was worn by men and women. Indeed, freemen often wore nothing else, and, like the tebenna of the Etruscans (Chapter 5) and the toga of the Romans (Chapter 6), it was worn as a symbol of status. The grace with which the free-hanging end of the body-swathing himation was handled indicated the sophistication of the wearer. Even the manner of casually carrying the himation was an indication of status and breeding. By their manner of draping, manipulating, and walking in these wound cloaks, the males of ancient Greece were able to project the image of themselves that they desired. Young men,

**Figure 4.13.** One of many wearing styles of the female **himation,** worn here over a **chiton** which has been pleated. *(Statue of Maiden,* Roman adaptation of a Greek work. Metropolitan Museum of Art, New York City.)

**Figure 4.14.** Enveloping drape of the **himation** completely conceals the **chiton** worn beneath. *(Tyche of Antioch,* Eutychides,
c. A.D. 295, Roman copy. Galleria dei Candelabri, Vatican.)

garment. The ancient Greek women, who went out in-
frequently and when they did were considered a specific
male's property, concealed their beautiful forms from
masculine admirers. The himation, donned by men or
women of Greece, was a highly refined, aesthetically
ordered body covering created from a simple rectangle of
fabric.

The **pharos,** a casually draped, narrow scarf of thin
fabric wound about the body, was worn by women. Possibly it was adapted from the Mesopotamian covering and
was used more for decoration than for any other purpose.
Unlike the diplax, a utilitarian garment for minimum
warmth, women wore the pharos for much the same reason
as the men wore the himation, that is, for status. The
pharos has often has been mislabeled as the himation. The
manipulation of this garment served to identify the most
sophisticated women of ancient Greece.

## DEPLOS (1100–146 B.C.)

The **deplos** was contrived to envelop the female
figure in an even more concealing manner than the himation. Also made from a three- or four-yard length of
material, the top edge of the deplos was folded down to
form a cape effect for added warmth about the shoulders.
This overfold could be brought up over the head as added

protection. As was the himation, the deplos was handheld
to keep it gathered tightly around the body. *The Dancing
Girl* (Figure 4.15) shows that the deplos was used as an
enticing garment by entertainers. Figures 4.15 and 4.18
illustrate the ways in which the deplos could be arranged.

Because the statuette in Figure 4.18 wears the curi-
ously fashioned **tholia,** it is thought that this terra-cotta
figurine depicts a lady out on a summer day. Fair skin was
highly regarded so the wearer has drawn the overfold
closely around her face and donned the tholia as added
protection from the sun's rays.

The deplos used for a winter wrap was made of woolen
material, generally left in its natural color, although there
are artifacts which suggest that himations and deplos worn
in the winter were deep brown or Mars red. Summer styles
of the deplos were made of delicate linen fabric. After the
introduction of "flower colors," these wraps appeared in
pale pinks and soft yellows with overall floral patterns
embroidered in delicately colored threads.

**Figure 4.15.** Dancing female swathed in a head-concealing
**deplos.** *(Dancing Girl,* collection of Walter Baker, New York City,
by permission of Mrs. W. Baker.)

**Figure 4.16.** In the foreground, a young man wears a draped, short **chiton** and **chlamys.** On the right, a male figure is clad in a **himation.** (Redrawn from the Cat stele, c. 410 B.C. National Museum, Athens.)

The deplos appears to have been made of different widths of material which, in turn, determined the length of the wrap. Not always worn as a concealing garment for warmth, it could be used as an accessory to emphasize the graceful movements of the wearer.

## CHLAMYS (1100–146 B.C.)

The **chlamys** was a practical garment made of rough woolen fabric for men. It was worn primarily by warriors, travelers, and young lads (Figure 4.16). Warriors of Greece used this practical, simple wrap for much the same purposes as the Roman sagum was used by the foot soldiers of that later civilization (Chapter 6).

Made from a length of fabric, perhaps a yard wide and a yard and a half long, it was fastened on the right shoulder with a fibula. The left arm was completely covered, while the right was free to wield a sword or hold horses' reins. Naturally, there were instances when the fastening

slipped to center front. However, this garment was always pinned on the right shoulder when arranged on the body. The activity patterns of the wearer ultimately determined the final positioning of the chlamys. Figure 4.16 illustrates that, although the left arm was covered, the chlamys was not a confining garment.

## PALLIUM (500–146 B.C.)

The Greek wardrobe often contained several outer wraps in addition to the himation and chiton. The **pallium** and the **tribon** were fashioned from a circular piece of material. The pallium (Figure 4.17) usually had an attached hood and was open in the center front. The tribon, made from the same general pattern, had no attached hood. Both were fastened at the throat with ties or fibulae. The tribon, made of coarse material, was worn by the lower class and slaves.

**Figure 4.17.** The **pallium** was a hooded cape generally used for travel during unseasonable weather.

The variations achieved by the draping and girdling of rectangular lengths of fabric for body coverings are remarkable. These garments projected a dignified image of the wearer, and the versatility with which they were arranged attests to the imaginative and creative nature of the ancient Greeks.

Unfortunately, there are few examples left that show the range of pattern motifs or the range of colors available to them. The hems of chitons often were trimmed with the Greek fret. Dot patterns and repeated geometric shapes were used and sometimes combined with decorative border treatments. Palmettes and other floral derivative designs were employed to add splendor to the female garb. These applied designs did not surpass the girdling and draping of the chiton or the wrapping of the himation and the deplos which were employed as the primary designs in Greek dress.

Elegance was achieved through simplicity. Complexity evolved during the Ionic and Classical periods; however, grace and elegance were not destroyed. The verticality of the pleats lent dignity to the images of the personages depicted in commemorative sculpture. The severity of these vertical design patterns was softened by the swag draping developed in the sleeves fashioned with fibulae. Femininity was accented by the deep, V-draped décolletage. While the bust often was emphasized by underbreast girdling, a gracefully clad body in its totality was the emphasis of Greek dress.

# Accessories (1100–146 B.C.)

## HEADWEAR

An early hat form worn primarily by men of Greece was called the **petasus.** This head covering, made of felt, consisted of a round, bowl-shaped crown and a rather wide brim made in two sections. A V-shaped slit was formed where the two halves of the brim met over the ears. Thin cords, tied under the chin, held the hat in place. When not on the head, the ties were loosely knotted, holding the hat on the person but allowing it to rest on the back. The felt **pileus** was a tall-crowned skull cap, a male hat form common to all ancient peoples.

Women seldom wore any hats, but on very sunny days they would don the **tholia** (Figure 4.18), a hat worn on top of the drawn-up himation or the overfold of the deplos. This rather amusingly shaped hat had a small brim and a tall, pointed or cone-shaped crown. It was placed rather precariously atop the head, possibly held in place with a long stiletto pin driven through the crown and into the chignon hair arrangement.

The **Phrygian cap** was an oddly shaped hat made of leather or woolen cloth. It was designed rather like a hood with a rounded point that projected forward (Figure 4.19).

**Figure 4.18.** Woman wears a **tholia** on her head and an intricately draped **deplos** over her flowing, floor-length **chiton.** The brimmed tholia was a form of sun hat seldom used unless the day was excessively hot. (Terra-cotta figure: *Woman with Fan,* Tanagra, fourth century B.C. State Museum, Berlin.)

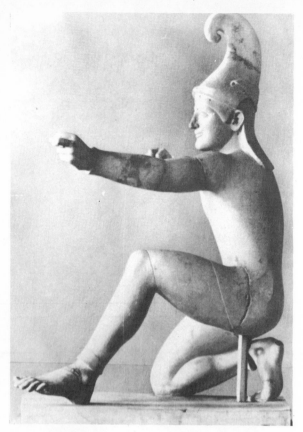

**Figure 4.19.** One of several forms of **Phrygian caps** used by the Greeks. (Figure from West Pediment, Temple of Apaia, Aegina, sixth century B.C. Munich.)

When the cap was made of stiff material, the point stood up, curving toward the front. A pair of falls covered the cheeks in front of the ears, and a veil or neck sheath covered the back of the neck and extended to the shoulders. If it was made of softer fabric, the point was worn crushed down, almost disappearing into the cap section.

The **sakkos** was a pointed cap with a tassel trim. This cap covered much of the head and had a small brim or visor in front that stood semierect.

Women covered their heads with a variety of veils made of wool or linen. Earlier versions were small and were draped over the head simply, reaching no farther than the shoulders. Later versions were sheer, gossamer trims encircling the head like a misty cloud. These diaphanous veils were usually white, although saffron, blue, and purple hues were used also.

The **snood** and **sphendon scarf** doubled as head coverings and chignon supports. The sphendon scarf cradled the bun of hair in back (Figure 4.2), partially covering it, and was drawn forward over the brow where it was secured by winding the ends together and tucking them into the back section. The snood was primarily a hair support. It was a loosely woven net, made of linen cords or gold wires. This coif decoration was held in place by a tiara worn rather low on the forehead.

## FOOTWEAR

The earliest shoes worn by the Greeks were made with felt, leather, or wooden soles bound to the feet by thongs. Later, straps were attached to the soles, arranged in a variety of crisscrossed patterns to form the traditional Grecian sandals. Boots and shoes that covered the foot were laced over the instep and were tied at the ankle or at the calf of the leg.

High boots worn by warriors or slaves had wooden soles and wide, leather-strap laces. These rugged boots had leather tops and an enclosed heel. Boots referred to as **crepida** were made of a heavy leather sole that was somewhat larger than the foot. The excess sole was brought up over the foot and attached over the instep by thongs laced through large slits cut into the edge of the sole. These afforded a means of securing this basic style to the foot and protecting the sides of the foot as well.

By the year 400 B.C., shoe and sandal making had attained a high degree of sophistication. At this time the classical sandal became an elaborate form of footwear. Men of wealth and high rank wore sandals made from soft leather of natural or gold color.

## JEWELRY

The necklaces of Greek women consisted of golden forms elaborately embossed and engraved. Repoussé and plaited gold wires were combined by skillful goldsmiths to create ornaments. A typical necklace design consisted of small gold animal forms, blue or green enameled rosettes, and pendants in vase shapes, arranged alternately. Deep fringe, made of minute chains or twisted gold wires, was often added to the vase forms of the pendant necklace. Stone cameos and small vials filled with sweet scents were worn suspended from long golden chains.

**Figure 4.20.** Greek and Roman **fibulae.** (Metropolitan Museum of Art, New York City.)

Bracelets were fashioned in much the same manner as necklaces, using chased and engraved motifs on gold.

Rings were believed to have magical powers. Their charms were thought to insure health, love, wealth, and happiness. Rings were made of precious stones, jasper, rock crystal, and chalcedony set in gold with gold shanks. Intaglio and cameo engravings were used as settings in many of these rings.

The **fibula** was a functional and a decorative accessory used by men and women (Figure 4.20). The early form was simply a bent wire with a sharp point on one end and a hook latch on the other. As Greek culture became more sophisticated, fibulae developed into elaborately decorated, large pins fashioned in many diverse shapes. They were made of precious metals with intricate, chased designs and became important costume accessories.

Earrings were given protective attributes to drive away spirits and were worn by both sexes. The earliest forms were simple loops; later designs included single ball shapes, single pearls, vase pendants, and the long, fringed pendants. Figures of humans or cupids, as seen in Figure 4.21, also were used as earring motifs. All of these ear ornaments were suspended from a small metal loop inserted in pierced ears.

Large bodkin hairpins were used to hold the elaborate Grecian coiffures in place. The designs of the heads of these pins ranged from geometric shapes, to stylized floral forms, to intricate insect motifs.

## HANDHELD ACCESSORIES

The staff or walking stick carried by the men of Greece was a sign of distinction, although it was a simple form with a small crook at the top.

The Greeks are credited with introducing the umbrella into Europe. It, too, was a symbol of importance and was carried by a slave for the comfort of the master. It was made in several styles, including one designed with a round shade section supported by reed ribs attached to a long handle. Another design consisted of a semicircular shade section supported by ribs, with the handle attached to the straight or back edge. An umbrella fashioned in this semicircular style shaded only the person for whom it was carried.

Fans were used by individuals or were wafted by slaves. Those used by women were small and made of linen in triangular or leaf shapes. The larger, slave-manipulated fans were made of peacock feathers.

Combs of boxwood and ivory were used only in a functional rather than a decorative sense. Metal and ebony combs came into use later. The comb usually had two functional sides, one with fine teeth and the other with coarse teeth.

Men and women used perfume profusely. Elaborately designed perfume vials of alabaster, set into three-legged stands when not in use, were important toilette acces-

**Figure 4.21.** Grecian jewelry was delicate in its intricacy but often bold in size. Figure *A:* a gold and silver earring made of disc and pendants from Madytos on the Hellespont, fourth century B.C. Figure *B:* a pair of earrings, *Ganymede and the Eagle of Gold,* fourth century B.C. (Metropolitan Museum of Art, New York City.)

**A**

**B**

sories. Vials made of white glass with glass inlay were another type of these cosmetic accessories.

Greek women clutched or carried small linen handbags made from either a gathered circle or a square of cloth, often decorated with embroidery. The drawstring may have been used as a handle.

Hairnets made of a lacy golden network, strung with beads or laced with enameled figures, were worn over a chignon.

The elaborate girdling effects used in establishing the drape of the chiton were created by winding long lengths of ribbon around the figure.

The Greek figure-controlling girdle, called a **strophion,** was made of three rather wide bands of cloth. These were wound snugly about the body, one just under the bust, one at the waist, and another around the hips.

## COSTUME TRIMS

Greek women attained great skill in the art of embroidery. Favorite motifs included stars, floral patterns, zigzag, fret, key, spiral, guilloche, honeysuckle, palmette designs, and simple parallel bands. Often stars or floral forms were scattered all over the chiton fabric. The more rigid designs were used as hem borders. Although it is not known for certain, it is believed that the overall patterns were painted rather than embroidered.

# Hairstyles (1100–146 B.C.)

Men and women took care in grooming their hair. Men's hairstyles have been divided into four categories: **kepos**, curls tumbling over the forehead; **Hectorean**, combed back from the face and curled in back; **Theseid**, short bangs over the forehead with long locks in back; and the **monk cut**, ear-length locks cut round, with no part. Trinkets and ribbons or metal bands decorated the male coif. Ribbon hair trims were worn low over the forehead, usually tied at the back. Very early styles included braided plaits of hair bound around the head, holding a crown of curls on top. Carefully arranged bangs covered the forehead in this style.

Women regarded their hair as a crowning glory. Early styling included wearing the hair in a knot on the top of the head with ringlet curls masking the brow. Later hair fashion dictated that a large bun be projected outward from the back of the head. This bun was bound by a snood or sphendon scarf and was wound with ribbons. The chignon was a vast bun of hair worn at the nape of the neck or projecting some distance from the back of the head. The scarf or snood also secured the knot of hair featured in this coif. Cascading locks of hair hung from the end of the bun, distinguishing it from the snood-covered style. The simplest style permitted the hair to fall free with a flattened pompadour pushed well over the forehead. Athenian women generally wore their hair in a knot at the nape of the neck, while Spartan women pulled the hair to the crown of the head and tied it in place with ribbons.

Brides of the Doric period shaved their heads as a sign of submission. A husband often shaved the head of an unfaithful wife as punishment. Wigs, false hairpieces, and gold, silver, and bronze bands also were used in caring for hair. Other hair-grooming aids were a bleach of potash, a rinse of yellow flowers crushed in water, perfumes, and pomades. Washing procedures are not known, but oils were used to add luster to the hair.

FOOTNOTES
1. C. M. Bowra, *Classical Greece*, p. 31.
2. Alexander Eliot, *The Horizon Concise History of Greece*, p. 28.
3. Bowra, *Classical Greece*, p. 32.
4. Ibid., p. 114.
5. Ibid., pp. 79–87.
6. Gisele D'Assailly, *Ages of Elegance*, p. 24.
7. Millia Davenport, *The Book of Costume*, vol. 1, p. 71.
8. D'Assailly, *Ages of Elegance*, p. 25.

# Chapter 5

# Dress of the Etruscans (1300–251 B.C.)

**Figure 5.1.** Etruscan male wears a sleeved **exomis** and **tebenna.** (Clay tablet: *Worshiper in Front of a Statue of a Goddess,* detail. Louvre, Paris.)

Precise statements concerning the origins of the people who settled in the low, marshy lands of Tuscany along the east coast of Italy cannot be made. Contemporary archaeologists have determined that they were immigrants from the Near East. This agrees with historians of the ancient world. The Greek historian Herodotus asserted that the Etruscans came from Lydia, an ancient civilization of western Asia Minor. Modern authorities are unable to pinpoint the Etruscans' origins exactly.[1]

The settlements of a stable society were made during the last years of the ninth century B.C. The first communities were probably located at Tarquinia (then called Tarquinii) and Vetulonia. Dates and sites have been determined from excavations of Etruscan tombs, which greatly predate others in the area and are totally different in style. The artifacts which have been found have a distinct character indicating the influences of cultures of Asia Minor and of Egypt.

As their society became more advanced and more powerful, the people of Etruria expanded their territory. At the height of its power, this loosely bound city-state society stretched from the Alps in the north to the Tiber River in the south. Between 600 B.C. and 400 B.C., it ruled over Rome and established an alliance with Carthage. The Etruscan naval victory over the Phoenicians about 535 B.C. not only enlarged Etruscan territory to include the island of Corsica but it gave them visions of grandeur. Colonies were established in widely separated regions across the Apennines reaching to the Adriatic Sea. Their vision of controlling a large landmass was dimmed when the Gauls destroyed these colonies.

After the rape of Lucretia in 509 B.C., the Romans rebelled against Etruscan rule and expelled King Lucius Tarquinius. Rome became more powerful and defeated the Etruscans in the Battle of Lake Regillus in 496 B.C. This began a century of battles between Rome and Etruria, culminating in a ten-year seige of the city of Veii, which fell to Rome in 396 B.C. Etruscan naval power ceased to be a force of consequence with the defeat of its fleet by Syracuse in 474 B.C. Rome completed the conquest of Etruria in 281 B.C.[2]

The base of the Etruscan political structure was the League of Twelve Cities. These loosely confederated city-states had self-rule and were headed by annually elected magistrates who were selected from the Etruscan nobility. As in many other ancient cultures, the political structure was supported by an economy which depended on trade. As early as the eighth century B.C. the Etruscans plied the waters of the Mediterranean, carrying on commerce with the Phoenicians and the Cypriots and harassing commercial fleets of other countries. In time these trade routes grew to include most of the nations of Asia Minor and the Aegean region and areas as far west and north as Marseilles.

The Etruscans' chief products included cattle, grain, wool, timber, and wine which they traded for essential materials that they could not produce. Like their contemporaries, they were primarily agrarians; however, they also worked copper and iron mines in the interior. The inhabitants of Tuscany were farmers and town merchants who performed and supplied all services needed by the cities' inhabitants. Being a militaristic society, many male citizens served in either the army or the navy.

While the Etruscan city-states were powerful militarily, they seldom if ever aided a neighboring city-state engaged in a conflict. Each had strong walled fortifications surrounding its city. The double-gated city

entrances were flanked by watchtowers. The center city
had a quadrangle around which were probably arranged
shops and businesses, with the family dwellings beyond.
The walled cities were architecturally sound and well
engineered. These well-planned cities were compatible
with the Etruscans' strong, well-established social order.

The overriding unifying force of the Etruscan civilization was its religion. Temples were constructed in which
were held elaborate ceremonies honoring their anthropomorphic deities.[3] Within their walled cities were
tombs and necropolises (cemeteries). These, too, exemplified the dogmatic religious belief that life as they knew
it continued after death.

Although this civilization left no written documentation of its civil laws, there was a strict set of religious laws.
These were recorded in three volumes, with an inclusive
title of *Etrusca Disciplina*, which were concerned with the
interpretation of natural phenomena, the art of divination,
and social and political standards. *Libri Hanuspicini*, the
first volume, interpreted the meanings of the entrails of
sacrificial animals. Divination by lightning and the art of
interpreting this natural phenomenon were taken up in the
second volume, *Libri Fulgurales*. Ritual practices and
social and political standards were outlined in the third
volume, *Libri Rituales*.

The Etruscan religion was a multigod religion, some
of whose names are familiar, including Uni (Juno),
Menrva (Minerva), and Tinis (Jupiter). They worshiped
the sun (Catha), the moon (Tiv), and the dawn (Thesan).
Their god of love bore the name Turan. Still another group
of gods with nameless powers were personifications of
Fate, while others were underworld deities. In contrast to
the Etruscans' ribald daily life-style, the Etruscan religion was sombre and ridden with superstition. It involved
such extremes as revelations through mystical signs and a
belief in eternal life after death. Worshipers bound by the
religion of Etruria had faith that through observations of
flights of birds, lightning storms, and matches between
fighting cocks they would discover the will of their gods.[4]

Little is known of the daily activities of these ancients, but Roman historians such as Livy have left written records which give rise to some speculation. In general, the Etruscans were believed to have been moody and
cruel. The fact that they were militaristic and marauding
pirates, often unmerciful to their victims, attests to this.
These two negative qualities were hidden by a false gaiety. Both men and women attended bawdy banquets.
Livy, shocked by the freedom and equality Etruscan
women enjoyed, is said to have remarked that "they went
abroad unblushingly attending banquets, reclining on
couches, relishing the repast with their male compan-
ions."[5] Both sexes also enjoyed concerts, boxing matches,
foot and chariot races, and other spectator sports.

This was a society that preferred to appear nude in
public. There are records indicating that their behavior

**Figure 5.2.** As adapted by Etruscan women, the **chiton** was
snug-fitting, made of patterned fabric, and had inset sleeves.
No girdling was used during the earlier periods. Though the
sleeves were sewn into the garment, fibulae were pinned into
the sleeves to imitate the chiton draping. Note **tutulus** or
pointed hat. (Redrawn from statue of *Aphrodite,* fifth century B.C.
Louvre. Paris.)

was often shameless and obscene. Overindulgence was the rule, particularly among intellectuals, artists, and musicians. Some men were exceedingly effeminate, while, conversely, many women were dynamic and had masculine characteristics.

Oddly, these vigorous people were borrowers rather than innovators. Their clothes and luxuries evidenced influences of Egyptian, Greek, Phoenician, Cypriot, and Mycenaean peoples. As has been noted, they were excellent builders and developed a sophisticated system of highways which was remarkably well engineered. They built an excellent sewer system, the *Cloaca Maxima*. They were adept at metal working, using bronze and copper to create utilitarian objects and gold to make jewelry to flatter their persons. They excelled in boot-, shoe-, and sandal-making, creating foot coverings unique among those of their contemporaries.

Architectural decorations had a lively virtuosity, making use of colorful wall paintings in interiors and terra-cotta tiles on exteriors. Though they were skillful ceramicists, the sculpture they created indicates that they had been strongly influenced by the Greeks.

Many authorities claim that the Greek influence on Etruscan costume was very powerful. However, the stylized images that remain of these people clearly illustrate that the arrangement of the Etruscan female chiton

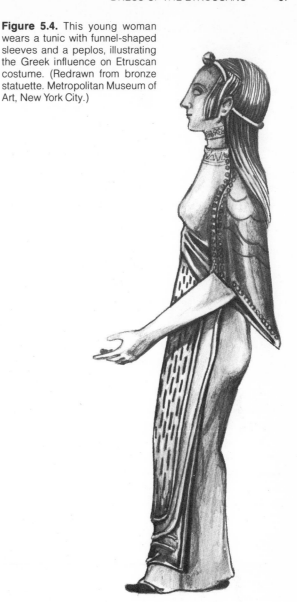

**Figure 5.4.** This young woman wears a tunic with funnel-shaped sleeves and a peplos, illustrating the Greek influence on Etruscan costume. (Redrawn from bronze statuette. Metropolitan Museum of Art, New York City.)

**Figure 5.3.** Lad wears the wound **tebenna** over a short, sleeveless tunic. Note cross-laced sandals. (Redrawn from *Musicians Group*, Tomb of the Leopards, detail, 470 B.C. National Museum, Tarquinia.)

was less cumbersome and confining than that of the Greeks. The female garments were slim, revealing the limbs and ending at the ankles. Often, over the chiton was worn a small shawl which merely covered the shoulders. Large fibulae were used in the sleeve treatment as shown in Figure 5.2. However, unlike the Greek female chiton which had sleeves with deep, cumbersome draping, the sleeves of the Etruscan version were generally snug to the arms.

Male Etruscans were often depicted wearing nothing other than a **tebenna** (Figure 5.7). This was an oval or rectangular scarf larger than the scarf worn by women. Both males and females wore the tunic, or **exomis** (Figures 5.1 and 5.3). The exomis was styled in the same manner as the tunics worn by the Greeks and, in the late ages of this civilization, was worn only by the lower classes.

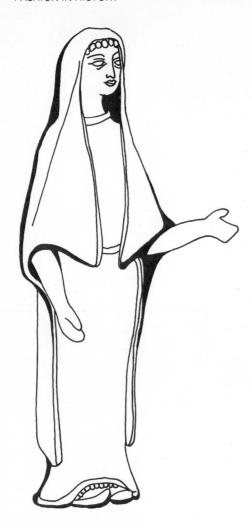

**Figure 5.5.** While some authorities suggest that the Etruscan women wore a shaped cape which was longer in back than in front, it is diagrammatically suggested that it was nothing more than a rectangular length of cloth with the shorter dimension draped over the head and shoulders with the remaining fabric falling down the back. (Diagrammatic sketch: tomb statuette, sixth century B.C. Perugia.)

The funnel-sleeved tunic worn by women was ankle length (Figure 5.4). The skirt width of this garment was sufficiently broad to allow easy movement, providing further evidence that women of this civilization were allowed to behave and move about with self-determination and equality with men. This is not to suggest that, when weather or ritualistic canon required it, the females did not cover themselves completely as in Figure 5.5.

The League of Twelve Cities and its outlying colonies, after many defeats at the hands of the Gauls and the Romans, were subdued by ancient Roman authority. The lasting contributions made by the Etruscans were few and, except for their influence on Roman customs, little af-

fected succeeding cultures. Those that were incorporated into the Roman life-style included certain religious rites; the gods Juno, Minerva, and Jupiter; and engineering fundamentals of their architecture, particularly the arch. Some authorities credit them with evolving a rudimentary alphabet which served as a base for the Roman alphabet, but this is doubtful. Their shoe forms were adopted by the Romans, and, after minor modifications, the tebenna became the Roman status symbol known as the toga.

# Basic Garments of the Etruscans (1300–700 B.C.)

## EXOMIS (1300–700 B.C.)

The **tunic,** or **exomis,** a simple, short-sleeved garment common to all early people, was also worn by both sexes of Etruscans. Because of their concern for revealing the human form, this basic costume of Etruria was narrow, close-fitting, and short, though ankle-length versions were also used (Figure 5.6). Bas-reliefs and wall paintings indicate that some of the snug male tunics barely covered the posterior. Generally, peasants wore the simple exomis, made in the same manner as that worn by the Greeks.

## PERIZOMA (1300–700 B.C.)

The **perizoma,** or tight-fitting trunk, was worn with a waist-length tunic (Figure 5.6). Made as any simple pants form, this brief costume covered the figure from waist to buttocks, outlining the latter because of its extremely close fit. The short legs of this clothing item had small, inverted V-shaped side vents. Occasionally these vents were curved and quite large, the opening extending almost to the waist. Bands of contrasting color trimmed this style, bordering the leg opening and the curved vent. This garment may have been simply a length of cloth worn between the legs and tucked into the girdle to secure it.

## LOINCLOTH (1300–700 B.C.)

These people wore the scant loincloth so common to the costume forms of all ancients. It was made from a long, thin length of cloth and was worn between the legs and secured about the waist with a belt, or simply tied about the figure with the ends falling down in front.

## TEBENNA (c.1200–700 B.C.)

Said to be the forerunner of the Roman toga, the semicircular **tebenna,** or **trabea,** was an Etruscan garment innovation for both sexes (Figures 5.7, 5.10, and 5.12). The knee-length tebenna was wrapped around the figure in the same manner as the Greek male himation.

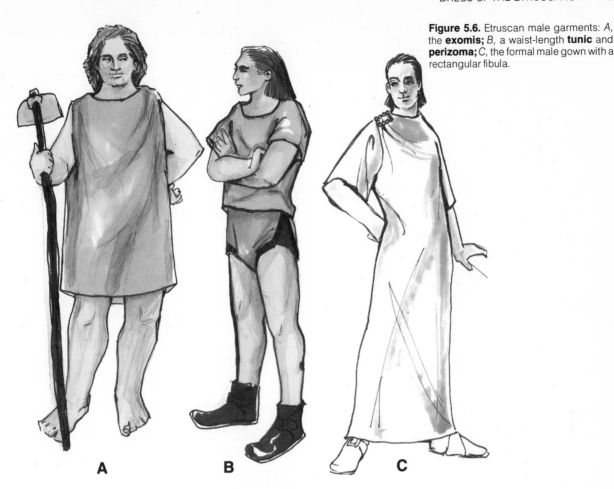

**Figure 5.6.** Etruscan male garments: *A*, the **exomis**; *B*, a waist-length **tunic** and **perizoma**; *C*, the formal male gown with a rectangular fibula.

The oval or circular form was folded in half. It was placed under the left arm with this fold at the top and wound about the body in a spiral fashion, with the curved edges creating interesting draped effects. It was made of woolen cloth which was usually white and had gay decorative borders of red or blue. A black bordered tebenna was worn exclusively during a period of mourning. Many young men wore only this garment, casually tossed over the chest with the loose ends falling down the back.

## CHLAMYDON

The **chlamydon** was a simple, wound garment of lightweight patterned fabric (Figure 5.8). While rather formless itself, it was pulled taut about the body, revealing the natural curves and forms of the figure. This was a garment worn primarily by young men, perhaps for festivals only. It had decorative borders as well as the overall, random patterns embroidered or painted on the cloth from which it was cut.

## SKIRT AND BLOUSE (c.1100 B.C.)

Women wore a decorative, full, bell-shaped skirt around 1100 B.C. (Figure 5.9). The fabric of this garment was covered with an ordered pattern of crosses or dots.

Skirts made of striped material arranged to create horizontal bands about the figure were also worn. Bands of contrasting color decorated the hem. This garment was ankle length and was similar in many ways to the bell skirt worn by Cretan women, though it was much fuller.

An elaborately styled blouse with a yoke was worn with the full, gathered skirt. It was made of intricately cut pieces, particularly the sleeves. These were designed with curved cuffs, bands of contrasting colors encircling the arms, and long, floating ribbons attached at the cuffs. Sleeves were elbow length and often bell shaped.

## CHITON (c.1100 B.C.)

The Etruscan **chiton**, worn extensively by men and women, was an adaptation of the Greek chiton (Figure 5.10). Women's styles were made of very thin, transparent fabrics dyed in extremely dark hues. These fabrics were covered with random or ordered patterns of geometric or floral designs. The female chiton was also decorated with bands or geometric borders at the hem.

Men also wore the chiton, but the male style fitted the figure closely. Warriors wore leather chitons of scant length under their armor, patterned after the Archaic style of Greek chitons for men.

**Figure 5.7.** Young Etruscan man wears naught save a **tebenna** and a fillet to keep his hair tidy. (Redrawn from *Youth with Drinking Cup,* 470 B.C. National Museum, Tarquinia.)

**Figure 5.8.** Reclining youth wears wrapped **chlamydon** used for festival occasions. (Redrawn from statue of *Reclining Youth.)*

**Figure 5.9.** Etruscan dancing girl wears an intricately cut blouse with inset double sleeves of patterned fabric bound with a contrasting color. Dots and stripes pattern the gathered skirt. Wound about her arms is a thin scarf with bell tassels on lengthy cords. Her feet are clad in soft leather boots which extend above the ankle. (Redrawn from illustration in B. Payne, *History of Costume.)*

**Figure 5.10.** *A,* Etruscan male in the wound garment called the **chlamydon.** *B,* Etruscan woman wearing **chiton,** of Greek origin, with **tebenna** overgarment closely resembling the peplos. *C,* figure illustrates the female tunic which often was tied in back. (Redrawn from bas-relief of *Orestes Avenging His Father,* Carlsberg Glptotek. Copenhagen, Denmark.)

## OVERTUNIC

The **overtunic** worn by women was made in much the same way as a tunic but with inset sleeves (Figure 5.11). These sleeves were somewhat flared at the cuff. The longer-sleeved styles had cuffed sleeves formed by rolling full-length sleeves to the elbows. The neckline was broad but shallow. When worn for added warmth over the blouse and skirt costume, the high-standing blouse collar projected above the broad, low neckline of the overtunic. This overtunic was seldom if ever belted, and it covered the figure from the shoulder to mid-calf. An ankle-length overtunic was also used. This longer version had a band of trim around the neck which sometimes extended down the center front. Both men and women are depicted wearing this style. Insets in the side seams were pleated, adding fullness to the skirt at the hem of the overtunic.

## SCARF (1300–1100 B.C.)

The Etruscan scarf was made from a long, rectangular length of cloth and was an adaptation of the Greek himation. This wrap was brightly colored, often red, yellow-orange, or royal blue. A saw-toothed border design of yellow or brown was the distinctive decorative element of this wrap. The manner of wearing the scarf differed for each sex, corresponding to that established in Greece.

## LACERNA

The **lacerna** was a short, circular cape worn by men and women of the lower classes. It was made of rough, heavy woolen cloth and had a center front opening extending from the simple round neck to the thigh-length hem. This too was a borrowed garment form based on the Greek tribon.

# Accessories (1300–700 B.C.)

Few people wore hats; however, the conical **tutulus** was used by some women (Figure 5.2). This oddly designed hat form had a tall, cone-shaped crown with a small, turned-down knob at the top. The small brim was

**Figure 5.11.** The **tunic** and thigh-length **overtunic** were customarily worn by older women in Etruria and Rome. The wrist-length sleeves generally were rolled to the elbows when the wearer was working. This was a utilitarian form of dress and the added overtunic was for warmth only.

worn upward, framing the face. The back of the head and hair was covered with a long, sacklike sheath or a gold net. This hat was perhaps a poor copy of the Phrygian cap. It was worn well back on the head and probably was made of rather firm material such as felt or leather, for it held its shape even though projecting precariously outward from the back of the head.

A draped and wrapped head covering was used by women, particularly older matrons (Figure 5.12).

## FOOTWEAR

Etruscans were accomplished shoemakers. Three basic forms of footwear predominated: the slipper, the sandal, and the boot. The slipper was made of one piece of felt or cloth in a simple shell form that covered the sole

and the top of the foot (Figure 5.13). The fabric colors included red, green, and brown.[6] A variation of this slipper had instep laces and was open at the toe and heel. Etruscan sandals were rather delicate footwear with thin straps and binding laces attached to a leather sole. Boots were sturdy and were made with leather soles and tops. The body of the boot covered the foot and the lower leg. The section that covered the foot and the back of the leg was laced together with thongs.

## JEWELRY

Much of the Etruscan jewelry was imported, though the Etruscans too created handsome body ornaments. They are credited with the lost art of soldering powdered gold to jewelry. In an affluent society, the female Etruscan aristocracy possessed great casks filled with gold rings, brooches, fibulae, bracelets, clasps, and earrings. Earrings were an important accessory, and they dominated the costume by their enormous size and length. There were three-inch long pendants with snakes or human heads as the design theme. Gold and precious stones

**Figure 5.12.** Dancing girl wears a wrapped **tebenna** over a ceremonial gown, perhaps a **chiton,** with a deep border of contrasting color and center-front vertical stripe. Her feet are clad in soft leather Etruscan boots. The draped and wrapped head covering was later adapted by Roman women. (Redrawn from fresco in Ruovo tomb, fifth century B.C. Museo Nazionale, Naples.)

etched with images of small birds or animals, arabesques, and floral volutes were used extensively.

# Hairstyles (1300–700 B.C.)

The earliest female hairstyle was simple, with the hair falling about the head and body to the waist. Later the hair was trained into corkscrew curls about the face and arranged into small pencil braids in back. Hair was also formally waved over the brow and drawn back, plaited into a floor-length braid that was then encased in a long cloth sheath. The hair in back also could be enclosed in a gold net that was secured just behind the ears. In this coif a jumble of curls, originating from waves drawn smoothly over the forehead, fell in front of the ears. Coronets and wreaths of golden leaves were the primary head decorations. Blonde hair was much admired and Etruscan women used bleaches to attain it.

Men wore their hair rather short, with curls over the entire head and with sizable sideburns. In a very early style, they also pulled the hair back from a center part and formed two club pugs behind the ears. Some men wore a chin-fringe beard or a sparse jawline beard ending in a stiletto point at the chin.

FOOTNOTES
1. François Boucher, *20,000 Years of Fashion*, p. 113.
2. *Funk and Wagnalls New Encyclopedia*, edited by Joseph Laffin Morse, vol. 9, pp. 198–202.
3. H. W. Janson, *History of Art*, p. 45.
4. *Funk and Wagnalls New Encyclopedia*, vol. 9, pp. 198–202.
5. Mila Contini, *Fashion, from Ancient Egypt to the Present Day*, p. 45.
6. Ibid., p. 48.

**Figure 5.13.** Many of the Etruscan clothing forms were borrowed from other cultures. Young girl wears a sleeved gown over which is placed a decorative, thigh-length version of the Grecian **peplos,** bordered with a wide band and patterned throughout. The shoes have turned-up toes reminiscent of the footwear of Asia Minor. (Redrawn from bronze statue, Etruscan, c. 550 B.C. Metropolitan Museum of Art, New York City.)

# Chapter 6

# How the Romans Looked

## (700 B.C.–A.D. 476)

Horace's statement, "Captive Greece took Rome captive" is a truism of antiquity. The centuries of Roman influence over vast areas of land extended from hundreds of years before the birth of Christ to well into the Christian era. The growth and rise of Rome to power can be divided into three parts: the Kingdom (750–509 B.C.), the Republic (509–30 B.C.), and the Empire (30 B.C.–A.D. 476).

The Roman Empire was carefully constructed upon conquest, diplomacy, and citizenship for the conquered. Intelligent management of the people that Rome defeated served to make this far-flung domain cohesive. The Romans respected what progress had been made by those they conquered and fused the foreign concepts of politics, art, and engineering with their own. The more gifted intellectuals and artists were given honored positions within the social structure dictated by Rome. Captured Greek scholars were brought to the capital on the Italian peninsula to teach offspring of the highborn. In Gaul, schools with Latin curricula ultimately surpassed the quality of the schools in Rome.

The Romans also demanded much of the inhabitants of conquered provinces. Heavy taxes were imposed, and the bureaucrats who administered the tax collection were often unfair and incompetent. In turn, however, Rome gave much to the provinces. This influence created a bond that lasted for centuries and through the two diametrically opposed religious philosophies of the pagans and Christians.

Rome provided those she conquered with laws, the philosophical and aesthetic concepts of Greece, the religion of Jupiter, and the philosophical concepts of Christ. Roman citizenship, which was granted to provincials, enabled some to become greats of Roman literati. Roman military might protected the provinces against invasions by barbarian hordes. Throughout the empire, Roman engineers improved crude provincial roads and built aqueducts. Trade between widespread provinces made it possible for an exchange of goods and products. By treating the people they conquered moderately and with tact,

**Figure 6.1.** This funeral stele depicts a Roman gentleman and his wife formally garbed in the clothes of their time. (*Roman Couple*, 50–40 B.C. Capitoline Museums, Rome.)

the Romans were able to win them over and eventually to civilize them.

The military writer Vegetius wrote the maxim, "He who desires peace should prepare for war." This was the basis of Roman foreign policy. Roman might lay in the loyalty of the men who served in the army. Aristocrats served as generals, and all Roman boys were raised to revere the state, to serve it, and to protect all that it stood for.

Originally Rome developed as a trade center. Located on the Tiber, it became the meeting place for Sabines, Romans, and Etruscans. City-states situated on the seven hills were merged, forming a loosely knit coalition which also included the nearby plains areas. About 509 B.C. a patrician-dominated state evolved to form the Roman Republic, which was ruled by consuls who eventually gave more status to plebes or commoners.

The Roman people, spurred by their leaders, were encouraged to expand their lands by tireless conquest. They sacked Gaul and Greece and subjugated the Semitic people. By the third century B.C., Rome controlled most of the areas of the Mediterranean.

Although often torn by internal conflicts, the Roman people were temporarily united in 60 B.C. when the First Triumvirate was formed by Pompey, Crassus, and Julius Caesar. In the ensuing rivalry between the three leaders, Crassus was killed in battle, and Caesar emerged victorious in the power struggle with Pompey. Caesar became the sole ruler of Rome and, although he generally used his power well, was assassinated by conspirators in the Senate.

After Caesar's death there was another period of turmoil as Mark Antony and Octavian struggled for supremacy. In 27 B.C. Octavian triumphed and became the first emperor of Rome. Adopting the name of Augustus, he consolidated the Roman Empire. Emperors Tiberius, Caligula, and Claudius enlarged the empire until it spanned from the British Isles to the Orient.

Under the rule of Marcus Aurelius, Rome prospered and was at peace. Art flourished during the reign of Nero.

**Figure 6.2.** This dignified Roman wears a toga **(amictus)** and **tunica exteriodum.** The border on the hem indicates that he is a person of status and is garbed in a **toga praetexta.** (Statue: Aulus Metellus, detail, 100 B.C. Archaeological Museum, Florence.)

By A.D. 313, before Rome was divided again by internal strife, Germanic invaders plus the power of Byzantium and countless other factors contributed to the downfall of the power that once was Rome's.

No matter how sophisticated Rome became, its beginnings were humble. The basic naivety of the Romans allowed them to accept the legend of Romulus and Remus. Remaining true to the soil and their heritage, they accepted discipline and respected strength. Rigorous Roman discipline taught them to be always loyal, frugal, and tenacious. *Mos Maiorum,* "always of the fathers," was an inbred concept and pervaded the Roman citizens' outlook on life.[1] Their loyalty to their gods, to their state, and to their families was a paramount attitude governing their life-styles.

The pattern recognizing the domination of the family head over its members had been established early in this culture. By law the head of the family, *pater familias,* had absolute power over all its members. Therefore, it was not difficult for these ancients to accept the authoritarian state and, ultimately, the all-powerful emperors.

The chief authority of the land was called *pater patriae,* father of the country. Great power and influence were bestowed on individuals who served the state. This service to the state was given as an extension of the obligation each person felt for his immediate family and was thus given, with equal loyalty, to the state.

Dignity is another key to understanding Roman character (Figure 6.2). Cicero's works clarify this facet of the Roman personality. He explains that dignity meant to them, "weightiness, a weighty quality, sobriety, monumentality, endurance." Possibly these qualities fortified the Roman character and allowed them to perpetuate their rule over so many people for 800 years. The Roman Empire was built on the credo of strength, not delicacy, of power instead of agility, of mass rather than beauty.

The heavy swathing of the human body in the toga was an outward visible symbol of this weightiness, massiveness, and hence strength (Figure 6.1). Men of ancient Rome never hurried because, encumbered by their heavy status-identifying cloaks, they were forced to move with weighty dignity. Unlike the Grecian women who glided about gracefully despite their cumbersome garb, Roman patricians and citizens strode slowly and emphatically to give credence to an expressed concept.

Fond of ceremonial fetes, the pompous Romans never stooped to bawdy or frivolous festivals.[2] Ceremonial celebrations were organized to show the importance of a person or event. The festival's importance was a constant reminder of the eminence of their forebears. The dominance of Roman lives by public and private rituals conditioned the Romans for acceptance of the ritualistic liturgy of the Roman Christian church. The new faith vanquished the old pagan faith but did not eliminate the ceremonial aspects. Thus, a continuum was established between the old and the new religion. The new Christian religion affected the concepts of many Roman citizens, which in turn changed the tide of the Roman Empire.

The pre-Christian Roman religion was abstract, based on ethical concepts and fundamentally associated with worldly conditions. Formal worship ceremonies were brief, dedicated to such dieties as Saturnus, god of planting; Fides, god of faithfulness; and Terminus, the god of territorial limits. Oracles and other means of foretelling the future were an integral part of the early Roman faith. Of great importance was the god of the home. Six vestal virgins in the Forum attended the sacred fires of this god, which were kindled anew each year. Then the home fires were relighted by a flame brought from this sacred fire. In time Greek gods were adopted and renamed. A female underworld god, Matura, represented with a child in her lap, was to become the Madonna of Christianity.

The Romans were so ritualistically oriented that even declarations of war followed a precise format. A priest of their pagan multigod religion was charged with formally presenting a list of specific grievances to the offending nation or territory. He also presented a demand for compensation to assuage the grievance. These demands were often exorbitant, and, if not met, war was officially declared. Before military retaliation, a justification for the grievance was always outlined with great care.

Roman lives were as orderly as their governmental structure. Private life, as in public life, was bound by ritual and ceremony. On the day of birth a Roman infant was ritualistically laid at his father's feet. As a sign of acceptance into the family, the father gathered the child up in his arms. In early Roman times, infants rejected by their father were put out in a public place to die.

Because the family was the ministructure of the whole social order, marriage was important. Proper grooms were sought so that the right marriage might be arranged. The family members, or a matchmaker who was generally a family friend, sought out the most eligible young man. At a festive ceremony the betrothal was announced, a ring given to the bride, and the dowry set. In time the marriage took place but, unlike Greek weddings, a Roman woman could choose one of three forms. In the *confarreatio*, generally the form selected by patricians, the wife's property and person were given wholly to the husband. The *coemptio* allowed wives more freedom and the ceremony of this type included the husband symbolically buying his wife from herself. The *usus* allowed the wife to keep all her property as long as she held to the stipulations of this form.

A Roman bride planned her wedding with great care. Days and months were selected after due consideration, for neither March nor May were thought lucky. The first half of June and certain days throughout the year were assumed to be inopportune also. On the night before the selected wedding day, the bride offered her toys and childhood garb to her father's house gods. The morning of her marriage day was spent in dressing for the occasion. Freshly bathed and anointed with scented oils, the bride donned a tunic which was girdled about the waist with a woolen sash.[3] Knotted in a Hercules knot, this sash could not be untied save by the groom. A saffron yellow palla was placed about her figure in the customary manner. Her hair, carefully plaited in six braids, was covered with an orange veil. She was then crowned with a wreath of orange blossoms or other delicate flowers.

The ceremony was performed by two priests while the bride and groom held hands and sat on two sheepskin-covered stools. The event was solemnized with the eating of special wheatcakes while the rites were read and the marriage witnessed and sealed. Then banqueting and entertainment followed until darkness fell, at which time the wedding party progressed to the groom's house. There the bride was lifted over the threshold by a friend after she had anointed the doorway. In the Roman rite, carrying the bride indoors was performed to prevent her from tripping, a bad omen. Once inside, the bride received from her new husband a water vessel and a lighted torch, the most necessary tools of homemaking. Having lighted the hearth fire, the bride would fling the torch out to the assembled well-wishers. Good luck was supposed to come to whomever retrieved the torch. The tossing of the bride's bouquet is a remnant of this tradition.[4]

Family formalities changed slowly over the centuries. Ancient Romans were reluctant to institute instant changes, but by A.D. 100 *pater familias* no longer had absolute authority. Instead, the clan gathered in conference to solve problems which arose.

During the earlier stages, families were required to educate their children at home. In time this too changed, and boys and girls were sent to school to be taught, often by a Greek intellectual. Training was divided into several phases. Primary education for both sexes was presided over by a *literator* and continued until the age of twelve or thirteen. At this age, a girl of high social status returned home and was given special tutoring. Boys continued formal group education in the *gramaticus* to learn Greek, Latin grammar, history, geography, and astronomy. They concluded their formal studies at the *gramaticus* at sixteen and attended the Roman equivalent of college, the *rhetor*.

Boys came of age at sixteen and exchanged their red-bordered **toga praetexta** (Figure 6.3) for the **toga virilis.** This was an important advance for a boy, and it was celebrated elaborately in the Roman fashion with a liberation feast. He also was given a shave and the haircut of an adult male. After the rites of liberation were observed, the lad, now a man, was formally recognized as a member of the clan. The son of an extremely wealthy family continued to expand his knowledge through travel to centers of ancient cultures, primarily Greece.

**Figure 6.3.** Lad wearing the **toga praetexta** without a tunic. The twist over the abdomen could be used as an elementary pocket. (Redrawn from statue of *A Boy of the Julio-Claudia Family,* first century B.C. Metropolitan Museum of Art, New York City.)

Roman males, in this highly structured society, were governed by a strict code. Trades and professions were divided into two categories—liberal and vulgar. Again, Cicero's writings explain these terms. The term *liberal* was applied to such professions as medicine and law, etc. He relates that the *vulgar* classification included customs officials, usurers, and unskilled laborers. The wages paid to the workers in these ranks were the badge of slavery to the class. Other occupations listed under the vulgar classification were mechanics, and those which ministered to pleasure such as fishmongers, butchers, cooks, sausage makers, perfumers, and performers. Many businesses classified as vulgar were beneath the dignity of an upper-class Roman. But, just as the Romans tricked offending nations into war, so they deluded themselves into vulgar businesses. This was accomplished by turning over a vulgar business to a hired agent. Romans, unlike the high-minded Greeks, were not overly concerned with ethics.

Highborn Romans were limited in their choice of acceptable liberal professions although approval was granted for the practice of law or politics. Service in the army, usually as an officer, or management of large family-owned farms were also appropriate occupations.

Unlike the females of Greece, a matron of Rome often acted for her husband if he were absent or ill. Class lines in Roman times were strictly drawn. The aristocrats (patricians or *nobiles*) held office through hereditary succession. Occasionally, wealthy and influential plebeians were allowed to hold certain offices as well. Businessmen were the next highest class and were referred to as *equestrians*. Patricians and equestrians had full rights of citizens, but plebeians, freemen, and liberated slaves did not.

All classes were distinctly visible, for the style and decoration of their costumes were strictly prescribed. Athletes strode about nude while commoners wore the rough wool garments of their class—the **tunica** and **toga sordida**. A candidate for office wore a white chalked **toga candida**; a boy under sixteen wore the red-trimmed *toga praetexta*; and only an emperor could wear a royal purple toga.

In this stratified social structure there developed a complex system of patronages for which there is no modern equivalent. Each class above the plebeians was obliged to look after its inferiors. In a way this system took the form of protection and assistance. The recipients, in gratitude, were required to be loyal to their patron and to give support and respect as prescribed. Begun during the period of the Republic (509–30 B.C.), by the latter years of the Empire in the third century A.D., every Roman male citizen was obligated to someone whose station was higher.

A woman was not a part of this complex patronage, for though more liberated than her contemporaries in other countries, she was primarily a housewife. She had charge of the provisions and all household wares and efficiently managed the children. She oversaw the cooking and weaving but she did not actually perform these arts if she were a patrician. Even those of modest circumstances had two or three slaves, while the most affluent had hundreds of slaves to perform these tasks.

Slavery markets were supplied by victims of Roman conquests. A slave's lot varied from that of utter wretchedness to that of a comfortably situated slave in the city. Slaves who worked in mines were poorly fed, scantily clad, and left to die when they could no longer work. The lucky slave might manage to buy his freedom or be given freedom, as in the case of Tiro, who received his freedom from his owner Cicero.

A slave was allowed to enter into business, although from its profits he was forced to pay his owner a royalty. A slave with business acumen was able to amass a *peculium,* a fund with which he bought his freedom. Once a freeman, he in turn might own slaves.

With slaves to provide a luxurious life-style, it was easy for Romans to indulge in lavish entertainments.

Banquets of the wealthy were eaten in the *triclinium*, or formal dining area. This adjoined the large reception area, or atrium. Well-to-do homes in ancient Rome were built around an open courtyard with sleeping quarters and dining areas opening off the reception area. The atrium had a covered colonnade while the center was open to the sky. The focal point of the atrium was a shallow mosaic pool which was decorative and functional since it was used to collect rainwater for household use.

Roman fare was more varied than that enjoyed by their contemporaries. Three-course meals included salads, shellfish, honey, and eggs as appetizers (*gustus*). Lobsters garnished with asparagus, capon, and boar with truffles and apples often were served as the entrée or *cena*. Cakes and fruits in abundance were eaten during the dessert course. However, peasants and slaves ate bread spread with olive oil and honey. Fruits, including grapes, were also part of the commoner's food staples.

Feasting, festivals, religious ceremonies, and games in the Colosseum or Circus Maximus occupied much of the time of the leisure class. They enjoyed gambling and simple games for their quiet evenings at home. A favorite individual pastime was reading. Book stalls full of scrolls of novels, histories, and other forms of literature abounded.

Bathing at the huge *thermae* was another daily diversion. These creative comfort accommodations might be likened to modern shopping centers. Ringed by shops and offices, the large inner courtyard contained the bathing areas plus libraries, gymnasiums, and sports arenas.

The bathing ritual was as formalized as all the other activities. Exercise, bathing in hot pools (*calidaria*), tepid pools (*tepidaria*), and cold pools (*frigidaria*) were followed by massages.[5] In the morning men enjoyed conversation, carried on business transactions, and listened to lectures or musical concerts. Women, who arrived with their slaves in the afternoon, had their bodies rubbed down with a curry comb of ivory, one side coarse and one side smoother.

The public gathering places, such as the Baths of Caracalla or Baths of Constantine, were another material expression of the Roman love for luxury and grandeur. The Forum, the Colosseum, the Circus Maximus, the arches of Titus and Constantine, and the Palace of Septimius Severus are additional examples of their fondness for massive structures built to honor or commemorate a person or event. These and the great system of aqueducts, Roman roads, and Hadrian's Wall in northern England still stand as testaments to Roman engineering skill.

The art of Rome was not inspired directly by its religion. The ideal of individual service to the state was a paramount concept contributing to their art forms. Decorous behavior was significant in their lives and was transformed and represented as beauty in their art. These qualities also influenced the form of Roman architecture.

The vast structures such as the Baths of Diocletian, the Basilica of Maxentius, the buildings of the Forum, and the House of the Fawn in Pompeii are representative of their skill and mastery as architectural designers. Wall paintings used as interior decoration were well drawn and beautifully organized spacially. The sculpture of Rome was dominated by portraiture which attained a remarkable degree of realism and grace, for Greek art was their ideal.[6] They borrowed perfection from the Greeks and used it to their own ends.

The Roman character and interests were reflected in their costume. Elegance and luxury were lavished on their garb as in all aspects of their life-style. Wealthy women vied with one another in the fashions they wore. Hairstyling became so intricate and changed so swiftly that marble busts of Roman matrons were made so that the hair sections might be removed.[7] Thus, even the marble portraiture of prominent patricians might always be in fashion.

Before the fall of Rome, even males of high rank were caught up in fashion. The **tunica lati clavi** with its purple vertical bands was worn by every important male and was arranged with meticulous care. The ponderous toga was draped by attending slaves so that the wearer might appear in all his dignity. Late in the Roman period of power, garments to identify rank and office were created for special occasions.

Many early garments of Rome had been adapted from those worn in other countries. The early cloak called the **amictus** served as a wrap by day and bed coverlet by night. Made of a semicircular piece of material that was eight feet in diameter, this body covering was common to Romans, Greeks, Etruscans, and Macedonians. The Gauls and the Celts wore a similar style of cloak. The **trabea**, a short toga; **femoralia**, or **feminalia**, the short pants worn during the winter; and the stola had origins in other cultures.

At a casual glance the attire worn by the Romans closely resembled that of the Greeks. But Rome was a latecomer in the power struggle of ancients. When it did gain ascendancy over most of the world, it became heir to many resources, not the least of which were technical advances and textile sources. The needle had been refined and dye processes perfected. Trading centers provided a wide variety of textiles ranging from rough wools to cotton brought from India, linen from Egypt, and silk from the Orient. Fabrics were dyed in many colors including sea green, azure blue, flesh pink, dark blue, red, yellow, and orange.

Roman women, particularly after the period of the Kingdom, preferred soft, flattering silks and cool, delicate cotton garments. Color was also important to Roman patrician females, and they selected a wide range of hues.[8] They were also daring in combining colors, using flesh pinks with saffron yellows, oranges with reds, deep purples with azure blues.

The **stola,** the adaptation of the chiton, had inset sleeves which were pinned to match the fibulae-fashioned sleeve facsimile of their Greek counterparts. Because females of Rome were not as housebound or subservient as Grecian women had been, they wore less cumbersome garments. Both stola and **palla** were arranged to allow more freedom of movement. Women wore the palla more as a decorative, colorful accessory than as a figure-swathing cloak. The toga and smaller trabea (tebenna) were their protective wraps. These were worn for travel, and the entourage of a wealthy patrician woman would include an extensive wardrobe and was attended by a large retinue. Living comforts of luxury, lavish linen, tents for rest stops, cases of rich clothes, gold and silver plates, and items for her toilette accompanied these tours.

Women and men wore several layers of clothing during the Imperial era. While the Romans were not prudish, the fashion of appearing in the nude was going out of style. Also, the Italian climate was less temperate and more clothing was needed for warmth. Romans seemed to adhere to the adage, "clothes make the man."

The undergarments for men were labeled the **indumenta.** The indumenta consisted of a lower-body covering—either the waist-to-mid-thigh **subligaculum,** or the **licinium,** the official garb of athletes—and the *tunica indumenta.* In the earliest Roman period, the subligaculum, a loincloth knotted at the waist, was the only undergarment. The *tunica indumenta*, a torso covering, was added later. This tunic was generally made of linen for patricians and plebians. However, coarse wool was used for these garments when worn by slave laborers, field hands, and miners. The tunic was sewn on shoulder and side seams after the manner of the Greek exomis.

On top of these two garments the men wore the *tunica exteriodum.* During the early days of Rome both men and women used the amictus as an outer wrap. The amictus closely resembled the himation. Late in the first century femoralia, short pants, were worn beneath the *tunica exteriodum.*

Beneath the stola or *talaris insita* (a long gown), women wore a breast band called either the **strophium, zona,** or **mamillare,** and the fitted pagne (loincloth).[9] The stola and talaris were held smoothly about the hips by a band girdle called the **succincta.** To take off the chill in the home women often wore the waist-length **sapparum,** which had half sleeves. The shoulder shawl or cape, called an **olicula,** was worn for the same purpose. The palla replaced the amictus as the sophisticated female's outer wrap. These items were the basic garments worn by the Romans, who developed a large variety and elegant style in their clothing.

Elegance in costume was achieved by using precious and semiprecious jewels. Jewels were sewn to the stola and tunic in intricate patterns. This was an Oriental influence, and pearls were the preferred decorative trim on body coverings and footwear, which was created of white leather. While diamonds were available and given great value, they were seldom used, for the method of faceting diamonds was unknown. In addition to the wide use of pearls, which covered the clothes of men and women, emeralds, aquamarines, and opals were most commonly used. Pearls were not only embroidered upon garments, but were used to fashion necklaces and earrings. One earring style was created by hanging a pearl inside a golden form. When these were worn, the swinging earring gave off a musical sound as the head turned. This double-pendant earring was sometimes called **crotalia.** Techniques of jewelry making were possibly acquired from the Etruscans who were proficient in this art. The sumptuous quality of the apparel and the bejeweled and golden accessories, however, was an Oriental influence. Strangely, the engagement ring, given to the prospective bride during the betrothal ceremony, was an iron ring, occasionally gold washed. It had symbolic rather than intrinsic value.

There were several variations of the female outer wrap or scarf (palla). The earliest form was a simple rectangle of fabric draped about the figure and fastened at the breast. Later, a double length was used which was arranged so that one end fell down in front, the other in back (Figure 6.4). Another seamed style was created by drawing a slender length of fabric over the chest and thence the shoulders. The two ends passing over the shoulders were brought together in back and seamed, creating a neck opening. The trailing ends fell down over the back of the figure.

The most lavish apparel was worn during the period of the Empire (30 B.C.–A.D. 476). Important events such as banquets, celebrations of victorious conquests, and religious ceremonies demanded the most elegant attire. Preparation for such occasions was attended to with great care. The Romans were concerned daily with fastidiousness, and great public and private occasions demanded even greater care with their toilette. Hair and skin were of utmost importance. Women dyed their brunette hair red or blonde in imitation of Britons and Germans. Brassy yellow hair, however, was not favored by patrician ladies, as this color was a form of advertising used by the courtesans. A slave hairdresser daily spent hours arranging her mistress's tresses. This was a thankless task for, if the coif developed a stray lock or did not flatter the face, the mistress might fly into a rage and subject the slave to pummelings, pinchings, or jabs with pins.[10]

Facials made from ill-smelling concoctions were administered at home and during journeys. These ointments were made by combining sheep fat and breadcrumbs soaked in milk which quickly became rancid. Ovid, an enthusiastic observer of female fads and fancies, suggested that face packs be made from barley, eggs, powdered stag antlers, narcissus bulbs, gum, and honey.

**Figure 6.4.** Female wears a Roman **palla,** arranged so that the loose ends trail down the front and back. (Detail from wall painting, Pompeii. Naples Museum.)

elegantly adorning the human figure. This elegance was the result of the refinement and sophistication of a culture.

Perhaps it was overindulgence, political intrigue, and licentiousness in the latter days of the Empire that caused Rome to succumb to the barbarian hordes from the north in the fifth century A.D. Before their destruction they had hammered out a system of laws, developed a mighty social structure, erected monumental architectonic structures, spread learning and culture to once uncivilized people, and bequeathed the new religious philosophy of Christianity to many whom they conquered. Rome's imprint is as indelible on Western civilization as is that of Greece. In fact, it was the Romans who transmitted Greek philosophical thought and aesthetic perfection to the inhabitants of Roman provinces.

# Basic Garments of Ancient Rome (500 B.C.–A.D. 400)

## TOGA (800 B.C.–A.D. 400)

The huge, enveloping toga, first known as the **amictus,** was the primary garb of the earliest Romans from 500 to 27 B.C.[11] Possibly it was derived from the Etruscan tebenna (trabea) and made from a length of fabric which at first was rectangular. Later, copying more closely the Etruscan tebenna, it was of semicircular shape, and then an oval worn double. The early semicircular amictus had a border of contrasting color, or a border of the same color as the main body of the garment, corded or of slightly different texture (Figure 6.2). The oval toga often had an inset of contrasting color through the center in addition to a border when it was worn to identify emperors, priests, or magistrates.

The toga in its earliest form was made of a length of fabric measuring in excess of three or four yards. During this period it was the only garment worn. Wound spirally about the figure, it bore a striking resemblance to the scarf skirt of the Mesopotamians. Our knowledge of the exact origins of the amictus is primarily speculative. Its evolution was probably the fusion of many garments of the same style from different cultures.

While wearing patterns differed according to individual preference, the amictus was generally placed about the figure with the straight edge at the top and the border at the hem. The left corner was placed under the left arm and positioned so that the lower edge reached to the ankle. The remaining length of fabric was wound about the figure, rising higher at each wrapping. This allowed the border trim to spiral up the figure. With about fifty inches remaining, the fabric was brought up over the shoulder. At this point it might be left to fall free or was bound about the left arm. The right arm was always exposed.

In an attempt to sweeten these mixtures, rose petals or myrrh were added. White skin was greatly admired, and lupine, broad beans, and white lead were lavishly ladled on the face to achieve the desired gleaming whiteness. Cheeks were given color by applying red nitrate.

Although the greatest extravagances developed during the Empire, even during the Republic personal adornment had become so dominant in the minds of Romans that Cicero was called to remark upon it. He was supposed to have said that Roman women were conspicuous in dress and actions. Cicero also remonstrated Catiline for shaving his legs and wearing transparent garments. Excavations of Herculaneum and Pompeii have revealed the greatest knowledge of the lavish dress of the Romans. The murals found at these two sites, many now housed in the Museum of Naples, provide visual evidence of the latter-day Romans' excessive interest in personal adornment.

Captive Greece thus captured Rome—and the Roman interpretation of perfection was visualized by

The gesticulations of the left arm manipulating the hanging end clearly identified the wearer's social sophistication. By winding the trailing end firmly about the left arm, the padded arm could be used to fend off the blows to the head delivered by an adversary if a confrontation occurred during a heated discussion in the Forum.

Many ancient Roman males fashioned a pouch pocket from the excess layers of fabric over the chest, rolling it downward and exposing the breast. Into these primitive pockets might be stuffed book scrolls, daggers, or money pouches.

The initial donning of the toga was arranged with the help of a slave. It was quite impossible for an individual to swath himself alone and produce the desired silhouette of grandeur and solemn dignity. In time the toga was reduced in size and made of rich fabrics of silk decorated with palmata (leaf shape) designs, shot with gold or silver thread and bordered with a color which identified the status of the wearer. These togas were loosely draped about the figure, acting more as an accessory than as a body covering.

As togas evolved to connote rank and social status, they were assigned specific names. The **toga praetexta**, perhaps developed in the middle years of the Republic (400–100 B.C.), identified emperors, priests, certain magistrates, and censors (Figure 6.2). The *toga praetexta*

**Figure 6.5.** A Roman general wearing the **toga picta** and **tunica exteriodum.** (Statue: Marcus Aurelius, A.D. 165. Piazza del Compidoglio, Rome.)

worn by these individuals was white with a purple border woven into the fabric on the straight edge. The curved edges were formed with shears. The *toga praetexta* worn by children until they were sixteen (or until married in the case of young girls) was bordered with a red trim.

The **toga picta** was an elegant wrap made of purple cloth, usually silk. This toga was worn exclusively by victorious army officers (Figure 6.5). It was embroidered with stars stitched in gold thread for generals, or palmata designs for captains. These designs were geometrically arranged in repeat patterns.

All freemen, citizens of Rome in the urban capital or in the provinces, wore the **toga virilis** (800 B.C.–A.D. 400). The *toga virilis* was generally made of unbleached woolen or linen fabric. This toga was adopted by young males upon completing the manhood rites.

Running for political office was one of the chief acceptable occupations of patrician males. During a political campaign for office, seekers chalked their bodies and their togas. Then, as now, white was the color which symbolized purity and integrity. These ancient campaigners must have been startlingly visible with chalked faces and their gleaming white **togae candidae** (500 B.C.–A.D. 400). So garbed, they were easily recognized as they moved among those wearing the mute-colored *togae viriles* and the drab *togae sordidae*.

The **toga sordida**, made of rough spun wool of a drab gray or brown color, was the wearing badge of peasants and slaves.

The **toga vitrea** was a more decorative body covering, not a specific office-identifying symbol. Most assuredly, it set the highborn apart from the low, for it was made of transparent silk fabric. The transparent toga with palmata patterns was a favorite style selected by the more effeminate men of the late period of the Empire.

The **toga gabiana** was worn by soldiers in the Roman cavalry. It was worn from the waist down and tightly secured at the waist so that it would stay in place while on horseback. Foot soldiers wore togas to protect their lower limbs; at night, they used them as blankets.

## TUNICA (700 B.C.–A.D. 476)

Roman males wore many more garments at one time than their Greek or Egyptian contemporaries who lived farther to the south. The **tunica indumenta** was a short-sleeved undergarment. It was cut in a T-shape if there were any sleeves, and the sleeves and body were cut in one piece. Shoulder, side, and underarm seams were sewn together.

Undergarments were covered by the **tunica exteriodum** (Figures 6.2 and 6.5). Made in the same manner as all tunic forms but cut much fuller, the *tunica exteriodum* was thigh length, girdled at the waist, and the bodice section bloused over the belting. The sleeves were full and reached the elbow.

Women wore a floor-length tunic. The female *tunica intima* generally had elbow-length sleeves. However, the ladies' style was definitely an undergarment worn for warmth, not decoration. The patrician intima (**interala,** or **indusium**), was generally linen or silk, while the intima worn by lower-class women was made of wool cloth. At first, the female tunics were either natural linen color or dyed yellow. The silk undertunics, worn by women during the latter days of the Republic and the entire Empire period, were often sea green, flesh pink, or azure blue. *Coan,* a fine, transparent silk fabric from the Aegean island of Kos, was popular during the Imperial period.

Just as a toga with a specific trim designated social status, so did specially decorated tunics. Vertical bands called **clavi,** appliquéd on either side of the neck opening and extending from the shoulder to hem in front and back, were significant of rank, and were usually purple in color. Generally, individuals of greater rank were entitled to wear wider clavi. The *tunica lati clavi,* with the widest bands of all, was worn by members of the consul, the senate, or the priesthood. Military equestrians were entitled to two narrow bands, the *augusti clavi,* which ran from each shoulder to the lower edge of the tunic.[12]

The width and color of the vertical bands served to establish the wearer's place in the structured Roman hierarchy. The same was true of the tunics worn by members of highborn families. The width of the clavi on these garments indicated the political importance, affluence, and rank of the wearer within the patrician class.

A general in the Roman army wore the distinctive *tunica palmette.* This ceremonial garment, embroidered with gold thread in palm-leaf designs and bordered at the hem with gold bands, was used only for celebrations glorifying military victories.

Another festival garment was the *tunica tularis,* which had a hem trimmed with the Greek fret motif embroidered with gold thread. Gold-embroidered stylized animal forms arranged in a random pattern decorated the body of the *tunica tularis.* While the male tunic was generally knee length, the *tunica tularis* was often floor length during the latter days of Imperial Rome. This floor-length style was the wedding garb of the groom.

All *tunicae exterioda* were cut very full. In many cases the body of this outer garment was so wide that before it was carefully gathered and girdled, it would cover the wearer's outstretched arms to the elbows. The sleeves of the outer tunic were also cut quite amply. A tunic with long sleeves was called a *tunica manicata.*

## STOLA (500 B.C.–A.D. 400)

Roman women wore a garment strikingly like the Grecian chiton in appearance but it was far different in cut. The Roman **stola** (Figure 6.6), was a true dress form—cut, shaped, and sewn—while the cleverly cre-

**Figure 6.6.** Simple **stola** is draped off the shoulder and made of such sheer fabric that the female form is readily recognized. The large jewel-encrusted fibula on the right shoulder is typical of the excessive size of these pins used by the Romans. (*Sabina as Venus,* c. A.D. 130. Museum, Ostia.)

ated chiton was made of a single length of fabric. In most cases the stola, the female outer dress, was made on the same pattern as the *tunica intima.*[13]

Sleeves were either snug or loose, and, depending on the season, were either short or long. If the *tunica intima* had elbow-length sleeves, a stola without sleeves might be worn over it. If the sleeves were inset, they were sewn to the body of the garment so that the sleeve seam was on the outer arm. The fabric of the sleeve was often gathered at this visible seam in such a way that it closely resembled the Greek chiton sleeve which was formed by pinning. To further create the illusion of a chiton, chased or jewel-encrusted fibulae were placed at intervals along the sleeve and on the shoulders.

Stolas of silk, often shot through with silver or gold thread, were further embellished with pearls and jewels. Gold braid was used to enhance the neckline. Hems were trimmed with fringe or bands of contrasting color.

The full-cut body of the stola was draped and girdled in a number of ways. The length was altered by blousing the bodice section over the girdling. When the girdling was visible, the belt was not the simple ribbon or cord used by the Greeks. Roman patrician ladies selected rich braids studded with pearls and jewels. Often the back of the stola was cut longer than the front to create a train. A wide variety of styles was achieved by careful attention to the arrangement of pleating, or draping and girdling, which was done by a slave taking instructions from her mistress. The girdle encircling the hips was called the **succincta** and that just under the breasts was labeled the **cingulum.**

## TALARIS (510 B.C.–A.D. 400)

The **talaris** worn by women was basically a stola with a pleated inset added in the back. This pleated gusset, the **insita,** created a train and added fullness to the skirt. Generally, the main body of the talaris was of slender cut and more figure revealing than the stola. Opulence was given to this garment by sewing fringe at the hemline. It was made of a variety of textiles ranging from wool to fine transparent *coan* silk.

The *talaris dalmatica* was a long-sleeved version of this same gown and was popular late in the period when the capital of Imperial Rome was moved to Byzantium. The *talaris dalmatica* usually was made of white silk heavily embroidered in gold.

## SYNTHESIS

Romans, fond of feasting as they lounged on couches, developed a garment particularly suitable for such a posture. Quite logically, this garment was called a **synthesis** for it synthesized the tunic and the toga into one garment. It was worn by the more sophisticated males in Roman society when attending lavish eating orgies. The exact construction is unknown. However, Boucher describes it as a garment which combined the "simplicity of the tunic in its upper half with the fullness of the toga below." It was imperative that a dignified Roman, when dining out, wear a special outer wrap since the toga, draped about the entire figure, was quite cumbersome to wear when eating in a reclined position. It not only hampered consumption of the repast, but also became disarranged.

## DALMATIC

The *tunica dalmatica*, a garment popular in the Roman provinces of Asia Minor, was a late arrival on the Roman costume scene. The dalmatic, similar to the *tunica manicata*, was a floor-length overgarment with full-length sleeves which opened wide at the wrists (Figure 6.7). This utilitarian garment, considered bizarre, was often bordered at hem and cuffs with contrasting bands. Clavi were sometimes added as decoration. While primarily a male garment, older women also adopted it as a useful piece of apparel for extra warmth. It was usually made of wool, for it was used as a protective rather than a decorative garment.

**Figure 6.7.** Roman citizen wearing the sleeved, floor-length **tunica dalmatica** popular during the fifth century A.D. Wrapped over the dalmatic is the **paenula.** Note **clavi** on the tunic. (Composite redrawn from statues of Tiberius and an aedile.)

## OUTER WRAPS (509 B.C.–A.D. 400)

The **casula** was a very early cape-style garment designed much like a Mexican poncho. A square of woolen fabric, folded on the diagonal, was cut on the fold for a neck opening and a slight slit extended down the center front. This slit allowed the head to pass through, but kept the neckline snug about the throat. Truly a cape, the casula had no sleeves and was worn hanging loose, an ideal wrap for travelers on horseback.

Another simple cape form worn primarily by Roman foot soldiers was the **sagum.** It was the Roman version of the chlamys, made from a rectangle of fabric and fastened on the right shoulder with a fibula. For the troops of the

Roman legions, it was a functional wrap which could serve as a cape, a tent, a blanket, or a knapsack. Not as cumbersome as the toga, it was used on long marches as a light wrap. Slaves and peasants recognized its practicality for they too wore the sagum.

A larger version of sagum, the **paludamentum,** was a wrap used by male plebes or commoners when traveling. It was a rugged wrap of coarse wool, either gray or brown in color, and fastened with a fibula either on the shoulder or on the clavicle.

The **laena** was a large calf-length, circular cape. Designed as a decorative wrap for men, it was made of heavy woolen material and lined with a brightly colored fabric. The large variety of warm wraps was needed because of the chill winters in Rome and its northern provinces. The laena was a voluminous garment which would easily cover a figure swathed in multilayers of the *tunica interiodum* and *tunica exteriodum*.

Roman women wore a shaped toga called the **pulla** during the earliest period of Roman history. They soon discarded this garment and adopted the **palla,** a derivation of the Greek himation. Created from a rectangular length of fabric, it was made of woolen material for a short period after its introduction into the female wardrobe.

A similar garment for men was called the **pallium.** It was made of a rectangle of cloth and was sometimes used by those of lesser rank.

The palla worn by patrician women became a decorative accessory. Variety and elegance in this wrap were achieved through fabric, deep border trims of contrasting color, and embroidered patterns worked throughout the length of the material. The eyed needle of bronze or iron, having achieved a refined form, made possible intricate embroidery of gaily colored thread or threads of gold and silver. Fringe, frequently golden threads, also was used to heighten the elegance of this wrap.

Widths of the palla varied from narrow to wide, figure-swathing pieces. The proportions of the palla were dictated by the wearer's whim and whether it was worn as a practical wrap or a decorative accessory. When used as a warm wrap, Roman women bound it about them in much the same manner as the Greeks donned the deplos or himation (Figure 6.8). In time the type of fabric from which the palla was made ranged from woolen material to the gossamer *coan* silk.

For extra warmth within the home, women used the **sapparum.** This was a loose-fitting, short jacket with elbow-length sleeves. The body of this garment probably was gathered at the shoulder seam to create the desired fullness. In appearance it resembled a modern-day bed jacket and possibly was worn only in a matron's private apartment.

Another light wrap was the **clicula.** It was also an at-home garment in the form of an elbow-length circular cape with a center front closing which was tied or pinned at the throat.

**Figure 6.8.** Here the **palla,** worn in much the same manner as the Grecian deplos, is drawn over the head for warmth or protection from the elements. (Redrawn from statue of *Livia*, 10 B.C. Antiquareo, Pompeii.)

The **caracalla** was the Roman version of an overcoat with an attached hood. It was used by men and women only when the weather was extremely cold. The caracalla was cut after the same pattern as the dalmatic, but was open from neck to hem in the center front. Resources do not explain the manner in which this garment was fastened. This large cloak, made of heavy, warm wool, covered the body from head to ankles when the hood was drawn up.

Romans used capes of many different patterns. The largest cape was the **bardocucullus,** which had a circular shape with side slits for armholes and an attached hood. Some authorities have suggested that it was designed originally for wandering bards, since a smaller cape with an attached hood was called a **cucullus** (Figure 6.9). Bard and cucullus were combined to identify this as a garment worn by wandering travelers of the lower class. It was made of rough, homespun wool in drab colors of brown, rust red, or gray.

The **lacerna** was also a hooded, sleeveless cape, but it did not cover the entire figure as did the bardocucullus. The lacerna extended only to the thighs, and generally it was made of a finer, natural-colored wool fabric than the serviceable cloak of travelers. The same style, when made of red material, was called a **birrhus.**

The **paenula** was yet another voluminous cape worn by travelers. The paenula was made from a full circle of woolen cloth with a hole cut on the shoulder fold for a neck opening. Sometimes this cape was made with an attached hood and often was designed with a slit extending some distance down the front from the neck opening.

**Figure 6.9.** Rider wears a hooded short cape **(cucullus)** over a dalmatic, beneath which are **feminalia.** The foot is clad in a **crepida.** (Redrawn from an illustration in B. Payne, *History of Costume.*)

For centuries Roman men were forbidden by law to wear any form of trousers. Indeed, older men, who suffered from cold during the winter months, were forced to wind their legs with strips of wool. Neither hose nor pants of any form were accepted until the end of the Empire period. No one knows why **feminalia** were held in disrepute (note the name of these pants). Perhaps it was considered effeminate to yield to the chill of a winter's day and cover the limbs, or perhaps it was their barbaric origin. In any case, it was not until the Emperor Augustus began to use feminalia as winter wear that they were accepted. Male pant forms originated in Asia Minor. By migrations northward they were adopted by tribesmen encountering the Persians because of the satisfactory leg protection which the trousers afforded. In turn, feminalia were introduced to the Romans during their conflicts with the warriors of Gaul.

Feminalia (**femoralia** or **braies** as they were known to the tribesmen) were knee-length, tight-fitting britches of simple cut (Figure 6.9). At first they were adopted by common Roman foot soldiers and were used only as part of the military apparel until acceptance by Augustus. Up to that time, only foreigners were allowed to wear them on the streets of Rome. Eventually the knee-length feminalia were replaced by the fuller ankle-length **braccae.** However, they continued to be garments for warmth or horseback riding.

The rather rude cut of these garments did not add to the quality of dignity so necessary to the image that Roman males wished to present and to which the toga contributed. Of the toga, however, Tertullian wrote in his treatise *De Pallio,* "It [the *toga puris* or *virilis*] is not a garment but a burden." There are no statues showing males of Imperial Rome wearing both the *toga puris* and feminalia, though these garments appear on human figures of equestrian statues.

## UNDERWEAR (146 B.C.–A.D. 300)

Beneath the male tunic or toga, the **subligaculum,** or loincloth, was worn. If weather demanded, the **subucula,** a close-fitting, short tunic, was used. The loincloth of linen worn by men was known as the **licinium,** which, like the subligaculum, was worn between the legs and held in place by knotting the ends together. The licinium was the official garment of the Roman athlete, who wore no other costume, weather permitting.

Underwear for women consisted of a loincloth (pagne) and the **mamillare.** The mamillare was a band of leather bound under the breasts to lift them and add voluptuousness to the female figure. The **strophium**, also called a **zona,** and pagne were garments worn at the public bath beneath the stola, while participating in exercises which were part of the bathing ritual, or gymnastic events (Figure 6.10). When combined, these garments made a very

After the flammeum became a popular female head decoration, the name was changed to **ricinium**. This accessory was a near necessity for, as its popularity grew, no *grandame* of Rome would be seen in public without a ricinium draped over her carefully coiffed head. It was arranged in a variety of ways and usually was pinned to the head with a hairpin. The flowing ends fell loosely over the bosom or trailed down the back. The ricinium was made from elegant fabrics which often were transparent. Many colors were fashionable including saffron yellow, orange, and azure blue.

### FOOTWEAR

Footwear of this period was designed to suit the demands of the occasion, ranging in style from high boots to silk or white-leather bejeweled slippers. For the most part, Roman shoe forms covered the foot. The earliest of these was the simple, soft leather **carbatina** made from a sole cut two inches larger than the foot size and drawn up over the foot by a thong which laced through slits, crossed over the instep, and tied at the ankle.

The street shoe, or **cacei**, which had a separate sole and top, also covered the foot. It laced over the instep and tied around the ankle with a knot at the back. Patricians wore these shoes made of elegant leather encrusted with gold or silver ornaments and pearls.

The spike-soled soldiers' boots were called the **caligae**. Another rugged high boot, the **pero**, had many variations, one of which identified senators. The senatorial style was made of black leather decorated with a silver *C* placed behind the ankle on the heel.

Women wore white, soft-leather footwear laced with colored silk straps called the **phaecassium**. At home, they wore a simple slipper, the **solea**, or sandals with four straps, one of which was worn between the first and second toes. About the house men wore a shell-shaped slipper called the **campagus**.

The many boot forms developed in the latter years of the Roman civilization include: the **calceus**, a high boot laced on the inside of the lower leg and fitted with a tongue; the **muleus**, similar to the calceus but laced with red thongs and worn only by emperors; the **gallicae**, a knee-high closed boot; the **espadrille**, a boot with the straps laced through eyelets, and **crepida**, similar to those used by the Greeks (Figure 6.11).

The **soccus** was an elegant and decorative slipper that appeared during the last years of this civilization when trade with the Orient introduced fabrics made of silk fiber. This colorful shoe in red, green, yellow, or white fabric was a delicate shell shape and was trimmed with pearls and emeralds.

### JEWELRY

In a society that was so fond of sumptuous personal adornment, jewelry items were numerous. Pins in the

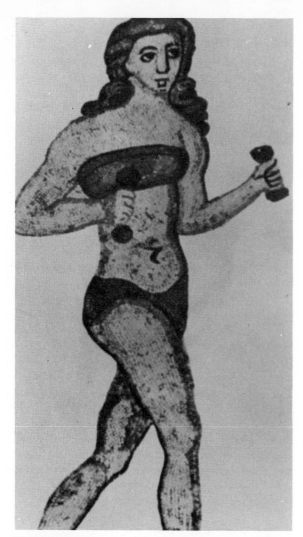

**Figure 6.10.** A Roman woman dressed in **zona** and **pagne** for her exercise session at the thermae. (Mosaic, detail, Piazza Armerini villa, Sicily.)

early version of the bikini bathing suit. The strophium was a simple band brassiere, and the pagne was similar to brief trunks, shaped to fit the figure smoothly.

# Accessories (500 B.C.–A.D. 400)

## HEADWEAR

Roman hats and headcoverings developed in many forms which included the **galarus**, a close-fitting cap; the **causia**, a hat with a low crown, ear flaps, and broad brim; the **pileus**, a cone-shaped cap worn by plebeians and slaves; and the **petasus**, a straw sun hat worn by women and senators to outdoor sports events.

The ceremonial wedding veil, the **flammeum**, was worn by a bride "atop six pads (or braids) of hair and covering the brow," encircled with a wreath of marjoram, verbena, myrtle, or orange blossoms.

**Figure 6.11.** *A* is a heavy-soled **crepida** worn by men and women when traveling. *B* and *C* are Roman sandal forms.

B

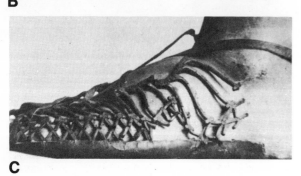

C

with colored paste or enamel; and highly polished stoneware set in a tracery of gold filigree.

Roman bracelets were equally massive and made of the same materials as the necklaces. The serpent bracelet wound about the arm was a popular form. Nero awarded bracelets to heroes of the state, much as chest medals are given today for meritorious acts. Pompey has been credited with initiating the popularity of these arm decorations which ranged from the single circle of metal to the massive, jeweled, hinged, and clasped forms of later periods.

The ring was one of the most unique jewelry items of this era. The iron ring was perhaps the original Roman accessory and later was made of gold. During one period, after a defeat, the wearing of rings was banned, but when the ban was lifted, iron rings again were worn as a sign of mourning. Other fashionable rings were gold-washed iron rings given to prospective brides during the betrothal ceremony, seal rings, key rings, thumb rings, summer and winter rings, and poison rings, which were functional and extremely lethal when used to get rid of foes or to commit suicide.

Poison rings were made with a minute vial which held poison and had a hinged lid. The lid could be surreptitiously lifted, and the lethal contents slyly poured into a victim's goblet.

All rings were decorative, and the effect was enhanced when worn in multiples. Summer rings were small and winter rings were massive. Often those worn on the thumb were as long as three inches. Key rings were worn most often by women who used them to gain access to the household store of supplies in their charge.

## HANDHELD ACCESSORIES

Umbrellas, fans, mirrors, watches, and gloves were popular accessories used by the Romans. Gloves were worn during a meal or lavish banquet for sanitary purposes because guests dipped their hands into common bowls of elegantly prepared food. Watches, while not the complex spring-run devices of modern times, were carried or worn suspended from a chain, and were nothing more than miniature sundials.

form of fibulae or stiletto pins were richly decorated. The Roman fibula had three dominant shapes: the *T*, the harp, and the arrow. The Romans were perhaps the first to create the brooch pin form and to use jewel-encrusted buttons as costume decorations.

Much of the heavy, massive Roman jewelry was imported from the Near East and was less graceful than that worn by the Greeks. Necklaces were set with diamonds, sapphires, garnets, and opals, and were also fashioned from cylindrical beads of amethyst and chrysoprase. Other neckwear designs were ropes of pearls; heavy gold plates encrusted with pearls and inlaid

# Hairstyles (500 B.C.–A.D. 400)

During the early periods, Roman men wore long hair and beards. Later, hairstyles were short and carefully curled by *tonsors*, as Roman barbers were called.[14] Beards, generally worn by older persons of status and dignity, were also short and carefully waved. The hair usually was clipped to lie in flat curls or waves and golden wreaths of laurel were used as head decorations.

Female coiffures evolved from the simple, free-falling, waved, or plaited fashions to rather high pom-

**Figure 6.12.** Ovid is credited with stating that ladies' hairstyles were so numerous that it was easier to count the snails in the sea. (Bust of unknown matron, first century A.D. Capitoline Museum, Rome.)

padours made of corkscrew curls (Figure 6.12). The hair in back was caught up in nets or cauls of gold, or wound with ribbons which bound it in place. During the period of the Empire, hair was parted in the center, waved and puffed out, circling the head. Wigs were formed in the same style. During one period late in the third century B.C., the hair was arranged into shallow waves from a center part, drawn to the nape of the neck, and plaited into three flat braids. These were then brought up over the back of the head toward the front, covering the part. For another popular style of the same era, the hair was formed into two small buns on the neck and held in place by a large, oval clip. A fashion of the second century was to wind braids into a coronet form atop a mass of closely waved hair brought well over the forehead.

Cauls, diadems studded with diamonds and emeralds, or a jewel-encrusted **stephone,** a cloth hair decoration much like a diadem, added elegance to a wide variety of female hair fashions.

## FOOTNOTES

1. Moses Hadas, *Imperial Rome,* p. 36.
2. Ibid., p. 45.
3. François Boucher, *20,000 Years of Fashion,* p. 124.
4. Gisele D'Assailly, *Ages of Elegance,* p. 31.
5. Hadas, *Imperial Rome,* p. 87.
6. H. W. Janson, *History of Art,* pp. 153–54.
7. James Laver, *The Concise History of Costume and Fashion,* p. 42.
8. Mila Contini, *Fashion: From Ancient Egypt to the Present Day,* p. 50.
9. Boucher, *20,000 Years of Fashion,* p. 120.
10. D'Assailly, *Ages of Elegance,* p. 24.
11. Boucher, *20,000 Years of Fashion,* p. 119.
12. Carl Köhler, *A History of Costume,* p. 116.
13. Laver, *The Concise History of Costume and Fashion,* p. 42.
14. D'Assailly, *Ages of Elegance,* p. 31.

# Chapter 7
# Dark Ages and Before
## (8000 B.C.–A.D. 1000)

Wild, fierce men with intrepid spirits braved the last remnants of the Ice Age as it retreated from the northern territories of Scandinavia, Germany, and Jutland. Jutland, Sweden, Norway, and Finland once were joined, but, as the ice retreated, the land rose slowly and fingers of the sea rushed into the low places creating islands and peninsulas.[1]

Authorities believe that members of a Germanic tribe moved to the Danish landmasses about 2000 B.C. The settlers in the Jutland area of Denmark were still hunters using flint tools and weapons. The more adventurous moved on to settle in Sweden. Alvastra, a small, Stone-Age Swedish community based upon a farming economy, was established at this time. Archaeologists have excavated this site and found evidence that the inhabitants fished, farmed, and domesticated pigs, cattle, and dogs. Tribal skills were refined as the Bronze Age (1200–600 B.C.) advanced and new migrants from Hungary, Spain, and France came northward. Cliff paintings of this period illustrate people plowing with oxen, going to sea in oar-powered boats, and riding in horse-drawn wagons.

During the first century B.C., Scandinavia of the Iron Age was making rapid progress. The adventurous Celts of Jutland, who had originally come from Central Europe, again drove south, engaged in battle with the Romans, and were defeated. Operating from a home base in Jutland, these wandering plunderers were in constant flux, making raids into Roman provinces and then returning to their own lands. By A.D. 700 the formidable Norwegian coast was thinly populated, and Finland had a few settlers from the Baltic region.

Strong and rugged, these early ancestors of the Vikings, Visigoths, Celts, Ostrogoths, Franks, Picts, Scots, and Huns withstood the rigors of the climate and the scant food supply to produce the proud, individualistic hordes called barbarians. This name was given to them by the Romans because of the fierce and loyal way in which they fought in battle.

These very early people of the Irish Sea and the North Sea islands, and northern Europe were undoubtedly ruled by chieftains as they were in later centuries. Their first

**Figure 7.1.** Many Roman garments were adapted and worn by barbarians. Shown here is the hooded **bardocucullus.** Ties at the throat end in what may have been spherical metal bells. (Redrawn from bronze statuette, second-fifth century. Musée des Antiquités Nationales, Paris.)

clothing was fashioned from skins of animals and primitive felts. Later, immigrants from the south taught them to create colorful woven fabrics.[2] These people are known to have gone nude during the short, but pleasantly warm summers. Males of the early settlements continued to fish, hunt, sow, and reap food. Females attended to the preparation of food, the care of children, and the making of the rude garments which they wore.

There is evidence in southwestern England that the climate of the southern coast of England was once more temperate than it is now. Palm trees grow there today as living proof of a once milder climate. Many believe that Stonehenge on the Salisbury Plain was a temple erected to honor the gods for granting good crops. Others speculate that this monolithic ruin was built to determine the right time for planting the fields to bring yields of grain in the greatest abundance. The ruins of Stonehenge indicate that the engineering capability of these island people was remarkable. How they mastered the placement of the immense stones into such precise positions remains a mystery.

The Celts, thought first to have inhabited Jutland, and then England and Ireland, had been an organized tribe since the second millennium B.C.[3] They spread their political and cultural leadership into Central and Western Europe between 1200 B.C. and 400 B.C.

The religion of the Celts was based on worship of the sun and a belief in immortality. It was the druid priests of this cult who, through their political power, pressed for invasions of the Italian peninsula.

Picts and Scots were fierce men of northern Britain, whose harassment of the Roman outposts resulted in the construction of Hadrian's Wall to protect the outermost boundary of the Roman Empire in Britain.

The modern-day Scottish kilt evolved from the body coverings of these ancients. Having learned the art of

**Figure 7.2.** The modern-day Scottish kilt design evolved from the ancient draping practices of the **tartan**.

weaving, their first and only garment, the **tartan**, was a length of plaid fabric draped similarly to the himation (Figure 7.2). In time a skirt and upper-body-covering cape were fashioned from a single length of fabric. This garment was created by laying the fabric flat on the ground over a long leather strip which served as a belt and carefully pleating the full length of the fabric. Then, the individual for whom this curious garb was intended lay down on the material, seeing to it that his waist and the belt corresponded. Bringing the two side pieces over the front, he secured the skirt (**kilt**) with the belt and arose. The excess material fell down all around his body from waist to thigh. If it were cold, the excess material of the tartan was brought up over the shoulders and fastened at the clavicle by pinning or tying. In time the cape section was separated from the kilt, and the tartan once again served as a cloak, or merely as a decoration if the weather was warm.

The barbarians' origins were widely separated geographically. Goths, of which there were two dynamic tribes, the Ostrogoths and the Visigoths, swept southward from the Scandinavian peninsula in the fourth century A.D. The Ostrogoths moved eastward into Russia, then turned west, and finally south to settle in Rome. The Visigoths followed a parallel route for a time and then split off, ultimately settling in the Pyrenees region after having traversed much of the lands adjacent to the Aegean, Adriatic, and Mediterranean.

The Huns from the Volga, also searching for better living conditions, penetrated Gaul and met with military disaster which forced them to retreat.[4] For several centuries Gaul had harassed Roman provinces, but ultimately they were brought to submission, first by the Celts and then the Romans. The Franks from Burgundy invaded Normandy. The Jutes, Angles, and Saxons from Jutland crossed the North Sea to Britain.

The most auspicious migrational invasion was made because of a natural phenomenon which occurred in December of A.D. 406. That winter was unnaturally frigid, causing the Rhine River to freeze over at a point where the city of Mainz is now located. In that area, on the easterly banks, awaited a band of 15,000 Germanic nomad warriors plus their women, children, and their domesticated animals. On the eve of A.D. 407 this band crossed the frozen river by moonlight and began an invasion which changed the course of Western history.[5] The independent, individual spirit of these people, though dormant for many centuries, made Western democracies possible. They are seldom credited with this fact, for their invasion and conquest totally obliterated the cultural majesty and military might of Rome. It was this small band which perpetrated the Dark Ages.

While the capital of Christendom flourished in Byzantium, Western Europe and Rome, in particular, were in a state of uncontrolled chaos. Rome was sacked, and a few hardy souls from Rome and its provinces made their way to an island in the Irish Sea, taking with them their skills and their new religious beliefs.[6] Religious zealots and members of the priesthood saved the centuries of learning for subsequent generations. For several centuries the barbarians from the north plagued coastal villages. Britons, inhabitants on the Seine, Carthaginians, and those beyond the Bosporus felt the keen edges of their highly prized and powerful swords.

While the Norsemen plied the oceans well beyond the established trade routes, a group of Europe's refugees from the barbarians huddled in their wood and dry-mortar, dome-shaped huts on the precipitous Isle of Skellig Michael in the Irish Sea. These wanderers, while not builders, formed a community made up of craftsmen and scholars. They had traveled first to France from the eastern Mediterranean and thence to Cornwall. By A.D. 550 fifty scholars sailed to Cork and established a semistable society.

Two groups, with different human characteristics, led Western Europe into and eventually out of the Dark Ages. One group was the fearless, seafaring warriors of Scandinavia; the other group was made up of locals and refugee scholars who adopted a tranquil, scholarly life-style with an agrarian base. The manner in which the two groups organized their life-styles was quite different.

Life in Norway, Sweden, and Denmark was harsh. Norway's coast was pierced by deep fjords and precarious cliffs. Its tillable soil was a scant few inches deep. Winds from the North Sea swept the western coast. The way of life in Norway demanded that people be sturdy. They cleared the land of trees and boulders, and planted crops.

With the stones and lumber they built one-room shelters and roofed them with sod. The floor plan of most Viking homes was oval.[7] The roof was supported by wooden pillars, and in the center was a hole to allow smoke from the fire to escape. Although rude, these dwellings were snug. The chieftain's hall was of similar construction but much larger, and it was the most impressive building of the village, able to hold over 100 retainers attending a feast. As time passed, houses assumed a rectangular shape. They were often nestled close to the side of a steep mountain, and were made of logs with a steep, beam-supported gambrel roof. Over rudely trimmed logs, sod roofing was laid. Sheep and goats rambling over the mountainside trod and trimmed these sod-covered roofs, not caring whether they fed off of the ground or off of a dwelling's naturally insulated roof.

Inside, the domestic activities revolved around the fire pit placed in the center beneath the chimney hole. A trestle table and crossed-legged stools or trestle benches stood in one area. Along one wall were built-in sleeping quarters with built-in beds enclosed with curtains and placed well above the earthen floor. From another wall was suspended a strong, shaped pole. Hanging from the pole on an iron chain was a large iron caldron in which food was boiled.[8] A low door was the only opening in the facade. A constant fire inside kept the room bright and warm.

Food consisted of fish, wild game, and bread if the grain crops were successful. Even in times of good harvests, grain often rotted because of the dampness. When this happened, a bread substitute was made from tree bark. To this day Norwegians hang hay and grain to dry on rows of laddered fences made from sapling limbs stripped of the bark.

The conversion of some of the northern tribesmen to Christianity in the tenth century inspired them to erect houses of worship. Of those built in Norway in the tenth century, one still stands in Bergen. Built high on a mountainside surrounded by pine trees, this particular church evidences the reluctance of these once pagan people to discard their protective past gods. The roof beams extending beyond the patterned shingle roof are tipped with dragon-head images. At the top of the steep, three-tiered, four-sided roof a cross is placed on the center-set belfry.

The early pagan religion was a result of the struggles these early tribesmen had against the forces of nature.

**Figure 7.3.** The fierce visages of these chess pieces illustrate helmet and crown forms of the North Sea region during the Dark Ages. (*Morse Chesspieces*, Isle of Lewis, Scotland, twelfth century. British Museum, London.)

Their pagan deities were depicted in carved ivory as fierce images with human visages (Figure 7.3). The Celtic god Cernunnos, magnificently bewhiskered, was typical. The heads of these gods were patterned after the tribesmen themselves and record quite accurately the hair and beard styles. Christianity became infused with their mystical and superstitious cults. Transitional statuettes of gods combined pagan-god attributes with Christian symbolism. The Christian religion gained acceptance only after the Pope and the bishop of Avignon promulgated a constancy of religious doctrine.[9]

Because the barbarians' survival depended on weapons, their swords became prized possessions. They endowed their swords with magical powers and gave them names that corresponded to these powers. Their nature-dominated life-style was reflected in weapon and jewelry decorations. They loved clothes and used vibrant color in their weapons and jewelry. As the barbarians settled among those they conquered, the skills of the conquered were assimilated. These skills included goldsmithing, and their jewelry became resplendent with a blend of pagan and Christian symbolism embellished with precious and semiprecious stones. Symmetry of design was offset by variety in shapes which added vitality to these decorative accessories.

By the ninth century A.D., 400 years after the first barbarian invasion, the European inhabitants had begun to re-establish a stable society. The greatest contribution to this social reorganization was the improvement in farm implements which made possible a greater abundance of edible produce. Survival and adequate food supplies were insured by successful crop rotations. Trade and industry prospered, contributing to an economic revival. A British monk created a series of drawings which depicted some of the eleventh-century tradesmen including blacksmiths, weavers, and merchants of necessities and frivolities. With the advent of the twelfth century, occupations in banking, building, baking, and the commodity market also had developed. Armorers and farmers were equally important in the Dark Ages.

Though life was settling into a more viable living pattern, Vikings continued to strike, plunder, and sack villages, taking material and human prizes. Returning from conquests ranging from Byzantium to Cork, the Vikings brought fine silken fabrics, gold, jewels, and trinkets to their wives. The Vikings' earliest attempts at writing took the form of a series of diagonal lines in groups up to five, or equal to a five-finger communication system. Later, the runic alphabet evolved from a refined form of Mesopotamian cuneiform.

New prosperity brought with it a more luxurious life for the wealthy. Stone castles replaced wooden manor houses, and wealth permitted leisure. During the day the upper class indulged in the sport of boar hunting with

falcons; at night the lords and ladies attended lusty banquets. Jugglers, musicians, and wandering players provided the entertainment at such lavish affairs.

Embroidery became a popular pastime for women of wealth who had serfs to attend to the manorhouse and castle chores. Spinning and weaving of linen and wool remained a female occupation, although, by the eighth century, the silk fabrics used by the nobility were imported.

Male costumes were a combination of garments derived from the intermingling of many peoples. The Germanic tribes at the time of the first northward migrations in 2000 B.C. wore the same basic body coverings used throughout the geographic areas of their origin. Many of these garments have been uncovered in the peat-bog burial sites of Jutland. These are examples of very early forms, for at a later date, prior to the acceptance of Christianity, bodies were cremated. Thus there are no known examples of the garments worn during the transitional period between paganism and Christianity.

The earliest garments were made from woolen fabric, often woven in colorful striped patterns. A pair of **braccae** found at Marx-Etzel in Denmark was made of two pieces of rough woolen fabric sewn together on the side

**Figure 7.4.** Bronze-Age male wearing apparel of northern Europe illustrates the **paenula,** the tunic shirt of patterned fabric, and the simple foot covering made from an oval of untanned hide and tied to the foot with thongs. (Reconstructed from garments found in peat-bog burial grounds of Marx-Etzel, Bernuthsfeld, and Obenaltendorf.)

**Figure 7.5.** Female tuniclike frock, or **gunna,** indicates that the fabric for this body covering was made by stitching together smaller lengths of material. (Reconstructed from a garment found in the peat bog of Bernuthsfeld. Inset shows a photocopy of the original garment's remnants.)

seams with another seam on the inside of the legs and crotch. The pattern for these knee-length breeches was an inverted U-shape. The length from waist to crotch was equal to the length of the crotch to the lower edge of the legs. The waist was gathered by a drawstring or was rudely pleated and belted. A simple **singlet** (exomis), shoulder-to-thigh length, was worn to cover the upper body. **Paenula, rhino** (animal skin), and **sagum** served as warm outer wraps (Figure 7.4).

The basic female costume was a frock called the **gunna,** which appears to have been made from a length of fabric composed of many smaller pieces of woven fabric (Figure 7.5). The body of the garment was shapeless, with slender wrist-length sleeves and a small, round neckline. The first female settlers wore few basic garments. Centuries later, after sorties into more technically and culturally sophisticated areas, the dress of these barbaric groups altered, and women were decked out in rich silks brought back from Byzantium. Love of color did not diminish, and this aesthetic factor, combined with increas-

ing technical sophistication, produced garments of elegance. Females adapted the Roman flammeum. Thus began a fashion of concealing ladies' hair which lasted well into the Renaissance (Figure 7.6).

Common people of the Dark Ages continued to wear simple costumes made of leather, coarse wool, and unshaped fur cloaks for warmth.

Stratified society became distinct as the feudal system of the Dark Ages stabilized. New styles were created for the pleasure of kings, vassals, and their ladies. Multilayered clothes made of rich fabrics in gay colors were decorative and practical.

Such dress was a far cry from the manner in which the Picts had originally decorated their persons. The Romans gave them the name *Picts* because these wild people painted their bodies or, as the Romans said, the Picts were "picturing their bodies." However, their love of color never diminished from the period when the Celts used the pastel plant to create a deep blue dye and the leaves of the woad tree to whiten their early woolen material.

**Figure 7.6.** Typical female garments of A.D. 900 include the **gunna, wimple, chinstrap,** and **headrail.** (Redrawn from Claudius manuscript IV, folio 66ᵇ. British Museum, London.)

# Basic Garments of the Barbarians (1200 B.C.–A.D. 1000)

## LOINCLOTH (2000–1200 B.C.)

While visual documentation is not extant, it is assumed that, prior to 2000 B.C., the earliest barbarians used some form of loincloth. Because of the inclement climate, it is considered to have been primarily an undergarment. Figure 1.2 illustrates forms of skirt loincloths or kaunakes loincloths. Because greater body protection was required, the wrapped skirt was preferred. The doeskin loincloth, at first unshaped, and later rectangular, was worn between the legs. It was held in place by a thong or woven strip of braid tied about the waist. The animal skin was looped over this girdling with the ends falling free in front and back. Possibly this was summer wear. Later inhabitants were from regions where body coverings were somewhat refined. It is assumed that, after 2000 B.C., a modified loincloth was used by men and women as an undergarment and continued to be worn for some time.

## FUR TUNIC OR EXOMIS (2000 B.C.–A.D. 700)

In the frozen north, the earliest inhabitants depended upon animal fur for garment materials. The developmental advances of the people were somewhat retarded after their migration, and readily available materials were substituted for more sophisticated fabrics previously used. Figure 7.7 shows an early resident of the thawing north in an exomis (fur tunic) made from bearskin. This was a simple, sleeveless garment which men used to cover the body from shoulder to thigh.

## BRACCAE (1200–30 B.C.)

The **braccae**, a crude trouser form for men, had been introduced by northward-moving migrants from Asia

**Figure 7.7.** Simple tunic or male **exomis** of northern Europe. (*Torŝlunda Plaque,* seventh century. Museum of National Antiquities, Stockholm.)

Minor (Figure 7.11). The barbarians fashioned them from deerskin or a crudely woven woolen textile. The braccae (braies, feminalia, femoralia) were patterned after an inverted U-shape. At first, though ill fitting from the waist and over the buttocks, they snugly fitted the leg and ended at the knee. They were gathered about the waist with a drawstring or simply gathered and girdled.

From 700 B.C. to A.D. 1000, cloth or doeskin strips called **tibialia** were wound around the calves of the legs in extremely cold weather (Figure 7.8).

In time the leg-covering sections of the braccae were lengthened.[10] These were known as **paison** (1200 B.C.-A.D. 1000) and were often fastened snugly about the ankle or cross-bound up the leg to the knee (Figures 7.10 and 7.16). These trousers were extremely ill fitting. The Romans thought them ridiculous and dubbed those worn by the men of Gaul, *Gallia Narbonenis* or *Gallia braccata* (Figure 7.11). Versions of these pant forms continued to be used by all classes of males for several centuries. The lower classes wore them well into the Middle Ages.

## SINGLET (1200 B.C.–A.D. 600)

From 1200 B.C. to A.D. 600, men covered their upper bodies with a sleeveless tunic called the **singlet,** which

**Figure 7.8.** A king wears a royal **paragaudion** and **chlamys** with legs bound in **tibialia.** (Bohemian king from illuminated manuscript, c. 1085. University Library, Prague.)

**Figure 7.9.** Garments of the second century A.D. include the **colobium** (vestlike form), the **singlet** with narrow sleeves, and a linen undertunic with a gathered neckline and seemingly full sleeves. (Redrawn from *Hunting God of Mont Saint-Jean,* Sarthe. Musée des Antiquités Nationales, Paris.)

was worn tucked in or hanging loose (Figures 7.9–7.11). The singlet was made of a patterned coarse woolen textile and sewn on the shoulder and side seams. The lower hem was often notched into decorative V-shapes called toothed edging. Fringe trims were also popular on hems, the result of using the ends of the warp at the lower edge of the singlet. In some instances the singlet was made of furred animal skins, with the skin worn outside and the fur inside during periods of extremely cold weather. This practice was reversed during warmer months, when the fur side acted as insulation against the heat of the sun. The singlet was worn with a belt on occasions or allowed to hang free.

**Figure 7.10.** The **colobium, paison,** and **singlet** with toothed edge are typical garments of the barbarian male.

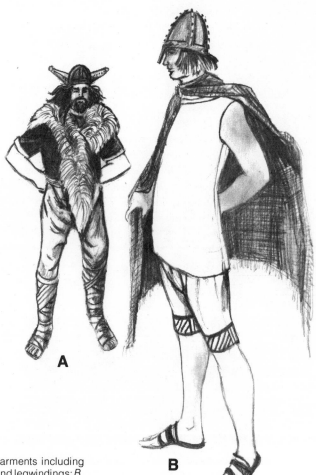

**A**

**B**

**Figure 7.11.** *A,* barbarian garments including the **singlet, rhino, braccae,** and legwindings; *B,* the **singlet, feminalia** (or *Gallia braccata*), and **sagum.** (Reconstructed from descriptions and illustrations in C. Köhler, *A History of Costume.*)

Belts were an important accessory during this period and they became very decorative with chased buckles and studded rosettes or bosses of precious metal. Simple braids were also used for belts, often as double girdling during the early periods. Perhaps this style was a remnant of double-girdled chitons, or an imitation of the girdling of the Roman tunic.

In A.D. 700, sleeves were added to the singlet, and it became a highly decorative garment called the **gonelle** (Figure 7.16). A band of embroidery was added across the shoulders and around the lower edge. These rich embellishments were the influence of contacts with Byzantium where an Oriental luxuriousness dominated fashion. The gonelle was cut with a full body, reaching to the middle of the thigh or to the calf, and had wrist-length, funnel sleeves.

Peasants wore either a gonelle with elbow-length sleeves or a long-sleeved smock (A.D. 400–600). When at work, field hands often drew the back of the gonelle skirt between their legs and tucked it into a belt.

## PARAGAUDION (A.D. 400–600)

The **paragaudion** was worn by men of the ruling class and commoners (Figures 7.8 and 7.12). It was worn outside the paison and belted at the waist, with the upper section bloused to conceal the belt. The sleeves were long with decorative cuffs of embroidery or contrasting colorful bands. Royalty generally wore a purple paragaudion richly trimmed with gold-thread embroidery. The paragaudion was worn over knee-length braccae and tibialia or paison. Beneath the paragaudion, or gonelle, a singlet was used for extra warmth.

**Figure 7.12.** Male figure is dressed in **paragoudion** and mantle clasped at the throat with a large brooch. (*Battle of Hastings,* detail from Bayeux Tapestry, c. 1073–1083. Bayeux Town Hall.)

## TUNIC (1200–300 B.C.)

Floor-length tunics made of reindeer hides were worn by the earliest settlers of Norway (1200–300 B.C.), both male and female. These garments were fashioned with short or full-length sleeves. Hems were trimmed with fringe or were tooth edged. At first men usually belted their tunics, but women seldom did so. In time female outer tunics were amply cut and double girdled with an extremely long, braided cord. The first winding of these cord belts was placed at the natural waist while the second was wound about the figure at the level of the hip bone. The belt was knotted at mid-abdomen, with the trailing ends falling almost to the lower edge of the tunic.

## SKIRT (1200–200 B.C.)

Barbarian women formed a simple skirt by pleating a length of fabric about the waist (Figure 7.13). This was secured by double girdling made from a woven braid with fringed ends.[11] Examples of this garment and the short blouse worn with it have been uncovered in Jutland's bog burial grounds.

## BLOUSE (1200–200 B.C.)

The example of the female blouse or bodice shows that this Bronze-Age garment covered the upper torso from the shoulders to the bottom of the rib cage (Figure 7.13). The narrow sleeves were elbow length, and the neck opening was broad across the shoulders and rather shallow, with a slit extending down the front, slightly off center. These two rather crudely assembled garments were made of coarsely woven sheep fibers. A skirt with attached halter top was presumably for summer wear (Figure 7.14). The top closely resembled the latter-day design of the Egyptian procardium. It was attached to the slender skirt at the center front, passed between the breasts, had a deep V-opening at the neck, and was secured to the skirt in back.[12]

## GUNNA (A.D. 200–900)

As the social structure stabilized, female garments became more form fitting and assumed the characteristics

**Figure 7.13.** Bronze-Age cap, short blouse, and skirt. (Reconstructed from illustration in C. Köhler, *A History of Costume.*)

**Figure 7.14.** Young girl of the Bronze Age wears a summer skirt and halter quite like some styles of the Egyptian procardium. (Redrawn from Quennev's *Everyday Life in the New Stone, Bronze and Early Iron Ages.*)

upper classes were richly decorated, indicative of the affluence of the wearer's spouse.

## OVERGOWN (A.D. 700–1000)

In the far north, females of the Dark Ages wore an **overgown** covering the gunna and kirtle. While the kirtle was generally linen, the gunna and overgown were made from handsome woolens, rich ribbed satin, or heavy silk. Linen was used to make all of these garments for summer wear. Peasant women also wore a layered costume consisting of the same garments, but they were made of rougher woolen fabrics and were less decorative.

## DALMATIC TUNIC (A.D. 700–1000)

Between A.D. 700 and 1000, men who were of more advanced years or who held an authoritative position wore the long **dalmatic tunic** (Figure 7.15). The length of this garment, made from colorful silken or woolen fabric, and the rich trims at neck, cuffs, and hem added dignity to the wearer. It was patterned after the Roman counterpart and was worn by kings and noblemen of the Dark Ages. Characteristically, this apparel of status was of slender cut in the body, and side slits were often introduced to permit greater ease in walking. These slits and the blouse

**Figure 7.15.** Legal garments include the dalmatic and judicial mantle. Note pointed-toed shoes. (Detail from *Lawgivers*, illuminated manuscript, c. 690. Bibliothèque Nationale, Paris.)

of a dress or gown. The **gunna** was a slender, figure-revealing gown which had a low, square neckline (Figure 7.6). It was girdled (often double) below the normal waist with a handsomely jeweled leather belt when worn by a member of the upper classes. The gunna was styled with exceedingly long sleeves, which in time increased in length and width. At first the gunna sleeves were twenty inches in diameter at the opening and extended some length beyond the hand. The additional sleeve length served as a substitute for gloves in the winter. They were worn crushed up on the arms during warm weather, thus often revealing the slender sleeves of the female under-tunic, or **kirtle.** The side-seam slits and the low, square neckline of the gunna revealed the hem and drawstring round neckline of the kirtle. The gunna and kirtle of the

**Figure 7.16.** Leige lord wears a coronet, **gonelle, sagum,** and cross-laced **paison.** (Redrawn from illustration in C. Köhler, *A History of Costume.*)

sections were also decoratively embroidered with gold thread or with thread of a color which contrasted that of the garment.

## OUTER WRAPS (2000 B.C.–A.D. 1000)

Before and during the Bronze Age from 2000 B.C. to A.D. 1000, **capes** served both men and women as outer wraps. Tribeswomen wore a semicircular cape of coarsely woven wool. The straight edge was worn around the neck with the edge rolled or folded back to form a crude collar.

The **sagum** was a male wrap of woolen cloth worn around the shoulders and fastened at the throat with a fibula (Figures 7.11 and 7.16). Other simple wraps were the **lacerna** and the **paenula** (Figure 7.4), which were long shawls draped around the figures in the same manner as the Greek himation. The hooded cape of this time was the **bardocucullus** (Figure 7.1). The animal-skin wrap, the earliest of all cape forms, was called the **rhino.** During warm weather the skin side was worn inside, while during winter months it was reversed for added warmth.

Cloaks, mantles, and rectangular capes continued in the same styles as used for several centuries (700 B.C.–A.D. 900). Women wore the ancient palla and men the chlamys (Figure 7.8). The **sale,** or shoulder cloak, later fitted with a hood, was elbow length and more decorative than functional. It often had the toothed or serial cuts at the cape edge and face opening of the hood.

If weather permitted, the **colobium** (Figures 7.9 and 7.10) was used by the tribesmen of the north (1200 B.C.–A.D. 500). This was a fur vest which had no fastenings at center front and varied in length from hip to mid-thigh, depending on the size and number of skins available at the time of fabrication.

## UNDERWEAR (2000 B.C.–A.D. 500)

Underwear remained very simple between 2000 B.C. and A.D. 500. In time women discarded the loincloth and wore a waist-length shirt, or **camisia.** Men wore it with or without the loincloth for added warmth.

Originally, the sleeveless stola of the Roman culture had first been a basic female outer garment during early migrations. It was either pinned on the shoulders or sewn there and at the side seams. Later it reverted to an undergarment and eventually was discarded. By that time it was amply cut and was visible when the kirtle skirt was hooked or pulled up in front. Often the stola was used for a sleeping gown.

# Accessories (2000 B.C.–A.D. 500)

## HEADWEAR

Between 2000 B.C. and A.D. 500, many Gallo-Roman people wore the round **pileus** (Figure 7.17); Celts and

**Figure 7.17.** Viking seamen are wearing **singlets,** and pointed caps similar to the Greek **pileus.**

Teutonic tribesmen wore a round cap made by using an early form of crochet; and seafaring males adopted a two-tiered cap, similar to those worn by men in present-day navies. Women used the larger, more protective, broad-brimmed hat styled much like the **petasus.**

The period of A.D. 700 to 1000 saw the beginning of unique hair-concealing headwear for women. Veils were used extensively in many shapes and sizes. Long rectangular veils were draped over the head and wound around the neck; small shoulder-length veils made from a square of cloth were held in place with a coronet; and elbow-length veils were placed over the head and allowed to fall free. The **wimple** was a square or circular veil which was often made of transparent fabric, although wimples worn by the poorer classes were always opaque.

In time the **chinstrap** and **headrail** were added. The chinstrap was a folded piece of cloth, usually linen, long enough to bind the head from under the chin to the top of the head where it was securely pinned. The headrail was a similar piece that was bound around the forehead and fastened in back. A silken veil, or **guimp,** was worn over all of these face-framing bindings.

The style of head coverings for men remained constant, consisting of a form of cap with variously shaped crowns, round or pointed, and usually brimless. Hoods attached to short capes also served as protective headwear. The hoods could be worn pulled well down over the face, pushed back, or crushed about the neck and shoulders.

The first hoods were made by forming a cone shape out of woolen fabric, sewing up the seam, and cutting a round hole in the fabric some distance from the edge. Then it was slipped over the head, and the face poked through the hole. Another early hood was made from a rectangle of cloth by taking the two top corners and folding them to the center of the lower edge. By making a seam where the corners met, a crude hood was fashioned.

## FOOTWEAR

The earliest foot coverings were made by binding animal skins to the feet with strips of leather. Later styles (A.D. 400–1000) were made in the same way as the soft leather Roman slipper. The sole, cut larger than the foot, was held on by a thong laced through a series of slits arranged over the toes, laced over the instep and through the leather that covered the heel. **Gallicae** were simple boots made of two pieces of leather shaped like the profile of the foot, large enough to allow for the foot's width. These were worn with crude gaiters, crude woolen hose, and paison.

Shoe making and boot making became more advanced, and a wide variety of new forms and perfected older styles was used. **Brodequins,** or high leather shoes with laces, were heavy boots worn by the lower classes. The upper class wore **heuze,** a boot made of soft leather, which laced and was fitted with a tongue beneath the center opening. Soft slippers made of silk were worn indoors by the nobility, and women wore soft leather slippers tied or buckled at the ankle.

Hose for the period between the fourth and tenth centuries were made of knitted material in a tube shape. Tapes sewn to the top were simple garter supports which possibly tied to a cloth belt worn around the waist under the gonelle or kirtle. Men wore their hose either under their breeches or pulled up over them. In warm weather the working classes wore their stockings crushed down over their boot tops.

## JEWELRY

Jewelry between 2000 B.C. and A.D. 500 included rings, bracelets, and lucky amulets made of bronze which were enameled or set with bits of coral. Rings were worn on the fingers between the first and second joints. Fibulae were usually disc-shaped with an open-work design. Metal headbands or coronets set with large stones were worn by tribal chiefs, by members of their families, and by warriors of proven loyalty.

The most distinctive jewelry in northern Europe from A.D. 500 to 1000 was created in England. Rings, bracelets, and pins were fashioned by twisting golden wires together to the desired width and thickness. Stiletto pins with large decorated heads, buckles made by using a pierced technique, and fibulae of similar design were jewelry accessories that remained in style throughout this period.[13]

# Hairstyles
# (2000 B.C.–A.D. 1000)

Hairstyles from 2000 B.C. to A.D. 1000 were created originally to give the male wearer a ferocious appearance. One such awesome style was made by shaving the head smooth except for a topknot which was bound by a thong at the crown and a long, trailing lock streamed out from behind the head. Long corkscrew sideburns and a thin mustache added to the fierce appearance. Full, uncombed heads of hair with full beards, long hair brushed back from the brow, and long locks falling from a rough center part, were other hairstyles of these early men.

Women wore their hair long, often reaching to the ground, and fashioned in long plaited braids starting from a center part and brought forward to be braided with strips of colored fabric or caught up in a net snood. The snood was placed beneath the hair in back, tied over the crown with thin cords, and then drawn up over the hair. The net was held in place by another pair of cords tied low over the forehead. Women also allowed their shoulder-length hair to hang free and uncombed. Later coiffures were more carefully arranged and often were topped with a circlet of bronze set with stones.

Women's hair fashions changed little until around A.D. 500. Then women bound their hair close to the head in braids, or twisted ropes wound into small pugs at the nape of the neck and covered them with guimps.

During this same period, men's hairstyles altered drastically. For some time, they continued to wear their hair long, but it was combed and parted in the middle. The nobility added a coronet to keep stray locks from interfering with sight or concealing the face. By the end of the tenth century, men began to wear a shoulder-length bob, often with bangs covering the forehead. Beards, which once added to the ferocious appearance of the wearer, began to be carefully trimmed and shaped, and finally went out of style. Younger men were clean shaven well into the Renaissance. Hair continued to be shortened as the Crusade period commenced, perhaps as a convenience in maintenance.

## FOOTNOTES

1. Gerald Simons, *Barbarian Europe*, p. 11.
2. Carl Köhler, *A History of Costume*, p. 124.
3. Ewan Butler, *Scandinavia*, p. 11.
4. Simons, *Barbarian Europe*, p. 41.
5. Ibid., p. 11.
6. Kenneth Clark, *Civilisation*, pp. 6–7.
7. Folk Museum, Oslo, Norway.
8. Folk Museum, Stockholm, Sweden.
9. Simons, *Barbarian Europe*, p. 81.
10. François Boucher, *20,000 Years of Fashion*, pp. 137–138.
11. Köhler, *A History of Costume*, p. 122.
12. Ibid., p. 122.
13. Boucher, *20,000 Years of Fashion*, p. 161.

# Chapter 8
# Elegance of Byzantium
## (A.D. 330–1453)

For many centuries scholars of the Western world discredited the contributions Byzantium had made to modern civilization. One English writer, William Lecky, crossed off eleven centuries of this Eastern European civilization with the remark, ". . . a monotonous story of the intrigues of priests, eunuchs, and women, of poisonings, of conspiracies, of uniform ingratitude, of perpetual fratricide." True, the years of powerful Byzantine emperors were full of grizzly acts and strange behavior patterns.[1] Yet this empire, with its capital at Constantinople, developed on a base of Greek culture, Roman law, and the new religion, Christianity. While Imperial Rome was disintegrating under the onslaught of barbarian invasions led by Alaric, Attila, Clovis, and Theodoric, Byzantium flourished and grew in power.

First under Constantine, crowned emperor in A.D. 324, and then during the reign of Charlemagne, Byzantine influence spread throughout the Balkans, western Russia and parts of Germany. The rise to power of Byzantium was an indirect result of Diocletian's attempts to salvage the Roman Empire. It was Diocletian who gave new authority and importance to the Roman dominions in the East.

This heightened influence combined with the force of a new emerging power, Christianity. The downtrodden people of the world were receptive to the teachings of this new religion, hoping that from it would come improvement in their lot. Just as the Romans permitted the practice of Judaism, so at first they allowed this new cult to survive. But Diocletian's edict that Christians must accept the new emperor as god was not palatable to those who had committed themselves to the new faith. The old Roman Empire with its pagan dogma survived the rule of Diocletian by only a few years.

Four leaders struggled to succeed him after his abdication, one of whom was Constantine. Son of one of the former emperor's western governors, Constantine was acclaimed Augustus in 306 by the troops under his generalship. Having been successful in several conquests, he arrived in Rome and declared himself to be a Christian, a decision that was to affect the course of Western civilization. In 323 he successfully eliminated all competitors

**Figure 8.1.** Fine draping, like that of Roman garments, was incorporated for a time into Byzantine garments such as this **saccoz.** (Redrawn from manuscript illumination of the period.)

and became the sole emperor of Rome. With a Christian ruler, the new religion was assured. In 330, to escape the political intrigue in Rome, he moved the capital to Byzantium where he built the city of Constantinople. However, his first choice for the new capital had been Troy, and perhaps this factor contributed the strong Grecian influence. Although faithful to the new religion, Constantine's court discussed Greek philosophy, read and recited Homer, sent forth missionaries to convert the Russians, and maintained the law of Rome.

Constantine ordered many churches built, a number of which still stand. Byzantine architecture is noted for the use of brick and scintillating mosaics. Roman structural-engineering skill was applied to the construction of these monuments. The human images on walls, in domes, and within the vestibule visually record personages of the period—the elegantly garbed priest-kings, and the members of court. The most noteworthy Italian Byzantine church is in Ravenna, Italy, a province of the Eastern Empire until A.D. 751. Byzantine architecture and art were admired by much of the known world, including Persia.

The people residing in Constantinople were very chauvinistic and considered themselves God's chosen people. The emperor declared that he ruled by divine right and was God's earthly spokesman, and therefore had dominion over clerical and secular life. For this reason, an emperor was depicted in mosaics in royal raiment, with a golden nimbus glowing about his head.

As the new religion flourished, missionaries, orders of monks, and hermits dedicated to the teachings of Christ proliferated. Fearless and dedicated to their faith, these new servants of the Lord became the conscience of the empire and spread its influence as they traveled, zealously gathering converts to the fold.

The beautiful site of Constantinople was strategically located, having not only a fine port, but natural fortifications. Because it was protected and yet accessible to trading vessels, Constantinople did a lively business in slaves, salt, wax, gold, honey, corn, caviar, furs, and grain. Products from India, Ceylon, and China included ivory, amber, silks and damask, jewels, porcelain, and many savory spices. Overland routes from the Far East terminated at the port of Constantinople, located at the narrowest water barrier between East and West. By land, exotic treasures from the Orient were transported to commercial centers on the Mediterranean Sea and thence to those on the North Sea and landlocked points between.

For years this naturally fortified center of trade and elegance was a showcase of the Byzantine emperors' priest-king power and the city's orderly urban planning. The city walls were penetrated by golden gates.[2] There were six forums within the city walls where merchants and lawyers conducted their business. Triumphal parades were held in the largest, the Forum of Constantine, amid teaming throngs and waving silken banners. Other forums were given over to selling bread, food products, and meat. Crowded together in tenements were those of the less fortunate lower class who bought from or manned the stalls of canopy-shaded bazaars. Craftsmen huddled in small, dark shops where they manufactured their wares. The huge Hippodrome situated near Hagia Sophia offered diverse entertainment for poor and rich alike. These offerings ranged from violent combat on horseback to mystery (miracle) plays.

The city contained many churches and luxurious palaces, some of which had their own yacht basins. Interior walls of the palaces shown like jewels, for they were covered with mosaics. Fountains played in the beautifully landscaped gardens. Also included within the palace's walls were shops which manufactured fabrics, shoes, golden service plate, and elegantly chased weapons of war. Twenty thousand slaves and servants were needed to provide for the demands of the royal household.

Evening meals were a ritual duplicating the Last Supper. Woe betide the awkward slave who inadvertently spilled a beverage or dropped a serving dish. For such clumsiness the servant might be decapitated.

While opulence and tranquility graced the palace, an opposite life-style prevailed among the lower classes. Roman urban planners wasted no space on those whose lot was humble. Alleylike streets were heaped with refuse. Noise rose and fell from the streets, adding to the discomforts of crowded conditions, filth, and hunger. A plan was put into practice for feeding the hungry, and as many as 80,000 loaves of bread were distributed daily among the tenement wretches. The monks and the monasteries also cared for the poor and gave temporary shelter to the homeless.[3]

The trade within the city walls of Constantinople was strictly regulated. Silk drapers were forbidden to sell linen. Exact records were kept of the fishermen's catches, for each boatload of fish was registered. Those who worked at the leather crafts were not allowed to tan hides for use in what they manufactured. Locations of shops were carefully specified. In this planned economy, laws regulated specialization, and excellence was demanded under penalty of punishment for sloppily produced wares. Travelers and tradesmen from the West marveled at the goods in the marketplaces. Success and prosperity abounded for the fortunate few in this society. Greek influence demanded perfection; Roman influence demanded order and law; and the new mystical religion demanded piety. From the fourth century until the twelfth century the elegance of Byzantium held the world spellbound.

The Byzantine influence, in turn, altered Eastern and Western thought, art, and politics. For eleven centuries the boundaries of Byzantium were in constant flux. Justinian controlled lands from Spain to Mesopotamia in the sixth century. The last emperor, Palaeologus, controlled only the city of Constantinople and the southern part of the Greek peninsula.

Islam's zealous warriors of Allah and the Pope's dedicated Crusaders had put Byzantium to the test. Western Byzantium, between the fourth and sixth centuries, had felt the onslaught of the barbarians. The dream held by Justinian of revitalizing the Roman Empire was extinguished by the early seventh century. The Eastern Orthodox Christian doctrine began to stabilize and direct its efforts of conversion eastward. The political fate of Byzantium, as well as of its philosophical concepts and standards of excellence, waxed and waned with each successive emperor. Infidels and Crusaders, originally motivated by their ideologically different faiths, soon succumbed to greed and coveted Byzantium for its materialistic potential. The rift between the Western Church in Rome and the Eastern Orthodox Church grew wider after 1054. The landed Byzantine aristocrats became increasingly independent of the state, and smaller landholders suffered at their greedy hands as the social structure began to crumble. Thus weakened, Byzantium was ripe for conquest by the Seljuk Turks.

Preoccupation with the new faith and its concepts were reflected in the costumes of the emperors, empresses, and nobility of Byzantium. Because emperors were priest-kings by divine right, much of the attire of the court had liturgical characteristics. The feigned piety of emperors and their courts is seen in the mosaic friezes in such churches as San Vitale in Ravenna. It was believed that by wearing figure-concealing garments, each individual subordinated his or her own identity to the higher identity of the church.[4] However, the colors and opulent decorations on the paraliturgical garments which emperors, bishops, empresses, eunuchs, and court members used, clearly marked class, status, and individual power.

The garments of the priest-king and his court were rigidly prescribed in the *Book of Ceremonies*.[5] The offices held by members of the Byzantine court were defined by a meticulous list of garments specifying the cut, fabric, and decoration to be used. On ceremonial occasions, court garments took on a quality of liturgical vestments. Thus, the hierarchy of the court was defined, and the costumes had neither utilitarian function nor seductive characteristics.

All of Byzantine clothing reflected influences of aesthetic concepts of other cultures. The melding of many cultures occurred during this period because of the far-reaching trade routes. The Byzantines borrowed from the Huns, Persians, Assyrians, and Medes. Oriental elegance in textiles, fashions, and accessories was brought to Constantinople by the barbarians, although, for prestige reasons, the Eastern seat of Imperial Rome credited Persia with contributing most to its innovations in apparel.

During Constantine's reign, garments retained the styling of earlier Imperial Rome. While the cut remained unchanged, color and jeweled decorations were added. These additions greatly altered the older garment forms.

The development of the shuttle, a technical advance attributed to the Syrians, added to garment elegance by allowing woven patterns to be introduced into fabric. This weaving technique eliminated the need to embellish elegant silks with embroidery and was possibly borrowed from the highly skilled weavers of the Orient.[6] The overall patterns were derivatives of those used by the Greco-Roman, Oriental, and Near Eastern civilizations. The introduction of this new technology into Byzantine fabric production occurred during the fourth century A.D.

Silks gradually replaced woolens and linen.[7] Silk was so sought after that missionaries were sent to China secretly to bring back silk worms and mulberry leaves. Thus, the cost factor was reduced by producing the silk in palace factories. Byzantine production of silk from locally raised silk worms dates from the reign of Justinian (A.D. 527–565).

Still in use was the toga, which, during the Byzantine period, was emblazoned with a **tablion** of golden thread and jewels. The toga was still made of a semicircle but was cut of rich silk and worn like a cape or chlamys, rather than as a spiral wrap. The dalmatic worn by the emperor was made of white silk so heavily embroidered at hems, collar, blouse section, and wrists that it no longer was the gracefully draped garment that it had been. The color purple was used exclusively by emperors, but a full range of vibrantly colored silks other than purple was available to the rest of the court and aristocracy.

Two ivory plaques from the fifth century A.D., in which female figures personify the old and new capitals of the Roman Empire, dramatically illustrate the differing costuming concepts of Rome and Constantinople. In the one representing Rome, the figure is garbed in the draped stola patterned on the lines of the Greek chiton. A swag arrangement of a palla and helmet completes the representation. The figure representing the new Eastern capital wears a stola, a deep jeweled collar, and a crown patterned after the city's wall. A mantle or palla envelops most of the figure. The San Vitale mosaic frieze most

**Figure 8.2.** The courtiers of Justinian of Byzantium wear the figure-concealing **chlamys** with **tablions.** The emperor's tablion is jewel encrusted, as are most of his garments, which destroys the graceful draping characteristic of earlier Roman garments. (Mosaic: *Justinian and His Court*, detail, sixth century. San Vitale, Ravenna.)

**Figure 8.3.** Justinian's wife, Theodora, wears an elaborate crown, a **maniakis,** and large pendant earrings. (Mosaic, detail, sixth century. San Vitale, Ravenna.)

Once again, social status and affluence are established by the styling, trim, and fabric of the garments.

Theodora was probably the most notable of the Byzantine empresses. Justinian made his own choice for a wife, selecting from young maids, not for family connections, but for the fairness of their skin.[8] Theodora must have been fair indeed, for she belonged to the theatrical profession, which was severely frowned upon by the church. Nevertheless, she was granted clerical dispensation to marry Justinian, which later proved that Justinian had great perception and had seen in her something more than superficial beauty. In time she was to give him strength in battle, encouraging him to stand firm during the Nika riots (532). Though often cruel and autocratic, she is credited with establishing a hospital for the poor and converting an old palace into an abode for destitute females.

The texture of Byzantine life was vital and varied. The wealthy had a luxurious life-style full of amusement and elegance, but these early Christians also had a concern for the elderly and for those less fortunate. Plying a craft, participating in commerce, and practicing law were major occupations. The social and political status of

frequently is referred to for examples of Byzantine dress. In one panel, Justinian is depicted in a purple mantle and white tunic, or paragaudion (Figure 8.2). The mantle is fastened on the shoulder with a brooch set with a large ruby surrounded by pearls of enormous size from which are suspended three baroque pearls on golden chains. The mantle bears two golden tablions on which are embroidered green birds within red circles. His white paragaudion is knee length and belted with a red girdle. Gold braid edges the seam slit to above mid-thigh and decorates the cuffs. On his head is a crown studded with pearls, rubies, and emeralds. His feet are clad in purple slippers with pointed toes, trimmed with pearls and other jewels. White mantles, or chlamyses, with tablions are worn by the figures which surround him, representing members of his court.

Figure 8.3 shows Justinian's wife, Empress Theodora, who also wears garments which have liturgical significance in their designs. Her crown is much more elaborate than Justinian's, and from her ears hang large pendant pearl earrings.

Most of the people depicted in the portico dome frieze in St. Mark's Cathedral, Venice, are clad in the dalmatic and chlamys, or mantle, if male; and mantle and stola, if female (Figure 8.4). Since these images represented inhabitants of one of the Byzantine provinces and not the court, the garments shown, though rich in color and fabric, have a secular flavor. Borders and other embroidered decorative motifs are stylized animal or plant life.

**Figure 8.4.** Byzantine costumes were somewhat modified in the provinces. (Mosaic, detail, c. 1260. St. Mark's Cathedral, Venice.)

Byzantium, always swinging back and forth like a pendulum, affected the lives of the people, which were neither tedious nor uniform. Each year there were thirty official Christian festivals. Pageantry of Imperial Rome, adapted by Byzantium, lifted the masses out of their drab humdrum existences.[9] Their love of beauty was incorporated into the pageantry of the festivals. In the forums on these occasions, people gathered at many restaurants to eat and drink. For the wealthier urban dwellers, public baths, theaters, bear baiting, and sailing were available. Simpler entertainments such as watching wandering acrobats and jugglers or listening to street musicians were available to the people of lesser means. Most played quiet games of dominoes or checkers when evenings were spent at home. Chariot races were enjoyed by all in the enormous Hippodrome. For the most part, families were happy, well disciplined, and contributed to the culture now called Byzantine.

# Basic Garments of Byzantium (A.D. 300–1453)

## TUNIC (330–1400)

The Roman tunic was the common dress of most males by the fourth century A.D. As adapted by most of the citizens of Byzantium, the tunic, or **paragaudion,** had longer sleeves and excessive decoration (Figure 8.5). The gold and jeweled ornamentation altered the paragaudion dramatically when this garment belonged to a member of the nobility.[10] All of these garments were colorful. Originally made of wool, silken fabrics were used in later periods as trade with the Orient expanded. The paragaudion was belted at the normal waist with a leather belt, which added decoration, or was obscured by the blousing of the upper part of this garment (Figure 8.6).

## DALMATIC (330–1453)

The dalmatic (330–1453) differed from that worn in earlier periods only in color and the amount of heavy, stiff ornamentation. Worn alone or beneath the paragaudion, it was a garment which added dignity to the wearer and conveyed an illusion of piety by partially concealing the figure, and thus, the wearer's individuality.

## SACCOZ (1200–1400)

The **saccoz** (1200–1400), a long stiff garment, was a royal gown in the last centuries of the Byzantine Empire. Usually, it was purple or black in color with a moderately full body and long sleeves with cuffs which fastened snugly about the wrists (Figure 8.1).[11] As was all royal raiment, it was made of silk and embellished with gold-thread embroidery. This royal robe, like so many items of

**Figure 8.5.** The Byzantine **paragaudion** was often elaborately embroidered at the wrists, neckline, and hem. (Redrawn from illumination in *Chronicle of John,* thirteenth century. Bibleoteca Nacional, Madrid.)

apparel used by rulers of Byzantium, created the impression of an Oriental potentate because the earliest textiles brought from China were woven with Oriental designs. After silk was eventually produced in the workshops of the palace, the overall decorative designs continued to be patterned after those initiated in the Far East. In cut the saccoz retained the characteristics of the tunic, as did the priestly robe, the *tunica talaris*. Elegance in the gowns and robes of the Byzantine court was achieved not by intricacy of cut, but by the richness of fabric and by embellishments with jewels and embroidery.

**Figure 8.6.** The floor-length male gown, a version of the **paragoudion,** was either trimmed with a band on the upper part of the sleeve, or the simple round neck was faced with fabric which contrasted in color to the main body of the garment. (Redrawn from *Young Basil and His Family, Chronicle of John,* thirteenth century. Bibleoteca Nacional, Madrid.)

## STOLA (400–1100)

Men and women used the **stola** from 400 to 1100. This was a long-sleeved garment with styling features similar to the Roman female stola (Figure 8.7).[12] In time these styling features altered and assumed the characteristics of the garments mentioned earlier. Examination of visual resources, which other authorities have identified, indicates that the apparel depicted as stolae are difficult to distinguish from the dalmatic, saccoz, or tunic. Generally floor length, with inset sleeves, the stola was not as decorative or elegant as later garments. Banded

necklines and bordered hems were often the only decorative accents.

## CEREMONIAL AND ROYAL WRAPS AND SCARF FORMS (400–1200)

Because of the liturgical nature of royal costumes, many status-identifying scarves and wraps were used for specific occasions between 400 and 1200. In addition to the paragaudion and breeches, an emperor might wear the **trabea.**[13] This wide scarf was worn diagonally over one

**Figure 8.7.** This female of the Byzantine Empire wears a multilayered costume consisting of a **stola,** an **overtunic,** and a **lorum.** Jewel-encrusted silken **stemma** adorns her head. These are garment styles of the fifth to seventh centuries.

shoulder, across the chest and back, and secured on the opposite side. This style was the forerunner of the baldric, a belt worn over one shoulder and across the chest to support a sword or bugle. The trabea also was worn around the back of the neck and crossed over the chest with the ends hanging down just in front of the hip bones.

## PALUDAMENTUM

Constantine also wore a toga, or **paludamentum,** designed after the pattern of those used by Roman consuls. The emperor's paludamentum was purple silk with a gold tablion encrusted with pearls.

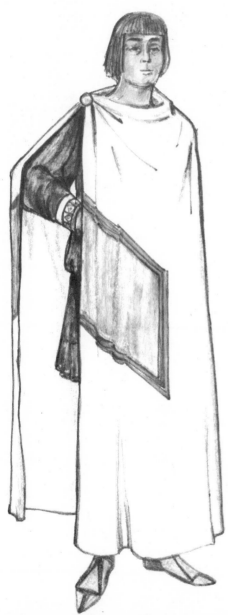

**Figure 8.8.** Byzantine **chlamys** is decorated with a **tablion,** probably green in color. These outer wraps are worn with a **paragoudion,** breeches, and boots.

**Figure 8.9.** This royal figure with orb and scepter wears a **chlamys** with an intricately decorated **tablion,** a **thorakion,** and a large, circular jeweled collar, or **maniakis.** (Ivory bas-relief: *The Empress Ariadne,* detail, fifth century. Museo Nazionale, Florence.)

The **chlamys,** or royal mantle when of semicircular cut, was worn by laymen and royalty (Figure 8.8).[14] When worn by royalty, the chlamys was fastened on the shoulder with elaborate fibulae in the same manner as that used by the ancient Greeks.

The **tablion,** a square or rectangle of heavy gold fabric with green embroidery and jewels, identified clerics and members of the royal court. A cleric's chlamys was white; a person of royalty wore purple; and those of lesser rank wore yellow ocher with a brown tablion.

Between 500 and 1400, the emperors and empresses of Byzantium framed their faces with a wide, circular collar called a **maniakis** (Figure 8.9). The maniakis was studded with precious stones, catching the light and attracting attention to the head and features. In design and focal-point characteristics, it was much like the Egyptian circular necklaces.

The loros and lorum were overgarments that were similar in use. The **loros,** introduced into the royal wardrobe during the tenth century, was a very long, narrow scarf emblazoned with jewels and gold-thread needlework (Figure 8.10). It was crossed around the figure in an

**Figure 8.10.** The **loros,** one of the Byzantine priest-kings' scarf accessories, is shown in the mosaic on left, accompanied by diagrammatic interpretation of the complex wearing arrangement (right). (Mosaic: *The Emperor as Builder,* detail, A.D. 330. Hagia Sophia, Istanbul.)

intricate manner, reviving one of the accessories used to identify a consul of Imperial Rome. The **lorum** was a rectangular overgarment made of a wider panel which had an opening for the head to allow the panel to hang straight down in front and back.

The **thorakion** was arranged in an intricate manner and appeared to be a shieldlike ornament (Figure 8.9). In fact, it was a thin scarf with the ends brought up through the belt. Because of the stiff, heavy material from which it was made, a shield effect was created.

During the Byzantine period, the **palla** (female) and **pallium** (male), now only slender scarves, continued to be used (Figure 8.11). They were colorful accessories made of silken textiles ranging in hue from brilliant greens and reds, to oranges and golds.

### GRANATZA (400–600)

The **granatza** (400–600), a figure-enveloping, coat-like garment with ample sleeves, was another royal garment which also was worn by the *archontes*, or chief magistrates (Figure 8.12). Of Assyrian origin, the granatza covered the figure from shoulders to floor. Emperors wore these garments hanging loose, but the *archontes* wore them belted, possibly as a means of differentiating between the two classes.

### TROUSERS (500–1000)

According to Procopius, the trouser forms worn by Byzantine men between 500 and 1000 were inspired by garments used by the Huns (Figure 8.13).[15] Pants during this period were very tight fitting and often made of patterned fabrics. Worn by the ordinary population, these pants covered the figure from waist to ankle and were worn

inside calf-high boots. In a figure represented in Oppian's *Treatise on Hunting,* Byzantine breeches or trousers are illustrated with horizontal patterned bands encircling the thigh, calf, and ankle. A mosaic in the Church of Sant'Apollinare in Ravenna shows men wearing tight ankle-length trousers made of fabric covered with floral and geometric designs. A sixth-century fresco depicts men wearing a looser style of trousers. Perhaps regional differences account for variations in style.

## Accessories (400–1400)

### HEADWEAR

On Constantine's royal head rested a **stephanos** (330-429), a fabric diadem encrusted with gems. This was a stiffened band tied at the back of the head and appeared to be a cloth crown of gold silk. Around 430, the altered form of the diadem was called a **stemma** and flared out at the top with chains of gold links dangling over the temples and along the sides of the cheeks. In time the stemma form was executed in a precious metal with mounted gems. Empresses wore an oval tiara called the **skiradion.** This style of headgear was a rich fabric circlet that was trimmed with pearls and topped with a plume. Its basic color ranged from white to scarlet to green.

At times, the emperor wore a **turban,** which had originated in Persia, or the **calyptra,** which was in the form of an arched polygon.

### FOOTWEAR

Calf-high, foot-encasing leather boots with pointed toes were worn by the general populace. Royalty wore soft

**Figure 8.11.** Common Byzantine women's garments included the **palla** and were plain and unexciting. (Manuscript illumination from the *Book of Job*.)

**Figure 8.12.** The body-encompassing **granatza** worn by a Byzantine dignitary is made of heavy, silken fabric. The **lorum** is encrusted with jewels and edged with heavy golden braid. These garments represent styles worn from 400 to 600.

**Figure 8.13.** This sword-wielding male wears the snug-fitting trouser form of the Byzantine period, a **rhino** shoulder wrap, and an animal-skin apron form as a protective device. (Redrawn from the *Chronicle of John Soylitzes.* Bibleoteca Nacional, Madrid.)

**Figure 8.14.** Scarf, **stola, stemma,** and large earrings of gold and pearls exemplify the sumptuous dress of wealthy Byzantine women. The hair fashion is similar to the coiffures worn by patrician women of Imperial Rome.

**Figure 8.15.** Byzantine soldiers wore armor over their **paragaudions** and a **chlamys** about their shoulders. (Redrawn from Byzantine plaque representing St. George.)

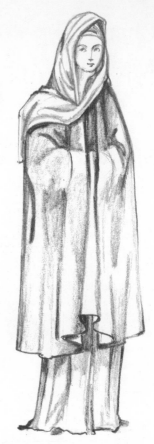

**Figure 8.16.** Average Byzantine women wore a **stola,** a capelike cloak, and a head-concealing scarf. (Redrawn from detail in the *Basil the Magnificent* saga.)

leather slippers trimmed with pearls and jewels. The slipper shoes were lowcut and were made of leather dyed in various colors including red and purple.

### JEWELRY

Opulence of dress was enhanced by ropes of pearls, heavy pendant earrings made of pearls, and gold chains (Figure 8.14). Bracelets which encircled the wrists were wrought of gold and mounted with gems. Equally elegant were large fibulae and large circular or oblong brooches crafted of gold and gems.

# Hairstyles (400–1200)

As a rule, men wore shoulder-length hair, parted in the center and drawn back behind the ears. Chin fringe and trimmed mustaches were worn by some men, others were clean shaven (Figure 8.15). Young men wore a short bob with bangs over the forehead.

A majority of the women wore their hair drawn back from a center part and twisted into a pug at the nape of the

neck. The pug, or even the entire head, might be covered with a gold-thread net decorated with pearls. Often the coiffure was topped by a transparent veil or flammeum.

### FOOTNOTES

1. Philip Sherrard, *Byzantium*, p. 13.
2. Alexander Eliot, *The Horizon Concise History of Greece*, p. 170.
3. Sherrard, *Byzantium*, pp. 31–40.
4. H. W. Janson, *History of Art*, p. 170.
5. James Laver, *The Concise History of Costume and Fashion*, p. 46.
6. François Boucher, *20,000 Years of Fashion*, p. 146.
7. Gisele D'Assailly, *Ages of Elegance*, p. 37.
8. Mila Contini, *Fashion: From Ancient Egypt to the Present Day*, p. 61.
9. Sherrard, *Byzantium*, p. 45.
10. Laver, *Concise History of Costume*, p. 48.
11. Boucher, *20,000 Years of Fashion*, p. 150.
12. Carl Köhler, *A History of Costume*, p. 119.
13. Boucher, *20,000 Years of Fashion*, p. 148.
14. Köhler, *A History of Costume*, p. 119.
15. Boucher, *20,000 Years of Fashion*, p. 147.

# Chapter 9
# More Medieval Modes
## (A.D. 1000–1499)

The later years of the medieval period were rife with paradoxes. With the exception of Charlemagne, there was no lasting emperor or king who dominated vast geographical area and united the people under one authoritarian head. Most people lived in their own small village world, accountable to the lord who oversaw the locale's feudalistic establishment. Successive dynasties sought power through military conquest, and popes and petty kings struggled to control people and land. Great cathedrals were built while the masses dwelt in hovels. Although secular and clerical corruption abounded, pious and holy souls struggled to establish moral and ethical standards. Kings were often as ignorant as the peasants over whom they ruled, while priestly scholars and intellectuals founded universities which still are renowned for their erudition. Chivalry flowered, yet even those who took the chivalric oath were capable of perpetrating bestial tortures. In this potpourri of contrasts, art, architecture, literature, and music began to develop a new creative aesthetic.[1]

If there was a unifying force in medieval Europe, it was the common bond of Christianity. Though never absolute, *Republica Christiana* did indeed transcend other factors at play during this complex time. A person who was not baptized into the one religion was without legal rights, and had neither political nor social identity. The clergy controlled the minds of the masses and were advisors to and teachers of kings and emperors. The church succored the ill, housed the wayfarers, fed the poor, gave sanctuary to troubled souls, and provided refuge in time of military crisis. The church also sustained a link with the classical past throughout the Dark Ages.[2] Church missionaries Christianized the pagan barbarians, making possible a more stable social structure.

The individuality of a person was recognized by the church, if only in the medieval sense, whereby each person had a place and a function in the feudal order. Earthly good works determined the fate of the soul. Medieval people, taught by morality plays, allegorical biblical tales, and verse, sought to overcome evil by good deeds, for to them there was an earthly and a spiritual

**Figure 9.1.** Dancing girl wears a **kirtle** with decorative wrist bands and, over this garment, a fur-trimmed **gunna**. The gunna sleeve trim assumes **tippet** proportions and the outer garment might be a **garde-corps**. (Redrawn from mosaic of *Salome*, c. 1200. St. Mark's Cathedral, Venice.)

reality. By far the spiritual reality was more comfortable to contemplate.

The earthly reality was a bustling cesspool. Houses of wood were crowded in close proximity on narrow streets. The streets, alleys no more than six to ten feet wide, were muck-covered with slops and swill tossed out for the pigs. While there was beauty in the forests and countryside, usually the only uplifting sights in the urban centers were the cathedrals.[3]

Though filth and disease surrounded them, and their diversions were brawls and drinking at a local alehouse, medieval men and women were beginning to assess their life-styles. The very nature of the environment fostered concepts which would alter the whole of Western political and social thought and, ultimately, the condition of humanity itself.

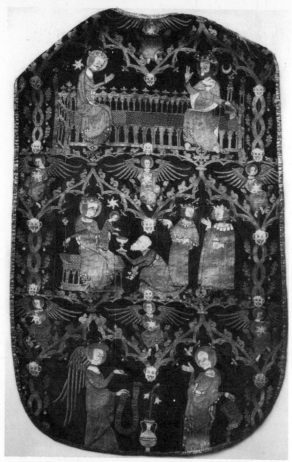

**Figure 9.2.** This fourteenth-century **chasuble,** a liturgical garment, is embroidered with scenes of *The Enthronement, The Adoration of the Magi,* and *The Annunciation,* using metal threads and silk on red velvet. The biblical figures are represented wearing clothing typical of the early fourteenth century. (Chasuble, English, fourteenth century. Metropolitan Museum of Art, New York City.)

Several other factors contributed to lifting the dark veil which obscured Europe after the barbarian invasions. These factors were social, political, and technical. Politically, the lethargy that enveloped the continent and adjacent islands was given new stability as early as 768 by the ascendancy of Charlemagne to the Frankish throne. This larger-than-life, earthy Frank, who also possessed extraordinary vision and enterprise, assumed imperial leadership of the Western Empire in the year 800. He was said by contemporary chroniclers to have been "the chief and the father of Europe," leaving all of Europe, upon his demise "in the greatest happiness." This so-called happiness was due to Charlemagne's prodigious efforts to stabilize government, to improve education, and to expand his territory. The concepts of Europe with the common culture which became Western civilization were given impetus and implementation by this great king of the Franks.

During the eighth century, the western geographical area of the European continent and Asia Minor were politically tripartite. The three socially and politically separate units came into being because of three different theologies. These were the Islamic faith, and Eastern Orthodox and Roman Catholic views of Christianity. The Roman Catholic religion fostered a unifying emotional appeal in its concept of spiritual union and a worldwide commitment to the conversion of pagans, infidels, and other nonbelievers. It was Charlemagne who used this appeal, after as many as sixty military engagements, to bring Europe into being. After much intrigue involving Pope Leo, Byzantium, and Rome, Charlemagne was crowned the Roman Emperor. However, until his death in 814, the title of emperor made little impact on the rule of this mighty organizer of the Dark Ages.

Under Charlemagne's rule, trade improved to a degree, but routes often were plagued by marauding bands of Moslem warriors, and European economy remained primarily agrarian. In time traders and merchants of Jewish origin made these occupations respectable. By the eleventh century, a new, financially stable merchant class emerged.

The tenuous life-style, dependent on limited food supplies, became more secure because of several technical advances. Animals were fitted with harnesses, enabling horses or oxen to pull heavier plows as men guided these creatures to till the land with deeper furrows. Rich subsurface soil was turned up, which increased fertility and yielded larger harvests. Excesses of grains and foodstuffs created a surplus of produce for trade. Crop rotation on a three-field system also developed. A new invention, the windmill, helped dredge bogs, turning them into useful farmlands. Forests were cleared, releasing more acreage for cultivation. Estates belonging to the church and nobility increased in wealth from the abundance of produce being offered on the commercial market. The introduction of the swiveling front axle on the wagon made this trade carrier more functional. The rediscovery of the water-wheel was another influential technological breakthrough. Mills for grinding grain into flour or mash were constructed along rivers and streams. Increased production contributed to a better fed human population, and, in time, the birthrate balanced the death rate. Periods of famine and plague continued, but the population of Europe was never to sink to the low ebb of the period of barbarian activists. Peace at home and only "good Christian wars" on the borders of the Western Roman Empire created a favorable environment for human advancement.

The villages of the Dark Ages had developed around the area of the lord's manor house in sight of his keep and bailey.[4] The keep, motte (mound), and bailey were the keys to the defense of the medieval feudal community. To this day in England, the mottes of medieval castles are visible even though the castles have disappeared. The motte was built by digging a ditch around the area which would be occupied by the keep and bailey. The keep was constructed on a still taller mound, and the entire area enclosed by a wall. The ditch, or moat, surrounding the sheer peripheral walls eventually filled with rain water. One fixed bridge, which evolved into the drawbridge, was the only access. The keep was several stories high. The submound areas contained the well, the next level was used for storage. Living spaces were on the next level up, and the top floor was reserved for sleeping quarters. Castle guards stood continual watch atop the tower. Twelve-foot-high walls surrounded the bailey where the stables, wine and grain storage sheds, and living quarters for the lord's vassals and soldiers were located. In times of siege the lord's household and all villagers occupied the keep and bailey, the most protected refuges.

The village itself was nestled just outside the keep, and beyond the village lay the farmlands. Country peasants dwelt in rude wood-and-wattle huts with thatched roofs and earthen floors. They earned their keep by tending sheep and cattle and tilling their allotted acreage. The wealthier villagers owned a few head of cattle, an ox, pigs, and chickens. Peasants and serfs worked the lord's farmlands, receiving produce as payment for their labor.

The lord and his family resided in the manor house, discreetly set apart from the huts of the peasants. It was quite substantially built of stone or brick and had quiet, expansive living spaces. The lower floor, with a ground-level entrance, served as a storage area. Above were the living, sleeping, and dining areas with wooden floors.

At the heart of the medieval village stood the church, which often was the only completely stone structure. The church tower and the keep tower dominated the landscape. As the life-style became more sophisticated within the manor's encircling walls, additions to the original living area were made. In time castles became quite elegant and, after a country's unification when petty lords were no longer self-determining, became centers of hospitality during "royal progresses."

The lord-ruled village was a sign of the return to an orderly social system. The lord levied taxes and demanded loyalty of his vassals and serfs. The lord of a small principality was lord protector of his "people's persons."

The church was the keeper of the lord's, the vassals' and the serfs' spirits. Monks established either clerical communities or monasteries. Within the walls of these establishments were abbeys, hospitals, cell rooms for the ordained, and dormitories for the novices. Hospital and hotel facilities also were maintained by the monks at monasteries. The cloisters were the private colonnaded areas where monks walked or meditated. Shops, libraries, stables, storage areas, and latrines were peripheral support areas. An abbey was self-sufficient and could meet the needs of 100 monks, 200 wayfarers, and 100 craftsmen and monastery laborers. The surrounding farmlands were controlled by the monasteries and were used to grow the foodstuffs and grapes for wine to supply the earthly needs of residents and guests. Ecclesiastical orders also had long been engaged in preserving the literature and history of the past by carefully creating artful manuscripts which are some of the great treasures from the Dark Ages.

Charlemagne encouraged learning, but, although he was able to read, he was never able to master the writing system which was used throughout this period. Before Charlemagne's ascendancy, secular education had been totally obliterated. Often even priests and monks were illiterate. Educated men were necessary if an orderly social structure, administered by imperial appointees, was to succeed. It is indeed remarkable that amid numerous other problems, Charlemagne was able to inspire his subjects with the will to learn. This is particularly true since many writings of classical scholars had been destroyed and multilingual problems further complicated educational processes. Scholars and teachers formed a cadre of educators and received handsome rewards. The Palace School, which had been founded in 714, became a center for aspirants to official administrative posts. The Palace School in Charlemagne's capital, Aachen, had a curriculum which consisted of the seven classical liberal arts. The students were bearded men and callow sons of the nobility. The court of Charlemagne came to be known as "the second Rome" or "second Athens" as the members of the royal family became caught up in the pursuit of knowledge. In turn, this eagerness for education spread from Aachen to the surrounding villages and neighboring countries. Libraries were established as repositories of the written language. Because of their scarcity and value, books often were chained to the shelves in these libraries.

When Charlemagne died in 814 his empire fell apart. For a time, all progress ceased and a frontier system prevailed. The village with its castle protection and land supports for food again became the center of life for people of the early Dark Ages.

The Norman invasion of England in 1066 heralded the end of the first phase of civilization's struggle to recoup the losses it had suffered at the hands of the barbarians. Upon reaching his majority in 1048, the Duke of Normandy, later called William the Conqueror, began to rebuild his dukedom. The Bishop of Bayeux, his liturgical vassal, aided and abetted him. After two decades William the Norman had established the best organized state in Western Europe and had total control over knights, self-serving vassals, and recalcitrant serfs. Duke William's social order was based on a complete feudal system, and, after the conquest of England in 1066, he imposed this system on the whole of that land.

The eleventh century was a turning point in history. Church reforms were undertaken, self-confidence returned to the people, and secular education increased among the nobility, even extending to the peasants in some areas. Led by the church, a new strength and moral consciousness evolved. Romanesque art and architecture developed and was known as the Norman style in England.

Most important of all these factors of change was the growth in economic prosperity. Hard money, not barter, was responsible in part for this economic expansion as trade increased and became a complex structure in itself. Market sites were selected along trade routes outside lord-controlled villages or monasteries. Chosen because they were along major water routes or overland roads, the markets ultimately became suburbs and were self-ruled.[5] These in turn were drawn into the local village administrative system, but only after much struggle. The often transient residents were known as burghers as opposed to those who dwelled in the "old burg" who were called castellani, or castle-dwellers. When supplies of trade items appeared in these market villages, the already bustling settlement of burghers became a beehive of activity.

In England, to limit the proliferation of market towns, certain requirements for their establishment were laid down. No village might be designated a market town unless it could boast a cathedral. Hence, in Canterbury, Exeter, Winchester, and Salisbury, great ecclesiastical edifices were built.

However, cathedral building abounded not just to satisfy the market-town requirements, but to satisfy the resurgence of faith in the church. Fostered first by the Abbot of Cluny, who is credited with establishing the Cult of the Virgin, great structures were begun by the faithful.[6] Noblemen, their ladies, and artisans of the new stone-cutting craft all worked together, endlessly giving of wealth, talent, and human effort. Chartres is an example of such a cathedral. One cannot stand in the nave of any of these magnificent Christian structures without a feeling of awe at the prodigious accomplishments of these people who had only crude tools by today's standards.

The church and the spirit of the Teutonic people, the idealization of manhood and individualism, injected the quality of chivalry into the waning days of medieval Europe. The goal was knighthood, but a three-part probationary period preceded the knighting ceremony. A lad aspiring to knighthood entered the service of a knight as a page, advanced to a squire, and ultimately, if he qualified, was knighted. When a candidate was dubbed a knight, he took an oath to "defend the church, to protect his lord and lady, and to succor the poor and the meek." Thus dedicated, it is no wonder that so many "faithful" men became involved in the Crusading expeditions.

The effects of the eight Crusades on the life-style of the Dark Ages were far reaching. The First Crusade, perpetrated by Pope Urban II in 1095, introduced Europeans to the opulent excesses of Byzantium and Asia Minor. Knights and kings, as well as younger sons of nobles, entered into the great effort to free the Holy Land of infidels. At first they were dedicated to this principle in order to attain eternal glory. Later, personal glory, wealth, and lands were the unnamed aims.

The signing of the Magna Carta at Runnymede in 1215 was another social and political factor which altered many facets of human and social relations as medieval feudalism, strongly influenced by the church, drew to a close. The cessation of the Crusades marked the turning point. Economic status of princedoms and kingdoms had been altered by nearly two centuries of provisionary Crusade expeditions. Rich merchants had become more wealthy and vied with the nobility to attain status.

By wearing elegant clothes and practicing courtly manners, the merchants sought recognition and respectability. The nobility strove to keep ahead of their contemporaries of lesser rank by garbing themselves in innovative costumes. Men, who during the early Dark Ages had worn the knee- or thigh-length gonelle, abruptly adopted longer, fuller-cut garments. The **bliaud**, or **bliaut**, was a tunic style with a semifull, floor-length body and long funnel sleeves. In the twelfth century, the garment was shortened to calf length and the name generally associated with this item of apparel was **cotehardie.** It was made from a variety of fabrics: Alexandrina paile, a silk brocade from Egypt; asterin, a purple silk; siglaton from the Cyclades; and fustian, cotton corduroy or velveteen. For warmth, woolens were supplied by the weavers of Flanders, Champagne, and Picardy. The returning Crusaders brought with them samples of delicately woven taffeta, or cendal, which was later exported to Europe from Byzantium via the busy port of Venice. Men's wardrobes consisted of several items of apparel, the whole of which was called the **robe.** The separate items comprising the entire costume were the bliaud, surcoat, boldcoat, dust sheet, or cape, and, in cold weather, the necklet, a short mantle.

The impression made upon Crusaders by the opulence and formal etiquette of Byzantium altered many attitudes, including their relationship with women. During the formative period, women were held with little regard. Ribald behavior, strong language, cursing, and other crude acts were not curtailed if women were present. The first tentative step toward respecting womanhood was an odd law which concerned touching a woman's arm. Quite "suddenly" women received respect and admiration, and being placed on a pedestal even changed women's attitudes toward themselves.

During the twelfth century, the female cotehardie and other gowns of the *robe à six garnements* were of rather simple cut. The paintings and woodcuts of the period indicate that, while there was some fit to ladies' garb, usually the outer gowns fell rather simply from the shoulders and had snug sleeves, plain necklines, and slit skirts. The generalization of female clothes, which lacked the complex brocade fabrics and were made in rich, mellow, but dull colors, further exemplified the low status of women. It was not until the adulation of "ladies fair" that women's garments began to show any complexity in cut and fabric as documented in the paintings of the period. Once clothed in loose-fitting, rather drab apparel, women now realized that their costumes might aid in attracting the attention of the opposite sex. The gunna was exchanged for the figure-molding **bliaud, cyclas, sorquenie, chainse,** and **cotehardie.**[7] They were fashioned from the same rich materials as those used for garments of the men.

The high regard for femininity changed not only women's costumes, but male costumes as well. Serious doubts were raised by churchmen and others concerning the increased effeminacy in men's clothing, hair fashions, and posturing.

Fur was used as trims and lining. **Gules,** made of dyed red fur and flecked ermine, were the most popular. The less prosperous patterned themselves after the affluent nobility and burghers, using rabbit, squirrel, and even dog furs as substitutes for ermine, sable, and fox. Pearls and ostrich feathers, worth a king's ransom, trimmed hats, belts, shoes, doublets, and even armor.

Choice of costume colors had symbolic significance as well as family identity. As courtly love, *l'amour courtois,* progressed through the formal and prescribed stages, colors identified each phase.[8] The languishing knight donned green garments when smitten but unable to declare himself. A white costume indicated that the knight had declared himself but had not yet received words of encouragement from his lady fair. Declaration that his heartfelt hopes were gratified was proclaimed by wearing bright red garments. This chivalric sign language in color also was used by ladies of the court in making their replies. Pastel colors of many differing hues invited a lady's knight to watch or assist her in going to bed. She declared the return of his affection by choosing robes of yellow. The entire process of courtly love-making was in recognition of the new status women were achieving during this period. It was a fundamental social change which elevated ladies of the court to an idealized position. Manners of the court were altered, as were male and female fashions, because of this feminine influence.

Head coverings such as the chinstrap, headrail, and wimple (Figure 9.3), were discarded. Heads were crowned with decorative circlets (Figure 9.4), or a brow-encircling **guirlande,** a string of decorative beads. Coiffures were fashioned by braiding the hair and rolling it into buns positioned over the ears. These braided buns were held in place by **amices,** or cauls. The back of the neck was covered with cowls of cloth, often made of velvet and lined with fur.

Hairstyling for men also paid heed to head coverings and careful grooming. At the time of the Crusades, men's hair was carefully arranged. Beards, out of fashion for some time, came back into favor during the twelfth cen-

**Figure 9.3.** Veils, or **wimples,** with **headrail** and **chinstrap** (right) were the chief type of female headwear during the early fourteenth century. (Master Heinrich of Constance: *The Visitation,* statuette group, c. 1310. Metropolitan Museum of Art, New York City.)

tury. Beards of the men of the courts were shaped, parted, fluffed, and decorated with golden threads.

Attention to matters of personal toilette was given new importance. A pamphlet was written concerning the proper etiquette for care of clothing. These written instructions advised that, upon retiring, one's clothes should be "poled," perhaps on a wooden hanger, or the first silent valet, in the following order: "pole . . . coat, surcoat, cloche, and doublet." This paper recommended that skirt and breeches be folded neatly "beneath the bolster." Donning instructions in the same pamphlet were equally explicit, ending with the phrase "tighten your braces and wash your hands."

**Figure 9.4.** The **reticulated hairstyle** took several forms and was used for many years. The fillet is missing from this bust. (Jean de Liège: *Bust of Marie of France,* c. 1382. Metropolitan Museum of Art, New York City.)

foam was used as a skin freshener. Hair dyes were concocted from a combination of cinders, horse fat, and other ingredients. Sweet scents became very important. At first, golden balls with perforations were filled with musk and hung from a lady's trinket-laden belt. By 1300 a flexible ball to hold an herb called cyprus oyselet had been invented. A simple squeeze of this flexible ball emitted a sweet, aromatic scent through the perforations in the ball. The first perfume, distilled in 1370, was called "Hungarian Water," and was composed of alcohol, turpentine, and rosemary. Women also used ointments on their bodies and depilatory creams to remove unwanted hair. A toothpaste of unknown composition is mentioned in some contemporary chronicles. Daily baths, group bathing, and sauna baths ultimately were forbidden by the church. This may account for the popularity of nosegays, scent apples, and perfumes, as well as head-encircling garlands of sweet-smelling flowers.

Bathing before dressing apparently was not thought necessary, but later in the day men and women went to public baths. Here they "steamed and sweat" in a sauna, later lolled "coeducationally" in large wooden tubs arranged in long rows. Oddly, while bathing, women wore their hats (the hennins). Music was provided and light refreshments were served on small tables constructed in the centers of the tubs.

An English lady who lived during the Middle Ages, Mrs. Trot, set forth a list of beauty suggestions for the women of her day. She recommended that baths be taken in seawater and offered a recipe for afterbath deodorant made from bay leaves, calamint, abseneke, and hyssop. Quicklime was the chemical proposed to use for removing unwanted hair. She thought honey rubbed on the lips would keep them firm, and suggested that white skin would be achieved and wrinkles prevented by using leeches. For tooth care, she recommended a mouth rinse of lukewarm wine.

Pity the poor lady who was obese, for Mrs. Trot's reducing plan must have been odoriferous if nothing else. She called for "applications frictions" made of combined cow dung dissolved in wine. Next, she prescribed sitting in the "stove," an early sauna made of a ring of stones, with a fire beneath a platform. In the center of a platform, the obese lady was seated on a stool. A sheet was wrapped about the person and draped outside the ring of stone. After this treatment the lady was placed in a "sand grave."

Some of the cosmetic habits of the medieval period were quite unusual. Eyelashes were darkened and the illusion of length was achieved by applying soot. Beer

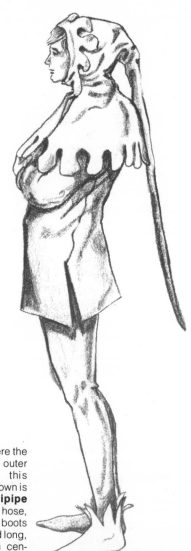

**Figure 9.5.** Young men were the first to introduce shorter outer garments such as this **supercotehardie.** Also shown is a streamer-trimmed **liripipe** hood with dagged edge, hose, and "crabbed," ankle-high boots called **estivaux,** which had long, pointed toes. (Fourteenth century.)

Foot coverings first assumed their ridiculously long points during the late twelfth and early thirteenth centuries (Figure 9.5). These shoes with the long points, variously called **crackows, pistachios,** or **poulaines,** became the fashion after the pointed, upturn-toed shoes were introduced by returning Crusaders. The points, in their extreme form, extended twelve inches beyond the foot. To keep from tripping the wearer when walking, the toes of the shoes were reinforced with whalebone staves or hay. This style remained in fashion until the early fifteenth century. The crackow shoe form, so the story goes, was introduced into England by gentlemen from Cracow, Poland. They had come to the court of Richard II to pay their respects to the king's new bride, Anne of Bohemia. Poland then was a part of that princedom. These courtly gentlemen were shod in the first long-pointed shoes the English court had seen. Language barriers complicated the spelling, hence the term for this footwear—*crackow.*

From the time the Crusaders returned to their homelands, interest in apparel made of elegant stuffs and fanciful trims reached new peaks. By the end of the medieval period, individuality and signs of group identity abounded. The male figure was revealed, clad in tight hose and short, chest-padded doublet. The fifteenth-century North Italian artist Pisanello is given credit for creating this fashionable silhouette. Hems of garments were shredded, marbled, and dagged, or dragged (Figures 9.8 and 9.39). Lead tatters were fringed trims for edges adopted by the Germans. Gold coins were sewn on hems to identify the wearer as a prosperous character. Cutouts of many shapes—stars, butterflies, or straight slashes—were introduced. Undoubtedly the expression "by my stars and garters . . ." came from this period. Women and men adopted particolored clothes. Badges also were used as class or group identification. An example is the badge worn by those who had made a pilgrimage to Canterbury Cathedral. In this period good Christians, rich and poor, were expected to make pilgrimages to religious shrines. Those who had completed such pious trips felt it important to let the world know of their accomplishments by wearing something symbolic of the feat.

Peasants, Jews, heretics, and convicted witches were required to wear special attire. A Jew was forced to wear the **rowel** and a pointed hat. The rowel was a spiked wheel of iron fashioned much like that in the center of a horse's bit. This was worn from a chain around the neck. A witch convicted of practicing her craft was required to wear a special marking on her clothing similar to the scarlet *A* imposed on Hester Prynne in Hawthorne's novel, *The Scarlet Letter*. A witch's hair was cut in a symbolic way to identify her position in society.

Indeed, from head to toe, the fanciful dress of the Middle Ages was a colorful, imaginative means of self and group identity. Peasants, while garbed in clothing made of lowly homespun, enjoyed color in their apparel. Not affluent enough to own more than one set of robes, they washed their clothing and themselves at the same time. The penalty for affluence and a large wardrobe was taxation. Sumptuary laws and taxation of garments owned in excess of a specified number were the means used by impoverished princes for raising revenue. Princes of church and state reviled against excesses in clothing by the privileged few, but to no avail. In the Renaissance, even more elegant and complex apparel was created.

# Basic Garments of the Medieval Period (1000–1400)

## BLIAUD (1000–1200)

Between 1000 and 1200, the gonelle and the paragaudion (Figure 9.6), the basic garments of the early Dark Ages and Byzantium, were slightly altered and renamed the **bliaud,** or **bliaut** (Figures 9.7 and 9.8). Still a tunic shape, innovations in design changed the overall silhouette of this item of outer wear. The body section of the male bliaud was cut quite full and extended to midcalf when not girdled. However, its length was shortened

**Figure 9.6.** Loose-fitting **paragaudion,** typical of the easy comfort of these often embroidery-trimmed outer garments for men, and full-length **braccae.**

**Figure 9.7.** Funnel-sleeved **bliaud** with hose, **crackows,** and four-piece bonnet with ear flaps and under-the-chin ties. (Sixth to tenth centuries.)

**Figure 9.8.** Dagged-edge **bliaud.**

**Figure 9.9. Braies** of the tenth century were still ill-fitting trouser forms but were shortened to knee length as the shorter **bliaud** or knee-length **paragaudion** came into male fashion.

**Figure 9.10.** Male **chausses,** or hose, under **braies** gathered tightly around the waist with a drawstring. Chausses are tied to tapes attached to braies. (Tenth to thirteenth centuries.)

**Figure 9.11.** Female **bliaud** of the Middle Ages. The German version was intricately cut with a bodice made of several pieces designed to emphasize the bust. (Redrawn from C. Köhler, *A History of Costume*.)

**Figure 9.12.** Female **bliauds** of the medieval period were figure concealing, covering the body from neck to toes. There were styles, however, which accented the female form by snugly encircling the upper torso. The form fit was achieved by side or back lacings (figure on left).

**Figure 9.13.** Fitted **bliaud** typical of German styles between 1066 and 1154. This embroidery-trimmed garment was cut in several complex pieces designed to accentuate the bust.

by blousing it over a leather belt, thus revealing the knees. Sleeves were altered also and, instead of having tight wrist bands, were designed in a funnel shape, flaring modestly at the wrist. Sleeves were quite often longer than the arm, extending well beyond the hand, which served as a means for keeping the hands warm. Peasants and nobility alike wore the bliaud, and the wearer's country of origin and class status were identified by the trimming or lack of it.

By 1150 a distinctly new innovation developed in the cut and styling of the male bliaud. During the second half of the twelfth century, the body of the bliaud was designed with a close-fitting waist section and a rather full, knee- or thigh-length skirt. The excessive width at the cuff of the large, funnel sleeves of this male garment was discarded. Trims on hems, cuffs, and embroidered bands on the upper arms were retained. The bliaud was worn over the floor-length undertunic with band and hem trim, or with only **braies** (Figure 9.9), and hosen (hose), the latter being poorly devised leg coverings. There is some doubt about whether hose were separate apparel items or slim trousers (Figure 9.10).

Women's bliaud styles worn by the nobility were more fancifully created. At first a floor-length version of the male costume, the bliaud soon acquired sex-differentiating characteristics (Figure 9.11). It was worn over the stola, or **cotte**, gunna, and **chainse**. The flaring, long, hand-covering sleeves were occasionally eliminated, and the female bliaud became an overgown without sleeves. The skirts of this gown were made of many gores and were long in front and back. The bodice laced on the side or in back and was more intricately cut and shaped over the bust than earlier robes to reveal the curves of the female form (Figure 9.12). There was a deep V-shape in front of the bodice to which the gathered skirt was attached.[9]

Before the long sleeves were discarded, regional differences in sleeve treatments were apparent.[10] In the eleventh century, the German bliaud sleeves were styled in two patterns. The first style was the wrist-length funnel shape, with geometric border trims at the wide cuffs (Figure 9.13). The other sleeve design had a snug-fitting upper section with a band trim encircling the upper arm. The cuff was slender and trailing from a point about midway between elbow and wrist. This trailing cuff was decorated with repeat lozenge-shape designs, geometric patterns, or embroidered and decorated with braid. The funnel-sleeved style reached just below the calf. During the twelfth century, the German funnel sleeve reached such excesses in length and width that ladies were obliged to knot them to keep these cumbersome sleeves from interfering with hand movements.[11]

French female bliaud fashions for the same period were designed with narrow, banded cuffs which were quite long, perhaps trailing thirty inches beyond the sleeve width. The French style included belting with a soft, wide girdle (Figure 9.14).

The English sleeve version was styled in a scoop shape which created the illusion of a trailing cuff, but was more complex in cut. However, less intricate trimming of braid rather than embroidery was used.

Isabeau of Bavaria, a rather stout, thickset princess, initiated the practice of collecting all excess fabric from the skirt front into a bunch over the stomach to conceal her bulk, and ladies of her court were quick to imitate her mannerisms (Figure 9.15). The normal, diminutive belted waistline was discarded with this new profile innovation. An under-the-bust bandeau replaced the cinch belt made of golden plaques, often weighing two pounds, which had been popular during the twelfth century. Excessively long skirts retained their fashion popularity well into the fourteenth century. When walking, posturing, or standing, ladies gathered their skirts deftly in one hand. Some of these long, full skirts had two vertical slits placed rather low on the skirt front. Instead of holding the skirt with her hand, a lady simply ran her arm through both of the slits and, by resting her arm on her stomach, the hem was elevated to achieve the desired silhouette (Figure 9.16).

**Figure 9.14.** The belted **corset,** with center front tucks from neckline to waist, worn over a **chainse.** Also shown, a tall turban hat form, c. 1400.

**Figure 9.15.** During the early fifteenth century, gown skirts were extremely long in front and back. They were gathered over the abdomen to accentuate the stomach. (Jan Van Eyck: *Giovanni Arnolfini and Wife,* detail, 1435. National Gallery, London.)

**Figure 9.16. Steeple hennin** with veil, and short-bodice gown with long skirt, front and back, which was held up by thrusting arms through skirt slits. This revealed the instep-length chemise beneath, which also showed at the elbow, having been puffed out between the tied-on gown sleeves. (Late fourteenth century.)

## DALMATIC (1000–1100)

During the eleventh century, the dalmatic, generally reserved for royalty, assumed a complex cut. The sleeves were inset well into the body of the garment and were truncated shapes with deep cuffs. The hemline, cuffs, and a deep V-neckline were banded with a wide, patterned braid. The body of this garment was made of purple or lavender silk damask. Over the dalmatic, an **alba** (mantle) was worn as an outer wrap. The name of the alba refers to white color of this decorative, rank-defining wrap which was emblazoned with a rampant heraldic symbol of the emperor's family.

## COTEHARDIE (1100–1300)

The most significant clothing innovation during the twelfth century was the development of the **cotehardie, cotte hardie,** or **cotes-hardi,** the first true coat to be designed. The men's version was knee length, with a tightly fitted body and inset sleeves (Figure 9.17). As in the evolution of any garment styling, changes occurred and pockets became an integral part of this costume. Long, vertical slashes, bound with braid or embroidery,

placed thigh high on the center of each of the front panels formed the openings for pockets.

The lady's cotehardie had a fitted bodice and a long, many-gored skirt. This sumptuous garment with its excessive skirt length and width was held up in front, giving the wearer a pregnant profile and a swayback contour. Some of these gowns had two vertical slits, similar to those on the bliaud, placed low on the skirt front which allowed the wearer to slip her arm through the slits to catch up the bulk of the skirt and lift the front hemline. This made walking easier and eliminated holding bulky quantities of fabric in the hand to create the desired silhouette. Sleeves in the female cotehardie were snug and sewn more tightly about the wrists after the garments were put on. Women carried small scissors suspended from a cord attached to the girdle in order to snip these wrist stitchings if the need arose. When out walking or playing in the woods, they frequently cut the threads at the wrists and "went about with unsewn sleeves," to quote one chronicler. The cotehardie is believed to be the first coat form with fitted, shaped, inset sleeves. The body of this outer garment was also more figure revealing and it became quite snug during the fourteenth century. It had no collar until 1375 and was

**Figure 9.17.** The **cotehardie** illustrated here is slit from hem to crotch, front and back, to give more comfort while horseback riding. Pockets were an innovation introduced into the design of this garment. Duck-billed slippers and bonnets made in four segments were also popular during the thirteenth century. The brim could be turned down to cover the ears for added warmth during cold weather. (Redrawn from C. Köhler, *A History of Costume.*)

fastened in the center front with many small, closely set buttons. Some cotehardies had bateau necklines, others had hoods.

Early in the thirteenth century, the fit of clothes, particularly the cotehardie, became very important. Snug fit emphasized the more masculine attributes of robust chest and broad shoulders. In court circles more formality began to appear in male attire, though activity patterns continued to be natural. It was only after the shorter styles came into fashion, revealing men's legs encased in the snug, movement-restricting **chausses,** that stilted posturing typified male activity patterns.[12]

In the late thirteenth century, young clothes-conscious men of the Middle Ages altered the silhouette. This alteration was achieved by the introduction of the short cotehardie, or **supercotehardie,** which scarcely covered the posterior and was exceedingly tight fitting through the upper body and sleeves (Figures 9.18 and 9.19). To achieve a better fit of the sleeve at the underarm, a small gusset was inserted. In addition, a small standing collar was added. Bands used for trimming generally were discarded. The entire effect was one of tall, slim masculinity, depending on the severity of the tailoring. Elegance depended on the quality of the fabrics used.

## GARDE-CORPS (1300)

The **garde-corps,** a variation of the cotehardie, was a fad which grew out of a chivalric custom (Figures 9.1 and 9.20). During jousts and other field meets displaying masculine prowess, a young lady of the court was apt to give her admirer a token symbolic of good luck. These tokens, or charms, were either veils or sleeves. The sleeves, loosely attached or tied to the female bliaud, were stripped off and tossed to the favored combatant in the field to "guard the person." These tokens were swept up

**Figure 9.18.** Styling of the **supercotehardie** appeared in 1375 when a standing collar and a snug fit to give the illusion of broad masculine shoulders were added to characteristics of the **cotehardie.** Note pouch purse tied to the low-slung belt. (Redrawn from fresco of the period.)

**Figure 9.19.** Young swain of the fourteenth century in **supercotehardie** and **chausses** with flop-crowned bonnet. Lass wearing a **gunna** with tight sleeves. (Detail from woodcut of the period.)

by the knight and tucked into the sleeve articulation of the armor, or attached to the helmet.

Ultimately, a facsimile of the veil or sleeve amulet was reproduced on everyday wear as a permanent part of the garment. This appendage was attached to the sleeve just above the elbow and was called the **tippet** (Figure 9.20). In time the narrow tippet became a wide, long panel, two or three feet in length. The cotehardie, thus altered, became known as the garde-corps. The garde-corps often had four slits in the skirt—front, back, and on the sides. These slits made horseback riding more comfortable when wearing this garment as it was usually calf length, and without the slits would have been cumbersome and confining. Other hem trims employed in elegant garde-corps were dagged edge trims, **trails,** or slashes in the hem, facings of a contrasting color, and braid borders around the skirt slits, neckline, and cuffs. The trim of trails was introduced by Philip Augustus and was a German tailoring trait.

**Particolored** garde-corps also were worn during the thirteenth century (Figure 9.20). Because families were identified by crests and specific colors, clan identity was established by incorporating family-identifying colors

**Figure 9.20.** Particolor **garde-corps** with **tippet** and "devil's fingers" **crackows.** (Thirteenth century.)

**Figure 9.21.** Male garments include the short **houppelande, chausses,** and **crackows,** with heads covered by caps and **roundlets,** or a **liripipe** arranged to form a **chaperon** (right). The lady's headwear is the **heart-shaped hennin** and she wears the high-waisted **houppelande** with bandeau. (Tapestry: *Courtiers with Roses,* fifteenth century, Franco-Flemish, Arras or Tournai. Metropolitan Museum of Art, New York City.)

into wearing apparel. This practice was begun by servants of noble families and later adopted by the members of court themselves.

Both cotehardie and garde-corps were designed with pockets set low on the skirt section. The female version of the garde-corps often was worn beneath the **cyclas,** a floor-length surcoat. During the twelfth and thirteenth centuries, multilayered costumes of four garments were worn by married women, while spinsters and young girls wore but one outer garment. This practice did not preclude additional wraps worn for warmth.

The early fourteenth century saw the addition to the garde-corps of another, more practical body-protecting device. This was a hood attached at the neckline. The hood was drawn up in inclement weather, or thrown back if not needed for protection. The center front of the neck opening was designed with buttons and buttonholes so that it might be fastened snugly about the neck.

Sleeve designs of the garde-corps varied from snug to full. The fuller style was pleated to the armhole. This sleeve was a simple rectangle, sewn on three sides, pleated to the shoulder seam, and gusseted at the underarm. A long, vertical slit was cut in the upper-sleeve section allowing the arm to pass through. The female garde-corps with this sleeve style was an outer garment.

## HOUPPELANDE (1380–1450)

The garde-corps evolved into the houppelande, a voluminous outer garment with enormous, conical sleeves, which was worn by both sexes (Figures 9.21–9.23

and 9.44). The neckline fitted snugly about the throat, and the skirt, which was sometimes calf length for men but always floor length for women, was slit in front and in back. The distinctive design feature of this bulky costume was the deep, sausage-roll, or organ pipe, pleats that radiated from the tightly belted waist upward to the shoulders and downward to the hem. The bodice was extremely full in some versions and only slightly bloused in others. The long, funnel sleeves were trimmed with fur (Figure 9.23), or the dagged design, a series of deep scallops or deep V-shapes. These designs were modifications of the toothed edge of earlier times. A belted or unbelted short houppelande was worn by younger men. The sleeves of this garment were often short in front and long in back. Made of elegant fabrics, often particolored, and on rare occasions emblazoned with heraldic designs, these long or short costumes were worn primarily by the upper class. Simpler versions in rough wool were later adopted by the middle and lower classes.

Another name change occurred because of the sleeve detailing of this voluminous coatlike garment. Made after the houppelande pattern, it was called the **corset** (Figure 9.14), and was styled with flaring wing sleeves or large, full sleeves gathered to cuffs but left open at the underarm seams.

## SURCOAT (1100–1400)

The **surcoat,** or **surcot,** was a fashionable garment for a long period of time.[13] First used by crusading knights, it served to deflect the sun's heat and eliminate

**Figure 9.22. Chaperon** with short **houppelande** and particolored **chausses.** (Late fifteenth century.)

the deep armhole. Often it was entirely lined with fur, which showed at neckline, hem, and armholes.[14] Heraldic symbols, widely used after the Crusades in the late twelfth century, were incorporated into the front and back panels. The use of these intricate group-identity symbols had their origins in Oriental blazonry. From 1300 to 1500 they were incorporated into particolored clothes worn exclusively by the members of the royal court. Once a slender garment, the surcoat increased in fullness and opulence, and men of court wore long and calf-length versions.

**Figure 9.23.** Woman is clad in a **gamurra,** a combination of a **surcoat** and **houppelande.** She wears the gamurra over a houppelande. On her head she wears the bubble-shaped headpiece, the **balzo.** The man wears a belted houppelande with funnel sleeves, and a **chaperon.** (Redrawn from *Jewish Wedding,* detail, Jacob ben Essen, fifteenth century. Vatican Museum.)

its blinding reflections on armor (Figure 9.24). In its simplest form, the surcoat was a calf-length rectangle of fabric of shoulder width, having a slit for a neckline along the shoulder fold. It had no sleeves at first and there were no side seams. Later, though still worn belted at the normal waist, the knights' surcoats had elbow-length, or shorter, tab sleeves. The sides were sewn together from waistline to hem with center front and back slits. Red crosses originally decorated this simple covering in front and back.

After it was introduced into the civilian wardrobe, deep armholes continued to be a characteristic feature of this garment. Adaptation of the surcoat by members of the nobility turned this utilitarian accessory into an elegant outer garment. As a noble's garment, it was made of heavy, brocaded Arabian silk or velvet. It often was lined with silk of a contrasting color and edged with fur around

**Figure 9.24.** Armor was a definite part of male costume for many years and was distinctly nationalistic. These twelfth- to fifteenth-century examples illustrate the individualism injected in the design of the helmet. By the sixteenth century, soldier's headgear was decorative and fearful, often styled to resemble fierce animal heads. Center figure wears the **surcoat,** first used by Crusaders. (Sketched from the Wallace Collection, London; and the Metropolitan Museum of Art, New York City.)

**Figure 9.25.** Colorful garments of the thirteenth century include the hérigaute, shown here worn over a suit of armor. (Redrawn from illustration in the thirteenth-century Capodelesta Codex, Padua.)

**Figure 9.26.** The female version of the surcoat became known as the **cyclas**. In this sketch, the young lady wears the button-decorated cyclas over a **sorquenie** with snug sleeves, which were probably sewn after the garment was put on. Hairstyling is reticulated, topped with a coronet of fresh leaves. This garment continued in fashion until well into the fifteenth century. (Redrawn from *Jeanne d'Armagnac*, (or *Isabeau of Bavaria*), sculpture, c. 1388. Palais de Justice, Poitiers.)

The shorter, fuller style called a **hérigaute** was gathered at the shoulder seams, and the side seams were sewn only a modest distance up from the hem (Figure 9.25). The **tabard** was a variation of the surcoat used primarily by pages but also worn by adult males. Short in length, rigid in form rather than gathered or draped, the tabard had semicircular tab sleeves which stood out stiffly beyond the points of the shoulders. Highly decorative gold braid and gold thread defined the heraldic affiliation of the wearer, either his own or that in whose service he was employed. The tabard is still the official ceremonial costume of the guards of The Tower in London.

The ladies of the court also wore a floor-length surcoat called variously the **cyclas,** or **pellotes** (Figure 9.26). The pellotes of Leonore of Aragon, who died in 1244, is one of two garments extant from this period. Leonore's pellotes, made of Arabian brocade, had a high, round neckline, the usual deep armholes, and, though badly damaged, appears to have had side lacing.

Some members of society ridiculed the cyclas with its deep armholes which revealed such undergarments as the sorquenie or tunic. The derogatory term "windows of hell" was used when referring to this female version of the surcoat.[15] The skirt of the cyclas was long and trailing, made up of many gores to add fullness and elegance. Braid trims on the hem and wide strips of elegant fabric were inset in the upper section of the skirt. The front panel, or **plastron,** often was completely covered with fur, or was edged with fur, and imitation buttons were attached down the center front. This garment, when styled for winter wear, was lined throughout the upper section with fur. Fur trims were referred to as **gules** when dyed (Figure 9.27), and red was one of the preferred hues. Flocked ermine, reserved for royalty, was also a favored trim and lining.

An undergarment, the tunic, or **tunique,** was designed in a fashion similar to the cyclas, but the armholes were not as deep nor the skirt as full. An example of this garment was found in the Tombs of Ferdinando de la Cerda, a sarcophagus sealed in 1211, on the remains of the original owner. It was a fine linen garment made with a six-panel skirt and a small, round neckline, and it laced on the right side only, for a snug fit. This garment continued to be worn well in the fourteenth century. It often was visible when ladies draped up the cotehardie skirts, and it might also have shown through the cote's side vents.

The **sorquenie** usually was worn beneath the cyclas (Figure 9.28). This snug, buttocks-length garment with very tight sleeves was quite figure revealing. The sleeves were form fitted by using closely set small buttons and were exceedingly long, extending over the palm, leaving only the fingers exposed. The section covering the hand was called the **mitten.** During the fourteenth and early fifteenth centuries, the sleeves were attached to the main body of the tunic or cotehardie by pins or ribbons when

**Figure 9.27.** Generally, elderly men retained older styles of garments, preferring the un-belted sausage-roll **houppelande** trimmed with gules. The figure here also wears a tiered bonnet of the early Renaissance period. (Late thirteenth century.)

donned in the morning and "ripped off at night" (Figure 9.16). These separate sleeves served to add variety to the costume and carried out the heraldic symbols or family-identifying color schemes.

## ROBE (1200–1400)

During the later years of the medieval period, opulence in dress and group identity increased as style-determining forces. Richness of costumes was achieved through fabric, jewel and feather trims, and many garments worn simultaneously. The multilayered set of garments was referred to as the **robe.** As few as two and as many as six different pieces of clothing were worn at once, comprising *robe à six garnements* (Figure 9.29). There was no prescribed grouping but garments were selected from the following list: tunic (chainse), surcoat, cotte, cotehardie, dust sheet (short cape), necklet (short mantle), and braies. Kings' and queens' robes consisted of the bliaud or cotehardie, doublet, dalmatic, and mantle.

Until 1340, gentlemen of the nobility wore courtly, floor-length costumes. The short **doublet** and other jacket forms were worn for two centuries thereafter. All of these waist-length garments were padded with wadding, as was the late twelfth-century **gambeson,** or **gamboisée.** The

**Figure 9.28.** Thirteenth-century women wore a thigh-length **sorquenie** over a rather full floor-length **chainse.** Some authorities suggest that the chainse was also used as night apparel.

**Figure 9.29.** Multilayered costumes, or **robe à six garnements,** were typical in European regions with cold climates. Shown here is a fifteenth-century adaptation of the **surcoat,** fur lined and trimmed. This is worn over a **houppelande,** which conceals the main part of the square-necked **doublet.** The head is covered by a turban of figured material and a large beaver hat. (Redrawn detail from a painting by F. Ratgerb.)

**Figure 9.30.** Fourteenth-century female costumes featured reticulated headdresses and the **houppelande-**style robe with high waist. The headdress was called variously **horned hennin, templers,** or **escoffion.**

Present-day academic regalia had its origins in the thirteenth century. During that century, Rome granted the medieval universities the right to set their own gown patterns, which were generally more sombre than court dress and had specific sleeve styling and cut, intended to denote dignity and authority. These floor-length robes called **gens de robe longue** were quite a contrast to the fashionable, figure-revealing short dress of the nobility. Undergraduates wore short versions of the university-identifying gowns. Medical doctors also wore **robes longues** of bright colors and doctors' caps of specific cut. Surgeons, called surgical workmen, however, were required to wear short gowns for they were not as highly regarded as professors, dons, and doctors.

Knights and military men had a prescribed set of garments which consisted of the bliaud; gambeson; **broigne,** a leather jerkin with metal or horn frame; **hauberk,** a cap and neck protection of mail; coat of mail; and a **baldric,** a sword belt. By 1350, plated mail was introduced. Heraldic symbols were emblazoned on the leather covering of shields, and feathers, ostrich plumes, and aigrettes as well as deer antlers decorated helmets.

Peasants wore clothes of rough wool and coarse linen. Men wore the ill-fitting braies; a gonelle; a **cotteron,** a

doublet gained its name because it was made of two layers of fabric with an interlining. The wadding was used to fill out the chest and to extend the shoulder width by padding the upper sleeves. The broad-shouldered appearance, achieved by leg-of-mutton sleeves, and the long-legged look took over the male fashion scene during the mid-fourteenth century.

Other short padded jackets comprising the *garnements* included the **pelicon,** a fur-lined garment with snug sleeves and a high, round neck made in the same style as the quilted or tufted doublet. The **gipon, jupe,** and **justaucorps** were other names given to similarly styled waist-length jackets (Figure 9.31). Ladies often adapted a form of the doublet as an undergarment for extra warmth. The **houqueton,** used first by knights beneath their armor, was a padded waistcoat, perhaps styled without sleeves. This garment was adapted for civilian use late in the thirteenth century. When the male fashions became shorter—a fad believed to have been of French origin—some of the cut trims were eliminated. Hems no longer were fringed with lead tatters, trails, or dagging. The term *robe,* which referred to outer garments in the late thirteenth century, was later the label given to undergarments.

**Figure 9.31.** The **gipon,** or **jupe,** was a quilted undergarment worn for extra warmth. It was made of many layers of fabric, none of which were elegant or intended to show. (Redrawn from description in C. Köhler, *A History of Costume.*)

**Figure 9.32.** Costumes of common men during the Dark Ages and well into the Gothic period were of simple cut. Shown here is a tuniclike shirt, ill-fitting breeches, or **braies,** and leg windings, or **tibialia.**

**Figure 9.33.** Typical garments used for protection in stormy weather between 1154 and 1272, include the **balandran** and hooded cape with dagged edge trim.

smocklike garment, or a blouse or shirt of coarse linen; **chausses,** or linen hose; and heavy, tied shoes (Figure 9.32). Women wore many apparel items of the past, including the chemise as an undergarment, **cotte, cotella,** stola, linen hose, and the **sayon,** or **frieze** cape, an outer wrap used by both sexes.[16]

## OUTER WRAPS (1095–1400)

Until the mid-fourteenth century, wraps for warmth were considered as part of the *robe à garnements.* They were elegant in fabric and trimmed with gules, jewels, heraldic symbols, and gold-thread embroidery. Some had hanging sleeves or attached hoods.

During the eleventh and twelfth centuries, cape or mantle wraps continued to be used as garments for warmth and protection against inclement weather. The most common were the **chape** and **chasuble,** circular or rectangular cloaks without collars that were fastened with ties or brooches at the throat and lined with fur. The **balandran** was a full-circle mantle used as rainwear (Figure 9.33). It was often fitted with a shoulder cape and a deep face-hiding hood. The shoulder cape was edged about the hem with the dagged design. The *à parer,* derived from the bardocucullus, was also a circular cape that tied at the neck and had slits on the sides for armholes (Figure 9.34).

Other lighter-weight capes included the **housse** and **herigaute** (1200–1300), both variations of the surcoat; the **garnache,** with a full back panel and two long tabs in front crossed over the chest; and a small, hip-length, circular cape.

Jackets such as the cotte, gamboise, gambeson, and hoqueton were wadded or padded garments with high necklines, tight sleeves, and front closures with closely spaced fastenings. These latter styles came into use in the mid-fourteenth century as outer garments and continued in style for some time.

The **bold coat** was worn by men in Germany during the reign of Philip Augustus. It was designed much like a cotehardie but had side vents, wing sleeves, and the hem was fringed with trails. It fitted the figure easily but was not a loose, full garment.

The peasant garment, the **sayon,** was similar to the garde-corps used by the nobility. This garment had a hood attached to the body, but did not have the tippet trims on the sleeves.

## TROUSER FORMS (1100–1400)

While outer garments were long, men continued to wear knee-length braies and tube hose beneath the bliaud or cotehardie. After 1340, when shorter styles which added to allow for body movement. Young men, the first to adopt the hip-length cotehardie, wore closed hose and were rather restricted in their movements. Both secular and religious leaders demanded that, for the sake of male modesty, closed hose must be worn with the shorter upper garments.

As better knitting techniques were developed, **full-bottom hose** and the **codpiece** were introduced. The leg sections of these limb coverings were made to fit more smoothly by making a series of small darts around the ankles of the hose. The darts were hidden with fanciful embroidery. As the doublets and supercotehardies came into general use, the hose, or chausses, were first worn over the braies, but eventually these became only brief trunks and then were discarded in favor of the full-bottom hose. Both of these styles of leg coverings were attached to the doublets or jupes by cord laces with metal tab tips.

## UNDERWEAR (1100–1400)

Simple garments of fine linen lawn were worn as underwear. Called variously the **chainse, tunic, cainsie,** or **shift,** this undergarment was made after the basic tunic pattern with sleeves. The neckline was small and round with a slit down the center front. The chainse often was intricately embroidered with cross, chain, and feather stitches. There is an example of this type of chainse trim

**Figure 9.34.** Traveling wrap with hood, the **bardocucullus,** or **à parer,** adopted by many people from a similar garment used by the Romans.

revealed male legs came into fashion, **chausses,** or hose, replaced the tube hose. Tube hose were simply made from a folded rectangle of fabric, cut diagonally across the bottom to accommodate the foot and sewn from foot to upper hem. Tapes were attached to the top edge, which in turn were tied to tapes on the cotte hem or to an underbelt. The major difference between hose and tube hose was that the hose were cut into two duplicate pieces shaped like the leg and foot in profile. It is easy to understand how particolored hose were fashioned from this pattern using fabrics of contrasting colors. Hose, also tabbed and taped, were held in place by tying them to tapes on the inside of the doublet, gipon, or jupe. Beneath the hose were a shapeless pair of linen "legs" which were stitched through the crotch, hemmed at the top, and gathered by a drawstring around the waist.

In time, the outer hose were joined and called **closed hose** or a **"pair of legs."** This was an uncomfortable and impractical arrangement, for no extra fabric had been

**Figure 9.35.** Female **cotteron** with apron. Head is bound in **chinstrap** and **headrail.** A peasant costume. (Tenth to thirteenth centuries.)

on a sarcophagus effigy in the Victoria and Albert Collection in London. Minisized buttons made of crochet and loop buttonholes were used as fasteners for the chainse on the same funerary statue. Family crests were often worked in fine stitches on the body of this garment, placed to fall just over the heart. By the late twelfth century, Roman terms such as tunic were discarded and replaced by garment names in the regional tongue. For this reason, many garments of similar cut and function have a number of different names. The **kirtle,** with snug sleeves extending over the hand and belted low over the hips, was yet another undergarment still in use during the mid-thirteenth century.

The female cap-sleeved cotehardie, with its plain functional design, was worn by peasant women. It was made of rough linen or wool in a wide range of colors. The **cotella** generally was open on the side seams and worn belted. It served more as an apron than a garment for warmth. Many genre paintings of this period show the skirt of the cotella looped up and tucked out of the way, or serving as a pouch. The **cotteron,** used by male and female peasants, was a loose, long-sleeved smock which was thigh length with the skirt gathered to a deep yoke (Figure 9.35).

## Accessories (1100–1400)

### HEADWEAR

During a span of 300 years from 1100 to 1400, women's headwear and hairstyles altered radically. The long-used veils and wimples, which had been worn by women since Roman times, totally disappeared (Figure 9.36). They were replaced by individualistic and often ridiculous female head coverings. During the thirteenth century, women's hair continued to be concealed beneath a close-fitting cap called the **touret** that was introduced about 1280. The touret had a starched, face-framing band that was secured tightly about the head and fastened under the chin. When worn by noble women, this was topped by a golden coronet of graceful and intricate design (Figure 9.37).

The major fanciful head and hair decorations developed between 1280 and 1375. It was a natural evolution and became known as the **reticulated headdress.** Dating this style accurately becomes difficult, for it developed at different times in each country. The styling was governed by nationalistic design traits and personal preference.

The reticulated headdress followed the nebulated style, an English fashion which developed before English ladies adopted the reticulated style. The **nebula** was a pleated linen, semicircular head cover resembling a face-framing ruff, though it was not carried under the

**Figure 9.36.** Typical woman's costume with **wimple** of eleventh- and twelfth-century Britain. The curved cuff, extending well below the wrist, is characteristic of British sleeve treatment. (Redrawn from illustration in C. Köhler, *A History of Costume.*)

chin. The back of the head was draped with a veil, perhaps of velvet. Prior to the nebulated fashion, during the late thirteenth century, hair of noble ladies was parted in the center, drawn back into a thick, heavy plait and topped with a **fillet** of gold.

In styling the hair when the reticulated fashion appeared, the center part was used, but the hair was formed into two coiled braids which covered the ears. These buns of braided hair were encased in pearl-encrusted nets of gold called **cauls.** A fillet or **foliated crown** finished this headdress. The fillet, also called a **crispine,** was functional as well as decorative, for it served to hold the cauls in place. Reticulation took many forms, including the

**Figure 9.37.** These ladies of the fourteenth century are wearing **bliauds,** and chinstraps wound over coronets. (Velislav Bible, detail, c. 1340. University Library, Prague.)

fashion of forming the hair into two horn-shaped hair rolls called **templers** (1375–1400), worn at the temples (Figures 9.15 and 9.30). The back hair of this style was rolled up tightly into the horn buns set at the temples. Pointed cauls held the buns in place and a jeweled golden net covered the back of the head. Caul-covered hairstyles also have been called **truffles.**

Variety and change were the essence of hair and head-covering styles of the late fourteenth to early fifteenth centuries. Hair which had been fashionably revealed was suddenly confined beneath oddly shaped, veil-covered hats derisively called **hennins.** A wag of the period noted that ". . . the more the girls are young, the higher the stovepipes they wear." The hennins of this period were indeed extraordinary—pointed, veil tipped, mitered, heart shaped (Figure 9.21), or rolled.

The **butterfly hennin,** worn until very recently by a French order of nuns, was yet another style. This was called "gallows attire" and was arranged by piling the hair high off the forehead. Long stiletto pins were placed at strategic points in this pompadour and a starched, transparent veil was draped in a symmetrical manner over the pins. Another variation of Dutch origin had the starched veil arranged over a thin gold or silver wire frame (Figure 9.38). A pointed, truncated hennin also was worn beneath

the butterfly hennin. The variations were endless: **steeple hennin** with **frontals,** velvet cheek-framing tabs; **stovepipe hennin;** and **double-horned hennin (escoffion).**

The veil and circlet; the chinstrap, headrail, and wimple, or guimp; and the **gorget,** or **gorgerette,** were female head coverings which remained in use over a long period. The gorget, a throat veil, and the diaphanous wimple continued to be worn as late as 1325. The gorget was the last bit of veil draping to be added to a lady's headwear and was attached to the chinstrap below each ear. This veiling covered the neck, either falling free or tucked into the neckline of the gown. Older women used the gorget for a much longer time, doubtless out of vanity, for in the late fourteenth century, gown necklines were cut extremely low, concealing only half of the bust.

**Figure 9.38.** One of the many variations of the **butterfly hennin.** (Redrawn from studies by Albrecht Dürer.)

**Figure 9.39.** Throughout the Dark and Middle Ages, men wore hoods of many types. This hood is trimmed with dagging. As the dagging fad grew in popularity, the scalloped shapes became more fanciful and complex. Some attained such elaborate proportions that they dragged on the ground and were derisively dubbed "dragged edges."

The great number of styling changes and the personalized variations are almost incomprehensible to the modern mind. The noble laity was extremely fashion conscious and totally unaffected by the clerical admonitions that such earthly concerns were inspired by the devil.

Head coverings for men as well as women became more fanciful. During the twelfth century, however, men's heads were covered with simple cap forms, usually brimless with variously shaped crowns, either round or pointed. Hoods attached to short capes also acted as protective headwear for men and women (Figures 9.39 and 9.40). They could be worn pulled well down over the face or pushed back, or worn crushed about the neck and shoulders.

Cowls of cloth, a form of hood called **amices** were another head-covering fashion. These were made of cloth, usually velvet, and lined with fur. When not needed as head protection, they were crushed down about the throat.

The simple cap shapes for men included: the **cole,** fur-lined with ear-covering tabs but no chinstrap; the **calotte,** a skullcap made of four or six pie-shaped pieces; the **barrette,** a wool cap made of four rigid segments worn by clerics and professors; and the **bonnette** of the late fourteenth century.

The bonnette had a jaunty air about it and was designed with a tall, conical crown that came down well over the head. This crown was turned up in back and shaped into a pointed-bill brim in front. Feathers and embroidered headbands were used as trimming. Young men carried these bonnettes on their walking sticks. To show off their stylish graces, they would, with a flick of the sticks, deftly don these dapper hats (Figure 9.41).

The **aumusse** and **liripipe** were styles that evolved from the conical hood with the face hole (Figures 9.5 and 9.42). The aumusse was a peaked hood with a shoulder cape. An attenuated hood peak was called a **liripipe** and was often ten or twelve feet long. When excessively long,

**Figure 9.40.** Outer garments worn as protection against the weather, or as here, in mourners' procession, included the hood with shoulder cape and mantle. (Etienne Bobillet and Paul de Mosselman: *Mourner,* statuette, c. 1450-1453. Metropolitan Museum of Art, New York City.)

**Figure 9.41.** Young medieval dandy is shown in a **paragaudion** made of exceedingly heavy fabric, richly decorated with an embroidered yoke, with another embroidery motif on the blouse section, and still another on the hem. It is girdled at the normal waist, with a belt slung low on the hips to which is attached his drawstring purse. The lad spins his pointed-bill **bonnette** atop his walking stick. These male fashions continued until the twelfth century.

**Figure 9.42.** The **aumusse** was the most typical male headgear during the Middle Ages.

**Figure 9.43.** Female version of the prearranged **chaperon** and **roundlet.** The dagged edging is called triffling by some authorities. (Redrawn from statuette of the fifteenth century.)

the point was wrapped about the neck much as a scarf. This hood was made from two profile sections sewn together along the top for the full length of the liripipe, and down the center back of the shoulder cape. The front was left open so that it could be pinned snugly under the chin as protection against the winter's cold. Later versions were made with a profile-pattern hood and an attached cape that was closed in front.

It was from this style that the **chaperon** developed, which was worn by men and women (Figures 9.43 and 9.44). This was a type of turban made by drawing the cape section up to the head, carefully pleating it, and then winding the long point around and around. It was firmly secured by pulling the end of the liripipe through the binding layers. The scalloped edges of the cape made a

cockscomb effect if carefully arranged. Often topping off the liripipe-formed chaperon was a stiff, decorative, doughnut-shaped hat called a **roundlet,** which also was worn over a simple skullcap.

## FOOTWEAR

Footwear was greatly influenced by the Crusaders' contact with the Near East. Shoes known as **pistachios** were made of leather, waxed and decorated with braid, and had upturned pointed toes extending a modest length beyond the foot. In time the points of the shoes called **crackows** (1360–1410) greatly increased in length, a fashion believed to have originated in Poland. The toe section was padded with hay or given rigidity by inserting a strip of whalebone. Observers deriding others wearing

**Figure 9.44. Houppelande** with leaf-shaped dagged edge of deep funnel sleeves, late fourteenth century. The head covering is a combination of the **chaperon** arrangement of the **liripipe** with **roundlet,** which during this period were prearranged. (Redrawn from Dan Chimmey piece, Amsterdam.)

crackows called the long toe points "devil's fingers." Cork soles often were fitted into the feet of hose, and no other footwear was used indoors. Ankle-high leather boots, **estivaux,** with a snipped or "crabbed" design at the cuff were also worn in the twelfth and early thirteenth centuries (Figure 9.5). Serviceable knee-high soft boots were used and often worn with the upper section crushed down about the ankle. A **poulaine** was an ankle-high shoe with a pointed toe. It was tied at the junction of leg and instep. This style of footwear had a heavy, crudely fashioned sole.

In addition to the pointed-toed estivaux, crackow, and poulaine footwear, **pattens** and **chopines** were used as shoe protection. The patten, a forerunner of galoshes,

was first an oval of wood with a toe or instep strap with which to hold them to the foot. The shod foot was slipped into the patten, keeping elegantly styled footwear out of the muck and mire of the unpaved medieval city streets. As the devil's fingers increased in length, the patten also increased in size. A heel was added in front and in back, further elevating the wearer and protecting the shoes. The chopine, a pedestal arrangement with a toe strap, served first as shoe protection, but later was adapted by ladies of the Renaissance court to give the impression of greater height. The pedestal, an oval column spreading into the shape of a shoe sole, often reached a height of ten or twelve inches.

The phrase "rings on her fingers, bells on her toes," is believed to have originated during this period because of the practice of wearing bells on the tips of the pointed crackows. When the toes reached such excessive length that it was impossible to walk without tripping over them, a fad developed of attaching one end of a gold or silver chain to the toe tip and the other end around the leg below the knee. Thus the over-long devil's fingers were held out of the way. The long-toed crackows were originally introduced to create the illusion of longer legs and more height. Women's footwear never reached such outlandish proportions since their long gowns obscured the feet.

## JEWELRY

The most distinctive jewelry characteristic of this period in northern Europe was created in England. Rings, bracelets, and pins were fashioned by twisting golden wires together to the desired width and thickness. Stiletto pins with large decorated heads; buckles with punctured or cutout geometric designs; and fibulae of similar design were jewelry accessories that continued in use throughout this period. Belts and bracelets were ornately engraved with filigree, set with stones, or decorated with enameled designs. Brooches called **agrafa** and **fernails,** and stiletto and **tasseau** pins in many designs were used as mantle fastenings or as costume decorations. The tasseau was a hook-shaped pin over which the front of the gown skirt was looped.

# Hairstyles (1100–1400)

Throughout the fourteenth century, female hairstyles and head coverings were closely related. Women's hair fashions changed little until the end of this period when women bound their hair close to the head in braids, or in twisted ropes which were then wound into small pugs at the nape of the neck and covered with guimps.

Women dyed their hair blonde or black but never red, a color which remained symbolic of wickedness. Wigs were used by those not endowed with an abundant hirsute crown of glory. However, wigs were made of dead hair, for hair cut from the living was not used by wigmakers of this period. Small caps of golden net, tied under the chin, were used to hold the hair snugly against the head.

Men and women affected the **love-lock**, also called a **dorelot**, or **mollycoddle**, which was a curl in the center of the forehead. This affectation can readily be seen in pictures of ladies wearing the hennin. The love-lock is carefully arranged over the polled forehead. Women polled, or shaved, their hair in front to give the illusion of a high, curving forehead.

Shortly after the end of the Crusades, men let their hair grow long. By 1280, however, it had shortened to shoulder length and was turned up at the ends. By the fourteenth century young men wore a bowl-cut hairstyle. The sideburns were shaved up to the temples and the neck was shaved as high as the bulge of the cranium in back. Between these extremes, young men wore long, curled locks, drooping moustaches, and beards trimmed in the Spanish style. Then, as now, fathers railed at their male offspring because of their outlandish coiffures and costumes, but eventually followed suit. So incensed were the clergy during one period that they refused to serve Communion to those dressed and coiffed in the height of fashion.

FOOTNOTES

1. Anne Fremantle, *Age of Faith*, p. 11.
2. Ibid., p. 12.
3. Kenneth Clark, *Civilisation*, p. 33.
4. Fremantle, *Age of Faith*, pp. 71–78.
5. Ibid., p. 170.
6. Clark, *Civilisation*, p. 35.
7. Giselle D'Assailly, *Ages of Elegance*, pp. 55–57.
8. Fremantle, *Age of Faith*, p. 113.
9. Carl Köhler, *A History of Costume*, p. 141.
10. Ibid., pp. 138–39.
11. Louise Pickney Sooy, *Syllabus on Costume*, plate 24.
12. Margaret Hamilton Hill, and Peter A. Buchnell, *The Evolution of Fashion*, p. 31.
13. Köhler, *A History of Costume*, p. 169.
14. François Boucher, *20,000 Years of Fashion*, p.176.
15. D'Assailly, *Ages of Elegance*, p. 59.
16. Boucher, *20,000 Years of Fashion*, p. 181.

# Chapter 10
# Renaissance Elegance
# (1400–1600)

**Figure 10.1.** An excellent example of the manner in which puffs were created. The front lacing of the **vaquero** is also apparent. The bodice bows are part of the gown's decorations. (Ambrogio de Fredis: *Girl with Cherries,* late fifteenth century. Metropolitan Museum of Art, New York City.)

As the Middle Ages drew to a close, the progressive advances which had been made during the two preceding centuries seemed to falter. The force which halted the renewed vigor in commerce, agricultural production, technological advances, and revised social concepts was the Black Death. Rat-infested ships returning to home ports on the Mediterranean and North Sea brought this feared pestilence, and wave after wave of the plague swept from coastal port towns to rural hamlets. Highly contagious, the Black Death devastated the population as had not happened since the barbarian invasions. The depopulation by pestilence was so overwhelming that the few who survived were not sufficient in number and physical strength to accomplish the tasks necessary for survival. With so few to till the soil, crops were insufficient to sustain those who survived, and starvation further depleted the population.[1]

In the troubled minds of those who managed to survive, God and nature had turned against man. The church preached that God's wrath was being vented on the miserable survivors for their earthly misdeeds. Sermons of hellfire and damnation poured forth, filling peasants in the nave and princes in the choir with fear. Floggings and beatings were administered to discipline children, servants, and apprentices and to encourage rightful earthly behavior. Attendance at universities dropped too, thus combining ignorance with the other troubling factors of this devastated era.[2]

Once again the rural community became the hub of this dark century, the fifteenth. Weather determined the success of the agrarian efforts, and the life cycle of the provincial farming areas was governed by the four seasons. Successful crops and good harvests raised these poor people out of the doldrums. November, particularly St. Martin's Day, was the great fall festival. Drinking, feasting, and prayerful thanks gave this day a spirit not unlike festivals celebrated by pagans of the past or the American Pilgrims. However, the day's rejoicing was clouded by the question of whether the stored supplies of grain, root vegetables, and salted meat would last through the long winter.

Natural elements and the plague were not the only forces to be overcome. The male population had been decimated by the Hundred Years' War between France and England. In England there was strife to determine the rightful heir to the throne.

However, the Muslim conquest of Byzantium and the fall of Constantinople were blessings in disguise. Greek scholars fled the capital of the Eastern Empire and brought with them classical Greek philosophy, literature, and biblical texts. The Vulgate translation of the Bible by St. Jerome was made from the Aramaic scrolls. Through research and translations of the Greek texts, contradictions in the first translation were brought to light.[3] A major concept which had been lost in the earlier translation was the humanistic teaching of the early church. This humanism, coupled with the Greek philosophy of individual freedom, began to be infused with the slumbering concepts of human individual dignity held by thinkers of the late Middle Ages.

The Crusades had combined with the Hundred Years' War to set the stage for the period in human history called the Renaissance. The new spirit of this age was epitomized by a pledge given to elected kings by lords of petty states: "We, who are each of us as good as thou, and who together are far more powerful than thou, swear to obey thee if thou dost obey our laws, and if not, not." This oath expressed a new attitude, an attitude involving a humanistic philosophy and stressing the importance of individuals.

This age, in time, was dominated by the Medici family, who perhaps more than any other family at any time, directed and motivated intellectual concepts. Dante, Petrarch, and Savonarola had played important roles during the centuries prior to this intellectually explosive and humanistic period. Although theological dogma had controlled learning for centuries, as thousands attended the established universities during this period, an era of truth developed.

Dissemination of these concepts was made possible by the invention of movable type and the production of paper. The availability of books and the arrival of Greek scholars on the Western European scene gave new impetus to the desire to learn. These major technical, philosophical, and intellectual factors nurtured the rebirth of Western thought from which evolved the Renaissance. New thoughts and new attitudes toward people generated new social concepts. Humanism was the key word of the fifteenth and sixteenth centuries.

Intellectual concepts alone did not alter the age, though, at first, intellectual curiosity prompted some early sea exploration. Intellectual curiosity was wed to the economic necessity of finding sea trade routes to India and the Far East. Adventurous men who were visionary and persuasive managed to convince princelings, kings, and queens that sea exploration was necessary to the economic success of their kingdoms. Because of his own personal interest, Spain's King Philip II—the Navigator—gave impetus to the coastal exploration of West Africa. Soon the competitive necessity of kingdoms to send fleets on exploring expeditions sent many adventurous men in search of new lands, sea lanes, and gold. These voyages were arduous, hazardous, and highly speculative, for no charts existed and navigational principles were based largely on speculation. The success of Columbus was followed by the navigational explorations and discoveries of Amerigo Vespucci, Magellan, Balboa, Cortez, Cabrillo, Cabot, Hudson, and many more. Through their tireless chartings, navigational technology improved. Soon, it was apparent that the ruler of the seas also ruled the world, a fact proved by England's defeat of the Spanish Armada. Francis Drake and Walter Raleigh, who were sometimes pirates, gave England supremacy of the oceans.

Life was altered by churchly attitudes and questioning minds, such as those of Erasmus and Martin Luther, who challenged the church and began to push social concepts in newer, freer directions. To quell the impact of infidels in Spain, the cruel Spanish Inquisition was begun in 1480. As the forces of the Protestant Reformation gathered, the tide of Christianity was set to flow away from the power of papal Rome throughout the fifteenth and sixteenth centuries. On October 31, 1517, Luther posted his *95 Theses* on the north door of Castle Church in Wittenberg. By 1529 princes and peasants of Germany and Scandinavian Europe had risen to support him. In the first half of the sixteenth century, Protestantism in many forms had been developed by the Calvinists in Switzerland, the Anglicans in England, and the Huguenots in France. The Counter Reformation was given impetus by the Jesuit Order in 1545 when the Council of Trent first convened. Religion became a political pawn rather than a pious faith.[4] Many power struggles between kings and countries originated in differences of theological doctrine.

The governmental systems of city republics, in Italy particularly, developed when the simplistic administrative machinery of feudalism was dissolved. Philip IV, king of France from 1285 to 1314—also called Philip the Fair—was the first to establish checks on the rights of feudal barons. He devised a means of national taxation and divided baronial lands into districts. He won many military and diplomatic engagements through his cleverness in electing his councils from the lower classes and forcing the nobility into a state of dependence. Populations of many countries were developing a strong sense of nationalism. The papal and imperial controversies of the past had fostered these feelings. In France and in England there was a quiet rebellion against papal authority in temporal matters.

By the end of the fifteenth century, the Byzantine emperor in the East had been vanquished, and the one in the West reduced to a petty princeling. The Bishop of Rome, sensing change, had begun to withdraw from his militarily supported political activities. New monarchies grew powerful in Aragon, Austria, Denmark, and the Netherlands. It was because of these strong influences that the republics of Venice and Florence developed their hold on intellectual and political matters. Wealthy merchants and bankers acquired power and, with the increasing influence of the developing middle class in trade and banking, the role of the nobility diminished. The Italian families of Este, Scaliger, Visconti, and Medici were members of this important commercial class. Their power became so great that they were soon a tyrannical aristocracy, controlling much of Europe. The trading centers of Venice, Genoa, Marseilles, Bruges, and Antwerp functioned to establish a new, powerful capitalism. Gold currency was reintroduced, which for a time produced economic stability, followed by inflation.

The potential for improvement of social standing through economics was given impetus by several factors. The merchant class, once restricted to trading farm commodities, was able to expand its trading base with the increased production of man-made goods. With the diversity of items for trade, expansion of profits followed. Through the accumulated wealth from profits, tradesmen were able to loan out money at high interest. Banking systems developed as a method of holding or loaning funds to those interested in making investments in new enterprises which were opening up throughout Western Europe.

Italy, England, France, and finally Germany remodeled Roman law, developing a code suitable to their political systems. With the codification of laws came the professional lawyers. As the need for each new profession increased, those who practiced banking, law, medicine, and mercantile trade attained a more and more respected social status.

The ineffectiveness of the ruler of the Holy Roman Empire also contributed to social change. Though France and England had long been unified countries ruled by kings, the rest of Europe was a potpourri of princedoms, city-states, and duchies. Frederick III, Emperor of the Holy Roman Empire, was no more than a figurehead whose power and authority were given only ceremonial homage. Each man considered himself a citizen of his duchy, princedom, or city-state, rather than a member of a larger political unit. The fact that every man felt this type of independence was the result of increased education in contemporary, classical, secular, and religious literature.

Learning, expansion of trade because of surplus industrial production, and the diminished authority of the nobility combined in this new age. The middle class rose to a position of power and trust. Secular considerations raised doubts about clerical teachings of the Dark and Middle Ages. Some authorities suggest that the threshold

into the Renaissance was crossed during the first third of the sixteenth century. The advent of the Renaissance was implemented by the questioning of every aspect of the life-styles of the past.

Nobles, no longer able to collect taxes, sought other means of bringing in revenue. The elector of Saxony, Frederick, raised capital from his collection of 17,000 relics which included a bundle of straw purported to have come from the holy stable in Bethlehem. Pilgrims to Wittenberg paid substantial sums to view these churchly treasures. These fees swelled the elector's coffers and procured indulgences from the church for the pilgrims. In an increasingly materialistic society, people of the sixteenth century paid for God's grace with coins of silver and gold in lieu of doing penance by acts of fasting, prayer, and good deeds. This practice eventually brought about the schism between the Roman church and those who questioned the pious proprieties of buying indulgences as insurance for everlasting salvation.

It was a ribald age, full of penniless princes turned highwaymen. Supported by their action-hungry armies, they preyed on travelers and tiny towns. Work-weary peasants—underfed, poorly clothed, and living in rude huts with earthen floors and thatched roofs that were dark, dank, and forever cold in winter—saw little hope of improving their lot. During the many feast days, they took the opportunity to indulge their appetites for food, drink, dancing, and rude ceremonials. Though released from abject serfdom, freemen, tenant farmers, and artisans

**Figure 10.2.** Male field laborers wear leather **upper stock** with pronounced **codpieces,** leather vests, and rough-spun tuniclike shirts. (Peter Bruegel the Elder: *Summer,* sixteenth century. Metropolitan Museum of Art, New York City.)

*Iulius, Augustus, nec non et Iunius Aestas.* **AESTAS** *Adolet* *tenui imago* *Frugiferas aruis fert Aestas torrida meßeis.*

were still beholden to their lords. It was in the community-organized festivals that this stratum of society found camaraderie. Wedding ceremonies and the attending banquets and revelry were other means of briefly forgetting their weary lot.[5] The Flemish painter Peter Bruegel visually recorded the joys and sorrows of the common classes of his time (Figure 10.2).

Freedom from bondage of the feudal lord did not mean that freedom from want was eliminated. The need to care for the aged, sick, blind, and orphaned, once the obligation of the liege lords and the monasteries, was no longer the lords' responsibility. Wandering in bands made up of those with similar afflictions, the needy begged for food and alms, often dying from lack of either.[6] Peasants, however, were no longer subservient serfs. In 1524 German peasants rebelled against the harsh living conditions in which they were forced to exist. For many peasants, life was no longer as predictable as it formerly had been. Feudalism had firmly established the peasants' positions in life and those of their descendants. By the fifteenth century feudal authority was disappearing, and the serf, who had long been kept from social and economic advancement, now became free to move up the ladder of social status.

Members of the new monied class altered the economic processes and, at the same time, altered their own social status. With their new money, they achieved fame and power, and many were awarded titles. Hard money and the demand for it, while creating economic prosperity, also introduced new social problems. Cities, principalities, and kingdoms minted their own money. By altering the intrinsic content of coins, inflation resulted. Merchants and bankers united by pooling their financial resources, thus the concept of corporate business enterprise was born. So powerful were these corporate entities that kings were often hard pressed to raise money for military ventures and were forced to seek loans from these sources. Charles V of the Holy Roman Empire was beholden to a Jacob Fugger of Augsburg for an enormous sum. Fugger was so influential that the pope, kings, and even Martin Luther trembled when he spoke or wrote to demand payments.

Antwerp was the center of commerce, banking, and the stock exchange. All classes and a wide range of professions from all the nations of Western Europe were represented there. In the main mercantile quadrangle, every conceivable item was on sale, from utilitarian objects to paintings by the masters of the day.

Rome, though the center of Christian religion, was a jumble of crumbling ruins, crooked narrow streets, and medieval houses. The older Christian basilicas, such as Santa Croce and Santa Maria Maggiore, stood amid vineyards. The princes of the church lived in palatial splendor while commoners, prostitutes, beggars, and charlatans roamed the city streets.

The cities of southern Germany were prosperous business communities. Switzerland, naturally fortified by the Alps, achieved and maintained independence. It became the crossroads for European pilgrims on their way to Rome.[7]

With the changing intellectual spirit developed a changing aesthetic. Gothic architecture gave way to the Renaissance style in the so-called Italian manner. Florence, and later, Rome, became the centers of the Italian style in art and architecture of the Renaissance. In the Republic of Florence, where members of the Medici family were patrons of the artists, there was a rebirth of interest in Greek Classicism which soon permeated all of Europe. Pictorially, patrons were portrayed in idealistic perfection with fine features and elaborate garb. In Rome it was the pope, most particularly Julius II, who commissioned the rebuilding of St. Peter's and a sarcophagus honoring himself. Da Vinci, Michelangelo, Raphael, and Botticelli marked these two Renaissance centers of culture with their aesthetic stamps. Basilicas in Italy, châteaux in France, paintings in Flanders, and manor houses in England reflected the Italian influence, modified by the cultural concepts of specific countries of origin. The painters of northern Europe were more earthy in their portrayal of human subjects, in keeping with northern religious concepts and philosophy.

Subtle changes appeared in art and learning, leaning toward more secular subjects. People took pleasure in life and in the pursuit of learning. Pictorial manifestations of these attitudes were executed by such greats of visual imagery as Jan van Eyck, Rogier van der Weyden, Veneziano, Bosch, Bellini, Botticelli, Donatello, Michelangelo, Da Vinci, Raphael, and many others. Ideals of beauty were in transition, and trends toward individualism and human beauty set forth earlier by the Italian poet Dante and Giotto, a pre-Renaissance Florentine painter, were accepted, modified, and reshaped into the Renaissance style.

By the sixteenth century, all of Europe had felt the impact of the philosophical concepts of the High Renaissance. In the works of Marlowe, Bacon, Spenser, and Shakespeare, themes were developed that expressed the ideas of the age. Every aspect of life reflected the exaltation of the individual and the concept that human achievements were worthy of recognition in their own right, and not just as a reflection of divine will.

Within seventy years, these differing aesthetic considerations would develop into an international style which was reflected in the clothing worn during the Renaissance. At the time that the Renaissance began to bloom, women's gowns were long, flowing, and intricate. Nationalistic styling trends and individuality dominated. Men's fashions were equally diverse in styling, and within each country design preferences were expressed. Some of the more unique nationalistic trends were matters of detailing. In every country, principality, and dukedom, however, clothing was elaborate and sumptuous. While the dates of this period fall roughly between the years 1300 and 1600, the cultural impact and influences stimulated by intellectual curiosity began to gain momentum during the fifteenth century. The clothing concepts emphasizing individualism and individuality spread from Italy to other countries. Clothing, rich in fabric, jeweled, slashed, padded, and corseted, developed into a new silhouette.

Italian artists of the importance of Pesellino, Pollaiuoli, and Jacopo Bellini turned to designing costumes and textile patterns and may have been among the first fashion designers. During the last decade of the sixteenth century, Titian's grandson, Cesare Vecellio, produced innumerable fashion plates to inform all who were interested, and financially able, how to dress in the latest vogue. These styles from Venice appeared in *Degli Habiti antichi a moderni* and established style trends for many. Pietro Bartelli, in *Diversarium Nationum Habilia*, presented fashions to the people of England, Germany, Spain, and Hungary through handsome illustrations.

There were garments similar to those of previous centuries, there were styles that were international, there were details that were nationalistic, but they all were elegant. The High Renaissance, at least for those of wealth, was a flamboyant fashion period with the dominance of the individual evident in every garment. There were as many variations of design and detailing as there were persons to wear them. With the expansion of trade, wealthy families of commerce spread the wearing of elegant apparel from the nobility to the *nouveaux riches*.

The international character of costume came about primarily because of the political union of the royal houses through marriage. This, coupled with the slow transformation of the idealized figure visualized by the master painters of the period, altered concepts of dress. The wealthy personages of the Renaissance took great pride in their physical beauty. Rich fabrics and complicated designs served to embellish the physical person. Italian modes had influenced fashion from the thirteenth century to the mid-fifteenth century. Gradually, Spanish styles superceded this influence, though French and German fads were fused into costume designs as well.[8] After 1494 French fashions in hats and shoes dominated these accessories, but slowly other garments of French design appeared in Venice, Genoa, and Milan. The extreme décolletage of the Italian gown gave way to the high neckline and face-framing ruff, both Spanish fashion innovations.

The rejection of the opulent Medici court dress had had results, for in the first score of years of the sixteenth century, sumptuary laws were written and special controlling officers were established in Milan, Venice, Rome, and Genoa. Around 1512, Varchi wrote that ". . . men and women have acquired much elegance and grace."

Italians grew to appreciate the "full flesh" of excess weight on their elegant ladies. Costumes were laden with jewels, chains, pearl rope necklaces, and trimmed with fine laces and furs. Men, as well as women, were covered from head to foot in silk brocade and rich velvets.

Deep rust brown, subtle wine purple, gold, yellow, and bright pink gave way to the sombre dress of black, which was the fashionable color of the Spanish court. The pious King Philip II of Spain had declared black to be the acceptable dress color of his court. Spain's political power in Europe was visualized in the dress of courts of other countries controlled by or wishing favors from this Hispanic crown. The marriage of Mary Tudor to Philip of Spain brought black into the court costumes of England during her reign. Spanish gown styles as well were fashionable in mid-sixteenth-century England.

The new styles which emerged in the Renaissance were partially due to the successful manufacture of fabrics. Industries emerged which influenced silhouette changes. The production of softer serge materials and muslins made it possible to create close, figure-fitting garments. Refinements in embroidery techniques and braid making embellished the soft rich fabrics.[9] Tours in France produced yards of velvets, satins, and taffetas from 8000 looms with as many weavers employed to operate them. Lyons was noted for the production of brocade. Silk stockings were produced in Dourdan as the hosiery trade increased in importance. Local production of the "stuffs" of fashion was encouraged by heavy taxation of imported fabrics. Dyes, however, came from the far corners of the globe. Madder and henna were imported from Arabia, saffron from India, and indigo from Baghdad. Rich fabrics brought from China, and the gold and jewels captured by the conquistadors, enhanced the splendor of the opulent Renaissance costumes.

While the ancient Greek culture was faithfully studied, the simple draping of the chiton was not opulent enough for the taste of the time. Houppelande, gamurra, and the high-waisted gown gave way to a silhouette of the opposite extreme. The fashionable silhouette for men changed from the broad-shouldered, attenuated-limb look of the fourteenth century to a boxlike, bulky silhouette by the middle of the next century (Figure 10.3). Masculine dress had seen some alterations during the reign of England's Henry VII. Broad shoulders and expansive girth in the waist were visual expressions of the new bold masculinity. Even the long-toed crackow footwear was supplanted by square-toed, **duckbill slippers**.[10]

**Puffs** and **slashes** covered men's doublets, hose, and breeches. This style was introduced by German mercenaries, after the Battle of Grandsone in 1476. These soldiers of fortune had captured a prized booty of rich silks. Ever practical, they used strips of the rich fabrics to patch their tattered clothes by wadding bunches of it into the holes and slashes of their clothing. The Swiss and the

**Figure 10.3.** By the sixteenth century, the male silhouette had greatly altered. The long, attenuated figure gave way to one of bulk. Many garments worn at one time added to this broad, square, upper-torso look. (Redrawn from *Young Man in Red*, anonymous, 1548.)

grateful townspeople imitated this practice when the soldiers returned home victorious over the armies of Charles the Bold, Duke of Burgundy.

In the extreme, slashes were bands of fabric called **paning** with full silken breeches showing beneath. Puffs, slashes, and bombasting served to add extravagant embellishment and girth to male costumes. The stuffing or bombast, which gave the wearer an upholstered look, was made from horsehair, hay, or kernels of grain. A deftly placed slash of a rapier could cause a garment bombasted with grain to spill, which perhaps proved more embarrassing and serious than the blow itself. Predominantly a detail feature of menswear, women too used puffs and slashes as sleeve detailing.

As the silhouette became bulkier, the doublet tails increased in length. Breeches were altered also in length

and styling. **Stock, upper stock,** and **canons** were supplanted by **Venetians, pumpkin breeches, Spanish slops,** and **Venetians *en bourse*** (without padding). Colored hose in the German manner—each leg a different color, usually yellow and black—were a dominant accessory in continental male costuming by 1514.

Ladies' silhouettes also underwent radical changes, as can readily be seen by comparing Figures 10.4 and 10.5. Tortured figures with flat bosoms and constricted waists, farthingale-enlarged hips, and head-restricting ruffs dominated women's fashions of the late sixteenth century. Women's hairstyles were developing nationalistic modifications by the end of the fifteenth century. Belgian, Dutch, and Flemish women continued to use the towering, diaphanous butterfly hennin, while Italian women revealed their hair coiffed in intricate styles (Figure 10.6). In England, fashionable females wore head-encasing headdresses which were replicas of the flattened Tudor arch.

The early fifteenth-century dress of the north consisted of a kirtle, bodice, and skirt sewn together with a voluminous gathered overskirt. The bodice sleeves were

**Figure 10.4.** Ladies' gowns during the 1530s were designed with normal waistlines, deep, inverted V-necklines, and multiple sleeve treatments. Skirts were long with considerable fullness in back. Note the gabled headdress. (Hans Holbein: *English Lady,* c. 1535. British Museum, London.)

**Figure 10.5.** The rigidity of the clothing worn by Queen Elizabeth I reinforced her royal position. The **cartwheel** or **millstone** collar in England was often worn attached to the inverted V-neckline, rather than tied about the throat. (Crispin van de Passe: *Queen Elizabeth I,* engraving, detail, 1588. Metropolitan Museum of Art, New York City.)

**Figure 10.6.** One of the most startling changes in ladies' fashion was that hair was again considered a woman's crowning glory. Shown here is a coiffure arranged in a manner reminiscent of those worn by ancient Grecian women. (Redrawn from *Portrait of Margherita Gonzaga,* Pisanello, fifteenth century. Louvre, Paris.)

snug, and the undergarment, a high-necked chemise made of lawn, was seen above the lowcut, square neckline. Italian styles of the same period between 1530 and 1540 often had full, ample sleeves and a low, square neckline filled with lattice detailing. Square or bateau necklines were typical styles for costumes during the first third of the sixteenth century. Double sleeves, tied on at the shoulder, added elegant touches. The portraits of Helen of Bavaria (Hans Schöpfer, 1563–66) and of Jane Seymour (Figure 10.7), are excellent examples of the variety of sleeves and headwear used during the middle years of this century. The flat-chested look was achieved by severe corseting. Corsets of this period might be described as female armor, for they were made of iron. Although the lining was padded with quilted linen, they must have been exceedingly uncomfortable.

The low, square neckline was superceded by the high, round neckline topped by the face-framing **Spanish ruff.** In the later years of the reign of Elizabeth I, this ruff style increased in diameter and developed into the **cartwheel ruff,** famed in Frans Hals' paintings of the

Baroque period. The **Medici collar** allowed for a ruff of extreme décolletage and a head-framing enchantment of lace, pearls, and gold.

Men's doublets soon reflected the narrow waist and firm controlled look typical of female bodices. However, the profile of the **peascod doublet** projected in a curve, which bulged severely just above the waist. This change in male silhouette was introduced about 1570 and lasted for several decades.

Rigidity, dignity, pomp, and elegance of dress dominated the last years of the reign of Elizabeth I, when England's dominance of the sea, and eventually the world, began.

The **farthingale** was the most curious fashion of the late sixteenth century and early seventeenth century. This skirt support or hip extender took many forms and had regional styling differences. It first appeared in 1545 as a wire, whalebone, or wood frame over which the voluminous outer-gown skirt was draped and was called the **Spanish farthingale** or **verdingale.** The French introduced a variation about 1580 known as the **wheel far-**

**Figure 10.7.** The **gabled headdress** was a face-framing, hair-concealing style. Its shape perhaps was derived from the Tudor arch. Necklace and pendant brooch were characteristic accessories of this period. (Hans Holbein: *Jane Seymour,* detail, 1536. Kunsthistorisches Museum, Vienna.)

**thingale,** whose name describes its form. Wits of the era were known to remark that women wearing this style appeared to have a hobbyhorse beneath their skirts.[11] The **Italian farthingale** differed from the French style only in that it tilted up in back, making the front profile almost straight from bust to gown hem. **Roll farthingales** were round, padded-pillow skirt supports, referred to in the vulgar vernacular of the day as "bum rolls."[12]

However, for all the sumptuous dress, personal toilette habits were disturbingly neglected. Daily communal bathing, so popular during the Middle Ages and once banned vigorously by the church, was not thought to be necessary. Queen Elizabeth I is said to have had but three complete baths in her lifetime. It is no wonder that nosegays were carried to keep the offensive and odoriferous smells of streets and bodies from assailing the nostrils. Powders and perfumes, goat- or cow-milk facials and ointments, and compounds of curious ingredients were part of the Renaissance lady's toilette. There were many makers of perfumes and their products were used liberally. To quote one chronicler of the time, "Hair, shoes, fans, and gloves gave out sweet odors ..." for it was believed that "... strong odors refreshed the brain."

# Basic Garments of the Early Renaissance (1400–1500)

## ROBE (1400–1500)

By the fifteenth century the many visible layers of outer garments that had been worn by women for several centuries were slowly being replaced with the **robe** or **gown.** Designs for these voluminous, graceful gowns at first varied from country to country (Figures 10.8 and 10.9). General traits included a short-waisted bodice that flattened the bust; a deep square neckline; fanciful, elaborate sleeves; and a long, many-gored skirt with a train. The protruding stomach silhouette continued in fashion and was achieved by sewing small bags filled with horsehair, or other padding, in front just below the high

**Figure 10.8.** There were many design variables during the sixteenth century, most of which were nationalistic preferences. This costume of Venetian origin is styled with a deep décolletage and leg-of-mutton sleeves. The pleated chemise neckline projects into the décolletage, adding some modesty to this flamboyant **robe à six garnements.** (Redrawn from a portrait, sixteenth century.)

**Figure 10.9.** The **vaquero** of the Spanish **ropa,** or **saya,** characteristically had a very rigid bodice. This saya combines the overskirt, which has a bell shape, the vaquero, and the kirtle, or underskirt. Two sets of sleeves are also worn: the outer type is a tube sleeve; the undersleeve is a form of the **cuerpo baxo** with puffs and slashes made by drawing the bishop sleeves of the chemise through the slashes. The rigidity of the entire costume, including the French-style headdress, places this costume early in the sixteenth century. (Redrawn from portrait of *Princess Elizabeth,* Flemish School, c. 1547. Windsor Castle, Windsor.)

waistline. The deep, square neckline was modified by a filmy gauze insertion called the **gorget, gorgias, gorgerette,** or *touret de col,* or by a lattice of thin velvet ribbons trimmed with pearls at the intersections. A **bandier,** or wide belt, was worn around the figure under the bust. Embroidery was used extensively, particularly at the neckline. This colorful and artfully stitched decoration was called **parement.** The swayback silhouette continued into the fifteenth century and the forward curve of the figure was emphasized by the skirt, which was often caught up and fastened with a pin called a **troussoir** or simply gathered up by the hand.

The intricate sleeve designs were given names to designate their styling, such as *à la française,* full and straight with deep cuffs or revers; **mancheron,** tight elbow-length sleeve; and **brassard,** a half-sleeve extending from the wrist to the elbow. Flared funnel

sleeves, *à la française,* and mancheron were tied to the bodice at the armhole and were interchangeable. When both mancheron and brassard were worn, the full sleeve of the softer linen chemise was carefully puffed out through lacing at the elbow (Figure 10.1).

Ties of sturdy silk ribbon with metal tips called **points** were laced through eyelets at the edges of the parts of a garment to keep the parts together. Points were decorative and functional and were used on garments worn by both sexes (Figure 10.10). In addition to the cloth bandier, a second belt, or **demiceint,** made of hinged metal plaques, was worn low on the hips (Figure 10.21). From the long end that extended almost to the toes dangled keys, scissors, a mirror, or other accessories necessary in a lady's life.

The **chemise** neck opening was replete with minute and intricate embroidery. Over the chemise was worn the **corset,** which had a low neckline, short sleeves, and a rather full skirt. The long **blanchet,** or indoor coat, fur-lined and with full funnel sleeves, was worn for warmth, as was the cyclas, or female surcoat, patterned after those worn during the previous period. These wraps of warmth disappeared from the fashion scene late in the fifteenth century. Both of the overgarments were designed with long full skirts and trains. The blanchet was a dual-

**Figure 10.10.** Intricate sleeve lacing tipped with points was a typical feature of the Renaissance costumes. (Redrawn from pastel sketch by Raffaellino del Garbo: *Angel Holding Infant Jesus,* c. 1470. Uffizi Gallery, Florence.)

purpose costume, serving as a dressing gown as well as a housecoat.

The houppelande continued in use between 1400 and 1495 as an elegant, high-necked garment for either indoor or outdoor wear. The rolled organ pleats, so characteristic of this garment, were now stitched in place, accenting the high waistline and broader shoulder line of this period.

## POURPOINT (1400–1500)

The **pourpoint** developed from the doublet in the fifteenth century and became the major male garment (Figure 10.11). It was made from carefully cut pieces and, for the first time, armhole and sleeve matched accurately. During the first years of its use, the pourpoint accented the natural contour of the figure. It was designed with a high-standing collar called the **carcaille,** a center front closure, and a short or waist-to-hip *à grandes assiettes* (full-skirted peplum).

The doublet sleeve was also important in male costuming. These sleeves were varied and intricate, and, during the early phase of the pourpoint, were tight, wrist length, and slightly padded for warmth as was the rest of the garment. As styles changed and the pourpoint became very short, the sleeves were enlarged with padding to raise and broaden the shoulder line. This added to the silhouette illusion of long, slender legs and a masculine,

**Figure 10.12.** The short **houppelande,** or **haincelin,** was used for many years, perhaps as a serviceable, everyday garment. The lad uses a more decorative short-sleeved jerkin with **manches pertuisées** covering the lower arm. The lad's shirt is puffed out between the ties of the lower sleeve. (Domenico Ghirlandaio: *Francesco Sassetti and His Son Teodoro,* fifteenth century. Metropolitan Museum of Art, New York City.)

**Figure 10.11.** The **barrel breeches** shown here are another variation of **pumpkin breeches.** This 1542 style is widely paned with large, vertical puffs. The **peascod doublet** has a standing collar and slashes but no puffs. The **chamarre** is heavily banded with gold braid on deep wine silk. Even the modified **duckbill slippers** have slashes, though no puffs have been added. (Seisenegger: *Archduke Ferdinand of Tyrol,* 1542. Kunsthistorisches Museum, Vienna.)

broad-shouldered torso. Sleeves ranged in design from balloon shapes to inverted padded cones puffed at the shoulders to the slit sleeves called *manches pertuisées* (Figure 10.12), gathered at the wrist and shoulder with the underarm seam left open.

Under the pourpoint, men wore a linen shirt. It was a full blouse gathered to a round neck-line and tied with cords at the throat. The shirt sleeve was full and gathered to a narrow cuff. The **cotte** and **gambeson** were tuniclike undershirts worn beneath a pourpoint or a **jack (jaque),** which were heavily padded, loosely fitted doublets, often made with thirty inner layers of lining and very simple sleeves.

## CHAUSSES (1400–1500)

In time, the pourpoint and the jack became so short that the *à grandes assiettes* extended only a little distance below the waist (Figure 10.11). The long hose which, for some time, had been tied by tapes to the waistband over the braies, satisfied neither the church's demands for

**Figure 10.13.** This sixteenth-century male costume combines the **pourpoint** with **barrel breeches,** widely paned **hose,** visible **codpiece,** and a **Spanish cape.** The flat-brimmed bonnet is characteristic of this period. (Attributed to François Clouet: *Henri II,* 1550. Louvre, Paris.)

modesty nor the male's demands for a neat, smooth, long-legged silhouette.

The older *chausses à queue* were discarded and replaced by *chausses à plain fond*, or full-bottom hose. These were made by sewing a triangular piece of fabric between the legs of the hose in back and adding a small inverted triangle, called the **braye,** in front. The braye was tied on either side by points. Later, it was greatly enlarged by padding and called a **codpiece,** or **braguette.** This style of closing for full-bottom hose was used for many years in a number of different variations (Figure 10.13). The leg coverings, or chausses, of this period were adaptations of the hose of previous years, made with the portion covering the outer leg several inches longer, reaching almost to the waist, while the inner portion extended from toe to crotch. A two-part panel, or waistband, was attached, often by ties, to the longer outer-hose section. This was brought over the stomach and laced together. The codpiece was fastened to this band and to the hose at the crotch.

At first introduction, the codpiece was a basic triangular or truncated triangular piece of fabric similar to that used for the hose section. Later, this full-bottom hose closure, or hose-joining device, became very decorative and exaggerated. At the height of its elaboration, it was slashed and padded into a large crescent or bun shape suggestive, in some instances, of the male sex organ which it covered. [13] According to some authorities, but not Rudofsky, this larger, more prominent style, which was often used as a purse to carry small coins, was attached to the hose at the crotch and at the waistband by metal-tipped cords or ribbons. The codpiece joined the two stockinglike leg coverings in front, and the back was covered with two larger triangles of material. These triangles, sewn or tied to the longer side of the hose, were inset with the points downward and the bases at the waist. They were seamed together in the center back, forming a complete covering for the posterior.

As knitting techniques for hose were perfected, it was no longer necessary to have a small series of darts around the ankles so there was no longer any need to use decorative embroidery called **clocks** to hide the darts. However, these embroidered clocks of fanciful patterns extending from the ankle bone well up the calf of the leg were used as a hose decoration a long time afterwards.

The combination of the hose, triangular inset back panels, and the codpiece created a trouser form resembling present-day tights or the leotards worn by ballet dancers. The design of the codpiece was never affected by the strict edicts and criticisms from the church; only the evolution of fashion eliminated it as a prominent decorative and functional part of male attire. It continued to be used as a front-closing device until the breeches of later years, such as Venetians and Spanish slops, became so large and full that it was no longer functional (Figure 10.14).

Before the introduction of these larger, fuller breeches, men wore pants or a brief trouser-type garment. Often a small, padded crescent was tied over the full-bottom hose at a point on either side where the codpiece was fastened. This padded roll rose upward in front to the hipbone and then descended to be attached with points in back. **Lodier** and **boulevard** were other early types of **upper stock,** as the crescent pads were called. They were short, unpadded breeches made in the same manner as the full-bottom hose, but with legs that just covered the upper thigh. Made of heavy silk, or leather if worn by peasants, lodier were worn over the full-bottom hose. Under these were worn shapeless linen braies.

## HOUPPELANDE (1470–1500)

From 1470 to 1500, the male houppelande included a tall, standing collar; bag sleeves that were full and gathered at the shoulder and wrist; deep, radiating pipe pleats; and a tight belt (Figure 10.15). This garment was buttoned from the tight neckline to the waist, with the belt worn quite low about the figure. The full, floor-length style

**Figure 10.14.** This sixteenth-century gentleman wears a multi-minislashed **peascod doublet,** pear-shaped **Venetians** with a modest **codpiece,** and a **Spanish ruff** close under his ears. The **ropillas,** which hide the laced and tied-on sleeves, are flat. (Redrawn from portrait of *Francis, Duke of Alençon,* French School, c. 1570.)

**Figure 10.15.** Male dignity and importance were epitomized in costumes such as this bag-sleeved **houppelande,** tall-crowned hat, and heeled shoes. (Redrawn from sculpture of Dan Chimmey, c. 1405. Amsterdam.)

was usually worn by older men who preferred the *robe longue,* the knee-length cotehardie, or the houppelande to the hip- or waist-length pourpoint.

### CABAN (late 1300–1400)

Late in the fourteenth century, the **caban** had been introduced, prompted by a design called the **caftan,** brought from the Far East. It was an outer garment with "crossed fronts," (double breasted). This long jacket coat had a fitted waist, gathered skirt, and long, tight sleeves. A belt was sometimes worn with the caban, but this accessory was not essential to create the tight-waisted silhouette. In some versions it was made with an attached hood.

### ORNAMENTAL WRAPS (1530–1560)

Between 1530 and 1560, the people of the Renaissance devised a number of ornamental wraps for their elaborate ceremonial festivities. These wraps included: the **tabard,** particolored and embroidered with heraldic emblems; the **huque,** made of two fur-lined, decorative panels; the **paletot,** a jacket with *manches pertuisées* (slit sleeves); the **journade,** made with two floor- or ankle-length panels; and the **giornea,** or manteline, a two-panel, floor-length ceremonial costume with a deep V-neckline.

# Accessories (1400–1500)

### HEADWEAR

Hats and head coverings between 1400 and 1500 remained similar in style to those of the Gothic period. The chaperon; sugarloaf cap, a four-segment, square cap; hennin; and reticulated headdresses continued in vogue for women.

## FOOTWEAR

The pointed **crackows,** discarded for a brief time, reappeared from 1380 to 1410 with even longer pointed toes. They became so lengthy that walking was impaired, and again the tips had to be held up by a thin chain extending from the toe to the calf of the leg. These pointed shoes were also referred to as **poulaines. Heuze** were high boots with instep laces, buttoned or buckled at the ankle, and made of soft leather in a variety of styles. Women wore soft-leather, fur-lined boots indoors during the winter months. The **botte,** or *bottes à relever,* were simple bedroom slippers. **Pattens,** a simple wooden-oval shoe protection, and **chopines,** a tall, platform shoe protection with a wide toe strap, were used out-of-doors.

## JEWELRY

Neckwear for men became massive and two or three great chains, plaques, and pendant ornaments were worn around the neck at one time. Late in the fifteenth century jeweled collars that covered the shoulders were worn by men. Families of great wealth employed talented artists to do nothing else but create these elegant baubles. Belts were equally important to the look of the total costume during the Renaissance and were designed in a similar way to the neckwear. There were also wide leather belts fastened with large, jewel-encrusted buckles from which might dangle several trinkets including fans, keys, mirrors, scent boxes, or seals, attached by golden chains.

Rings, popular to the point of excess, were worn in multiplicity. Every finger was adorned with at least one gold ring. Diamonds, sapphires, and rubies were mounted in the settings. The Grecian charm ring was revived and believed to have magical powers. These charm rings were made with mystical words or symbols engraved on them, or set with animal teeth and worn on the thumb. Signet rings, rings of twisted gold, and those with stylized floral patterns were a few of the many fashionable ring designs.

## HANDHELD ACCESSORIES

Gloves of the fifteenth century were made of doeskin, sheepskin, and hareskin. Because of the demand for gloves, entire villages in France built their economies upon the manufacture of these accessories, and glove making achieved a high degree of sophistication. Gloves were made with individual fingers and thumbs, and with wide, embroidered cuffs of leather tanned in such a way that the scents added to the finished gloves were retained.

Walking sticks with carved heads and made of rare woods were a short-lived fad in the middle years of the fifteenth century. They were carried by women and were ornamental rather than functional.

**Escarcelles,** or purses, were carried or worn suspended from belts by men and women. Two forms predominated: a canvas bag made from a rectangular piece of fabric with tassels hung at the corners, and richly embroidered with animal designs or scenes of romantic tales; and a drawstring pouch, also heavily embroidered. These purses were first used to hold missals.

Fans were not an important accessory during the Renaissance and were either a round form which folded or shirred. They were often carried by a servant who whisked annoying insects away from his master. The servant carried the fan suspended by a chain or cord attached to his belt.

## BODY SUPPORTS

The **busk, busc,** or **busque,** introduced in Italy in the late fifteenth century, was the first in a series of garments designed to control the female figure. It was made by sewing several layers of fabric together which were then stitched or quilted to give stiffness to the simple body-encircling band. When it was worn, it laced snugly in back and assisted in creating the flat-chested appearance typical of the female silhouette of the period (Figure 10.16). This corset was made of rich, heavy silk, replacing the woolen material used in making the cotte, an earlier figure-forming garment. A still later refinement was the addition of whalebones which were stitched or quilted into the required positions between the layers of the busk. Thus boned, the busk had more rigidity and gave even more figure control, particularly in the area of the bust. The tight lacings pulled the body in at the rib cage, decreasing the girth of the figure in that area. Shoulder straps were usually formed from a pair of simple ribbon ties. These were attached to the top hem of the busk, with one pair of straps in front and one pair in back, which were knotted in bows on each shoulder.

# Hairstyles (1470–1500)

Hair and head-covering fashions changed very slowly for men and women during this period. Women's hair was generally concealed by hennins or other elaborate headwear. By the end of the fifteenth century, men wore their hair in shoulder-length bobs, discarding the round cap and shaved-neck style that had persisted for many years. Long bangs covered the forehead at this time, and the hair was worn straight or gently waved, curving inward at the ends.

# Basic Garments of the High Renaissance (1500–1600)

## DOUBLET (1500–1600)

During the High Renaissance men wore four types of short jackets: the **doublet,** the **jerkin,** the **vest,** and the

**Figure 10.16.** In this late sixteenth-century gown, the **vaquero** is front laced and the **stomacher** is used to obscure the lacing. The **busk** is sewn into the **stomacher** to insure the required flat-bosom look. The **farthingale** is emphasized by the addition of a cartwheel exterior farthingale. The English often did not tie the **ruff** tightly at the neck but wore it open as shown here. The hair is piled quite high in front, and in back it is caught in a golden, pearl-trimmed net. The transparent cap of delicate linen is a modified French cap or Mary Stuart cap. (*Portrait of a Lady*, British, anonymous, sixteenth century. Metropolitan Museum of Art, New York City.)

**peascod jacket.** The doublet, vest, and peascod jacket were made with two layers of fabric and an interlining of padding or **stuffs.** The outside of the **doublet** was made of heavy silk, and the lining was linen. The padding was usually horsehair, though sometimes it was straw. The thickness and position of these stuffs changed as the male silhouette was modified.

Early in this period, the upper part of the figure was made to appear square, bulky, and broad-shouldered by heavily padding the sleeves. **Puffs and slashes** in them increased the illusion of a strong, masculine figure. Slashes were made in the sleeves of outer garments with small, hot irons; the linen shirt-sleeve fabrics were then meticulously pulled through. In time the whole garment was covered with puffs and slashes, permanently created with rich fabrics. Scrutiny of a portrait in the Frick Gallery indicates that these slashes may not have been finished off, for the artist has painted raveling edges on each slash.

Men and women however, continued to arrange a linen shirt between the bodice of any outer garment and the tied-on sleeves.

The **vest** was a lightly padded doublet, with or without sleeves. It may have been merely vest fronts held together by a narrow band across the back of the neck and buttoned down the front.

The **peascod jacket** was a long-waisted, padded pourpoint or doublet worn during the last half of the sixteenth century (Figure 10.17). The upper-body section fitted the back and sides closely, while the front was heavily padded into a convex curve. In profile, the silhouette of the torso bowed into a low curve. This jacket had a high-standing collar in contrast to the earlier doublet and vest, which had either square or oval necklines that revealed the shirt worn underneath. The frontal view of this costume tapered from broad shoulders to a low, narrow, pointed waist. The fronts sloped to the fitted side seams. (Armor of this period had the same configuration, suggesting that the shape was developed as a defense against the thrust of a sword.) The peascod jacket had a small, stiff peplum extending three or four inches below the waist. Sleeves for most garments were tied on with points, which, for a time, acted as decoration as well as a means of holding sleeves to the main body of the garment. As the use of points faded from fashion, padded crescents, or **ropillas** (c. 1570–1600), were tied over the lacings that held on the sleeves (Figures 10.14 and 10.17).

There was a wide range of sleeve styles including the large, puffed or balloon sleeves of the bulky silhouette period; the padded, inverted, cone-shaped sleeves

**Figure 10.17. Spanish doublet** with high-standing collar, no sleeves, and **ropillas.** (Actual garment, c. 1570.)

gathered and puffed at the shoulder; the padded ball forms covering the upper arms and worn over slightly padded, full-length sleeves; and the slightly padded, full-length sleeves typical of the peascod jackets. Hanging sleeves called **cuerpo baxo,** which were long, wide, and fur trimmed, were also laced on with the doublet sleeves.

The **jerkin** (c. 1540–1550), was an intermediate evolutionary style of **haincelin,** or short houppelande (Figure 10.18). The haincelin, an outer wrap worn by young Renaissance dandies, had been designed with a variety of sleeves: the bag sleeve, the *manches pertuisées*, and the wide tube sleeve (Figure 10.12). The thigh-length outer wrap of the sixteenth century was made by gathering the main body of the garment to a deep yoke. Generally worn loose with the fronts folded back into deep lapels, the jerkin assisted in creating the square silhouette characteristic of the early sixteenth century. Sleeve styles were the same as those of the doublets, and there were also sleeves that had cross slits at the elbows or a long vertical slit on the outside. Arms could be withdrawn from the

**Figure 10.18.** This early sixteenth-century **jerkin** is very much like the earlier long-waisted **cotehardie** with its high collar and many-buttoned front closing. Below the waistline can be seen **à grandes assiettes,** also characteristic of the earlier **pourpoint** style. The soft brimless bonnet and cape are typical. (Tintoretto: *Portrait of a Young Man,* c. 1540. Metropolitan Museum of Art, New York City.)

long, cumbersome sleeves through these slits, allowing more freedom of movement. Fur collars, cuffs, and linings were an important part of these large coats.

Often the vest, peascod jacket, and jerkin were worn at one time. A linen shirt with bishop sleeves and a high, round, gathered neckline, or a square, embroidery-edged neckline, was worn next to the body. The round, gathered neckline eventually evolved into a small, ruffled collar, which in turn became the Spanish ruff.

## BREECHES (1500–1600)

Chausses (hose) continued in style until the middle of the sixteenth century. The **upper stock,** a small, padded roll, was gradually enlarged to cover the buttocks, and became known as **pumpkin breeches.** Below these brief, padded, slashed, and puffed breeches was worn the **lower stock,** which consisted of thigh-length tubes with hose covering the lower part of the legs and feet. Hose were made by cutting leg shapes on the bias until about 1590, when knitted hose came into use in increasing quantities.

The **codpiece** became an elaborate, functional protuberance, joining the two halves of the upper stock above the crotch. Throughout much of this period, this device seems to have been symbolic of some of the excesses in which men indulged. This puffed, slashed, padded, grotesque breeches closure continued in style, despite censoring and banning by the church, until breeches became so swollen with padding that the codpiece was lost from sight and discarded. Horsehair, straw, grain kernels, or bombast were used as breeches padding and to form the globe-shaped **pumpkin breeches,** pear-shaped **Venetians,** and balloon or oval-shaped **trunk hose** (Figures 10.19 and 10.20). Trunk hose were varied in styling by the addition of long strips of fabric attached at the waistband and at the breeches cuff. These were called **paned** trunk hose. **Canons,** or half-hose, were also worn with the trunk hose. Late in the period the padding and bombast were removed from the breeches. This calf-length style, known as **Spanish slops,** often was made more elegant by using paning of a contrasting color.

## GOWNS (1495–1620)

Gown styling during the late sixteenth century and early seventeenth century changed radically from the high-waisted styles of the previous period. In general, the gown was comprised of several separate items of apparel which were combined to form the complete garment (Figure 10.21). The **saya** was one three-piece costume made up of a **vaquero** (bodice); a bell skirt worn over a farthingale; and *cuerpo baxo*, separate or hanging sleeves (Figure 10.22). The bodice was a female version of the doublet or pourpoint with tight-fitting sleeves. The waist was long and tapered to a point below the normal waistline. An underbodice, called the **jubon,** was tight and worn be-

**Figure 10.19.** This nobleman from the turn of the seventeenth century wears **doublet, Venetians,** and a **Spanish ruff.** The **Spanish cape,** carefully arranged in a gallant but casual manner, is of deep purple velvet with gold braid on the hem. (Redrawn from *The Proxy Marriage of Marie de' Medici,* Peter Paul Rubens, 1600. Louvre, Paris.)

**Figure 10.20.** Early seventeenth-century dandy wears an elaborate costume of **doublet** with **ropillas,** paned **Venetians, hose,** and **canons.** The high-standing lace collar *à la Medici* is held upright by a delicate underproper. (Anonymous: *James I,* late Renaissance. University Library, Cambridge.)

neath the vaquero.[14] In time the vaquero was laced in front, with the lacing hidden under a **stomacher,** a decorative and functional device that tied over the lacings and held the busk.

The stomacher served to extend the waistline to well below the normal level. Around the turn of the fifteenth century the waistline had dropped from just under the bust to far below the natural waist and remained there for almost fifty years, from about 1530 to 1570. In the 1570s, a slight, pointed, frontal dip in the waistline began to appear. The exaggeration of the deep, pointed stomacher took over as the sixteenth century waned (1595) and continued as a gown characteristic until well into the seventeenth century. Research of available visual resources indicates that the stomacher had several variations. The sharp V-shape was often modified into a rounded V- or U-tab, which was used most often in Holland and Spain. Swedish noblewomen never adopted the extremely low waistline, preferring the modest front dip introduced first in France after 1570.

During this period the busk was a V-shaped piece of whalebone or wood used to flatten the bust and hold the figure erect. It was inserted between the two layers of fabric that formed the stomacher.

The **ropa, simarra** (Italy), **marlotte** (France), and **vlieger** (Holland) were names given to ladies' gowns. They all combined the three primary costume parts to form the gown. Some were styled with the Dutch waist which made the bodice appear square and short-waisted.

As feminine styles of the High Renaissance changed, the outer skirt was slit in the center front to reveal the kirtle skirt beneath. **Farthingales** (1540–1608), which were designed to add girth at the hips, were bombasted at first or consisted of deeply pleated cartwheels tied around the waist. Their shapes were a matter of nationalistic design preferences and they became elaborately constructed skirt supports made of tapes and whalebone, or tapes and reed bands, or bombasted, doughnut-shaped hip cushions.

The neckline was a truncated V-shape in England; a high, throat-encircling collar topped by a little ruff in Spain; and, in France, an inverted V-shape with a tall Medici collar that framed the head. Each country developed this detail to suit its taste.

**Figure 10.21.** During the first half of the sixteenth century, gowns were designed using conical shapes, including the bodice, funnel or tube sleeves, and the bell skirt. Textural combinations were startling, using furs, and different combinations of brocaded silks. The bandier has disappeared but note the new form of the **demiceint.** (Hans Holbein the Younger: *Portrait of Catherine Parr,* sixteenth century. Novarro Collection, Italy.)

**Figure 10.22.** The addition of **cuerpo-baxo** sleeve puffs gives the illusion of increased breadth to upper figure in this gown of the mid-sixteenth century. (Bronzino: *Lucrezia Panciatichi,* detail, 1550–1560. Uffizi Gallery, Florence.)

Starched, pleated **ruffs,** which developed from the drawstring-gathered neckline of the male shirt, became the dominant detail of men's and women's costumes (Figure 10.14). What originally had been a small lace ruffle encircling the throat, eventually grew into a vast, pleated wheel of lace. It was so large that a wire frame, or **under-proper,** was needed to support it. Poorer classes used a full circle of heavy paper with ties at the open ends.[15] The wide, stiff collars caused considerable problems when eating, and spoon handles were lengthened to facilitate getting the food over them from plate to mouth.

Large lace collars, standing high in back and attached to the corners of square necklines, also were supported by delicate wire frames. These collars were styled in fan, heart, and wing shapes, and often were studded with seed pearls and shot through with golden threads (Figure 10.23).

Beneath the three-piece gowns women wore **kirtles,** which were petticoats or skirts made of handsome fabric and attached to a bodice. The kirtle often had long sleeves which were visible beneath the tied-on sleeves. The kirtle skirts were visible through the inverted V-opening of the outer skirt.

Additional female underwear included: the **partlet,** a fine linen or silk underwaist with full, soft, gathered sleeves trimmed with lace cuffs; the **chemise,** a long, linen, one-piece tunic with tight sleeves; the **shift,** a long silk tunic; and **underknickers,** which were full, baggy pants. At first they were considered indecent because originally courtesans had worn gold or silver lamé underknickers beneath the split gown skirt without wearing underskirts or kirtles. It was Catherine de' Medici who made underknickers popular and proper.

Although the shift was sometimes used as a nightgown, the wearing of clothing at night was not considered respectable until Margaret of Navarre began to wear black silk shifts to accentuate her extremely fair skin when she retired.

## OUTER WRAPS (1400–1600)

The **gamurra** (1400–1495) was a woman's wrap made by combining the surcoat and houppelande. It was sleeveless, with full, floor-length skirts made of silken fabrics and lined with fur or contrasting colored silks.

**Figure 10.23.** Intricate combinations of lace braid and jewels typify the court costumes of Europe as the century turned the corner, leaving the Renaissance behind. (Peter Candido: *Portrait of German Duchess,* c. 1601. Louvre, Paris.)

**Figure 10.24.** This gentleman is clad for warmth in a **doublet** with an extra pair of sleeves. The fur-trimmed, floor-length **zornea** reveals at the shoulder that it is also lined with fur. The small ruffle at the back of the neck is part of the shirt, which is tied with a drawstring tightly about the throat. The cap is a sixteenth-century version of the **Canterbury cap.** (Giovanni Battista Moroni: *Bartolomeo Bongo,* sixteenth century. Metropolitan Museum of Art, New York City.)

During the early fifteenth century the **zornea,** a male outer garment, was fur trimmed and made of elegant material (Figure 10.24). It was much like a large cape, but was worn tightly belted at the waist and had wide, full sleeves. The **chamarre,** another masculine wrap made of silk lined with fur, was fashionable around 1530 (Figure 10.11). The sleeves of this short, full coat were made with large puffed wings attached at the shoulders, encircling the upper arm. The **casaque** was a thigh-length overcoat tied in the front with bows and with deep side vents or slits. The sleeves of the casaque were either closed and full length, or were designed with long slits that exposed the forearms, revealing the rich fabric of the doublet sleeves beneath.

Capes, the major decorative wrap during the last half of the sixteenth century, were either long or hip length and were known by several names: **ferreruolo, boemio, balandran, futera, capa,** and **Spanish cape.** The Spanish cape was hip length and of circular cut. Worn as an accessory, it was made of heavy velvet lined with a contrasting color of silk. The surface decorations included gold lace and complicated braids. It was worn, as were most of these capes, slung over one shoulder and tied with silken cords under the other arm, giving a dramatic, dashing accent to the total male costume. Ladies also selected this wrap form.

# Accessories (1500–1600)

## HEADWEAR

During this century head coverings changed radically. The hennin worn by women totally disappeared. It was replaced briefly by the **balzo,** or **rebalzo,** a large, dome-shaped toque which completely covered the hair and accented and slenderized the neck (Figure 10.25).

Hair-concealing hoods were introduced at the beginning of the sixteenth century. These were designed with many variations, all nationalistic in origin. Basically they consisted of a veil, or **touret,** of black velvet lined with contrasting silk, generally white or red. In the next form change, the veil was cut on the sides in front of the ears, forming **lappets** which fell over the shoulders in front, and the back of the head was covered by the remainder of this heavy veiling. Later these side pieces were folded up and pinned onto the top of the head. In the French variation of this hood, the veil was made of stiffly starched linen and arranged into large imposing wings. During the time of Mary Tudor, the English modified the hood into the **gabled headdress,** consisting of a veil and a pointed or gabled shape framing the face and covering

**Figure 10.25.** The **balzo,** or **rebalzo,** first worn in the fifteenth century, continued in popularity into the early sixteenth century. The gown has the shallow Dutch waist with ruching along the edges of the low U-shaped neckline and the brocade inset. The pearl necklace tucked into the bosom is a characteristic style of the early sixteenth century. (Redrawn from a portrait, c. 1530.)

the cheeks (Figure 10.7). A frilled and stiffened white or gold coif, which hugged the face and hair, was worn under this type of hood. The **French hood** was worn well back on the head revealing the hair in front. The back hair was caught up in the back in a caul or a black velvet bag. The cap section of this hood was made with a small curved or heart-shaped brim. The small white cap with a heart-shaped brim, the **Mary Stuart cap,** was the final hair-concealing hat form of this period.

Between 1550 and 1600, Elizabeth I popularized the wearing of tall-crowned bonnets with small brims decorated with plumes and ribbon headbands. Large, jeweled brooches held the feathers to the crown, standing erect or trailing off the brim at the back.

Men wore conical bonnets with puffed crowns and feather trims; flat, small-brimmed pancake berets; and, late in the High Renaissance, tall-crowned beaver hats with small snap brims. The pancake bonnets of the male nobility, rich with jewels and feather trims, had been popular since early in the reign of Henry VIII.

## FOOTWEAR

Late in the fifteenth century, the men's point-toed poulaine was discarded and replaced by the broad-toed, ankle-strap slipper known as the **duck's bill.** Just as crackows had once grown to ridiculous lengths, so the duck's bill became excessively wide, at one time measuring twelve inches across the toes. They were made of silks, brocades, and velvets, and were heavily embroidered, padded, slashed, and puffed. To keep from walking on their own shoes, men were forced to walk in a duck's waddling gait.

Women's shoes were soft, ankle-strap slippers with puffed-and-slashed round toes. Because women's footwear was neither visible nor as important to the total silhouette as men's, it never reached outlandish proportions. A shoe style with a raised heel attached was introduced late in the sixteenth century. The spool-shaped heel was placed well toward the arch, and the toes, while square at the tip, were rather narrow. The shoes were held to the feet with a T-strap and were sometimes decorated with large ribbon rosettes.

These shoes were a natural outgrowth of the tall, single-pedestal **chopines** worn particularly in Italy. The elevated-toe slippers were raised to extreme heights; often the platform was twelve inches high. They were worn indoors, and ladies using this decorative but awkward footwear had to have assistance when walking. Another late sixteenth-century shoe style was a T-strap, round-toed sandal raised by two heels, one under the ball of the foot, and the other under the heel. During the reign of Elizabeth I, a platform sole about one inch thick became popular.

Pattens, or **corned shoes,** which were worn to protect the shoes in rainy weather, altered somewhat between 1510 and 1540. The sole was foot shaped and was held to the foot by two shaped-leather straps tied together over the instep.

The invention of a knitting machine by William Lee revolutionized hosiery making and hose became less costly and better fitting. They were an essential item in the male wardrobe and, although hidden by the saya skirt, were an integral part of the female costume. The colorful leg coverings came in bright blues, reds, yellows, and greens, often embroidered with gold thread on the instep and up the shin.

## JEWELRY

Watchmaking attained perfection during this century in England and on the continent. Some of the types of watches carried included the *Nuremberg egg,* a fat, oval timepiece; finger watches; earring watches made with gold, crystal, or enameled cases; and many which were fitted with tiny chimes that "chimed sweet tunes" on the hour. These costly accessories were always worn where they might be seen and admired.

Ropes of pearls, gold chains with a series of large, precious stones, and large rings worn on the index finger, were typical neck and finger jewelry of the late sixteenth century.

## HANDHELD ACCESSORIES

Fans changed radically, particularly during the late sixteenth century. They were made in the shape of flags or weathercocks rather than the customary semicircular forms or pleated circles of the past. The small rectangular blades of these fans were made of plaited straw, painted linen, parchment, vellum, or silk. Disc or screen fans became popular about 1550, and the folding fan, made of leather with deep, permanent pleats, was also used. The handles of all these fans were made of gold and beautifully chased, or set with precious stones. When the circular, pleated fan was folded, the pleated sections were concealed in a silver, gold, or ivory handle. Fans were used so extensively that master gilders were kept constantly busy decorating them.

## MASKS

Prior to the late sixteenth century, masks were a prop used exclusively by theatrical performers. The masks made for cosmetic purposes in mid-century were small and colorless, and were first worn as eye shades while riding horseback. In France they were called **loup;** in England they were referred to as **loo.** However, it took little time for the charm and mystery associated with the mask to take this fashion accessory out of its totally utilitarian role. By 1558, and continuing to the end of the reign of Elizabeth I in 1603, the fashion mask was worn by all elegant women when they went outdoors. The short, eye-covering mask gave way to a larger oval mask made of velvet. Finally, a full, face-concealing mask of fine white cloth was introduced and was generally accepted.

Many devices were developed for keeping the mask in place after the original, handheld, smaller versions went out of style. String ties, velvet ties, and wire bands much like early spectacles' bows were used. One of the strangest devices was the stave-and-button arrangement attached to the inside of the full-face mask. The button was held firmly between the teeth, keeping the mask in its face-concealing position.

Women wore masks to prevent the detection of their identity when attending the bawdy and prohibited theatrical productions which were popular during the period, and on other occasions, such as an engagement with a secret lover, when mystery was paramount. There were also many who wore masks to protect their heavily rouged and powdered faces. Glass was sometimes fitted into the eye openings to keep out the dust and grime while "riding to hounds." The mask continued in vogue during these centuries of intrigue, serving both as a utilitarian and camouflage accessory.

## BODY AND SKIRT SUPPORTS

The busk was the V-shaped piece of whalebone or wood used in the stomacher. This "pair of bodies" also acted as an additional body support to mold the figure into the narrow, elongated torso considered the height of feminine pulchritude in the late sixteenth century. The **cotte,** an earlier figure-controlling garment, was made of quilted layers of silk or linen with whalebone sewn between these layers to insure that the proper female form was achieved. Later a metal cotte, or gambeson, lined with quilted silk or linen padding, was introduced. This diabolical, figure-forming garment was hinged on one side and laced with ribbons tied in bows on the other. Ribbon shoulder straps were used to further insure the proper positioning of this armorlike underwear.

There were several methods used to support the gown skirt: a **bourrelet,** a roll of felt tied around the waist with a **verdingale,** a hip-level hoop; a **farthingale,** a tape and wire hoop larger in the back than on the sides in the final stages; or a tray farthingale, a wire skirt support that held the gown out perpendicular to the waist, dropping the skirt in a straight rather than a belled line to the floor. National preference dictated the shape while acceptance of various styles generally depended on the speed of fashion communication between nations. Earlier farthingale styles had included a pleated and padded peplum form secured at the waist over the gown skirt. In later styles these skirt supports were composed of hoops that were flat in front, semifull in back, and extended well out beyond the hips at the sides.

# Hairstyles (1500–1600)

During most of the sixteenth century men's hair was styled in a close, head-shaped bob. Some men wore their hair in an ear-length bob, flared slightly behind the ears, with rather long sideburns. Thin moustaches and stiletto beards trimmed the face, but most men were clean shaven, and a lad's first shave was a matter of ceremonial festivity.

During the Elizabethan period, tight, crimped curls, shaped into a head-encircling bubble, were in vogue. Wigs made in the same style were also used, imitating Elizabeth I, who was forced to use wigs because she had lost her own hair due to illness and high fever. Earlier in the High Renaissance, females wore their hair parted in the center, pulled back, and covered with some variation of the hood.

## FOOTNOTES

1. Anne Fremantle, *Age of Faith*, p. 162.
2. Edith Simon, *The Reformation*, p. 12.
3. Ibid., p. 102.
4. Ibid., pp. 42–44.
5. André Chastel, *The Italian Renaissance*, p. 30.

6. Timothy Foote, *World of Bruegel*, p. 90.

7. John R. Hale, *Age of Exploration*, p. 30.

8. Ludmila Kybalová; Olga Herbenová; and Milena Lamarová; *The Pictorial Encyclopedia of Fashion*, p. 130.

9. François Boucher, *20,000 Years of Fashion*, p. 238.

10. Margaret Hamilton Hill, *The Evolution of Fashion*, p. 54.

11. James Laver, *The Concise History of Costume and Fashion*, p. 97.

12. Ibid., p. 98.

13. Bernard Rudofsky, *The Unfashionable Human Body*, pp. 58–59.

14. Boucher, *20,000 Years of Fashion*, pp. 240–44.

15. Victoria and Albert Museum, London, Costume Court.

# Chapter 11
# Opulence of the Baroque
## (1600–1700)

Two major factors served to alter the political, social, and aesthetic concepts which had given rise to the great age of the Renaissance. One factor was the new intellectual, scientific curiosity by which scholars of this period sought truth. The other factor resulted from the residual effects of the Reformation as princelings and kings sought to gain political dominance in Western Europe. The power struggle had a religious base, but it was not a clear-cut confrontation between Roman Catholics and Protestants. The intricate web of diplomatic intrigue allied Catholic France with Protestant Sweden to overthrow the Catholic Habsburg domination of the Holy Roman Empire. The lengthy Thirty Years' War was fought to determine which religious faction would establish its sovereign prince as emperor.

Most of the major battles raged on German soil.[1] Armies which fought there were at first easily raised. However, the drama and glamour of the first engagements soon faded, dimmed by the fierceness of the encounters. Food was scarce and battles were frequently lost because foraging, plundering soldiers were off hunting for food or booty.[2] Such sorties often turned into orgies of cruelty, for the brutality of battle had sucked from the soldiers the last drop of human kindness. If wounded in an encounter, their wounds were given cursory treatment. As the war slogged on, villagers and conscripted, poorly paid soldiers lost their verve for the conflict.

All armies were villagers' enemies regardless of the banner behind which they marched. Though vastly outnumbered, the villagers generally made an effort to protect their homes by putting up some resistance to the quartering of troops nearby. Homes, however humble or prosperous, were by now orderly living spaces with large heating-and-cooking fireplaces as the focal points. Pewter treasures and preserved provisions intended to sustain the household were worth a struggle.

Of course, there were officers who, on occasion, punished those who participated in these plundering exploits. Those caught in the act were made an example and punished by hanging. When war was finally concluded, the foot soldiers and the thousands of camp fol-

**Figure 11.1.** This male costume illustrates the masculine mode of the 1630s: slash-sleeved **doublet** with truncated, segmented peplum, **breeches** fastened with points and bunches, and heeled shoes with rosettes on the instep. The points which hold up the knee breeches can be observed at the waistline just to the right of the side seam. The cape draped about the figure is voluminous and circular in cut. (Anthony van Dyck: *Robert Rich, Earl of Warwick*, 1578-1658. Metropolitan Museum of Art, New York City.)

lowers found themselves miles from home. Without money, often suffering from injuries incurred in battle, they staggered and straggled homeward. Countless numbers died enroute; many who survived turned vagabond or highwayman. Children born to camp followers, many of whom had grown to adulthood during this prolonged war, had neither family, home, nor country. Generals fared better and one such successful officer, General Wallenstein, was awarded sixty-six large estates and the Duchy of Friedland.

The Treaty of Westphalia in 1648 put an end to this conflict by establishing independence from the Habsburgs for the 100 German princes. Ironically, this treaty provided that Sweden and France, whose rulers had sought to deprive their own nobility of power, were the protectors of the German princelings' independence and autonomy. The Thirty Years' War had been fought for the paramount reason of religious ideology. However, the freedom to carry on trade, the assurance of Swedish access to sea lanes from Baltic ports, and the insurance of German liberties were also motivating factors.

The continent was not the only geographical area involved in military struggle for religious reasons. In fifteenth-century England, the War of the Roses (1455-85) had eliminated the old nobility and subsequent generations of nobility were never able to acquire the power once wielded by this class. The British gentry and merchant classes continued to strengthen their social and political positions through newly amassed wealth of lands and money.

James I, who ruled England from 1603 to 1625, believed in the divine right of kings, but his power was questioned as no other English monarch's had been since John in 1215. There were rumblings among the rich merchant class which wanted representation in Parliament, and there was a growing belief in the rights of all people, not just the divine rights of rulers. Because the threat of territorial invasions had decreased, the English people felt there was little need for a strong king, much less for a despotic ruler. These concepts of the rights of commoners to determine the political directions, with their origins rooted in the reign of James I, had consequences that were felt in many European countries for centuries to come.

In 1625, Charles I succeeded to the throne upon the death of his father, James I, whose reign had closed amid political wranglings over the support and conduct of the Thirty Years' War.[3] Charles almost immediately quarreled with Parliament over the war he had initiated with Spain, so he dissolved the legal body that represented the British people. It was convened again, only to be dissolved twice more over the conflicts arising from the king's need for money and attitudes toward religious innovations. In 1649 the king was ordered beheaded. The fifth signature on his death warrant was that of Edward Whalley, son-in-law of the militant Puritan and first signator, Oliver Cromwell.

For more than ten years England was a commonwealth, until the royalists at last restored a Stuart king, Charles II, to the throne in 1660. During the Restoration, Charles II encouraged the establishment of the Church of England, and Catholic and Puritan dissenters were persecuted and prosecuted. This Stuart king cleverly managed his churchmen and his cavalier supporters during most of his reign until his death in 1685. His brother, James II, a Catholic by conviction, was summarily deposed. Elected to replace him and to rule jointly were his daughter Mary, and her husband, William of Orange.

Britain's civil war from 1642 to 1652, which resulted in the deposition of Charles I, was a fierce and bitter conflict. The Roundheads, passionate Protestants, ravaged many of the beautiful cathedrals that dotted the English countryside. Cromwellian soldiers rode into them on horseback, swords swinging. The targets were the statues of saints, Episcopal effigies, and any sculptural symbolism which was papist.

The cathedral close at Litchfield, for example, became the fortress for the defenders of the monarchy. During the siege, loyalists in the dark of night carefully dismantled the cathedral's organ and hid the pipes in the homes of the king's loyal followers. Even organs were destroyed by Cromwell's men, for great music of the established church was detested by the Puritans.[4]

The Restoration Period which followed did not bring peace or tolerance. The Quakers suffered grave abuses at the hands of Charles II and the followers of the Church of England. Quakers, Puritans, Roman Catholics, and members of other splinter sects were to be the first settlers of the American colonies.

In the seventeenth century Protestant Holland finally shook off the yoke of Catholic Spain. It was through the leadership of King William of Orange that resistance was organized which won independence. As Spanish might faded, England and France increased their political power. Wars, and murders of kings and influential members of the nobility swung the power pendulum of these emerging nations as they fought for supremacy. Struggles for the control of religious faith and philosophy perpetrated many diabolical acts of torture upon those who were believed to be heretics.

Out of these struggles new attitudes were to develop. The poet John Donne (1573–1631) deplored the passing of the old way of life, while Francis Bacon (1561–1626) lauded the new, based on the belief that the inherent creativity of people would build a new, more relevant system of human relationships.

With technologically improved scientific instruments, scientists of the seventeenth century challenged Aristotelian precepts on the nature of the universe as well as the functions of natural phenomena. In turn, relationships in the social structure were altered. A new social, political, and intellectual order grew out of the challenges raised against the established system. The ability to effect change rested on a base of power. Thomas Hobbes, the most perceptive political philosopher of the seventeenth century, succinctly put it when he wrote in the *Leviathan*, "So that in the first place, I put for a general inclination of all mankind, a perpetual and restless desire for Power after Power, that ceaseth only in death."

The restless motion of this Age of Enlightenment was symbolized in the undulating rhythms and countermovements of the artistic style evolved by masters such as Bernini and Rembrandt.[5] Artists and scientists sought new order because of their curiosity. Rulers sought new order because of a need to preserve their power over their subjects.

The Sun King, Louis XIV, who established the concept of a sovereign's *divine right* to govern, catapulted France into a position of political and cultural power that was never to be duplicated.[6] The ruling families of the Bourbons in France; the Stuarts in England; the Habsburgs in Spain, Austria, and the Holy Roman Empire all had divined themselves as having supremacy by God's will. The Protestant north, because of the personal charisma of the kings themselves, was also ruled by supreme monarchs. Tensions between the fiercely nationalistic Bohemians and Czechs against the Catholic emperor of the Holy Roman Empire were ultimately resolved and the emperor's power diminished.

The death of Charles II brought a Catholic, James Stuart, to the English throne. The significance of Protestant pressure in Parliament to depose him and replace him with Mary and William of Orange was profound. To this day, those who sit on the British throne are constitutional monarchs, as were William and Mary. Queen Anne, succeeding her sister Mary, reigned without issue for a few tortured years. Upon her death, the House of Hanover was placed on the British throne. The line of Georges and colonial dissatisfaction with the autocratic rule of the mentally incompetent George III laid the groundwork for the American Revolution.

The widely disparate life-styles of the kings, the patronizing nobility of their courts, the mercantile class, and the peasants continued apace. Trade and the agrarian-based economy altered with the expansion of new industries, which altered the occupations of the lower class. Interest in science and the search for truth in nature changed activities among intellectuals. The new intensity of the upper class in satisfying their insatiable appetites for pleasures of all sorts led to a vast array of enjoyable diversions.

The Baroque style of music and art, full of curvilinear embellishments and complexities, influenced the social manners of all classes. Self-indulgent kings had an endless number of mistresses, for royal marriages were contracted to expand landholdings and personal power, rather than for love. It was only during the later years of Louis XIV's seventy-two-year reign that Madame de Maintenon, Louis' second wife and the former governess to some of his illegitimate children, reinstituted pious attitudes in court and developed a new morality.[7]

Pleasure at the table and in bed were the major enjoyments of the seventeenth century. Wives of this period had no civil rights and functioned in society as organizers of the home to serve the creature comforts of their spouses and to bear and rear children.

The genre painters of the seventeenth century have left copious records of courtly and bourgeois daily life. From elegant living spaces in Versailles to modest or elegant, but always orderly, Dutch homes, artists such as Jan Vermeer have illustrated a cross section of daily activities, festive celebrations, and political conferences.

Card playing was a favorite pastime of the period and the four card suits represented the dominant ruling families. Hearts represented the French Bourbons, spades the Habsburgs, diamonds the Stuarts, and clubs the Swedish monarchs.[8] In addition to cards, those who were financially able enjoyed the theater, particularly the reinstituted ballet. Others became collectors of specimens of flora and fauna, ultimately establishing museums to house them. Masked and fancy-dress balls occupied the leisure hours of the upper class. Evenings were spent listening to chamber music played by court musicians, or playing flutes, lutes, clavicords, or *viole da gamba*.

Court life throughout Europe was a pale copy of the court of Louis XIV, who ascended to the French throne in 1643 at the age of five. He did not assume the reins of power until he was twenty-three, after the death of Cardinal Mazarin, his powerful prime minister, in 1661. The power of Louis XIV was absolute, and, in his determination to establish France as the political and the cultural leader of the world, he set the pattern of pomp and ceremony for his whole nation.

He took over the great tapestry works at the Gobelins factory in Paris. He brought Italian master artists, such as Bernini, from their homeland to design imposing buildings and to create masterful paintings and sculpture. He rebuilt the Louvre, constructed the Place Vendôme, and built the palace of Versailles at a cost possibly in excess of half a billion dollars. Versailles, overpowering, rambling, and elegant, with glistening pools of water and great fountains, provided a theatrical backdrop for his court. And his court, made up of intelligent bourgeois advisors whom he had selected to replace the hereditary noble advisors, responded to his every whim. They even vied for the honor of assisting him at his morning toilette.

Louis XIV was a man of prodigious vigor. Each day he hunted and played tennis; every night he entertained the court with banquets, games of chance, dancing, theatricals, and musicals. Those invited to these exhausting affairs were required to arrive at six-thirty in the evening. They were expected to stay until every sequence of the entertainment was concluded, often not leaving until eight the following morning. To offend the Sun King in the most minor manner meant banishment. To be part of this exclusive society meant to have power, and families used every possible means to gain the favor of the king. An attractive daughter would be presented to the king in the hopes that she would be chosen as a mistress.

The rigors of life in the Versailles court were countless. The bedrooms of court guests were cramped and stuffy. Bathing facilities and their companion appurtenances were almost nonexistent. To be a member of Louis

XIV's inner circle took great physical stamina: the royal apartments, the dining hall, ballroom, and the chapel were separated by miles of long spacious halls. Simply going from one place to another took time and energy.

The course which costume design took during the Baroque period cannot be disassociated from the aesthetic considerations inherent in the art and architecture of the time. The mobile twisting and counter-twisting of human forms in sculpture, the plastic organization of the two-dimensional painting plane, and the complex interaction between pier and decorative embellishment of architecture visually embodied the intellectual and social movements rampant throughout this era.[9]

Art concepts of the fourteenth century influenced the styles, silhouettes, and decorations of that period. With greater impact, the art of the seventeenth century governed garment shapes and embellishments. Spanish reluctance to abandon accepted court fashions of the High Renaissance and the rejection of Spanish influence gave rise to two new nations as style pacesetters. France and Holland emerged as the two countries which set the fashion patterns of the seventeenth century. England, though politically powerful because of dominance at sea, had neither the exquisitely refined taste of France nor the affluence of Holland. The great costume creators of this age were Messieurs Regnault and Gautier, and Mesdames Charpentier and Villeneuve.

Germans, particularly young men, slavishly adopted French male fashions. In localities where princes, burghers, and commoners were affluent, class barriers delineated by garment fabrics and trims were obliterated. To maintain preeminence as tastemakers, the style-setting nobility altered fashions continually.

The major fashion change was the elimination of padded and rigid clothing. The harsh silhouettes in the styles of both sexes were relaxed. Fabrics were softer in hue and texture, and trimmed with laces of intricate complexity and innumerable bunches of ribbons (Figure 11.1). Women's clothing never became as lavish during this period as the garments of their male counterparts.

Fashions of the colonial settlements in North America were, to a great extent, duplicates of those worn in Europe. The degree of difference from European styles depended on the social status of the immigrants, religious concepts concerning personal adornment, and geographical and nationalistic variables. Climate and availability of materials dictated the weight and quality of the fabrics used.

Spanish colonizers of St. Augustine were required to import all of life's necessities from Spain so their garb closely followed Spanish fashion. The Louisiana colonists were less slavish in their adherence to high fashion because most women in particular were from peasant stock. In turn, the refugees from Canada who fled to the French colony on the Gulf of Mexico brought a distinctive costume. The British colonists of Virginia were eager to perpetuate the styles of the upper stratum of English society from whose ranks many had been drawn.[10] Dutch-dominated New Amsterdam continued to wear the stylish garb of successful burghers of the Netherlands, while religious concepts limited the splendor of dress in the Puritan settlements to a simple, uncluttered look. Processed deerskin provided a sturdy material for outer wear for westward-bound settlers of the New World.

Court costume for men became so decorative as to be almost effeminate. The "farthingale breeches," as some called the padded and bombasted breeches popular among the British, were greatly altered. Long, full-legged **pantaloons,** introduced in the 1630s, followed by **rhinegraves,** or **petticoat breeches,** in the 1660s, replaced the more formal wear for men. A soft, short-waisted doublet with deep, front-slash sleeves, sloppy pantaloons, full-sleeved shirts, and decorative capes dominated men's fashions for some years (Figure 11.2). In turn, the breeches were modified in the 1680s, the doublet lengthened, and the ruff totally replaced by a falling collar made of fine lawn or lace.

The introduction of the **periwig** brought about the demise of the ruff because of this hairstyle's excessive length and fullness. Louis XIII and Charles I began the

**Figure 11.2.** Children's clothes were exact copies of the garments worn by adults. This lad wears **petticoat breeches** bedecked with bunches, a short **justaucorps,** and a **beaver** hat. His costume is made more ponderous by an immense cape. (Redrawn from *Young Lord,* detail, Jan Van Noordt, 1665.)

fashion of the full wig, but it was under Louis XIV's domination of fashion and all visually related creativity, that the design of the male wig became increasingly flamboyant. Head coverings also varied, ranging from the tall-crowned, wide-brimmed **beaver** hat during the earlier decades, to the befeathered and braid-trimmed **tricorn** popular very late in the seventeenth century.

Shoes, once as decorative as the rest of the costume, became more serviceable at the close of this period. The large heels of the shoes worn by Louis XIV were sometimes decorated with scenes depicting his supposed military successes. Boots with oversized, crushed top cuffs were the badges of the seventeenth-century cavalier (Figure 11.3). Court shoes of satin and "rabbit-ear" bows were worn with silk hose. Oddly, pictorial records of the hose indicate that they fitted rather poorly, and wrinkled horizontally about the leg. Perhaps this was an affectation of flamboyant casualness, but more likely it resulted from the lack of technical skill needed to produce snug-fitting hose.

**Figure 11.3.** The nobleman's costume in the seventeenth century was flamboyant in its fullness rather than in its elegantly textured textiles. Here, the nobleman wears **pantaloons,** crushed-top boots, and a **justaucorps** with shoulder rolls and full, gathered sleeves. The segmented peplum is quite prominent in this illustration. (Detail from etching of the period.)

**Figure 11.4.** The **hurluberlu** coiffure was a characteristic hairstyle of the seventeenth century. Spanish women did not discard the **farthingale** as quickly as did ladies of other countries. (Velásquez: *Marianna of Austria,* mid-seventeenth century. Prado, Madrid.)

Women's gown styles altered as radically as men's fashions during the seventeenth century, although the first decades saw only slight modifications. The popular skirt support, the farthingale (Figure 11.4), creating a dome-, drum-, or cone-shaped silhouette, lasted through the first twenty years of this century. Many variations of the ruff persisted. A painting by Santvoort clearly illustrates the many versions of fashionable collars (Figure 11.5). Nationalistic styling was dominant through much of this period. The Spanish court held fast to the past, and the tightly corseted bodice and drum-shaped skirt were retained for many years. Vermeer's many paintings detail explicitly the Dutch feminine modes of the middle decades of the seventeenth century (Figure 11.6).

When men donned loose-fitting doublets, justaucorps, and full, floppy pantaloons, women discarded boned bodices with stomachers and farthingale-supported skirts. By mid-century, most female gowns were soft and unboned. Only Marie Thérèse of Spain, wife of Louis XIV, persisted in wearing the farthingale which spread out sideways. After 1630 the light bodice and stomacher disappeared. Thereafter the bodice and skirt were allowed to softly reveal the figure. The waistline was raised during

**Figure 11.5.** These figures illustrate the variety of costumes during the first years of the seventeenth century. The older woman on left clings to the **cartwheel,** or **millstone,** collar, while the younger women have adopted the falling collar made of handsome, delicate lace. The gentleman's short-waisted **doublet** is decorated with bunches at the waist and he wears lace hose cuffs, a falling lace collar, and lace sleeve cuffs. (D. Santvoort: *Burgomeister Dirk Bas Jacobs and His Family,* detail, 1635. Rijksmuseum, Amsterdam.)

this middle period and the sash, so popular as a male costume trim, was incorporated into women's gown styling. Generally a two-part costume, gowns worn during the 1630s and 1640s created an ample silhouette. The large puffy sleeves served to add more bulk to the figure.

Necklines varied from high, modestly modish styles with falling collars of lace or white lawn to those with deep décolletage set off by face-framing standing lace collars. When fall collars were worn, they created a pyramid effect with the head at the apex, and the lower collar edge at the base, falling to just above the bustline.

By 1640 the female outer dress was made in one piece and worn over innumerable petticoats. The trims of golden lace and fine white lace, braids, points, and bunches were as popular for women as for men. However, buttons, which were used on thigh seams of men's breeches and justaucorps as decorative devices in the 1640s, apparently were not as popular with women. The puffed, modified, three-quarter sleeves with wide cuffs of lace and the lace neck trim dominated the decorative elements on women's apparel. The gown overskirt, often slit in the center front, revealed an equally rich underskirt.

In the 1670s, radical changes occurred in female dress (Figure 11.7). The snug-fitting bodice reappeared and skirts were given width at the hips to accentuate the newly fashionable narrow waist. The waistline, which had been moderately high, dropped to the normal waist level. Hair fashions also changed as the scatterbrain, or **hurluberlu,** mode (Figure 11.4) was replaced by the ribbon bow *à la Fontanges* in the 1680s, and later by the **sultana.**[11] The Fontanges caps took many forms of pleated lace and ribbons, and each variation had a name which identified it.

**Figure 11.6.** Tab peplum **justaucorps** popular with the women of Delft during the early seventeenth century. Paning was still used at this time for male and female sleeve trims. The **cartwheel ruff** was beginning to be replaced by lace or fine lawn falling collars. (Redrawn from *Young Woman with Water Jug,* Vermeer, c. 1650.)

**Figure 11.7.** Female costumes after 1670 developed a slim silhouette with some fullness, created by side draping over the hips. (J. D. de Saint-Jean: *Woman Walking in the Country,* 1675. Bibliothèque Nationale, Paris.)

with upturned ends graced dapper males' upper lips, and the pointed Vandyke beards so popular early in the century had vanished.

Colors ranged from sombre, dignified black to buffs, pale pinks, blues, yellows, and startlingly brilliant reds. Lyons silks and brocades with polychrome brocaded decorations invaded the fashion scene late in this period. Braids, lace, and loops of brilliant silken ribbons amplified the opulence of costumes of this period. The variety of sleeves, skirts, bodices, and necklines which appeared in this century deserves a volume, for the plethora of adaptations to the basic silhouette was altered by personal whim and national origin. Adults and children of the upper classes were all duplicates of one another. No quarter was given to activity patterns of children by the prescribed fashions of this century (Figures 11.2 and 11.8).

**Figure 11.8.** This child's gown embodies all of the characteristics of its adult counterpart. It is styled with a lowcut, oval neckline; snug, three-quarter sleeves; and boned bodice. The skirt falls into a slender silhouette but has some back fullness and a modestly proportioned train. She also wears a **Fontanges** headdress. (Largillière: *James Stuart and His Sister,* detail, 1695. National Portrait Gallery, London.)

By the 1690s, women's gown skirts had lost their girth (Figure 11.8). Sleeves had diminished in size and fitted snugly to the elbow, finished at the edge with a gathered, ruffled cuff of lace. The outer-gown skirts were drawn to the back, parting in front to expose handsomely decorated underskirts. Often the outer gown was a plain, delicate color while the underskirt was made of striped silk in a contrasting color. This was the style when the Fontanges headgear was the mode. The poufs created by this type of skirt draping foreshadowed the panier-supported skirt silhouette of the next century.

Many portraits of the 1690s show women wearing tailored justaucorps or copies of men's long coats over slender skirts with modest trains. Although an offshoot of men's garments, these tailored suits were totally feminine for they conformed to the upper torso very tightly, thus revealing all the attributes of the female form.

Women heavily powdered their faces to achieve a fashionable creamy-white complexion. Black patches were placed strategically on cheeks and brows to accent the skin's whiteness and to draw attention to features the ladies felt were their best. Men also wore patches on their clean-shaven faces. In mid-century, small moustaches

Garments worn by both sexes during this century were numerous. Unlike previous periods, changes occurred rapidly after the padded and restrictive styles associated with the High Renaissance were discarded. In paintings of large groups of people, the variety of acceptable styles is most apparent. This sense of individuality was not carried into the next century. At least the individual garment styles are not as prevalent.

# Basic Garments of the Baroque (1600–1700)

## DOUBLET (1600–1620)

Male doublets during the early years of the seventeenth century (1600–1620), retained much the same appearance as those worn during the previous century. The peascod silhouette continued with the *à grandes assiettes*, or short peplum, made of several small

**Figure 11.9.** The intricate patterns of embroidery decorating this **doublet** are so boldly worked that they create the illusion of having been worked over a quilted pattern. Shoulder hoops carry out the design motif used on the bodice. (Peter Paul Rubens: *The Artist and His Wife, Isabella Brandt*, detail, 1610. Pinakothek, Munich.)

**Figure 11.10.** Both functional and decorative, **aiguillettes** were used extensively during the first third of the seventeenth century. (F. Elle: *Henri II of Lorraine*, detail, 1631. Museum, Rheims.)

truncated sections accenting the small waist. The shoulder line was extended by crescent-shaped epaulettes. These crescent-shaped attachments were worn with pendant sleeves and sewn into the top of the armseye. They were often called **shoulder rolls**, or **shoulder hoops** (Figure 11.9). Embroidery trims of gold bedecked the doublet bodice, and the lines frequently were arranged in a V-pattern with the apex ending at the waistline. This *V* motif further served to broaden the shoulders and minimize the waist girth. Sleeves of doublets from 1600 to 1616 were snug, following the shape of the arm and finished with large funnel-shaped cuffs of handsome and delicate lace. A variety of lace-collar styles, including the ruff, cartwheel ruff, de' Medici, or soft cartwheel ruff without an underproper, were used to frame the face. The doublet and collar of this fashion were called the Spanish doublet or the French doublet.

There was a gradual change in the cut of the pourpoint, or doublet, from 1620 to 1630. The padding slowly disappeared as did the snug sleeves. The formal rigidity of the pourpoint was softened and the broadness at the shoulders was reduced. The skirts of the doublet were lengthened in front, the waistline was raised, and at the waist were positioned a series of evenly spaced holes.

Tapes or ribbons (bunches) with metal tips called **aiguillettes** (points) were threaded through corresponding holes in the breeches and tied into bows on the outside of the doublet (Figure 11.10). These bows became part of the ever more flamboyant costuming decorations of the seventeenth-century male garments.

If the embroidery embellishments were eliminated from the doublet, a heavily embroidered cape known as the **galler,** or **collet,** was added. Doublet sleeves also became more fanciful. They were often slashed from shoulder to cuff and lined with satin or brocade in colors which contrasted with the color of the doublet fabric. Many of these short doublets had small standing collars. At this time the doublet body, peplum, sleeves, and collar often were trimmed with gold braid instead of embroidery. Silk fabrics worked into quilted patterns also were used in place of brocade as a decorative motif for the male doublet (Figure 11.11).

## DOUBLET (1620–1650)

The loosely fitted doublet of the early seventeenth century was unpadded. It was designed with wrist-length sleeves, slightly puffed and slashed; a rather tall-standing, tight collar; and a front closure fastened with closely spaced, round buttons. When this garment was

**Figure 11.12.** This gentleman wears a fur-trimmed **justaucorps,** or long doublet, **Venetians en bourse,** and a broad-brimmed, plumed **beaver** hat. (Callot: *La Noblesse,* detail, seventeenth-century engraving.)

designed with a normal waistline, it often had a snug band section around the rib cage and a tab peplum. Later it was styled with a very short, square waist and a peplum that was shallow at the hips, extending into a deep *V* in the center front. Later the high collar was eliminated and the peplum was lengthened and made of trapezoidal sections arranged to overlap one another. The sleeves of the later variations of the doublet were large bishop sleeves; gathered full sleeves with deep, tight cuffs; or paned, gathered sleeves. Many times, arm-length slashes bordered with braid revealed the full bishop sleeves of the linen shirt beneath.

In the evolution of the doublet, it became a hip-length coat, with the skirt silhouette a truncated triangle.[12] This **long doublet** (c. 1670), was worn fastened at the neck with the fronts falling open in an inverted *V* (Figure 11.12). The sleeves were amply cut with slashes, points and bunches, or paned trims. More often, however, it was a serviceable rather than a decorative coat.

The **justaucorps** (1660–1690), was a decorative outer garment much like the long doublet (Figures 11.13 and 11.20). It was first designed with elbow-length sleeves slashed from the shoulder to the hem. They were

**Figure 11.11. Shoulder rolls,** or shoulder hoops, had somewhat diminished in size by the time this olive green, quilted **doublet** had been designed. (Actual garment, c. 1630-1640).

**Figure 11.13.** Near the close of the seventeenth century, the **justaucorps** sleeves were shortened and the body section lengthened. The bishop sleeves of the shirt were often tied with ribbons at the elbow. The ribbon loop **la braye** on the **Venetians en bourse** continued in use as a breeches closure. (Redrawn from C. Köhler, *A History of Costume*, c. 1650-1660.)

elaborately trimmed with ribbon fringe, and **points** and **bunches,** which were the typical decorations of the period composed of ribbon streamers with metal tips, ribbon rosettes, and lace or braid. The justaucorps gradually lengthened to the calf and was worn over a full linen or lawn shirt, veste, and flared breeches. There were slits or vents in the side seams, allowing this shapeless coat to cover the petticoat breeches.

The **veste** replaced the doublet late in the century. Worn as an accessory, it was often made of silk brocade or other rich fabrics that matched the justaucorps. At first it had narrow sleeves matching the fronts, and the back was made of linen. In time the sleeves were omitted.

The **rochet** was a very short bolero jacket with elbow-length sleeves similar to those of the justaucorps. It was square in silhouette, with a round, collarless neckline buttoned or tied at the throat beneath the large, falling lace collar characteristic of the period. This decorative, abbreviated jacket was trimmed with looped ribbon fringe or points and bunches around the hem, at the shoulders, and on the sleeves. The rochet was worn either in the normal fashion or tossed casually over one shoulder.

## BREECHES (1600–1700)

Male **breeches** developed into many ridiculous and strange forms during this century. The puffed Venetians of the sixteenth century continued or returned to vogue as **grègues**, which were pants forms made of two pear-shaped pieces covering the body from the waist to the lower thigh. **Pantaloon breeches,** or **Venetians *en bourse*,** (without padding) were also popular early in this century (1630). These were full and baggy, calf length or ankle length, and worn with the garment legs hanging loose or stuffed into boot tops (Figure 11.13).

**Petticoat breeches,** or **rhinegraves,** were one of the excessive styles of male attire during the seventeenth century (Figure 11.14). The legs were made with deep pleats or by gathering long lengths of fabric to form two shapeless tubes. At one time they appeared to be a skirt worn over puffed, padded, lace-trimmed upper hose, with the lace showing below the rhinegraves. The petticoat breeches were fully lined and were decorated with points and bunches or looped ribbon fringe around the waist, down the sides, and around the leg hems. Deep ruffles were also added at the waist and leg hems as an embellishment. The breeches' closure, *la braye*, was created by arranging ribbon fringe to form an inverted triangle where the two legs met.

**Knee breeches,** rather ill fitting at first, were introduced after 1680. They were gathered to a waistband and held tightly around the knees with a buttoned or buckled band. The front closure of the knee breeches was fastened

**Figure 11.14.** Male **habit** including **petticoat breeches** and short **doublet** with bunches at the hem. (Actual garments, c. 1660. Victoria and Albert Museum, London.)

with large decorative buttons which were elegant trimmings and functional closing devices.[13] Later the **bavaroise** *(la braye)* was buttoned unobtrusively with a set of small buttons, three on each side of this flap-type closing.

## LONG COAT (1680)

The **long coat** for men, which replaced the justaucorps when knee breeches were introduced around 1680, was a slope-shouldered coat with knee-length or calf-length skirts (Figure 11.15). It was made with a cardigan neckline or high, round neckline and was fastened with buttons and buttonholes set closely together on the straight edges of the front. The sleeves of this coat were of modest size with wide, deep cuffs elegantly trimmed with braid. The **waistcoat** of matching fabric, first with, and later without, sleeves, replaced the veste.

**Figure 11.15.** Male promenade costume of the late seventeenth century includes the **long coat,** feather-trimmed **tricorn,** knee **breeches,** hose, neckcloth, muff accessory, and hose with embroidered clocks. (Redrawn from *Male Costumes,* etching, Bonnart, 1693-1695. Bibliothèque Nationale, Paris.)

**Figure 11.16.** Gown styles varied little for some time after the turn of the century. The **cartwheel ruff,** modified **stomacher,** and bell-shaped skirt continued in fashion. Ruffs were not always white. This one is a dusky olive green in the original. (Van Dyke: *Duchess Doria,* 1625. Louvre, Paris.)

## SHIRT (1600–1700)

The men's shirt was made with a full body section; long, voluminous bishop sleeves; and lace, or lace-and-ruffle, cuffs extending over the hand. The sleeves and high, round neckline were trimmed with lace. The styles of shirt collars ranged from the large, cartwheel ruff to the beautifully made, shoulder-covering lace collar, to the square, lawn collar that covered the chest in front and the shoulder blades in back. The shirt sleeves were often bound with ribbon and tied with points and bunches for additional decoration. This was a popular arrangement during the height of the rochet and rhinegraves fashion. Many of these super-embellishments were discarded when the long coat was introduced with the cravat neck trim and the wide, waist-encircling sash with deep fringed ends.

## GOWNS (1600–1700)

Women's gowns during the seventeenth century were known by a variety of descriptive names, including: *friponnes, déshabillées, negligées, innocentes, battantes, robes de chambre,* and *manteaux.* The **manteau** was a rich, elegant, two-part dress. Gowns had changed radi-

**Figure 11.17.** The boned bodice had totally disappeared by the 1640s, though the head-framing lace collar persisted. This gown is made of eggshell white satin trimmed with lace made of golden thread. (M. C. Hiert: Margareth Bromsen, detail, 1641. Saint Anne Museum, Lübeck.)

cally in style from those of the sixteenth century, and the *manteau* with its soft lines was typical. The farthingale had disappeared by 1640, as had some of the firm corseting. The stomacher became part of the bodice, but for a time remained stiff and pointed (Figure 11.16). The bodice was short-waisted and slightly fitted, with a tabbed or slashed peplum (Figure 11.17). Decorations included a soft fall ruff, the cartwheel ruff, or other collars similar to those worn by men. Deep, turned-back lace cuffs trimmed sleeves that were slashed, padded, and puffed. The full, billowing *manteau* skirt was slit in front, revealing through the inverted *V* an underskirt of elegant silk. The gown was heavily decorated with swags of gathered ruffles, or ***prétintailles***—motifs cut out of different colored materials and appliquéd to the front of the gown—on the skirt, at the waist, and on the sleeves, which were also bound with points and bunches at many places along the arms, creating double or multipuffed sleeves. The neckline, high and round in the early decades of the Baroque period, changed to a rectangular shape about mid-century.

The gown of the 1680s later became more firmly corseted, and the farthingale skirt support of rather small

proportions was reintroduced. The bodice waistline was lengthened, and pointed in front and back. The extreme décolletage of the plunging neckline was often masked by a ruching of gauze or lace. The bodice, which was either pleated or gathered, appears to have remained separate from the full, bouffant skirt. In this period the skirt was drawn back from the center front opening, draped into large puffs, and held back with bunches of ribbon rosettes. The *manteau* gown characteristically had a long train throughout most of this period.

Unlike the *manteau*, the ***déshabillée*** and ***robe de chambre***, which were worn by elegant ladies in their homes, were designed with the skirt and bodice sewn together, or "cut in one piece" (Figure 11.18). They were loose fitting and had floor-sweeping skirts. The *robe de chambre* was said to have been designed by Madam de Montespan, an actress, to camouflage her pregnancy.[14]

**Figure 11.18. Robe de chambre** and **Fontanges** of the late seventeenth century. (Redrawn from sketch by Watteau, c. 1690.)

## JUSTAUCORPS (1600–1700)

For added warmth, women wore the **justaucorps**, or brief peplum jacket, with a center front closure and narrow sleeves. The sleeves had a cuff, often of swansdown, one of the many types of decorative trims used during this period. A cloak, or short cape with detachable hood called a **mantilla**, was often worn indoors and in the garden at home. It was made of a variety of fabrics. The pattern used was four quarter segments of a circle. A drawstring cord at the neck was used to close it snugly around the throat. The justaucorps and the mantilla added to the bulky and rotund silhouette typical of the middle years of this century.

Toward the end of the seventeenth century (c. 1650–1690), women chose to wear an adaptation of the male **long coat.** Sometimes referred to as the justaucorps, this garment and the accompanying skirt were perhaps one of the first sportswear costumes. Doubtless used for riding to the hounds, such a costume was not only more practical than the multiskirted *manteau*, but also provided more comfort when horseback riding on a hunt.

## UNDERGARMENTS (1600–1700)

The **jupe**, another name for underdress, was a handsome garment made of rich fabrics embroidered with silver and gold. The skirt of the jupe, visible through the V-opening of the gown skirt, became more important to the total gown design when the fashion of back-draping the overskirt came into vogue around 1690. The bodice, overgown skirt, and jupe should be considered the three elements that constituted the entire formal costume for women. The jupe skirt was often trimmed to match the overgown decorations.

During part of this century, the farthingale was replaced by wearing several petticoats beneath the gown and jupe to hold the skirt in the desired bouffant shape. As many as eight or ten underskirts were worn at a time. Although considered underwear, these billowing, gathered halfslips were decorated with ruffles and bows, all of which helped to add girth to the overskirt.

The *friponne*, worn about the home with the justaucorps, was also used as an underdress. It had a full, gathered skirt designed with a train and was worn as an underskirt in the last part of the century.

# Accessories (1600–1700)

## HEADWEAR

The high-crowned **beaver** hat was a luxurious male accessory of the seventeenth century (Figures 11.12 and 11.21). Though called beaver, the hats were made of taffeta, velvet, and "hair of particular fine quality." It is believed they first developed in Florence sometime during

**Figure 11.19.** Early in the seventeenth century, women affected tall-crowned hats patterned after gentlemen's **beaver** hats. (Peter Paul Rubens: *The Artist and His Wife, Isabella Brandt,* detail, 1610. Pinakothek, Munich.)

the previous century. These hats were costly, greatly admired, and considered an important part of the male wardrobe. They were so highly valued that they were packed into specially designed boxes when not in use and were willed to favored heirs on the death of the original owners. Samuel Pepys, the inveterate chronicler of the day, recorded that in such a way he received a hat which was valued at four pounds and five shillings, an impressive sum at that time.

Hats were worn indoors as well as out. They were decorated with great flowing plumes when worn by cavaliers or left extremely plain when worn by Puritans. These elegant and colorful broad-brimmed hats were an important part of a gentleman's posturing pattern. When "making a leg" (a deep, solicitous bow), the hat was swept from the head in an eloquent, practiced gesture. Between 1625 and 1640, the brim was rolled up on the side or in the front and held in this jaunty position by a clasp. A great feather was stuck into the roll, its long fringed elegance cascading over the wearer's shoulder. It was an honor to be permitted to retain one's hat in the presence of royalty, but few were accorded this privilege.

Women wore hats of similar shapes and trims during the early 1600s (Figure 11.19). Later, to accommodate fuller and more fanciful coiffures, women covered their heads with a simple hood or shawl with the ends tied loosely under their chins. One version of hood that appeared during the last third of the century combined a frilled cap with a hood. The cap section was often made of gossamer fabric trimmed with lace, contrasting colored silk, or even fur.

## FOOTWEAR

Shoes for men and women became important costume accessories during this century. This was especially true for women during part of the century because, for the first time, a woman's feet were somewhat exposed beneath her skirts. The raised heel continued in fashion and eventually became a large, clumsily shaped piece placed well back under the foot. The top piece covered the entire foot, with a broad square tongue covering the instep and extending a little beyond the curve of the foot at the ankle. The shoe was latched or tied over the instep with straps formed by extensions of the heel-covering fabric. Brocades, embroidered velvets, and fine leathers were used in making the shoe uppers. Square toes; ribbon ties through A-shaped instep straps; wide shoe bows with lace ends; "shoe roses," large ribbon pompoms; and "rabbit-ear bows," often twelve inches in breadth, were some of the features of shoes in this century.

Ladies of the court wore **mules,** high-heeled slippers with closed toe straps and fur trimming added to brocade fabric. Heels and soles, often colored red, were used on men's and women's footwear. The feminine **pump** was designed with an oversized tab that covered the instep and rose to ankle level.

Men's high boots with long, large leg-covering sections, were worn with the pantaloons. The tops of these boots were worn crushed down, with large, floppy cuffs folded over them. Over the boot cuff was worn a large lace ruffle which was either the hose cuff or a separate item.

Pattens and **pantoffles,** or heeled scuffs, were used as footwear and shoe protectors during inclement weather.

Hose were important to the male costume. They were made of linen with large lace cuffs, or of silk fiber knitted into smooth-fitting leg coverings. The latter were often embroidered with "clocks," decorative patterns extending from the ankle to the calf.

## NECKWEAR

Neckwear was modified with changes in the general costume. The cartwheel ruff and the large lace collar disappeared after the introduction of the periwig and the long coat.

The legend of the necktie's origin had its beginning in the seventeenth century. At this time, all members of a certain Croatian regiment, from the lowest soldier to the highest ranking officer, wrapped narrow scarves around their necks several times to fend off the slashing blows of the enemy's sword. When the regiment visited Paris, the cosmopolitan French were enchanted by the dashing ap-

pearance they presented. The style was adopted as a novel neck accessory which the French dubbed **cravat** from the term *cravates* used to identify the regiment. Soon the fall collar with neckband and tabs gave way to this innovative style.

In 1684 the cravat was again modified because of the wearing arrangements created by military personnel. The sudden and unexpected victory of the French at the Battle of Steinkirk caught the officers of the conquering regiment unawares. Unable to complete their elaborate toilettes, which included the meticulous wrapping of their cravats, they hastily put them around their necks, twisted the ends and tucked them through the buttonholes of their military jackets to secure the loose-hanging ends. This new wearing style was called the **steinkirk** and was quickly adopted by men and even by some women (Figure 11.20).

The unstarched, gathered **falling ruff** replaced the stiff cartwheel ruff after the death of Henry IV in 1610. This style and that of the semicircular, supported **carcan** (collar) remained in vogue until the reign of Louis XIV.

**Falling collars** (c. 1620–1640), made from squares of lawn, linen, or lace were designed to closely encircle the throat (Figure 11.21). They were tied at the neck with

**Figure 11.20.** The **justaucorps,** destined to become the suit or **habit** coat in the eighteenth century, was usually collarless when first introduced as a male outer garment. The **periwig** was excessively curly and the neck trim was the **Steinkirk.** (Redrawn from *Male Costumes,* etching, Bonnart, 1693-1695. Bibliothèque Nationale, Paris.)

silken cords finished with small tassels. Several examples of this style of neckwear are in the Costume Institute of the Metropolitan Museum of Art, New York. Sumptuous laces were used in making these neck trims worn by the nobility and upper classes. Venetian lace was the most highly prized lace of the many types produced during this period. Matching cuffs were also a necessary costume accessory.

After the succession of Louis XIV, the design of the falling collar was again altered, with the fronts becoming longer and the sections covering the shoulders shorter. This style of collar was tied under the chin by two or four tassel-trimmed cords. In general, during Louis XIV's reign, the falling collar was less elegant even when used by the nobility. Plain linen or lace-edged lawn were the two most often used materials. Matching cuffs, or **rebras**, were folded back over the justaucorps sleeves.

The **tab collar** was introduced into the male toilette some time after 1633. When he began to get bald, Louis XIV established the fad of wearing huge wigs which concealed the elegant falling collars. An obvious solution was the plain linen or lace-tab neck trim. These were worn high on the neck, tied with tassel-trimmed cords, and

**Figure 11.21.** Puritanical concepts influenced seventeenth-century Dutch modes. Stalwart burghers dressed in somber black **justaucorps** and **plunder hose.** The tall-crowned, broad-brimmed **beaver** hat was a symbol of status. Lace-edged falling collars and lace-trimmed, turned-back funnel cuffs were the only concessions to elegant decoration. (Frans Hals: *Portrait of a Man,* seventeenth century. Metropolitan Museum of Art, New York City.)

were no wider than the wearer's neck. A more narrow type was used by clerics and dubbed *petit collet*.

The **fan collar** worn by women, so typically pictured in portraits of Elizabeth I, continued in vogue from 1590 until about 1640. A **flat collar** which revealed much of the upper breast replaced the fan style of neck trim. A soft knotted kerchief often was worn with the flat collar. At first the kerchief was an ample square, folded diagonally and knotted demurely. Later it became a more provocative trim which accented the deep décolletage.

## JEWELRY

Earrings of pearls and gold, and the **earstring** were worn by men and women. The earstring, a silk thread with a ribbon rosette, was worn through one pierced ear only, dangling down for some length.[15] Ear pendants were highly prized baubles of precious jewels and metals. Charles I, as he dressed for his execution, carefully selected the earrings he would wear on his last day. Before he laid his head on the block, he removed each one with care and handed them to an attendant for safekeeping. Necklaces were extremely simple during this period of elaborate costumes and hairstyles. A single strand of pearls was preferred. Rings were also out of favor, though simple gold bands or gold rings with a single, small stone were worn on either the ring or index finger.

**Patches** of taffeta cut in star, crescent, and circular shapes were coyly pasted on the cheeks of men and women. These bits of black became the fashion late in the century and were to become a cosmetic necessity. At the height of their fashion, patches were made into intricate forms—ships in full sail, animals, and other more eccentric shapes. Because a patch was apt to fall off during an evening of revelry in court, a small, silver box full of replacements was carried. Patch boxes were fitted with tiny mirrors, a compartment for the extra patches, and a place for the adhesive needed to attach them to the face. The church, always with a wary eye on fashion excesses, failed once again to control costuming. The edict concerning patches did not eliminate the fad, and they continued in style for some decades.

## HANDHELD ACCESSORIES

Small feather fans with repoussé handles of gold; silken pouch bags with silk-cord drawstrings, used primarily for carrying missals to mass; and muffs were some of the handheld accessories of this period. The muffs used by women were small at first, while those worn by men were immense fur pieces (Figure 11.15). They were attached to a large silk sash and hung down in front of the body when not used to warm the hands.

## BODY SUPPORTS

Early in the seventeenth century, corseting was an integral part of the garment. The **corps piqué** was a firmly boned bodice, usually lined with heavy linen. The **gourgandine** was also an outer bodice stiffened with reed staves. For a brief time during the Baroque period, little or no figure-controlling support was used. Toward the end of the century, however, when gowns were again designed with small, longer waistlines, the metal corset with inside padding, shoulder straps tied or buttoned to the front panel, and hooks or laces in back was again worn. These metal prisons flattened the bust and the stomach. Full breasts were not fashionable, and little girls were strapped into tight-fitting bands that held lead plates over their breasts to retard development.

# Hairstyles (1600–1700)

The coiffure styles of the ladies of the seventeenth century were many and varied. At the turn of the century, the hair was braided and arranged into a pug or bun. In 1625 the hair was arranged into a pyramidal shape by parting it in the center and puffing it out about the head. It was tightly waved or frizzed and extended to the greatest distance from the head at ear level. After the puffed styles came a series of ringlet coifs called the **hurluberlu,** or scatterbrain (1630), a scatter of bunched curls from a center part; the **hurlupe,** a similar arrangement; *à la Fontanges,* or duchess (1680), in which the hair was piled into two peaks from a center part and decorated with ribbons and a pleated hair accessory; and the **sultana,** a tall puff over the forehead draped with a scarf or ribbon bows.

The Fontanges was supposed to have been created when the wind played havoc with the coiffure of a lady of the French court. In haste she tried to remedy the damage by catching up her loose curls with a garter of ribbons, to the immediate delight of the king.[16] The Fontanges style was in vogue from 1678 to 1701, despite criticism and later royal disfavor. **Fontanges caps** with a lace peak in front and, in some versions, a small cap covering the back of the head, were made in many ways and had many names, such as: *effronte,* revealing the ears; *guigne-galants,* worn with curls on the forehead; *guepes,* with precious stones in the hair; and *palissade,* a wide form, tilted forward (Figure 11.18).

For some time men wore their hair loose, long, and waved. This natural style may have been a reaction to more formal styles. During the reign of Louis XIII, formally arranged coiffures for men were again fashionable. Hair was combed from a center part and brushed into curls that fell over the shoulders. One lock was brushed forward and called the **moustache,** until the Duc de Luynes conceived the idea of tying it with a ribbon decorated with a precious gem. This added embellishment and the lock of hair were then called a **cadenette.**

Wigs became popular after Louis XIV lost his hair because of a severe illness. Wigs became long, flamboyant, and elaborate headpieces. Different styles of wigs included: the **peruke,** a formal, elaborately curled wig; the **periwig,** less formal and somewhat less curly (Figure 11.20); and the **campaign wig,** with twisted side pieces tied at the ends. Of the later style Rondle Holmes wrote in *Academy of Armor,* "... this wig is knots and blobs, a dildo or corkscrew on each side with a curled forehead."

Heated clay pipes were used to curl the hair. Elaborate and complex styles developed as wigs increased in popularity. One of these consisted of two tall, curly peaks on either side of the center part, with two "full-bottomed" side pieces and a back section that fell well below the shoulder blades. Powdering the wigs became the fashion about 1690.

Keeping the wig properly styled was a time-consuming task that required special care. It was first brushed, then pomaded, and finally powdered with white talc. Hair for wig making was in such demand that small street urchins were waylaid and "snatched bald." Even horsehair was used by wigmakers to meet the demands for wigs. The wig was worn over a shaved head for proper fit, but no attempt was made to conceal the fact that a person was wearing a wig. Combing and attending to the wig in public was an accepted practice, a proper activity according to the etiquette of the day. It was done with handsome combs and with great finesse.

FOOTNOTES
1. C. V. Wedgwood, *The World of Rubens,* p. 8.
2. Charles Blitzer, *Age of Kings,* pp. 43–49.
3. Ibid., p. 42.
4. Canon Residentiary John E. W. Wallis, *Litchfield Cathedral,* p. 20.
5. Kenneth Clark, *Civilisation,* p. 201.
6. Blitzer, *Ages of Kings,* p. 56.
7. Mila Contini, *Fashion: From Ancient Egypt to the Present Day,* pp. 152–53.
8. Blitzer, *Age of Kings,* pp. 19–29.
9. Raymond Somers Stites, *The Arts and Man,* p. 641.
10. Elisabeth McClellan, *History of American Costume,* p. 57.
11. François Boucher, *20,000 Years of Fashion,* pp. 262–63.
12. Ibid., p. 261.
13. Carl Köhler, *A History of Costume,* p. 298.
14. Boucher, *20,000 Years of Fashion,* p. 261.
15. Katherine Lester and Bess Oerke, *Accessories of Dress,* p. 263.
16. Boucher, *20,000 Years of Fashion,* p. 262.

# Chapter 12
# Elegance of the Enlightened Age
# (1700–1795)

**Figure 12.1.** This graceful **robe volante,** adapted to the English mode, has a deep semioval neckline and snug sleeves with cascading lace cuffs. The towering coiffure is powdered and combines natural hair in front with back and neck curls made by a wig maker. (Gainsborough: *Mrs. Grace Dalrymple Elliott,* c. 1770. Metropolitan Museum of Art, New York City.)

The eighteenth century was to produce more dramatic social and political changes than had occurred in the preceding ten centuries. The political situations in Europe involved much of the known world. England, Spain, and France had established colonies in the western hemisphere, and wars broke out between them in an effort to gain more territory. Frederick the Great of Prussia perpetrated a military struggle between the countries on the European continent. Marquis Joseph Dupleix, the French colonial administrator in India, attempted to seize an Asiatic empire for France. Peter the Great began the westernization of Russia after attempting to gain access to warm-water ports from the Black Sea to the Baltic Sea. In 1748 England succeeded in defeating France in the French and Indian Wars, the North American conflict related to the Seven Years' War in Europe. In what some historians have called the prelude to "The Second Hundred Years' War," battles were fought on many fronts in Asia, Africa, America, and Europe. Conflict finally ended in 1815 with the Battle of Waterloo when Britain again was victorious. Colonial wars and the American and French revolutions were part of the historic picture of this period that was to shape so many enduring social attitudes.

The intellectual ferment that had begun during the Renaissance continued in the eighteenth century. The Age of Reason expanded the European mind, as humanity enlarged its geographical horizons by exploration, conquest, and increased colonization. The political attitudes of the middle class during this century were influenced by John Locke, Jean Jacques Rousseau, and François Voltaire. Their writings, widely read in the English colonies of America, influenced colonists to perceive the feasibility of freedom from England.

During the Age of Enlightenment and Reason, many people at all social levels studied with renewed interest the concepts of individual freedom and democracy, first introduced by the ancient Greeks. Writers, philosophers, and other intellectuals often gathered in salons established by elegant ladies of the upper class. Here they discussed and refined new concepts of individual rights long before the American Revolution. By 1789, spurred by the courage of revolutionaries in the New World, these concepts were put to test in France.

The bloody and opulent years of the seventeenth century ushered in the Age of Enlightenment. Scientists carefully had examined the material world with new instruments and inquisitive minds. New theories developed from observations and culminated in new basic laws of biology, astronomy, physics, optics, and geology. Isaac Newton's theory of gravitation was but one of the scientific discoveries which would dominate the discipline of

181

physics for the next 200 years. Hooke and van Leeuwenhoek invented and refined the microscope. Pascal introduced the first mechanical calculating device. Astronomers, mathematicians, and inquisitive men of medicine projected concepts ranging from capillary circulation in the lungs to a method for determining a tree's age. Halley accurately predicted the reappearance of the comet that bears his name, while Hevelius explored the moon's surface through the multilens telescope he perfected. In the seventeenth century, people had turned from the dogmatic rationale of nature established by the church and Aristotelian theories to the true study of nature via scientifically provable practices.

Encouraged by Louis XIV, great strides had been made in the arts. Visual teaching aids of churchly doctrine, created by devout artists and commissioned by patrons of the religious hierarchy, were supplanted by more worldly images under the patronage of kings with the divine right to rule. On the continent, Dutch and Italian painters had reigned as visual recorders of the previous century.

England had gained prominence in literature, increased its political power, and prospered financially. The tide of political and aesthetic dominance had turned with the expulsion of James II in 1689. Social stability increased under William and Mary. The Golden Age of England was firmly established when London superceded Amsterdam as the world's trade center. The people's confidence in England's world position brought peace at home and an end to the bloody political struggles of the preceding century. England grew richer in material

wealth under two kings of German origin, George I and George II. George I, who had a totally Germanic outlook, was a constitutional monarch who was installed to reign upon the death of Queen Anne in 1714. The increase in wealth stimulated a new interest in cultural matters and a desire for improved education.

In France, belief in the divine right to rule diminished with the death of Louis XIV in 1715. The aging monarch had experienced the defeat of the French troops by Marlborough at Blenheim in 1704. In 1713, two years before his death, the Peace of Utrecht had ended the War of the Spanish Succession and had altered the entire political character of Europe.

In the early stages of the eighteenth century, the European social system was not much changed. The great English painter and printmaker, William Hogarth, recorded the social patterns of his time. As a visual commentator, full of morality and contempt for the life-style of commoner and aristocrat alike, he accurately depicted people's attitudes toward themselves and their ways of enjoying life. Hogarth's allegorical, moralizing etchings fascinated the Londoners of his time, and they reveled in his caustic visual commentaries.

Unlettered and unwanted, orphaned or illegitimate urban youth fended for themselves while others worked in fabric mills or mines. In this period of a highly stratified class structure, marriages were arranged for the social advancement of one family or the other. The hardworking youth sought the hand of the mill owner's daughter. To secure shaky finances, titled gentry bargained for the hand of a wealthy merchant's daughter. Merchants threw

**Figure 12.2.** Modes, manners, and morals of the eighteenth century were faithfully recorded by William Hogarth. (Hogarth: *The Toilet, Scenes from Marriage a'Mode,* mid-eighteenth century. Metropolitan Museum of Art, New York City.)

their daughters at the sons of aristocrats in hopes of gaining a titled grandchild. With a title went social status and great holdings of land. The banking and mercantile classes as well as newly created baronettes—the title awarded to generals for successful military campaigns—put into force a new, vigorous society. Royal and noble lines were strengthened by marrying into the rising middle class. The wealthy upper class built impressive townhouses and imitated the life-style of the aristocracy and nobility. It was a vigorous time, full of corruption in high and low places. The poignancy of "cottage life," drawn by Gainsborough, is an innocent contrast to the recorded urbanity in Hogarth's London etchings (Figure 12.2).

The politics of the age might be summarized by stating that continental governments were controlled by enlightened despots. In Spain the new Bourbon dynasty offered the hope of revival of that nation's supremacy. A shift in the ruling house meant a shift in trade centers, and Spain opted for the market of the New World.

Italy, on the other hand, experienced a severe decline beginning during the latter decades of the seventeenth century. The population, which had diminished by a third, was overtaxed and politically and economically impatient. Young men were unable to find vocations, save in the service of the church. Perhaps the most far-reaching consequence of the papal authority in Italy was the suppression of the Society of Jesus. These former champions of the pope's omnipresent control over the life-style of this ravaged land had sustained the old inherited order of nobility. The age-old suppression of learning by censorship of the classics had greatly affected Italian educational advances. Invasions and constant interference by foreign sovereigns had robbed Italy of a sense of nationalism. Authors and musicians delved into this problem with satirical prose and operas that, in turn, subtly affected the common people. Because of the efforts of Italy's creative minds, attitudes were altered, but Italians generally maintained loyalty to their hometowns and cities. In Italy the eighteenth century was an age of pessimism, not an age of enlightenment or reason.

Before King Louis XIV died in 1715, his position in the hearts and minds of those over whom he had reigned had reversed. Once called "the most loved," he was quickly forgotten after his death. In his last years, Louis XIV had turned from his old ways of joyful, zestful licentiousness to pious behavior and had worn only black clothes. The style he had set for his court, which had been imitated by all of Europe's upper classes, no longer seemed relevant.

The Regency period which followed was given form by the Duke of Orleans. Uncle of the five-year-old King Louis XV, the Duke had wit and intelligence and had been reared in a time when France led the world culturally, socially, and politically. While he was regent for Louis XV, there was a return to the gaiety of the past. Artists again influenced manners and social graces via the pictorial statements they created.

Jean Antoine Watteau (1684-1721) was chief among the French artists who set the style for the time, and he not only dictated manners but actually established the silhouettes for court gowns. His paintings, grouped under the title *fêtes galantes*, were pictorial manifestations of his prodigiously creative talent and were faithfully copied in real life by members of the court. Life was no less immoral, but the licentiousness was indulged in with style and elegance.

The Age of Enlightenment in England was equally concerned with festive activities and comfort-oriented amusements. Unlike France, burdened with inflation as a result of the introduction of paper money, the English commercial and financial position was sound. Although some financial speculation had gone afoul, for the most part, affluence was maintained.

The old Roman town of Bath became the social center for the ruling classes of prosperous England, and the affluent indulged themselves and "took the waters" in the spa there. The once sleepy village was suddenly a resort town for the first time since the Roman occupation.

Hundreds of elegant houses were built on "crescent" or "circus" streets stretching from the center city into the countryside. These soundly built structures were designed with neoclassic facades. There was a renewed interest in the Greek and Roman Classical periods because of the discovery of Pompeiian ruins by eighteenth-century archaeological expeditions; this interest permeated architectural design.

Each day visitors to Bath, clad in cumbersome bathing attire, went to sit in formal pools of hot (100°) water. Some came for health reasons, but more came because it was fashionable. After steeping in the ill-smelling waters while wearing so many layers of clothing that they scarcely got wet, the guests retired to the Pump Room. Here, sipping glasses of mineral water, they exchanged gossip which became more exaggerated with each telling. Nightly entertainments revolved around the expansive banquets, at which many overate, and the balls held in the Assembly Rooms. The fad of Bath faded in 1811 when the then English Prince of Wales and regent established Brighton as the fashionable spa in Southdown.

During most of the eighteenth century, England was ruled by Hanoverian kings. Electors of Hanover, George I and George II, were more concerned with their German domain than with matters of Great Britain. Neither was popular in England, and the Jacobites, supporters of the old Stuart pretender, James Francis Edward, attempted to replace George I. However, Sir Robert Walpole, a Whig, established the Hanoverian family firmly on the British throne through his wise foreign and domestic policies. George I was succeeded by his son, George II, in 1727, and Britain became sound in material matters. Though never popular, George II won the admiration of the English because of his conduct in the War of the Austrian Succession. During his reign the Jacobian rebellion was quelled and the Seven Years' War successfully concluded.

George III ascended the throne following the death of his grandfather, George II, in 1760. Though English born and trained, he lacked intelligence and wisdom, and he was no more popular than his grandfather. Blindness and insanity brought him down in 1820, but not before he had provoked the American colonists into the American Revolution. Under his royal authority, England fought France between 1793 and 1815 in wars that developed out of the French Revolution.

Louis XVI, born at Versailles, was the grandson of Louis XV. He came to the throne of France in 1774, a time of great French travail. Economically impoverished, with the population burdened by heavy taxation, Louis XVI managed some reforms. Wise counselors aided him, but these efforts fell short of complete political and social reorganization due to the pressures of the upper classes and the court. His wife, Marie Antoinette, whom he married in 1770, was no help for she was headstrong and extravagant and had no empathy for the miserable and oppressed commoners. Louis XVI's financial complications were compounded by the monetary aid given to the American revolutionaries between 1778 and 1781. To add to his difficulties, he was forced to take out loans to sustain the elaborate courts demanded by his extravagant

**Figure 12.3.** Male fashions altered drastically in the period between 1699 and 1790. The shapeless long **justaucorps** and **frac** at first were knee or calf length, *A*. The outer coat had no collar, primarily because the larger periwig was in vogue. In the next style phase, coat skirts were shorter, vest sleeves were omitted, and knee breeches were closed *a la bavaroise, B* and *C*. Later a standing collar was added to the suit coat. Buttons and buttonholes were added at the hemline of the coat so that front and back sections could be buttoned on the side, *D*. Outer graments for travel and warmth evolved from the **Brandenburg,** c. 1670, *E;* to the **redingote** with **retonne,** *F;* and the **roquelaure,** *G*. Wig styles include: *A,* periwig; *B,* pigeon wings; *C, vergette à la chinoise; D,* the bag wig; *E,* club wig; *F,* queue wig.

wife. He was a pious, simple man, but his true character was not reflected in the court dominated by his wife. The resultant financial burden imposed on the French population infuriated the people. On July 14, 1789, the Parisian populace seized the Bastille and imprisoned the royal family in the Palace of the Tuileries. The fate of Louis XVI and his family was sealed when France was declared a republic and the Assembly of Deputies was elected. After an abortive attempt to escape to Austria, Louis, his wife, and family were convicted of treason and were guillotined.

Louis was more a victim of circumstances than a traitor. He was never the despotic ruler that his predecessors had been, and his interests were simple. It was his wife who plotted the course of his court. She loved to give elaborate banquets in the Petite Trianon, some distance from Versailles. Pretending to enjoy the bucolic life, she and the ladies at court idled away their leisure hours playing at "milkmaid" in the pasture glade just beyond Petite Trianon.

These pastimes greatly influenced the fashions of the later decades of the eighteenth century, just prior to the French Revolution. Many changes in costume design had taken place in this fast-paced century wrought with revolution and social change. As the eighteenth century opened, men's styles included the long coat and knee breeches that had evolved from the flamboyant styles of the Baroque era. There were no radical silhouette changes until the second decade (Figure 12.3). Many men continued to wear Venetians *en bourse*, however, as well as the shorter, loose doublet. Puritanical influences in northern Europe persisted to reinforce the subdued styles preferred by certain Protestant sects. Louis XIV (1643-1715) brought elegance and formality to the French court. The arbiter of taste during the early years of Louis XV's reign (1715-1774) was the Duke of Orleans. Because the style of the court he established was more relaxed and frivolous, fashions became more elegant and the silhouette less restricted.

During this period, the artist Watteau dictated the course of beauty and "taught women to be pretty, not just beautiful." The prettiness he prescribed encompassed not only costume but accessories and manners. Watteau may have designed the back treatment of the popular gown that bears his name (Figure 12.4). The characteristic detail was the flared, fan-shaped deep pleating that fell from shoulder to hem in the back. The ***sack (sacque)*** and ***robe de chambre*** were equally popular A-shaped gowns made of soft silken fabrics, with elbow-length sleeves, low, triangular necklines, and billowing skirts. After Louis XV came of age, his mistresses, Madame de Pompadour and Madame DuBarry, influenced fashions of dress and behavior.

This period saw a refinement in the development of nationalism. France, the arbiter of European taste, subtly changed Baroque forms and refined them into the style

**Figure 12.4.** Two back views of the deep pleats used in the **Watteau gowns.** (1766. Gallery of English Costume Collection, Manchester.)

known as Rococo. Directions in art were controlled by kings, wealthy bourgeoisie, and, to some extent, the church of Rome. Rich merchants of Holland, England, Germany, and Flanders employed native artists and demanded a superrealism in their portraits. For the pleasure of their patrons, painters of the nobility developed a playful, flamboyant style involving sensuous, curvilinear compositional patterns and romantic subject matter. The paintings of Watteau, Fragonard, and Boucher depicted people cast in a rosy glow, participating in carefree activities in a misty, wooded environment.

The economic impact of fashion-related materials on the prosperity of European countries was far reaching. During the War of the Spanish Succession, England set up a sea blockade which had a crisis effect on the French textile industry. Nimes, Lyons, and Rheims, France's textile centers, were all but ruined. The 1713 Treaty of Utrecht reestablished French mills, but the struggle for textile markets continued through the century. Throughout this period, "cotton wars" were fought as each nation sought to control the cotton-textile market.

The technological development of a method to print cotton fabric was concurrent with the advances made in the sciences of physics and chemistry. Direct printing on cotton fabric replaced the older blotting method used prior to 1760. In that year printed cloth called *toile de Jouy* was produced at a small factory at Jouy-en-Josas. The textiles from this establishment outshown those produced in the previous decade called *toile d'Orange*. In both cases, Swiss emigrants had developed the techniques which made cheap, colorful cotton fabrics available to the poorer classes.

Science aided in development of new dyes. Newton's exploration of optics contributed to the creation of new dyes for textiles. Through his research, the possibility of tints and tones was realized, as well as that of combining dye hues to achieve a wider range of colors. During the reign of Louis XV, the range of tones was subtle, but the dyes developed during his successor's rule were more brilliant. A wide range of color and the possibilities inherent in bleaches were introduced in the eighteenth century. Costumes were affected, for designers could work with a greater range of color and a wider spectrum of contrasting tints and shades. In turn, these technological advances with a fashion base affected the economies of Spain, Belgium, Holland, France, and Saxony. Colors in costumes and in paintings became rich with near-musical overtones.

The styles of the first three decades of the eighteenth century were constantly changing, dependent on the whim of the French court. Other countries accepted the French fashion leadership and slavishly copied its modes. The demand for laces, elegant brocaded shoes, and rich silks for dresses and waistcoats established fashion as an economic factor in France. The dominant position occupied

by France in setting styles lasted until the outbreak of its civil conflict.

At that time England stepped into the breach, dictating male and female fashions. The superior British tailoring of menswear never has been supplanted. The tailors of Bond Street have ruled over male costuming from the late eighteenth century to the present. The British love of casual country living influenced changes in fashion.[1] The landed gentry and the newly prosperous mercantile class, which imitated the gentry, were exceptionally devoted to country living and outdoor sports. These interests governed costume, and designs were adapted to the activity patterns incumbent on their use. In turn, as changing social patterns evolved in the countries of the Western world, English interests and attitudes were preferred.

Men and women were slaves to the rich, cumbersome costumes that dictated their movements. Late in the century, fashionable ladies of the French court were often forced to ride in their coaches or sedan chairs with their heads projecting awkwardly from the windows because the ceilings of these vehicles could not accommodate their towering coiffures. Men of fashion were often subjected to ridicule as they were forced to adapt their habits and activity patterns to the whims of the fashionable modes.

The fashion directions set by kings and queens and the kings' mistresses of France were epitomized by the courtly and playful practices of Marie Antoinette. Gowns designed with apronlike accessories were worn while participating in pseudopastoral pastimes. These foolish interests and the costume excesses that accompanied them were but a few of the activities which enraged the general populace of France and caused them to revolt against the aristocracy.

The development of new machines for production and new methods of distribution of goods assisted in changing the social order. Indirectly, these advancements influenced clothing. Fabrics were particularly sensitive to the changes introduced by these new inventions and trading systems. There was an abundance of cotton imported first from India and later from the American colonies. Richard Arkwright's invention of the cotton-spinning loom in 1767, the flying shuttle invented by John Kay, and the perfecting of weaving looms by Strutt in 1785 contributed to the eventual industrialization of fabric making. Availability of cotton from Manchester, silk from Coventry, and wool from Norwich aided in creating a variety of garments in a wide range of fabrics. With machine-produced cloth, the newly affluent merchant class was mingling with the nobility, and laborers and workers were attempting to assert their rights affecting social, political, and fashion forms. These factors in turn combined to create new forms of garments and new modes of fashion.

During this century, the technique was developed to mass-produce spools of thread. With this English technological advance, cotton balls were mechanically carded, the fibers spun, and the thread wound on spools to be sold commercially in yardage shops. Prior to this contribution to the dressmaking and tailoring trade, cotton was carded, spun, and wound into balls by hand.

In this period embroidery became so accomplished that the rich, gold-and-silver thread embellishments worked into court gowns were signed, much in the same way as easel painters signed their creative works. In the Costume Court Gallery of the Victoria and Albert Museum are several examples of this style of ball gown.

Oddly, the consistency of perfect embroidering techniques was not carried throughout the garment. The overskirts with the V-front openings were more often than not carelessly fashioned to fit over the wide elbow paniers. The overskirt pattern used late in the eighteenth century was merely a straight length of material with deep complex embroidery on the hem. This was fitted to the waist by carelessly mitered pleats and gathers over the paniers. If the overskirt was not large enough, it was patched with mismatched gussets. These gussets, often made from what appeared to be odds and ends of fabric, served to attach front to back. This rather hastily contrived construction of an otherwise elegant gown is never evident in the great portrait paintings meticulously produced at this time. The bodice peplum usually covered these hodgepodge patches, obscuring them from the artist's penetrating eye. Idealized perfection was the prerogative of court painters who, though faithfully recording the elegance of garments and posturing, eliminated the imperfections which actually existed. Undoubtedly, the finishing of such gowns, commissioned for a specific grand fête, was completed in haste, for the actual time required to create the embroidery was endless. Three to four months were required for a masterful mistress of the needle to execute the intricate patterns that enriched these beautiful dresses.

Silhouette variables, which swept through female fashions, can readily be traced in the portraiture of the period. During the eighteenth century, the titans of portraiture were Gainsborough, Sargent, Watteau, Fragonard, Goya, and Boucher. Many examples of Boucher's creative productivity have been destroyed, but enough remain, particularly in the Frick Collection in New York City, to succinctly present an overview of the life, times, costumes, and attitudes of this monumental century. The study of costume without the visual records that these great court and upper-class painters left would be impossible.

The very emergence of new styles in painting, architecture, and sculpture influences the clothing fashions of a specific time. In no other period was this more true than in the eighteenth century. The visual records traced by artists point to the emergence of nationalistic preferences in fashion fads (Figure 12.5). To a great degree, the silhouette and detail variations are related to nationalistic personality and character differentials. The climatic dif-

**Figure 12.5.** In eighteenth-century Spain, gown skirts were never as full as those in other countries, and the custom of covering the head with a lace **mantilla** was introduced. (Goya: *Dona Narcisa Baranana de Goicoshea.* Metropolitan Museum of Art, New York City.)

ferences of widely separated geographical locales helped to determine the styles popular in different countries. The dominant religions of individual countries and the moral influence of the various dogmas also controlled fashion's forms.

The scene of St. Mark's, painted by Canaletto, is peopled exclusively by men dressed in knee breeches, silk hose, justaucorps, and tricorn. Many of the men wear voluminous, thigh- or ankle-length capes. Gentlemen of importance use powdered wigs *a-queque*. Legal dignitaries wear powdered, full-bottom wigs and long, legal gowns.

Two pastoral paintings done by Watteau in 1716 illustrate opposing points of view concerning attitudes of the sexes.[2] In the pastoral painting titled *The Shepherds*, young lasses and lads are gathered together in the shade of a tree, and two are dancing together. The lad is dressed in a short, silken doublet with slashed sleeves, striped-silk knee breeches with rosettes on each knee, silk hose, and a feathered bonnet. The lass wears a three-quarter-length sleeved chemise of white lawn, a boned, sleeveless bodice, a full, softly gathered, yellow-taffeta silk skirt, and a garland scarf of light blue silk. These styles are only

**Figure 12.6.** In portraits, many American women were shown dressed in elegant gowns which were often copies of dresses from engravings of portraits of great European ladies. American artists collected these engravings and their clients would select a style of gown, such as this **gown à l'anglaise.** (Copley: *Mary Turner Sargent,* detail, 1763. The Corcoran Gallery of Art, Washington D.C.)

slight variations of the garments worn during the preceding period. The group includes other young women wearing full skirts and oval-necked, white lawn blouses. In contrast are the elegant ladies and gentlemen depicted in the painting *Gathering in a Park*. The ladies wear luxurious Watteau gowns; the men are clad in doublets, knee breeches, silk hose, shoes decorated with rosettes, and cavalier-style beaver hats. One gentleman has a deep-blue brocade Spanish cape; another still wears pantaloons, in addition to other attire.

In the New World, the art of dressing fashionably was equally important. Because the first half of the eighteenth century was a prosperous and pleasant period in the new United States, women of financially successful families could indulge in a preoccupation with clothing styles (Figure 12.6). Worldwide sailing ships stopped at American ports, bringing cottons from India and silks from China. Names of these fabrics were incorrectly derived from the geographical locations where they were produced. For instance, *nankeen* was a fabric made in Nankin, China; *calico* was a colorful cotton first imported from Calcutta, India. The latest European modes were recre-

ated from the abundant supply of fabrics constantly being delivered to America's thriving ports.

In America, as in European capitals, the jointed fashion dolls, "Big and Little Pandora," were the devices used to report the most fashionable modes (Figure 12.7). Of course, the very latest styles were copied somewhat tardily, for delayed passage of the fashion dolls was frequent and women of quality fretted on their late arrival. Whispered gossip that a fashion doll had been delivered was known to have disrupted the Sunday devotions of even the most devout. The contemporary periodical, *The Spectator*, extensively quotes one such devastating interruption to the attention paid to a preacher's pious pronouncements. The extent of the latest fads displayed on the fashion dolls was complete. Hairstyles, jeweled accessories, and outer garments were detailed in full.

One of the innovations introduced in 1711 by the manteau-maker Selby was the hoopskirt support, or **panier.** Prior to this date, skirts had been looped up over contrasting colored underskirts. A hip fullness and bustle back resulted. The new skirt styling ultimately replaced the loose-fitting sack. This overdress had been worn open in front over petticoats. The hip fullness of the looped skirts was created by drawing up the sack skirts, some created with gathering tapes or pockets to achieve the desired silhouette. Panier-supported skirts added width to the frontal silhouette, while the depth, front to back, remained slim. Petticoats and beribboned stomachers became important elements in the total costume look. Necklines altered and changed in shape from low, truncated triangles to deep, curved U-shapes. A superabundance of flounces and *falbalas* added to the complexity of these fanciful gowns.

Hairstyles were altered too, for in his later years, Louis XIV ridiculed the ladies of court who still wore the Fontanges. When they disappeared, these towering caps were commented on by Joseph Addison, an English commentator on society and politics. He wrote, "I remember several ladies who were once near seven feet high, that at present want some five inches." Women's hair, complexly coiffed and bonneted, assumed a smooth, natural arrangement. However, late in this century, excesses in towering coiffures and powdered wigs again were in vogue.

The use of patches on the face was not simply to direct attention to some comely feature. In Queen Anne's day (1702-1714), the patches' shapes connoted political affiliation. Position on the face was also an indicator of the wearer's political preference. In England Whig ladies used patches on the left cheek; Tory women wore patches on the right. The fanciful shapes of patches and the fad of wearing several at once were French affectations late in the century. Men also used patches. The production of elegant patch boxes made of silver and gold inlaid with ivory or of tortoise shell increased as the demand for this

**Figure 12.7.** Fashion dolls illustrated eighteenth-century fashion changes. Near right, "Little Pandora" wears a daytime gown with articulated elbow paniers. Far right, "Big Pandora," always dressed in court attire, wears the **gown à la française** with gondola paniers.

cosmetic affectation became more and more popular. Patches were placed coquettishly at the corner of an eye or invitingly at the edge of the lips in contrast to the white powdered face and highly rouged cheeks. Patches of fetching design were used to conceal a mole or blemish; they were also placed on the expansively exposed bosom just above the edge of the square or triangular décolletage.

The charming posturing of Louis XV's favorite mistress, Marquise de Pompadour, painted by François Boucher, clearly depicts the garb and practiced grace of the ladies of the French court (Figure 12.8). From her neatly crossed ankles encased in pink mules with rosette trims to her neatly coiffed head encircled with flower garlands, Mme. Pompadour is pictured as the epitome of fashionable French femininity. Her gown of dull, aqua-blue satin is edged with rambling apricot-pink roses and leaves. The sleeves fit tightly over the upper arm, ending in voluminous lace falls bedecked with large bows in the same apricot pink. The stomacher, concealing the rigid and boned corset, is crowded with rows of bows of the same hue, diminishing in size to the tiny waist. Around her neck is a shirred apricot-pink **Betsy**, a small ruffle tied around the throat with a slender cord. Multirows of pearl bracelets encircle each wrist. For all the superabundance of figure decoration, the ears are left unadorned. While ropes of pearls hanging to the waist might be chosen by some in place of the Betsy, selecting just the right combination of decorations was the result of training in good taste nurtured since childhood.

Although clothing styles for men and women were decidely different during this century, there were remark-

**Figure 12.8.** The complex curvilinear rhythms of the Rococo were incorporated into this **robe à la française.** Rows of bows were used to conceal the front lacings of the bodice. The inverted V-neckline was a trait of gowns at this period. (F. Boucher: *Marquise de Pompadour*, detail, 1756. Maurice de Rothschild Collection.)

ably close parallels in head and figure silhouette adornments. This was particularly true during the reign of Louis XV. He was not a strong monarch and society's interest shifted from a "divine king." The debauchery of the Regency period faded and the listless Louis XV allowed Mme. de Pompadour, his beautiful mistress and the admitted queen of art and taste, to set the fashion pace. The mid-years of the eighteenth century might be labeled the era of divine femininity. Perhaps this is the major reason that male attire, with some masculine modifications, echoed female fads.

In this age of portraiture, the artists produced images of their subjects which displayed self-confidence repleat with practiced carelessness. Elegance, distinction, and social success were visualized in portraits of members of court and people of lesser rank. Even before the French Revolution, fashion caused a democratization of eighteenth-century life. Portraits of members of the French royal family show them dressed in street clothes, rather than formal royal robes. Youth and zest for life's playful pastimes were the keys of this age. Faces were doll-like and the clothes were those of fairyland princesses.

The alarming contrast to these attitudes descended with the civil war that saw hundreds of aristocrats trundled off to the guillotine. A change to humbler costumes was protection for the aristocrat and a badge of the political convictions of the citizenry of France. Gone were the days when a maiden of high social status could sail through the air on a velvet, cushion-covered swing as shown in a 1766 painting by Fragonard. The French mademoiselle flicks her pretty pink, ruching-trimmed mule at her swooning swain as a bishop pulls the ropes to propel her to and fro. Men discarded their powdered wigs and traded tricorns for bicorns and full-length trousers. Shoes were simple sandals, an attempt to imitate those worn by ancient Greeks. Much of the apparel worn during the last decade of this century showed the influence of ancient Greek and Roman fashions. These styles continued to be in fashion until the 1830s.

# Basic Garments of a Graceful Age (1700–1795)

### SACK GOWNS (1705–1715)

While authorities disagree over whether the great eighteenth-century artist actually designed the gown that bears his name, the A-shape of the **Watteau gown** (1705-1715) was typical of the first years of this graceful age.[3] At the request of the Duchesse de Berry, skilled

**Figure 12.9.** Standing or seated, the **sack,** or **andrienne,** was an enveloping gown with a center panel in front which made that section fall straight. The back had deep pleats set into the shoulder seam. The ample sleeves were sometimes designed with box pleats ending in a wide, deep, flat cuff. (Redrawn from a sketch by Watteau: *Costumes.* Bibliothèque Nationale, Paris.)

seamstresses and tailors met at her home in July of 1715, when she asked that the opera designer, Bertin, make radical changes in fashion. The large triangular silhouette was the result.

An apocryphal tale concerning the name of one of these gowns is linked to the contemporary play, *Andriana*, by Terence. Mme. Dancourt appeared in one scene in a shapeless gown of similar styling. This theater costume was adapted and dubbed *andrienne*, which later was corrupted to *adrienne*.

The **andrienne**, or **adrienne**, gown (1705-1715) was a one-piece, tentlike garment. The back was designed with several large box pleats that added fullness to the girth at the hem. The front had a center seam extending from the modified V-neck to the hem. Just under the bust in front were two additional pleats. The hem was held out in a vast circle by a hoop panier or hoop petticoat. There are many variations of this gown with similar general characteristics (Figure 12.9).

The Watteau gown in the Costume Institute Collection of the Metropolitan Museum of Art is typical of one of the variations. The back treatment with the Watteau pleats falling from the shoulders is consistent with those of

**Figure 12.10. Watteau gown,** the fashionable mode of the early eighteenth century. (Redrawn from a sketch by Watteau.)

the *andrienne* gown, or **sack *(sacque)*** gown of 1715. The design of the bodice introduces a variable, however. The bodice is boned and fitted by back lacings which are hidden beneath the Watteau pleats. This intricately cut gown with Watteau pleats, boned bodice, and slim, lace-edged sleeves was made of delicately tinted silk.

An engraving of a similar gown created from a series of Watteau sketches titled *Figures of Different Characters* (c. 1715) is a fine illustration of this styling (Figure 12.10). The sleeves in this illustration, however, are loose and vertically pleated with large cuffs decorated with buttons. The larger sleeves indicate that the gown shown here is of an earlier date than the one in the Metropolitan's Costume Institute Collection. Many of Watteau's paintings were created after 1720 when slimmer sleeves that were tighter in the upper arm came into vogue.

Many of these sack-style gowns were outgrowths of the **robe de chambre**, an earlier at-home gown of loose and comfortable cut (Figure 12.11). These style variations replaced the boned bodice and manteau (overgown) so typical of the court costumes from around 1680 to 1715. Some were open down the front revealing the underdress beneath.

Often the underdress was designed with slits on the sides, and the front corners of the full, open overskirt were tucked into them, creating a drape over the hips. This slit-skirt style was called **robe retroussée dans les poches** (gown turned up into the pockets), for pockets as well as slits were used to achieve the correct and fashionable hip puffs (Figure 12.12). These skirt arrangements were a prelude to the paniers of the gown *à la française*.

## GOWN *A LA FRANÇAISE* (1720-1760)

After 1720 the sack gown was modified into a pleated gown which, known by mid-century as the *robe à la française*, the formal gown of the French court (Figure 12.8). The pleats were arranged in two layers and allowed to hang loose in back.[4] The tight bodice was boned and fitted by front lacings (Figure 12.13) hidden by a stomacher, or **la pièce d'estomac**. This elegantly trimmed concealing device was V-shaped and embellished with bows and lace. In turn, the stomacher was replaced by rows of ribbon bows diminishing in size as the bodice narrowed to the tiny nipped-in waist. *Compères*, two small facings fastened on either side of the bodice, later replaced the rows of bows. The neckline was either a deep *U* or truncated triangle. A small ruffle or ruching was worn around the throat.

Sleeve treatments were altered as well. The early sleeves were a pagoda style ending in layers of lace at the cuff, which was cut shallow on the inner arm and deep at the outside. These were replaced by elbow-length sleeves that fitted snugly, although the multiruffled, graded layers of lace at the cuffs were retained.

**Figure 12.11.** The **robe de chambre** and **Fontanges** headdress, which appeared during the latter years of the seventeenth century, continued in popularity as at-home fashions. The costume on near right was in fashion between 1710 and 1730. The **sack** (far right) was another at-home costume worn extensively between 1700 and 1750. (Redrawn from sketches by Watteau. Bibliothèque Nationale, Paris.)

**Figure 12.12.** The **robe retroussée dans les poches** was a gown of many parts. A petticoat was worn over the shift, then the bodice was laced firmly about the body. Separate padded pockets were then tied at the waist, a pocket on each hip. Over this was placed the front-slit outer skirt with the fronts carefully draped and stuffed into the pockets. The coiffure on the far left figure was called **chiens couchants,** the other **coiffure à la flore.** (Sketched from actual garments, c. 1770, in the Costume Court, Victoria and Albert Museum, London.)

**Figure 12.13.** This illustration shows the bodice lacing without the stomacher. The skirt draping is created by tucking the overskirt into pockets. (L. Jacob after Watteau: *Departure of the Italian Comedians,* engraving, 1697.)

The overskirt encircled the figure to a point at the waist of the slightly elongated bodice which was covered by the stomacher. The smooth-fitting petticoat, with a multiruffled skirt decorated with *falbalas* and flounces, was revealed between separated front edges of the overgown. Paniers swelled the skirts out beyond the figure at the hips. These paniers, or hen baskets as they were derisively called, reached exaggerated proportions, often extending as much as six feet beyond the figure at the hips.

Nearly all of the gown skirts were supported by hoop paniers, or **criardes.** These gum-starched, ankle-length petticoats were also adapted from theatrical garments. The term *criardes* was derisive too, for these stiffly starched skirt supports created quite a rustling sound when the ladies wearing them moved. *Criardes* are believed to be of German origin, and the hoop petticoats were an English innovation.

Other late *à la française* designs include the gown *à la piémontaise* with a free-hanging panel attached at the back of the oval neckline. This totally free panel, pleated in the Watteau style, formed a floor-length courtly mantle or cape. As a characteristic posturing pattern, this pleated panel was held or carried at either side by the hand. The

gown *à la piémontaise* was introduced by the Princess of Piedmont in 1755. Just prior to the French Revolution, a gown similar to the *à la française* with a boned bodice was known as the **robe ronde.**

The underdress worn beneath the sack, *robe de chambre,* and similar overgowns was styled in much the same way as for these two gowns. All of the underdresses were elaborately trimmed with volants, *falbalas,* bows, and flounces.

## GOWN *A L'ANGLAISE* (1760s to 1770s)

The gown *à l'anglaise* typically worn by English women and wealthy women in the American colonies (Figure 12.6) was quite different from the French fashions. This style fully developed in the 1770s and was ultimately adopted by the anglophiles of France. An English woman's fashionable attire consisted of a snug, boned bodice and softly gathered skirt (Figure 12.14). The bodice was intricately cut of many pieces that curved outward from a narrow waist to the armholes. It was laced

**Figure 12.14.** After the French Revolution began, elaborate panier fashions were discarded. This British lady wears a **gown à l'anglaise** and cape. (Thomas Lawrence: *Elizabeth Parren, Countess of Derby,* 1790. Metropolitan Museum of Art, New York City.)

**Figure 12.15.** The **robe à l'anglaise** opened in front over a waistcoat formed of two *compères* (panels) and was designed with a boned bodice and a waistline which dipped to a point below the normal waist in front and back. (Redrawn from *The Martineau de Fleuriau Family*, detail, Roslin, 1785. Collection of the Marquis de Gontaut.)

in front to within a few inches of the low neckline. The skirt front opened in an inverted *V* to reveal a matching, highly decorated undergown, or skirt. The front edges of the overskirt were trimmed with ruchings and fringes (Figure 12.15). The neckline was often filled in with a fichu.

## GOWN *A LA POLONAISE* (1770s)

Although the gown *à la polonaise* was never worn in Poland, the name may have been derived from the three swags that were characteristic of its skirt styling and its appearance on the fashion scene at the time when Poland was partitioned into three parts.[5] The *à la polonaise* fastened high on the chest, had tight sleeves, and a unique overskirt which opened wide over an underskirt. The overskirt was drawn high over the hips into three swags: a short one on each side and a long one in back. Two drawstrings set on the inside of the skirt were used to form the swags.

Other styles of this period were given romantic names because of political events, the successes of a particular portraitist, or travels of ambassadors and their ladies. The

following are the names given to several gowns:, *à la circassienne, à la lévite, à la levantine, à la turque,* and *à la sultane.*

## *ROBE VOLANTE* (1780s)

A more formal gown, the ***robe volante*** of the 1780s, had a boned, fitted bodice that dipped to a point below the waist (Figure 12.1). Sometimes the bodice was pointed in the front and back. The skirt of the *robe volante* was full, supported by a hoop pettiskirt. This type of skirt support was constructed of thin circles of steel graduated in size—small hoops at the hips increasing to larger hoops at the hem—and suspended from the waistband by tapes. Hoop frames of this type were made in many shapes, each with a descriptive name. The elbow-length sleeves of the *robe volante* were snug and trimmed with lace cuffs that were narrow over the upper arms and dipped to wide, full cuffs at the backs of the elbows. The neckline shape varied from a wide square to a super-ellipse, plunging low into an extreme décolletage. Filmy lawn or delicately woven cotton fabric concealed the lowcut neck if the wearer were advanced in years or very modest (Figure 12.16).

**Figure 12.16.** Elderly women often wore little linen caps with their at-home gowns. Note the transparent **fichu** with a delicate leaf-and-dot motif and the mitts in place of gloves. (Copley: *Mrs. Thomas Boylston*, detail, 1766. Fogg Art Museum, Harvard University, Cambridge.)

**Figure 12.17.** As the eighteenth century drew to a close, women began to affect apparel with styling similar to male garments, such as this **chemise a l'anglaise,** or **robe Roslin.** The gown skirt is softly gathered at the normal waist and the deep V of the jacket neckline is filled with a **fichu.** (Redrawn from *The Optics Lesson,* L. Boilly, 1796. Private collection.)

This popular neck trim, which had a variety of names, was placed loosely around the neck, brought across the shoulders, crisscrossed over the bust, and the ends tied in a knot with silver cords, or buttoned to the waist in back. To achieve the desired fullness over the bust, flattened by the boned bodice, a wire frame support was worn under the kerchief. These supported neckerchiefs were given rather sarcastic names, such as **liars, caracasses, trompeuse, menteur,** or **lügner,** depending upon the country. **Fichu** and **mouchoir** were the more formal terms used to indicate this bouffant type of neck trim (Figure 12.17). After 1778, when the fichu became larger and framed the face, it became known as the **fichu menteur.**

**Tippets,** put on in the same manner as the fichu, were worn in the winter for warmth. These tiny capes were made of fur, velvet, or short black or white feathers.

## GOWNS (1780s)

Toward the end of the century each occasion had a special costume. Gowns became more slender and the **fourreau,** or sheath, was introduced in 1781. Some versions of this garment, with few or no bones in the bodice, had an apron skirt that was open in the back from waist to hem and was worn over a sheath that had a very modestly gathered skirt. The overdress with the apron skirt, called the **tablier,** was usually white with a flounce around the hem.

Other dress forms late in this period were: the ***robe redingote,*** a gown with a boned double-breasted bodice, gathered skirt, and long, tight sleeves; and the gown ***en chemise,*** or ***à la créole*** (1778), a simple, one-piece dress with slender sleeves and a narrow silhouette. The gowns *en chemise* and *à la créole* were created using the ever-fashionable Indian cotton textiles. This styling developed as a reaction to the rigid, figure-confining gowns with boned bodices and paniers. Simple in cut and slender in silhouette, the softer, less formal chemise and *à la créole* gowns were dubbed "false gown(s) without train."[6] These soft, sash-trimmed gowns could simply be stepped into or slipped on over the head. This was quite a contrast to the trussed-up bodices and cumbersome panier skirts of the more formal styles. The gown *à la créole* was of chemise cut with a wide sash, patterned after costumes worn by "French ladies in America," specifically by a traveling ballet troupe.

The acceptability of these simpler gowns reportedly developed after the exhibition of a portrait of Mme. Vigé-Librun in the 1783 Salon. These gowns also visually expressed new feminine concepts and attitudes toward motherhood, learning, humanity, and love of country. The chemise and apron styling reflected a simple peasant involvement by imitation. After 1781 the ease with which the cotton gowns might be laundered also reflected the interest in the newly discovered importance of sanitation and personal hygiene.

## WOMEN'S WRAPS (1700–1795)

A number of outer wraps, capes, and jackets were worn by women during the eighteenth century. These included: the **casaquin** (1700-1768), a simple hip-length jacket that was fitted in the front and hanging loose in back; the **caraco,** introduced in 1768, a short fitted jacket with tight sleeves and tails; the **pierrot,** a short jacket with a ruffled peplum in back; the ***à la polonaise,*** or ***à la française,*** a snug-fitting waist- or hip-length jacket; and the **spencer,** a version of a man's riding jacket without tails. Another jacket was the mannish, tight-fitting **juste** of 1785, designed with a full basque in back.

Capes were large and used for formal occasions. The **pelisse** (1770-1790) was a fur cape with half sleeves. The **mantilla** was a short velvet or taffeta scarf with many frills of the same fabric and small ruches used as decorative elements. This scarf style originated in Spain around 1721 and was replaced with the ***mantelet à coqueluchon*** in 1730 by the ladies-in-waiting to the Spanish Infanta. Other cape forms such as the **pèlerine**, were voluminous, circular styles that tied at the throat with ribbons and were made of a variety of silks, patterned velvets, and furs. The fabric capes, with slits for the arms, were fur trimmed.

## JUSTAUCORPS (1700–1795)

The long coat, or **justaucorps** (1660-1710), continued to increase in popularity as one element of the three-part male **habit,** or suit, which consisted of a justaucorps, a jacket, and breeches (Figure 12.18). Gradually the term *habit* was applied only to the men's outer coat and the term *justaucorps* was dropped from common usage. By 1770 only tailors referred to the suit coat as a justaucorps.[7]

At first the justaucorps had been a calf-length, shapeless garment, but it soon was modified and refined. Between 1700 and 1730, the skirt of this coat had flat side pleats over the hips. The front was straight with both of the open edges trimmed with braid galloons. Buttons and buttonholes were arranged close together from the collarless neck to the hem. Huge cuffs made from the folded-back, ample sleeves had a similar trim of buttons and braid. The coat was fitted in the back, and the skirt back had a deep slit to make it more comfortable for horseback riding. By 1730 the fan of flat pleats was enlarged and the total fullness of the skirt was increased "to imitate a panier," supported by horsehair panels at the hips (Figure 12.19).[8] Whalebone later replaced the horsehair padding. The fullness of the coat decreased and had all but disappeared by the 1740s.

The coat sleeves were rather full at first, but became quite snug when the hip flare increased. Large, decoratively embroidered cuffs or facings and big pocket flaps were characteristics of the coat for some time. There were three basic cuff styles: broad and deep, with the cuff open in back; narrow, and either open or closed in front and

**Figure 12.18.** This eighteenth-century gentleman's suit consists of a short **justaucorps,** vest, knee breeches, and cape with standing collar. The neckline is adorned with a lace neckcloth. (Actual suit of the Grand Master of the Order of St. Hubertus, c. 1720.)

**Figure 12.19.** A man's **justaucorps,** during the first third of the eighteenth century, was designed with deep side pleats and padding at the hips. (J. F. de Troy: *The Declaration of Love,* detail, 1731. Staatliche Schlösser und Gärten, Berlin.)

**Figure 12.20.** By the 1750s a gentleman's suit, or **habit,** consisted of a matching **justaucorps** and knee breeches combined with a richly ornamented vest. The suit coat was collarless and worn open although there were functional buttons and buttonholes. The breeches buttoned snugly about the leg just below the knee. (Copley: *Theodore Atkinson,* detail, 1757–1758. Lee Boltin Collection.)

back; and broad with modest depth, closed in back. The cuffs and lining were made of matching fabric.

In mid-century the name of this long suit coat was changed to **pourpoint** and it was slightly modified. The skirt became slimmer and the fronts were pared away to create an inverted V-opening. Braid, embroidery, and buttons, which were functional and decorative, continued to be used as trimmings. Buttons, made of silk, horsehair, or metal, were used so profusely on male garments that they became an important commercial commodity in England and France. For a time the bodice of the pourpoint was slightly boned and padded, but by 1750 this had disappeared and a more masculine silhouette developed Figure 12.20). A style change in the coat took place after 1760. The lower front corner of the skirt was folded front to side seam, and the back center corner of the skirt also was folded to the side seam and clipped together, or the lower front corners were folded to the center back and buttoned together. This created a very large inverted V-opening in the front. While this wearing style was used primarily for horseback riding, it was typical of military

uniform coats. Later in the 1760s, the skirt of the coat was cut in a curve starting at the chest in the center front and sweeping to the side seams. When the name changed to habit, a collar was added and it continued to increase in width over the years. Originally designed as a small, straight band, it developed into a tall, folded or doubled-down collar. Collar, cuffs, and coat fronts were embroidered with gold thread. These rich and elegant garments were made of velvets and brocades and often had embroidered panels on either side of the front opening. At times this needlework would follow the same elaborate designs woven into the fabric, making the design more pronounced.

## FRAC (1700–1795)

Essential to the overall appearance of the male habit, the **frac,** a frock coat or waistcoat, was at first a duplicate of the justaucorps (Figure 12.21). The only essential differences were proportions of the sleeves and skirts, which were narrower. In time the sleeves and the skirt in

**Figure 12.21.** Typical male garb of the eighteenth century includes simple waistcoat, puffed-sleeve shirt, knee breeches, and **habit** coat. (Redrawn from *David Garrick,* Reynolds, detail, 1773.)

back were eliminated. This new garment was known variously as *le gilet,* **vest,** or **veston.** When it was introduced, the frac was the same length as the coat, reaching to the mid-calf. Eventually, the vest was shortened, first covering the body to the thighs, then to the hip bone, and finally to just below the waist. The line of the lower edge across the front was modified, and the tabs extending below the waist were reshaped to create a small inverted *V*.

By 1785 the vest or waistcoat was decorated with printed braid or **cordonnet,** a triple-thread embroidery. Previously worn open, all coats and fracs were buttoned high on the chest if they were worn closed. Toward the end of the century, the waistcoat was buttoned at the waist only. The waistcoat originally had been designed with tabs, but toward the 1780s it was cut straight across at a point just below the normal waist. During the 1780s and 1790s, waistcoats were often designed with large revers. Men of lesser social station wore broadcloth versions of these garments.

Although formal wear, the *frac habillé* and the veston were seldom decorated with embroidery but were trimmed with large brass buttons and braid. The earlier justaucorps and pourpoint were made in a wide range of delicate pastel colors, but the *frac habillé* was made of fabrics more somber in hue and darker in tone. Court attire for men remained very formal and was sumptuously decorated with gold and silver embroidery.

## BREECHES (1700–1795)

Men's breeches were knee length and buckled or tied with a ribbon at the knee (Figure 12.22). At first they were cut full in the seat and semifull in the leg; the result was a poor fit. After the center-front button closure was discarded in 1730 and replaced by a wide front panel, the breeches were known as *culottes à la bavaroise.* Gradually the patterns for knee breeches improved, and they fitted the figure smoothly. By 1750 tabs and bands replaced the tie fastenings as a means of holding the legs of the breeches tightly over the hose. After the 1760s buckles or a row of small buttons were used as fastenings at the knees. Breeches were made of elegant satin for the aristocracy and of sturdy broadcloth for commoners. Originally two ribbon braces, or suspenders, were used to hold up the breeches; later, heavier fabric suspenders, or *les bretelles,* were worn. These were buttoned to the breeches on the inside of the waistband. Suspenders were not crossed in back until the late 1780s.

## SHIRT (1700–1795)

Men's shirts continued to be made of fine linen and had deep bishop sleeves, ruffled or deep lace cuffs, and a small standing collar or neckband. The body of the garment was gathered to a shoulder yoke. It was not open from the neck to hem, but had only a slit in front from the

**Figure 12.22.** Early eighteenth-century **justaucorps,** knee breeches, and **periwigs.** The periwig, as the century turned, was styled into two high peaks from a center part. (Tardieu: *Assis auprès de toy,* engraving, eighteenth century.)

neck to the chest. During the first decade of the eighteenth century, the **Cremona,** a simple neckpiece created from thin muslin folded into a narrow thin ribbon, was worn. Later it was trimmed with lace or richly embroidered.

The next neckwear accessory was the **jabot** (c. 1710), which was finely pleated and lace trimmed to create a cascade of ruffles covering the shirt front and falling over the waistcoat. In 1750 this was replaced by the **solitaire,** a black bow of ribbon. The military wore black silk neckcloths while civilians wore white silk ones. The **cravat,** which appeared late in the century, wrapped around the neck several times and tied in back. It was secured in front by a gold stickpin with a precious gem set in the head.

## SURTOUT (c. 1750)

The **surtout,** a heavy and serviceable broadcloth topcoat designed much like the justaucorps, was worn for travel or country wear in the 1750s. It had a flat collar, functional buttons, and generous pockets with large flaps. It covered the figure to mid-calf and was worn with broadcloth knee breeches, woolen hose, and heavy boots. This was the costume of the eighteenth-century English squire.

## MEN'S WRAPS (1700–1795)

The **balandran** was a heavy, full cape used as protection against rain and snow. Two side slits permitted the hands to be extended, and serviceable cords tied this cape at the neck. The **roquelaure**, a large overcoat designed by the Duke of Roquelaure, was an enormous, bell-shaped wrap created exclusively as a garment of warmth. Other warm outer garments worn between 1700 and 1795 included an overcoat with a shoulder cape and deep pockets on the skirt fronts; a long, wheel-shaped cloak with a shoulder cape and tie fastenings at the neck; and an overcoat that was thigh length and designed with an elbow-length cape, a high collar, and long sleeves with deep cuffs.

The **redingote**, styled with two collars, served as an overcoat, as did the **hongreline** (Figure 12.23). These garments had full sleeves with turned-back cuffs edged with buttons, and two flat collars. Made with ample body sections, they were used for travel and sportswear; later they were worn with formal attire as evening-dress overcoats. The **retonne** was a lighter-weight version of these overcoats (Figure 12.24).

**Figure 12.24.** Early eighteenth-century boy's long coat with side hip pleats and a broad-brimmed straw hat worn by young Russian lads. A large, soft bow replaced the lace **jabot** worn in Western European countries. (Redrawn from *Two Pupils from the Convent at Smolny,* Dimitri Lewizkij. Hermitage, Leningrad.)

**Figure 12.23.** The **redingote** and the **hongreline,** styled with double collars, were particularly snug overcoats. Atop his **queue wig,** this gentleman wears a **tricorn** with a rigid, cocked brim made of brushed beaver. (Redrawn from a 1730 men's fashion plate.)

The **wrap rascal,** another overcoat of the eighteenth century, was designed with a large double collar, voluminous body section, and large sleeves without buttons. The inner collar could be turned up for greater protection of the lower face and neck, in the same manner as the double collar of the redingote. The wrap rascal was closed with bands buckled across the front. The **tabarrino** was a knee-length cape. These wraps were often worn with scarves and a variety of hoods, the latter primarily by the lower classes.

# Accessories (1700–1795)

## HEADWEAR

Men of the late Baroque and Rococo eras wore the flat-crowned **tricorn,** which was carried rather than worn to prevent raising clouds of powder from the wigs. This established the custom of appearing bare-headed indoors.[9] The brim was cocked into three points and often trimmed with gold or silver braid, or plumes. The feather-edged brim was an early fashion. Around 1730 the tricorn was styled with a wide, wavy brim and an upturned peak. Its size diminished or increased as fashion dictated. By 1775 and through the 1790s, the tricorn *à la suisse* became the established headwear for men.

*Chapeaux-bras* were large tricorns with erect brims. They were almost completely flat and were carried rather than worn, for they were in fashion during the period of the high wigs. A rather silly, small tricorn, called the **macaronie,** was perched high atop the more pointed wigs by young dandies and fops in the 1780s. The precarious tilt of these ridiculously small hats made the wearers appear all the more outlandish, and they became the brunt of much ridicule because of their garish and flamboyant costumes.

Because of their elaborate, towering coiffures during much of this period, women seldom wore hats but they did wear other head coverings. The fan-fold hood, or **caleche,** of the 1780s was made of a transparent fabric structured over a collapsible frame that folded like a fan. The **gauzier,** also called the **Thérèse,** was another hood made in a similar fashion. The **capeauz** and bonnet were considered less formal types of head coverings and were nothing more than a circle of filmy fabric gathered into a great puff at the headband with a face-framing ruffle. These large, round caps were fancifully decorated with bows, flower garlands, and feathers. The puff bonnets sometimes had straw brims, but they were generally made with gathered self-brims. When the bonnet was made with a straw brim, it was trimmed with plumes. The softer, ribbon-decorated versions were worn indoors and were popular with older ladies well into the next century. Eventually, the bonnets decreased in size and were acceptable headwear for formal occasions, perched atop the towering coiffures that had become the mode of the late eighteenth century.

Floppy straw leghorns with the crowns piled high with feathers, flowers, and large bows were in style from the 1750s to the 1780s. These were worn for garden parties and for spring and summer wear. Broad, silken ribbons with long trailing ends were tied under the chin, either over or under the brim.

In the 1770s women, too, wore small beaver tricorns tipped forward over the right eye. Feathers and braid were used as trimming for this masculine type of hat, worn while riding to the hounds or for other activities on horseback.

## FOOTWEAR

High-heeled slippers of brocade, kid, and velvet in light hues were the foot fashions for women during much of the early and middle period of the eighteenth century. These delicate shoes were often embroidered with gold and silver thread. Buckles of gold and silver, set with paste imitations or precious gems, were attached to the instep. Satin pumps, with high spool heels and very pointed toes, were a mid-century style of female footwear. Then shoes became increasingly simple: the ribbon rosettes and the paste gems disappeared from the large instep buckles; the large bows and satin ribbon ties of the A-strap slippers and the high heels were eliminated. Plain kid or satin mules with rounder toes and lower heels became the dominant shoe forms for women between 1740 and 1790.

For most of the eighteenth century, men wore a closed, soft leather shoe that covered much of the foot. The long tongue over the instep was gone. Boots that were calf high were introduced in the 1770s. Dandies in tight-fitting chamois breeches, vest, long coat, and a *chapeau-bras* continued to wear metal buckles on their low-heeled, foot-encasing leather shoes. In the 1770s the **jockey boot** came into fashion. These knee-high boots were tightly fitted to the leg and were made of dark-colored leather lined with buff-colored leather. The tops were turned down to form a cuff of contrasting color. **Splatter dashes** were puttees or leggings that were buttoned on the inside of the leg and worn to protect silk hose during inclement weather.

Shoe forms for men and women during this period were made in a wide variety of styles that included: the spool-heeled pump, the buckled pump, the brocade or kid mule, the high shoe, and the jockey boot. Late in the century women began to wear an adaptation of the Grecian sandal.

## JEWELRY

Elegant jewelry was used sparingly for personal adornment. Chokers of rubies and diamonds, earrings with pear-shaped pearl drops, gold watches with enameled cases, and brooches covered with precious gems were common. The **Betsy,** or neck ruffle, and a wide throat-encircling ribbon replaced gold and jewel neckwear. The preference was for an expanse of white skin exposed by a deep neckline bordered with *tatez-y* (touch here), or pleated ruffles (Figure 12.25).

## HANDHELD ACCESSORIES

Oval and circular masks were essential accessories until about 1750. The **bauta,** a white half mask, and the **moreta,** a black round mask, were the most common forms. These were often decorated with ruching and attached to a slender dowel that was gilded and encrusted with paste gems. They were held in the hand or tied around the head by delicate cords. By 1750 the mask was discarded by most Europeans except the Italians, who continued the fads of masks and patches for much longer.

**Figure 12.25.** In the New World, women's gowns were seldom as elaborately trimmed with **falbalas,** but were decorated with bows of ribbons and laces. This gown has a lace **tatez-y** and a lace insert substituting for a stomacher. (Copley: *Ann Tyng,* detail, 1756. Museum of Fine Arts, Boston.)

Fans were an important part of female activity patterns through much of this era. Wafting a fan coyly with grace was an accomplishment signifying the user's artfulness and sophistication. The "language of the fan" was an important means of a coquette's communication. Fluttered, wagged, or positioned at eyes or lips gave a suitor specific information concerning the feelings of the lady he admired. Eighteenth-century fans were beautifully crafted in pleated half circles with ivory or gilded ribs inlaid with mother-of-pearl. The pleated section was made of silk or parchment and intricately painted with romantic pastoral scenes. The complexity of these delicate paintings is remarkable.

Muffs were ample puffs carried by ladies and gentlemen. This was an age with a fetish for small and unique animals. Grand and sophisticated ladies often carried toy-sized dogs, "dressed" in a neck ruffle, in their muffs. The muffs were made of fur or velvet and lined with satin. Men, on occasion, slipped the muff loop over the top button of their justaucorps, allowing the muff to dangle there when not in use.

Thin canes and decorative parasols were very necessary to the posturing and posing manners of eighteenth-

century society. Both had long slender handles and were carried point down at arm's length in an affected gesture. The parasol did have more purpose than the cane, for the flounce-trimmed shade section afforded some protection from the sun.

Men and women preferred to be drenched by a rainstorm rather than to carry an umbrella. It was thought that the use of an umbrella indicated that the person who carried one could could afford neither to own nor to hire a carriage. Finally the good sense of using an umbrella was realized and it became popular among all classes. Umbrellas were then sold in Paris streets by vendors for fifteen or twenty francs each.

Walking sticks became so fashionable between 1700 and the 1770s that they provided a source of revenue for the government, which taxed their owners for the privilege of using them. To carry one of these elegant sticks, a petition had to be submitted which was reviewed by the censor. At his discretion a license of use was granted and the stipulated fee paid.

By the middle of the 1700s, canes became a symbol of status. Doctors could easily be identified by the form of their canes. The general design of canes became more and more elaborate with the handles and the stick sections elegantly decorated. The heads were fashioned in the shape of a reclining *S* made of gold encrusted with jewels and set perpendicular to the ivory, ebony, or glass stick section. Slender daggers or stilettos were often concealed in the stick. Men of wealth possessed as many as forty walking sticks, sometimes valued in excess of $7000.

The handkerchief was another gesturing accessory during this posturing, elegant age. They were trimmed with deep lace edges and made of fine linen in a variety of shapes including ovals, circles, and rectangles. The square handkerchief of modern times is the result of Marie Antoinette's frustration over such a wide variety of shapes from which to choose. Her accommodating husband, ruler that he was, made one of his more lasting decrees—that from then onward all handkerchiefs must be square to be legal.

Silk gloves and silk mitts replaced the large cuffed gauntlets of the previous century. Red kid gloves were used for travel, while those worn daily matched the color of the costume or complemented it with a contrasting color.

The purse, formed by gathering a circle of fabric with a drawstring, was elevated to an elegant accessory item by adding needlepoint decorations.

## BODY AND SKIRT SUPPORTS

For most women, the upper torso was supported by the boned bodice of the gown. Corseting, an integral part of this garment, was made of whalebone stays around the rib cage and a whalebone or wooden busk in the stomacher. According to one writer of the period, "a plated or quilted thing" was worn to "keep the body straight." Late in the eighteenth century, the wasp waist and flat chest reached exaggerated proportions. The desire of all ladies of fashion was to span their waists with "their own two dainty hands" and to achieve, by corseting, a flat, narrow bosom in a "whalebone prison of littleness."

The farthingale skirt supports reappeared briefly during the middle of the Rococo period. At this time the band-and-tape device was used to form a hooped skirt. The bands of *le bout-en train* or *la culanta* increased in number as the skirt styles changed. Ultimately they were extended and held out the skirts in an ever-enlarging circular bell, from the hips to the hems. In time, with the form changes, they became known as **paniers**, or hen baskets. Specific names were attached to each type of panier construction which included: *à guéridon*, a funnel form that was narrow at the waist and wide at the hem; *à coupole*, a dome-shape curving from the waist over the hips and falling straight from the hip-socket level; elbow paniers that were flat in front and semicurved in back—constructed to fold up under the arms to make coach travel more comfortable—projecting in a horizontal line from the waist (Figure 12.26); paniers *à bourrelets*, a

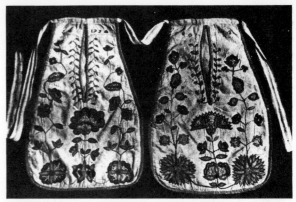

**Figure 12.27.** These pockets, or **dans les poches,** were tied over the hips at the waist, the outer skirt donned, and the draping arranged by stuffing the outer skirt into the pocket slits. (1774, Gallery of English Costume Collection, Manchester.)

round barrel form extending in a straight line from the waist-high panier to the hem at the sides, with puffs at the hips created by the overskirt; paniers *à gondoles*, extending two or three feet beyond the body at the hips and flat in front and back, or projecting only slightly in back; **criardes** paniers, using the same shape as *à gondoles*, but covered with oiled cloth and called "screechers" because of the squeaking noise they made when the wearer walked; and *dans les poches*, puffs and panier forms created by tucking the overskirt into pockets or skirt slits (Figure 12.27).

The chemise, or simple floor-length skirt, was worn beneath the paniers. It had long or three-quarter sleeves that were often visible below the elbow-length bodice sleeves. Men wore a similar undershirt, or waist-length tunic, the **sattana.**

# Hairstyles (1700–1795)

Usually, women's hair between 1700 and 1740 was brushed back from the forehead and gathered into a small twist at the back of the head. There were slight variations which included puffing the hair at the sides of the brow, then drawing it back into large sausage curls. Both of these styles were decorated with small bunches of imitation roses or tiny velvet bows. As more elaborately arranged and higher pompadour coiffures came into fashion, the hair was powdered extensively. The high pompadours were at first pulled taut from the brows and temples and secured high over wads and pads. Much of the hair in back was false, with only that in front being natural. The back was arranged into many small roll curls, large tubular curls, or a combination of all these plus a large bun at the nape of the neck.

After 1770 the hair was piled even higher and was supported by wire frames. Coiffures of this period were so

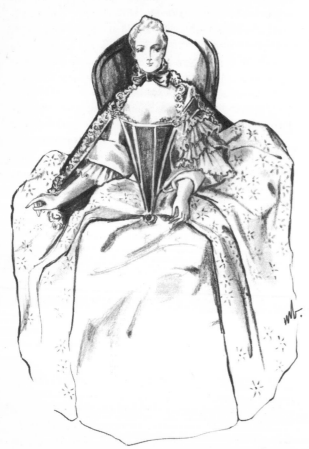

**Figure 12.26. Elbow paniers** were articulated so that these side skirt projections would collapse when a lady was seated. (Redrawn from *Adelaide Tatting,* J. M. Nattier, 1756.)

elaborately dressed that their height and complex decorations took hours to arrange. Hairdressers used ladders to properly attend to the decorations on top or tucked into the hair. These unique embellishments often included ships in full sail, horses, and carriages with passengers and footmen. In the 1770s and 1780s, each hairstyle of this sort had a name: *cheveaux à la conseillère,* historic events; *coiffure à la flore,* baskets of flowers; *à la victoire,* laurel or oak-leaf wreaths; *parterres galantus,* heroic events; and *chiens couchants,* few decorations but with the hair formed into an inverted pyramidal pompadour (Figure 12.28). Because of the time-consuming task of having these coiffures created, once they were finished they were left for weeks with only minor touching up and repowdering. Of course, this was not the most sanitary way of caring for the hair, and vermin quite frequently established healthy colonies in a lady's hairdo.

Hair was brushed and pomades used extravagantly so that the colored powder of white, blue, gray, buff, or pink would adhere. At first, flour was used to powder these elaborate coifs, and many of the peasants resented its use

**Figure 12.29.** This young lad coiffed his own unpowdered hair after the fashion of the **pigeon-wing wig.** (Chardin: *Soap Bubbles,* detail, c. 1731. National Gallery of Art, Washington, D.C.)

**Figure 12.28.** After 1850 ladies of fashion continued to use the **robe retroussée,** but styled their hair in a high **chiens cochants,** an inverted pyramid pompadour. (F. H. Drouais: *Marie de Verrieres,* 1761. Metropolitan Museum of Art, New York City.)

for this vain purpose while common people went hungry. Many contraptions were devised for powdering. One complex invention involved a large shaker under which the person sat, swathed in a voluminous combing jacket and holding a cone tightly over the face to keep the billowing talc out of the eyes and nose. Simple bellows puffed talc on the hair, but the cone was used even when this elementary system was employed if for no other reason than to keep from destroying the carefully applied cosmetics. For a time it was perfectly acceptable to have hair powder on one's suit coat or gown. It signified that the hair had been freshly done.

With the turn of the century, the large periwig was relegated to ceremonial status or to judges of the court. The campaign wig had demonstrated the need and desire for more practical hairstyling for men. At first this resulted in the hair being drawn back into a pigtail and tied with a wide, black silk ribbon. From the 1720s to the 1760s, natural hair and wig styles were created this way. Wigs and natural hair were next pulled back from the forehead and temples and held tightly in place by braiding the hair in a queue in back. The queue was finished by tying large, black ribbons at the head and again at the end of the long braid to form the **Ramilie wig.** Other wig styles included: loose, short curls in back, tied next to the head with a bow; club wig, or **catogan wig** (1770s), with the hair in back folded under and tied, often enlarged by horsehair; *le capaud,* a bag wig or purse-string wig (1750s), the hair in back stuffed into a drawstring pouch, the drawstring tied in back, and then the ends brought to the front and pinned with a brooch or cameo pin; and the **toupet,** hair tufted out over the ears with a queue in back. The ***ailes de pigeon***, or pigeon wings style (1770s-1780s), included the queue in back with the hair cut to ear length and brushed into a triangular shape over the ears (Figure 12.29). In 1790 the hair was rolled back from the forehead and sausage curls arranged in front of the ears. The rolls on the top of the head were next arranged into a point, or ***vergette à la chinoise*** as it was called, because it resembled a Chinese dusting brush used at the time. Commoners of both sexes copied these styles but dusted their own hair with powder rather than wearing wigs.

## FOOTNOTES

1. François Boucher, *20,000 Years of Fashion*, p. 320.
2. Pierre Schneider, *The World of Watteau*, pp. 63–64, p. 73.
3. Ibid., p. 69.
4. Boucher, *20,000 Years of Fashion*, p. 296.
5. Ibid., p. 300.
6. Ibid., p. 303.
7. Ibid., p. 308.
8. Ibid.
9. Ibid., p. 313.

# Chapter 13

# From Revolution to Empire (1790–1815)

**Figure 13.1.** During the late eighteenth and early nineteenth centuries, **sheath dresses** were gracefully draped and figure revealing. This lady has added a **fichu** around her neck, tucking it into the deep neckline. (Charpentier: *Mille Charlotte du Val d'Ognes,* early nineteenth century. Metropolitan Museum of Art, New York City.)

The American Revolution was a product of the Age of Reason. However, the French Revolution was given impetus as the Romantic Age came into being. The individual's inherent right to freedom was a romantic concept. As Kenneth Clark states in his book, *Civilisation,* ". . .philosophers had attempted to tidy up human society by the use of reason."[1] Rousseau had aroused the romantic spirit by appealing to the heart, not the head. Rational arguments were supplanted by more energetic assertions that wisdom and reason were confining. The old ways of prudence and rationality were no longer strong enough to answer the questions being raised by such men as William Blake, Jean Jacques Rousseau, and Robert Burns.

By June of 1789 the Revolution had gone through the first, more rational phase. The National Assembly was sealed to its former members, who then convened in the "tennis court session,"[2] depicted by the Revolutionary artist Jacques Louis David, to swear to establish a constitutional government. In turn the Constituent Assembly was dissolved and was replaced by the Legislative Assembly.[3]

Robespierre, who had helped bring down the old order, was fearful that, when this new body declared war on Prussia and Austria, a victory would bring new consequences. He had said that ". . .were we to be victors, the triumphant general would become the enemy of the people," thus predicting the rise to power of Napoleon.

The last decades of the eighteenth century and the early years of the nineteenth were fraught with cataclysmic military upheavals. England had earlier lost her thirteen colonial territories as the outcome of the American Revolution. France had engaged in a titanic struggle to rid herself of a monarchy which had ruined her population financially. Many lucky French aristocrats sought refuge on British shores where they were given support and sympathy. Louis XVI at first was sympathetic to the French revolutionaries' point of view but was surrounded by advisors who were jealous of their social position and power. Ultimately, they reversed the king's sympathetic attitude toward social reform.

The French Revolution was the culmination of previous uprisings by the masses of people deprived of civil rights and social privilege, burdened with heavy taxation and frustrated by precarious hand-to-mouth existence. Stirrings against the established nobility and aristocracy had begun as early as 1688 in England and had swept to an idealistic success in America in 1783. These revolts did not completely bring down the existing social structure, but they acquired for the people a voice in their government's activities. The French struggle against despotism began in 1789, and its consequences were not finalized until 1815. The beginnings of the French Revolution were liberal and sound; the original concepts were to achieve reform, not to bring about the devastation of the economy, the dissolution of the monarchy, and the demise of all the grandeur of France. As this social war progressed, power fell into the hands of the fanatics. It was this political and philosophical shift which eventually caused the emigration of many aristocrats to England and the execution of countless others, including Louis XVI, his queen, and most of the royal family. The proletariat seized the reins of reform from the bourgeoisie in 1792, which led to the dictatorial reign of Napoleon Bonaparte.

Much of Europe was prosperous when the revolt in France began. The Rhineland, northern Italy, and Belgium were outstandingly affluent. In Belgium, Verviers was an important cloth manufacturing center. Ghent, Lyons, and Rouen produced fine laces for Parisian consumption. With the call of liberty, equality, and fraternity, luxurious stuffs became the hated symbols of all that the citizens detested. As if by edict, but more as a means of erasing aristocratic identity, sumptuous and elegant costumes were discarded. Social distinctions were eliminated with the disappearance of silk knee breeches, tapestry and brocade pourpoints, silk hose, and lavishly trimmed silk gowns. The impact of these shifts in costume styles upon the economic structure of some of the luxury-producing areas in France was profound. This was particularly true in the lace industries and silk mills, and the resulting depressions that occurred in these towns and villages eventually played a part in the attempts to rebuild France. At first a few of the French aristocrats did remain in their homeland, clinging to the social patterns and elegance of the past. But their funds were soon depleted, and eventually even knee breeches, regardless of fabric, were also discarded. Even so tenuous an identity symbol was too dangerous.

The continental consequences of the French Revolution included the reorganization of the Swiss government into the Helvetian Republic. In Italy, rulers of small principalities were deposed, the pope for a time was driven from Rome, and new republican states were formed. Russia, Austria, and England, with pressure brought by the latter, formed a new coalition to stem France's new aggressive actions. The arrival on the continental political scene of a self-made ruler was the result of the machinations of civil war and the intricate workings of national and international governmental activities.

By clever manipulative actions, Napoleon Bonaparte became a military dictator. As his power increased, Napoleon sought more for France. During the Directoire period (1795–1799), France acquired Belgium from Austria in a trade for Venice, the Po region was conquered, and the Rhine was in French hands. However, French rule of much of Europe was continually challenged, and England and Austria incessantly sought to check her empire-building aspirations. France began a campaign in Egypt but British warships under Lord Nelson defeated Napoleon in the Battle of the Nile. Although Napoleon was forced to flee to Paris, he was received as a hero. He was a supreme opportunist who took advantage of public adulation and governmental corruption to seize control of France and ultimately crown himself emperor.

By 1804 the ambitious new king had developed a secret police. In time he gained power over the pope, who even consecrated bishops chosen by Napoleon. He controlled France militarily, politically, economically, and even in the area of fashion. His sway over these vast,

differing forces affected the whole of Europe. Wars with England, Austria, Prussia, Spain, and other countries continued. As long as he made kings and churchmen submit to his whims, the masses in the countries he defeated believed him to be a liberator. In time he miscalculated the attitudes of the populace in the countries he conquered. He pressed them into military service, kidnapped their country's artifacts, and disillusioned them with his despotic conduct. The fateful defeat at the Battle of Waterloo in 1815 ended his power, but not before he had organized the French government, codified French law, established a national system of education, reestablished the Roman church as the national religion, unified the country, and recreated the magnificent city of Paris. He gave to the French a national pride in their cultural attainments which has persisted well into the twentieth century.

While France was unsettled, the rest of Europe progressed economically. War profiteering, as well as the capture of markets once supplied by France, aided this growth. The trends in fashion modes, once established by the royal court in Paris, were set by England. There, a supremacy in men's tailoring was established which has remained unsurpassed for generations.

In the late eighteenth century, a reawakened interest in the governmental organization of ancient Greece led to the rediscovery of other facets of the classic Greek culture. Ancient Greek art forms and clothing styles gave impetus to eighteenth- and early nineteenth-century adaptations.

England developed a technique for weaving cotton fibers into a cloth so fine that it almost rivaled silk in texture and appearance. This new marketable cloth was easily draped in the style of Greek and Roman clothing. At this time the English introduced women's gowns patterned after the Greek chiton, and women attempted to appear as much like copies of ancient sculpture as possible (Figure 13.2). Other details of antiquity were copied in sleeves, necklines, and decorations. Attempting to achieve the maximum similarity, women drenched their cotton-draped figures with water so that the garments would cling to their skin. Men soaked their chamois trousers in an effort to create a figure-revealing appearance. Over these skin-tight trousers, some French men wore a copy of the Roman toga or himation. Going about soaked to the skin gave rise to severe colds and pneumonia, which in many cases resulted in death. Eventually French governmental officials decreed that it was illegal to wear drenched clothing.

After the Reign of Terror, there was a renewed interest in appearance. Marie Antoinette's designer, Rose Bertin, returned from exile, as did designers André Scheling and Duval. They became the dictators of female and male fashions. As in any age, social stratification soon began to be identified through clothing.

**Figure 13.2.** Borders, duplicating hemline trims of the ancient Greeks, were common **chemise** and **sheath** details in 1800. Scarf wraps were used in the same manner as the palla of Imperial Rome. (Fashion illustration of the early nineteenth century, Bibliothèque Nationale, Paris.)

The arts of the late seventeenth and eighteenth centuries, for the most part, were created to satisfy the desires of the courts of several European countries. The painters Fragonard, Boucher, and Gainsborough, the sculptor Houdon, dramatist Molière, and composers Bach, Haydn, and Mozart are representative of the vast group of artists who were supported by court patrons. Renewed interest in classical cultures and in the medieval tales of the Holy Grail and King Arthur gave rise to changes in the visual arts. The Neoclassical and Romantic styles spanned about a hundred years, originating in 1750 and fading out by the middle of the nineteenth century. The period involved a long-forgotten interest in the "Gothnick" past and developed from a growing revulsion toward the existing social order. Emotionalism, the expression of an experience, imaginary or actual, motivated many creative individuals. These were the Neoclassical concepts, while the Romantics who came later had a burning desire to return to nature. The bucolic pastoral paintings of the early eighteenth century had presaged these later attitudes. Architecture with columns and Ionic capitals and Roman domes supplanted the elegant but simple structures of Sir Christopher Wren and the complexities of the Baroque. Adam in England and Jefferson in America utilized the columns and capitals of Greek art in buildings and monuments. West, Copley, Stubbs, Fusell, and Blake created paintings typical of this new period. The social struggle controlled the visual expressions of the age, and costumes were affected also.

Bonaparte, although engaged in military conquests ranging from Egypt to Russia, found time, because of the economic impact, to issue pronouncements on fashions. He established in his court the elegance of Louis XIV. The fashion designer Leroy was commissioned to establish fashion with an emphasis on sumptuous dress (Figure 13.3). He was instructed to use rich fabrics, velvets, heavy silks, and brocades with laces and precious metal embroideries. All these materials were to be produced in France so that regions dependent on the fashion-related industries would recover economically. To insure that heavier fabrics were used, Napoleon ordered all fireplaces bricked up in the palaces frequented by his court. Of necessity, ladies ordered warmer gowns made of velvets, for nature had conspired to implement his decree. The mild winters of previous years turned severely cold and gossamer gowns were totally inadequate.

**Figure 13.3.** The **Leroy gown** was mandatory in the Napoleonic court. The separate train was royal purple velvet and the embroidery made of platinum thread. (David: *The Consecration of the Emperor Napoleon I and the Coronation of the Empress Josephine*, detail, 1803. Louvre, Paris.)

Fashion's silhouette changes were as striking as the social changes. While Napoleon influenced fashion for economic reasons, life in England and her dominance as a vogue pacesetter also had a profound impact on costume in Europe and in America. Technology, too, was advancing rapidly as it stood on the brink of the nascent Industrial Revolution.

George IV of England had established Brighton as the spa of England. There, the privileged were guests at the Royal Pavilion. They engaged in many diversions, including target practice with bows and arrows in the long narrow hall which led into the grand ballroom. Influenced by things Oriental, particularly Chinese objets d'art, the decor of the Royal Pavilion where George IV entertained was a fanciful combination of gilded rosewood turned on a lathe to imitate bamboo, and columns spreading onto the ceiling to simulate palm leaves. This interior-design motif was carried throughout the entire structure, even in the massive kitchen.

George IV made bathing in the sea popular. Unlike twentieth-century customs, bathers were clad in shapeless garments and seated in wicker, hooded chairs on wheels which were rolled into the surf. Here they sat, enjoying the gentle ebb and flow of the sea. Salt water was assumed to have curative powers, and, in his declining years, King George had many afflictions including obesity and gout.

The Royal Pavilion had originally looked out to the sea with an unobstructed view. However not all activities were centered in this elegant, kingly retreat, for broad boardwalks and piers were built to accommodate open-air entertainments.

The restoration of the Royal Pavilion was begun in the 1940s, and the Pavilion now contains some excellent examples of costume from the late years of the reign of George IV. Large hats with tall crowns and face-concealing brims bedecked with feathers, and wraps, such as redingotes, are laid out on chaise longues as if lady guests had only just doffed them. The complexity of the trims foretells of the braid-and-ribbon-encrusted gowns of the early Victorian era and belies the earlier, simpler styles that had resulted from the French Revolution and the interest in classical cultures of Greece and Rome.

Though the English are credited with the introduction of the classical style, it has also been suggested that France was the first country to promote styles based on classical garments. The rest of Europe clung to mildly modified versions of the older, more sumptuous French court costumes, believing that to imitate the earlier modes reflected their level of taste, that of monarchic France.[4]

In *Family Portrait*, Naigeon, 1793, the women are shown wearing soft, sheath gowns of white tied with wide ribbon sashes of contrasting colors in a bustlelike bow in back. The paniers have given way to softly gathered skirts supported by many petticoats. This soft, feminine, romantic costume had snug-fitting, elbow-length sleeves with lace cuffs of modest size. Fichu or ruching trimmed the modest oval or circular necklines. The hems of these sheath dresses may have been trimmed with horizontal pleats or a border of delicate lace insertions and embroidery as depicted in François Sablet's *Family Portrait*, created in 1794. The tricolor costume popular with female sympathizers to the French Revolution was of similar cut, but made of fabrics with a red, white, and blue color theme.

Hairstyles continued to be elaborately coiffed, waved, and bouffant with sausage curls in back until just before the turn of the century. After this period the styles imitated, if not precisely, the hairstyles depicted in Greek and Greco-Roman sculpture.

By 1797 the waistline of female gowns was lifted to a level just below the bust. A formal gown was shown in a fashion illustration which appeared in that year. This formal costume consisted of a chemise dress with a softly gathered skirt, puffed sleeves, and a separate train attached at the high waist, and decorated with a palmette design reminiscent of the military toga of Imperial Rome. Gowns created in the manner of the Greek chiton and Roman stola were given such exotic names as tunic *à la romaine* and chemise *à la grecque* (Figure 13.4). Usually made of white muslin, the day costume, or *toilette*, often was delicately decorated on the chemise skirt with scalloped horizontal bands from hem to thigh. The status of the wearer was indicated by the number and abundance of ribbon rosettes and trailing ribbon streamers. Pendant necklaces of gold chains with enameled brooches were worn in multiples.

French gowns between 1801 and 1806 were even simpler. Transparency of the outer chemise revealed a shorter **opaque** or underchemise. The wearer's lower limbs and feet were tantalizingly visible. Sandals *à la grecque* were secured about the lower leg with silken ribbons in the manner of the cross-laced style of Grecian sandals.

During this entire period, garments were styled according to the plasticity of available textiles. Because of the wars throughout Europe, embargoes and blockades determined the export and import of various fabrics. In Belgium, Verviers and Ghent became textile-producing centers, as did Lyons and Rouen in France. The latter two cities were famous for printed cotton textiles and were the primary suppliers to the Paris garment makers. Over 12,000 women worked in the textile mills of these cities. The Berlin Decree of 1803 blockaded British ports for three years, preventing the English importation of continental cotton cloth, nankeens, muslin, and even thread.[5] Of course, not all blockades were complete and smuggling was a lucrative practice, with trade not only in fabrics but dyes too. However, trade with the United States was brisk.

**Figure 13.4.** The **chemise à la grecque** was a simple garment with small, puffed sleeves, a high waistline, and a skirt section slightly gathered all around the figure. (Redrawn from portrait of *Caroline Bonaparte*, c. 1800, dressed in a gown designed by Leroy.)

France also extended commercial routes to include not only the countries over which she had dominion, but to several other republics.

England expanded its trade, making London a commercial world power. Implemented by great sea power, England's trade routes stretched from her own ports to North America, the West Indies, the Far East, and Africa. As the Industrial Revolution grew to dominate the world situation, the quantity and quality of garment-making supplies were affected, often adversely.

Political concepts continued to dictate garment forms. While the court costumes of France were abolished during the first phases of the French Revolution, costumes of elegance were reintroduced late in the reign of Napoleon I, but not until he had gained dictatorial authority over the French government. The French mode of the Empire soon spread to the nations whose "kings" had been enthroned by Bonaparte. After 1814–1815, French fashions were accepted by the British, many of whom had traveled to Paris at the time of the Peace of Amiens. The

occupation of Paris by allied armies did more to spread the Paris-created fashions than any efforts by the Consulate and Empire.[6]

Utilitarianism and individualism dictated changes in social concepts and patterns and struck down the elegant but cumbersome styles of the preceding century. Democratic attitudes and economic prosperity also had an effect on garment design. The centralized authority which royal courts and Napoleon's Imperial regime had held over costume styles came to an end with the exile of France's self-proclaimed emperor. To be sure, even in the early phases of the revolution in France, there had been established a sense of newfound freedom. This freedom was expressed in clothing which for men and women was more comfortable. After the Reign of Terror in 1793 and 1794, the "citizens" in France wished to forget the horrors of their civil struggle. In this mood they sought entertainment and a more frivolous life-style. Costumes reflected the will to once again enjoy life. The kings' mistresses, who had developed feminine costume patterns for men and women, no longer existed.

Although elegant, men's clothing was restrained in cut and decoration. As early as 1797, the black, tailed coat and leg-covering trousers were the basic French male costume. The trousers were often stuffed into boots reaching mid-calf, retaining in part the appearance of knee breeches.

Of course, not all countries costumed themselves in exactly the same mode, and peasant dress was much different from European city dress. American frontier women also were bound by the limitation of available textiles and even the knowledge of the explicit current mode.

In some of the early portraits by Copley, important American ladies are depicted in gowns of duplicate styling but different colors from those worn by the women of the Court of St. James.[7] Until the introduction of fashion books, knowledge of the latest Paris and London fashions was limited and gowns were often copied from engravings of European portraits. Two obvious examples are the portraits of Mary Toppan and Mary Turner Sargent. The former is in the Yale University Art Gallery and the latter in the Corcoran Gallery of Art.

Using the termination of Napoleon's reign in 1815 as the end of this period of radical style changes, it is again obvious that the mode had altered from the simple to the complex. By the year 1815 the spirit of freedom expressed through costume had disappeared. The elegance of the monarchy had been reintroduced by Napoleon. His court, wishing to establish its social status, had dressed in fashions that symbolized their importance and affluence. Financiers and wealthy tradesmen and their families, in turn, imitated their social superiors. In France the productive creativity of Leroy made it possible for women of wealth and rank to appear in totally individualistic costumes. Though the basic silhouette was constant, Leroy never repeated a gown.[8]

The resumption of a consuming interest in being fashionably dressed reached its height in 1814. Napoleon was retreating from Russia, but in Paris Josephine's daughter was ordering an elegant gown, said to have cost as much as 14,000 francs, made of rich fabrics and trims. Indeed, costume concepts had come full circle from elegance through the simplicity of the white cambric **gaulle,** or chemise dress, of 1780 to the elegance of Leroy gowns during the Empire.[9] During the 1790s excesses in dress of the *Incroyables* and *Merveilleuses,* sympathizers to the French Revolution, presaged a trend toward more complexity in costume. *Merveilleuses,* female counterparts of the *Incroyables,* had chosen gowns with such fanciful names from classical antiquity as Ceres, Minerva, Diana, and Omphole.

By 1794 white as the preferred gown color had been exchanged for a yellow called "pale canary," or a violet named "fly's backside."[10] The dressmaker Leroy and his partner, Mme. Raimbaut, introduced even more sumptuous colors in court gowns when they created modes for the Empress Josephine. The opulent fabrics increased the cost of gowns, and the average price was about $300, but royalty spent far more for a garment.

Napoleon was so concerned that his court be elegantly attired that an important painter of the day, Isabey, was hired to make the fashion sketches. These beautiful, short-sleeved costumes had revealing décolletage. With these female court costumes were worn long, perfumed gloves, diamond tiaras, and long trains. A far cry from Mme. Tallien, formerly Theresa Cabarus, who had appeared at the Paris Opera with, as a chronicler of the day said, "her arms clad only in the rings on her fingers."

Fashion changes were reported in periodicals: *The Ladies European Magazine,* London (1798); *La Belle Assemblée,* London (1806–1832); *Bell's Court and Fashionable Magazine,* London (1806); *Magazine des Modes,* Paris (first published in 1785); and *Galerie des Modes,* Paris (1797).[11] These replaced the fashion dolls of previous years which, for several centuries, had been sent out from the fashion capitals of Europe to one city after another. The earliest recorded use of fashion dolls occurred in 1396 when an English queen sent to Europe for samples of continental court dress.[12] Sometimes the dolls had to be transported through battlefields and, because of the importance of fashion, military engagements were known to have been halted so that the fashion couriers might pass safely.

In America, fashion was equally important to the landed aristocracy and the wives of wealthy tycoons of commerce. In 1801 *Port Folio,* created by Mr. Dennie, opened in Philadelphia and became a fashion center where Abigail Adams shopped for her clothes when she was the First Lady.[13]

Costumes and the homes of the influential populace underwent parallel changes. Early Empire furnishings imitated the simple beauty of ancient Grecian chairs, tables, and chaise longues, incorporating design motifs of that earlier period. A passion for stripes in textiles was carried over into wallpapers. **Mameluck** sleeves, swags, trains, and tiaras again were introduced in dress, and households were bedecked with accessories of comparable complexity. The aesthetics of the age again projected into garment styles of men and women. The organizational clarity of David and Igres, with its sense of classic, disciplined proportion, gave way to more plastic dynamic relationships of the romantics. Subject matter in literature, the opera, and painting also changed. The court music of Handel and Mozart was displaced by the romantic, ponderous compositions of Beethoven.

Many social changes had taken place during this period. The élégantes had become refugees in England and Austria. To earn a living, some turned to millinery while others became maids or darning women.[14] Another startling social change concerned contracts for marriage. Advertisements for marriage appeared in papers such as the *Indicateur*. Such announcements appeared on Tuesdays and Fridays, and from such lists lonely French republican couples were paired off. No church ceremonies were required; posting of the marriage in the town hall was the only requirement. A civil official wearing a tricolored sash joined the pair. After 1792 divorce was easily obtained by a decree which proclaimed incompatibility as reasonable grounds.

Life, its style, and the aesthetic sensitivity of those living in constant change influenced manners and fashion modes. The poor, however, continued to struggle. Social changes had been made, but a new aristocracy developed in France and even in the United States. The wealthy again set the styles that were copied in cut and fabric by their inferiors.

Textiles, save on the frontiers of the new world, were produced in factories. In the ever-growing cities and in tiny hamlets, shops were established for creating all the fashion materials and related accessories. The first such fashion-related shops made undergarments such as corsets. Ready-to-wear shops made their appearance in the last decades of the eighteenth century. Each shop was designed to sell one specific item such as hose, gloves, hats, laces, and textiles. However, in Paris at Leroy's, all accessories were available. Shops with similar merchandise were often grouped together and whole areas devoted exclusively to their manufacture. Centers of production continued to supply the shops at an increasingly rapid rate as technological advances were made in naval architecture, iron mongering, wagon making, and printing, which had been refined to visually report fashion's changes in fashion books. The agrarianism of the past continued, but the economic base was developing another facet which was to affect clothing in such a way as to ultimately industrialize it.

## Basic Garments from the French Revolution through the Empire (1789–1815)

### GOWNS (1780–1790)

While many women of the upper classes continued to use costumes comparable to those worn at the French court, others were adopting new style trends. The romantic and bucolic life-style, given impetus by Rousseau's writings, was translated into clothing by shortening skirts to just above the ankle. An apron was worn over the multipetticoat-supported skirts. The softly gathered skirts had the greater bulk of the skirt fabric drawn to the back. Adding a pad over the posterior resulted in a modified bustle. Overskirts were drawn up to reveal handsomely trimmed petticoats. This fashion imitated the peasant woman's practice of lifting the skirt of her outer garment to keep it out of her way while going about her chores.

When Benjamin Franklin was in France representing the United States, he introduced styles reminiscent of colonial Puritans into Paris fashion circles. These fashions were quickly dubbed *à la Franklin* and were accepted as symbols of republican freedom throughout Europe.[15]

The mania for all things British also influenced the mode of the day. In turn, English climate and interest in country living dictated the trend of female fashions on this prosperous island. A German chronicler, Helferich Peter Sturz, noted, "To some extent we are avenged by the anglomania of the Frenchmen of today. Everywhere one meets wandering riding coats with fragile, sketchy, and shadowy beings fidgeting in their folds . . . ." The styles to which he referred were called *mode à l'anglaise* (Figure 13.5). These consisted of gowns similar to those described above. For added warmth they were worn with a tailored jacket with tails or hipbone-length peplums in back. Multilayering of garments, which added to the silhouette's bulk, was necessary in England because of the generally chilly weather. Often gowns of this period were styled with slender but not snug-fitting sleeves, cuffed in contrasting color with ruching trims at the wrists. Others were fitted with more complex sleeve treatments including one called *à l'espagnole.* This type of sleeve extended beyond the wrist; a ruching edging was attached at this point, and an inset of contrasting fabric, slightly puffed, introduced just above the elbow on the upper arm. Waistlines of the gowns of this decade were positioned at the normal position in back and dipped in front, forming a *V* over the upper abdomen.

**Figure 13.5.** English ladies were less elegant than their continental contemporaries, often wearing their straw bonnets atop ruffled, brimmed mobcaps. The **chemise à l'anglaise** was designed with snug-fitting sleeves and was belted with a sizeable sash or belt. (Anonymous: *Madam Serezeat,* detail, c. 1800. Louvre, Paris.)

While many gowns were given exotic names, general classifications included: morning dress, court dress, and ceremonial dress. These terms referred to the entire ensemble including gown, wrap, hat, and accessories.

**Morning gowns** were, as a rule, plain with few trimmings except at the cuffs, and a fichu or kerchief about the neck (Figure 13.6). The major embellishment was achieved in draping the skirt.

**Court dress,** in countries where monarchs still ruled, was more elaborate and was designed with specific seasons in mind. For example, a court dress for winter might have been trimmed with swags of ermine, caught at the peak of the swag by twisted or braided frogs and dangling, fringed tassels or multilooped ribbon bows.

**Ceremonial dress,** or **grand ceremonial dress,** of the 1780s retained all the characteristics of earlier, less troubled times when royalty dictated fashion. Necklines were oval, revealing the shoulders and the upper bosom. Sleeves were snug to the elbows and cuffed with a lace puff over the elbow with lace gracing top and edge of the puff. Bodices were boned, and the body firmly controlled by corseting. While the stomacher no longer was in vogue,

**Figure 13.6.** Female undergarments and morning costume of the 1800s. (*Morning Toilette,* detail, print c. 1800. Bibliothèque Nationale, Paris.)

gold or silver braid was used to simulate this once needed accessory which served to conceal the bodice lacing. In England until 1800, skirts of grand ceremonial gowns were many layered, intricate, and panier supported. For example, the swag-edged overgown revealed an intricately trimmed underskirt through the inverted V-opening. Atop the overskirt might be a thigh-length, gathered peplum edged with rows of contrasting gathered trims. In some illustrations from fashion journals of the day, the overskirt was drawn back asymmetrically. Trims also were arranged in a similar organizational pattern which departed from the formal bilateral styling of the period between 1770 and 1780.

While France explored the potential of adapting the classical styles of Greece and Rome, the rest of Europe remained faithful to the so-called **chemise dress** in the 1780s. This costume was similar to the morning dress with the exception of the waistline treatment. It was now positioned at the natural waist and accented by a wide, silken sash of contrasting hue elaborately tied in back. Skirts were gathered to the waist and were not quite as full in the back as had been the vogue during the previous decade. The dominant color of the chemise was white as opposed to the deeper, richer hues popular in the preceding years, although pale yellows and other tints continued to be used by some.

## TUNIC DRESS (1793–1808)

The simple tunic dress or chemise *à la grecque* appeared early in the last decade of the eighteenth century. The adjustment from elaborate dress to simple lines was gradual. The major change was in raising the waistline to just below the bust and adding small, puffed sleeves (Figure 13.7). The first appearance of a raised waistline is credited to the Duchess of York at the height of the Albion fad in Europe. The Duchess, realizing that she was pregnant, introduced the new fashion line by moving the *cul de Paris*, the small horsehair bustle, to the front. The new silhouette line was called "false stomach," and predated the Empire line by several years. The false stomach was worn not only by pregnant, married women but by young girls and was the rage in Paris in the early 1790s.[16] Intended to be a facsimile or at least inspired by classical garments, it bore little resemblance to the beautiful drapery of the Greek chiton.

More closely related to these ancient garments was the tunic *à la romaine*, or *à la grecque*, of the Directoire period (1800–1808). A painting by Jacques Louis

**Figure 13.7. Chemise gowns,** generally made from fine, white cotton fabric, were styled with small, puffed sleeves and a low, straight neckline modestly trimmed with edging lace. Silk ribbons were tied just under the bust. (Redrawn from *Mlles. Mollien,* Rouget, detail, 1811.)

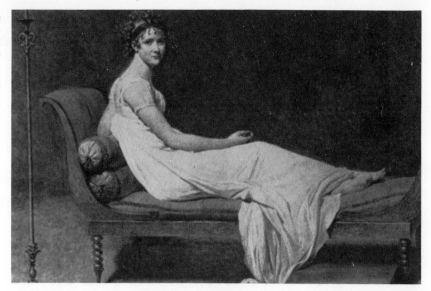

**Figure 13.8.** This **chemise** illustrates the box-pleated sleeve and hints of a complex design of the bodice back. The skirt fullness shifted to the back of the gown as the century turned, and developed into a modest train. The coiffure was called **Titus.** (Jacques Louis David: *Portrait of Mme. Récamier,* detail, 1800. Louvre, Paris.)

David of Mme. Recamier (Figure 13.8) more closely resembles the aesthetic sensitivities of the past, and the importance and appreciation of the beauty of the human female form. It was the physical beauty of Mme. Tallien which gave impetus to the fashion for revealing the female body in all of its sensuous attributes. For a gala ball at the Paris Opera, A. Duval created for Mme. Tallien an exotic, provocative costume, called by some the tunic *à la romaine*. It was a simple, sleeveless gown with a deep décolletage and a slightly gathered body. Mme. Tallien wore this tunic over a body-revealing, flesh-colored garment similar to the modern body stocking. Many immediately adopted this style, enlarging the neckline to reveal much of the bust. The tunic *à la romaine* was styled from the sheerest of textiles, generally made of cotton fibers. This simple gown dress with two side seams gathered to the rather large, round neckline was worn over an equally transparent undertunic (Figure 13.6). The female form was almost completely revealed, including the stocking supports, through these two thin layers of fabric. Some authors suggest that these tunic gowns were sometimes knee length; however, this supposition is contradicted by the portraiture of the period.

While the name of this dress was maintained for some years, the silhouette adjusted drastically. At first a simple garment cut in two pieces, it soon was devised from a more complex cut. The earliest style had a drawstring at the neck and another just beneath the bust. Depth of décolletage and draping of the rest of the gown were arranged according to the wearer's preference. This styling survived throughout the French Republic period, and the only changes made were to enlarge the neck opening and raise the girdling string. In the last phase of this mode, the sleeves were mere puffs over the cap of the shoulder, or nonexistent. One concession to sumptuousness appeared with the addition of ever longer trains.

**Figure 13.9.** As the first decade of the nineteenth century closed, the **chemise** silhouette was altered by placing a roll at the hem to hold the gown in a full circle at the ankles. Men's suit coats were designed with rather sizeable puffed sleeves and were slightly padded in the chest. Typical trouser forms were skin tight and worn with **Wellington** boots. (Fashion illustration, c. 1812–1815. Bibliothèque Nationale, Paris.)

At the turn of the century, a bodice, or *le corsage*, was added, made in only two pieces but of intricate design. The skirt section was arranged in large pleats and joined to the bodice, which was as brief as possible with deep décolletage in front and back.[17] By 1807 the fullness of the skirt had been eliminated and the skirts became so narrow that walking was difficult. Snug fitting and figure revealing, these gowns were labeled *robes en calecon*.[18] The next style change was the addition of a gusset at the hem and back pleating (Figure 13.9).

The revealing tunic *à la romaine* was introduced to American women by imported European fashion books and those published in the new world. A Mrs. Samuel Harrison Smith recorded the reaction to these gossamer gowns in 1801 when she wrote, "There was a lady here who afforded us great amusement. I titled her Madame Eve and called her dress the fig leaf." Generally, American women did not adopt the extreme décolletage of the tunic *à la romaine* or *grecque* except for evening wear. The fad of wearing a high-necked underchemise, introduced

**Figure 13.10.** *Merveilleuses*, female revolutionary sympathizers, wore the **negligee à la patriot, bicorns** decorated with rosettes, blue **redingotes** lined with red, and **sandals à la grecque.** (Redrawn from a political cartoon, c. 1795. Bibliothèque Nationale, Paris.)

in Europe about 1803, remained popular in the United States throughout the first two decades of the nineteenth century. This fad satisfied those with greater modesty than modishness and added a modest decorative element to the costume.[19]

The **negligee à la patriot** was a simple style around 1790 that identified the wearer as a supporter of the Revolution (Figure 13.10). Always made of white cotton fabric, it had tight sleeves, a tight, short-waisted bodice, a full skirt, and round neckline. The neck was trimmed with a red-and-white striped collar. This costume was worn with a blue redingote, carrying out the tricolor theme of the revolutionaries.

Both the tunic *à la vestale* and tunic *à la Diane* were introduced in 1790 as fine muslin replicas of the chiton. These exaggerated styles were worn by the Merveilleuses.[20] The Diane and vestal tunics had small set-in sleeves, deep oval necklines, and right-side openings to more closely resemble the Greek chitons, and were worn over flesh-colored tights. Posturing that extended the right leg from the side slit was a part of the wearer's technique of being fascinatingly feminine. Toe-rings and sandals with crossed, ribbon lacings further related the attire to antiquity. For convenience, women suspended from the high-waisted belt, a work bag, or balantine, which was an embroidered, rectangular pouch hung on the left side from a wide, decorative cloth band.

The **sheath dress** and the **chemise dress** were more conventional gowns with high waists, round necklines, and puffed sleeves (Figure 13.1). The sheath had a rather full skirt with a wide sash tied under the bust and sleeves that were either three-quarter length or long. A calico ruffle or muslin kerchief was used as a neckline trim. The chemise had a more slender skirt with the hemline treated in one of several variations including scalloping, or a deep, center-front slit with curved edges. Tiered skirts were also a characteristic of these dresses. The puffed sleeves had no standard size, varying from small, puffed cap sleeves to large puffs that covered half the upper arm. Skirt and sleeve trimmings included ribbons and garlands of flowers (Figure 13.11). Both of these dress styles were introduced in 1797 and each was made with a separate bodice and skirt, sewn together at the high waistline. The **constitution, camelle, indienne dress,** and **chemise grecque** were all chemise dresses with distinctive decorations. Some of the trimmings used were rosettes, wide fringed sashes, and hem embroidery. Authors often group all of these styles under the heading *à l'antique.*

## GOWNS (1800–1815)

Leroy, commissioned by Napoleon to design elegant female costumes, created gowns bearing his name (Figure 13.3). They were made with bust-length bodices and either small puffed sleeves or long, hand-covering, tight sleeves. The neckline of the **Leroy gown** was square and

**Figure 13.11.** French ladies, in an effort to create the illusion of Greek sculpture, wore transparent white **chemise** dresses trimmed with ribbons or floral garlands. (Redrawn from fashion plates, c. 1800–1804.)

typical high-waisted bodice, slender skirt, and puffed sleeves of various lengths comprised the major elements of the sheath. The high waist was marked by a slender ribbon belt tied in a crisp bow. The square neckline was extremely décolleté, revealing the upper half of the breasts. The skirt was plain in the front, with greater fullness in back. Usually, the sleeves were draped and elbow length or full length in **mameluck** style. The mameluck sleeve consisted of several puffs from the shoulder to the wrist created by tying ribbons at several places along the arm (Figure 13.12). In many instances this type of sleeve treatment was reminiscent of the puffs and slashes of the Renaissance. Elbow-length sleeves were often buttoned into graceful drapes called *à l'anglaise* sleeves. During the second decade of the nineteenth century, sheath dresses appeared in many variations. One sheath from about 1815 in the costume collection of the Victoria and Albert Museum was made of a subtle blue velvet with intricately trimmed mameluck sleeves. Braid of a dark navy blue edged the scalloped sleeve trim which overlaid the multipuffed mameluck sleeve.

There were many neckline trims also reminiscent of the Spanish ruff of the Renaissance. The V-necklines of

very low in front with a deep round curve in back. The waist seam was hidden by fringe. The skirt fell straight over the front and created a conical silhouette with a slight flare at the hem. A padded roll was added at the hemline to hold the skirt out in the required form. A drape that became a modestly proportioned train in back was also characteristic of this gown.

The **gala gown,** or **gala dress,** was designed exclusively for wear at Napoleon's court. It was a richly embroidered chemise with small, puffed cap sleeves, a low bust-revealing neckline, and a slender, floor-length skirt. This court gown was designed with a mantle extending into a train which was fashioned from heavy velvet and platinum-thread embroidery. Platinum thread was used rather than silver, because these dresses were ceremonial garments, seldom worn, and the silver or gold embroidery would tarnish during the periods when they were not in use. The mantle train was separate from the gown and tied around the figure just below the bust with heavy silk cords that ended in decorative tassels.

Between 1810 and 1815, the term *sheath* was applied to all gowns made of heavy fabrics (Figures 13.1). The

**Figure 13.12.** An example of **mameluck** sleeve treatment. The gown is of British origin. (Redrawn from an actual costume in the Victoria and Albert Museum Costume Court, London.)

gowns or sheath day-dresses were trimmed with ruching or braid. A ruff, similar to the Betsy of the previous century, was worn with the V-necked gown as an added throat accessory.

The female figure emphasis of this period centered around the head and bust. Tantalizing hints of the figure's form beneath the rather snug-fitting, instep-length skirts added a high sense of femininity to these gowns. By the end of the second decade of the nineteenth century, the transparent mode had ended. Petticoats, sometimes in multiples, were worn beneath all gowns, if not for modesty, at least to extend skirts to the desired circular form at the hem.

An elegant variation of the sheath and the chemise was the formal **theater gown** of satin in which the bodice and skirt were cut together. A design imitating the high-waisted styles of the period was achieved by folding in diagonal darts starting at the point of the bust and slanting to the side seam. These folds were held in place and fastened at the seams with four or five small, covered buttons to maintain the desired short-bodice effect. The folded darts merged into unpressed skirt pleats that originated below the last button and extended to the floor-length hem. This rolled pleat added fullness to the hemline of an otherwise slender skirt silhouette which, by 1810, had no train. These handsomely designed gowns were made from brocade or patterned taffeta fabrics. In some cases small fur pieces of ermine or marten were worn, repeating the décolletage of the neckline. A formal theater gown was styled with a low, ruffled neckline and puffed sleeves laced to the armseye. Two thin belts were bound around the figure to create a high-waisted dress with a clinging skirt which was often caught up in front with a brooch. This draped opening extended from the knee to the hem, exposing the sandaled feet.

The chemise retained the typical lines of all dresses of this period except that about 1804 a larger, fuller skirt was added which eventually developed into a rather long train that extended the skirt six to fourteen feet in back. Simple in general styling, the chemise was worn over a taffeta petticoat.

The tunic *à la grecque* reappeared in fashion briefly around 1810. Like the chemise, it was made of transparent material for summer wear.

Velvet tunic dresses with contrasting mameluck sleeves or short puffed sleeves were open from the high waist to the hem. They were overdresses usually worn with the chemise. The tunic with the longer, more complex sleeves was called **tunic *à la mameluck*** (1810-1815), and the short, puffed-sleeve style was known as **tunic *à la Juive*** (Figure 13.13). Yet another style of tunic evolved into an **apron-gown** (1789-1790). It had a full skirt which opened down the back from a point originating at the base of the high-waisted bodice. More elaborate decorations began to appear about 1804, and the apron gown

**Figure 13.13.** By 1810 women were wearing several petticoats beneath a softly gathered, high-waisted **chemise** dress, or **tunic à la Juive.** Long mitts extended from just below the small, puffed sleeves to the palms of the hands. Face-concealing bonnets, such as the **cabriolet,** were also in fashion. (Redrawn from a fashion plate of the period.)

was trimmed with an embroidered border around the hem and along the edges of the back opening.

The **classical gown** was a simplified chemise with draped or puffed sleeves. The skirt was full in back and smooth in front with weights used to maintain a straight, vertical skirt silhouette. Fringe or a pleated ruffle was added at the hem as a simple decoration. Other gown details included **Betsies** and **collarettes,** basically neckline trims. The Betsy, an English innovation reminiscent of the Renaissance ruff, was composed of a ruching or small ruffle tied under the chin with a slender

**Figure 13.14.** Typical lady's bonnet, **Betsy,** and collar treatment of the female **redingote.** (David: *Madame de Tangry and Her Daughters,* detail, c. 1816. Louvre, Paris.)

gathering cord (Figure 13.14). Collerettes were made in two styles: *à la Gabrielle,* a high-standing, pleated, and starched collar that nearly obscured the head; and *à la Cyrus,* a somewhat flatter collar attached to the neckline of the dress. The corrupted name for this neckline trim became *chérusse,* then *chérusque.*

## JACKETS AND SKIRTS (1790–1799)

The skirts of the early Revolutionary period were rather full and gathered to a waistband. They were worn by most women with a simple blouse or mannish shirt. Later, the skirts were a wraparound style, trimmed on the open edge with braid which also edged the hem. Braid frogs were used to outline the darts in the skirt front, in imitation of the male trouser closure. A white waistcoat was often worn with the wraparound skirt as a blouse. It had a center-front button closure, high, winged collar, and a wrapped white cravat. The **ecrouellique,** or lady's cravat, was the only neck treatment. The waistcoat sleeves were rather snug fitting and wrist length.

The **caraco,** also worn with the wraparound skirt or the chemise *à l'anglaise,* was the feminine version of the frock coat. It was made from an intricate pattern and fitted the figure to reveal the female form. The back was snug

across the upper torso and flared into a peplum formed by deep pleats or shirring. Some versions had mannish coattails. The sleeves of the caraco were tight and wrist length, and a fichu was worn about the neck to fill in the deep neckline. These jackets often were made of tricolor-striped fabric with the stripes arranged horizontally across the diaphragm and vertically from shoulder to bust. Sometimes, different fabrics were used for the back and the sleeves, contrasting either in color or texture to the front. If this jacket wrap were worn with a long-sleeved sheath, the ruffled cuffs of the sheath were allowed to show below the caraco cuffs.

The **coureur** was a little jacket similar to the caraco. It was designed in two styles: one was very tailored and masculine with a high-standing collar and wide, crisp revers; the other was softly feminine with bow and satin trimming. The more severe style, with a military air, was often part of the negligee *à la patriot* costume of 1795, and had long, tight sleeves with cuffs of contrasting color, matching the button-down revers. The feminine, frilly style had three-quarter sleeves with lace cuffs and a fichu at the neck. This style was usually worn with dresses; the former was worn with a bell-shaped skirt. Both styles had a peplum in back.

The spencer jacket of 1797 was hardly more than a pair of sleeves held together in back by a band that barely covered the shoulder blades (Figure 13.15). The scant front consisted of two bust-encircling lapels. As derivatives of the longer caraco, some of these brief jackets had minute peplums in back. What the shorter spencer jacket lacked in length and body-covering potential, it made up for in sleeves which were amply cut, often puffed at the shoulder, and knuckle length. The curved cuff extended over the greater part of the back of the hand but exposed the palm and fingertips.

**Figure 13.15.** The female version of the **spencer** jacket was extremely abbreviated to conform to the high-waisted **chemise** mode. This lady wears a **spencer** and a mannish jockey cap. (Print detail, c. 1796. Bibliothèque Nationale, Paris.)

## WOMEN'S WRAPS
## (1780–1799)

The **palatine** scarf was the most common lightweight wrap. It was made of swansdown and wrapped casually around the neck and shoulders with one end trailing down the front. The **bayadere** scarf was a late eighteenth-century version of the Greek himation or Roman palla. It was hardly a good facsimile since it was rather narrow, made of striped silk fabric and decorated with fringe. It was worn high on the shoulders in the manner of a kerchief or fichu.

The only coat worn by women in the 1790s was the redingote, which was a slim, high-waisted garment. The sleeves were snug fitting and often trimmed with velvet cuffs that extended slightly over the hands. A matching, rather deep band collar stood up around the neck. Frog closures were used, bringing each front together without an overlap. Other details of the redingote during this period were a small capelette lined with velvet to match the cuffs, a tall, straight collar, and a velvet belt gathering the short bodice snugly under the bust. This was not a full-length coat for it ended about twelve inches above the skirt or dress hem.

Capes, shawls, and other wraps of the past that had enveloped and hidden the figure were almost never worn in France, but women of other countries, not engulfed by a national social struggle, continued to wear them for added warmth.

## WOMEN'S WRAPS
## (1800–1815)

The velvet overcloak made with silver embroidery on silver brocade and an ermine lining was the wrap worn by women at Napoleon's court between 1804 and 1815. It was a large cape fastened on the left shoulder with a brooch and on the right hip by bringing the back left edge across the front and securing it at the hip with another brooch. Variations of this overcloak were many, including a contrasting lining and the addition of puffed sleeves that covered only the upper arms.

The first fur coats appeared in 1808 and are believed to have been introduced by Russians visiting Paris. Two names were used for this garment, each described the use made of the fur. If the exterior were fur and the lining silk, it was called the **witzchoura** and was of Russian origin. However, when spelled **witchoura**, it was of Polish design and was a heavy woolen coat with a fur lining. In both instances, this warm outer garment was styled like a redingote.

The redingote had for some time been considered as a warm woolen gown worn for walking excursions. In 1808, the redingote became distinctly an outer wrap, a coat, to be worn over sheath or chemise dresses (Figure 13.16). It was made of worsted fabric, retaining its long sleeves that were lengthened to cover the hand to the first knuckle,

**Figure 13.16.** Back view of Marino redingote of 1813 with a three-tiered cape around the shoulders. The intricate hat combines a cap of uncut velvet and a tall-crowned bonnet trimmed with an ostrich plume and trailing ribbons.

ending in a fan-shaped cuff. This coat was shortened to three-quarter length, but retained the extremely short bodice and cape around the neck and shoulder area. The redingote was single breasted and fastened by frogs in the center front. Another name given to this coat late in the period was **capotes**, but its design elements were the same, including the slightly flared skirt gathered to the high-waisted bodice.

Other female wraps of the period included: the **palatine**, a small cape; the **canezou**, a sleeveless version of the spencer, with a tall collar that slipped on over the head; the **guimp**, of similar cut with short tippets extending from the collar and worn tucked into the belt; and the **spencer**, an extremely short jacket which had long sleeves with the characteristic curved, hand-covering cuffs of the period. Very similar to the canezou, it differed in that it no longer had the small peplum in back. Many of these smaller wraps had details adapted from Renaissance styles, such as crescent puffs at the point of the shoulder, ruffle trim around the bustline hem, and variations of the puffed and slashed mameluck sleeves.

## TROUSERS (1790–1799)

In 1790 trousers replaced the rejected, court-favored silken knee breeches. The trousers were often loose fitting and quite short. The slightly longer than calf-length leg was slit up from the hem for four or five inches and the front closure was usually a wide flap buttoned on either side at the waistband. They were made of a fabric called king cashmere and other types of cloth. The *sans-culotte*, or trousers of the working class, were baggy with loose, large legs that were calf length or ankle length. Made of rough, red-and-blue striped material, these pants were the badge of a wearer's station and his political affiliation (Figure 13.17).

**Casimir** breeches were a transitional style, and, though revolution was running wild in France, men in other countries had no reason to radically change their fashion preferences. These breeches continued to be knee length but became very tight in the body section and the legs. A drawstring tape was used to hold the leg down

firmly below the knee (Figure 13.18). The waistband was very deep and decorated with three buttons that fastened at center front. By 1798 trousers were cut to fit the legs skin tight, while others were modified and styled with somewhat larger or wider legs. The looser style of trousers was bound twice around the ankle with ribbon and tied securely. They were usually worn with low-cut slippers and white hose. The very close-fitting trousers were worn with knee-high jockey boots.

## WAISTCOAT (1795–1799)

From 1795 to 1799, the **waistcoat** was designed as a close-fitting garment with the tight fit accentuated by deep lapels trimmed with braid or piping (Figure 13.19). Corded braid fastenings, called **hussard** buttonholes by some authorities, closed the coat. These coats were made of king, or kingfisher, cashmere, the major garment fabric for male attire of the period. This fabric may have been a rough, woolen twill.

## FRAC (1793)

The **frac**, which served as a vest, was reintroduced in 1793 by Robespierre before his demise at the end of the

**Figure 13.17.** Near right: French protesters often wore the **tricorn** backwards, plus striped hose, a **frac** of intricate cut, and a variation of the older **justaucorps** styled with large lapels and turned-up collar. Far right: Costumes of the *Incroyables* also included the **bicorn, demi-converti,** and **sans-culotte.** Activists also affected **dog-ears** coiffures and shallow slippers. (Redrawn from political cartoons, c. 1795–1799.)

**Figure 13.18.** English country costumes for men were composed of a tucked shirt with a high collar and cravat, **spencer** jacket, **casimir** breeches, and **Wellington** boots. (Redrawn from a fashion plate, c. 1798.)

**Figure 13.19.** In 1798, **à l'anglaise** breeches were used in countries other than France. These tied at the knee and had four buttons on either side of the center opening. Colored **waistcoats,** particularly red, were popular with young men. A tall-crowned, wide-brimmed hat called **en bateau** and a full cravat completed the male costume. Fur trim was used extensively by the wealthy. (Redrawn from *Bertrand Andrieu,* Delafontaine, 1798. Musée de la Monnaie, Paris.)

Reign of Terror. This late-century frac was made of white material, and had a double-breasted front and wide, pointed lapels but no sleeves or tails (Figure 13.20). The buttons, placed in a double row, each showed an engraving of the guillotine if the frac was worn by a Revolutionary. An angled closure with an intricate button arrangement was also introduced as an alternative detail.

## HABITS (1800–1815)

Men's clothing appeared to be settling into a pattern forecasting the suits of modern times. Called the **habit,** it consisted of trousers, waistcoat, and coat, and was made of woolen cloth in dark blues, greens, and browns with trims of pea green and tobacco brown (Figure 13.21). French men with Revolutionary sympathies wore an entirely black habit for a time.

Trousers of this period were lengthened but remained slim. If worn with lowcut shoes, they were crushed over the instep. The nineteenth-century trousers were made of many different types of fabric including fine cotton, usually striped; stockinette, an elastic material; buckskin; and nankeen, a fabric with a soft sheen imported from

Nanking, China. Nankeen trousers were usually buff or yellow. Diagonal pockets or side-seam pockets and a slightly crossed-over center closing were details typical of these trousers.

Breeches, again in style, reached below the knee and were buttoned around the calves with deep cuffs which had scalloped trim around the buttonholes. The breeches also had a center-front closure and slash pockets and were worn over knee-length stockings or hose with boots or slippers.

Coats were waist length in front with tails in back. The **claw-hammer coat,** introduced in 1811, was typical of suit coats at this time; the name describes the shape and styling of the tails, which were cut rather straight with only a slight curve where the tails joined the bodice at the side seams. They were square cut at the tail hem and extended from the waist to mid-thigh. The body of the claw-hammer coat was cut to fit the figure easily and was designed either with a deep V-neckline, shawl collar, and a double row of buttons arranged in a triangle forming a double-breasted style or with a single-breasted front without lapels but with a rolled collar that rose to the ears.

customarily used for cravats. The **col-cravat** of the Empire period was attached to a collar that could be put on top of the shirt collar and fastened in place with a button or spring pin. The **royal cravat** was trimmed with cascades of Alençon lace and was worn without a collar.

## MEN'S COATS (1795–1799)

The **demi-converti** was an outer coat that was worn either with the fronts buttoned back or closed in a double-breasted style. It had a tall, doubled-over collar, sleeves that were slightly puffed at the shoulder, and narrow tails in back that extended well below the knees. The front of the coat was waist length and straight at the hem. The tails originated at the side seams and tapered in a gentle diagonal to the back hem.

**Figure 13.20.** In the 1790s, men on both sides of the English Channel wore the **spencer,** shown here with a necktie style called **à la Byron.** The knee **breeches** are fastened with ties and buttons. The **frac** is double-breasted and cut straight across the normal waist. (Jacques Louis David: *Monsieur de Sériziat, 1795.* Louvre, Paris.)

The suit-coat sleeves were long with deep, folded-back cuffs and were slightly puffed at the armhole.

Waistcoats became an important and decorative part of the habit. Styles varied because of the many collar treatments, which included the shawl collar and the high-standing collar with deep lapels. The front of the waistcoat was lengthened and cut straight. The back and front were made of different materials; the finer, more decorative fabric was used for the front. This vest was usually double breasted and sleeveless. This garment was made of white pique, or colored percale, or patterned fabrics which were often quilted.

Shirts were made of linen and styled with a modestly full body section, a yoke, and large sleeves (Figure 13.22). They opened down the front and were trimmed with flat pleating or ruching on the edges. Shirt collars were high with points worn flat against the cheeks. A **neckcloth** was wrapped around the throat, sometimes so high that the chin was hidden, and a **cravat**—often two, one white and one black—was wrapped over the neckcloth and knotted once. Madras and foulard silk were

**Figure 13.21.** Young men wore exaggerated versions of the prevailing modes. Note puffed sleeves of the **habit's** coat, the ruching-trimmed shirt, and striped vest. A beribboned watch fob hangs out of the watch pocket on the left. Lowcut slippers and ill-fitting hose were typical of this period, c. 1802.

**Figure 13.22.** During the Romantic period, casualness was a studied attitude. Hairstyles were carefully rumpled, sideburns were in style, and ruffles replaced lace for shirt trimming. Vests or waistcoats were generally double-breasted and cut straight across the normal waistline. (Goya: *Don Tiburcio Perez, the Architect,* 1820. Metropolitan Museum of Art, New York City.)

Many men wore the simple, loose-fitting **carmagnole** or workmen's coats (Figure 13.23). These were shapeless, boxy coats with large lapels, broad collars, and a double row of buttons that could be fastened snugly around the neck.

The **crossed redingote** was a long, double-breasted overcoat which buttoned down the front to a point several inches below the waist where a small, straight, horizontal notch separated the coat skirt fronts. The skirt fronts were slightly rounded, or cut away, to create an opening eighteen or twenty inches wide at the hemline, which exposed the legs. The sleeves were narrow but had a slight trace of a puff at the shoulder and the cuffs were held back with a button-trimmed tab. Because this was a double-breasted style, the fronts could be folded back to create deep

**Figure 13.23.** Men of the laboring class who sympathized with the revolutionaries wore **sans-culottes.** The jacket, designed in much the same manner as a modern pea jacket, is called a **carmagnole.** The hat is cocked into a **bicorn.** (Redrawn from *The Actor Chenard as a Sans-Culotte,* L. Boilly, 1792, Musée Carnavalet, Paris.)

revers. The crossed redingote collar was modestly proportioned but stood up, framing the neck.

The excesses of the late eighteenth-century dandy can be recognized in the ***Incroyable* coat**, which had an eccentric cut with every detail exaggerated (Figure 13.24). It was basically patterned after the demi-converti, but the lapels were excessively wide, the points extending four or five inches beyond the figure. The cuffless sleeves covered most of the hands and only the last joints of the fingers were visible below them. The front of the coat waist was cut to a point and buttoned at the waist. Lapel facings were made of patterned material and their borders were edged with braid. The tails of the *Incroyable* coat extended almost to the ankles.

**Figure 13.24.** This *Incroyable* costume includes a single-breasted **demi-converti,** a striped waistcoat with lapels, knee breeches, striped hose, and boots. The hairstyle is a **Brutus** cut. (c. 1799)

**Figure 13.25.** After the French Revolution, children's clothes became more suited to their activities. The lad on the pony wears a **spencer** jacket, trousers which extend to just above the ankle, white lisle hose, and lowcut shoes. The little girl is dressed in a calf-length **sheath** which reveals her ankle-length **pantaloons.** (Raeburn: *The Drummond Children,* c. 1800–1810. Metropolitan Museum of Art, New York City.)

The velvet or king cashmere **spencer,** a waist-length jacket, had an accidental beginning. Lord Spencer, an inveterate horseman, was galloping over the fields in pursuit of a fox when suddenly he and his horse ran into difficulty. Neither was hurt, but the tails of the lord's riding coat were partially torn off when they were caught on brambles and branches as he fell. Half in anger and half because he could not continue the hunt in comfort, Lord Spencer ripped off the dangling tails and proceeded on his way. He was so pleased with the comfort of the coat without tails that he had several made for riding and for casual at-home wear. He was greatly admired by many gentlemen of the time and they, too, adopted his new innovative fashion.

The spencer was designed to fit the figure easily with rather loose sleeves, wide lapels, and a high, round neckline with or without a collar (Figure 13.25). Other details included cuffless sleeves with a seam slit at the wrist, nonfunctional button trim, and tab-trimmed pockets set rather high on the jacket fronts.

In the 1790s, in an attempt to recreate costumes of antiquity, the French wore a loose-fitting **tunic coat** with a wide sash belt. Over this style was worn a square cape which was draped around the figure after the fashion of the toga or male himation. Both of these outer wraps were worn with long stockings made of coarse yarn, thigh-length tight breeches, and boots much like the Roman crepida or jockey boots. They also wore a short jacket tunic, floppy breeches, and high shoes.

## MEN'S WRAPS (1800–1815)

The male **redingote,** during the Consulate and Empire periods, became a narrower garment, though it continued to be of double-breasted design. Russian frogs made of braid were used as fastenings and as trim. The back was made of four sections with a slit in the center of the skirt. A decorative button marked the waistline at the end of the curved seams on each side of the center back. The collar—only one collar instead of the two of previous styles—pocket flaps, and sleeve cuffs were of contrasting color to that of the main body of this garment. Buttoned bands were an alternate sleeve trim. Sleeves were slightly puffed at the armhole. This top coat was also called the **cossack,** or greatcoat.

The **carrick,** styled after the livery of coachmen, was a large, full, ankle-length coat with a double-tiered cape; double collars worn high around the neck, almost obscuring the face in profile; and long, cuffless sleeves. Some carrick coats had two high pockets in the form of vertical slits, placed well above the waist, which were trimmed with an inverted, scalloped, and buttoned-down flap. The carrick was generally made of heavy woolen cloth in somber colors.

## WOMEN'S UNDERWEAR
## (1796–1799)

During the period of interest in Greek and Roman styles, women wore knitted figure-revealing undergarments made of flesh-colored lisle yarn. Tights covered the lower half of the body and the legs, while vests of cotton were worn as undershirts. A sleeveless thigh- or floor-length undertunic made of finely woven cotton fabric was worn beneath the chemise or *à la grecque*. In England, lisle hose were held up by garterlike suspenders attached to an unboned corset. During this fashion phase, the body was not restricted. The new corset encircled the figure below the waist and functioned only as a support for the knitted lisle hose.

## WOMEN'S UNDERWEAR
## (1800–1815)

Undergarments reappeared after the demise of fads revealing the figure and imitating antiquity. The petticoat, or gathered half-slip, trimmed with lace, was worn beneath chemise, sheath, and tunic, and held up by knitted braces or suspenders.

Some women wore pantalettes, two tubes formed into shapeless underdrawers and made of flesh-colored cotton. Most women did not wear drawers before 1830, but there were some who did, and these garments were oddly constructed indeed. In the *Language of Fashion* between 1806 and 1813, three styles are represented in drawings. The earliest was made of two funnel shapes with the widest section sewn to a waistband which had a single-button closure. The small opening, encircling the knees, was sewn up from the hem about five or six inches. The crotch seam was left unsewn. The next style was made of two tubes of material gathered to a band at the waist and sewn through the crotch. By 1813, the panty hose of the nineteenth century were much the same in design as the male full-bottom hose of the thirteenth and fourteenth centuries. The hose were made to fit over the buttocks by two inverted, triangular gussets. All these drawers were made of muslin. The pantalet legs were tied below the knee with ribbons, and they were gathered around the waist with a drawstring. Lace occasionally trimmed the legs, but not much attention was given to this garment, for it was thought by many to be indecent for any woman to wear a form of trouser. Also, the ribbons binding the pantalets to the legs often came loose, dropping them below the skirts, which was embarrassing, and it was not until after 1830 that pantalets became an acceptable item of underwear.

Other pieces of underclothing included a slip, slip chemise, smock, and underpetticoat. Basically, these garments were simple tubes of cloth made of cotton or silk taffeta with a variety of shoulder straps, and worn next to the body, singly or in multiples depending on the weather and the modesty of the wearer. The **bandeau** held the bust firm and flat. It was made with a knitted stitch that created an elastic quality and was worn over the chemise slip. Braces, used to support the half-slip or petticoat, were also made with the elastic knitted stitch.

After some years of freedom from body-binding corsets, they were reintroduced in 1804. This figure-controlling garment was a linen bodice that covered the body from the shoulders to below the bust. In 1806, a busk and some boning were added, and, by 1808, the corset was extended to cover the stomach, hips, and the breasts. All of the corset variations were laced tightly by crossed lacings slipped over hooks in the back of the garment. The **corset à la Ninon,** used during the latter part of 1808, was less rigidly boned and the busk was eliminated.

Up to the time of the development of the elastic knit stitch, hose had been held up with ribbons. In 1811, knitted garters replaced the ribbon ties and were used not only to support hose but also to hold long gloves firmly on the upper arms.

# Accessories (1795–1799)

## HEADWEAR

Men's hats were designed with low crowns and large brims and, during and after the French Revolution, they were cocked into **bicorn** shapes. The brims were folded up front and back, set squarely on the head, and decorated with a colorful cockade. In France these were usually tricolored. Pleated rosettes, of the same or contrasting colors, placed just below the topmost curve of the brim in front were also used as hat trims. The *Incroyables,* the most outlandish dressers of the day, wore **bicorns** with great brims or large hats cocked into **tricorns.** They wore tricorns with one point in back, and decorated all three points with tassels. Men also wore tall-crowned beaver hats with wide headbands, cockades, and feather trims.

This was an age of individuality and hat forms for men and women took a wide variety of shapes. The **turban** and **toque,** hat forms worn by both sexes, were prewound and decorated in front with aigrette-feather brushes. Women's turbans were made with a filmy layer of tulle over the

crown and trimmed with a large ostrich plume in front. Women also wore large caps, or mobcaps; the **cordey** cap with a large, puff crown and wide, lace brim trimmed with cockades or ribbon bows; and bonnets made of straw with tall crowns and wide, deep brims set well back on the head (Figure 13.26). Bonnets had falling plumes and standing aigrette *esprites* as decorations. The **casque** was a puff-crowned bonnet with a long bill visor and feather trimming.

## FOOTWEAR

Lowcut slippers replaced the high-heeled pumps during the last years of the eighteenth century. Men's slippers were made of soft, black leather or striped fabric. Ladies' slippers were little more than leather shells laced over the instep and up the legs to the calves. **Sandals *à la grecque*** were worn by women with their pseudo-Grecian gowns. These sandals were made of a leather sole and crossed thongs of leather or ribbon laces. The thongs were attached to the sole at the great toe, then passed between the first and second toe and across the instep. The heel was closed and, in some instances, a drawstring was passed through a hem made at the top of the heel closing and tied to the instep thong on the top of the foot. The sandal sole was slightly longer than the foot and came to a modified point beyond the toe.

Men continued to wear **jockey boots** that had first been introduced in the 1790s. These fold-top boots reached to just below the knees when the cuff was turned down. The cuffs were lined with contrasting colors and, when turned down, gave a colorful accent. Other boot styles came into vogue at the very end of the century: decorated with tassels at the front, fringed tabs on the sides, and with the high fronts curving to a lower point at the back of the calves.

## JEWELRY

During the Revolution, Republic, and Directoire periods, jewelry was scarce and very simple. The denial of the aristocracy of France was symbolized by discarding these forms of personal adornment. Brooches functioned as fastenings, and patriotic buttons, engraved with the images of revolutionary figures or the guillotine, or enameled with the tricolors, were worn as decorations and as badges of loyalty to the new order.

Ribbons were tied around the neck instead of gem or pearl necklaces. Red ribbons were worn by citizens as a gleeful commentary and to celebrate the number of aristocrats who had been beheaded. In contrast, the upper classes work black neck ribbons to symbolize mourning for those of their number who had met death during the Reign of Terror.

The one jewelry excess was the use of toe and finger rings. Ankle bracelets became a brief fad, particularly in

**Figure 13.26.** This gown has a high waist, **mameluck** sleeves, and a collar patterned after the Medici collar popular during the Renaissance. The bonnet has a small rolled brim, a pillbox crown capped with a puff of silk, and an ostrich plume. (Constable: *Mrs. James Pulham, Sr.,* c. 1820. Metropolitan Museum of Art, New York City.)

France. Watches, in countries not torn by civil strife, were a prominent fashion accessory made in many unique shapes and were key or stem wound. These timepieces were usually designed with hinged face covers that were deftly painted or decorated with enameled designs.

## HANDHELD ACCESSORIES

The **buskin,** or **balantine,** was a rectangular purse, sometimes called a "work bag," perhaps because it was the revolutionaries' version of the "keep" carried by Roman matrons to hold the household keys. This purse was worn suspended by a woven band from a belt placed around the figure above the waist. It and the suspending devices were elaborately decorated in contrast to the simplicity of the tunic dress.

Long gloves of kid or satin were replaced by half gloves of cotton net or lace. Knitted mitts which were gloves without full fingers, were worn for warmth. The mitts may well have been symbolic, representing the worn, tattered, and fingerless gloves of the poorer classes. With the introduction of the dresses with puffed cap sleeves, long arm-covering gloves returned to fashion.

# Accessories (1800–1815)

## HEADWEAR

Women's bonnets and hats changed many times between 1800 and 1815. Bonnets with large face-concealing brims *à l'invisible* and tall crowns were tied under the chin with wide ribbons (Figure 13.27). The **pamelas** were smaller bonnets which also tied with ribbon streamers into great bows under the chin. Straw variations of these bonnets, called **capotes,** were first introduced in 1806. The capote, with a much shallower crown than that of the other bonnet forms, was held on with a triangular kerchief arranged over the top and tied under the chin.

Typical male headgear included stovepipe hats, often made of beaver with tall, slightly flared crowns and rolled brims; boat-brim hats with the brim rolled, scooping forward and back; and tall-crowned hats, conical in shape with a dip in the top and a modestly scooped brim.

## FOOTWEAR

Boots of several styles were in fashion for men: The snug-fitting English boot with turned-down cuff; the jockey boot, that fitted more loosely over the leg; and **Hussars,** also known as **Hessians** or **Souvaroff,** knee high in front curving to a point in back below the knee. Men also wore lowcut shell slippers with no heel. Later these shoes were styled with higher tops that covered much of the foot over the instep. **Gaiters** worn with the slipper shoes protected the upper part of the feet and the legs. These stout, canvas leg coverings were fastened by laces on the outside of the leg.

**Figure 13.27.** These young girls of the early nineteenth century wear the same styles of high-waisted **chemise,** straw bonnet, shawl, and **redingote** as those worn by adult women. (c. 1815)

Women's shoe styles included: **escarpins,** pumps cut very low, with slender toes and a slight heel; and the simple, cross-laced flat slipper. They were both made of soft leather or a striped fabric. A small rosette or slender bow decorated this slight slipper at the side of the foot. Men and women wore stockings of white silk or wool. Women's hose often were made with decorative open work over the instep or with horizontal stripes and a random pattern of rosebuds.

## JEWELRY

Jewelry fashions at this time were unique and included toe-rings, earrings set with tiny watches, finger rings, ankle bracelets, wrist bracelets, and long pendant earrings. Men often wore two watches, each with a fancy fob. In the courts of Europe, women preferred diamond tiaras to grace their heads, and heavy necklaces made of precious gems to cover the deep décolletage of the court gowns.

## HANDHELD ACCESSORIES

Men carried bamboo walking sticks or riding crops in place of the slender canes that had concealed stilettos or the swords of earlier periods. Women adopted the drawstring bag in which so much was carried that it soon became the brunt of many jokes and much ridicule, hence the name **reticule.** These rather small bags were decoratively embroidered and often had a small tassel dangling from the bottom. The drawstring was used as a handle. Umbrellas for men and parasols for women, trimmed with small ruffles, were used for protection from sun and rain.

# Hairstyles (1789–1800)

The towering, bedecked hair fashions of the 1770s had been complex coiffures. Hairstyles of the 1780s and 1790s were equally complex, although the head silhouette altered greatly. Instead of towering coiffures, the fashionable hairstyle consisted of ringlets and frizzes poofed out on either side of the temple with long sausage curls falling down in back. Powdering the hair was discarded, and wigs of natural hair were arranged into poofed side curls in a variety of colors.[21] In fact, women were not satisfied with owning one wig, but had several of different colors such as yellow, black, red, or brown. Fashion dictated that the color of the wig be the opposite of the wearer's natural hair. Just as a special style of dress was required for each activity pattern, necessitating several changes of clothes a day, so it was with wigs. Madame Tallien owned no less than thirty in graded shades when, at a later date, she revived the fad for wigs. These hair fashions, popular primarily in England, were given rather silly names including **fiddle-de-de, passionate heart, young-lovers-gone,** and the rakish **risky-roll-me-over.**

In France this was a period of revolt against all things related to formal conduct, and a casual appearance was popular. The short, curled bobs of the ancient Greeks inspired some styles, while other styles were merely untended, snarled messes. These attested to the disgust which the revolutionaries felt toward the elaborately cared-for coiffures of the immediate past.

Women's styles included: **dog ears,** a pair of tangled puffs at the sides of the head looking like two dog ears and an unkept pug in back; **Titus,** shaved neck with short curls covering the head; **caracalla,** a mass of crimped curls; and **infanta,** a closely cropped, shaggy, uncombed coiffure typical of the Directoire period.

Men's hair was equally unruly (Figure 13.28). Powdering and wigs were abandoned swiftly and, though men tied their hair in back, it was untidy and the hair came loose from the ribbon or string, falling over the face. The major hairstyle change was in the cut. The hair was snipped into uneven lengths and arranged into ragged

**Figure 13.28.** During the French Revolution, many adopted the **dog-ears** hairstyling as a symbol of their resistance to the old order. A disheveled look was popular as was the throat-encasing neckcloth and casually-tied full **cravat.** (c. 1801)

tufts in front with longer, shaggy hair straggling over the shoulders or around the neck. The cut, called either **victim** or **guillotine,** was shorn in an uneven manner with the hair clipped off higher in back than on the sides like the hair of victims prepared for the guillotine.

# Hairstyles (1800–1815)

During the early part of the nineteenth century, men wore a tousled hairstyle called the **Brutus** cut. The hair was combed in the style of a Roman general, with waves over the forehead, rather long and sometimes bushy sideburns, and long locks brushing the top of the high collar.

Women also wore more casual hairstyles, many cutting their hair to resemble the styles worn by ancient Greek males. These coiffures acquired many picturesque names including: ***à la Titus, en porc-épic, à la Caracalla,*** and others, some of which were retained from prior years. False switches, called ***cachefolies,*** were also used in an attempt to recreate the coiffures of the women of Greece. Snoods were worn to hold these wigs or switches in place, but no attempt was made to match the *cachefolies* to the natural hair color, which often resulted in startling effects. Triangular kerchiefs were also tied over the hair. These were made of transparent materials and worn loosely tied under the chin.

## FOOTNOTES

1. Kenneth Clark, *Civilisation*, p. 293.
2. Marshall B. Davidson, *Concise History of France*, p. 163.
3. Ibid.
4. François Boucher, *20,000 Years of Fashion*, pp. 335–36.
5. Ibid., p. 334.
6. Ibid.
7. Alfred Frankenstein, *The World of Copley*, pp. 76–79.
8. Gisele D'Assailly, *Ages of Elegance*, p. 160.
9. Ludmila Kybalová; Olga Herbenová; and Milena Lamarová; *The Pictorial Encyclopedia of Fashion*, p. 142.
10. D'Assailly, *Ages of Elegance*, p. 152.
11. Elisabeth McClellan, *History of American Costume*, p. 273.
12. Antonia Fraser, *Dolls*, pp. 29–30.
13. McClellan, *History of American Costume*, p. 274.
14. Mila Contini, *Fashion: From Ancient Egypt to the Present Day*, p. 212.
15. Kybalová, *Encyclopedia of Fashion*, p. 178.
16. Contini, *Fashion*, p. 213.
17. Carl Köhler, *A History of Costume*, p. 392.
18. Ibid.
19. James Laver, *The Concise History of Costume and Fashion*, p. 396.
20. Kybalová, *Encyclopedia of Fashion*, p. 240.
21. Köhler, *A History of Costume*, p. 401.

# Chapter 14

# Romanticism and the Industrial Age (1815–1870)

With the failure of the First Empire and the downfall of Napoleon Bonaparte, the economic stability of Europe faltered. The United States, having prevailed in the War of 1812 against England, began to examine her role as a newly emerging, stable nation. The greatest concern in the United States involved a "search for the bonds of social, economic, and intellectual ... loyalty" which would cut across the many differences of the several states and territories.[1]

Following Napoleon's exile, a period of reaction swept over Europe. The two great principles of the eighteenth century—the democratic principles for the individual, and nationalism—were ignored by the Congress of Vienna (1814-1815), and fought by Prince Klemens von Metternich, the Austrian chancellor of state from 1809 to 1848. It was Metternich who proclaimed, "Sovereigns alone are entitled to guide the destinies of their people...."

From the time of the Battle of Waterloo in 1815 to the end of the American Civil War in 1865, political and social forces again took new directions and reshaped Western civilization. During the first decades of the nineteenth century, many nations of Europe, spurred by such politically oriented poets as Lord Byron, were in revolt. Liberals were impatient and indignant with the delays of their leaders to establish some form of constitutional government. Delays in progress were in part due to the earlier pronouncements made by political agitators who had declared that crimes against existing forms of government, even the assassination of leaders, were justified in order that the reforms necessary for a more representative government might be made. Chancellor Metternich formulated a policy that united the four allies—England, Russia, Prussia, and Austria—with their one-time foe, France, to counter the activists' threats.

The unrest felt by the general populace was given further impetus by the general lack of employment. Wages for those who had employment were low and the

**Figure 14.1.** By 1825, carefully planned casualness was the mode for young romantics. The **col-cravat** topped by a flat necktie; two vests, one with lapels, one without; a **claw-hammer coat,** and trousers with front gathers creating fullness below the waist, were characteristics of the most modish.

working hours long. To solve the economic problems and quell the unrest, a struggle for dominance in trade was begun by the commercial giants of the age. Maritime countries fought for trade, and industrialization, growing at differing paces in different countries, compounded the efforts to secure export trade. France countered England's free-trade policies with laws which established a protective attitude toward its industrial productivity. The United States, having increased its cotton output tenfold in the years between 1815 and 1830, was able to compete successfully with the East Indian cotton output. Industrialization altered living patterns and workers moved from the country to city centers involved in exportation or manufacturing. The export of textiles and fashions were two of the main commercial endeavors which helped to stimulate the lagging economy of the world.

Technological advances supported the production of the stuffs for fashion. Bauwens' loom revolutionized the production of woolen fabrics in Flanders. Jacquard further modified the mechanized loom to mass-produce laces which made Calais a successful boomtown. Successive improvements in knitting looms had great impact on the production of knitted garments, even making it possible to produce a one-piece corset. The introduction of the stitching clapper added strength as well as lightness to silk textiles and, in turn, improved the economy of Lyons. The sewing machine, invented in France by the tailor Thimonnier, then perfected and refined by Elias Howe in 1846 and by Isaac Singer in 1851, further revolutionized the garment-making industry abroad and in the United States.[2] Heilman's embroidery machine, developed in 1834, also altered the industry by taking lace making and open work out of the hand-crafted phase and into industrialized mass production (Figure 14.2).

None of these inventions, however, would have revolutionized the garment industry without the introduction of innovative banking concepts. During the first decades of the nineteenth century, the principles of capital investment made it possible for speculative financiers to establish vast textile mills using the new mechanized looms. The mass production of these looms had, in turn,

been financed by the same new banking concept of capital investment.

Inventions related to textiles and fashion trims were not the only contributors to the fashion production industry. The invention and building of steam-driven railroads facilitated land trade by improving transport time and the volume of shipments. Invention of new and cheaper presses allowed for daily newspapers to be printed at reasonable cost and afforded a means of mass advertising. Through the news media and fashion books, visual merchandising reported fashion news and simultaneously created a customer demand for the new modes. Garment making had improved immensely through the publication of books on tailoring. In 1852 Elisa Le Monnier established a successful school for tailors, the first such school in Paris, though the Duc de La Rochefoucauld had started one in Liancourt as early as 1780.

Demand for the latest in fashions and accessories gave impetus to the establishment of the first department stores. Merchandise once sold in separate shops was consolidated under one roof. The first such venture in Paris was *Belle Jardinière* in 1824, followed by the *Galeries du Commerce et de l'Industrie* in 1838, which, upon

**Figure 14.2.** Ladies' gowns were overly decorated, perhaps due to the invention of the embroidery machine. (Godey's *Lady's Book,* 1835, author's collection.)

its failure in 1841, was replaced by the *Palais Bonne-Nouvelle*. The first fabric store opened in 1805 in the *Palais Royal*.[3] These were followed quickly by the appearance of shops with such odd names as Little Red Riding Hood, Magic Lamp, and The Unfaithful Page. These department stores, with their windows artfully dressed, have been credited with creating the middle-class costume.

During the Restoration period in France, tailors began to stock their shops with various lines of fabrics. Prior to this time, clients had purchased fabrics and trims elsewhere, and brought them to the tailor to be made into new costumes. The range of textiles available included poplin, zenzolin, stokolmic, canegou, and bazazinkoff. The quality of fabrics varied, of course, between England, France, and America, due to the different sources of raw materials and dying processes.

Fabric colors were given bizarre names in keeping with some of the concepts derived from Neo-Gothic literature popular during this period. Light green was dubbed "lovesick toad" and dark green was called "startled toad." Velvet, dyed pale gray, became "frightened mouse" and a darker gray taffeta was named "spider meditating a crime."[4] This practice of giving odd cognomens to fabric colors persisted from 1820 to 1870, well after Romantic, Neo-Gothic, and Neo-Renaissance interests had waned.

The social attitudes which also greatly affected fashion might be divided into several opposing groups. While the emerging upper-middle class sought to attain position through affluence, the young generation was devoted to Romanticism and rejected everything connected with money and material possessions. With the restoration of Louis XVIII in 1814, the reestablished French nobility vied to regain its social position, countered by the social-climbing, newly rich bourgeoisie. In England the wives of bankers and industrialists imitated the landed gentry. For many throughout this age, key words were sobriety, solidarity, industriousness, and propriety. This was especially true for the hard-working middle class.

In contrast were the socialites of the day who never awoke until eleven in the morning. They avoided going into the streets until well after the working classes were hard at their labors. The idle rich strove to attain serenity, luxury, and tasteful elegance, and were connoisseurs of elegant food. If they were French, they had a passion for the new English harnessing systems, the opera, the theater, lazy morning walks, and posturing in languid poses to gain attention. The English rich, on the other hand, retired to their vast country estates where their houses were copies of Gothic structures. Banks, stores, and Parliament buildings also copied Gothic architecture.

Not only Europeans of wealth were striving for social recognition, but so were those establishing vast fortunes in the United States. Association with titled nobles and landed gentry legitimized the bourgeoisie. They copied the aristocrats' manners, often with mediocre results, but they attempted to behave like the idle rich. As the affluence and power of the middle class increased, they turned their interests to poetry, music, and collecting rare books and paintings. Between 1830 and 1850, this newly elevated class, which had amassed great sums of money, set fashion's modes.

This was a period of extreme feminism in the upper and middle classes, and women dominated the society of the day, ruling over the home like martinets. Looking pale, fainting frequently, or suffering from the vapors were sought-after afflictions by the majority of females. In contrast to these concepts were women such as George Sand, the writer, who wore a trouser costume called the *lionne* style (Figure 14.3), smoked cigars, drank, rode astride, and spoke the "slang of the turf."

The conspicuous consumption of all available goods was practiced by nearly the entire population, from the grisettes (working girls), who spent their meager earnings on fashions in the many stunning shops, to the financiers

**Figure 14.3.** The first ladies' pants suits were introduced in 1840. All femininity was not discarded, for the hat, ruffled cuffs, and shirt collar added a touch of softness. This style was presented a decade before the introduction of the Bloomer dress. (Fashion plate, detail, 1840. Bertarelli Collection, Milan.)

and their wives, who bought rare paintings and lavished large sums to attain an elegant life-style.

Interest in Romanticism, or the nature cult, Neo-Gothic art, architecture, and literature, and a revival of concern for things of the Renaissance occupied the creative minds between 1820 and 1860. Horace Walpole, Beckford, Byron, and Rogers were among the many literary lions. Keats and Shelley, masters of odes and sonnets, had many Gothic novelists as counterparts, including Mary Shelley, who wrote *Frankenstein* in 1818. Maturin's dramas filled the theater and Victor Hugo became a literary titan in his own time. Taglioni and Fanny Essler staged and danced exquisite ballets. Chopin, Liszt, Tchaikovsky, Beethoven, and Brahms were the romantic masters of musical composition and concertizing. Turner, Constable, Delacroix, and Daumier were but a few of the painters of the Romantic School whose aesthetic innovations were precursors of Impressionism.

These giants of the arts were no longer bound to record royalty; they were sophisticated, well-traveled intellectuals and their creative expressions set the pattern of the age. Kenneth Clark, in his book *Civilisation*, states that, to the activists of the Romantic period, movement meant escape. Even the new industrial giants sought

individualism. The Romantics clung to a statement in Nietzsche's *Zarathustra*, "The road to excess leads to the palace of wisdom." Since excesses lead to eccentricity, eccentricity and ostentation combined to become the style of this age.

Not all changes were technical, commercial, or aesthetic. Wells, Jackson, and Morton discovered the effectiveness of chloroform as an anesthetic. Applied first in tooth extractions, Queen Victoria used it in childbirth, after which many women used the *à la Reine* technique, following the queen's example. Also it was discovered in this period that the death rate of mothers was reduced if sanitary conditions prevailed during childbirth. A vaccine, too, was discovered to lessen the danger of smallpox epidemics.

In the United States, following the end of the Civil War in 1865, living patterns in the defeated South were totally disrupted. Once affluent plantation owners were left destitute. Financially ruined, many Southern men were forced to take employment at whatever tasks they were capable of performing. Some opened academies and finishing schools. Still others became workers for the expanding transcontinental railroad system and the telegraph network. Many veterans of the Civil War looked

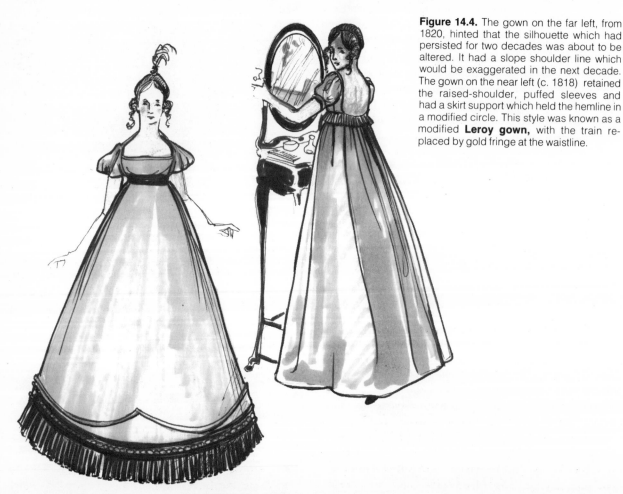

**Figure 14.4.** The gown on the far left, from 1820, hinted that the silhouette which had persisted for two decades was about to be altered. It had a slope shoulder line which would be exaggerated in the next decade. The gown on the near left (c. 1818) retained the raised-shoulder, puffed sleeves and had a skirt support which held the hemline in a modified circle. This style was known as a modified **Leroy gown,** with the train replaced by gold fringe at the waistline.

westward for means of recouping their former wealth. Large cattle ranches were established, and vast wheat farms and small family farms increased in number.

In the North, industrialization continued to grow at a rapid pace, and, with the completion of the first transcontinental railroad in 1869, the East and West were joined. Although much of the mid-continental landmass was still wilderness territory, the United States boasted of states on both coasts. With a renewed spirit of pioneering, the United States began a series of ventures that would bring it to world domination and again alter living patterns in the Old and the New worlds.

The years between 1815 and 1870 saw an incredible acceleration in political, social, medical, and aesthetic innovations. Fashion trends reflected the accelerated pace of the period; never again would a single silhouette dominate costume styles for a prolonged period of time. Each season produced a new fashion silhouette. With the return to France of the monarchy and the nobility, the bourgeoisie was determined to compete. Designer Leroy artfully jumped to the royalists' side and continued to dress both the reinstated nobility and the rising middle class.[5] During the restoration period from 1815 to 1820 and until 1825, costumes in France retained the classical features introduced during the Empire (Figure 14.4). The slender or "beanpole" silhouette slowly gave way to the slightly full, rounded skirt in women's dress. By 1825, with Romanticism thoroughly entrenched, new skirt lengths and girths appeared. During this period of forty years, no European court dictated fashion's modes. Because of the need to forget the events since 1789, the people of France reverted to the pleasurable pastimes associated with Marie Antoinette's court. These attitudes were assimilated by other continental countries, principalities, and confederations. The people of the archaic German Confederation quite readily returned to the *Ancien Régime*. Anglomania disappeared as the Albion influence—English costumes as accepted on the Continent—diminished and was contained almost entirely within the limits of Britain.

Fashions in France catered to the sophisticated Parisians who attended the theater, ate breakfast at Tortoni's, danced endlessly at balls, and went to racing meets. In contrast, English clothes were more practical and adapted to country living. English daytime wear consisted of stiff jackets *à la malakoff*, blouses with jabots, and skirts. Accenting these costumes were tight, yellow-leather gloves.[6] Evening dress was made up of lowcut gowns with "Turkish sleeves," and "Grecian" bonnets worn over hair coiffed in falling curls at the nape of the neck (Figure 14.5). As costumes became more complex, with lower, thicker waists, and fuller, gathered skirts, hairstyles also became more complex.

For a time, wigs remained popular and those who could not afford full wigs used front twists or partial wigs.

**Figure 14.5.** By 1831, formal attire again had become luxurious. This robe of silk has flat silk embroidery on the collar. The mantle is made of cashmere with crushed astrakhan trim. The costume is completed with a matching cashmere turban decorated with jewels and aigrette.

Since there were neither permanent-wave machines nor curling irons, women puffed out their hair over steaming water.[7] Eugénie de Montijo, who married Napoleon III, launched the fashion of bleaching hair blonde. This empress, misunderstood by many French people, was nicknamed *falbala première* because of the frivolous complexities of her hairstyling.

The classical influence in women's gowns had been eliminated by the 1820s, but the skirts did not increase appreciably in girth at the hem until the end of the decade. From then until the 1860s, fullness increased yearly. The skirt fullness ranged from all around to exaggerated fullness in the back. Crinoline underskirts in multiples were added, culminating in the invention of the articulated hoop skirt. Puffed sleeves, which had derived from cap sleeves, evolved from the many-puffed mameluck style.

The varied sleeve fashions from the wrist-length mode of the early nineteenth century to the awkward balloon sleeves of the 1830s and back to the easy sleeves of the late 1850s showed the inventive aesthetic character of this period. One authority describing sleeve treatments of these years stated that "They were swelled hams or legs of mutton" attached to a snug-fitting bodice (Figure 14.6). During the 1860s dresses were trimmed so elaborately that they looked like the overstuffed furniture so typical of the same period.

The styles during the years of the French Restoration from 1825 until the end of the long reign of Victoria in 1901 are believed by many to have been some of the ugliest fashions of any age. Leroy was the leading designer early in this period. Victorine and Palmyre were the significant designers during the reign of Napoleon III

**Figure 14.7.** Formal attire during the 1840s shed the excesses of proportion common during the previous decade. (Gavarni, fashion plate, detail, 1845. Bertarelli Collection, Milan.)

**Figure 14.6.** The complex sleeve treatments during the 1830s included **à l'imbécile** shown here. This styling combined puffed sleeves covering the upper arms and transparent, puffed over-sleeves fastened by large buckles at the wrists. (Redrawn from *Mme. de Mirbel*, Champmartin, 1831. Museum, Versailles.)

(1852–1870). Palmyre created a thirty-garment trousseau for Eugénie de Montijo for her wedding to Napoleon III. Queen Victoria, upon ascending to the throne in 1837, shook off the influence of her domineering mother and was guided in her selection of costumes by Princess Charlotte, wife of the king of Belgium.[8] This gracious lady, known to Queen Victoria by a complex set of circumstances, was a frequent visitor to Paris. She was considered to have superb taste for the time and made the dowdy young queen aware of clothes for the first time. In *Queen Victoria* by Cecil Woodham-Smith, excerpts from the queen's diary frequently mention the pleasures of new dresses and theater gowns.[9] On ascending to the throne, Victoria was at last free to enjoy life, unencumbered by the domination of her mother, the Duchess of Kent. She did this with zest, going to operas, giving balls and state dinners, and always appearing in exquisite gowns. In adulation, her subjects imitated the fashions she wore. At last England's modes were changed and updated to the elegant attire worn on the continent (Figure 14.7).[10] After that time style trends became international and national characteristics in fashion vanished.

**Figure 14.8.** Men's fashions altered subtly between 1810 and 1835. Lapels of the **claw-hammer coat** varied from sharp, pointed lapels to lapels with gently curved points. Trousers, at first ankle length, became full and covered the shoes, bringing the return of the instep strap. Shirts with attached collars which framed the cheeks continued in style for several decades. (Redrawn from a series of fashion plates in *Modes d'hommes,* 1810, 1829, 1835.)

Men's costumes during these years eventually developed the uniform, drab, and uninventive look which was typical for the next 100 years. However, during the twenty years between 1820 and 1840, the Biedermeier gentleman's look and the influence of Beau Brummell prevailed (Figure 14.8). Those in society adopted a *habit* which was conservative to the point of being inconspicuous.[11] The Biedermeier gentleman dressed in long frock coats, tight trousers, waistcoats, shirts, and slippers. The fit of coats by 1820 had been greatly improved by cutting the bodice and tail sections separately. Sleeves were still styled with two seams (Figure 14.9).

Men's shirts after 1820 were of two styles: the London style with fancy front trims was still worn in Paris; Englishmen, busy with commerce, discarded this romantic fad earlier than men on the continent and wore a shirt style with a plain front, full sleeves, and a yoke with gathers in the back.[12] Disraeli was said to have remarked, "... an Englishman's income impressed people more than his shirt."

Just as the breadth across the shoulders increased in the women's costumes during the 1830s, so it was with male coat styles. The chest girth also was increased, the waist nipped in, and the coat skirt flared. Ankle-length topcoats with hand-covering sleeves and low, velvet collars, had appeared by 1818. Broadcloth cloaks, lined in contrasting colors and tied with cords, were worn as formal outer accessories. Tall-crowned hats, appearing early in the nineteenth century, persisted in male fashions for many decades.

Beau Brummell, born George Bryan Brummell (1778–1840), is credited with drastically altering the neckwear modes of his day. So fascinated were men with the lower, starched collars and the intricate tying of cravats that Brummell instituted the publication of booklets containing tying instructions. Under the pen name of Baron de l'Empese, Honoré de Balzac wrote *The Art of Putting On One's Tie*. The Beau took as long as two hours to dress, spending much of that time tying his cravat. The starched collar he introduced soon eliminated the use of the chin-hugging col-cravat, a pleated piece of linen five or six inches wide with tab ends (Figure 14.10). Buttons on one tab and buttonholes on the other secured the col-cravat firmly about the neck and chin. Pleated to the

**Figure 14.9.** Gentleman's overcoat, c. 1820, worn over suit with knee breeches. The high, standing collar and wide lapels are fur trimmed.

**Figure 14.10.** Dandies of the 1820s were much concerned with the tying of cravats. The pamphlet, "The Art of Tying a Cravat in Sixteen Lessons," included illustrations duplicated here: *A,* col-cravat; *B,* Americana; *C,* and *D,* colletti Russi; *E,* colletti Jatto di balena; *F,* caccia; *G,* sentimentale; *H,* in Valigia; *I,* in Cateratta; *J,* Alla Talma; *K,* all'italianna. (Redrawn from *The Art of Tying a Cravat in Sixteen Lessons.* Bibliothèque Nationale, Paris.)

tabs and buttoned at the nape of the neck, the col-cravat could be spread out to the desired position covering chin and throat.

George IV, a friend of Brummell's, helped him launch the popularity of the impeccably cut suit.[13] George Brummell was always seen in a blue frock coat, white trousers, waistcoats of conservative colors and a narrow black tie. In the booklet *Fashions and Costumes*, published in 1840, H. Hauf wrote: "The frac, or frock coat, is a symbol of present-day civilization: it is the uniform that the man of culture has to wear." Thus, menswear was standardized. Prince Albert popularized the *habit* coat which to this day bears his name. Minor modifications of lapels and collars were introduced, but the basic *habit* remained constant, somber, conservative, and inconspicuous. One authority, observing the static design qualities of menswear, said that, as Prince of Wales, Edward VII provided the only two significant style changes, those of "trousers with creases and turn ups (cuffs)."[14] Kings, generals, tradesmen, and titans of commerce all wore the same costume.

During these years, children's wear ceased to be the miniature versions of adult fashions. Little girls were dressed in frocks whose silhouette, though similar to the adult style, had raised hemlines (Figure 14.11). Little boys wore long, uncreased trousers and short spencer jackets, or the style known as Eton jackets. In the 1850s and 1860s little girls' dress hems were further lifted to reveal their lace and ribbon-trimmed pantaloons.

As hemlines for women and girls were raised, stockings became a decorative accessory. They were knitted in stripes, stripes alternating with floral patterns, or with triangular clocks over the ankles. Slippers, popular during the first decades, were exchanged for high shoes or boots for day wear. Men, too, discarded the slender slippers of the Romantic period in favor of more practical boots or high shoes. Of course, the more decorative slippers and pumps were appropriate for formal attire.

By 1870 many fashion periodicals were being published. In America, Godey's *Lady's Book*, *Patterson's Magazine*, and Frank Leslie's *Ladies Gazette* reported the latest modes, political happenings, and social events. Sarah Josepha Hale, the editor of Godey's *Lady's Book*, not only reported fashions but influenced the president on women's rights, which were spurred by periodicals catering to females.

With the end of the American Civil War, the influence of the burgeoning middle class increased. Tastes changed radically, given impetus by the aesthetics of the Impressionists. With the changing aesthetic, fashions again were to radically alter.

# Basic Garments of a Romantic Period (1816–1870)

## GOWNS (1816–1830)

The pencil slim or "beanpole" silhouette began to disappear during the second decade of the nineteenth century. Exotic names for particular styles also ceased, and women's garments were classified as morning dresses, walking dresses, afternoon gowns, and ball or bridal gowns. The waistline was gradually lowered and, by 1830, was positioned at the normal waist. The effect of a high waistline was retained, for a few years, by wide belts or sashes, which had been used since about 1817 and were particularly popular on formal gowns. As the waistline was lowered, skirts increased in girth at the hem, supported by a padded roll, a design characteristic

**Figure 14.11.** Tiered, ruffled skirts were in fashion for women and young girls during the 1850s. Youngsters seldom used the hoopskirt support but they wore many petticoats. The younger the girl, the shorter the skirt. Ruffle- and lace-trimmed pantaloons were always visible below the skirt. The lad's costume was the Scottish kilt, jacket, and tartan. (*Modes Parisian*, c. 1850–1855, author's print collection.)

**Figure 14.12.** Formal morning dress was worn by ladies when making calls. Note the cloth-top boots with squared-off toes. (Fashion illustration from *La Mode,* detail, 1830.)

introduced by Leroy. This gently swelling, bell-shaped skirt persisted until 1828. Fullness was added first to the back of the skirt, then, after 1830, the gathering encircled the entire waist. During this period, the bodices of the dresses were soft, giving the figure a full-bosomed appearance.

The sleeves from 1815 to 1820 continued to be fashioned in cap puffs; slender, full-length sleeves ending in a cap puff at the shoulder; or mameluck sleeves. Thereafter, for nearly thirty years, the puffed sleeve continued to grow, reaching an enormous size (Figures 14.12 and 14.13). There were many different sleeve shapes with strange names such as *à l'imbécile,* balloon, beret, elephant ear, and jockey sleeve. The *à l'imbécile* style was made with a large, puffed, rounded upper section, covered by another full-length loose sleeve which fastened snugly at the wrist (Figure 14.6). The **balloon** sleeve was a great round, arm-concealing puff, gathered to a dropped shoulder and ending in a cuff at the wrist. Both the **beret** and **elephant-ear** sleeves were flattened puffs, their horizontal width often exaggerated by a wide collar.

A sloped shoulder line was the mode in the 1830s and 1840s. Ball gowns had very wide shoulder-revealing necklines cut straight across the front and back. Daytime dresses accented the sloped-shoulder look by insetting the sleeve below the point of the shoulder. Day-wear

**Figure 14.13.** Daytime gowns of the 1830s had enormous sleeves, including this **leg-of-mutton** style, a recurring sleeve treatment. Demure off-the-shoulder necklines and drop-shoulder bodices were also typical, fitted atop voluminous, multipetticoat-supported skirts. (Redrawn from *Portrait of Young Girl,* Payne, 1835.)

**Figure 14.14.** Dresses, such as this carriage dress, were created for every occasion for the affluent. (Fashion plate, 1845, author's print collection.)

costumes had modest V-necklines trimmed with lace and ruching-edged collars. The variety and variables of dress designs during this period were as great and as many as the number of women who wore them (Figure 14.14). In the 1840s the bodice section of daytime dresses was often rather rigid. The general silhouette included a full, crinoline-supported skirt and overskirt with a V-front opening.

In the mid-1850s and continuing for several years, the **tiered skirt** became fashionable. Made up of rows of ruffles or layers of fabric, with each layer shorter than the one below it, a tiered effect was created.[15] By the 1860s voluminous, hoop-supported skirts appeared, decorated with rows of ribbons, lace insets, ruching, fringes, braid, or flowers. These were arranged in every conceivable manner and combination of trimmings. Yardage stores stocked fabrics and a wide variety of matching trimmings so that gowns and decorations might be color coordinated. The skirt fullness was adjusted to the back late in the 1850s and this skirt silhouette persisted up to the end of the next decade. Waistlines, dropping to a V-point over the abdomen and worn over firm corseting, became another mode of the 1850s. The bustline was accentuated by the narrow waist and V-neckline (Figure 14.15).

In ball gowns there was extreme décolletage; morning dresses had modest neck openings, but the *V* décolletage was always simulated by a ruffle or ruching trim on the bodice. Bodice necklines varied from a wide boat-shaped style that was very shallow over the bust but exposed the tops of the shoulders, to a style which dipped to a deep, wide V-line extending from the tip of one shoulder to the other. Flat fichu drapes, the **chemisette** bodice, and decorative **collarette** often filled in the deeper necklines. The modest, high round necklines of daytime and walking dresses were trimmed with small flat collars.

The differences between day wear and formal gowns during these years were mainly in the depth of décolletage and fullness of the skirts. Gowns for evening were slightly longer, revealing only the tips of the slippers. The total frontal silhouette from 1830 to the end of the 1860s resembled two triangles with the apexes joined at the waist, for gowns were buckled snugly with wide firm belts. Floral cotton prints, heavy silks, velvets, and striped or plain satins were used for these dresses and gowns.

Toward the end of the 1830s and during the early 1840s, the bodice lost its cocoonlike appearance and was cut in several pieces to fit the feminine form more snugly. The waistline was dropped even lower in front, forming a point much like the bodice silhouette of the late Renaissance. Sleeves continued to be bulky, but the wider girth was shifted to the area of the lower arm or wrist. Funnel sleeves, with lace-edged, gathered cuffs, reminiscent of the eighteenth century, were introduced in the late 1840s. Skirts became fuller during the 1840s, and the hemline dropped slightly. Day-wear gowns were particularly influenced by this change, though formal ball gowns had had full, gathered skirts since the 1830s. The skirt fullness was created either by gathering or deep, box pleats. The layered or tiered skirt made its first appearance at this time. The ruffles on tiered skirts were often scalloped at the hems, or trimmed with braid or fringe. In elaborate "visiting" dresses, all three types of decorations were used.

Late in the 1850s, while the general proportions of bodice and skirt remained constant, the emphasis of the gown shifted to sleeve treatments. The new form, called *à la jardinière* but derisively dubbed the "jug sleeve," was designed with tight upper arm and a puff encircling the lower arm. A variation of the jug sleeve was created by two truncated cone shapes. The top of the longer truncated

**Figure 14.15.** Ball gowns were elegant creations. The two on the near right are modified versions of the **Marionette** featuring a short overskirt with center V-aperture. Coiffures during the 1850s and 1860s were modified revivals of the **hurluberlu** mode of the seventeenth century.

cone fitted into the armhole, while the shorter cone was inverted with the smaller opening ending in a cuff at the wrist. The two cones were sewn together at a point midway on the forearm.

Many day dresses in the 1850s had deep yokes which extended across the shoulders and dropped to a point well down on the upper arm. Most daytime dresses had modest, round necklines with small, demure collars. The **Bertha** collar was an innovation during this period and was the reverse in design to the neckline treatment just described. The Bertha was a wide, shoulder-covering collar with an inverted V-opening at the center front. It was trimmed with flat bands of lace or ruching and was generally white in color. The simple versions of these daytime dresses were made from fabrics of printed calico, small checks, or dainty floral patterns in subdued colors (Figure 14.16). Pioneer women in the United States wore no hoop-skirt supports other than several underpetticoats. They preferred serviceable fabrics in darker colors, for little else was available to them.

The **double-skirt gown**, popular during the 1860s, was similar in design to those worn during the eighteenth century. The bodice was close fitting, the sleeves were

**Figure 14.16.** Gingham fabric in small, check patterns was used extensively between 1850 and 1869 to make daytime dresses for those of modest means. (San Diego State University photo collection, gift of Patti Patterson to the Department of Art.)

snug or funnel shaped, and the full skirts were floor length. The overgown and the front of the matching pettiskirt, revealed through the V-shaped front slit of the overgown, were covered with flounces, garlands of flowers, ruching, and lace ruffles. The double-skirt gowns, made of elegant fabrics and elaborately decorated, were generally worn on formal occasions. Ostentation, visualized by an excess of trims, displayed the wearer's wealth, for prosperity had returned in the 1850s and early 1860s.

In an issue of Godey's *Lady's Book* dated September–December 1859 (page 105), fashions forecast for the upcoming year included large sleeve supports or **undersleeves,** yet another form of decorative ostentation, illustrated in Figure 14.17. For these sleeves, a sizable length of fabric was gathered to a band the size of the armhole at the top and a tie cuff at the bottom. This balloon-shaped, puffed undersleeve was tied at the cuff in a large decorative bow, for this support sleeve was visible under the funnel-shaped oversleeve.

In the same issue, plain, detachable at-home sleeves for the Marionette gown were shown. Detachable sleeves for "this full skirted" dress with drop shoulders were attached beneath a shawllike trim. According to Godey, decorative funnel, puff and ruffled lace, or eyelet cuffs also attached to the drop shoulders, were the height of fashion during that same year. Just as in the Renaissance, when detachable sleeves were popular and used to change the garment's styling, so in the late 1850s and 1860s detachable sleeves were used to make quick alterations in a gown's appearance. By the 1860s, the funnel sleeves modified slightly, becoming more slender. Sometimes called pagoda sleeves, they were often three-quarter length, revealing the soft, full bishop sleeves of the chemisette beneath them.

In this period, the more formal gowns were made with the bodice and skirt attached; morning and walking dresses were usually two-piece garments. In 1840 the **redingote dress** returned to fashion as a dress rather than as an outer wrap. The inverted V-opening of the double-skirt dress adapted easily to the dress style. Ladies wore less decorative dresses at home during the 1850s and the redingote style was described by a fashion reporter of the time as a dress "of sober cut." Darker tones of blues, browns, and black in plain, checked, or striped fabric were the colors selected for these daytime costumes. Formal gowns were made of velvets, fine cottons, crepes, taffetas, and delicately woven silk gauzes. The formal robes, as they were often called, were elaborately decorated with linen hand embroidery, lace, and ruching. Ruffles at the hem and midskirt were typical detail features.

While gowns for day wear were not frequently given fanciful names, in 1859 one picturesque style for at-home wear was called the **Marionette.** Retaining the dominant two conical forms joined at their apexes at the waist, the

**Figure 14.17.** The **Marionette** gown, featured in Godey's *Lady's Book,* was shown with two styles of undersleeve supports. The one on the near left was called an at-home sleeve and was visible below the wide, cuffed, funnel sleeve. The Marionette gown characteristically had a short overskirt. (Sketched from Godey's *Lady's Book,* September–December, 1859.)

Marionette was indeed a feminine, doll-like dress. The small, round neckline, accenting shawl trim over the drop shoulders, funnel sleeves, and double, gathered skirt created a demure picture of femininity (Figure 14.17). The bodice and attached outer skirt of plain fabric were worn over a full, gathered underskirt made of patterned fabric, often a stripe.

While traveling in Switzerland in 1850, Libby Smith Miller visited a sanitarium where the women who were recuperating wore loose trouser-and-short-overdress uniforms. Much impressed with the comfort of this costume, she stitched up for herself a travel costume patterned after these convalescents' uniforms. Upon seeing this two-piece pants-and-short-overdress costume on Mrs. Miller, her cousin Elizabeth Cody Stanton—also traveling in Europe—was much taken by its design and comfort. As Mrs. Miller extended her European tour, she added a mantle to this outfit for more warmth, but attracted few converts to this revolutionary costume. Mrs. Stanton, long a fervent advocate of women's rights, returned to the United States and told Amelia Bloomer of her cousin's startling and practical traveling costume. Mrs. Bloomer was equally impressed. The cumbersome crinoline- and hoop-supported dresses agitated some women, particu-

larly those who were actively working for women's rights and detested hoops and restricting boned corsets. Amelia Jenks Bloomer promoted the style, first writing of it enthusiastically in *Lilly,* a contemporary periodical. Erroneously, Mrs. Bloomer is credited by many authorities for having designed it.

The typical Bloomer dress, a modification of Mrs. Miller's design, was a two-piece costume consisting of a knee-length jacket dress and full, gathered, ankle-length Turkish trousers (Figure 14.18). The trousers were fastened around the ankle by small, buttoned cuffs and gathered at the waist by a band. The sleeves of the bodice were only slightly puffed and inset to a deep yoke. Very tight cuffs held the sleeves firmly around the wrists.

A more daring hip-length jacket and full-trouser costume known as the **trouser suit *à la lionne*** was introduced in Italy around 1840 and was perhaps the style worn by George Sand, the writer. Its trousers had very wide legs and were gathered at the waist. The jacket was worn over a mannish shirt with ruching-trimmed neckline and cuffs (Figure 14.3).

Both of these innovative styles, though daring to incorporate trousers, were very modest, covering the female form from the neck with snug, high necklines to the

**Figure 14.18.** Even the **Bloomer dress** was fashioned in different styles. The figure on the left shows a belted version. The one on the right is worn loose, topped by a short triangular coat. (Redrawn from engravings of Mrs. Amelia Bloomer, c. 1850.)

ankles. Of the two, the Bloomer dress was the least attractive, for its proportions were quite awkward and ugly. Neither gained wide acceptance, though some venturesome women were still trying to establish Bloomer dresses for everyday wear as late as the 1870s.

As a radical reformer of women's outer garments, Mrs. Bloomer failed, but the term *bloomer* in reference to gym clothing and female underpants lasted for years. Undoubtedly, the failure of the Bloomer dress might be attributed to the Empress Eugénie. She had become the epitome of French taste, and European nobility and affluent commoners dressed in imitation of the fashions she chose to wear. In the United States, from the growing metropolises in the East, to southern plantations, and to western cities such as San Francisco—booming because of the Gold Rush—women preferred to dress as ladies of society.

The dresses of the late 1860s took on a slightly different side silhouette. Skirts were still overloaded with decorations, but there was greater fullness in the back, the **turkey back,** and a short train was added (Figure 14.19). Braid replaced ruffles on the **town gown** of the late 1860s, and sleeves were reduced in size and were less puffed (Figure 14.20). Town gowns were made in two

pieces with a snug-fitting bodice and a full skirt that was less gathered or pleated in front than in back. Braid trim encircled the round, collarless neck and extended down the center front opening. Braid, applied in a similar pattern to that which decorated the bodice, bordered the hem. The toothed design of the Gothic period and flat scallops were also used on the hems of the bodice jacket and skirt. The jacket was lengthened by a hip-length peplum attached at the nipped-in waist. Cords and tassels were attached to shoulders, cuffs, and upper sleeves for additional decoration.

Gowns for formal balls and cotillions were designed with no sleeves and very deep necklines extending off the shoulders. The bodice and skirt were trimmed with multiple rows of lace ruffles, bands of patterned fabric inset above the hem forming a geometric border, and fringes (Figure 14.20). Bands of ribbon encircling the skirt at several levels, multiruffled skirts with scalloped edges, and ribbon bows were added lavishly to ball gowns to make them even more elegant. The general shoulder-revealing neckline shapes were those of an inverted heart, a deep *U*, or wide-angle *V*. A long sash was tied in back, adding to the bulk of the skirt. The sashes were edged with ruching and finished at the ends with long beagle-ear tabs that were circular or oval.

The **tunic dress,** introduced about 1865, was an overdress draped to expose a decorative petticoat. There were buttons at the waist and buttonholes or tab loops on the tunic hem so that it might be fastened up to create a draped effect. This costume was said to have been inspired by the French couturier, Charles Frederick Worth, who became prominent as a designer for the very wealthy in the 1860s. Mr. Worth, an English immigrant to Paris, had been a clerk in a fabric house, and, after his marriage, his wife encouraged him to design clothes. His first creations were made for the empress of France, but in time many ladies of wealth on the continent and in America wore his gowns. The great reputation which he established lasted for decades, and the House of Worth became synonymous with elegant, chic, and innovative clothes.

The **skirt** and **basque bodice,** cut like a man's jacket with several gored and shaped pieces, became a popular costume during the 1860s (Figure 14.21). The jacket was quite long, with the peplum slit in several places around the hem. The sleeves were amply cut but neither full nor puffed and ended just above the wrist. These outfits, made of heavy fabrics such as velvet and wool, were the forerunners of women's suits. They were less lavishly trimmed, but were by no means plain. The snug-fitting jackets had round, high necklines with or without collars, making them cozy and warm, for these were costumes for winter wear.

The influence of the couturier was strongly felt, and, from the 1860s onward, dresses, gowns, coats, and sportswear garments were to change radically almost

**Figure 14.19.** Tiered skirts with the **turkey-back** treatment became fashionable in the late 1860s. (Author's print collection.)

every season. The most important styling innovation introduced in the late 1850s was the **princess gown.** This dress was cut in many sections or gores, but the individual pieces had the skirt and bodice cut together. The lines of the princess gown were slim with few decorative trims. They created a slender, triangular silhouette and formed a smooth circular shape at the hem with slightly more fullness in the back. In 1869 the skirt of the princess gown was pulled up on the hips. This draping was supported by padding or flounces and was the beginning of the **style tapissier,** or upholstered look.

## WOMEN'S WRAPS (1820–1870)

The **capelette,** a gossamer cape for women that had long tab-shaped fronts, appeared to be a large shawl collar (Figure 14.22). The tab ends were either square or rounded and usually were worn under the wide buckled belt so typical of the early 1800s. The **canezou,** popular from 1826 to 1839, was another version of this light-weight summer shoulder wrap, a decorative frothy bit that added to the roundness of the bodice.

The **carrick coat** replaced the redingote as a warm outer wrap during the second decade of the nineteenth century. It was intricately cut to fit the figure smoothly, with duplicate capes over the shoulders and a double-breasted buttoned closure. The **witchoura,** or fur coat, continued in fashion, although the design of the sleeves, bodice, and skirt were modified to correspond to the changing silhouette of the gowns worn beneath.

The **spencer** bodice of the 1820s was fitted snugly around the waist and had a low V-neckline and multipuffed sleeves. This style of spencer was very short-waisted, giving the appearance of a bolero with three-quarter sleeves.

Except for a brief eclipse during the 1830s, the cashmere shawl was in fashion as a lightweight wrap from 1820 to 1860. It was made in large and small sizes from a square of fabric that was finished with a wide fringe.

**Figure 14.20.** Visiting dresses and formal gowns of the 1860s were lavishly trimmed. (*Peterson's Magazine,* hand-tinted fashion plate, 1860, author's print collection.)

**Figure 14.21.** Women's suits were introduced in the late 1860s. Designer John Redfern is credited with this innovation. Although tailored, they retained feminine qualities by use of curvilinear braid trims.

**Figure 14.22.** Summer visiting dresses in the 1840s often were made of delicate cottons and worn with ruffle-edged capelettes. (Author's print collection.)

Folded on the diagonal, it was worn either around the shoulders or loosely about the upper arms.

The **visite** was one of the many cape garments used during these decades of full skirts and heavy puffed sleeves. It was a small cape with armholes and ruffles arranged in tiers from the neck to the hem. The ruffles were made of lawn or tulle if the visite was made of a lightweight fabric, or of velvet if the visite was made of heavier or warmer fabrics. Lace trimmed the edges of the summer visite ruffles, while fur or braid decorated the velvet versions. This little cape was introduced in 1845 and remained in vogue with only slight modifications for nearly forty years.

The **pelerine** was a three-tiered capelet with long front tabs that often extended to the knees. This wrap was similar to the canezou which, in the 1840s and 1850s, became a very fussy bodice cape with shirred sleeves, lace and eyelet trim, and many forms of shirred decorations (Figure 14.19). Usually it was made of very lightweight transparent cloth.

The voluminous **pelisse,** or circular cape, with vertical armhole slits, returned to fashion between 1840 and 1869 as the gown skirts increased in size. Fur trimmed this formal velvet cape at the neck, slits, hem, and front opening. The pelisse and the ample **double capes** or **mantles** of the next decade were designed with many varying details. Crushed astrakhan was used as trimming on the large, flat collar and deep, circular yoke to which the flared cape body was attached. Some of these formal evening wraps had great wide sleeves which, if left hanging, extended to the knees. These great figure-enveloping capes swept the floor and often had the three-tiered pelerine effect about the shoulders to create an even more elegant wrap. Embroidery, braid, and balls bound with silken thread were all used to enrich the appearance of the mantle. Many of these garments had slit panel skirts so that they might be arranged over the vast hoop-supported skirts of the formal gowns.

The **tippet** was an extremely long fur piece, one pelt wide, that was worn loosely around the neck and shoulders, or looped over the arms at the elbows. The tippet varied slightly as time went on and was designed with a short cape in back, retaining the long slender tippets in front. Marten or fur of other small animals was used in creating this wrap.

The **basquine jacket** presented in an 1854 issue of Frank Leslie's *Ladies Gazette* was more like a double cape than a jacket (Figure 14.23). Braid trimmed the double collars which accented the drop-shoulder line. The lower collar was circular while the upper collar was a modified tuxedo cut. Both collars and the hem of the upper double cape were scalloped and outlined with double or triple

During the 1860s outer wraps took many forms, each designed to meet the demands of the occasion. The basic styles included: the **pardessus,** a semifitted jacket; the **mantelet,** a small cape; **zouave** and **Garibaldi,** small, tight-fitting jackets; semicircular scarfs; and the cashmere shawl, a large square with or without fringed hems. The Spanish bolero replaced the spencer bodice during this period.

The fichu returned as a neckwear accessory and as a lightweight summer wrap that could be worn over the shoulders and upper arms. Its revival was due to interest that the French Empress Eugénie had in Marie Antoinette, her costumes, and her activities. This interest also gave impetus to the reintroduction of the double-skirt gown and the longer, pointed waistline.

House robes, the **piccolomoni,** made of quilted velvet with hanging sleeves and a fitted bodice, were worn in the boudoir by ladies of elegance and wealth. A robe of this style, with an overskirt and hanging sleeves of contrasting velvet, was depicted in Godey's *Lady's Book* for the latter months of 1859 (Figure 14.25).

## WOMEN'S UNDERWEAR

As women's skirts became more bouffant, the **pettiskirt,** an undergarment that went over the petticoat, became an important accessory to the female costume. At first this gown accessory was a simple halfslip made from a

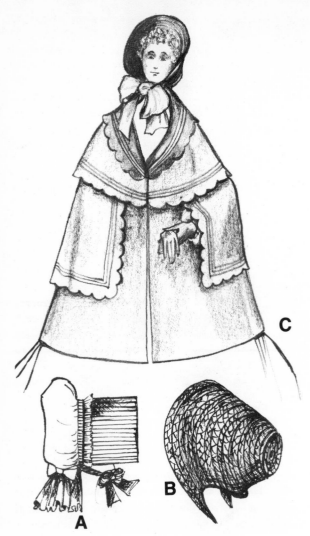

**Figure 14.23.** Hats and wraps during the 1850s embodied many demure qualities. Shown here: *A,* the slat bonnet; *B,* royal-braid straw hat; *C,* **basquine jacket** with gypsy straw hat. (Redrawn from illustrations in the 1854 fall issue of Frank Leslie's *Ladies Gazette.*)

rows of braid. The upper cape served as arm protection while the lower cape had no trimming. The lower cape extended to mid-thigh while the upper cape reached to the hip bone.

Popular around 1859, the **mathilde,** or **mantilla,** was cut in a style reminiscent of the paenula; however, it was open in front. For decoration, a broad braid hung down the back in a V-shape and was often embellished with three large, puffy tassels (Figure 14.24).

The **full paletot** of 1859 was an intricately trimmed outer garment that was more of a hip-length jacket than was the basquine jacket. The one shown as chic garb for ladies in an 1859 Godey's *Lady's Book* had funnel sleeves with braid and button trim. The bodice was fitted with the characteristic wide *V* trim extending from shoulders to center front waist. The skirt was flat in front, but had deep box pleats on the sides, giving fullness to the back of the garment.

**Figure 14.24.** The **Mathilde,** or **mantilla,** was a fashionable about-the-home cape. (Sketched from Godey's *Lady's Book,* 1859.)

**Figure 14.25.** Elegant ladies of leisure during the 1850s wore such house gowns as the **piccolomoni,** or *robe de chambre,* illustrated here. The design of this quilted garment was styled in the Renaissance manner. (Sketched from Godey's *Lady's Book,* September–December, 1859.)

length of material gathered to a tight waistband with a back placket. Then it increased in size and required many yards of material.

The **petticoat** was worn in multiples, sometimes as many as eight or ten, and each was trimmed with deep ruffles to further increase the girth of the skirt at the hem. During the popularity of the double-skirt gown, the pettiskirt, made much like the petticoat, was worn on top of these many halfslips.

The development of the **crinoline,** a stiff horsehair underskirt, eliminated some of the petticoats. The crinolines were made in a wide range of styles, and while they functioned adequately to support the gown skirt, they often led to rather embarrassing consequences for the ladies who wore them. Because of their stiffness and hooped hem, they were likely to stand straight up when a lady seated herself. They not only obscured her view but revealed her underwear. These underskirts changed in style each year as the fullness of the skirt shifted from all round, to the sides, and to the back. Each year these skirt extenders were given new names to identify their hooped form, such as: **The Parisien,** (1857), a tiered, ruffled, circular style; **"D.D.",** (1858), petticoat with gathered pouf bands and an inverted V-opening in front from waist to hem across which bands were tied together; and **Patent Medicis,** (1865), flat in front with side and back fullness.

Many detested the awkwardness of these skirt supports and French critic Hippolyte Taine said that the ladies at the Court of St. James lacked grace and were

outrageously crude in them. Though one group attempted to have them banned, they remained in style, modified by hoops, and finally were **hoop skirts** only. These were constructed by attaching steel bands of graduated sizes together with cotton tapes. Technical advances in the production of steel made possible the fabrication of light, thin hoops of steel; hence, these hoop skirts were lighter and more comfortable to wear. The hooped pettiskirt was first patterned by Tavernier in 1856 and resembled the eighteenth-century farthingale that was used just prior to the introduction of the panier. An articulated version was introduced in 1860 and, by late 1867, the hoop skirt consisted of a fabric halfslip with a hoop or boning at the hem only. These styles were more easily managed, and they swayed gracefully, following the movements of the body.

Though not accepted until the 1830s, once in vogue underpants became an important fashion accessory. By 1830 these **pantaloons, pantalettes,** or **bloomers,** were visible below the full gown skirts when women walked and were readily seen below little girls' dresses. They were made with wide tube legs and trimmed with ruffles and lace.

Between 1840 and 1870 many women wore rather shapeless, bifurcated undergarments called **drawers.** Given this name because they were "drawn on," the design of the 1860 drawers was much the same as those worn during the preceding period. The 1870 styles continued to be made of plain white muslin, silk, cotton, or merino. These more utilitarian garments of the late nineteenth century were not as elaborately trimmed as the pantaloons of 1840, which were trimmed at the leg cuffs with Broderie anglaise lace, or those of 1860, which were utilitarian and were made of scarlet flannel with tucked and frilled lace cuffs. By 1860 women's bloomers were no longer visible. They were merely an awkward pair of underdrawers, similar to a knee-length halfslip sewn together across the hem and fastened below the knees with tight bands. A placket extended below the buttoned band at each side.

Corsets, worn over a simple, slender undertunic, were less restrictive during the early years of the nineteenth century. A laced belt, or basque belt, sufficed. These were worn to cinch in the waist and were made just like their male counterpart. The boned bodice corset, which laced in back and had ribbon- or lace-trimmed shoulder straps, returned in the 1860s when the wasp waist came into vogue. Oddly enough, for an age that many consider most discrete, the basque belt and the corset were displayed in the windows of department stores. These displays were realistically set up with wax dummies clad only in undertunics, bloomers, and corsets for modeling the garments on sale.

Hose made of cotton lisle were either white or striped. The feet were not visible beneath the dress skirt so there was no need for decorative hose.

## MEN'S SUITS (1816–1870)

The most significant change in menswear between 1816 and 1870 was the acceptance of long **trousers.** The snug, leg-revealing trousers of the Empire period, made of chamois or knitted fabric, were discarded in the 1820s. Men now preferred the fuller, longer trousers that covered much of the instep and were held down with a strap under the instep. In 1830 men's trousers were gathered or pleated at the waist, increasing the width across the hips. They were made of many different types of fabrics, often very large and bold stripes or plaids in a variety of colors. The plain and patterned fabrics used for trousers contrasted to those of the coats (Figure 14.26). The legs were cuffless and the pants pockets were either diagonal slashes or half-moon slits placed at the front of the trousers rather than on the sides. The center flap continued to be used as a trouser closure.

For a brief period during the restoration of the French monarchy, men wore silk **knee breeches.** In time, and in countries other than France, knee-length breeches made of sturdy materials were worn primarily for horseback riding, morning wear, country activities, and hunting.

The rather loose trousers gradually became more narrow until, in the 1830s, they again "fitted like a glove,"

though the general styling characteristics remained constant. The full, easy-fitting legged trousers of the early decades of the nineteenth century were called cossacks.[16] This trouser form was styled with gathering over the hips, rather large legs with instep straps, and a tight-fitting waistband. The front closure was a square flap, buttoned with the large buttons arranged horizontally across the top of the flap. The trousers were cuffless and the instep strap helped to keep the trouser legs taut (Figure 14.27). The legs of more formal styles, which were sometimes cut away over the instep, fell well below the top of the slipper in back and retained the instep strap. The cutaway areas revealed the decorative, striped stockings worn by many men. After awhile, the trouser legs became quite long and were worn crushed over the tops of boots at the insteps. The instep strap continued in style from about 1820 to the 1860s.

During the years just before mid-century, trousers and coats either matched in color and fabric texture or were mix-matched. However, in the 1860s, the **ditto suit** was introduced, and it consisted of matching trousers, coat, and vest, all made of the same fabric and the same color. This suit was later called the **sack suit** because of the looser fit of the coat.

**Figure 14.26.** A wealthy gentleman's wardrobe included, left to right: formal wear consisting of tailed coat, knee breeches, waistcoat, hose, and shell slippers; cape and suit; town costume; promenade attire; formal tail suit; and short overcoat with Chesterfield treatment. (1852, author's fashion-plate collection.)

**Figure 14.27.** English fashions for men were admired by French gentlemen, and continental dandies set the fashions by wearing light-colored trousers with an instep strap, a carefully tied cravat, and a tall-collared suit coat, sometimes called a **claw-hammer coat.** (c. 1835)

Before the introduction of the ditto and sack suits, men wore a variety of jackets and coats. The **bucksain,** a short jacket, was introduced in the 1830s when women's dresses were styled with a full, rounded bodice. It, too, was a garment with a full bodice section achieved by padding the chest area. It had a tight waist, rather full, thigh-length skirts that were pleated in back to add fullness at the hips, and a single vent in the center back. The sleeves were rather snug but slightly puffed at the shoulders (Figure 14.28). The padded coats and pleated trousers of men's clothing in this period reflect design concepts similar to those of women's costumes.

The **coat jacket** of the 1820s and 1830s, a casual garment padded in the shoulders and the chest, was cut with straight, boxlike lines and slightly puffed shoulders.

Like the bucksain, it had no tails but a straight, thigh-length hemline. Side vents on the seams added a slight flare to the lower portions of the coat jacket. The **frac,** or frock coat (suit coat), of the early nineteenth century fitted snugly at the waist and had chest padding to emphasize this silhouette detail.

Fashionable gentlemen of the period achieved a smaller waist with a **basque belt,** worn beneath the shirt and cinched tightly. Large, rather decorative basques were worn over the shirt. This type, which extended from the armpits to the waist and wrapped around the figure, was pulled tightly with three tab and slip-buckle fastenings to control the shape.

The suit coat had waist-length fronts and thigh-length tails, which in time were elongated to strike the leg just above the back of the knee (Figure 14.29). The tails sloped from the side seams to the back, ending in a straight hem. Other variations had tails attached slightly to the front and curved toward the back. In this style, padding was inserted between the lining and the coat over the hips. Sleeve styling was similar to that of the coat jacket, although the sleeves were somewhat fuller over the upper arm and had a larger puff at the shoulder. Shawl collars that rose quite high at the back of the neck were characteristic at this time, though the rolled lapels were narrower than in the previous fashion period.

While trousers and suit coats were either matched or mix-matched, they were considered to make up the suit.

**Figure 14.28.** Male fashions in the 1830s emphasized the breadth of the shoulders and accented the small waist. (*Summer Dress, 1835. Modes de Paris.*)

**Figure 14.29.** The studied casualness of the Romantic period is shown here in a knee-length **frac** with large lapels and one center seam in back rather than the multipiece cut of coat backs more characteristic of this period. (Redrawn from Valentine, *Un coup de filet* in "Tableau de Paris," detail, 1853.)

Beginning with the 1830s, the shoulder line of the coat was sloped, though the chest padding and slender waist continued in style. The thin-waisted look was exaggerated by side fullness in the coat skirt, created by pleats or slight padding. The coats of this and the next decade were either single or double breasted, with tails or with a complete knee-length skirt. The single-breasted style was never buttoned; in fact, it was designed to be worn open. The rolled lapels of the single-breasted coat were often velvet or fur and extended almost to the hem of the coat skirt. The shoulder puffing was eliminated and the sleeve was set smoothly into the armhole. Narrow cuffs at the

wrists which matched the collars, and a breast pocket high on the left side were typical details. Collars of tailed coats were wide and flat and the roll of the triangular lapels extended into the sweeping line of the square-ended tails.

The **cutaway** and new styling of the frock coat were introduced in the 1840s. The cutaway was designed with the fronts sloping into a rounded tail in back, a flat collar, and high-set lapels. The shoulders sloped into sleeves of average width with no cuffs, but with a button trim that has been a characteristic of men's suit coats for many years.

Originally, the button decorations were added at the wrist slits on the outside of the arm for a functional

**Figure 14.30.** Men's coats during the mid-nineteenth century had tall, standing collars, cuffed sleeves, and coat tails which were full and flaired. Tall-crowned, brushed-beaver hats were also popular.

purpose. An unsupportable tale suggests that sleeve buttons were retained after their usefulness as a fastening had ceased, not only to be decorative but to discourage men from using their sleeves as handkerchiefs. During one phase of men's suit coats, the number of buttons on the cuffs indicated the quality of the suit—the greater the number, the better the suit.

The **frock coat** of the 1840s and 1850s was a snug-fitting coat with the waist-length fronts cut to a point at the side seams (Figure 14.30). The square-end tails were attached to the body of the frock coat at this point. The back waist section was cut in several parts to make the coat fit the figure smoothly. A two-button trim at the waistline seam in back, where the tails were pleated toward the deep center slit, was a distinctive feature of this coat, which has been retained to the present. Frock coats of the 1860s were single-breasted and had knee-length skirts with two pleats in back to add flare to the coat hemline. This style of frock remained in fashion for some years with only minor modifications of the collar and lapels to coincide with the changes in detailing which occurred in other suit coats.

**Waistcoats,** a very flamboyant accessory during the early nineteenth century, were made of patterned silks, velvets, or striped pique (Figure 14.1). They were tailless with shawl or rolled collars, and were double or single breasted. The single-breasted style had a V-shaped front. Two waistcoats were often worn with formal evening suits, one of white pique over one of black velvet. The rolled or shawl collar of the black waistcoat was turned over the one of white. Gold buttons decorated the single and double-breasted waistcoats for formal or everyday wear.

During the 1840s and 1850s, the **vest** replaced the waistcoat. The vest was decorative and double- or single-breasted, but had no collar. This garment had a V-neckline and the vest front was cut straight at the lower edge. As an accessory to the suit, it was made with decorative fronts and a plain, silk back. To insure a smooth fit, a half belt with a slip buckle was attached in back and adjusted to the correct size when worn. During the 1860s the vests were usually double breasted with small shawl collars or collars with small, notched lapels. A white vest was worn with a black, tailored tailcoat and tight-legged trousers for formal balls.

Introduced in the 1850s by Queen Victoria's consort, Prince Albert, the **Prince Albert** coat that bears his name was a full-skirted coat which extended from the shoulders to just above the knees. The bodice section was close fitting, the skirts flared slightly at the hem, and the lapels were either of modest proportions or very slender, ending midway between shoulders and waist. Three buttons generally closed this single-breasted coat. The back skirt section of a Prince Albert coat featured two box pleats that were placed equidistant from the center vent, which was open from waist to hem. A button was placed on

either side of the vent in the center of each box pleat. This style of coat, worn with matching black trousers, persisted as the business suit for executives until well into the 1870s.

Men's shirts of this period were tailored garments made of fine cambric or imperial cotton. The ruffles on the shirt front became smaller and smaller as did the ruffles on the tightly buttoned cuffs. Until the 1860s the shirt collar was large and worn standing up with the points projecting above the chin line. A wide neckcloth was wound around the throat and a cravat worn on top of it.

The wound neckcloth was replaced by the *colletti Russi, colletti Jatto di balena*, or **col-cravat** (Figure 14.1). The col-cravat in Figure 14.10 was sketched from the Victoria and Albert Costume Court Collection. The other two were redrawn from a pamphlet published in this period. These various prefabricated neckcloths were easily donned and the desired neck trim readily achieved. These colletti, or col-cravats, created the appearance of fullness around the neck without the many layers resulting from the wound style.

In 1827 a pamphlet was issued, titled "The Art of Tying a Cravat in Sixteen Lessons," in which thirty-two ways of tying a cravat were carefully illustrated (Figure 14.10). The simple looping of the ends and pulling the half knot up to the throat was called the Americana, while the large, floppy bow tie was called *à la Byron*. The importance of tying styles increased as shirt ruffles diminished. By the end of this period, neckties were made of silk in subtle or somber hues.[17] No longer were they given the same amount of attention as a male accessory nor was the tying style vital to the totally fashionable male look. The cravats of the late 1850s were sometimes called **regate**, or **plastron**. Pointed collars were worn with a standing stock, or col-cravat, and a tie.

The false shirt front, or **dickey,** first introduced in the 1840s, continued as a male accessory to the shirt until the end of the following decade. It was worn with a "practiced, crushed" look, in keeping with the romantic and casual air men affected, and was made of a strip of satin, ten or twelve inches wide, fitted with a neck strap.

Individuality was asserting itself, and men's shirts during the 1860s were designed with a wide variety of collars. There were high-standing, overlapping, flopping, fold-down, winged, and rigid shapes. With each collar style, the cravat size and knot changed. Soft, loop bows were worn with soft, pointed collars left slightly open at the throat. String ties that were either knotted once or arranged in a long bow; crisp tailored bows with a wide flat knot; and loose, looped, single-knotted ties, chin hugging or neck revealing, were the wearer's choice.

## MEN'S WRAPS (1820–1870)

During this fifty-year period of 1820 to 1870, men wore a wide variety of warm, heavy wraps. The double-breasted topcoat with ankle-length skirts, a high fur collar, and lapels was typical of the overcoat styling for this period (Figure 14.31). The waist of the topcoat was intricately cut in back, and the pleated skirt section added slight hem fullness to an otherwise slender coat. Made of heavy woolens, these coats were usually purple, green, buff, blue, or bronze in color. Between 1820 and 1830 the greatcoat was worn like a cape, although it was a double-breasted style with a tall fold-over collar and deep, wide lapels. During the early part of the century, the male redingote was knee length, double breasted, and had very full skirts.

Other wraps included: the **raglan,** a large circular cloak; the **talma,** a large semicircular cloak, introduced long before Talma became famous as an actor; the **dustcoat,** a traveling coat of gray alpaca; and the **burnous,** a very full, knee-length coat with an attached tassel-trimmed hood that was more decorative than functional.

Shoulder capes on a coat were a characteristic feature throughout much of this period, and often two or three capes in graduated sizes were used with a piping of contrasting color on the hem. The **MacFarlan,** introduced in the 1860s, was a knee-length wrap with two side capes. These capes were thigh length, covering the full sleeves but not the back of the shoulders. They were attached to a point about four inches from the back center seam and on the front about the same distance from the

**Figure 14.31.** Men's topcoats during the early nineteenth century were almost ankle length. The collar of velvet lay flat across the back. The beaver hat and the suit trousers were gray. (*Costume Parisien,* 1819. Bibliothèque Nationale, Paris.)

opening. The **Chesterfield,** also introduced in the late 1860s, was a calf-length, fur-lined greatcoat, with a flat fur collar, lapels, and cuffs.

During the 1830s and 1840s, innovations in men's fashions were launched by the dashing Englishman Beau Brummell. This dandy and his followers, who included the Prince of Wales, wore elegant clothes of perfect cut, and wraps were no exception. The **pardessus,** an ample, black formal cape, was typical of the elegant man's evening attire. This large semicircular cape had a deep, broad, sloped-shoulder yoke to which the body of the cape was gently gathered. The cape hem and the deep back vent were edged with braid arranged in a complex series of looped patterns. A wide velvet collar, worn either turned down or standing, added flair to this evening wrap.

The black **opera cape,** gathered and smocked beneath the large **krimmer,** or Persian lamb collar, was another elegant formal wrap which was often lined with the same fur as the collar, or with white satin. This voluminous garment reached to the ankles and remained popular into the twentieth century.

# Accessories (1820–1870)

## HEADWEAR

Women's bonnets became exaggerated versions of the earlier *à l'invisible* and **cabriolet,** which had been tall-crowned hats with vast, cheek-hugging brims festooned with feathers, flowers, and bows of ribbon (Figure 14.32). The ribbon ties were made into great bows under the chin or to the side of the cheek. There were many variations of these bonnets which concealed ladies' faces and protected them from sun or rain. The **slat bonnet** was styled in the same way except that the brim was made of slender slats of wood. These thin articulating slats were bound together with nearly invisible threads (Figure 14.23).[18] The slat bonnet and the **poke bonnet** of 1846, a large, head-covering semicircle without a crown, were serviceable headwear. They provided protection from the heat for many American pioneers traveling overland and farm women throughout the middle years of the nineteenth century.

By the 1850s, a wide variety of headwear was available to the city dweller. In a summer issue of Frank Leslie's *Ladies Gazette* of 1854, hat frames were shown in a wide range of shapes. These carried odd and romantic names which apparently described the weave of the straw used in their construction. Some names were, for example: **Empress Eugénie,** a wide, plaited straw with soft brim; **Blonde Lace,** lace combined with Swiss-twisted hair to create an airy, gossamer, semitransparent brim; **Royal Braid,** a coarse, braided straw (Figure 14.23); and **Gypsie,** fine Milan straw with a smaller, face-revealing brim. The trimmings for these hats were selected by the

**Figure 14.32.** The rounded silhouette of the 1830s continued into the next decade, particularly for young girls. Note the bonnet, high-topped boots, shoulder-enveloping collar, puffed sleeves, and voluminous skirt. (Redrawn from sketch of the period, 1840–1843.)

customer and secured to the frame by the millinery shops' nimble-fingered grisettes. For afternoon wear, caps and bonnets were worn well back on the head. These items were lavishly trimmed but much smaller than the bonnets of previous years. The small styles lasted for several years when once again larger, face-shading brims returned. The dressy bonnets of the 1860s framed rather than concealed the face. In many instances, ladies with less than luxuriant hair of their own pinned "frizzes" of false hair just inside the brim to frame their faces with curls. **Turbans** laden with feathers and **toques *à la russe*** and *à l'espagnole* covered with satin puffs and clusters of lace added width to the head to counterbalance the large skirts and big sleeves of dresses and gowns.

Cashmere shawls and filmy veils were used as head coverings. The shawls were either plaid or paisley. They were draped over the head and shoulders and—depending on their size—enveloped the figure. The small, square veils were folded diagonally, draped over the head, and knotted loosely under the chin (Figure 14.33). The general hat or bonnet shapes remained the same for some time, but became somewhat smaller.

Men wore tall, flare-crowned beaver hats in white, fawn, or gray, and black silk hats of polished beaver. The

collapsible, high silk top hat was invented in 1823 by **M. Gibus** and was the prototype for the matt satin opera hat of more recent years. Hat styles for men changed little during the first half of the eighteenth century except that beaver hats were called **stovepipe hats** when the crowns became taller. The width of brims remained constant although some were rolled; by the late 1850s many men preferred the flat-brim style. The soft, wide-brimmed, round-crowned felt hat was worn by men in rural areas.

During the 1860s, many hat forms were introduced for men including the **bowler**, the **boater**, the **Figaro**, and the **cap**. The Figaro was a broad-brimmed hat with a wide, slightly flared, flat crown made of Angora rabbit fur. The boater was much the same design but was made of straw. The bowler was aptly named, for it was shaped much like a straight-sided bowl, trimmed with a black hatband, and featured a rolled brim of very rigid fabric.

## FOOTWEAR

Footwear was as varied in types and styles as the rest of the garments during the first half of the nineteenth century. Some of the available forms included: boots (1820s–1830s) such as **Hussars, Hessians,** and **Wellingtons;** high shoes for men and women with leather vamps and cloth tops of nankeen; slippers; splatter dashes; and gaiters. The soft leather slippers of the 1820s had very narrow toes with square tips. In the 1830s the high shoes with cloth tops and side lacings on the inside of the foot were replaced by little boots with leather counters and toes, and elastic side gussets. This type of footwear

**Figure 14.33.** Nationalistic costume styles often fused with contemporary modes as in this traditional Scottish triangular head covering. This style was superceded by the **cornette** headdress, which in turn was altered into the **lingerie cap** of the 1820s. (Redrawn from *Portrait of Mrs. John Hutcheson Ferguson,* Raeburn, 1800.)

was used for daytime wear and leather slippers were worn for formal occasions. By the 1860s, women's footwear was created to suit the activity. Laced boots and high-topped shoes with side gussets were worn for daily duties; slippers of colored kid or satin were worn with ball gowns. Women's formal footwear after 1830 had slight spool heels and ruching or bow trims. Men's boots and shoes for daily wear were styled with rather broad, square toes but the other contrasting details remained constant. Men's dress slippers were made of black leather and trimmed with black flat bows or black ribbon rosettes. Turkish slippers, promoted in Frank Leslie's *Ladies Gazette* of 1854, were scuffs or heelless mules with pointed, upturned toes. The instep section was made of quilted red satin with diamond shapes at the intersections of the diagonal lines. On the instep, silk ribbon rosettes further embellished this elegant evening slipper.[19]

## JEWELRY

Neckwear for this era of extreme décolletage was rather heavy and was made of rubies, diamonds, and pearls. Necklaces appeared to be brilliant, large, gem collars encircling the throat and had pear-shaped, jewel pendants suspended from a matched row of gems. Round, multigem rosettes were strung alternately with swags of pearls. During the period of Empress Eugénie, the bare décolletage was fashionable and few necklaces cluttered the throat or the exposed shoulders and upper bosom.

Brooches set with one large jewel surrounded by small diamonds were worn at the lowest point of the neckline or were fastened to a neck ribbon. For much of this period, ladies' coiffures covered the ears and the need for earrings was minimal. Those that were worn were made of gold and precious gems of a pendant design and attached by means of a small gold wire inserted through pierced earlobes. Rings were small, if worn at all. Bracelets were wide gold bands often worn in multiples and many had small gold discs dangling from them.

Men wore pocket watches with gold fobs attached to the timepieces with wide ribbons. Cases were chased gold and had lids which opened to reveal glass-covered faces. They were either stem or key wound. In this age of excessive sentimentality, watch papers with loving phrases were inserted under the lid beneath a disc of thin glass. Watchmaking was a fine art and often the maker signed his name on these watch papers.

## HANDHELD ACCESSORIES

Mitts of lace and leather or silk gloves continued in fashion. Mitts were worn more often than gloves, and lace, silk, or net mitts were even worn indoors while performing sedentary activities such as knitting.

Just as the gowns of this Romantic age were superembellished, so also were the hand-carried purses. The reticule continued its popularity throughout the late nineteenth century. This drawstring pouch was trimmed with jet beads and tassels at the base of the reticule's pouch and on the drawstrings. In an 1859 Godey's *Lady's Book*, the **protection purse** was announced. Described as being thief proof, the protection purse bore a close resemblance to the clutch purse of the 1960s. A wide, inverted U-shaped frame with hinges and a snap closure was the newest feature of this handbag. On either side of the frame, where the gathered pouch section was attached to the frame, were two macramé tassels. This purse had no carrying handles and was either carried tucked in the crook of the arm or clutched in the hand.

Needlepoint bags, made in the same pattern as the reticule although some were square- or shield-shaped, were called **gold-dollar purses.** These little drawstring purses of 1859 were usually red, white, and blue, with tasseled drawstrings of gold cord and gold-cord loops trimming the bottom.

The year 1859 was a year for a variety of purses, and one of them was dubbed the **watch pocket.** The carrying section was made of two full circles beaded in contrasting colors. To these two circles was attached a gathered section with a ribbon drawstring.

Fans were as decorative as they had been during the eighteenth century. Now they were made of elegant lace attached to ivory or mother-of-pearl spokes and folded into pleats when not in use. Segmented fans, made of paper-thin sandalwood and strung together with tiny ribbons, were brought from the Orient. Both styles were held together at the base with a metal ring to which was attached a silk, tassel-trimmed cord or ribbon. Cords or ribbons were slipped around the wrist to carry the fan when it was not being coyly used.

The technology of the Industrial Revolution was producing an excess of superembellishments for manufactured goods, and the dainty parasol was an example. It was elaborately trimmed with ruffles and lace stretched over a complicated rib construction.

Men carried thin wandlike canes with round knob heads, usually made of ebony. After mid-century the bamboo cane was introduced for summer use.

# Hairstyles (1815–1870)

During this age of romantics and dandies who mimicked Beau Brummell, men's hairstyles were casual and often tousled. The Beau had three hairdressers, however, and took fanatic pains with his dressing. Men wore their hair short, as a general rule at the turn of the eighteenth century. However, Giacomo Perollo of Palermo preferred his long, and for wearing it that way he was arrested and sentenced. His punishment consisted of being locked into the public stocks while his hair was cut off. In time men's hair was styled in a long bob, parted on the side and slightly curled. Beards were either chinline whiskers, full brush beards, or long, flowing ones. By the 1860s, men's hair was again short, and sideburns and beards were worn.

Interest in the fashions of the past influenced the female coif. Hair was dressed high on the head into large loops by pulling the hair up from the back following the head contour. Puffs and frizzes were arranged on either side at the temples. Asymmetric arrangements of sausage curls and braids piled high on the head were called *à la girafe* or *à la dona Maria*. Hair worn smooth and taut, covering the forehead and lying snugly over the cheeks in front of the ears *à l'anglaise*, had a triangular part. During the 1830s and 1840s, some women affected the Renaissance **ferronnière**, a fine gold chain worn low on the forehead with a pearl pendant in the center. Flowers, ribbon bows, large decorative combs, and pleated lace ruffles adorned the female head when she was dressed for a festive ball.

In the 1840s, the hair was parted in the center, dressed into a tight pug at the back of the head, and the

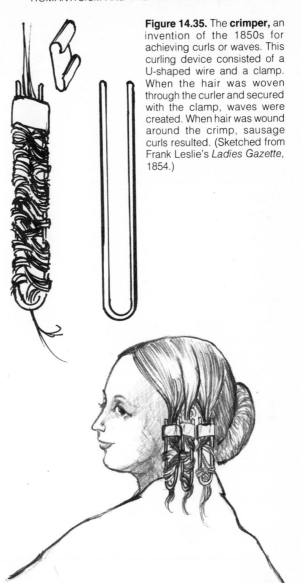

**Figure 14.35.** The **crimper,** an invention of the 1850s for achieving curls or waves. This curling device consisted of a U-shaped wire and a clamp. When the hair was woven through the curler and secured with the clamp, waves were created. When hair was wound around the crimp, sausage curls resulted. (Sketched from Frank Leslie's *Ladies Gazette,* 1854.)

**Figure 14.34.** The Romantic Age reached its zenith of expression in the modes just after mid-century: wan looks framed by sausage curls, and delicate fabrics and colors gathered and ruffled in the most feminine ways conceivable. (Redrawn from *Duchess d'Aumale,* Winterhalter, 1846. Museum, Versailles.)

sides fashioned into long curls originating at the temples (Figure 14.34). During the next two decades, the side curls were eliminated and the hair was drawn to the back of the head and gathered at the nape of the neck. Curls cascaded over the shoulders or down the back from this point. The hair at the side of the cheeks was pulled taut, then puffed out over the lower part of the ears, forming a pyramidal head silhouette. Large ribbon bows or garlands of flowers worn like a halo trimmed these coiffure styles.

Many women used a curl- and wave-creating device frequently called a **hair crimper,** which was advertised in Leslie's *Ladies Gazette* during the 1850s and 1860s (Figure 14.35). The crimper was a long U-shaped piece of rigid wire with a cufflike clamp. The wet or dampened hair was wrapped in a figure-eight pattern from the curved end to the opening. The detachable cuff clamp was snapped in place at the top of the *U,* and the crimper was left on until the hair was dry and firmly set.

FOOTNOTES

1. Charles Austin Beard, *Basic History of the United States*, p. 225.
2. François Boucher, *20,000 Years of Fashion*, p. 358.
3. Gisele D'Assailly, *Ages of Elegance*, p. 167.
4. Ibid., p. 172.
5. Ibid., pp. 172–73.
6. Mila Contini, *Fashion: From Ancient Egypt to the Present Day*, p. 231.
7. D'Assailly, *Ages of Elegance*, pp. 172–73.
8. Cecil Woodham-Smith, *Queen Victoria*, p. 260.
9. Ibid.
10. Boucher, *20,000 Years of Fashion*, p. 360.
11. Carl Köhler, *A History of Costume*, p. 403; and Ludmila Kybalová; Olga Herbenová; and Milena Lamarová; *The Pictorial Encyclopedia of Fashion*, p. 261.
12. Boucher, *20,000 Years of Fashion*, p. 360.
13. D'Assailly, *Ages of Elegance*, p. 177.
14. Kybalová, *Encyclopedia of Fashion*, p. 256.
15. Boucher, *20,000 Years of Fashion*, p. 370.
16. Mary Brooks Picken, *The Language of Fashion*, p. 11.
17. Boucher, *20,000 Years of Fashion*, p. 384.
18. Frank Leslie's *Ladies Gazette*, Fall 1854, p. 36.
19. Picken, *The Language of Fashion*, p. 65.

# Chapter 15

# Impressionism and the Edwardian Era (1870–1910)

**Figure 15.1.** The **Polonaise** gown, introduced in the 1870s, was often designed with an extremely décolleté inverted V-neckline. A close-fitting neckband decorated with a brooch or bow added modesty. (Renoir: *Madame Charpentier and Her Children*, 1878. Metropolitan Museum of Art, New York City.)

After the French Revolution, the British Empire dominated the world political scene until the reign of Edward VII (1901–1910). During Edward's brief reign, international activities were at a quiet ebb and the British Empire encompassed one-fourth of the earth's landmass. The strength of the sprawling dominion lay in the ability of the English prime ministers to control international diplomacy. The leaders in Commons and Peers, however, were unable to cope with the internal problems caused by the expanding Industrial Revolution.

English workers, inspired for some decades by the French citizens who had sought their rights, began to agitate more aggressively for their franchise. Reform was slowly formulated and grudgingly passed. Suffrage was not granted to the majority of British males until 1884 with the passage of the Third Reform Act. This did not relieve the problems of unemployment and deplorable working conditions. Because no cotton fiber was shipped from the United States during much of the Civil War, English mill workers were unemployed. The lamentable working conditions of children were brought to the attention of Queen Victoria by author Charles Dickens.

As a result of problems brought on by rapid growth of the Industrial Revolution, English politics shifted from Liberal to Conservative. Disraeli and Gladstone were the two forceful prime ministers of Victoria's reign. Disraeli instigated a vigorous foreign policy. The intervention of Britain after the defeat of the Turks by Russia preserved Turkey's European connections and blocked Russia's access to the Mediterranean. Gladstone was progressively more liberal and clashed with the Tory Disraeli. Gladstone was unpopular at home because he supported Irish dreams of independence.

In the United States, the Reconstruction program floundered because Andrew Johnson, who became president following the assassination of Lincoln, had neither the wisdom nor the Congressional backing to bring it to a successful conclusion. Before the Civil War, the industrialization of the United States had been responsible for a

few radical changes in the production of food, clothing, and shelter. Handcrafted commodities ceased to contribute to the economic wealth of the country, and major and minor inventions modified transportation and communication.

Agriculture lost its dominant role, and young Americans were attracted to burgeoning industrial centers. Under this new system of industrialization, the laborers worked for someone else. They owned no tools, nor did they have a real interest in the establishment in which they worked. Young women flocked to the fabric mills in New England and to the sweat shops of the garment industry. In time, as overworked women, small children, and male laborers were able to arouse interest in their plight, protective legislation was passed and labor unions were formed. The union struggles made the established two-party system in the United States look briefly at reforms, at least to the point of making promises. It was not until 1911, when 146 workers—most of them young girls—lost their lives in a fire in New York's Triangle Waist Company, that steps were taken to improve the miserable working conditions in the garment industry.

Government, particularly in the United States, was forced to do more than levy simple taxes and maintain a volunteer army and navy. With expanding commercial and industrial frontiers, legislation was passed to regulate railroads and utilities and to oversee the relationships between business and labor. Oil, steel, coal, and railroad tycoons in the United States secured a place in the history of industrial development, and in doing so amassed vast fortunes.

More refined and orderly medical and scientific research contributed to the elimination of some dreaded diseases. Education, because of social evolution, was modified and improved.

The gaslight, the electric light, the phonograph, the wireless, and forced air or steam heat changed the living patterns of rich and poor. Electric trollies provided inexpensive transportation for many; the horseless carriages, or "machines," were transportation for a fortunate few. Revisions of environmental conveniences such as indoor plumbing served to modernize the living conditions of the American population. New devices that freed women from heavy household duties included an elementary gasoline-driven washing machine in 1909, and the electrically-powered vacuum cleaner in the following year.

In this period families with great wealth pursued pastimes with elegance and grace. American financiers and their wives dressed, acted, and entertained as if they were royalty. Fortunes made in gold and silver mining were spent lavishly to build replicas of European palaces in remote western villages or in small thriving state capitals.

In the United States and England, contrasts between economic levels were pronounced. There were laborers struggling to live, those in the middle-income group, and those with great wealth. The decorous, genteel behavior patterns of the socially elite filtered down to all economic levels, and were admired and emulated.

Only Edward VII seemed indifferent to the restrained behavior that originated during his mother's rule, and his amiable personality served to establish favorable relations with other nations on the continent. His rather flamboyant actions did hint of the abandoned approach to life that was to become a characteristic of the years following the first great war.

During Victoria's last days as reigning monarch of Great Britain and Edward's brief rule, American society was untroubled by political maneuverings and sought to establish a cultural identity. Small mining towns such as Central City, Colorado, villages of the western plains like Dickinson, North Dakota, and cities such as San Francisco and New York built opera houses patterned after the elegant houses of musical theater in Europe. Many still stand, and some, such as the Central City opera house, continue to mount performances. Others, like the New York Metropolitan building, have vanished. The latter was built because the original "400" of New York would not sell box subscriptions to the *nouveaux riches*.

On opening night of the Met, the elegant wife of a business tycoon entered wearing a diamond of enormous weight suspended from an ankle-length gold chain. As she mounted the stairs, it was tossed into glittering view with every step, but once seated in her box in the "diamond horseshoe" it was obscured from view. Undaunted, she hauled up the gem by its precious chain and dangled it over the protective railing, displaying to all the evidence of her husband's success.

Appreciation for the quality of the production was not always the primary motivation behind the construction of the elaborate, gold-encrusted great halls. Their plush, red seats and draped private boxes were filled with the newly rich who had risen to prominence through clever financial manipulations.

Displays of cultural sophistication were given added visibility by the elite and affluent with the purchase of paintings from Europe. In these collections, the owners left a magnificent visual legacy, a tribute to their astute judgment, if not always to their aesthetic awareness. These private collections were made up of portraiture by Gainsborough, landscapes of the Barbizon School, the innovative studies of light by the Impressionists, and the work of young artists who would one day be leaders in the modern movements.

Corot, Turner, Constable, Manet, Monet, Toulouse-Lautrec, Degas, Van Gogh, Gauguin—the list of the creative masters of these years is endless. The Impressionists' concern for the effects of light evolved into the Expressionists' concern for self. Ensor, Munch, and many others explored on canvas and in various media the reactions of the inner self to experience. In the early years of such dynamically influential painters as Cezanne, Renoir, Matisse, and Picasso, Maurice Denis wrote, "A picture before being a force, a nude form, or some story, is in essence a flat surface covered with a certain arrangement of colors." This statement is a synthesis of many of the concepts of these artists. The church had lost its power to dictate the pictorial content of a painting. At last the choice of subject, color, shapes, and message was in the hands of the artist.

Musicians and literary figures also brought about changes by breaking with tradition. Innovators in music during these years included Wagner, Verdi, Moussorgsky, Rachmaninoff, Ravel, and Debussy. Debussy was expelled from the conservatory when he produced on the piano "such sounds of overwhelming discord and terrifying progressions" that it was thought he was unfit to continue.

It was a disquieting age among those gifted with creativity. Artists, no longer bound to patrons, were making choices. Every man was striving for a chance to choose. Led by artists, this was an age when at last it seemed that humanity might achieve this goal.

Architecture of the future was to be lastingly affected by the vision of the French engineer Gustave Eiffel, the innovative genius of architect Antonio Gaudi, and the techniques of Joseph Paxton encompassed in the Crystal

Palace with its vast expanse of glass walls and ceiling. Paxton's mid-century concepts of glass and steel construction were to be imitated in many structures for years to come.

The productive capacities of several nations were showcased in a number of great expositions. The Great Exhibition of 1851 in London, for which the Crystal Palace was built, was the first of such extravagant displays of a nation's wares. In Paris, Vienna, St. Louis, and Chicago, great expositions were mounted during the years between 1878 and the turn of the century. The impact on the economy of fast and economic transportation was given recognition in 1893 at the Columbian Exposition in Chicago. The entrance to this world's fair was an arch colonnade facing a Statue of the Republic. Its most famous building architecturally was the Transportation Building designed by Louis Sullivan.[1] This structure epitomized in concrete and glass an aesthetic philosophy held by Sullivan that would dominate the next century. This concept held that "form results from function."[2]

The expansion of the department store, in size and range of merchandise, began with Liberty's in London, Lord and Taylor in New York City in the 1870s, and Marshall Field in Chicago in the 1880s. Parissot had sold garments to workers in his store, *la Belle Jardinière*, as early as 1824. The large department stores of the 1870s, 80s, and 90s made simply cut clothes available to many. These stores, with many items under one roof, also made shopping convenient.

After the turn of the century, the syndrome of "made-to-measure" was at last broken, and even the affluent demanded simpler styles from couturiers. The lower costs of ready-made clothes were due, in part, to cheap labor and increased output of raw materials needed in garment making. Between 1900 and 1914 cotton production rose thirty-eight percent. The spinning machine was improved, which contributed to a larger output at reduced prices. Roberts and Parr Curtis's self-acting loom, Madsley's continuous loom, and American Northrop's automatic loom helped to make ready-to-wear more economical.

Fashions now were always changing; new fashions were presented annually, even seasonally, for the next 100 years. Clothing styles for women were constantly altered and adjusted, or former fads were reintroduced. Between 1870 and 1895 clothes were aggressively overdecorated and almost gauche (Figure 15.2).

The decorative arts rather than the fine arts gave impetus to fashion's decoration but had little impact on its outer forms. The shimmering light of the Impressionists and its resulting defused compositional order gave no sense of organizational concepts, nor did this painting school establish space relationships as had those during previous eons. Color alone, used by such *avant-garde* painters as Manet and Gauguin, was incorporated into

**Figure 15.2.** Ball gown with the overstuffed silhouette of the last decades of the nineteenth century. (c. 1879, author's collection.)

fashions, but not until the early twentieth century. Strangely, the musical hue harmonies of Monet and Renoir made no impact on the color fashions during their zenith periods of creativity.

Between 1900 and 1910, *Art Nouveau* precipitated considerable influence. The curvilinear tendrils of *Art Nouveau*, its melting tones, sensuality, and naturalization became part of costume-design concepts during the first decade of the twentieth century (Figure 15.3).

Materialism and lavish display continued to be hallmarks of couturier-created costumes between 1870 and 1895. It was Charles Frederick Worth who, from 1860 to his death in 1895, was the master of fashion. His designs and sketches, shown to Princess Pauline de Metternich by his wife in 1858, were an immediate success. Princess Metternich, an influential Parisian noblewoman, ordered several of Worth's designs made up for her at the time of the first interview. Worth, displaying his characteristic ego, took credit for the radical change in the gown silhouette when he said in 1870, "I dethroned the crinoline!" Worth not only eliminated the large-skirt look, but introduced the innovative idea of producing many models of the same design and distributing them worldwide.

**Figure 15.3.** The tailored suits of 1902 hinted that the days of abundantly trimmed ladies' costumes were numbered. Note modish waistline and dipped belt, often held down to a point with a belt pin. (*Robes de Luxe,* c. 1902. Author's print collection.)

As early as 1848 there were 109 garment manufacturers in Paris producing thirty million dresses and forty-five million male garments each year. A substantial percentage of these garments bearing the Parisian label were distributed internationally and established Paris as the world's fashion center. Paris retained that position until the German occupation during World War II.

From the end of the Second Empire to the beginning of World War I, fashions developed in three stages. In 1870 the crinoline skirt supports and the huge, conical cage covering the lower female figure disappeared. This romantic silhouette was replaced by the Worth-initiated

**Polonaise** gown which featured an overskirt drawn up to the back, supported by an oval **pouf** revealing a decorative underskirt (Figures 15.1, 15.4 and 15.5). Concurrently, there were two other dominant styles: the **tunic** with the skirt draped at the sides, revealing the underskirt (Figure 15.6); and the **apron** overskirt draped horizontally below the waist in front, drawn to the back and embellished with puffy bows and scarves which added to the size of the bustle. The **pouf**, or *cul de Paris*, (also called the **tournure**), helped create the fullness in the skirt back below the waist. It was made of horsehair at first, but later was a spring device sewn into the skirt.

For a brief period during the 1870s, women dressed in a mode which created the illusion that they were pregnant, a strange fad, for prior to this period expectant motherhood had been concealed as long as possible.[3] However, so fashionable was the expectant look that gowns such as *ventres a trois*, *quatre*, and *six mois* were in great demand.

The second phase of the continuing alteration of female styling appeared in the 1880s. The figure was

**Figure 15.4.** The **Polonaise** gown, introduced by Worth, featured a double skirt. The outer skirt was swagged horizontally across the abdomen and swelled into an oval **pouf** in back. (Redrawn from *A Young Woman*, Tissot, c. 1875.)

**Figure 15.5.** Most modish fashions were in cosmopolitan centers, and there was a fashion lag in remote communities. This sketch of an 1880s portrait illustrates a young woman dressed in a **Polonaise** gown introduced in the 1870s. (Redrawn from a portrait, anonymous, c. 1882–1883.)

completely encased, sleeves were tight, the bodice was snug, and the skirt bound the legs at the knees, forcing the wearer to take small, mincing steps. The only width in the skirt was at the floor-length hem which flared and swept into a small train in back. By the mid-1880s, skirts rose slightly, drawing attention to the feet. Consequently, shoes and hose attained new importance and were elegantly fashioned with complex tops and high, slender heels. Hose were created in delicate, lisle stockinette with decorative patterns worked on the instep in front. Stripes or lacy clocks trimmed the legs on the sides.

While day wear was becoming simpler for the lower classes, the use of as many as five or seven petticoats added to the overstuffed, pleasingly plump silhouette featured by most females (Figure 15.2). However, in 1885 the number of underpetticoats was reduced to one. The pettiskirt, truly part of the gown, remained an important part of the toilette. Styling, length, and fullness of petticoats had had as varied a history as the outer-gown

design. During the Directoire period, petticoats were tight and clinging and made of stockinette. The Biedermeier period featured full, long petticoats with long, full trims, and, at the end of the nineteenth century, petticoats were shortened and had only a gathered ruffle at the hem. The famous sketches created by Toulouse-Lautrec of the ladies of the night in Paris brothels are an excellent visual resource for many kinds of underwear used during this period.

Hats were an imperative part of the total costume look throughout these years. The face-framing hats and demure bonnets were replaced by the **bibis,** either small or with towering decor, perched squarely on the head; the *chapeau paré,* a full-dress hat worn by chic matrons; and the round hat for morning use which was generally considered a young girl's head covering.

Of course, Worth was not the only couturier of note during the last three decades of the nineteenth century. Redfern, an English tailor with shops in London and Paris, introduced women's tailored suits in 1885; later he presented the walking suit and the tailored coat. Others of this period include Paul Poiret, who began with Worth; Jacques Doucet; Mme. Madeleine Vionnet; Révillon, a designer in furs; Mme. Paquin; the Callot Soeurs; Jeanne Lanvin; and the milliners Caroline Reboux, Verot, and

**Figure 15.6.** Late nineteenth-century tunic gown with styling similar to the *robe retroussée dans les poches* of the previous century. (Author's collection.)

Lewis, who held sway over head-covering fashions for three generations.

Of the designers who were to attain the reputation for styling innovation enjoyed by Worth, Paul Poiret is worthy of note. In 1904 he established his own fashion house.[4] He revolutionized color in costumes, working with fabrics dyed in rich hues such as violet, vibrant reds, warm oranges, bright blues, and greens. Although he denied it, Poiret was probably influenced by a successful tour of the Ballets Russes to Paris in 1909. The costumes for the repertoire of this skilled ballet company were designed by Bakst and Benois, who used color to aid in identifying the personality of particular ballet characters. Perhaps because of this influence, Poiret created clothes "of fire and joy." He promoted the Oriental influence when he introduced his **turban *à l'orientale*** and altered the walking patterns of elegant ladies with his **hobble gowns.** Equally significant were his sultan skirt gowns, sumptuous tunics, heavy capes covered with fringes and tassels, cockades of multicolored feathers, coils of pearls, and white fox stoles.

One of his elaborate, heavy cape coats was exhibited in 1974 in the Metropolitan Museum of Art at the Costume Institute's significant exhibition, "The 10s, The 20s, The 30s." Few garments, past or present, have been executed to match its sumptuous elegance, magnificent color, and creative sculptural engineering of fabric.

Poiret also commissioned renowned painter Raul Dufy to design textiles to use in his couturier collection. Though many couturiers since have created perfumes to be sold in their boutiques, Poiret was the first to do so when he produced a scent called *Rosine*.

Mme. Madeleine Vionnet also began her career at the turn of the century and, for years after, was renowned for her faultless talent in cutting and draping fabrics. It was she who first explored the possibilities of the bias cut.[5] The first collection she presented, while still working with Doucet, introduced mannequins "barefoot" and "in their skin," meaning without corsets.

Jacques Doucet, a couturier with a great interest in Watteau paintings and costumes of the eighteenth century, was perhaps responsible for the profusion of laces, froufrou, and ruffles used from the 1880s until the end of the century.

Techniques of mass production of garments during the last third of the nineteenth century were such that

**Figure 15.7.** The profile silhouette in the 1890s had a straight line in front and a bustle in back. **Leg-of-mutton** sleeves, introduced during the decade, increased to enormous proportions before this mode was discarded. (*Les Modes Parisiennes: Peterson's Magazine,* December 1890. Author's print collection.)

consideration of aesthetic concepts was nonexistent. Clothing was produced for expediency and mass consumption by the lower classes. Even the superembellished garb of wealthy society showed little true aesthetic sensitivity. One fashion authority stated that costumes were a "jumble of shapes and colors" and fashion counselors' articles appeared in every periodical dedicated to the day's modes. Statements of advice made such suggestions as "... blondes can ... always wear blue to advantage" and "pale blondes ... a delicate shade of green is highly recommended."[6] On enhancing the complexion, one fashion counselor advised, a "sweet and rose hue ... can be effected by the reflection from red tints ... will be found suitable."

Yet it was in this period that dress designers, or more correctly *Haute Couture* or *Couture-Création*, became as respected by women of society as the creators of the fine arts. It was undoubtedly Worth's assessment of himself that perpetrated this attitude. He is said to have remarked, "I am a great artist. I have the color sense of Delacroix and I create. A gown is worth a painting. Art is God and the bourgeoisie are made to take our orders."[7]

It is no wonder that at the International Exhibition in Paris in 1900 the Haute Couture of that city exhibited

**Figure 15.9.** Tea-gown styling in 1904 combined soft ruffles and precise, vertical pleats. The pouf hairstyle complemented the face and, when a hat was worn, acted as a transitional linear movement from a large hat to the face. (*La Mode Illustrée*, 1904. Author's print collection.)

extravagantly and extensively.[8] In the same year a new decorative influence appeared on the scene and penetrated the design concepts. As a result, one fashion writer was wont to say, "Only the flowing lines of *Art Nouveau* at the turn of the century indicated that the thorough-going economic, technical, and political changes had not been without their repercussions on women's fashions."[9]

Prior to the flowing tendril lines of the 1900s, the silhouette of the Gay Nineties was again transformed (Figure 15.7). The bustle, eliminated for a time in the early 1880s, appeared again in 1883. In the 1890s the cushion rear-skirt support, or **strapontin,** held the skirt perpendicular to the upper back of the figure. The gowns were generally more simple, with slim skirts and leg-of-mutton or balloon sleeves (Figure 15.8). Types of capes called **collets** became the rage. By 1897 bouffant sleeves

**Figure 15.8.** In 1896 women were pleasingly plump, but their waists were nipped to a minimum by sturdily laced corsets. This costume was described in a Marshall Field and Co. ad as a **Promenade Toilette.** It was made "in novelty goods of mixed wool and silk impressed in a chain design." The waist was made of *mousseline de soie.* (Author's print collection)

were typical treatments in formal gowns, while **semigigot** (smaller leg-of-mutton) sleeves were characteristic of town dresses. Harking back to the Renaissance, the Medici collar reappeared and eighteenth-century Watteau pleating was reintroduced.

Throughout these forty years, women's clothes retained the high sense of femininity which had returned during the Empire period (Figure 15.9). Characteristically, as women's fashions were simplified, they became more comfortable and convenient. A new interest in participating in sports activities, if only with ladylike decorum, made the greatest impact on feminine fashions. Of course, the growing acceptance of the conceptual developments toward sexual equality, which received its greatest thrust between 1848 and 1914, created styling repercussions too. Theater greats, including actresses Sarah Bernhardt and Reéjane, injected additional influences on fashion during their years of stardom.

Conversely, men's clothing became logically and predictably plainer and more practical. The businessman's standard garb in the 1870s was made up of a jacket, tail coat, or frock coat, frac or waistcoat, and trousers (Figure 15.10). At the end of the century the cutaway was a popular coat cut. The dinner jacket was added to various suits for formal wear in 1900.[10] Sport clothes for every type of activity from tennis to boating to spinning about in the motorcar appeared for males of the leisure class. Overcoats were available in four dominant styles: the double-breasted **Ulster;** the velvet-collared **Chesterfield** with a concealed button closure; the tailored **paletot;** and the **raglan** coat. By the end of the century, the peacock had shed his tail, and fashion interest focused principally on the ladies, whose elegant gowns and extravagant ball dresses were highlighted dramatically against the severe, black-and-white garb of their escorts.

**Figure 15.10.** Dressed in the dapper mode of the late 1870s, this young gentleman wears an ascot tie, a waist-length vest cut straight at the hem, a braid-trimmed jacket, and cuffless, tubular trousers. (Courtesy of the Whaley family.)

**Figure 15.11.** Suits of the 1870s and 1880s were designed to accommodate a large bustle in back. (Redrawn from *Woman in Town Dress*, Degas, 1871–1872. Fogg Art Museum, Harvard University, Cambridge, Mass.)

# Basic Garments of the Impressionist and Edwardian Eras (1870–1910)

## GOWNS (1870–1910)

The forty years considered here introduced innumerable fashion changes. In 1893, a group of stockholders listed in the Social Register launched the prestigious American fashion periodical, *Vogue,* to report the social activities of the elite and the latest modes to entice these leaders. It was an exuberant period, and the stunning gowns reported in *Vogue* then, and until this day, have been presented under the editorial guidance of Josephine Redding (who gave *Vogue* its name), Marie Harrison, Edna Woolman Chase, Jessica Daves, Diana Vreeland, and Grace Mirabella. Much of the fashion history included in this chapter was researched from the pages of *Vogue.*

Hoop skirts disappeared totally during the 1870s. From the Worth atelier came a gown that was responsible for the revolutionary changes in women's dress styles. This designer, whose previous experience in fabric shops, a London accessory shop, and a fashionable Parisian boutique had given him an understanding of women's fashion wants, knew that a new silhouette was long overdue. His **Polonaise** gown was an immediate success (Figures 15.1, 15.4, and 15.5).

The Polonaise gown modified the **turkey back** by adding a "saddle," an oval-shaped **pouf,** and draping the sides of the pleated gown skirt (Figure 15.11). The pouf at first was a low-set pad of horsehair or very full, double ruffles. Other Polonaise gowns of the 1870s consisted of outer dresses swept up and back over bustle frames, revealing a decorative underskirt (Figure 15.12). The overskirt was draped in a swag across the front of the figure, puffed into an elongated puff in back, and trailed on the ground in a short train. Overskirts and underskirts were trimmed with frills, ruchings, and passementeries (Figure 15.13).

The introduction of the **princess gown** in the 1870s influenced the female silhouette dramatically. The princess gown was patterned after that of the previous decade. The graceful lines of the skirt, created by back draping, were somewhat fuller over the hips than the Polonaise gown. The profile silhouette with the low-set pouf was similar to the Worth creation, but the front of the skirt was arranged into a semihobble effect. The twelve-inch ruffle trim of the princess underskirt was an important detail called the **balayeuse,** or sweeper. This ruffle was either gathered or accordion-pleated, and braid often trimmed the seam where it was attached to the skirt.

The dust ruffle, which was not decorative but functional, was sewn inside the skirt hem and attached by simple basting stitches so that it could easily be removed and laundered. This ruffle was intended to keep the skirt hem clean and provided a slight skirt-hem support as

**Figure 15.12.** Garments worn in 1883 include, left to right: visiting gown with **pardessus;** ball gown with **Polonaise** skirt; **Polonaise** at-home gown; walking costume; tea gown. (*Les Modes Parisiennes: Peterson's Magazine,* December 1883. Author's print collection.)

**Figure 15.13.** Afternoon gowns of the leisure class in the late nineteenth century were designed with emphasis at the neck, elbows, and skirt from hemline to just below the knees. (Munkacsy: *The Music Room*, c. 1880. Metropolitan Museum of Art, New York City.)

well. It was made of coarsely woven, heavily starched cotton. Later versions of this ruffle were made of box-pleated buckram about four or five inches in width.

A princess gown appearing in the June 1893 issue of *Vogue* contained hints of *Art Nouveau* in the design of the trims on the skirt and leg-of-mutton sleeves. The skirt fell smoothly over the hips, flaring into a bell shape as it extended to the floor. The ample leg-of-mutton sleeves were overlaid with leaf-pattern shapes reminiscent of the dagged designs employed on Renaissance costumes. The skirt seams of this multigored gown were accented with a peacock-feather design and twelve-inch accordion-pleated ruffles at the hem. The neck-encasing collar extended from chin to clavicle and was embellished with lace insertions. The full-bosom, pouter-pigeon effect was belted by a sash pinned down in the center front. See Figures 15.14 and 15.15 for variations of the princess style. Many of the gown bodices of this period had center openings in back which were decoratively treated, rather than being concealed. The skirts generally had trains which were artfully manipulated by the gracious ladies who wore them. The semigigot sleeves were often enlarged with gathered **shoulder wings** laid over them forming a V-line on the bodice in front and in back.

Blouses for daytime and formal occasions were decorated in some manner. In the same June 1893 *Vogue*, a formal **toilette**, including a collet and white princess gown, was illustrated and described as having "black velvet ribbons" stitched over the gore seams to about eight inches above the hem. Here they ended in tailored bows, and the lower edge of the skirt was decorated in inverted V-shapes outlined with black ribbon.

**Figure 15.14.** Afternoon gown with **princess** skirt and **leg-of-mutton** sleeves. (*La Mode Illustrée*, 1905. Author's print collection.)

**Figure 15.15. Princess-line** ball gown with complex **leg-of-mutton** sleeves, which were made of many layers of fabric lined with crinoline to retain the desired shape. (Redrawn from *Portrait of Mrs. Joseph Chamberlain,* Sargent, c. 1895. National Gallery of Art, Washington, D.C.)

The **tunic dress** of the 1870s, with the skirt drawn to the sides (Figure 15.6), continued in style. As an added innovation it was often designed with an apron effect in front, and was sometimes called an **apron dress.** This draped skirt trim was edged with ruching and tiny pleats. Scarves were also worn over the tunic dress, draped across the front to create a shallow apron and tied in back with the scarf ends draped over the pouf. The necklines of daytime dresses were round and quite high with small lace or braid-trimmed collars.

Evening and ball gowns had an extreme décolletage with the bosom emphasis exaggerated by the addition of lace frills and ruching (Figure 15.16). The heart-shaped neckline exposing the shoulders, or off-the-shoulder styling, was a common characteristic of formal gowns. Ball gowns were styled with no sleeves but other gowns and dresses had slender elbow- or three-quarter-length sleeves. All of these dresses—tunic dress, princess gown, and Polonaise gown—had an overabundance of scarves, braid, ruching, and flounces which directed the emphasis to the back, although the very tight bodices accentuated the curves of the breasts.

During the 1880s women's dresses were modified by the introduction of very slim, vertically-pleated skirts which were so narrow at the knees that women had to take mincing, birdlike steps. The bustle was eliminated for a brief period, and a slim, columnlike silhouette was popular. This styling did not last, and by 1883 the bustle was again in vogue (Figure 15.17). A version of the crinoline skirt called the **crinolette** replaced the narrower skirt but it was a short-lived fashion.

The **bustle** of the 1880s changed in shape and position on the back of the figure. It protruded at the waist in a line at right angles to the body. Poufs, sashes, and flounces assisted in enlarging this posterior embellishment to excessive proportions. Great lengths of yardage were used to make these decorative rear appendages variously called "pipe pleats," "butterfly wings," and other descriptive names. These exterior frills and the

**Figure 15.16.** Ball gowns in the 1870s were designed with intricately styled skirts and with or without sleeves. Note the paisley shawl on the figure on the right, and the complicated rows of ruffles and horizontal bands on the figure to the left. Coiffures of this period featured frizzed bangs and large buns at the back of the head. (Stevens: *After the Ball,* 1874. Metropolitan Museum of Art, New York City.)

**Figure 15.17.** Suits, gowns, and coats emphasized the roundness of the female figure when pleasing plumpness was in vogue. *(Les Modes Parisiennes: Peterson's Magazine, 1883. Author's print collection.)*

**Figure 15.18.** Tailored crispness and soft, gathered laces emphasized the skirt back, **mono-bosom,** and sleeves in costumes of the early 1900s. *(Robes de Luxe, early 1900s. Author's print collection.)*

gown skirt were given added size by the whalebone or wire-cage skirt support often called the **dress improver,** which changed in shape with each new fashion dictate.

The draped gown skirt was often slit in the back so that the poufs on the underskirt might be seen. Below their enormous, ballooning shapes, the poufs of the underskirt were decorated by ribbons and tiered rows of pleated ruffles, ruching, and lace. Ladies, from the side and back, looked as if they were wearing the tail feathers of an exotic bird.

Most dresses and gowns during this decade had very snug-fitting bodices that emphasized the rounded bustline, and the waist was at the natural position. The sleeves were rather tight in daytime dresses, and either elbow, three-quarter, or wrist length. Toward the end of this ten-year period, the sleeves had added fullness over the upper arm or slight puffs at the shoulders.

Skirts continued snug in front but were lengthened in back. The resulting train, which became quite long in formal or ball gowns, was often added as a separate element, attached at the waist and spread over dress improvers or bustles.

Simplification of dresses and gowns developed during the 1890s. By 1899 the bustle had completely vanished as a skirt support (Figure 15.18). The new slim silhouette was a startling innovation. Daytime dresses were designed with graceful, flared skirts. The bodice front took on a new shape, and the emphasis area shifted from back to bosom. The female bodice of the late nineteenth century resembled the peascod jacket of the male Renaissance costume (Figure 15.19). The **monobosom,** or **pouter pigeon,** bodice was ample and voluminous, tapering into a narrow, tiny waist somewhat lower than the normal position. The bell-form skirt with a hemline flare was created by pleating or several gores. Attached to the narrow waist, it lay flat over the front of the figure but had side and hip fullness (Figure 15.20). In 1893 sleeves were immense **leg-of-mutton** styles, extending and raising the shoulder line. The oversized sleeves, tiny waist, and flared skirt established an hourglass silhouette with a wasp waist.

Skirts and shirtwaists (blouses) with large, full sleeves and high, throat-encasing collars—severe in line yet feminine in trim—were day wear for most women in the 1890s (Figure 15.21). The billowing leg-of-mutton sleeves were given added breadth with the addition of **pinafore wings** which were laid over them, attached at the armhole, and often extended to the waist. Tight, tube sleeves encased the lower arm and were trimmed with lace

**Figure 15.20.** Visiting dress with **princess-line** skirt. Throughout this period, day gowns were heavily embroidered in rococo motifs. (*Robes de Luxe,* c. 1903. Author's print collection.)

**Figure 15.19.** The throat-encircling collars of the early 1900s are reminiscent of the late Renaissance men's doublet. This one is finished with a small lace ruffle, indicating influence from the past. The rest of the garment is typically Edwardian. The skirt style is called the **tulip** silhouette. (*Robes de Luxe,* c. 1908-1910. Author's print collection.)

or lace insertion. The high collars were similarly decorated. Belts, held in place around the wasp waist by belt pins, were fastened to the skirt below the natural waistline to create a long-bodice look in front. These belts rose over the normal hip line at the sides and followed the natural line of the waist in back.

Between 1890 and 1910 the lined and interlined **bell skirt** worn with the shirtwaist was quite plain in contrast to the gown and the dress skirts. Because of the slender lines of these skirts and the lining, the number of petticoats was reduced. The dust ruffle of buckram helped to hold the hemline out to give the required silhouette. No other skirt support was used.

During the two decades between 1890 and 1910, ladies' dresses and gowns attained an ever-increasing

**Figure 15.21.** Casual wear for women during the 1890s generally consisted of a gored skirt, shirtwaist, and jacket. The only touches of masculinity were the high collar, necktie, and straw boater. Male clothes of this period continued to be the **sack suit** with large lapels and creased trousers. (Redrawn from *Mr. and Mrs. Newton Phelps Stokes*, Sargent, 1895.)

simplicity when compared to the costumes of the past several centuries. They were by no means plain, and daytime and formal wear had a variety of carefully placed ruffles, ruching, and lace decorations. **Ball gowns** were made of elegant, heavy satins and velvets. They were styled with large, puffed sleeves lined with buckram, or no sleeves; deep heart-shaped, or V-necklines; tiny waists; and long, flowing skirts (Figures 15.22 and 15.23). The skirts emphasized the hips, falling straight and smooth in front with long, graceful, elegant trains in back. They were lined with rustling taffeta and made from elegant textiles including delicate sheer fabrics, moiré, damask, patterned satin, and tulle.

Formal gowns worn after the turn of the century were elaborations of those worn during the day. Deep, square, off-the-shoulder necklines trimmed with large, Bertha collars and tighter skirts with knee-to-toe ruffles and trains were typical of this period.

By 1907 most female costumes had reedlike silhouettes. The bustline was raised and flattened. The collar

remained high and boned, coming well up on the back of the neck and dipping down under the chin. Bishop sleeves and slender tubes replaced the high, shoulder-widening, leg-of-mutton styles. To counter the more masculine styling of women's suits, Jacques Doucet designed elegant dresses with deep, lace yokes and sloping shoulders.

The Haute Couture houses of Worth, Redfern, Doucet, Vionnet, and Poiret were prominent in establishing fashions during the years after the turn of the century.

## TAILORED SUITS (1885–1910)

Introduced by Redfern and also created by Worth, the tailored suits of 1885 to 1910 consisted of jacket, blouse, and skirt. The versions of the female habit of the 1870s had a swag-bustle skirt and a hipbone-length jacket. As time went on, women's suits more and more closely resembled menswear, although in the 1890s the jackets were designed with the characteristic leg-of-mutton sleeves. However, the tailored suit sleeves were created with large, tailored box pleats rather than being gathered into the armhole.

**Figure 15.22.** In 1900 ball gowns were elegant creations, designed with deep décolletage, flowing trains, and complex sleeve styles. Gowns fell smoothly in front and the bodice was snugly fitted to the upper torso. (Sargent: *The Wyndham Sisters*, 1900. Metropolitan Museum of Art, New York City.)

**Figure 15.23.** While the exact cut of this diaphanous ball gown cannot be determined, its elegance is very clear. The small boy is dressed in an Edwardian suit composed of knickers, coat, shirt with four-in-hand tie, black silk hose, and dancing slippers. (Boldini: *Consuelo, Duchess of Marlborough, and Lord Ivor Spencer-Churchill*, 1908. Metropolitan Museum of Art, New York City.)

**Figure 15.24.** A cross section of ladies' outer wraps worn during the 1870s includes, left to right: froufrou **paletot, casaque,** camelia **paletot.** The right background figure wears a **mantelet.** (*Harper's Bazaar,* summer 1870, detail.)

A tailored suit featured on the cover of the 1893 *Vogue* summer issue showed that the suit jacket had been abbreviated by that year. A large sailor collar was attached to the jacket in back, and wide lapels bordered the unbuttoned front which revealed a cascading jabot. The neck was encased in a high, wing collar worn with a mannish, spotted bow tie. The waist was encircled with a wide belt drawn tightly to diminish the waist and accent the curve of the hips. The skirt was simply cut in front, straight on the sides, but full in the back. A flat, sailor straw hat was shown with this suit to carry out the masculine theme of its design. Many variations existed but the one described above is a typical example.

## WOMEN'S WRAPS (1870–1910)

Wraps between 1870 and 1910 were many and varied in design according to the fashion whim of the year or decade (Figure 15.24). Capes and jackets with a back vent that made room for the bustle pouf dominated the 1870s. The floor-length, fur-trimmed **pelisse** coat had wide sleeves that were designed to create a cape in back. The **paletot** was another popular coat worn in the next decade. Designed primarily for travel wear, it was floor length with a tight waist, box-pleated back, elbow-length cape, and small attached hood.

Coats generally reflected the design traits of other costumes. In 1900 collars were tall, flared, and frequently made of fur. The coat skirts flared as did the dress skirts and were often elaborately decorated with braid or fur trim or both (Figure 15.25). Lapels and shoulder capes in multiples were the significant coat details between 1900 and 1910. Typical evening wraps with deep dolman sleeves were made from heavy velvet fabrics and trimmed with lace or fur. Doucet was the first to treat fur as fabric and made an otter coat for women that imitated the design of a Prussian officer's fur coat. The **charmeus,** a jacket with deep dolman sleeves, was introduced into the female wardrobe about 1908. This jacket had curving, cutaway fronts sloping to a rounded point in back and sleeves that were full over the upper arm but snug from elbow to wrist. Marten or similar fur edged this jacket all around the hem, fronts, and neckline.

Boas featured fluttering feathers. Long fur stoles and calf- or floor-length astrakhan capes with tall, standing collars created an air of elegance. Double capes of velvet with silk fringe and beaded braid trim, enhanced with many intricate sleeve effects, were worn for many occasions.

The double-breasted **redingote**, which had been popular for many decades, continued in fashion. It was

**Figure 15.25.** Costumes for ladies and gentlemen in 1907 were formal and dignified, even for street wear. (English fashion plate, detail. Bertarelli Collection, Milan.)

styled with princess lines, a snug, high collar, ample lapels, and tab pockets.

With the advent of the automobile, the enveloping **duster** made of white or buff-colored linen was an essential part of the touring costume. This coat was usually unbelted, buttoned from throat to hem, and had tabbed wrist cuffs with buckles to tighten the cuffs.

## SPORTS COSTUMES
## (1890–1910)

As women became more active and participated to a limited extent in sports, special costumes were devised for these pastimes. Tennis dresses, yachting suits, riding habits, and the rather daring, calf-length hunting dress were all part of a leisure-class lady's wardrobe. Generally, these costumes included severely tailored skirts and shirtwaists worn with short jackets. The shirtwaist had a high, mannish collar and tucked bodice front. It usually was worn with a black four-in-hand tie.

Yachting suits had nautical collars and were trimmed with red, white, and blue braid. The correct costume for horseback riding consisted of an ankle-length wraparound skirt, tailored jacket, and shirtwaist with an ascot about the neck. Gym bloomers and middy blouses with sailor collars were used for the more strenuous physical exercises of lifting dumbbells and Indian clubs. For bicycling, a woman might wear knee-length knickers, a shirtwaist, lisle hose, and rubber-soled shoes with canvas tops, or high leather shoes with modest heels (Figure 15.26). However, many women simply wore their daytime garb, a shirtwaist and gored skirt.

Bathing dresses concealed the figure with long, baggy, ruffle-edged bloomers worn beneath a calf-length, belted dress that had elbow-length sleeves and a high, round neckline. The bathing dress was worn with black stockings and high-topped bathing shoes.

In the July 1893 issue of *Vogue*, the latest fashions in swimwear were illustrated in many styles. The most modestly styled swimsuit had a knee-length gathered skirt with a deep kick pleat in front. The bodice, with elbow-length, leg-of-mutton sleeves, was very much like the seventeenth-century justaucorps, and the neckline was décolleté. Other modish suits had full skirts, no sleeves, and large sailor collars. One illustration showed a deep V-neckline filled in with a horizontally striped dickey. This particular swimsuit was trimmed on the shoulders with large tailored bows. The hair was generally bound in a bandeau or a bandana type of head covering worn in much the same manner as that worn by a female slave before the Emancipation Proclamation. Tight-knit pants were worn beneath the swim dress, and the legs were clad in black lisle stockings.

For individual sports, a woman never exposed more of her body to the sun than face, neck, and forearms. Most of these sports costumes retained a considerable degree of femininity. The hunting dress was an exception. This costume consisted of a calf-length skirt much like the

**Figure 15.26.** Cycling costume of 1890s included shirtwaist, jacket, and bloomers. (*Les Gens Chics*, detail, 1895. Bertarelli Collection, Milan.)

Scottish kilt, a tailored blouse, and mannish jacket. Boots, gaiters, and long, heavy stockings were worn with the hunting habit, primarily an Englishwoman's style.

## UNDERGARMENTS (1870–1910)

Petticoats decreased in number and fullness as the skirt was modified to a narrower silhouette. Bloomers, underdrawers, and pantalettes were in general use during the 1870s and 1880s. Corsets were mid-bust-to-waist designs with gussets over the bust and intricate boning and back lacings to mold the figure into the prescribed small-waisted form. By 1905 the corset was restyled into a longer foundation garment which covered the figure from just under the breasts to over the posterior. This style hooked up the center front with large steel hooks and eyes, and laced in back. Two garter stocking supports were attached near the center front.

Umbrella drawers; lace-trimmed knee-length underpants with full, flared legs; or knee-length bloomers or knickers, gathered snugly at the knee by an elastic band, were worn next to the body beneath the corset. The available visual evidence in drawings and paintings of Toulouse-Lautrec and José Guierrez Solana supports the order of sequence just stated for wearing these garments.[11] The same wearing sequence is reported in *The Pictorial Encyclopedia of Fashion* and is shown in the many corset advertisements of the day, which illustrated that a corset was worn on top of the chemise and other undergarments. Since the crotch of underdrawers worn during this period was not seamed, the wearing sequence seems not the least out of order.

In 1877 an innovative undergarment, the **combination,** was introduced. The vest (chemise) and drawers were made in one piece, the forerunner of the twentieth-century step-ins.[12] A waist-length **chemise** with a ruffled front or a **corset cover** was worn to add fullness to the bust during the period when the pouter-pigeon bosom was in vogue.

During the colder winter months, lisle or woolen underwear was worn beneath the chemise and umbrella drawers. These items of winter wear were shapeless, one-piece garments with long legs and cap or long sleeves and were buttoned up the front to a high round or V-neckline. The **union suit,** made for winter wear but worn by many year-round, was a bifurcated garment which was worn next to the skin, covering the body from neck to ankle and shoulder to wrist. There were two styles of these one-piece undergarments. The "elastic ribbed union suit" advertised in the November 1896 issue of *Vogue* shows both styles. One version had a long-sleeved, long-waisted vest section with a truncated V-neckline. At the base of the V was a horizontal row of buttons and buttonholes, making it possible to step into this garment. Different types and sizes of ribbing were used for better fit at the waist, from hips to knees, and over the lower legs. The other style had the same step-in neckline design, small

ribbing at the cuffs and ankles, and was buttoned along the crotch opening.

Between 1870 and 1910 a gored petticoat with ruffles, ruching, and lace trim around the hem was worn singly or in multiples, depending on the shape of the dress skirt. A gusset of lace insertion was extended from knee to hem to act as a skirt support during the period of the princess gown and flared-hem bell skirt. These petticoats were usually waist-to-ankle length and gathered or sewn to a band that buttoned on the side or in back. By the 1890s some women were wearing a calf-length version. The full-length slip did not appear until sometime later. The upper body was covered by a knitted undervest or the chemise.

## MEN'S SUITS (1870–1910)

Men's suits after the Civil War became standardized and had little or no decorative innovations. Even the one touch of individualism, the waistcoat, was discarded. For a time, younger men wore mix-matched trousers and jackets, but the male suit in general was a somber dark costume consisting of trousers, matching vest, and coat (Figure 15.27). The number and position of the coat

**Figure 15.27.** Modish gentlemen of the 1890s affected canes and wore winged collars and suits with matching vests styled with shawl collars. Stiffly starched shirt cuffs were fastened with cuff buttons. (Boldini: *Count Robert de Montesquieu,* Museum of Modern Art, Paris.)

buttons, the size and shape of collar and lapels, and coat length were all that changed, and these only moderately. In the 1870s the lapels and collars were small and braid trimmed. Coat fronts were moderately curved, and the rather narrow trousers were uncreased.

In the 1880s the more formal and distinctive **lounge suit** was introduced. This was a single-breasted suit with a hip-length coat that had sloping shoulders, full sleeves, and buttoned quite high on the chest. It later became a less formal suit than the swallowtailed morning suit. The **ditto suit**, with the coat jacket following the general lines of the male figure, dominated the men's fashion scene.

Until the mid-1890s older men continued to wear the longer Prince Albert or frock coats. The cutaway and swallowtailed coats, styled with collars and lapels to correspond to the detailing in the sack suits, were in time relegated to Sunday-morning wear or morning formal

**Figure 15.29.** In 1904 boys' suits were very much like men's, except for short pants or knickers. Like his father, the boy on left has a pocket watch which is worn in the vest pocket. (Courtesy of the Schmidt family.)

**Figure 15.28.** Typical male **sack suit** of the turn of the century, worn with matching vest and striped, broadcloth shirt. The detachable, stiffly starched high collar was attached to the neckband with gold collar buttons. Ties were held in place by decorated stickpins.

functions. These coats were patterned after the suit coats of the 1830s with waist-length fronts and tailed backs cut straight down from the side seam, diagonally downward to the back, or in sweeping curves to the back. They were usually worn with black-and-gray striped trousers.

Trousers, full and creaseless in the 1870s, became more and more slender and finally were pressed with a center leg crease after the turn of the century (Figure 15.28). Two side pockets, two hip pockets, and a small waistband watch pocket were characteristic details. One of the hip pockets was usually buttoned with a small tab. The fly-front trouser closure was fastened by concealed buttons. The instep strap was discarded by the end of the 1870s and cuffed trouser legs appeared a little before the turn of the century.

**Knickers,** an adaptation of the knee breeches of the eighteenth and nineteenth centuries, were worn with a sack-suit jacket for spectator sports (Figure 15.29). These continued in vogue for many years, and the **Norfolk** jacket was designed especially to be worn with knickers, primarily as a country or hunting costume. This jacket was quite long, as were all men's suit coats when they first were introduced in 1890. The Norfolk was hipbone length, belted, and had one narrow, inverted box pleat in the center back that acted as a belt guide. Later this sporting jacket had two such pleats in front and back, one on each side of center, which continued to act as belt guides.

Men wore white flannel trousers with striped or plain **blazers** for boating, tennis, and other summer activities from 1890 and through 1920. As were the sacksuit coats, these blazers were styled with a looser fit, larger sleeves, lower-set button closures, and slightly larger lapels by 1910.

The formal attire for men developed into a selective number of costumes, depending on the hour of the day and the type of function. The most formal was the tailed-coat, black opera or ball costume worn with trousers which had braid or satin trimming down the side seams, "boiled shirt," and white waistcoat. In the 1890s the trousers of this costume were very narrow, and the tail-coat lapels were narrow and shallow. The waistcoat was made of white pique or linen to match the white tie. Stiff winged collars or stiff tall collars and deep, stiffly starched cuffs were details of the formal shirt. The center front of the shirt was boiled to retain its whiteness and very stiffly starched (hence "boiled shirt"), or a heavily starched U-shaped dickey held with a diamond stud was worn to give a full-chested masculine silhouette to this formal male attire.

**Figure 15.30.** Characteristic wing collar of the 1880s and 1890s. Note the fold of the breast-pocket handkerchief and the hairstyling. (Courtesy of the Whaley family.)

By the 1890s **morning suits,** composed of swallow-tailed coats, gray-and-black striped trousers, and gray waistcoats, were worn with unstarched white shirts which had winged collars and were worn with an ascot. The least formal of morning clothes was the **lounge suit.** This semiformal costume was made up of a black sack coat, striped trousers, and gray double-breasted waistcoat. It was also worn with a soft white shirt, which had a fold-down collar, and a four-in-hand tie.

The tuxedo, first introduced in the 1880s, was a more elegant version of the sack-suit coat made with quilted lapels and collar. It was usually double breasted and worn with braid-trimmed trousers. The tuxedo costume was completed with a black silk tie worn around the starched collar of the tucked-front white shirt. The tailless evening coat was an innovation for evening wear.

Men's shirts were altered in design about 1880 to resemble the basic cut of more modern shirts. They had a shoulder yoke, modestly proportioned sleeves, and either curved cuffs or French cuffs fastened with large, swivel-shank links. Usually, collars were detachable and heavily starched. At the turn of the century, rounded or pointed collars were white, matching the shirt cuffs. The bodies of the shirts were either white, a plain color, or striped. There were many collar styles ranging from winged collars (Figure 15.30), to high, straight, standing collars to stiff, tall, fold-over collars. They were worn with ascots, string ties with large loop bows, big bow ties, and the more modern four-in-hand ties which were made of silk fabric with small patterns or diagonal stripes.

## MEN'S WRAPS
## (1870–1910)

During this forty-year time span many topcoats and overcoats were worn. The modified **Chesterfield,** styled with a fly front and concealed-button, single-breasted closure was most popular after 1880. The body of the coat, usually made of heavy black wool with a black velvet collar, was designed with straight boxy lines, amply cut to fit easily over the sack or ditto suit.

Great ankle-length coats of buffalo fur or beaver were worn during the 1870s and 1880s (Figure 15.31). These straight-line coats had rather large cuffed sleeves, wide flat collars, and a single row of buttons in the front.

The **Inverness coat** was one of the more unique topcoats of this period. Introduced in the 1880s, it was sleeveless, mid-calf length, and had an elbow-length cape attached beneath a tall "square" collar. The Inverness was worn firmly belted at the waist; when worn unbelted, it appeared more like a buttoned cape than an overcoat. Considered a lightweight wrap, it was generally made of fabric with a shepherd's plaid weave. Some people call this wrap the Sherlock Holmes coat.

The **walking coat,** a knee-length garment with large flapped pockets, was often worn with matching cuffless

**Figure 15.31.** Long, buffalo-fur overcoats with fox collars and sealskin hats were popular winter wear in the plains states in the 1890s. (Courtesy of the Carter family.)

trousers. It was usually worn in the country and made of tweed materials or other rustic fabrics. The knee-length skirt was sewn to the waist section at the normal waist. This seam acted as a belt and waist demarcation, and as a trim, for it was a prominent welted seam. As the masculine image became more sturdy, the length of the coat skirts became shorter. Raglan sleeves and less bulky coat bodies came into fashion. The male overcoat was suddenly a serviceable garment with few flamboyant details. The shoulder capes and braid trims disappeared. Double-and single-breasted, knee-length coats of heavy woolen fabric in a limited range of colors of buffs, tans, browns, and black were worn. Greatcoats with fur collars and cuffs were worn by the wealthier men, but topcoats were usually conservative garments, cut with collars and lapels following the modifications made in the suit coats.

## Accessories (1870–1910)

### HEADWEAR

Women's hats between 1870 and 1910 underwent yearly styling changes. The trimmed bonnets of earlier years totally disappeared and were replaced by small felt or straw hats which were elaborately trimmed. These were perched forward, their tilted and rolled brims covered with ruffles, bows, and curled plumes. In keeping with the back interest created on gowns, these hats were more intricately decorated in the back.

By the middle of the decade and continuing through the 1880s, hats began to gain height and were worn farther back on the head. Throughout the next years and continuing until after the turn of the century, hats were structured into towering forms and decorated with flowers, feathers, lace, and ribbons. Hat frames and the decorations were purchased as separate items at a millinery shop. A lady, called a trimmer, would hold the bits of lace, feathers, or flowers in different places on the hat frame as the lady customer sat before a mirror giving approval to the suggested arrangement of the decorations. The hat was then left in the shop for the trimmer to secure the desired frills in place.

In the 1890s hats became somewhat lower and broader. The **chapeau paré**, a small bonnet with wide sashes that covered the ears and tied under the chin, was introduced. Major styling trends dictated a narrow, swooping brim and a shallow crown with whole, stuffed, spread-wing birds perched on top. The round hat was a more tailored style worn in the morning or for informal occasions. It had a wide flat crown, round brim, and was often trimmed with a circlet of gathered silk under the brim. The **tam-o-shanter**, a wide, flat beret with a puff tassel on top, was worn either pancake style or pulled down over the ears. The latter wearing mode was in keeping with the belief that it was unhealthy to go out in very cold weather with the ears exposed. This was the same reason for the use of the wide, ear-covering streamer ties on the *chapeau paré*.

The flamboyant hat styles introduced after the turn of the century were monumental in size and trim. Flowers, feathers, and brim veils covered the wide, swooping brims and large crowns. The face veil of the 1890s all but disappeared. These hats were worn high on the pompadoured coiffure. A bandeau on the underside of the brim helped raise the hat and functioned as the area through which the long stiletto hatpins were thrust. Although elegant, these large, fanciful chapeaus, often called **Gainsborough hats**, demanded that ladies stand erect in a haughty pose. The hats achieved maximum size in 1907 and were decorated with heron feathers, bird-of-paradise plumes, and tied "flues."

The **automobile bonnet** was a large, brimmed hat with a net or tulle scarf placed over the crown and tied under the chin. The brim was stiff and the scarf made a gossamer triangle from the big chin bow to the hat-brim edge. Straw **sailors' hats** were worn for tennis matches, bicycling, and croquet games. These flat-crowned, round-brimmed hats were trimmed with a wide grosgrain-ribbon hatband with a bow on the side.

Men's hats included: the **bowler**, the **derby**, the felt **fedora**, the **Homburg**, the **cap**, and the straw **boater**.

These hat styles for daytime and sports wear continued in style throughout this forty-year period. The tall, silk hat, the collapsible opera hat, and the gray top hat were used for formal wear (Figure 15.32).

## FOOTWEAR

Shoes for ladies were serviceable for day wear. They were high topped, made of fabric or leather with leather toes and counters, and buttoned on the side or laced over the instep. During the 1870s the toes were pointed, but squared at the tips; the heels, while raised, were not high but rather thick. Tops and counters often were made with leather of contrasting colors, and, as the turn of the century approached, the toes became more pointed.

Formal shoes and dressy shoes for daytime wear were made in a variety of pump styles with bow and rosette trims. According to page 378 of the December 1894 *Vogue*, toe shapes of formal pumps altered over the years. By 1896 they were pointed and the heels were wedge shaped and of modest height.

In the 1890s the low shoe or laced oxford was introduced. These often were worn with gaiters during colder weather or for sporting activities. Page 9 of the July 1893

**Figure 15.32.** Gentlemen of the 1870s wore stovepipe opera hats, gloves, large neckties, and white satin vests, or waistcoats with small lapels, and carried walking sticks. (D. Morelli: *Portrait of Bernardo Celentano,* detail, c. 1875. National Gallery of Modern Art, Rome.)

supplement of *Vogue* describes a lady's "canvas summer shoe" as being "cool and natty." The type of footwear was the oxford styling with a modest heel of the spool design. These rubber-soled low shoes, the forerunner of the tennis shoes with canvas tops and rubber soles, were first introduced in 1893.[13]

Shoes and boots for men continued to be made in approximately the same styles for many years. The changing shape of the toes was the only variable. These were square-tipped in the 1870s, rounded during the 1880s and 1890s, and became more pointed after the turn of the century. Tie oxfords, two-tone or plain, replaced the high-topped male shoes in the 1890s. Pumps with flat bows or rosettes were made of black patent leather and were correct for formal footwear.

## JEWELRY

Pearl necklaces, drop earrings, and bar pins with chased designs on gold were the popular pieces of jewelry worn by women early in this period. Diamonds, garnets, pearls, and semiprecious stones were mounted in gold settings. These pieces were not large, but the filigree settings were often intricate. Between 1900 and 1910 long pearl necklaces and diamond, emerald, or ruby sets mounted in gold or platinum were made into throat-encircling dog collars.

The first earrings with screw fastenings were introduced in this decade. Until that time, all earrings had been worn through pierced ears. Women's fob watches were worn pinned to the bosom or to the snug skirt belt of garments. The watches had closed faces and the gold cases were decorated with chased patterns or handsomely enameled. A watch also might be worn suspended from a long, heavy watch chain with a small chain guide that assisted in arranging the large chain into a variety of draped swags. Rings were usually single-set gems in gold mountings. Wedding rings were simple, wide gold bands, and engagement rings had sunken diamond settings or the raised Tiffany setting.

Men's jewelry included pocket watches with closed or open faces, carried in the vest pocket. The watch was attached to a heavy gold chain strung through the vest buttonhole and anchored in the opposite pocket with a gold-cased penknife. The closed-face watches went out of style before the turn of the century. Gold cuff links, stickpins with gem heads, and gem or signet rings were popular pieces of jewelry for men. Not only was the stickpin decorative, but it served to keep the tie inside the vest. The stickpin was a stiletto type with a curve near the head. Pin heads were precious or semiprecious gems, often with unique mounts, emblems of fraternal orders, oval discs with the wearer's initials, or even images of small insects. The jewelry wardrobe of the socially elite male also included diamond shirt studs and gold collar buttons.

## HANDHELD ACCESSORIES

Hand-painted folding fans, fans with incised ivory segments, and printed paper fans in semi- or complete circular styles were carried by coquettes and frantically fluttered by ladies suffering from the "vapors."

During the 1880s purses were little velvet bags which had semicircular metal frames with snap-closing devices and strap handles. The pocketbook, introduced in 1910, was styled in the Empire mode and carried for afternoon social functions. Pocketbooks were sacklike pouches with drawstring closings, or small pouches attached to arched metal frames with snap fastenings. The fitted-leather purse was designed with a number of small compartments, each with snap fastenings. It usually had leather-strap handles.

Short, wrist-length gloves of kid or cloth with radiating tucks on the back and buttons at the wrists were used for daytime wear. Long kid gloves that covered the entire arm were worn with formal gowns. The gloves had small, covered buttons on the underside of the wrists to make them fit snugly above the hands.

# Hairstyles (1870–1910)

Throughout these years of rapidly changing fashions, hairstyles were modified many times. Women's coiffures for the most part were pulled up off the neck and arranged in curls, frizzes, bangs, and bouffant pompadours in front. Small head shapes with face-framing small curls were typical during the 1870s and 1880s. Frizzed bangs, curls over the ears, and twisted knots of hair on the crown were popular during the latter part of the 1880s and into the 1890s. The next coif fashion added breadth at the temples, created by soft waves. After the turn of the century, coiffure height was attained by combing the hair over "pads" or "rats." A chignon was sometimes worn at the nape of the neck or the hair was upswept, held in place by

decorative tortoise-shell combs set with rhinestone brilliants.

The first permanent **hair-wave machine** was invented in 1906; however, it was not used in the United States until 1915. This cumbersome device, which combined ill-smelling lotions and electrically heated curl irons, made it possible for those with the straightest hair to have curls. The process was long and tedious; often scalps were seared, hair singed by the heat, and skin irritated by the lotions. This "beauty treatment" was also costly, but it was more convenient than the nightly use of the crimper, or curl papers, or the time-consuming use of a curling iron which had to be heated on the range or over a lamp.

Men's hair was gradually cut shorter, and faces were clean shaven except for flat sideburns and mustaches. The hair was combed from a side part, or a center part, or in a slight pompadour. Mustaches ranged from thick walrus styles to neatly cared-for waxed mustaches. By the turn of the century, the wearing of sideburns and mustaches was completely out of style and men's hair was clipped short in back and parted on the side.

## FOOTNOTES

1. Helen Gardner, *Art Through the Ages,* p. 673.
2. Ibid.
3. Ludmila Kybalová; Olga Herbenová; and Milena Lamarová; *The Pictorial Encyclopedia of Fashion,* p. 281.
4. Ibid., p. 393.
5. François Boucher, *20,000 Years of Fashion,* p. 391.
6. Kybalová, *Encyclopedia of Fashion,* p. 282.
7. Gisele D'Assailly, *Ages of Elegance,* p. 193.
8. Kybalová, *Encyclopedia of Fashion,* p. 293.
9. Ibid., p. 282.
10. Ibid., p. 286.
11. Ibid., p. 463.
12. Les Costumes Historique, Musée d'Artillorie de Paris.
13. *Vogue,* July 1893, p. 9.

# Chapter 16
# Costumes of the Modern Age of Change
## (1910–1939)

The cultures of all ages of humanity have been marked by social changes, but no developments were more dynamic nor involved more people than those instigated between the early 1900s and the beginning of the great twentieth-century depression. Following the death of Edward VII in 1910, new philosophies of humanitarianism were explored. Through educational and legislative measures, social reformers sought to promote a higher standard of living, better physical and mental health, and a consciousness of the plight of minority groups. The theories of economists, sociologists, and political scientists pointed up the inadequacies of the social structure in the United States and in some European countries.

After the Civil War the United States had developed under a burgeoning system of plutocracy. The labor forces were swelled by immigrants who lived in squalid tenements and worked long hours in factories with machines that often were not safe. Thousands of acres of free land, vast quantities of rich oil and mineral deposits, and recently invented labor-saving, work-creating machines were used to generate wealth which was controlled by a few people.

Social activists felt that these enormously rich families had stifled the restructuring of the living conditions for the greater mass of the population. American sociologists Lester Ward and Anna G. Spencer proposed that the government of the people was responsible for regulating congested conditions in the urban slums and factories and for controlling the spread of contagious diseases. They felt that the negative factors that contributed to many intolerable conditions had to be recognized and eliminated if living standards were to be positively altered.

Others attacked the lot of the poorer members of society in different ways. Carry Nation, convinced that she was divinely appointed, went about smashing saloons and agitating for temperance. She initiated the movement that later resulted in the addition of the Prohibition Amendment to the American Constitution.

**Figure 16.1.** Leneif created this exciting evening ensemble of black velvet, kelly green satin, and marten fur in 1913. The sleeve treatment is reminiscent of the late Gothic period. (Sketched at *The 10s, The 20s, The 30s* exhibition, 1974. Metropolitan Museum of Art, New York City.)

As early as 1815 Lucretia Coffin Mott, a Quaker, began to work for women's rights. During the nineteenth century, many feminists continued to promote her free-thinking attitudes, including Margaret Fuller, Clara Barton, Susan B. Anthony, and Esabella Beecher. In the twentieth century, such firebrands for women's suffrage as Victoria Woodhull in the United States and Emmeline Pankhurst in England organized parades, published monthlies, and enlisted the aid of many of New York's wealthiest women. In 1920 the Nineteenth Amendment to the United States Constitution gave women the right to vote, although some states and some foreign countries had done so earlier. Margaret Sanger sought to raise living standards by organizing the birth-control movement. She established the first clinics in the United States in 1921 and held the first international conference on birth control in 1925.

In addition to social reforms, the second decade of the twentieth century was shaken by the cataclysmic upheaval of World War I. The assasination of Archduke Francis Ferdinand of Austria-Hungary in June of 1914 touched off the conflict between the Allied forces of the British Empire, France, Russia, Belgium, Serbia, Montenegro, and Japan, and the Central Powers of Germany, Austria-Hungary, and Turkey. The Allies were joined by Italy in 1915, Rumania in 1916, and the United States and Greece in 1917.

Between September and November of 1918, the beginning of the end came when first Bulgaria, then Turkey and Austria, surrendered. All fighting ceased when Germany capitulated on November 11, 1918, with the signing of the armistice at Compiegne, France. The Peace Treaty of Versailles in 1919 outlined the terms of settlement which finally ended the First World War.

A period of postwar enthusiasm for life encouraged the concerns for self rather than for social reform. Business, money, and pleasure became the gods in the United States.

Blocks of stock were bought and sold with little or no real backing. In September 1929, the New York Stock Exchange went on a selling rampage and prices fell to new lows. Few were able to withstand the force of the financial catastrophy. Businesses failed, banks closed, and the worst depression since the 1830s enveloped the United States and Europe.

Paper wealth for a few had meant poverty for many others, which resulted in such demonstrations as the 1932 Veterans March on Washington, D.C., to demand immediate payment of war bonuses. Beneath the surface there was unrest in many countries which was manifested in events such as the Irish Rebellion in the 1920s against Northern Ireland and English rule, ever-increasing inflation in postwar Germany, and labor strikes in England.

The world of the arts reflected the changing face of the international scene. Radical artists of Expressionism, Cubism, Dada, and Fauves expressed their reactions in works exhibited at the Armory Show which opened in New York on February 13, 1913. Picasso, Braque, and Matisse were the innovative artists of the era.

Classical and popular music developed new thematic tonal systems and rhythmic beats. Schoenberg, Bartok, Berlin, and Gershwin created new sounds for concert halls and the mass medium of radio.

Moving pictures were a new creative force, and radio provided home entertainment as an inexpensive diversion. Radio and movies, at first experimental novelties, shortened distances and created new theater art forms.

Architecture, its innovative forms given impetus by the Bauhaus in Germany, was stripped of its extensive ornamentation and became direct and functional. Miës van der Rohe, Frank Lloyd Wright, and Walter Gropius were the leaders in this field.

No thirty-year period had ever seen such rapid changes in social order and the arts, which, in turn, altered fashion. As Diana Vreeland stated in the introduction to the catalog of the 1974 Costume Institute exhibition at the Metropolitan Museum of Art titled *The 10s, The 20s, The 30s: Inventive Clothes 1909–1939*, "The twentieth century came in fresh as paint and by 1909 started to roll."[1] Before the First World War everyone was intoxicated by the new life-style, new art forms, new musical tonal qualities, and new dance forms in social dancing and theatrical interpretation. Paris once again was the artistic and social center of the Western world. The Haute Couture of Paris, including Poiret, Vionnet, les Callot Soeurs, and later, Chanel, cut dresses in ways that had never before been seen. Interest in fashion was revitalized and *Vogue* magazine instituted the first fashion show in 1914 to meet this heightened enthusiasm.

The Oriental influence, *Art Nouveau*, and the native costuming of the Balkans were dominant fashion themes during "The 10s." The newest modes were the ***robe de nuit*** and the **cassock gown** with kimono sleeves made in nansook fabric. Hats were styled with large crowns to be compatible with the modish coifs of the period. Hair was worn pushed forward on the brow, a style which was to become the helmet cut by the late teens. Shoes for street and formal wear had pointed toes and Louis heels. The suit was a popular daytime costume created for specific activities and named appropriately the **walking suit** or the **traveling suit.**

The figure was controlled by corsets made of rubber elastic to mold the figure or "reduce your flesh" as one *Vogue* fashion editor reported in a 1910 issue. The new rubber-elastic corset replaced the style popular from 1903 to 1910, which was recalled in the December 1943 *Vogue* (page 41). This article, a remembrance of fashions and corsets past, described earlier figure-controlling garments as "corsets laced to the fainting point, hips are padded, petticoats costly, dress bodices boned, skirts billow and makeup is rice powder and a touch of rouge."

The fresh, startling styles of society during the 1910s were as dramatic as the exhibition installation of the 1910s fashions in the 1974 Metropolitan Museum of Art display. For example, an evening ensemble designed by Leneif in 1913 consisted of a tunic jacket of black velvet, green satin, and fur (Figure 16.1). The low U-neckline swept into the center opening which in turn faded into the jacket's curved skirt-front opening. The sleeves, tight over the forearm, had deep cuffs which were three feet long and made of green satin edged in fur. The waist was bound with a bulky girdle of metallic lamé over which a thin, gold cord was tied in a loose bow. This evening jacket was worn with a "kelly-forest" green satin "trouser skirt" which extended to the floor and had center-front fullness. At the hem the front and back of the skirt were seamed together except for an opening at each side seam which allowed just enough space for a foot to slip through.

deep, bag sleeves (Figure 16.3). The proportional relationship, the linear quality of the silhouette, and the soft textural elegance of the velvet fabric created a sense of simplified elegance.

This dominant trend toward simplicity contrasted sharply to the **tonneau** silhouette of a theater wrap designed by Paquin in 1912. The complexly cut, deep yoke of black velvet supported an equally complex body section of patterned orange, vermillion, and black silk created with a heavily draped blouson back, nipped in around the thighs by a black band a half-yard deep. The batwing sleeves were red trimmed with vermillion tassels, carrying

**Figure 16.2.** The Renaissance greatly influenced Poiret when he designed this 1917 evening wrap of deep royal-purple velvet with a forest-green satin lining. (Sketched at *The 10s, The 20s, The 30s* exhibition, 1974. Metropolitan Museum of Art, New York City.)

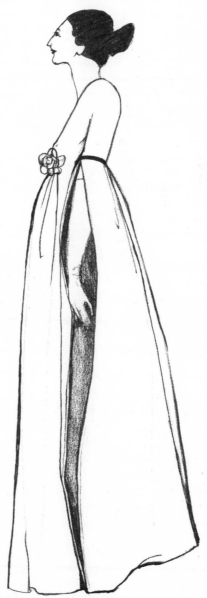

**Figure 16.3.** Poiret's 1917 evening wrap of wine-red velvet with an empire waist and an adaptation of the hanging sleeves of the Renaissance. (Sketched at *The 10s, The 20s, The 30s* exhibition, 1974. Metropolitan Museum of Art, New York City.)

Nor did elegance of trims and the carefully planned proportional relationships between them and the cut soon disappear. In 1917 the great couturier Paul Poiret created two theater wraps which displayed a remarkably close relationship to Renaissance female outer garments. From a deep royal-purple·velvet he cut a shoulder-to-instep wrap lined with green satin and trimmed with gold fringe, covered buttons, and a complex, looped shoulder fastening. In the 1974 Metropolitan Museum of Art exhibition, this sumptuous wrap was shown with an aigrette-trimmed turban created by the same couturier (Figure 16.2).

That same year Poiret created an extremely simple theater wrap in wine-red velvet with an empire waist and out the color theme of the patterned textile used in the body section. The patterned fabric was further enhanced in strategic areas with embroidery of silk thread and beads. An exaggerated and elaborate tasseled frog secured the asymmetric front closure (Figure 16.4).

Poiret apparently derived many of his design ideas from past periods of dress. In 1919 or 1920 he created a red-and-black silk crepe evening ensemble with a paenula-type cape for a wrap (Figure 16.5). Extremely simple, the paenula cape had a high-cowl, horizontal drape across the throat. Cape and skirt were bordered in black, accenting the subdued, deep red which was the dominant hue of this evening ensemble.

Poiret designed daytime costumes as well, including an intricate jumper and blouse with yellow grosgrain trim of ivory, pale dull yellow, and black crepe. The bishop-sleeve cuffs were quite complex, with the yellow grosgrain-ribbon trim tied over the cuff return. The ankle-length skirt was accordion pleated. The dull yellow upper bodice or jumper section was multitucked; the ivory blouse beneath had tucks also, but these were much narrower. Again, the proportional relationships and the

**Figure 16.5.** In 1919 or 1920 Poiret designed this evening ensemble with a cape wrap patterned after the paenula. Note the asymmetrical gathers on the skirt. (Sketched at *The 10s, The 20s, The 30s* exhibition, 1974. Metropolitan Museum of Art, New York City.)

**Figure 16.4.** An example of the **tonneau** silhouette created by Paquin in 1912. (Sketched at *The 10s, The 20s, The 30s* exhibition, 1974. Metropolitan Museum of Art, New York City.)

textures creating the detail were meticulously calculated. The colors were studies in value and hue relationships. This care in evaluating the elements of design was also visible in Poiret's coats, suits, promenade costumes, and traveling coats.

The 1910s were years of great change in etiquette and the manner in which women viewed themselves. The fashion word was a "no-figure silhouette," and in 1919 the Callot sisters created a model all the more chic because of its daring simplicity (Figure 16.6). It was made of four slender duplicate kite shapes sewn together part way down the long edges. The shorter edges created armholes and a deep décolletage. On the shoulders were two rhinestone clips. The hemline was uneven, draping into four points. The kite shapes were cut on the bias, which aided in the perfect draping of this garment when it was worn.

During the 1920s the new art form, Art Deco, was a dominant factor which influenced fashion forms and the drawings which visually reported them. The music of the

**Figure 16.6.** In 1919 The Callot sisters created this strikingly simple dress which was the beginning of a totally new female silhouette. (Sketched at *The 10s, The 20s, The 30s* exhibition, 1974. Metropolitan Museum of Art, New York City.)

The fashion world reflected, relished, and rejoiced in the taste and actions of the daring darlings of this decade, bent on having fun with style. There was no stereotype, only a general acceptance of the figure-freeing silhouette which denied both bust and buttocks. The detailing variables were the design factors which brought individuality to the costumes of this era. In the past only a few could afford a number of gowns; by the twenties, more people were able to enjoy the good life of affluence, and the size of wardrobes increased at all levels of society (Figure 16.7).

It was decidedly an era of individualism; even collars and cuffs gave expression to this individualism. For example, in a 1924 issue of *Vogue*, more than a half-dozen illustrations of collar and cuff details were shown. Included were a shawl collar, "supplemented with a double-pleated jabot," in a V-neckline; a pleated "frilled cream net" filling out a deep U-cut neckline; and a linen batiste stock with a black ribbon and pleated jabot. The article stated that a frock was as "new as its neckline and cuffs."

Neck scarves were also important fashion accessories. Made of plain-hued or floral-patterned chiffon,

**Figure 16.7.** Mail-order merchandising made it possible for those living in provincial areas to wear clothes somewhat in the fashion originated by Poiret. (Women's wear page from a 1919 Sears, Roebuck & Co. mail-order catalog.)

era was the blues and the poignant musical systems of Gershwin. The popular dance was the energetic Charleston danced by all levels of society. Women rouged their cheeks and lips, lacquered their nails, suntanned their skin, wore nude-colored silk hose, and shingled their hair in imitation of the Dolly Sisters. These actresses were the first to bob their hair and have it finger waved, giving up the curling iron for the marcel wave.

This period was rife with action, fun, and money; everyone acted as if the bubble would never burst. These attitudes were a reaction to the dismal years of the First World War. It was no wonder that the excesses enjoyed by those of the flapper era were engaged in so gleefully.

these neck scarves were tied to one side, close under the chin in large bows. This style was known generally as the **cravat collar** when the scarf was worn with a gown with a U-shaped neckline. This accessory fashion lasted several years and was shown with a Louiseboulanger creation, a restaurant gown designed in 1928, in the Metropolitan Museum exhibition (Figure 16.8).

The creative fashion designers of the period rose to meet the challenge of insatiable appetites for new and exciting costumes. The Callot sisters moved successfully from the previous decade to become the dominant couturières of the 1920s. Influenced by factors other than a swift

**Figure 16.8.** Short chiffon evening gown with single ostrich feathers attached at the hem and small glass beads, in an arched pattern, acting as a transitional device from the simple sheath top to the rich hem embellishment. Designed by Louiseboulanger, 1928. (Sketched at *The 10s, The 20s, The 30s* exhibition, 1974. Metropolitan Museum of Art, New York City.)

change in morals and interests, and guided by many innovative art forms, Chanel, Vionnet, and the Callot sisters liberated women from the confining female clothes of the decades just past.

The full meaning of the flapper era did not take shape until 1925. Prior to that date, hems modestly revealed the ankle; suits and dresses were intricately cut but not revealing. The loosely styled garments used for street wear were made with matching fabric textures of contrasting colors. Many evening-gown designs harked back to past ages.

For example, many copied some of the features of the eighteenth-century shepherdess gowns. Gilbert Clark created a handsome powder-blue taffeta dress with silver embroidery on the skirt. The major motif of this elegant decoration was the fleur-de-lis. The skirt had a plain panel in the center front with hip fullness creating a panierlike appearance. The bodice was simple and had silver-lace cap sleeves. An illustration of this gown can be found in the June 1, 1924 issue of *Vogue*. The cover of the June 15, 1929 issue of *Vogue* featured another adaptation of the panier treatment (Figure 16.9). Again the bodice was understated with a deep V-shaped décolletage and no sleeves. Three deep twelve-inch pleats jutted out from the waistline. This overskirt was made of white crepe with gold braid and gold fringe trim. The underskirt was green satin and fully gathered beneath the crepe overskirt.

Possibly for the first time the innovative minds of this period's designers consciously organized each of the garment's distinctive features with attention to the elements and principles of design. This is not to say that designers of previous periods were not aware of the governing factors of design. However, the aesthetics of the age, reflecting the cultural attitudes of the period, directed the design characteristics incorporated into garments.

The 1920s were vigorous times, filled with the exuberance of being *modern*, and aesthetically *modern* was interpreted to be functional. Léger, Mondrian, Diego Rivera, Dove, and Stewart Davis had introduced a machinelike quality into the images of people and still-life subjects. Decorative embellishments were forced to reflect this rigid functionality of the new machine age. Necklines were generally crisp, geometric shapes: bateau (oval), rectangular, square, or deep super ellipses. During the early years of the decade these harsh shapes were softened by ruching and chiffon bindings.

By the end of the decade the leading designers were firmly established. The fashion houses which were "... good indicators of chic" included such designers as Chanel, Paquin, Patou, Chéruit, and Lanvin, whose beautifully made and thoughtfully proportioned creations were considered conservative.

Skirt interest dominated fashions of the twenties. In 1929 special skirt treatments were given style-identifying names. The **princess** style (*Vogue*, April 27, 1929) con-

**Figure 16.9.** Formal ball gown with wide side projections, an updated version of the panier styling of the eighteenth century. (Redrawn from the cover of *Vogue* magazine, June 15, 1929.)

sisted of a high-waisted bodice with the fit over the hips to the thighs skillfully molded by "cutting and flat tucks" in the front of the garment. So flat was the silhouette thus created that the figure appeared to be "nearly concave." The high waistline gave the princess gown an empire flavor. In fact, many of the formal gowns from that period exhibited at the Metropolitan Museum Costume Institute were directly influenced by the Leroy gowns of the court of Napoleon. Patou was one of the leading designers who incorporated the separate train effect so typical of the court gowns of the First Empire.

The **mermaid** skirt style was form fitting to the knees, then flaring from that point to the floor. Lanvin

inventively adopted the peplum effect. However, instead of encircling the figure, the peplum was more of a back interest applied to the skirt.

Evening wraps during this period were equally flamboyant while adhering to the Art Deco aesthetic. Often created with fur at the neck and hem of the three-quarter-length versions, the bodies were made from a wide range of fabrics. Such combinations as crepe with fox, or sable with gold and cream moire, were used. These were, of course, the fabric weights used for summer evening garb.

As stated in *Vogue*, April 27, 1929, "Individuality is outstanding in the present mode ... feminity has completely replaced uniformity." The great creative couturiers were equally individualistic and used design concepts in a personal manner "to sign their models." The garments they created for each fashion season's opening were masterpieces of sculpture in fabric.

The decade of the 1930s presented to fashion designers a challenge far greater than the dynamic, insatiable appetite for innovation demanded during the flapper era. Caught between the Great Depression and World War II, the affluent society was plunged into despair by the stock market crash. Financially defeated and clad in raiment indicative of their former social position, many fashionably elite leaped from multistoried skyscrapers or sold apples on street corners. Churches, the Red Cross, and other agencies with a social conscience organized soup kitchens and welfare stores where day-old bread and old but clean clothes could be purchased.

Reflecting the changes in social status, clothes changed in silhouette. Hemlines dropped, waistlines assumed their normal level, and detailing returned to symmetrically organized embellishments.

In 1932, Franklin D. Roosevelt was elected President of the United States. With his inauguration, hope was renewed, spurred by his innovative proposals for reform. By 1934 this hope was reflected in the creations of the French and American fashion designers (Figure 16.10). In the 20s Chanel had stripped all superfluities from the clothes she designed. In the early 1930s Schiaparelli introduced wit and whimsy into apparel. Noted for her startling innovations, she designed accessories and costumes slavishly devoted to a sense of proportion and design excellence.

Evening-wear and day-wear silhouettes for a time continued the sheath line. Colors were more subdued, with grayish blues, black, forest greens, browns, and grays predominant. Designers had sensed the psychological impact of the stock market crash and used hues symbolic of the humor of the time. However, their optimism was given visual form in the projections and forecasts for fall 1934. Sealskin capes, tippets, stoles, and full-length coats were presented as fashion's best.

Patou's fall collection presented dinner suits of lamé cut in a severely tailored manner. Lamé turbans of green

**Figure 16.10.** Between 1933 and 1935 Chanel abandoned the simplicity for which she had become famous and designed this intricate theater ensemble with a mermaid skirt trimmed with ostrich feathers. The bodice front has myriad minitucks. (Sketched at *The 10s, The 20s, The 30s* exhibition, 1974. Metropolitan Museum of Art, New York City.)

and gold were recommended accessories with these dinner suits. A handheld accessory was presented as a "huge gold metal case which would hold quantities of cigarettes as well as powder and lipstick." The tailored dinner suit was made more feminine by adding shirred, draped, and tucked gloves.

The fashionably knowledgeable dictated that daywear accessories had to match. Gloves, bag, and shoes matched in color as well as in texture. Pliable antelope and calfskin were popular accessory materials. Suede and alligator were described as "in" for "semisport" shoes. Sewn suede swagger gloves and ribbed woolen gloves were popular handwear accessories.

The fall accessory which changed most radically was the hat. In the October 15, 1934 issue, *Vogue* stated that hats "were as important as a revolution." Headwear was styled with high-peaked or pointed crowns; squared-off crowns were considered the most chic (Figure 16.11). The designer Agnes created clown caps and talbot conical

caps. That year turbans, pillboxes, and toques were styled with a "universality" and worn tipped precariously over the right eye or back over the brow. "Sharp and tailored" or "soft and feminine" shapes and fabrics in hats ran the full range, and Lilly Daché made fur, velvet, and quill trims popular.

Because of the increased popularity of daytime suits, blouses became an important costume accessory. Skirts and blouses without jackets also became popular daytime casual wear. In an October 1934 *Vogue*, an article with the titillating title of "The Upper Half" emphasized the importance of the blouse in the fashion scene.[2] It recommended that designer Jodelle's green velveteen blouse should be worn with a black skirt. Presumably, black wool skirts were most chic when worn with an "afternoon blouse of grayish-blue satin" or with Schiaparelli's handknit, wide-rib blouse and scarf. Designer Mainbocher devoted much creativity to blouse design.

The skirts on formal gowns returned to floor lengths for ladies of fashion. The figure was adorned in a form-revealing sheath trimmed with silk fringe. Often the fringe assumed the appearance of a scarf, its sheen contrasting to the dull black crepe texture of the body of the garment. Blacks and browns were popular hues for evening wear.

Daytime coats were created from a wide variety of fabric textures with tweeds predominating. Bulky fox coats dominated the fur-coat silhouette.

The intricacy of shoe design continued throughout this period. Footwear had become an important facet in the total-costume look as soon as the dress hemlines were raised. The importance of shoes to the aesthetic appearance of a costume has not diminished in recent times. The fanciful combinations of straps, tabs, exaggerated tongues, and multitextured, multihued footwear was most inventive. Shoes advertised in September of 1937 were equally fanciful but more thoughtfully designed. There was a wide range of styles adapted to the activity patterns

**Figure 16.11.** Schiaparelli's twist top and pointed-crown hats of the 1930s. (Sketched from a 1937 copy of *Vogue* magazine.)

of the wearer: low shoes, oxfords for sportswear, and high-heeled shoes for more formal functions. The spike-heeled pumps called **black sheep** were first made in Switzerland from French antelope. The shoes of the late 1930s and early 1940s were designed rather high over the instep. In the 1940s the open-toed, open-sided shoes with elastic side straps to hold the shoes snugly on the foot became popular.

The Paris opening in the fall of 1937 proclaimed that the "women of 30" were "the new idols." To be chic for the winter season of 1937–38, women must assume a worldly look. Elegance, opulence, and luxury were the key words used to describe the season's fashion. A "studied look" replaced the casual air of the preceding time. Ladies of fashion were admonished to be fascinating women. No more "crazy dresses but styles which had an allure men would understand." Molyneux presented his **décolleté dinner gown.** Marcel Rochas (Rosha) reintroduced back

**Figure 16.12.** In 1938 Alix designed the "newly narrowed" evening dress in clinging crepe. (Sketched at *The 10s, The 20s, The 30s* exhibition, 1974. Metropolitan Museum of Art, New York City.)

skirt interest with the creation of his **bustle-back evening dress.** Schiaparelli devised the alluring **uplift bra bodice.** Alix and Vionnet draped the figure sensually to reveal the natural curves of the female body (Figure 16.12). Again recollections of things past were recalled by Francevramant's empire gowns "with charming exposure." Mainbocher reintroduced a panier-styled gown. Paquin and Chanel believed that allure depended on the wearer's veiled eyes.

The zipper closure was presented to the high-fashion world by Molyneux in his **tube jacket.** He was one of the first to use the zipper as other than a placket closing. The first zippers were rather bulky metal devices, given to jamming and running off their tracks. Bakelite—the forerunner of plastic—zippers were used, unconcealed, on side plackets. Even in the chic gowns shown in the 1974 Metropolitan Museum Costume Institute exhibition, they were clumsy and awkwardly installed.

Sewing-machine technology had not kept apace with the adaptation of this clever closure to costumes. The special sewing-machine foot which allowed the machine to ride next to this bulky innovation had not yet been invented. Not until 1939 did dress designers devise a placket detail which concealed zippers. Prior to the zipper, snaps or hooks and eyes were used to fasten plackets. The side placket itself was a twentieth-century invention which evolved in the thirties when slinky gowns were designed to be form fitting. Prior to the thirties, the loosely falling sheaths of the twenties did not require a side opening. The side placket became necessary to add girth at the waist so that the garment might be put on over the head with room for the shoulders to pass through. In previous periods blouses opened in the center back as did skirts or dresses.

Aside from the Molyneux tube jackets, Lanvin created the bulky **full-fronted day coat.** Suits and coats had similar details with mannish collars and large revers of a contrasting color or texture. Shoulders were broad, and sleeves, narrow in the arm, were amply puffed at the shoulder. Broad shoulders, snug-fitting sleeves, hipbone-length jackets, moderately full skirts, and contrasting insets or trims predominated in the most chic suits. The skirt length for daytime suits, coats, and dresses generally fell to mid-calf. Large buttons were decorative and functional. These design systems were employed by Vera Borea, Creed, Maggy, Rouff, Lelong, Lanvin, and Chanel.

Suit and coat fabrics included wool tweeds and plaids. Textures dominated in the color combinations of purple and pink, black and red, brown and gold. Jacket and coat linings were often made of patterned fabrics. Furs which were popular late in the 1930s included wild sheep and shaved beaver combined with suede.

The thirty bemusing years, which included one World War and the eruption of another, encompassed an amazing variety in costume design. The first phase saw the female figure denied, and closing years saw the bra halter top emphasize the bust.

By contrast, men's clothes became less and less interesting. There were fewer changes following the standardization of the sack or business suit, white collared shirt, and vest to match the coat and trousers. Denial of the male's peacock role would last until the end of the 1950s.

# Women's Basic Garments of the Modern Age of Change (1910–1939)

## DRESSES (1913–1939)

Women's dress styles changed from season to season, as they had since 1910. The innovation of 1913 was the **flounced skirt frock** that was a derivation of the eighteenth-century panier skirt treatment. In the same year, Poiret introduced the **lampshade tunic,** a dress designed with a thigh- or knee-length tunic over a pencil-slim, ankle-length skirt. The tunic was supported by a wire in the hem to hold it out beyond the figure and often was trimmed with a plissé frill, a circular flounce, or ruffle. The **Persian drape tunic** was another dress style popular in 1913. All of these dresses were designed with soft, full lines in the bodices and slender, draped skirts. They were patterned after the **kimono sleeve dresses** that were in vogue in 1910 (Figure 16.13).

Frocks of that year and for several years thereafter were designed with rather loose, bloused bodices and skirts that became increasingly narrow. The smaller girth at the hemline first appeared in 1911 as a band trimming that drew in the skirt at the hem, creating a **peg-top** silhouette. The hipline fullness was achieved by slanted pleats originating at the waist and draped in a curved line to the sides. The **hobble skirt dress** resulted by decreasing the hemline circumference to ridiculously small proportions. Slits extending from the ankle-length hem to midcalf were cut in the skirts so that women might walk rather than hop. Just prior to World War I, hemlines were raised, revealing the foot and the ankle.

Another silhouette modification introduced in 1911 was the raising of the waist. **Empire gowns** with high, wide waists and shallow bodices eliminated the corseted, longer-waisted lines of the gowns of the preceding decades. Ladies' costumes were more comfortable, designed with loose-fitting kimono or dolman sleeves and oval or V-necklines. The fan collar, echoing the late Renaissance neck treatment, was attached at the shoulder seam and stood up in back, flaring slightly and framing the head. Large, wide belts accented the high waistline, and hip and thigh width was created by skirt draping. Peplum and

**Figure 16.13.** Gown softness appeared as early as 1910 as shown in this afternoon dress styled with a peg-top skirt and kimono sleeves. Hats retained their femininity and exaggerated proportions.

tunic skirt effects, lace and ribbon trims, and bands or piping of sharply contrasting colors were characteristic details of the frocks of this period (Figure 16.14).

The chemise frock introduced in 1915 was the result of a designer's interest in medieval costumes. It was designed with a long, straight, sleeved blouse worn over a slender **slip dress.** The loose tunic blouse was gradually lengthened and worn with a belt placed low, on or below the hips. The under, or slip, dress was designed with a straight skirt attached to a sleeveless bodice.

The afternoon frocks of 1916 used fabrics with interesting textural combinations. Velvet and georgette crepe were the most popular of these combinations, but chiffon broadcloth, crepe de Chine, dovetyne, suede cloth, and

**Figure 16.14.** This graduation frock of 1912 was trimmed with lace insertions and handmade crocheted lace. (Courtesy of the Whaley family.)

soft twill gabardine were also used extensively. The skirts shortened first by the designer Lanvin in 1914, continued to have hemlines eight inches from the floor.

A short-lived silhouette was proposed in 1917 called the **tonneau** silhouette (Figure 16.4). This was a barrel shape with great fullness in the skirt between the waist and the knees. Tonneau silhouette dresses were never generally accepted although bulky coats styled with these lines were.

The **tea gowns** of 1919 were short-sleeved frocks with a wide girdle or sash (Figure 16.15). They were originally designed by Vionnet as a simple, tubular dress made to fit the figure comfortably with the sash as the accenting detail.

The **handkerchief frock** of the same year was a variation of the Vionnet tea gown. It was styled with the same simple, tubular one-piece dress with an overskirt made from squares of soft fabric which were sewn to the gown by one corner. This arrangement created a series of free-hanging panels, the lower points extending below the gown hem in an uneven line. A fashion periodical of September 1919 suggested that the feminine silhouette should have a softness that is "not the curves of restriction but the softly rounded curves of the natural figure trained to emphasize its feminine roundness rather than its boyish slimness."

*Jeune fille* (young girl) fashions of this year listed frocks with such lyric names as: **Minette, Elice, Cordia,** and **Azure.** These dresses had loose-fitting bodices, rather full skirts, and waistlines slightly lower than the normal waistline. Trimmed with a large sash, the Cordia, for example, had a straight-line, bloused bodice, long slender sleeves, and an accordion-pleated skirt. The modest necklines of these frocks were usually round and trimmed with neat, small, round collars.

Asymmetry was a typical skirt-design theme during the 1920s. The handkerchief frock had initiated the uneven hemline, which became a typical trait of dresses of this decade. One fanciful dress of the frivolous postwar period designed by Chéruit, the **Broderie anglaise,** was created with a round-neck bodice, lampshade sleeves of chiffon and crepe, a crepe underskirt, and ruffle-trimmed chiffon pouf overpanels.

During the first half of the 1920s, dresses were styled with rather shapeless, long-waisted bodices, pleated or straight ankle-length skirts, and long, straight sleeves or lampshade sleeves. Often, two fabrics of contrasting textures and colors were used for the sleeves and the skirt swags, draped skirt panels, and hanging vertical ruffles on the bodice. Throughout this period the straight, trim lines introduced in the creations designed by Chanel

**Figure 16.15.** Garden teas were popular in 1922. Tea gowns were of plain or floral chiffon trimmed with ribbon bows and streamers. Essential to the tea costume was the flop-brimmed leghorn. (Redrawn from *Lady in Pink,* a photograph by Etcheverry, 1922. Photo Archives Photographiques, Paris.)

influenced all costumes. Three-quarter jackets and slender skirts, often with side pleating as a skirt detail, emphasized the asymmetric design theme of this decade. The clothes and the mood of this period were succinctly summed up by a leading fashion magazine editor who noted that the 1920s "was scarcely an age of nostalgic charm" but one which was hectic, lacked poise, and was full of "slap-happy optimism" and that the **chemise frock** had irresistible charm only in retrospect.

The extremely short skirts for which this era is noted were first presented in the 1925 couture fashion shows. In that year the female frocks were styled with slim, shapeless, boyish silhouettes (Figure 16.16). Hemlines were

**Figure 16.17.** Collars and cuffs were popular trims for afternoon frocks of the early 1920s. (Courtesy of the Schmidt family.)

**Figure 16.16.** In 1925 skirt lengths were raised drastically, as shown in this design by Poiret which is made of black wool with a red inset placed below the gathered beige net at the round neckline. There are scallops at the hem and at the joining of the elbow-length sleeves with the gathered, beige-net cuffs. The band down the center front is white with printed red buttons. (Sketched at *The 10s, The 20s, The 30s* exhibition, 1974. Metropolitan Museum of Art, New York City.)

knee length, necklines were either low V-shapes or high turtlenecks. Blouses of dresses were created with long, wrist-length sleeves for the winter season and no sleeves for summer. Daytime dresses for those of average means during the early 1920s were simple but retained the major characteristics of the mode with low waists, straight bodice sections, and straight skirts with just-below-the-calf hems (Figure 16.17). After 1925 the only major adjustment was in hem length, which was raised to knee level.

Costumes reflected the somber economic conditions of the world. Designers such as Schiaparelli, Molyneux, Balenciaga, Paquin, and Mainbocher dominated the couture scene. They reintroduced puffed sleeves, the leg-of-mutton sleeves, and, late in the 1930s, created a change in silhouette when they presented the raised, divided, and rounded bustline. Costumes were designed for all occasions to meet the demands of many different activity patterns. Tea frocks, cocktail dresses, beach pajamas, shorts with halter tops, daytime frocks, and evening gowns all became necessary items in the feminine wardrobe.

During the 1930s, **summer frocks** were made of light, printed chiffons with full, circular skirts, loose-fitting bodices, and no sleeves. Squares of fabric were attached at the shoulders as sleeve substitutes. Skirts, which remained long for some time, became quite slender in 1931, as did the entire figure outline. Necklines were round and modestly proportioned. Complex geometric designs were used as skirt and blouse decorations. Bows made of the dress fabric were tied in a tailored manner and trimmed blouses and skirts. Soft gathers or pleats on one side of the skirt added some fullness to the skirts. The generally restrained appearance of dresses during the early thirties was heightened by the use of long sleeves and simple necklines with a variety of collars and narrow, tied or buckled belts.

By 1935 more flair in dress design was introduced. Bishop sleeves, uneven hemlines, modestly raised and puffed shoulders, and side draping created more imaginative costumes. Pleating, minute tucks, and diamond smocking were typical detailing features of blouses worn over a slip-top skirt.

Made of wool jersey for winter, silk or cotton for summer, the **run-about dress** of 1939 was designed in a shirtmaker style. A simple pointed collar, V-neckline, center-front button closure, and long, short, or three-quarter sleeves were the basic styling traits of this casual frock. The shoulder line was given added breadth by a variation of the leg-of-mutton sleeves. The raised puff of the sleeve was eliminated and a smooth, squared pleat at the sleeve top extended the line across the shoulders well beyond the normal contours of the figure.

The **little black dress** became an integral part of the female wardrobe during the latter years of the 1930s and remained in vogue for several years. Designed with simple lines, this frock was suitable for daytime, cocktail, or theater wear. It had short or cap sleeves, a full-busted blouse, and a slightly flared, gored skirt. The thin **wafer waist** accented the broad shoulders, full bust, and flare of the skirt.

For a brief period, some of the dresses of this period were designed with back skirt fullness reminiscent of the 1890 bustles. This skirt effect was created by unpressed pleats placed in the center back. Braid and bead braid were often used to trim the neckline or sleeves.

Late in 1939, shoulder padding replaced the puffed and flat-pleat sleeves as a means of extending the shoulder line. This construction innovation was used in the basic black dress, daytime dresses, suits, and coats. With the introduction of the shoulder padding, bodices were cut with a longer shoulder seam. Sleeve puffs were completely eliminated, and the sleeves were set in flat and flush. The added bodice fullness was slightly draped, placing emphasis on the bust and creating an extremely feminine silhouette. Skirts at this time were also draped, soft, and flowing.

## EVENING DRESSES
## (1920–1939)

**Formal gowns** of the 1920s carried out the figure themes of daytime dresses. The easy, uncorseted look

**Figure 16.18.** The short evening gown was introduced in the mid-1920s. Hair was bobbed, and makeup on lips, eyes, and cheeks greatly exaggerated. (Redrawn from *Madame Alsin*, Van Dongen, 1925.)

persisted, and extreme décolletage was the marked difference between day and evening wear. An extremely simple formal gown was usually a straight, long-waisted chemise with thin shoulder straps, deep V-shaped armholes and a plunging V-neckline front and back. Swag sashes, side puffs falling into a train, and an uneven hemline which was short in front and dipping to the floor in back, or handkerchief skirts, were characteristics of the early-twenties evening gowns.

The most significant change in formal gowns was the introduction of the **short formal** in the mid-twenties (Figure 16.18). The hemline was raised first to the calf of the leg and then to the knee. A new emphasis on back interest was created by a deep V-neckline in back and a draped girdle placed low on the hips and tied into a loose bow with the sash ends trailing down behind to the ankle. The designer Paquin is credited with originating this style which also included softly fluted skirts.

Informal **dinner dresses** worn during the summer of 1929 had large capes with ruffled trimming. The design of the gowns was simple and extended to the floor (Figure 16.19). They were worn with small hats.

Many costumes during the 1930s were influenced by the female stars of the cinema. The **dinner gowns** of 1935 were no exception, and they imitated masculine formal attire preferred by one of the popular movie queens. These dinner costumes were designed with a jacket with wide lapels which were sometimes faced with satin, and a pencil-slim, floor-length skirt. They were usually made of black crepe, severely tailored, and extremely simple.

A semiformal, floor-length gown, often worn at informal country-club dinner parties, was styled with an elbow-length bolero jacket. When worn without the jacket, this bare-shouldered gown was appropriate for informal dances. The bodice was intricately cut with a

**Figure 16.19.** Molyneux designed this evening gown with a modified **mermaid skirt** in 1929. The transparent jacket carries out the straight line of the upper figure. Red cabbage roses cascading down the back of the skirt create the mermaid silhouette. (Sketched from the April 27, 1929 issue of *Vogue* magazine.)

fullness over the bust, a snug fit over the rib cage, and had ribbon shoulder straps. The floor-length skirt flared gently at the hemline. Many of these informal evening gowns were patterned after the 1880s Polonaise gown. A draped apron effect was created between the waist and thigh, curving back and upward to the center back. The softly fluted skirt was attached to this pseudoapron. The apron and bolero jacket often were trimmed with rather wide ruching.

The influence of the halter top, originally designed to be worn with sportswear, was applied to the design of formal gowns. There were several variations of this styling including: the backless bodice with two fitted panels extending over the bust; an elaborately fitted brassiere form that fastened around the neck and the rib cage, leaving the midriff bare; and the short bodice, with or without sleeves, that covered the figure from the shoulders to just under the bustline. These various bare-midriff tops were worn with a separate flared skirt that extended from the normal waistline to the floor.

A more formal **dinner suit** was first introduced in 1939. It was composed of a high-necked jacket with long, tight sleeves, slightly puffed at the shoulder, and a pencil-slim skirt that had a modest flare at the feet. This was a floor-length costume which often was designed with a bustle treatment created by large, soft puffs in back below the waistline.

Throughout the 1930s, an interest in classical Greek costumes resulted in an increased use of skirt draping. The transition from soft, smoothly flowing lines to more rigidly controlled and contrived shapes occurred during the 1930s.

## WOMEN'S WRAPS (1910–1939)

The large dolman sleeves, increasing the apparent width above the hips and around the waist, dominated women's coat fashions between 1910 and 1920. Fur coats, often made of two furs with contrasting textures, carried out the sloped shoulder and middle-figure bulk of the cloth-coat styles. Russian sable and Hudson Bay seal were the most popular furs of this period. Fabric coats were often trimmed with elegant furs at the neck and cuffs.

During the Depression years, American designers dominated the fashion scene in the United States. The consequences of the 1929 financial cataclysm affected and controlled the import of French couture designs. Adrian, Fogarty, Mainbocher, Greer, Galanos, Zuckerman, and Simpson designs became the sought-after creations of the 1930s. There was less contrast in clothing between different social and economic strata. Good styling was available inexpensively because of technical improvements in garment-making machines and refinements in production methods. A leveling of the social strata and the generally poor economic situation caused fewer marked design changes to occur each season. The sub-

**Figure 16.20.** Dress-skirt and coat hems were drastically raised in 1925 as this sketch illustrates. Fur trimming on coats was popular. Note **cloche** hat and **T-strap** shoes.

**Figure 16.21.** For the continental traveler, a traveling coat was a must, such as this Poiret design in beige wool with vertical bands of darker beige and brown stylized roses. Ankles were kept warm and dry with **spats,** a dashing female accessory during 1919–1920. (Sketched at *The 10s, The 20s, The 30s* exhibition, 1974. Metropolitan Museum of Art, New York City.)

dued Depression years were given visual expression in clothing. Coats were a distinct part of this visual reflection of social and economic conditions.

Coats were styled in tweeds with simple princess lines. Black and other dark, dull colors were used for making cloth coats that were either single or double breasted. Puffed sleeves, fitted bodices, and gently flared skirts were the basic characteristics of coats during the early 1930s.

By 1937, however, a certain confidence in the recovery programs developed and this mood was reflected in all garment designs. More imaginative use of textured materials, lighter and somewhat brighter colors, plus more originally designed details appeared for coats of that

year. The slope-shouldered, full-bodied coat with lantern sleeves was introduced in contrast to the conservative coats of the previous years. Large bell-shaped sleeves were a typical detail of coats created with a full bodice, tightly belted waist, and full, circular, calf-length skirts. Gored coats in colorful tweeds with tailored puffed sleeves and bell cuffs were popular casual coats in the late 1930s.

Monkey-fur capes, coats of sable, mink, chinchilla, baum marten, broadtail, and Persian lamb were worn as the countries of the world recovered from the economic slump. Lesser furs such as dressed goat and lambskin were also considered chic. Leopard, beaver, and plucked muskrat skins were used in creating casual and sports coats. These coats were often styled with a straight-line, almost boxy silhouette. Collars that could be turned up for warmth or laid flat over a single-button closure at the neck, and sleeves that echoed the general styling trends of a season were details of fur garments during this period.

Velvet and sable in combination were used for formal wraps. Similar in design to the Victorian coats, evening wraps in 1939 were designed with huge leg-of-mutton sleeves, long floor-length skirts with back fullness and amply cut bodices. They were trimmed with shawl collars and deep sleeve cuffs.

## WOMEN'S SUITS (1920–1939)

The more comfortable costumes of the late 1910s continued in vogue, and suits for women were designed with the same silhouettes. They were styles with a tail-

Figure 16.23. Blue and dusty pinks, green-blues, and golden hues were used extensively during the 1920s to establish the strong proportional relationships shown in this walking suit of 1922. (Redrawn from an illustration in *Gazette du Bon Ton*, 1922.)

Figure 16.22. This striking suit with a wide, tassel-trimmed sash is typical of the no-figure look popular from 1913 through the late 1920s. (Redrawn from a 1914 issue of *Journal des Dames et des Modes*.)

ored, masculine overall design but had very feminine detailing. Suit skirts were ankle length, and the jackets echoed many of the styling traits that were typical of a particular season's fashion (Figures 16.22 and 16.23). There were cutaway jackets, lampshade jackets, snug-fitting, thigh-length coats, and high-waisted jackets following the empire style.

Chanel, who greatly influenced women's fashions of the 1920s, introduced the jersey chemise and **dressmaker suit** in 1918. This costume had straight lines with a loose-fitting bodice, a wide waist, and a slim skirt that created a boyish silhouette. Major detailing features included georgette embroidery, beads and metal brocade, gold and silver fringe, and grosgrain ribbon.

The **town blouse,** often worn with women's suits during the late teens and early twenties, was a long overtunic with a very low V-neckline and short sleeves. Some of these blouses had a deep V-neckline formed by crossing one front over the other and buttoning it at a point on the hipbone.

During the early 1920s, suit jackets were knee length and called **seven-eighths coats.** They had masculine detailing such as the large notched lapels on double-breasted jackets with button and braid trims. These suits had slender skirts and were worn with blouses designed with high, standing collars.

Suits of the thirties were made of menswear flannel or tweed, and designed with hip-length jackets. They fitted the body snugly, were nipped in at the waist, and designed with slightly puffed sleeves. The three-piece suit, or **ensemble,** introduced in 1932, consisted of a skirt and jacket with a matching cape or three-quarter-length coat. Late in this decade, blouses became an important suit accessory and were styled with bow-tie necklines that softened an otherwise tailored costume. Insets of two or three colors were used in making the intricately cut suit jackets as the general styling trends in women's costumes became more complex. The calf-length skirts of these suits were plain and straight, with a box kick pleat in the back.

## WOMEN'S SPORTSWEAR (1910–1939)

For some time the conservative, "covered-up," participation-sports clothes for women persisted in fashion. Although sleeveless, seaside suits still consisted of an overdress and knee-length bloomers. As the emancipated woman of the 1920s found the excitement of her new freedom, she engaged in a number of different outdoor sports. These active women created a demand for more comfortable and practical sports costumes.

The **exercise suit** replaced the old-fashioned and bulky black-bloomer-and-middy-blouse sports costume of previous years. It consisted of a sleeveless middy blouse and knee-length shorts that were designed with a deep center pleat. These shorts had the appearance of a very short skirt.

**Beach pajamas** were another 1930s sports- or casual-wear innovation (Figure 16.24). Originally, this costume was designed as a one-piece pants outfit. The trousers had large, flared legs and the bodice was loose fitting with shoulder straps that were tied into large knots or bows.

The **pajama suit,** forerunner of the very tailored and masculine-looking slack suit, was introduced in the 1930s by Jacques Heim. These suits had bell-bottom trousers and matching blouses often designed with sailor collars. Tricolored pajama costumes with flared-leg slacks, matching blouses, and boxy jackets became the

**Figure 16.24. Beach pajamas,** introduced in the late 1920s, were softly tailored and many had V-shaped panels over the abdomen, or gusset-trimmed flaring legs.

fashion as casual outdoor or patio entertaining became popular.

During the 1930s and into the 1940s, very tailored woolen **slack suits** were designed with single- or double-breasted jackets. The trousers of these suits had slender legs with deep cuffs, wide waistbands, and a fly-front zipper closing.

**Bathing suits** were radically altered in 1922. They were one-piece, knitted woolen costumes with thigh-length, tight-fitting shorts, covered with a shorter tight skirt. The tops of these suits had deep oval or V-necklines and thin shoulder straps. Many people thought they indecently exposed the female body, and plainclothes policewomen were stationed on some eastern beaches to measure the depth of ladies' bathing-suit necklines to see if they met the code of decency. This style of swimsuit replaced the two-piece suit with a sweater top and knee-length shorts of previous years.

Suntans first became the rage in the 1920s, and sun suits were devised to expose much larger expanses of flesh. Although earlier bathing suits had been modest cover-up garments, they had not been functional as swim wear nor as sunning attire. A June issue of a fashion periodical of the 1920s advertised the following items for swimming and sunning: **beach frocks** of black taffeta with ruffles and white piping, rubberized silk bandanas, and rubber beach slippers with over-the-instep straps. By 1929 the necklines of swimsuits exposed the back by a deep U-shaped opening. Midriff suits in a variety of halter styles were popular throughout the 1930s. Suits were made in a wide range of gay colors, rather than black or dark blues, with contrasting red or white bands on the skirt hems or around the bustline. Short shorts with halter or blouse tops were worn for patio lounging or sunbathing during this decade.

**Tennis dresses, slack suits, snowsuits** with tight ankle bands holding the amply cut legs snugly, and **culottes** were some of the many casual wear and sports costumes adapted to specific activities. Golf, skiing, tennis, bowling, boating, and badminton were the popular sports, and costumes were created specifically for them.

## WOMEN'S UNDERWEAR (1920–1939)

Some of the radical changes that had been made in women's apparel were introduced into female underwear. In 1915, corset covers, camisoles, and petticoats were replaced by the **envelope combination,** a one-piece undergarment with ribbon shoulder straps, a drawstring neckline, and a buttoned front closure. The **combination with knickers** had gathered legs rather than the loose style of the envelope combination. Both of these 1915 underwear innovations were discarded for the **step-in.** This one-piece undergarment of the 1920s was advertised as "comfy as brother's." It was given a variety of names, each with minor design differences, such as: **vanity, thora, vest chemise,** and **combination.** Underslips with slender bodies and ribbon shoulder straps were worn instead of petticoats.

Because of the more loosely fitted dresses and suits, figure-controlling garments were seldom worn. The **scandal belt,** or simple below-the-waist band with elastic garter supports, was introduced in 1933. Later in the thirties, when busts and slender waists were in style, the **foundation garment** was developed as a firm figure support. It were designed in a variety of ways, often combining corset and brassiere into one garment. Tight, bust-flattening brassieres were worn when the boyish silhouette was in vogue, but with the return of emphasis on feminine curves, bras were designed to raise and separate the breasts. By the end of the 1930s, women's underwear included some form of gartered corset, a bra, long-legged or very scant underpants, and a slip. At this period they were usually very tailored garments, decorated only with a lace trim on the slip hem.

# Accessories for Women (1910–1939)

## HEADWEAR

Hats took their shapes from the design demands of the major costume elements. They remained large through 1913, when smaller, head-hugging shapes were introduced. The famous dancer, Irene Castle, popularized the hat which bears her name. The Castle hat was made with a crushed crown and an asymmetric tilted brim, and trimmed with "numedie feather fancy" on one side for a perky decoration. Bandeau **beehive** crown hats of velvet with ostrich plumes plucked from live birds replaced the exotic feather decorations of previous styles. These hats with their turban shapes were worn squarely on the head and quite low over the brow.

Feathers such as ostrich or aigrettes were eliminated as hat trims when the Audubon Society forced the passage of legislation protecting "rare birds from careless and indiscriminate killing."

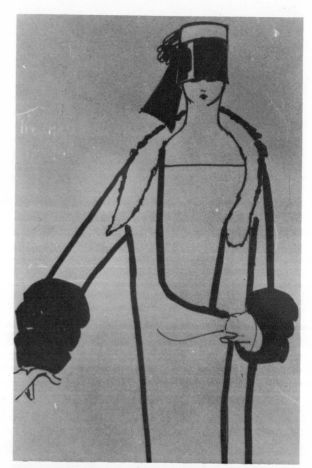

**Figure 16.25.** The face-concealing **cloche** and a loose, fur-trimmed coat combined to make a straight-line silhouette during the mid-1920s.

Hats of the 1920s were designed in a broad range of styles although the head-concealing **cloche** is the style which is closely identified with this period (Figure 16.20). Asymmetry was incorporated into hats as into other garment forms by trims, upturned brims, and other devices. However, there were large-brimmed hats such as the one illustrated in Figure 16.15 made of beige hemp straw and designed by Caroline Reboux. The off-balance asymmetric look was developed by the pleated ribbon-band trim and large off-center brim. The cloche emphasized the small-head look introduced by the boyish bob coif. These hats had very deep crowns and small brims that snugly framed the face (Figure 16.25). They were pulled well down on the head, obscuring the forehead and the cheeks.

During the 1930s hats were styled with shallow crowns, snap brims, and severely tailored bows. They were worn slightly tilted over the right eye. Toward the end of this decade, a style attributed to Schiaparelli evolved when the designer "clapped a stocking on her head." This **corkscrew turban** had a towering crown and was usually made of decorative printed fabric. Hats with tall crowns and snap brims were derivatives of this creation. The floppy-brimmed, round-crowned hat of the twenties, worn usually to garden parties, was modified until it resembled a gentleman's felt fedora. Other hat styles of the 1930s included: the skull cap, the pancake beret, the Schiaparelli knotted cap, turbans, and small-brimmed bonnets inspired by the movie version of *Gone with the Wind* and similar to those worn during the American Civil War.

## SCARVES

Scarves of many textures, patterns, and shapes entered the 1920s accessory scene. For evening, Chéruit created a gown with a deep-V décolletage in front and back. The scarf-accent accessory was a "mouchoir scarf encircling in the neck, tied in back to make a charming décolletage," as a fashion accessories editor remarked in a 1929 issue of *Vogue*.

## FOOTWEAR

Shoes became a significant costume accessory as skirts became shorter. Minor changes that appeared during the first decades of the twentieth century included: **mules** of white kid with strictly tailored satin bows, **pumps** with "little Louis" heels, **oxfords** for summer, and high-top shoes for winter wear. **Tweedies,** or gaiters, were a winter fashion fad in 1916. The most radical innovations in female footwear occurred during the twenties. The **T-strap sandal** with high, thick heels; the dress oxford with eyelet cutouts arranged in decorative swirl patterns; and two-toned **spectator pumps** originated in the twenties and were modified slightly during the 1930s, but remained the basic daytime styles for several years.

**Playshoes,** made of colorful heavy canvas fabrics and wedgie soles, were introduced to be worn with the wide variety of casual costumes.

## JEWELRY

The basic jewelry items remained constant for several years. The ladies' wristwatch had been the most startling innovation until the introduction of inexpensive costume jewelry by Chanel. During the 1920s, great ropes of glass beads and plastic bracelets were the most common types of neck and arm decorations. Long drop earrings were also popular. During the Depression, inconspicuous strings of beads were worn in keeping with the somber mood of the times. Women's wristwatches changed from small, round shapes to small oblongs and were made even smaller. Costume jewelry gained wide acceptance, and one fashion-magazine accessory editor wrote, "... to a girl with a born-to-the-purple feeling and a pinched pocketbook ... wear fake jewelry." Artificial roses intricately made of fabric or delicately tinted wood fiber also were used as dress accents.

## HANDHELD ACCESSORIES

Leather, fabric, or beaded bags and functional leather pocketbooks persisted throughout the 1920s. More serviceable forms were carried in the thirties and were made of leather with hinge-snap closings and leather strap handles. When women entered the business world, they discarded the more fanciful and decorative purses for fitted leather pocketbooks. The tapestry, beaded, and embroidered small bags were used for evening. The innovation in purse design in the 1920s was the **envelope pocketbook.** This purse had no handles and the flap closing was latched by slipping a projection of the flap through a small strip on the front. This style was the immediate forerunner of the more recent clutch purse.

# Hairstyles for Women (1910–1939)

The large bouffant pompadours of the Edwardian period were flattened and pushed well down over the forehead. The hair remained long until the 1920s when the first short bobs for women came into style. These boyish bobs were daringly short, combed from a center part with spit curls framing the cheekbones. At first the hair was the same length on the sides and in back, but during the flapper era it was shingled in back.

During the thirties, the marcel wave and then the permanent wave brought back longer hair and feminine curls. The invention of the permanent-wave machine made it possible for women to have curls that would last, if they were willing to suffer through the long, electrically "cooked" hair treatment. This eliminated rolling up the hair in curl papers, curling rags, or using the heated curling irons of the past. Hair was arranged to follow the natural contours of the head, with waves falling from a side or a center part. A small roll of sausage curls controlled the hair at the back of the neck, and the hair in front was pulled off the face and up over the ears. Late in the 1930s the pageboy bob was introduced. This was a shoulder-length style with the ends of the hair rolled under and allowed to hang free or caught up on each side over the ears. There was a variety of acceptable and fashionable ways to wear the hair at this time, and women went to the beauty shops to have their hair styled to suit features, faces, and personalities.

# Men's Basic Garments of the Modern Age of Change (1910–1939)

## MEN'S SUITS (1920–1939)

The sack suit retained the general design characteristics that had been established before the turn of the century (Figure 16.26). The concave shoulder line with the padded chest and **spider silhouette** of the teens disappeared totally by the 1920s. A looser coat with emphasis on broader shoulders and greater chest girth was introduced.

About 1927 the suit trousers were styled with a high waistband and rather full legs. The trouser cuff increased in width and depth. The trouser waistband returned to normal proportions and position in 1934, but front pleating was introduced, creating a **peg-top** effect.

The double-breasted **business suit** of the early 1930s consisted of a modestly proportioned coat, trousers with waist pleats and large legs, and a matching vest. Handpicking, small handsewn stitches, replaced machine stitching along the edges of the flat collar and notched lapels. Two side pockets on the coat fronts and a breast pocket on the left were typical functional details of the business suit coat. A vent in the center back, buttons on the sleeve cuffs, and a buttonhole on the left lapel were also major styling features of these suits. Pinstripe patterns, plain dark blues, browns, grays, and light browns were the colors of the gabardines, flannels, Harris tweeds, and serges used to make most men's suits during this decade.

Summer-weight washable fabrics, such as seersucker, were used for the first time in the late 1920s and early 1930s. The summer **seersucker suit** was the same style as the sack suit, or included a pair of trousers and a jacket with a belt in the back and deep center or side back pleats.

**Figure 16.26.** Men's suits retained the basic cut established in the Edwardian period. The sack suit was a popular style. (Courtesy of the Whaley family, c. 1913.)

In 1927, the **golf suit** combined a Norfolk jacket and **plus-fours,** a variation of the design used for the sports knickers and knickerbockers. They were called "plus-fours" because the legs were lengthened to extend four inches below the knees. These baggy pants were worn with argyle socks visible on the lower leg. In addition to the plus-fours and jacket, the properly clad golfer wore a shirt and sweater, and topped off this costume with a crushed fedora or billed cap.

Other male casual garments included: **sports slacks,** which in the twenties had a wide, high waistband; **peg-tops; Oxford bags,** with a high waistband and wide legs trimmed with deep cuffs; and **bell-bottom trousers** with large, flared cuffs that were often two to two-and-a-half feet in diameter. Casual **sport coats,** or jackets, with a half belt in the back were worn with various styles of casual trousers. These jackets were generally made of tweed fabrics.

The long-legged, two-piece **bathing suits** were replaced in the 1920s by thigh-length trunks and sleeveless shirts with deep armholes and U-shaped necklines. One-piece suits designed with large necklines, armholes, and two oval cuts on the sides in the area of the rib cage were popular male swim attire late in the twenties. Bathing trunks, or knitted shorts, worn alone were introduced in the 1930s. Woolen knitted swimming apparel persisted until the 1940s for men and women.

Evening clothes of black or dark blue included: the formal **dress sack suit;** the formal **lounge suit** with a black coat and gray and black trousers; the **tuxedo,** a black coat with satin lapels and trousers with a satin band trimming each side seam; and the formal **evening suit** with a black tailcoat, white waistcoat, and trousers with satin bands down the side seam. The formal evening suit was worn with a white shirt that was stiffly starched in the front, or with a stiff, white dickey.

Winged collars and white ties were other formal-attire accessories. The height of the collar was an indication of the period. They were very high during the years just after the turn of the century, and became gradually lower during the late 1930s.

The **mess jacket,** styled after the cut of formal military jackets, was introduced in 1930. This jacket was waist length, tailless, and cut with a deep *V* across the back hem. It had moderately large lapels and buttoned with shank buttons below the lapels. The mess jacket was worn with a cummerbund rather than a waistcoat. The cummerbund was a wide, horizontally pleated, sashlike belt that buckled in the back.

The white **dinner jacket,** patterned after the single-breasted sack-suit coat or the double-breasted business suit coat, replaced the mess jacket in the mid-1930s. The dinner jacket, worn with tuxedo trousers, was a summer or informal evening costume. The size and shape of the lapels were modified to conform to the prevailing design for these details on daytime suit coats. Lapels, except on mess jackets and dinner jackets, were faced with satin and were rather wide during the 1920s, gradually growing more narrow during the 1930s.

## MEN'S WRAPS (1910–1939)

Men's overcoats such as the **Inverness, Ulster,** and **Chesterfield** continued in popularity until the 1920s.

**Figure 16.27.** Young men often wore billed caps with topcoats and suits. (Courtesy of the Whaley family.)

The Chesterfield was reserved for more formal occasions, replacing the large opera cape. It was a single-breasted, straight coat with a black velvet collar. The bulky raccoon coat, popular with university and college men, was introduced in 1928. The polo coat of camel hair; the double-breasted, knee-length trench coat; and the topcoats with raglan sleeves were all belted coats typical of overcoat styles of the 1930s (Figure 16.27).

## MEN'S UNDERWEAR
(1920–1930)

The long-legged union suit of wool for winter or cotton lisle for summer was discarded in favor of the one-piece BVD. This was a sleeveless vest and thigh-length shorts combination which was replaced later by the sleeveless lisle undershirt and broadcloth shorts.

# Accessories for Men (1910–1939)

## HEADWEAR

Men's headwear from 1910 to 1939 continued to include the **fedora, boater,** and **Homburg.** Brims and crowns were large and the fedora crown was pinched into a three-cornered shape or creased on the top. The straw Panama and the straw boater were worn in the summer. Until the middle 1920s, caps were popular for younger men. The height of the crown and width of the brim were modestly proportioned during the 1930s.

## FOOTWEAR

Shoe styles changed only slightly during these decades. Most men wore plain or two-toned oxfords. The toes of men's shoes were more rounded with a straight cap, stitched or perforated trimming, and large, shallow heel lifts. Sport shoes were styled with "wing tips," a fringed flap covering the laces, or with intricately designed perforations on the toe tops. Formal shoes were black patent-leather pumps with flat grosgrain ribbon bows.

Shoe accessories called **spats** were worn until the end of the 1920s. Spats were either white, gray, or buff and covered the tops of the feet and ankles. They fastened with buttons on the outside of the feet and were held in place under the foot by instep straps.

## CLOTHING ACCESSORIES

Suit and shirt accessories included wide leather belts with large buckles during the 1930s; elastic suspenders or thin, light leather braces; detachable shirt collars, discarded by 1930; and plain, diagonally striped or patterned ties. Tie pins and tie clips with spring hinges were fastened over the tie and under the front opening of the shirt. Shirts, after 1930, were made with soft, fold-down collars, shallow shoulder yokes, straight sleeves with rounded cuffs, and plain, buttoned fronts. Hose were silk or cotton lisle about calf length and supported by garters. In the 1930s ankle socks with elastic ribbed cuffs were introduced.

# Hairstyles for Men (1910–1939)

In 1910 hairstyles for men included side parts, pompadours, and ear-length hair combed from a center part.

During the 1920s, men's hair was styled with a "patent-leather look" created by using brilliantine and combing the hair flat against the head from a center part, a side part, or brushed back from the brow. During the thirties, the hair was combed back and parted on the side; it was quite short and trimmed in back to follow the contour of the head. Throughout this period most men were clean shaven, although during the 1920s some wore long, straight sideburns and pencil-line moustaches.

FOOTNOTES
1. Diana Vreeland, *The 10s, The 20s, The 30s: Inventive Clothes 1909–1939*, p. 1.
2. *Vogue*, Oct. 15, 1934, p. 44.

# Chapter 17
# Costume Revolutions of the Recent Past (1940–1970)

**Figure 17.1.** Traina-Norell designed this afternoon dress described as "another long, long look" in silk taffeta, "bound at the hips" and "breaking into a wide skirt." (Gruan: illustration for *Vogue*, August 15, 1949. Permission of Condé Nast Publications Inc.)

One of the consequences of the post-World War I boom-and-bust economy was an uncontrollable inflation in Germany. The mark was valueless and the German government inept. Conflicts between the socialist and communist political philosophies developed which enabled Adolf Hitler to manipulate these economic and political circumstances to his advantage. Soviet Russia was still reconstructing its government following the Bolshevik Revolution and civil war of 1917–1920. England and France were in the process of recovering from the effects of the protracted depression that had begun with the stock-market collapse in 1929. By 1940 the United States, under the leadership of President Franklin D. Roosevelt, was at last achieving economic stability.

By the end of the 1930s Hitler had totally reorganized Germany and sought to expand his influence. Only a few months after the "peace for our time" meeting with England's Prime Minister Neville Chamberlain in 1938, Hitler began his relentless march across Europe. The fall of Czechoslovakia and Poland in 1939 marked the beginning of another total war in Europe.

The Axis powers of Germany, Italy, and Japan vowed to control the world. The Allies, primarily England and France, battled on many fronts in an effort to stop the Axis armies. Belgium, Holland, and France were overpowered by the Nazi blitzkrieg in 1940. Russia joined the Allies in 1941 after being invaded by Germany, a one-time ally. The United States did not enter into the conflict until the Japanese attack on Pearl Harbor in 1941.

After a long series of battles in Africa, Europe, and the South Pacific, the Allies managed to turn the tide. Although occupied, France, Belgium, Holland, and Norway continued their resistance against the German military through the operations of the underground. In May of 1945 Germany finally surrendered, trapped between the Russian armies on the east and the Allies on the south and west. After the atomic bombings of the Japanese cities of Hiroshima and Nagasaki in August, Japan was forced to sign an unconditional surrender.

After the war Europe was in ruins materially and economically. The United States supplied financial aid to allies and former enemies to help rebuild their countries. By 1947 President Harry S Truman and Secretary of State George C. Marshall had organized a successful plan to restore the economy of Europe.

In 1950 South Korea was invaded by North Korea, and United Nations forces, spearheaded by the United States, intervened.

Dwight D. Eisenhower, popular general of World War II, was elected President in 1952, and he negotiated a tenuous armistice in Korea in 1953. The Eisenhower years from 1952 to 1960 were a relatively stable economic and social period.

The United Nations, an organization formed after World War II to maintain peace between member countries, became powerless to maintain harmony in the world. Emerging nations, many freed from the colonial controls of England, France, Belgium, and the Netherlands, struggled with the problems of independence. Israel and the Arab nations engaged in border battles and outright war. Russia and the Western Powers were confronted with the trials of the Cold War.

Civil rights and the continuing war in Vietnam were major issues of the 1960s. There were many indications that minority groups felt the need for new social reforms. In response to civil rights activists, President John F. Kennedy and the Supreme Court took steps to integrate the public schools in the South. Riots, civil rights marches, strikes, and sit-ins on college and university campuses erupted in America and Europe. Violent hostility broke out over involvement of the United States in the Far East, directed by disenchanted youthful peaceniks. Economically affluent America was challenged and rejected by dedicated, youthful social reformers, impatient at the slowness of change. They denounced the establishment for its conservatism and violence either by rioting or by the use of drugs. A highly paid and skilled work force produced an economic boom reminiscent of the period following World War I.

It was a science-oriented age, but there was also great interest in cultural pursuits. Major cities erected great centers for the performing arts and renovated existing art museums or established new ones. Artists explored the visual philosophies of surrealism, abstractionism, abstract expressionism, nonart, Pop, Op, happenings, constructivism, minimal art, and conceptual art. In the early 1960s, many artists looked backward to the works of Blake and *Art Nouveau*, the funny-paper cartoonists of the 1930s, and Art Deco. Television offered to the public a wide range of programs from significant cultural presentations to mediocre entertainment. Via ever-improving visual communications, people around the world viewed coverage of the coronation of Queen Elizabeth II; the somber funerals of an assassinated president, a senator, and a civil-rights leader; man's first steps on the moon; and the investiture of the Prince of Wales.

As a dynamic age full of social concern, it was impatient for change and glorified its zestful, activist youth. Moral attitudes were in a state of flux, and many old taboos were discarded. Religion struggled to be relevant by modifying old liturgies, and the clergy worked actively for social reforms. Youth became involved in astrological mysticism, witchcraft, and back-to-nature cults. Individ-

ually motivated experimentation in music, art, theater, movies, and literature was explored by socially aware artists in these fields of creativity. Nonart, theater of the absurd, underground movies, and "four-letter word" poetry arose as creative expressions. Many attempted to be involved and relevant but few offered viable solutions.

As in earlier periods, costumes reflected the times. They became symbolic of an alliance with specific groups—establishment, reformer, or escapist—none of which understood nor wanted to understand the other.

Prior to the outbreak of World War II, speedy fashion reporting of Paris modes had been aided by the invention of the wirephoto. First used to report the Italian-Ethiopian conflict in the 1935, this technique was quickly utilized by the *avant-garde* editors of American fashion periodicals.

During the 1940s and 1950s, greats of the fashion illustration world recorded styles with verve. Fashions of this age were reported and recorded by artists like Carl Erickson, who had no peers throughout the 1930s and 1940s, although he had many imitators.[1] As Bettina Ballard stated in her book, *In My Fashion*, ". . . he had the most honest eye . . . his drawings never cheated; they showed true elegance when it was there and vulgarity even when it might escape the casual eye." He drew famous women in Louiseboulanger gowns or Reboux turbans with imperial magnificence. He caught the haughty elegance of a renowned actress or a member of international society. Thus Ericson, Willaumez, and Bouché created fashion sketches which evoked a beauty and elegance "that photographs could never equal."[2]

The fashion sketches of this era now hang handsomely framed in the new quarters of Condé Nast on Madison Avenue in New York City. In the fixed, technical age of the 1970s, such sensitive hand-created records of chic clothing are seldom recognized for their handsome evocative report of the elegant couture creations of the 1930s and 40s. These men, all creative geniuses, replaced the visual reporters of 1910 through 1929, including George Plank, Helen Dryden, Lepape, and Benito, who were influenced by *Art Nouveau* and Art Deco styles.[3] The years before the war also produced great photographers of fashion such as Horst, Durst, Penn, and Beaton.

The first years of the 1940s might have been disastrous for the couture if these creative artists in Europe and the designers in the United States had not recognized the predicament and reacted. In the United States, Adrian, Irene, and Sophie capitalized on the war-caused trade isolation and became leaders in American fashion design. Costume designers for the films had many Seventh Avenue copyists. Irene did both, working for MGM as a film costume designer and creating exclusive models for the chic Bullock's Wilshire department store in Los Angeles. Adrian established his own shop in Beverly Hills. Sophie, connected with Sax Fifth Avenue in New

York, was the mistress of mode for that renowned emporium.

In England the situation was more complex. Clothes rationing was soon imposed, but not before English designers attempted to respond. Not since the Napoleonic Wars had England and France been so widely separated; the German occupation had cut off all Anglo-French fashion intercourse. During the early years of the war in Britain, the Fashion Group of Great Britain, founded in 1925, banded together to form the Incorporated Society which produced a unified fashion opening in 1942.[4] The notable designers of this group were Hartnell, Russell, Molyneux, Cavanagh, Creed, and the House of Worth. Considering the wartime restrictions under which they worked, some attractive, practical garments were produced.

Italy was also cut off from French fashion exports. A number of talented Italians with fashion-oriented businesses turned their hand to designing for domestic consumption. Some of this group included: Biki, granddaughter of the composer Puccini; Farcioni, who became the Italian "king of fashion" during and after World War II; the Fantana sisters; Emilio Pucci of Florence, whose designs still command a significant position; and Enzo, couturier of the nouvelle vogue.

Not to be outdone, French couturiers Balenciaga, Balmain, Dior, Carven, Fath, Dessès, Nina Ricci, Costello, and Patou met the challenge of military occupation.[5] The Paris population resisted the presence of their German conquerors in many diverse ways: through the costumes they donned and, as a friend, Nanine van Toff, related, even by stealing rides on Paris buses. "Resistance" dresses were made from as many as thirty yards of ersatz fabric used in making full, gathered skirts. The cocottes during the Paris forties wore huge earrings that were designed after those worn by Portuguese donkeys and were almost as big in size. Reboux created "fiber cloth hats" and Gilbert Orcel fashioned a satirical head covering dubbed "bonnet-cum-haircurlers." This was a creation combining a scarf, paper, and curlers, commenting in costuming on the frequent incidents when ladies were caught at the hairdressers during electrical blackouts. Silk hose were a thing of the past in all countries. Rayon hose were available in the United States, but they were subject to runs, and "repair" shops for hose were set up in dime and department stores. Leather in Europe was not available, and shoes with cork or wooden soles and rabbit-skin tops appeared; even cardboard shoes were used. In the United States shoes were the only items of apparel which were rationed.

Clothing coupons were issued in England, but, in the last stages of the war, no garments could be purchased even with coupons. One chronicler of the period wrote that "King rabbit saved the day," for rabbit-fur coats were substituted for the more costly furs. Fox, weasel, mole, and marten fur were also used in place of sable, ermine, seal, and mink.

Clothing was also adapted for safety; white trims were used to protect the wearer during blackouts. Large white revers and flaring cuffs were available to be worn with plain, dark dresses.[6]

After the Liberation, clothing again took on a symbolic flavor, particularly in coloring. Jacques Fath introduced costumes in red, white, and blue, symbolically thanking the United States for freeing France from the Germans' tyrannical yoke. However, it was some time before the war-imposed silhouette disappeared. The padded shoulders of the late thirties, which evolved from the puff and leg-of-mutton revival of the previous decade, were squared off and held in place by shoulder pads in proportions of a football player's gear. Dress skirts were knee length and draped with folds radiating from center front. This design theme was repeated in the blouse, with the folds radiating upward in the opposite direction. Hips were full and rounded, though the dress skirt fell straight on the sides. The dolman dress with front gathers in the skirt, a loose blouse with a normal waist, and a deep V-neckline was so popular in 1941 that it almost seemed to be a uniform. Summer formals of the same year had the nostalgic look of a modified 1860s gown.

Throughout the war years, because of defense work, many women wore slacks and simple, mannish Henden shirts. These shirts were made very much like little boys' short-sleeved dress shirts of the 1930s.

For evening, dresses were soft, with full or semifull skirts and padded shoulders, creating a straight-line silhouette. The blouses of these evening gowns had high necklines and tight or bishop sleeves, and often were trimmed with sequins.[7] The feminine coiffure for evening chic was "demure and feminine," swept back in a slight pompadour with the shoulder-length hair in back turned into a curled page-boy fashion.

Day wear for the fashionably correct was "The Classic Look": two-piece suits with cardigan jackets, classic coats, and classic two-piece dresses worn with a wound "echo" scarf made of the same fabric, creating a turban head covering. Casual wear, and that of working women, consisted of dirndl skirts and blouses (Figure 17.2), play coats, beach skirts, cuffless slacks, and "sawed-off slacks," forerunners of pedal pushers.[8]

Jacques Fath emerged as the leading postwar designer with his barrel-skirt dresses, printed dresses, and princess dresses in muslin organza or brocaded taffeta. As early as the middle months of 1945, the couture were preparing for peace. Balenciaga, Balmain, Dior, Fath, and Givenchy showed their new models in "Le Théâtre de la Mode," presented in 1945 at the Musée des Arts Décoratifs. Designers of note in the brief years before the turn of the decade included the talented Mille Carven, who gracefully introduced wit and taste into her creations,

**Figure 17.2.** Coeds of the mid-1940s wore a "uniform" which included the **sloppy-joe** sweater, boyish shirt, or blouse with jewel neckline, and knee-length skirts. (Bartlet photo.)

**Figure 17.3.** In 1947, Dior presented the **New Look**, the most startling fashion innovation of the forties. He introduced the rounded bust, wasp waist, and flared skirt, and dropped the hemline to within eight inches of the floor. (Sketched from examples in the Photo Collection, L'Union Francaise des Arts du Costume, Paris.)

and Jacques Griffe, Piguet, and Lucien Lelong. Pierre Balmain "discovered *Jolie Madame,*" and Rochas presented gowns with wasp waists, round shoulders, and wide, knee-length skirts.

It was Christian Dior who reversed the fashion trends. In 1947 textile tycoon Marcel Boussac asked Dior to cut his exquisitely fitted gowns, dresses, and suits from materials Boussac supplied. In this collection Dior presented the **New Look** which startled the fashion world (Figure 17.3). The hemline was lower, the waist nipped, and the shoulders slanting and lowered. Dior had long been known for the meticulous care that he took in cutting and fitting garments. The models he designed while working first for Piguet and then for Lelong had gained him a reputation for "straight-thread classic" (on the straight of the fabric) and "slant-thread broque" (on the bias) creations. His new models were described as supple, slinky, and a "little precious" while he created a total outfit, combining the right jewels, hats, gloves, and stockings to complement the dress.[9] Dior so totally created the whole costume that he designed a foundation garment which hollowed the stomach and "lifted and rounded" the bust.

The "Generation of Vipers," as some called the malcontents of the 1940s, were supplanted by the beatniks who were to give impetus to an era of nonfashion, but not before fashion's face altered once again in the 1950s. Some of the costume creators of this decade included Larry Aldrich, Molly Parnis, Charles James Molyneux, Balmain, Paquin, Schiaparelli, Lanvin, Rochas, Bruyère, and Dessès.

Labels which identified the silhouettes created by specific designers can be listed as: Castillo—"elegance"; Lanvin—"cockleshell"; Lafaurie—"roly-poly"; Schiaparelli—"stop and go"; Dior—"scissor line"; Fath—"gushing line"; Rochas—"looping"; Paquin—"torpedo"; and Bruyère—"Eiffel Tower." Other silhouettes of this era were created by Vramant—"breath of spring"; Carven—"Holy Year"; Piguet—"mushroom"; and Heim—"helicopter." Some of these titles may have been derisive, others the work of imaginative fashion editors, but all of them bring to mind an identifying style. They all applied to the individuality of costume shapes available to women whose major concerns were fashions.

Molly Parnis created conservatively elegant shirtmaker dresses. Larry Aldrich created formal gowns with draped bosoms and slit skirts with stiff asymmetric projections (Figure 17.4). His dresses for street wear were complexly cut, emphasizing hips and bust, and often accented with large buttons (Figure 17.5). Simple woolen fabrics worked by other designers fell into straight skirts from form-fitting blouses with snug, three-quarter sleeves ending in large, crisp cuffs. A popular 1953 cocktail suit in black velvet was styled with a slim skirt, vented at the center back, topped by a snug-fitting jacket. The suit jacket may have had tight, three-quarter sleeves accented

**Figure 17.4.** In the 1950s formal gowns were complex costumes made of heavy silken fabrics with asymmetric projections and swag draping. (Sketched from *Vogue* photograph of a Larry Aldrich creation.)

with large cuffs, a nipped waist, and the front dominated by revers of white bengaline.

Generally, day clothes for men and women had a chic decorum. Men did begin to wear pink shirts with gray flannel suits. Trousers were tight and bow ties of modest proportions identified those who were succeeding within the perimeters of the establishment.

Feminine evening wear was sparkling and romantic; the fashionable ballerina-length gown had full skirts and was often strapless, an innovative style for formal occasions.

In 1956 Balenciaga introduced the sack dress which harkened back to the 1920s silhouette. It was straight and, unlike the figure-freeing flapper sack, was snug over the buttocks. In general at this time, suit jackets were

**Figure 17.5.** Aldrich (left) and Fath (right) created feminine day dresses, using modifications of the silhouette that Dior had introduced in 1947. (Sketched from *Vogue*, November 15, 1950.)

shorter and styled with complex collars. Other details included suit coats with three-quarter sleeves and slim skirts, gathered slightly over the abdomen. Fabrics of this period were heavy and the greatest emphasis in the costume was created through intricate weaves.

From 1961 to 1963 President Kennedy was the embodiment of youth and vigor to the nation. His untimely death in 1963 plunged young and old into despair. During his presidency, his wife Jacqueline set the fashions of the jet set. The 60s had opened with a burst of hope, and the theme "moving ahead" included not only political and social advancements that would provide justice for all, but also came to mean changing moral patterns, cultural interests, and a shift in aesthetic standards.

The dance crazes included the gyrations of the frug danced to the tumultuous throbbing and tuneless tones of rock and roll. The big-band sounds of the forties, playing haunting melodies from *Carousel* or *Oklahoma*, were gone. The romanticism of *Brigadoon* in the late forties and the elegance of *My Fair Lady* were replaced by musicals with social messages, and even *Camelot* ended on a note of sorrow.

Rejection of the establishment resulted in a shift in moral standards and a polarization of age groups and life-styles. To identify with peer groups, members of the youth cult introduced costumes of bizarre combinations bought at welfare stores, and unusual headwear and hairstyles.

Onto this scene came the jet-set designers, money oriented and supported by established fashion magazines, all capitalizing on the new craze of the provocative "topless" go-go dancers. Rudi Gernreich introduced the topless swimsuit, followed by "see-through" dresses and blouses. Pierre Cardin in 1961 presented the **miniskirt;** Mary Quant of Carnaby Street, André Courrèges—called by some "king of the mini"—and Yves Saint-Laurent followed suit. Saint-Laurent had come to Dior's notice, and, after the great innovator's death, Saint-Laurent took over Dior's business and role as the world's fashion pacesetter.

In time fashion consumers were confronted by **hot pants,** denims, dungarees, the layered look (often imitating ethnic minority costuming), hip huggers, and unisex clothes, all of which created a no-style style. Women wore ten-year-old dresses, and no one but those in the fashion world knew or cared. Handsome, tailored **pants suits** for women replaced the skirt and jacket suit.

By mid-1974, the youth cult which had dominated fashion, morals, and manners for nearly a decade retreated (Figure 17.6). Lower skirt hems for day wear were again tentatively introduced in the fall fashion shows of the mid-seventies. Floor-length gowns for evening had been enthusiastically accepted by 1970, though the **maxiskirt** was a dismal failure when it first appeared in 1968.

A great wave of nostalgia swept the college and university youth in 1974. The Big Band sounds were favored by the *avant-garde* of the mid-seventies. The film *The Great Gatsby* enchanted the college-age group, reviving fashions of the thirties and shorter hairstyles for men. The Jesus-movement freaks and followers of East Indian religions went quietly about, "doing their thing," but did not insist that others do the same.

The mid-seventies closed on a note of apprehension about the uncertainty of the future. Doomsayers abounded, but in fashion, seemingly always optimistic, gowns and garb of all sorts, from formal to leisure wear, evidenced a return to elegance with attention given to design elements and principles.

The direction of the future years will be determined by economic, social, and political considerations as well as philosophical and moral attitudes. The face of fashion will reflect these attitudes and factors, for a person's attitude and personality are formed by them. In turn,

**Figure 17.6.** By the mid-1970s, the youth cult had influenced the acceptability of many styles. Some wore bell-bottom pants or jeans dotted with patches and T-shirts emblazoned with silk-screened images of long-dead composers, the U.S. flag, or other visual commentaries. Others chose floor-length dresses with mameluck sleeves, high waists, and embroidery-trimmed necklines.

these same factors also will influence the future shapes of fashion.

# Basic Garments of the Recent Past (1940–1970)

### DRESSES (1940–1970)

Women's costumes during the 1940s were greatly affected by World War II. Although invaded and occupied by Germany, Paris maintained for a time its tradition as the fashion leader. Drawings of the latest styles were allowed past the censors and were reproduced in leading American fashion magazines. René Bouet-Willaumez's sketches of Alix, Creed, and Balenciaga designs indicated the major silhouette and detailing trends. Large white areas were used as trims. These were bold decorations that served a good purpose during the dark nights of the blackouts. Fashion-magazine editors rationalized their continued interest in chic styles in a policy statement which suggested that handsome fashions lifted women's spirits and helped them to persevere. The couture carried on also, sometimes under grave handicaps. Many couturiers left Paris and, in self-imposed exile, created costumes for a war-oriented society.

Many of the dresses of the 1940s were very tailored with broad, shawl collars; short, slender skirts; and broad, padded shoulders. Shirtmaker-styled bodices with V-necklines trimmed with pointed and notched collars were common. The straight skirts were given width at the hemlines by deep kick pleats. Cap sleeves, three-quarter sleeves, and long, slender sleeves, similar to those of men's shirts, were typical of casual daytime dresses. Street dresses were plain with a masculine simplicity and austere detailing. The shoulder line increased in width accenting the full bust, small waist, and narrow hips.

Afternoon frocks and dressy dresses for semiformal evening wear accentuated the full bosom. These frocks

**Figure 17.7.** The **New Look** hemline persisted for several years, but the flare of suit and dress skirts diminished. Muffs and asymmetrically designed hats were very much in vogue. (Willaumez: illustration for *Vogue*, September 15, 1952. Permission of Condé Nast Publications Inc.)

**Figure 17.8.** By 1955 the **sheath** had returned as the fashionable silhouette. This late-day or little-evening dress was designed by Jobere of black-ribbed silk with a close-draped, matte jersey cummerbund. (Bouché: illustration for *Vogue*, November 1, 1955. Permission of Condé Nast Publications Inc.)

were made with intricately cut bodices that had gathers radiating from a center vertical seam to over the bust. The sleeves were either cap or three-quarter length. Waists were small and the short skirts were slightly draped over the hips. Slit side pockets were also used to add emphasis at the hips. The deep V-necklines were trimmed with sequins, as were the sleeves, bodices, and skirts around the hips. By 1944 the skirt styling for afternoon dresses were flared at the hem. Front skirt fullness was retained but the back was smooth, creating a slender silhouette.

The most startling development of postwar fashions was the **New Look** introduced by Dior in the spring of 1947. The costumes had narrow sloping shoulders, nipped-in waists, rounded bodices, and the season's surprise, a lowered hemline (Figure 17.7). Skirt hems plunged from knee length—the standard length throughout the war—to within eight inches of the floor. Later New Look hems were twelve inches from the floor, a length which was more flattering to most women of average height. Skirts were not only long but also rather full. One fashion editor reported these costume innovations as "seemingly new," a lovely look, that had polished rounded lines but gave no impression of heaviness. The female silhouette had changed from a stiff, masculine, triangular shape set on its apex to a completely feminine form. The influence of the New Look **A-line** silhouette dominated women's fashions for several years. Dresses with long, full skirts, tight waists, and full bodices remained in vogue until 1953.

New fabrics of synthetic fibers and interest in fabrics with interesting weaves contributed to the design characteristics of women's garments. Fabric, rather than involved and contrasting shapes of bodice and skirt, hinted at a renewed interest in the straight-line silhouette of the 1920s. Simple straight dresses with bodices slightly bloused over a low waistline, straight sleeves, and much shorter skirts were known variously as **sack** dresses, **sheath** dresses and **chemise** dresses (Figures 17.8 and 17.9).

The straight-line dresses continued to grow in popularity and were made interesting and exciting by the wide variety of textured fabrics and startling color combinations. Exterior influences such as the interest in space science, Pop and Op art, and a renewed attention to *Art Nouveau* contributed to the development of elaborately curvilinear and strictly geometric detailing. Décolletage was broad with standing circular collars. Sleeves were modified bell shapes, straight, three-quarter sleeves, or elbow-length straight sleeves. Skirts became startlingly short; most hems were knee length or above, with the **miniskirt** covering only the upper thigh (Figure 17.10). Simple waistless and sleeveless **minidresses** were decorated with contrasting horizontal and vertical bands echoing the perpendicular linear themes of Mondrian paintings or projecting space-travel costume stylings.

**Figure 17.9.** Knee-length formals· or cocktail dresses of the early 1960s depended on the texture or pattern of the fabric for design interest. Left to right: gold and ivory brocade cocktail dress, c. 1961; brilliant red, upholstery-fabric, two-piece theater dress, c. 1963; vermillion, pink, and green evening dress of chiffon, c. 1967.

**Figure 17.10.** The daring **minidress** was often made more provocative by large see-through shapes introduced into the body of the garments. Some of these innovative clothes were made of transparent plastic materials.

During the late 1960s, a number of skirt lengths were proposed including the **midi, maxi,** and **mod** hemlines. The midi length touched the leg at mid-calf, while the **maxidress** hemline touched the floor. Only the very young, or young at heart, wore extremely short or extremely long skirts. Late in 1968 a nostalgic look backward to the fluff and lace-ruffled Edwardian period occurred. The severely plain silhouette made elegant by intricately-cut patterns, however, dominated the styles of the 1960s. Fashions for casual wear, tea frocks and formal occasions were all styled along the same lines.

## WOMEN'S SUITS (1940–1970)

Women's suits during the 1940s imitated the severe tailoring of men's clothing. They had short, pencil-slim skirts and jackets with broad shoulders, flat collars, and notched lapels. The suit jacket was nipped in at the waist and smooth around the hips. It was quite long and made in single or double-breasted styles. Dressy suits were made with intricate diamond-shaped insets that emphasized the bustline of the jackets, which were often collarless and were worn with a decorative blouse.

The New Look suit was designed with a long, full skirt and a short jacket. The deep dolman sleeves of suits of the early 1940s were replaced by straight, more slender

**Figure 17.12.** Boxy jackets and skirts that accented the hips were some of the suit styles of the early 1950s. Large buckles on wide belts that curved down in back were accessories. The darker, understated blouse was simple in design with a semi-Chinese collar. (Sketched from a 1953 *Vogue* by the author.)

sleeves. Suits of the late 1940s and early 1950s retained the *A* silhouette and were styled with peplum jackets nipped in at the waist and full, gored skirts (Figures 17.11 and 17.23). Gradually, the silhouette was modified to a more slender outline. Short, waist-length jackets and shorter, narrower skirts became the dominant styling features (Figure 17.12). By the mid-1960s, suits were quite bulky and made from heavy textured fabrics. Short, boxy jackets with large, away-from-the-throat collars were combined with straight-line skirts which had a slight fullness below the waist in front.

**Double-knit suits** became extremely popular in the late 1960s. These were handsomely tailored costumes consisting of a jacket, a skirt, and a matching blouse. They were either plain colored or two toned, and sometimes trimmed with large, oversized zipper fastenings, big brass hooks, or cleverly designed metal chain and button closures.

**Pants suits** for women were introduced in the late 1960s. These were styled from a variety of fabrics including velvet, wool, double knit, orlon, or quilted cotton prints. The more elegant, velvet pants suits were styled with jackets patterned after the eighteenth-century just-

**Figure 17.11.** For the proper look in 1947, suiting fabric had to be gray flannel and the neck bound with a figured and colorful scarf tied ascot fashion. (Courtesy of the Schmidt family.)

aucorps and worn with lace-trimmed, white blouses (Figure 17.13). Those of wool or woollike, synthetic fibers were designed with Nehru jackets and presented a very masculine appearance. The pants were at first very tailored with extremely slender legs. Later these were modified to a flared leg or bell-bottom style. Pants suits were worn for formal and casual occasions.

## FORMAL GOWNS (1940–1970)

Women's formal gowns, during the war years of the 1940s, were designed with softly flowing skirts or full bouffant skirts. Floor-length **dinner dresses** and **ball gowns** were styled with the typical bust emphasis of daytime costumes. Bodice backs were sometimes slit from the high round necklines to the waistlines. Dinner dresses had either full-length dolman sleeves, cap, or three-quarter-length sleeves; slightly flared skirts; and small, round necklines. Ball gowns were designed with strapless bodices, bodices with a single shoulder strap, or with two thin shoulder straps. Necklines of some formal gowns were deep V-shapes while others were small, round shapes.

**Cocktail dresses** duplicated these bodice and neckline treatments, but were made with street-length skirts. The feminine curves, typical of the New Look, were used in the designs for formal costumes of the late 1940s and early 1950s. Hemlines of these gowns were often styled to reveal the feet in front but dipped low in back, giving the appearance of a short train. The **ballerina-length formal** was designed with a slightly above-the-ankle skirt, a nipped-in wasp waist, and a variety of sleeves.

During the late 1950s and early 1960s, formal gowns were designed with intricately cut bodices, often trimmed with large bows with side streamers reaching to a floor-length hem (Figure 17.14). Tulip- or lily-shaped collars, loose-hanging panels, and large shoulder puffs added elegance to the slim, floor-length formal sheaths of these years (Figure 17.15).

Late in the 1960s the **see-through** costume was introduced for formal evening wear. This consisted of a long-sleeved blouse made of gossamer fabric and designed with a deep décolletage, which was worn without concealing undergarments, and a slim, floor-length skirt.

**Figure 17.13.** From the time of its introduction, the **pants suit** was accepted, but the **knickers suit** was not. Shown in some fall 1970 collections, the knickers suit, far left, was a fashion only the most daring would choose. (Sketched from *Vogue* magazine photographs.)

**Figure 17.14.** Formal gowns for women during the late 1950s were complexly draped and combined slender underskirts with asymmetrically swagged overskirts, accented with stiff bows. Men dressed conservatively in dinner jackets for summer and tuxedos with satin lapels or tail suits for formal occasions. (Sketched from a Saks Fifth Avenue advertisement in *Vogue*, c. 1958.)

Other formal gowns were designed with plunging necklines that extended below the navel, sleeveless bodices, and tight skirts slit from knee to hem (Figure 17.16). At-home formal costumes were designed with full transparent harem pants worn at hipbone level, and elegantly bejeweled gold brassieres.

A variety of novelty cocktail dresses were suggested for the holiday season of 1968. Some of these were made with several shapes of silver tabs hinged together to form a metal sheath or minidress (Figure 17.17). Another unique cocktail dress proposed for that season was decorated with battery-operated lights, which, when switched on, declared provocative, one-word answers to spoken or implied questions.

Late in 1969 a one-piece **jumpsuit** with bell-bottom trousers, an empire waistline marked with a wide belt, and a bust-outlining bodice with long, bishop sleeves was introduced. This too was a formal at-home costume made of "lunar white" crepe.

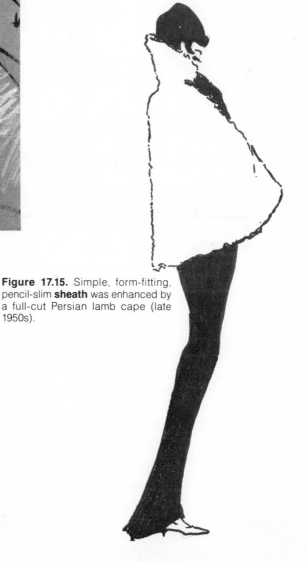

**Figure 17.15.** Simple, form-fitting, pencil-slim **sheath** was enhanced by a full-cut Persian lamb cape (late 1950s).

**Figure 17.16.** Languid drapes and deep, provocative décolletage were introduced for at-home gowns in the late 1960s. (Sketched from a 1969 *Vogue* magazine.)

**Figure 17.17.** Daring designers of the late 1960s created **mini-dresses** in silver or anodized aluminum. This minidress was made of plaques of metal hinged together. (Sketched from an example of that period in the Costume Institute exhibition in the Metropolitan Museum of Art.)

## WOMEN'S SPORTSWEAR (1940–1970)

Sport clothes for women were supplied in a wide variety of shapes and styles. Slacks, swim suits, and shorts dominated the scene until the 1950s. During the next two decades of ever-increasing casual living, a wide variety of sportswear developed: pedal pushers; calf-length tight pants; stretch pants; long pants with an instep strap made of form-fitting bonded fabric; Bermuda shorts—thigh-length, tight-legged shorts; hip huggers; pants dresses; culottes; and skimmer dresses.

Swim suits were made of cotton and designed like short-skirted dresses or were bikini suits with narrow breastbands and minute pants. Knit suits were much like those of the 1920s: two-piece suits consisting of a modest top and short trunks worn low on the hips with a delicate gold chain around the waist from which dangled a solitaire pearl in an appropriate position.

Slacks changed radically during the late 1960s, particularly in the leg size. At first slacks were form fitting and tight from waist to ankles, then the flared cuff was introduced toward the end of 1968. These were called **elephant-ear pants,** if very large and floppy; or **bell bottoms,** if only moderately flared. Slacks were no longer simply a female version of male trousers, but were often trimmed on the leg seams with lace, open shapes, or appliqué. Blouses worn with shorts or slacks ranged from short-sleeved tailored shirts to fussy lace and eyelet-trimmed styles.

**Ski costumes,** composed of pants and matching jackets, were severely tailored and made of bonded stretch knit. During the late 1960s, they were worn with turtleneck knit blouses. A variety of **car coats** with attached hoods, made in materials ranging from fleece-lined wool to nylon, were used extensively for winter sports events or sport-car racing.

## WOMEN'S WRAPS (1940–1970)

Masculine cut in women's coats and the inclusion in nearly every coed's wardrobe of the black **Chesterfield** with a flat velvet collar and wide lapels carried out the broad-shouldered styling themes of the forties. The **shorty coat,** a boxy, hip-length jacket with wide, three-quarter or full-length sleeves, was designed with a cardigan neckline. This light-weight shorty coat was often trimmed with nonfunctional buttons, though later styles were double breasted. This style remained in fashion for several years.

After 1947 long, full-backed coats with modestly puffed sleeves, bell sleeves, or straight sleeves with folded back cuffs reflected the *A* silhouette of the New Look. Shoulders were made more narrow and sloping. Sleeves were set-in, dolman, or raglan styles. The masculine types of coats—Chesterfields and heavy, double-breasted greatcoats patterned after men's coats of the early nineteenth century—were replaced by more feminine wraps (Figures 17.18 and 17.19). Voluminous, pyramidal coats with large, full sleeves and shawl, tuxedo, or tie scarf collars were made of handsome textured woolens. **Three-quarter coats,** so popular during

the 1940s, with full bodices, tight waists, and flared skirts were discarded totally in the 1950s.

Raincoats, chemically treated and made of colorful fabrics, replaced the reversible rain or casual-wear coats of the previous decade. The **reversible coat** was designed with a tailored woolen side and a chemically treated gabardine side. They could be turned inside out and worn as protection against the rain, and yet retained the same design. The chemicals applied to these coats made them water repellent.

Coats during the 1950s ranged from cape shapes with modified batwing sleeves to wraparound cashmeres with design traits similar to those of the 1920s polo coat. Large, head-hugging collars, shawl collars, and wide-standing circle collars (in the late 1960s) followed coat modifications from cape shape to bulky barrel shape. Coat hems rose with the dress hem, to minilength (Figure 17.20). In 1966 a **greatcoat** with calf-length skirts was introduced and continued as a chic winter style for some years.

Fur coats during the 1940s were designed with square shoulders, bell-shaped sleeves and round or shawl collars. The **chubby** was the fur version of the shorty coat.

**Figure 17.18.** Not all women's clothes of the 1940s had a masculine design. This three-quarter coat of soft, suede cloth with dolman sleeves, nipped-in waist, and flaring skirt was particularly feminine. The tiered hat with draped snood and the gathered fabric clutch purse were also typical accessories of the mid-1940s. (Redrawn from a fashion illustration in *Vogue*.)

**Figure 17.19.** The empire line, reintroduced by Costello, was described by the *Vogue* fashion editor: "Properly done, it is subtle and distinguished." (Bouché: illustration for *Vogue*, November 1, 1948. Permission of Condé Nast Publications Inc.)

**Figure 17.20.** Hooded **minicoats** of the 1960s were reminiscent of the Roman cucullus. Textured fabrics or smooth, synthetic woollike fabrics were the textiles used to create a bold silhouette. (Sketched from a photograph in a 1968 *Vogue* magazine.)

It was made from fox fur with the pelts arranged with a dominant vertical line. During the 1950s and 1960s, mink shoulder capes patterned after the nineteenth-century canezou were often called **clutch capes** (Figure 17.21). Mink capes, coats, and stoles were the most popular fur wraps for a number of years; however, sable, leopard, and fox with the pelts arranged in a horizontal pattern, were also worn. Cloth coats with dyed mink collars were styled with simple straight bodices and amply cut straight sleeves.

**Imitation furs** were worn by men and women during the late 1960s. Synthetic furs had reached a high level of perfection, and their simulation, in the expensive versions, was difficult to detect. The imitation furs, often seal or beaver textures and designed with simple straight bodies and sleeves, were worn either unbelted or girdled with thin leather belts or large-link chain belts. They were thigh, knee, or calf length, warm but light weight, and quite elegant in appearance.

**Formal wraps** during the 1950s and 1960s were flamboyant or luxuriously sophisticated and made of rich velvet or silk fabrics for formal winter functions. Great tiered capes, with wide ruffles arranged horizontally from the neckline to the floor-length hem, were made of vividly colored taffeta. Gossamer synthetic fabrics were used for summer formal wraps which were often styled with rows of bouffant puffs creating a billowing A-line silhouette from the shoulders to the ankle-length hem. Straight floor-length coats, made of velvet or brocaded silk with severe lines, had small standing collars and side-slit skirts, and were elegantly tailored evening wraps. The evening wraps of these decades were more intricate than the broad-shouldered capes and three-quarter-length wraps of the austere war years.

## WOMEN'S UNDERWEAR (1940–1970)

Styles of the undergarments worn by women remained more or less constant from the late 1930s through the 1960s. Minor innovations were the introduction of the half-slip in the 1950s and refinements in brassiere design, including a thin, padded interlining.

The introduction of the body stocking and textured or plain panty hose were two of the more significant changes of the late 1960s. The body stocking was a one-piece,

**Figure 17.21.** The coveted mink cape or mink stole, similar to the nineteenth - century canezou, was a popular evening wrap in the sixties. (Author's photograph of cape from her collection.)

flowers and trimmed with a fine net puff. Many of the hats of this period had coarse-net face veils and were made of felt for winter wear and straw for spring and summer. Hats during the mid-1940s were much larger with rolled brims and topless crowns. The gathered and draped fall trims of the previous years were replaced by more tailored decorations. Pancake and cartwheel straw sailors were the spring and summer hat fashions of the late forties, while evening hats were sequin- or flower-trimmed skull caps (Figure 17.22). Hats for daytime wear during the 1950s were made of velour and trimmed with a variety of feathers and veils. Brims gave an asymmetric line by being tilted up on one side and hugging the cheek on the other. Pleated and

stretch-knit garment of nylon fabric or other synthetic fiber. Panty hose were a combination of hose and briefs made into a single garment. While hose were relatively subordinate to the rest of the costume, they were smooth and beige or brown in color. Nylon hose were introduced in the early 1940s, but were replaced during the war with stockings made of rayon. Silk totally disappeared as a fiber for hose and, after the war, was replaced by nylon, stretch nylon, and, in the 1960s, by cantrece. When dresses, suits, and coats became very short, legs and leg coverings were considered part of the total look of the costume. Textured and patterned hose of mesh stretch material and hose made in a wide range of colors were worn.

Corsets and foundation garments were worn by some women to support hose and to control the figure. The **wasp-waist** or **Merry Widow** corset was introduced at the time of the New Look to control the waist size. Panty girdles, garter belts, and thigh-length elasticized underpants with detachable garters were also worn as hose supporters and for minor, light-weight figure control.

# Accessories for Women (1940–1970)

### HEADWEAR

During the first years of the 1940s, hats were small and were worn cocked over one eye. Styles included: the turban; tailored beret; small, tipped-brim hats; turban and snood combinations; pillbox hats with a ruffled fall or snood in back; and small hats composed entirely of fabric

**Figure 17.22.** Small hats, with pleated, rolled, and face-framing brims, befeathered or button trimmed, were modish headwear for fall 1948. The *Vogue* editor captioned these, clockwise from top: Directoire bonnet; Directoire postilion; Directoire, softly; and Directoire, slightly. They were designed by Albouy, Legroux, Orcel, and Saint Cyr respectively. (Eric: illustration for *Vogue*, September 1, 1948. Permission of Condé Nast Publications Inc.)

draped pyramidal crowns with feather trims were worn well back on the head (Figure 17.23).

From the mid-forties on, hats were set squarely on the head, a suitable position for the masculine derby forms with tall crowns and rolled brims that were in vogue during the 1960s. High-crowned fedora styles, space-age felt helmets, leather caps with tall crowns and large bills, hair-concealing tams, and fur hats made with dome-shaped crowns and no brims, or imitative of the fur hats worn by Russian men, were some of the winter hat fashions of the late 1960s. Floppy straw hats and cloth hats patterned after the 1930s beach hats were popular for summer wear during this period.

By the 1960s hats were not the fashionable accessories that they once had been. Hats were worn primarily for protection in the winter, and only the most chic or most conservative women continued to wear them except for warmth. Even the custom of women covering their heads when attending church was discarded, and small, round lace veils or large lace mantillas were worn instead. For tea or cocktail parties, dome-shaped crowns formed with

**Figure 17.23.** Softness and femininity were the mode in the early 1950s. Small waists were accented by suit jackets that nipped in at the waist and flared into short peplums. Hats, worn off the face, were pleated velours. Choker necklaces of imitation pearls and pearl-cluster earrings were stylish jewelry accessories. (Sketched from a 1953 *Vogue* magazine.)

net and trimmed with velvet or grosgrain ribbon bows and small, artificial flowers were substituted for traditional hat forms. Frivolous, beehive-shaped feather or cloth-flower hats that completely covered the head were a casual style. Mesh-net bonnets with rows of ruffles were transparent caps similar to the eighteenth-century mobcap and were worn about the house in a half-hearted effort to hide hair-curlers.

## FOOTWEAR

Shoes in the 1940s were heavy and clumsily designed. Leather was scarce during the war years, and shoes were designed to conform to available materials. Counters and heels were often leather, and the area over the instep was an elastic fabric. Shoe toes were round, heels were thick, and soles were raised. These platform soles often were made of cork and were quite thick. **Pumps, shanks mare, wedgies,** and **baby-doll** ankle-strap sandals were among the more common shoe forms of the forties.

During the 1950s, shoes gradually became more pointed with very high, slender heels. During the 1960s, heel shapes changed each season, ranging from stiletto heels set well back, to Louis heels placed toward the instep, to large, thick heels similar to those worn during the seventeenth century. Shoe tops were very shallow during the 1950s, and became increasingly heavy and foot concealing as the end of the 1960s approached.

**Boots,** which appeared briefly in 1947 as ankle-high, flared-cuff, feminine forms, became an important part of the total costume by the 1960s. With the advent of the minidress, suit, and coat, leg emphasis demanded rather startling leg coverings. Women's boots ranged from ankle-high duplicates of the nineteenth-century male boots, to calf-high Hessian or riding boot styles, to thigh-high boots with thick heels and square toes reminiscent of seventeenth-century boots. These latter boot styles, formed of stretch vinyl, were tight and form fitting.

Sandal forms for summer and casual wear ranged in design from the Japanese one-thong styles to Grecian thong styles which laced up the legs to the knees or thighs. The sandal designs were almost limitless.

## JEWELRY

Costume jewelry was generally accepted, and necklaces, bracelets, and earrings were accessory items that changed each season. During the 1960s, plastic was used extensively for much of the costume jewelry, including large rings, bracelets, and necklaces. Hand-crafted, individually created silver jewelry in either rigidly geometric shapes or organic forms became the vogue during the same decade. A renewed interest in the small rings of the early nineteenth century resulted in the wearing of rings on every finger in much the same way as they had been during the Renaissance. Charm bracelets, first popular in the 1940s, were revived during the 1960s, but were usually gold rather than silver as the earlier versions had been. Band bracelets, worn in multiples around the wrist or upper arm, were made of plastic, silver, or gold, and were wide or narrow.

Women's watches, round and tiny during the 1940s, became small, square shapes. Finally, in the 1960s, costume-jewelry watches were made with giant faces and large numerals and worn on wide wrist bands. Pendant watches, pin watches, and ring watches were other forms popular during a period of great variety in jewelry.

Elegant jewels were also worn by those who could afford them, and diamonds and precious gems set in platinum or gold were designed in styles similar to those of the French Empire period.

Body jewelry was introduced in the late 1960s. These exotic jewelry forms included: silver and gold bras, huge shoulder-to-breast collars, and large silver lorums composed of wide, circular silver collars and ankle-length front panels of silver.

## HANDHELD ACCESSORIES

The variety of handheld accessories was limited to purses, pocketbooks, clutch purses, and umbrellas. Purses or bags ranged from soft, modestly proportioned cloth styles of the forties to envelope shapes and large satchel forms or small clutch purses of the 1960s. They were made of leather, plastic, or straw. There were shoulder-strap styles with ample pouches during the 1950s and minute purses with long chain straps during the 1960s.

Umbrellas were functional as well as decorative rainwear accessories. They were made of plain or patterned fabrics or transparent plastic. Some of the latter types were made of opaque plastic with transparent "portholes." There were styles with long handles, short handles, and those which collapsed in half with handles that telescoped. Many women carried the longer-handled styles neatly furled, using them as walking sticks.

# Hairstyles for Women (1940–1970)

During the first half of the 1940s, women's hair was very long and worn pulled off the forehead into a high **pompadour.** These pompadour arrangements were often divided into two sausage rolls that terminated in two facing curls in the center front. The hair in back was allowed to fall free or was brushed up to the crown of the head and arranged into several curls behind the pompadour. More mature women wore modified versions of these two styles, but generally wore their hair somewhat shorter.

Hairstyles dictated by the New Look were short and demanded a **feather cut.** This was a controlled version of the nineteenth-century infanta coiffure. These styles were gently curled and remained in fashion from the late 1940s until the early 1950s.

Women's hairstyles changed radically during the next decade. The gently curled, skull-conforming feather bobs were abandoned and giant beehive coiffures, stiffly lacquered after much torturing and back brushing, became the vogue. Straight hair was the fashion, and women with naturally curly hair had it straightened. The **bubble** hairstyle, also large and bouffant but without waves or curls, was followed by a closely cropped cut combed from the crown over gently teased hair at the back, with forehead-concealing bangs and long, pointed, sideburnlike locks in front of the ears. Long straight hair, falling over the cheeks, was also worn with long bangs. There were towering coifs made up of large round curls, fantastically arranged loop braids, and straggling corkscrew curls worn for festive formal occasions, and severe styles with the hair pulled taut from the face and arranged into an inverted roll high on the back of the head. This type of coif was held in place by a broad flat bow placed beneath the roll at the base of the skull. Curls with a forehead-encircling bandeau, long braids, waist-length falls of hair, **infanta,** and **Brutus** coiffures were fashioned from the wearer's natural hair or carefully attended wigs.

**Wigs** became the vogue in the early 1960s and were carefully matched to the natural hair or made of synthetic fibers in garish colors. False hair pieces or **falls** were also used extensively. Wig shops, like the shops of the seventeenth- and eighteenth-century perruquiers where wigs could be purchased, shampooed, and set, appeared in shopping centers and major department stores.

Another fad of the 1960s was changing the natural hair color with the use of dyes. Henna rinses and peroxide had been used throughout the three previous decades, and, in the mid-forties, a lavender rinse was used to give life to gray hair. During the late 1950s and on into the 1960s, every conceivable hair-dye color was available, and many women, young and old, used them. **Frosting,** touching dark hair in random spots with bleach, was yet another fad.

# Men's Basic Garments of the Recent Past (1940–1970)

## MEN'S SUITS (1940–1970)

Men's business suits of the 1940s had very broad shoulders which were heavily padded to add breadth. The suit coats were long, single or double breasted, and

**Figure 17.24.** Male costumes during the years of the Vietnam conflict took forms which identified peer groups. Beards, moustaches, and hair length were also group identifiers. Adaptations of ethnic garments were worn by many young people. By mid-1970 hairstyles for men were carefully coiffed and shoes were fancifully designed with high, thick heels and often with platform soles.

extremely conservative in styling and color. The **gray flannel suit** became a uniform of young executives for nearly a decade. The double-breasted coat style disappeared in the fifties to be reintroduced during the late 1960s. Trouser legs became very slender when the Edwardian or Italian cut was in fashion (Figure 17.25).

During the individualistic period of the 1960s, flared cuffs, longer suit coats, **Nehru suits**—single-breasted suits with small standing collars (Figure 17.26)—and

**Figure 17.25.** Men's suits in the mid-1960s took on an Edwardian look. Suit coats were single breasted with narrow lapels and buttoned high on the chest. Male costumes changed little, but details such as tie width and the fold of the handkerchief worn in the breast pocket were modestly modified.

buttoned at the waistline or slightly above. They were designed with turned-down collars and broad lapels. Trousers were full in the legs with rather deep pleats on each side at the waist that extended into the center trouser crease.

An exaggeration of the double-breasted business suit called the **zoot suit** was affected by some of the more eccentrically dressed young men. This suit consisted of a thigh-length, double-breasted coat with large pointed lapels and peg-top trousers. These were very full at the waist and tapered to a cuff so narrow that it was difficult to get the foot through the opening. Zoot suits were usually made in rather garish colors, but the average man's business costume was more conservative in coloring.

While retaining the same general characteristics, men's suits during the 1950s and 1960s were modified in breadth of trouser legs, size and shape of lapels, and width of shoulders (Figure 17.24). In the 1950s men's suits were

**Figure 17.26.** The **Nehru suit**, introduced in the late 1960s, had a short-lived popularity. The main features of the Nehru jacket were the standing collar and the buttons from throat to just above the hem. The popular shirt used with the Nehru suit was the dacron-knit turtleneck.

other innovative details were introduced into men's costumes. The waistcoat reappeared and was as decorative as its predecessors. It was single or double breasted and designed with a plain, collarless V-neckline or trimmed with a small collar and lapels. The revival of vests and waistcoats followed a decade when neither were worn except by older men. Color, which had originally been reserved for men's sports clothes, was introduced into all types of men's wear in the 1960s and ranged from rich, subdued hues to brilliant and vibrant colors. Business suits and sports or casual clothes were styled from colorful synthetic fabrics.

The more flamboyant dandies of the "In Group" or the "Beautiful People" in the sixties affected velvet suit jackets and shirts with ruffled fronts, cuffs, and jabots. These were cut either like the eighteenth-century justaucorps or the Nehru jacket. Trousers were worn low on the hips and were trimmed with wide leather belts with large decorative buckles. Striped, plain or patterned materials in brilliant blues, dark wine reds, and burnt oranges were used to make these trousers. A jumpsuit with a sleeveless sack-suit coat was proposed for airplane travel. The total effect of this costume was that of a conservative sack suit. The long-sleeved bodice section of the one-piece jumpsuit created a waistcoat when worn with the coat.

During World War II, when fabrics for suiting were in short supply, the sport coat and slacks were introduced and accepted as business and street apparel. These garments continued in fashion after the war and were modified in cut and tailoring as the detailing of the standard business suits changed. The jackets were usually tweed and the slacks were gabardine or other smooth-finish fabrics of natural or synthetic fibers. Slim trousers or sports slacks were worn low on the hips, creating a long-waisted appearance. Belts were slender or nonexistent accessories for these styles by the mid-1960s. The center trouser-leg crease was eliminated during the period when the very tight trousers were in fashion. Trouser cuffs, which had been discarded during the war, were reintroduced during the 1950s and again eliminated for a time during the 1960s.

Men's shirts were altered slightly in design, and the long, pointed, turned-down collars were the details that changed most noticeably. During the fifties, collars were smaller and were either rounded or pointed. These Ivy League shirts were made of a wide variety of fabrics from madras to drip-dry blends of natural and synthetic fibers. They were styled with button-down collars, short sleeves, or long sleeves with plain or French cuffs. The casual shirts were styled in a number of handsome and intricate designs including: the conventional type opening in front; turtleneck styles; polo or golf shirts made of knit material; deep-yoked shirts with an unbuttoned, diagonal neck opening; and colorful plain or horizontally striped T-shirts.

Sport shirts were generally worn without ties, although the wide, long ties of the 1940s were featured when sport shirts were introduced. Ties of the 1950s became quite slender and were elegant accessories. Other style variations included: the thong tie with sliding guide; the bow tie, which was very narrow until the late 1960s; the early nineteenth-century string tie; the crossed and buttoned simplified version of the neckcloth; and the square or pointed-end knit or figured tie, tied either in a large Windsor or four-in-hand knot. Soft, loosely tied scarves and ascot cravats were also worn by some men.

Formal clothes, tailored to conform to current fashion detailing of the collar, lapels, trouser size, and coat length, included: the tuxedo, formal tail suit, lounge suit, and dinner jacket. The morning suit with cutaway, striped trousers and gray waistcoat was used for formal morning functions. Toppers worn with formal clothing included the tall, pearl-gray hat worn with the morning suit; the silk hat; the tall, collapsible, formal black hat; the black Homburg or black fedora. During the 1950s and 1960s, men's tuxedo jackets were made from a variety of dark, decorative fabrics. Lapels were faced with watered taffeta or brocaded material, and tuxedo coat sleeves were often styled with small cuffs that matched the lapel facings. Cummerbunds with matching ties and ruffled and tucked dress shirts were some of the evening-wear innovations of the 1960s.

## MEN'S SPORTSWEAR (1940–1970)

Men's sport clothes were functional and decorative. The swim trunks of the late 1930s were modified in leg length and ranged from thigh-length boxer-shorts swim trunks to calf-length surfers. Men also wore the abbreviated bikini swim trunks. All these styles were made of plain-colored cotton fabrics or synthetic fabrics in gay, bright patterns.

Sports costumes, made of either nylon or woolen fabrics, included: slacks and jackets; jumpsuits, one-piece cotton suits in a wide range of colors; ski suits; Levi's; jeans; golf sweaters; and intricately cut windbreakers with attached hoods.

## MEN'S WRAPS (1940–1970)

Men's overcoats during the 1940s were long, straight, knee-length coats with raglan or set-in wide sleeves. They had turned-down collars and single breasted fronts. As suitcoat lengths were shortened, men's overcoats were also made with shorter skirts. During the late 1950s and 1960s, car coats, with or without attached hoods, became popular. These were often fleece-lined, thigh-length coats fastened with large buttons, brass hook devices, or heavy commercial zippers. Men's cold-weather wraps for formal wear continued to include the Chesterfield with a velvet collar. During the 1960s, overcoats with beaver collars and fur coats made

**Figure 17.27.** By the 1970s male costumes expressed individuality and elegance. Full coats of real or synthetic fur with large collars and lapels of a contrasting fur, and leather shoulder-strap purses for men were introduced. Suit coats lengthened and were double-vented on the sides, or designed with a single deep vent, often well above the waist. The coats were single or double breasted with pleats in back, pocket flaps, and turned-back sleeve cuffs.

from skins of real animals or imitation furs became the fashion (Figure 17.27). The detail styling of these overcoats was similar to that of the cloth overcoats.

# Accessories for Men (1940–1970)

## HEADWEAR

Hats worn by men during the 1940s included such conventional styles as the felt **fedora,** the **Homburg,** and the **straw boater.** These hats had smaller brims and more shallow crowns than those of the previous decades. During the 1950s, the straw boater was replaced by a tall-crowned, small-brimmed straw hat much like the felt fedora. The felt fedora, the Russian-style fur cap, the leather-billed cap, and the ear-flap billed cap were worn for warmth. Most young men did not wear head coverings in the summer, but during the winter months of the 1940s and 1950s, they wore the shallow, flat-crowned **porkpie** hat. Later they wore brush-trimmed Tyrolian felt hats, caps, and Russian-style fur hats.

## FOOTWEAR

Throughout the 1940s men's shoes remained conservative and were either lowcut oxfords or variations of the saddle shoe. During the 1950s and 1960s, a wide variety of types were available, ranging from the casual moccasin-type loafer to calf-high boots. Toes were round during the forties, gradually becoming more pointed in the fifties, and changing to squared-off toes during the latter years of the 1960s. Formal shoes were lowcut slipper styles made of black patent leather with flat bows on the instep. The soles were made of leather. Other types of shoes had leather soles, rubber crepe soles, smooth rubber soles, and rubber soles with deep V-grooves.

Men wore a variety of sandals including: single-strap types; complex, multistrap styles patterned after Mexican sandals or ancient Roman footwear; and woven, leather-strip or straw-toed scuff sandals.

### JEWELRY

During the 1940s, wristwatches replaced the larger pocket watches and continued in fashion for the next two decades. They were stem wound or self-winding and some were made with calendars and alarm devices. They were generally made in thin, oblong shapes. Stretch-metal bracelets or leather-strap watchbands were used to hold them around the wrist. Late in the 1960s, watchbands increased in width to two or two-and-a-half inches wide. Identification bracelets made with a rectangular plate and large link chains were accessories for younger men.

During the era of the hippies and flower children, men wore **love beads,** a single strand of small stone or glass beads, or pendant necklaces. The pendant necklace was made of a leather thong with a stone or metal pendant, or a heavy chain and pendant of metal. The popular symbol or emblems of various ethnic religious movements were the design devices frequently used for the pendants of these bold, masculine accessories.

Most men wore rings of conventional designs, and a few wore small gold earrings, usually only one, in pierced ears.

# Hairstyles for Men (1940–1970)

For the greater part of this three-decade period, men wore their hair short, brushed from a part or in a slight pompadour. During the 1950s, younger men wore the closely-cropped crew cut. However, at the end of the 1960s, many men let their hair grow longer and grew long sideburns and beards. Many hippies let their hair grow to shoulder length, never cutting or shaping it, and seldom combing it. More fastidious young men had their hair professionally groomed by hairstylists who curled it, shaped it, and lacquered it with the same care used for women's coiffures. Many of the longer hairstyles for men were evocative of those worn during the romantic period of the nineteenth century; others were reminiscent of the seventeenth century.

### FOOTNOTES

1. Bettina Ballard, *In My Fashion*, p. 25.
2. Ibid., p. 26.
3. Edna Woolman Chase and Ilka Chase, *Always in Vogue*, p. 209.
4. Mila Contini, *Fashion: From Ancient Egypt to the Present Day*, p. 308.
5. Ibid.
6. Ballard, *In My Fashion*, p. 47.
7. *Vogue*, May 1, 1941, pp. 56–60.
8. *Vogue*, May 15, 1942, pp. 46–47.
9. Gisele D'Assailly, *Ages of Elegance*, p. 234.

# Chapter 18

# Summary: The Later Years Coupled to the Past (1930–1970)

**Figure 18.1.** In 1937 Schiaparelli created this evening gown of beige net and black velvet which incorporates the basic lines of the Gothic female cyclas. (Sketched at *The 10s, The 20s, The 30s* exhibition, 1974. Metropolitan Museum of Art, New York City.)

In reviewing fashions which followed the introduction of the Worth Polonaise gown, one is presented with a kaleidoscopic range of changes. The problems of annotating the myriad fashion variations of the 1920s and 1930s are compounded because designers created new styles and drew from fashions of the past. Paquin, Louiseboulanger, Patou, Cheruit, and Lanvin, along with Chanel, "a good indicator of chic,"[1] altered the very concept of how women should look at clothes and their bodies in them.

Clever and daring use of the bias cut skillfully revealed thighs and molded the garment for day wear, sportswear, and formal wear. The rounded yet constricted feminine form first was freed and flattened, and then slimmed with flaring at the ankles. Late in the twenties, the **mermaid gown** was introduced; the skirt was slim as far as the knees and then flared to the ankles. Hips were made to appear narrow but less restricted, and the waist, chest, and stomach appeared to be concave; then peplums (Lanvin), or "fantails," were added to create back interest. The three-quarter evening wraps with ample fur collars were created by Chanel from white crepe and white fox. Augusta Bernard also fashioned similar evening elegance by using an abundance of fox, sable, and other fur trims. Paquin created in gold and cream moiré. Printed chiffons abounded in 1929. Shawllike scoop collars revealed vast expanses of the figure from shoulder to waist in back. Modest cap sleeves were introduced for day wear.[2] Gilbert Clark used delicate blues in taffeta embroidered with silver and trimmed with silver lace for feminine evening attire. A resurgent interest in motifs of the French monarchy brought back the fleur-de-lis as a popular decorative device.

Caroline Reboux introduced hats made of beige hemp straw with large brims to counter the asymmetrically trimmed, dominant cloche styles. The Reboux straws were similar to the eighteenth-century Milan straws. The **envelope pocketbook** replaced the chain-handled, beaded bag.

The mermaid styling was adapted to day wear from striped fabrics cut on the bias and intricately put together to create exciting contrasts of linear direction, calling attention to new areas of figure interest—the knees and hips. Suits were low waisted, often with three-quarter-length jackets worn with blouses which had asymmetric front openings.

For all the easy simplicity of day wear, decorative embellishments made the evening gowns of 1929 exciting. Blouse sections remained straight and were cut with sliplike, narrow shoulder straps which bared the shoulders and deep, straight V- or U-necklines. Trailing panels swept to the floor as in Worth's gown #214 shown in the April 27, 1929 issue of *Vogue*. The underskirt hem of this black satin and chiffon gown was scalloped with shallow dagging. See-through jackets were introduced by Molyneux, who also decorated the mermaid skirt of his #93 model (1929) with "... huge flowers of chiffon ... to weight the trailing skirt and accent the shoulders,"[3] As *Vogue's* fashion editor summed it up, "Individuality is outstanding in the present mode, and femininity has completely replaced uniformity. The great creative artists use a dozen different ways to sign their models."[4] Signatures of the artists of fashion design included complex cuff treatment, imitation flowers of velvet or chiffon, low front and back décolletage, scarves, shawl collars, double-pleated jabots, linen batiste stocks, and draped or free-hanging fringes that fell to the floor or were swagged across the front and back of gowns.

Swim suits—designed more for sunning than aquatic activities—were called **beach frocks,** and often were made of black taffeta with small, flared skirts over trunks. Beach slippers and rubberized silk bandanas were *must* beach-wear accessories.

Modest adjustments continued after the financial crash of October 1929. The general costuming presented a somber look, but, by 1934, a new verve in clothing began to make an appearance. The new emphasis was "the upper half" or, more accurately, blouses. Jodell introduced the **afternoon blouse;** one example, featured in the October 15, 1934 *Vogue*, was of "grayish-blue satin worn with a green velveteen and black wool skirt."[5] The blouse had loose sleeves, a center-front opening fastened with oversized buttons, and a large tailored bow at the base of the throat. In the same year, Schiaparelli presented a line of knit blouses, many styled with wide ribbing and matching knitted scarves. Mainbocher also styled handsome afternoon blouses, many featuring bow treatments at the neck. Tucked blouses, with stitched ribbing and smocking and tight waistbands, were worn over slip-top skirts. Bolero jackets reappeared, styled with face-framing collars and simple sleeves. Fur wraps popular in the early thirties were sealskin capes, tippets, stoles, and full-length coats. Schiaparelli's tall, twisted hat forms were copied in "Eskimo seal."

Tailored suits of lamé with small matching turbans or backless halter-top formal gowns done in stark black crepe were effective wear for formal dining. The winter fashion predictions for 1934 recommended that elegance, opulence, and luxury should reappear. The "look" was to be a "studied effect rather than casual." Women were admonished to be fascinating, and fashion editors announced that the new mode included "no more crazy dresses" but styling "with an allure he will understand." Gowns with masculine appeal included Molyneux's décolleté dinner gown; Marcel Rochas's bustle-back evening dress; and Schiaparelli's dresses and gowns with uplift bra

bodices (Figure 18.1). Alix and Vionnet draped the figure to reveal feminine curves. Directoire-type evening gowns were also fashionable by 1937.[6]

Coats and jackets became full and bulky (Figure 18.2), as was Lanvin's bulky full-fronted day coat. Molyneux created tubelike jackets employing the new closure—the zipper. Furs included wild sheep and shaved beaver, often combined with suede. Mink with antelope was popular for hats which were fur trimmed after the modes of the 1860s, probably influenced by the release of the movie, *Gone with the Wind*, based on the Civil-War era.

The elegance of the late thirties was derived in part by the styles of the past, widely separated in times and cultures. For example, Alix's resources ranged from the Egyptian era to the Directoire period. One of his gowns of white crepe had fluid box pleating, a modern adaptation of Egyptian goffering, and was described as having been

**Figure 18.2.** Voluminous winter coats, often trimmed with fox fur, were introduced in 1937. Sleeves were still puffed but took on a bishop-sleeve style. (Redrawn from a fashion periodical of that year.)

"profoundly simple."[7] Multicolored full skirts reflected the influence of early Cretan fashions adapted to the contemporary slim silhouette of the thirties. Neck and back treatments showed a clear relationship to the double-strap Egyptian *procardium*. The straps, however, were gathered or draped, rather than flat, with the flowing ends falling down the front to the hemline.

Elegance was combined with wit in Schiaparelli's couture designs, all created with her "infallible sense of proportion." Often using shocking pink, her trademark for these years, she created necklines with new daring that were as startling as the colors she chose (Figure 18.3).[8] The trains she added to formal gowns were reminiscent of the Roman *talaris* gown with *insita*. Intricate mitering of the skirt's diagonal pieces where they joined the bias-cut bodice made the skirt fall suavely over the hips and form into a "shockingly long train" in back. Witty innovator that she was, Schiaparelli employed a drawing by Jean

**Figure 18.4.** This evening sweater with a nipped-in waist and dolmanlike sleeves was designed by Schiaparelli in 1937, using a Jean Cocteau drawing of a face as the pattern for embroidery work on the bodice and sleeve. (Sketched at *The 10s, The 20s, The 30s* exhibition, 1974. Metropolitan Museum of Art, New York City.)

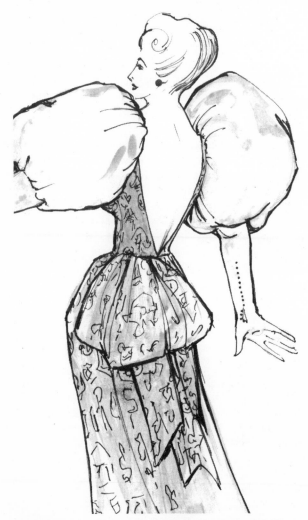

**Figure 18.3.** In 1939 Schiaparelli created shoulder-to-fingertip gloves made of lush velvet with giant leg-of-mutton puffs. They were shown in *The 10s, The 20s, The 30s* exhibition with a gown she had created from fabric designed by Dufy, who had used a circus for his fabric-pattern motif.

Cocteau on a broad-shouldered, houppelande-collared sweater of supercotehardie cut (Figure 18.4). The sketch, a female face with flowing hair, was hand-embroidered in multicolors and positioned so that the embroidered face covered the bust, the hair rippled down the right sleeve, and the embroidered hand—complete with rings— seemed to hold the sweater closed at the waist. Whimsical and semisurrealistic, a number of these models seemed to have been created in different color harmonies, for two were on display in *The 10s, The 20s, The 30s* exhibition in 1974 at the Metropolitan Museum of Art.

Schiaparelli's suits, like her other creations, were designed with complete understanding of the elements of art. Use of color was the most startling aspect as she combined purple and pink, black and red, or brown and gold, depending on strong value contrasts as a design principal. Variation was introduced by contrasting textures in fabric and fur: smooth broadtail and rough woolens, patterned linings in tweed suit jackets, and numerous other imaginative combinations. She was not limited to body garments, but designed hats as well. An apocryphal tale alleges that the witty wonder, pulling a silk stocking onto her head and giving it a twist here and there, originated the towering crown and turban hat styles of the late thirties. This turban had all the spontaneity of the chaperon of the Renaissance.

Suits with broad shoulders, snug-fitting sleeves, hip-bone-length jackets, modestly full skirts, and contrasting trims were typical of the late 1930s. These design systems were employed by Vera, Borea, Creed, Maggy Rouff, Lelong, Lanvin, and Chanel. "Exaggeratedly huge" buttons served as decoration and closing devices. Chanel employed the gored skirt and short or bolero jacket typical of the princess gown and bolero of the Edwardian years. But she retained the simplicity for which she had been noted since the 1920s.

Many of these great fashions, the "High Points of Paris Collections," were visually recorded by Bouet-Willaumez. With his infallible draftsmanship he sketched the elegant worldliness which Vogue prescribed as the mode of the day. During these years he drew the intricately fashioned evening gown by Chanel (Figure 16.10) with cross-laced sleeves and a slim, thigh-hugging skirt that swirls into a cascade of ostrich feathers at the hem and combines a deep V-inset over the abdomen with an uplift-bra bodice in black crepe.[9]

The "look" for the late thirties offered many possibilities from which to choose. Some suits of these years recalled the turkey-back or Polonaise styles of the previous century, with skirts horizontally pleated in front and gathered to the back. Nutria, marten tails, or fox cuffs and collars trimmed smooth-fitting suit jackets. The neck-encircling trims of fur held the head haughtily erect, reminiscent of the encircling Spanish ruff which created the same self-possessed posturing of people during the High Renaissance. Mainbocher and Molyneux, creating equally elegant evening attire, devised sophisticated silhouette variations that bespoke personality differences, adding to more individual choices. Mainbocher's creations were more feminine, while Molyneux's were feminine but with a tailored air. The thrust of the Molyneux's designs was achieved with appendages attached to parts of the female body which called attention to its femininity. Mainbocher's creations were "all of a piece" as a fashion editor for Condé Nast noted.

The return to the time of Velazquez with farthingale hip interest was presented over and over in variations, especially in Paquin's models. The total costume look created by the greats of fashion design seemed to be the product of total involvement with creativity and the visual arts of the past and the then (1930s) present. There was not just shocking innovation, but an innovation controlled by a supreme aesthetic sensitivity, not unlike the artists and architects of ancient Greece.

Accessories as well as major garments were governed by this same sensitivity, but were used to enhance the total costume. Accessories with frivolous characteristics all bore the stamp of Schiaparelli wit, though not all were introduced by her. Nearly theatrical in their flamboyant playfulness were her blue pumps cross-laced up the leg with pink ribbon ties. Blouses had Peruvian folk designs at the waist and elbow-length sleeves cut in the cuerpo baxo style of the Renaissance in size and length. Lavender slippers, or kid cocktail pumps to more accurately describe them, drew attention to the feet dancing the fox trot or tango. The attention-getting devices were large bow ties, or rosettes much like those of the seventeenth century, encircling the ankle, and cutouts or decorative eyelets in triple rows edging the opening around the instep, perhaps a contemporary adaptation of slashing. All the whimsy was not just Schiaparelli's, for Maggy Rouff, Chanel, Marcel Rochas, and Julienne contributed their share of playful costume accents. Chanel's "feather and Watteau veil nothing-of-a-hat charms and alarms" for it perched precariously, tilted forward on the head, a remarkably cantilevered bit of "chapeau-ery."[10] Such tentatively perched bonnets bring to mind those worn in the late nineteenth century.

The remainder of the 1930s was dominated by Molyneux, Chanel, Mainbocher, and Schiaparelli. A new silhouette was introduced, using as a prominent feature the leg-of-mutton sleeves not seen since the Gay Nineties. It hinted that fuller skirts would soon replace the reedlike grace of previous years, which had allowed the human form to establish the silhouette much as it had during the Egyptian, Greek, and Roman times. The return of the coyness of the 1830s to 1860s was suggested in sketches by Bouet-Willaumez in a late 1938 issue of Vogue, a sign that the "utter worldly" posturing would be supplanted by soft femininity. This change of female actions, attitudes, and face can also be attributed to the movie, Gone with the Wind, for films of this period had a significant impact on fashions and manner. However, an equal number of slinky, figure-clinging gowns for dinner and evening wear continued in vogue to counter the full antebellum skirts that were also shown.

As the 1930s gave way to the 1940s, the daytime fashions shown in the advertising sections of modish periodicals seemed to have a dull hausfrau look. The skirts were gored, pleated all around, or full in front. The simple dress bodices buttoned in front and had wide shoulders and unimaginative sleeves. The zipper, used first in jackets in the 1930s, was replacing the snapped or hooked fastenings of underarm side plackets.[11]

No doubt the cessation of production in the couture houses in Paris in 1939 affected the look of clothes during the early years of World War II. For generations Paris had been the arbiter of all fashion. From Parisian couture shops had come the most beautifully styled and designed garments, while other nations and other manufacturing centers parroted designs and produced pale imitations. In spite of all the grim horrors of the war in Europe, fashions continued to be created in France and America and faithfully cataloged in fashion periodicals.

Chiffon was declared *the* fabric, and dresses were romantically described as having "wind-snaring sleeves." Hemlines of gently full skirts were just below the knee. Harlequin lounging pajamas, with bare midriff and tight, cuffed pants, were made in particolor reproductions of the multicolored costumes of the Gothic period. Platform shoes of top designs recalled the high, platform-soled chopines. The range of styles included ankle-strap sandals, oxfords, brocade and gold-strapped evening models. Platform shoes for men and women appeared again in the early 1970s.

The dexterity and subtlety of the great Paris designers had been eclipsed by the war, and the war's ugliness was reflected by insensitively proportioned garments. Cloth was scarce; the fabrics available were made of inefficient synthetic fibers; and the amount of fabric to be used in a costume was dictated by the government. Masculinity entered female garb for day and evening wear. Shoulders were broad, hips narrow, and only in evening wear was there the slightest sense of femininity in costuming.

By 1942 fashion editors were calling for women to assume a new "aliveness" as opposed to the 1939 through 1941 "languid look." They proposed that sleep, good diet, exercise, and relaxation would help women attain the desired alert and alive appearance. Dressing modishly to meet this new look, fashions for women included hats with modestly tall crowns and wide brims scooping down in front and back. "After-dark" dresses became more narrow and were styled with skirt fullness only in front. The haughty seductiveness of evening dresses, first introduced by Nettie Rosenstein in her fall collection of 1940, continued to dominate the night scene. These gowns were broadly draped in the bodice and skirt, often radiating from a central point at the waist similar to the draped and goffered gala gowns of elegantly dressed women of ancient Egypt. Day dresses were casual and the "night suit" was popular with the nightclub set. Exercise and play clothes were available in a wide range of garments, including: dirndl skirts and blouses, play coats, beach skirts, cuffless slacks, sawed-off slacks, and flared-leg shorts. Long page-boy bobs that imitated the styles of medieval males were replaced by up-swept coiffures often dressed in a French roll similar to that used extensively in the 1890s.

Because nylon had "gone to war," women "painted" their legs with leg makeup. Shoes were toeless and backless. The summer fad of lacquering toenails to match long and brilliantly red fingernails developed with the introduction of open-toed shoes.

By 1943 the restrictions of the L85 law, which dictated the amount of fabric that might be used in clothes, radically affected evening gowns and resulted in the short evening dress. The "classic" look evolved in the first half of the forties. Two-piece suits with cardigan jackets, classic coats such as the masculine Chesterfield, and classic two-piece dresses worn with wound turbans and "echo" scarves were characteristic of women's attire during the war years.

During the early postwar years many of the same silhouette concepts persisted. Suits for women continued to be cut with broad, heavily padded shoulders. Sleeves were intricately cut, and jackets were designed with front fullness worn over slim skirts. Some coats had a semimilitary air, and others duplicated men's double-breasted overcoats of the early 1830s. Sequins were scattered over bodices and skirts of the just-below-the-knee cocktail and evening dresses. Dresses and suits with dolman and bat-wing sleeves were available in the newly established "French Rooms" of major department stores as the "made-to-order houses"—the French couturiers—resumed their places as fashion leaders. Now, however, buyers of the major United States mercantile establishments frequented the openings of the French collections, buying the rights to several models to have them copied and mass-produced in the United States, making authentic French fashions available in stores from Dubuque to Portsmouth, from Atlanta to Phoenix.

The dramatic silhouette revolution occurred in 1947 with Dior's collection which presented the New Look. Skirts dropped to within eight inches of the floor, shoulders were rounded, and waists were tiny. A new feminine look appeared as the emphasis shifted from the shoulders to full hips and wasp waists (Figure 18.5). Hair was coiffed in the new **feather cut,** much like the infanta coif of the French Revolutionary period. Big, tall, standing collars were also a new neckline treatment. Many of these had the design of the ear-tip, tall collars of men's coats of the Directoire and Empire periods. Nettie Rosenstein's greatcoat featured in *Vogue,* for November 1, 1953, retained the collar height but altered the shape into a face-concealing, circular collar. The coat itself created the popular A-line silhouette adapted from the early Renaissance gown.

Ball gowns of the 1950s also were designed with early Renaissance styling features. However, the adaptations of the late Gothic and early Renaissance did not neglect current modes, and bare shoulders in ball gowns added to the totally feminine look which dominated the first years of the fifties.

Maurice Rentner introduced the wrapped skirt which developed a modified bustle treatment, yet another resurrection of Worth's first Polonaise gown. Other prominent designers in the 1950s were Hattie Carnegie, Ceil Chapman, Dior, Mainbocher, Balenciaga, Larry Aldrich, and Traina-Norell. During these years Larry Aldrich and

**Figure 18.5.** The mixed-pattern boldness of the 1970s layered look (right) contrasts sharply to the softly feminine silhouette of the Fath design (left) introduced in the October 10, 1950 issue of *Vogue*.

Molly Parnis preferred skirts which reached mid-calf and were slim at the hemline, imitative of the hobble gowns of the early teens. The asymmetry of the late teens and early 1920s was also a prominent design feature of the 1950s.

Late in the fifties, styles of the 1920s were featured. Straight-line sack dresses with knee-length skirts and dropped waists had appeared as early as 1953; however, acceptance of this return to the past was slow. Variations of the twenties silhouette were introduced, some echoing the blousant bodice and slim-skirted gown which Chanel had created for a Roman princess in 1920 (Figure 18.7).

However, the delicately subtle, figure-revealing drape was utterly absent. Instead, the straight, knee-length skirts of these mass-produced replicas of the past, nipped in under the buttocks, hobbled the step and were generally gauche in design. The trims were obvious, not the gracefully drawn embroidery which subtly accented the fabric patterns of the ball and dinner gowns of the 1920s.

In the early 1960s these same styles persisted and were refined; cocktail dresses were created in elegantly textured, synthetic textiles. Generally, clothes of the late 1950s and 1960s depended for their chic on the colors and

**Figure 18.6.** Called an "evening turnout," this gown by Mainbocher features a "flounce-on-flounce" styling. It appeared in *Vogue,* April 15, 1969. (Permission of the Condé Nast Publications, Inc.)

**Figure 18.7.** This gown of white satin was created by Chanel in 1920. The skirt is cut on the bias and subtly but intricately draped into a sweeping train in back. At the exhibit, it was shown with a long cape train of purple velvet with gold braid and embroidery trim. (Sketched at *The 10s, The 20s, The 30s* exhibition, 1974. Metropolitan Museum of Art, New York City.)

**Figure 18.8. Car coats** and tall-crowned, small-brimmed hats were day-wear garments worn with **gray flannel suits** during the 1950s and early 1960s. Trouser legs became very slender, and dandies wore such snug pants that zippers were placed on the inner-leg seam so that the foot could be gotten through the trouser leg at the cuff. Belts and ties also were quite narrow.

textures of the cloth from which they were cut (Figure 18.9). Necklines were broad or bateau.

Balenciaga was one of the reigning designers during this period. The retrospective exhibition in the Metropolitan Museum of Art's Costume Institute in 1973 graphically illustrated the reason. Here, seemingly simple straight silhouettes were achieved by complex draping and cut. His wedding gowns designed for several European princesses conveyed all the fairy-tale feeling of royal weddings. These gowns were sprinkled with brilliants, seed pearls, and single ostrich feathers, many of the same decorative devices of the 1920s. The decorative, jewel-encrusted gowns of the Elizabethan Renaissance also provided inspiration for these royal wedding garments.

During the early years of the 1960s, Jacqueline Kennedy, the First Lady, influenced the attire of her faithful followers. Simple in shape, figure concealing, her extensive wardrobe had a chic elegance copied by many others. Helmet-crowned hats, big necklines with stand-away collars, loose-sleeved coats and suits, short-skirted daytime dresses, and slim shoes were characteristics of these years.

In reviewing this period, there seems to be no reference to modes of the past. Rather, there was a forceful projection into the future with clothes that might be worn on flights to outer space.

With the assassination of President John F. Kennedy, all this changed, but not until Mary Quant of Carnaby Street, Pierre Cardin, André Courrèges, and Yves Saint-Laurent had totally altered female apparel. Adapting to the developing new morality, Pierre Cardin in 1961 promoted the **miniskirt,** an innovation that followed the **balloon** dress which he had introduced in 1957. However, it was André Courrèges who became "lord of the miniskirt" and Mary Quant the mistress of minipants.

At the height of the mini garb, coats, suit skirts, and dresses had hemlines just below the curve of the derrière.

**Figure 18.9.** The flamboyance of the 1960s took many bold forms. Textures and patterns were combined in multilayered costumes. Thigh-high boots of imitation leather were necessary leg coverings in colder climates when **miniskirt** dresses were worn. (Sketched from a photograph in *Vogue.*)

Women were obliged to adjust their activity patterns—particularly stooping—so as not to reveal more than they desired of what little was concealed by these scant skirts. These provocative mini clothes were a far cry from the feminine couture costumes featuring the rounded slim suit by Balmain, the wrapped skirt and masked sheath of Paquin, the asymmetric chic of Fath, the dinner costumes by Heim, and the enveloping, tentlike late-day coats by Lanvin.

By mid-1960s the youth cult and the subcultures, in reaction against the establishment, created yet another revolution in clothing. The most daring accepted some of the topless and see-through styles for females introduced by Rudi Gernreich, reminiscent of the Cretan toplessness of ages past. The bare midriff of the 1930s was recalled late in the decade and carried on into the 1970s. The hip-hugger denim pants and below-the-bust sweaters ex-

**Figure 18.10.** The **maxicoat** had a brief popularity during the mid-1960s.

posed rib cage and navel. Pants dresses resurrected the culottes of the 1930s, but were short hot pants in length and divided skirts in cut. Of course, the culottes of the thirties had evolved from the divided riding skirts of the late teens.

Ankle-length **maxiskirts** and coats caused a slight ripple when first introduced in 1968 (Figure 18.10), but by 1974 floor-length dresses for day and evening wear were generally accepted. Many long day-wear dresses worn by antiestablishment females harkened back to the simple dresses worn by America's pioneering women. Others were styled with complex mameluck sleeves and below-the-bust empire-waist styling. Elegant evening gowns made of fabrics with overall patterns reviving designs created by *Art Nouveau* and Art Deco, in colors once thought to clash, were worn by young and old alike. Fashion editors catered to the youth cult, and couture and mass-market designers vied to capture this new market. Women of all ages appeared in clothes more suitable for the young.

In 1950 *Vogue* had announced that clothes for that year would be "convenient, simple, better than before." By the mid-1970s that statement was a fact, for women seemingly were no longer slaves to fashion. Pants suits in polyester fabrics were available in every conceivable combination of jacket length, sleeve length, and trouser design—cuffed, bell bottom, or straight. Pants-suit costumes in elegant velvet, lace, or brocades appeared at the opera, and those made of woollike cloth were worn in the office or schoolroom. The craze for Levi and denim pants, bib overalls, and patterned Levi's encouraged shop owners to open stores devoted exclusively to the sale of these garments. These shops supplemented the mod boutiques which sold funky clothing and accessory items. A phenomenon of the 1960s and early 1970s was the part played by the young in demanding clothes that identified them and their rebellious defiance of the establishment. This group seemed to revert to the Dark Ages in their garb. They adopted clothes which duplicated costumes worn by the barbarians, including the colobium and the paenula; females donned dresses as simple as the gunna. Men let their hair and beards grow and seemed neither to shave nor comb their tangled locks. Many affected the dog-ear coif of the French Revolution for they too were in revolt against the established order.

Women's Lib dominated the female scene. To reinforce the female personal status, women of all ages took to wearing pants. Young females wore jeans and Levi's after carefully twisting, tying, and soaking them in strong bleaches to achieve a worn and faded look. A brisk business in used clothes developed, and shipments of tattered, faded, and patched jeans were sent to England to meet the demands for such garb by young British activists.

With the termination of the United States involvement in Vietnam, new social and political concerns arose.

The ending of the draft in the United States also affected male fashions and fads. Long hair was trimmed and shaped, and men began using hair sprays long used by women. Beards were groomed and long sideburns extended to chin level. Urban men became quite elegant in their costume, donning suits, vests, or patterned waistcoats (Figure 18.11). Only older men retained long hair and beards, as the younger men assumed a new elegance with romantic tones of the early nineteenth century.

Yet another subculture was the motorcycle set which originally had been only a few rough daredevils identified by black leather jackets decorated with lettering and group-identifying symbols. With the increase in au-

**Figure 18.11.** This **pea-coat suit** was shown at the advanced fall style show in the late summer of 1974. (Sketched from a San Diego Union photo.)

tomobile prices and the gasoline crisis, more and more people took to motorcycles. Ralph Nader's emphasis on safety for all modes of transportation transformed motorcycle garb noticeably. Safety helmets were introduced, and these rider accessories were as colorful and as personalized as the jousting helmets and armor of the knights of old. More affluent riders adopted colors in helmets and nylon jackets that matched the colors of their motorcycles.

Late in 1974 a new fashion trend was waiting in the wings. Predictions for the fall of that year included the continuance of the layered look for, as in the medieval times, multigarment costumes were necessary for warmth because of the energy shortage (Figure 18.12). Also projected was a return to dresses and skirts similar to those worn in the late 1940s. Dubbed **big dresses,** they were styled with full, gathered or pleated skirts which had hemlines ranging from just below the knees to mid-calf—a choice of lengths was available. Bulky sweaters in ribbed, cable, or plain stitch recalled the sloppy-joe sweaters of the 1940s. Pants and pants suits were also in, and, for the first time, fashion editors admitted that the liberated women of the seventies were also liberated from the strict, seasonal changes of fashion dictates outlined in modish periodicals.

Men, too, were freer of fashion's prescriptions. The car coat, golf sweater, slacks and sack jacket, jumpsuit, and myriad other variables had altered men's attitudes toward dress. Color had been reintroduced in menswear, and the somber blacks, browns, and navy blues, even in semiformal dinner jackets, had been replaced by reds, brilliant lime greens, and powder blues as well as patterned fabrics.

Attitudes toward society, the new thrust of the importance of individuals, the acceptance of the dignity of persons regardless of ethnic origin also governed costume modes. The Russian-American detente brought back Russian styling details which had not been employed since the beginning of the Cold War. For the fall/winter season of 1974-75, *Prêt-à-Porter* reported that "the big skirt is a **look** not a length...a consciously *arante* fashion change. There is a desire...for an alternative ... a more romantic way of dressing." The same paper predicted "Folklorics," combining ethnic styles of many cultures into one total costume. Thus fashions in the mid-1970s developed a sensitivity to the social and philosophical concerns of the people of the Western world who were to wear them.

Romanticism of the neo-Gothic period may return, the elegance of the Gay Nineties may reappear, but most assuredly the practicality of mid-twentieth-century technological advances in fabrics of synthetic fibers, the comfort of figure-freeing styles, and the options of garments for varying activity patterns will not be abandoned, unless the contemporary life-style is radically altered by a cataclysmic social revolution of international scope.

**Figure 18.12.** Nostalgia for the 1930s was reflected in the costuming of 1973–74. Complex and different patterns in fabrics were combined, the layered look continued, and skirt hems dropped to calf length or just below the knee.

*Mademoiselle* predicted that these designers would retain the lead as the world spins into the last quarter of the century: Miyoke, Saint-Laurent, George Rech, Cacharel, Kenzo, and Sonia Rykiel. American designers whose Fall 1974 collections received kudos include: Adele Simpson, Leo Narducci, Oscar de la Renta, and Ilie Wacs. Some of the key summer-season designers of the mid-1970s were: Kolodzie, Evert, and Maxime de la Falaise, as indicated in the June 1974 *Vogue*. The only sure phenomenon in fashion is change—great or slight—depending on the economic potential of fashion consumers, their social standing, and their philosophical attitudes.

FOOTNOTES

1. *Vogue*, April 27, 1929, p. 59.
2. Ibid., p. 60.
3. Ibid., p. 71.
4. Ibid., p. 72.
5. *Vogue*, Oct. 15, 1934, p. 40.
6. *Vogue*, September 1937, p. 95.
7. Ibid.
8. Ibid.
9. Diana Vreeland, *The 10s, The 20s, The 30s: Inventive Clothes 1909–1939* exhibition catalog, p. 15.
10. *Vogue*, September 1937, p. 98.
11. Vreeland, *The 10s, The 20s, The 30s*, p. 17.

# Bibliography

Ackermann, Rudolph. *Changeable Ladies: Being an Assemblage of Moveable Human Features*. London: R. Ackermann, 1819.

Adams, James D. *Naked We Came: A More or Less Lighthearted Look at the Past, Present and Future of Clothes*. New York: Holt, Rinehart & Winston, 1967.

Adhélmar, Jean. *Toulouse-Lautrec, His Complete Lithographs and Drypoints*. New York: Harry N. Abrams, 1965.

Allemagne, Henri René d'. *Les Accessoires du Costume et du Mobilier depuis le treizième siècle jusqu' au milieu du dixneuvième siècle*. Paris: Schmit, 1928.

Amrams, Barney. *The Technique of Fashion Layout*. New York: Harper Brothers, 1949.

Anspach, Karlyne. *The Why of Fashion*. Ames, Iowa: Iowa State University Press, 1960.

Aretz, Gertrude. Preface to *The Elegant Woman from the Rococo Period to Modern Times*, by James Laver. London: G. G. Harrap, 1932.

Badawi, Dr. Ahmad. *Le Costume Dans L'Egypt Ancienne*. N.d.

Baker, Blanch Merrit. *Dramatic Costume Bibliography*. New York: H. W. Wilson, 1933.

Ballard, Bettina. *In My Fashion*. New York: Davis McKay, 1960.

Barfield, T. C. *Longman's Historical Illustrations: England in the Middle Ages; Drawn and Described*. Six portfolios. New York: Longmans, Green, 1915.

Beard, Charles Austin. *Basic History of the United States*. New York: New Home Library, 1944.

Beaton, Cecil. *The Glass of Fashion*. Garden City, N.Y.: Doubleday, 1954.

Benet, William Rose. *The Reader's Encyclopedia*. New York: Thomas Y. Crowell, 1948.

Bertin, Celia. *Paris à la Mode*. Translated by Marjorie Deans. New York: Harper Brothers, 1957.

Bigelow, Marybelle S. *Alphabets and Design*. Minneapolis: Burgess, 1970.

Blanc, Charles. *Art in Ornament and Dress*. Translated from the French. New York: Scribner, Wilford & Armstrong, 1877.

Blitzer, Charles, and the editors of Time-Life Books. *Age of Kings*. New York: Time, 1967.

Bonney, M. Therese. *Remember When: A Pictorial Chronicle of the Turn of the Century and of the Days Known as Edwardian*. New York: Coward McCann, 1933.

Boucher, François. *20,000 Years of Fashion: The History of Costume and Personal Adornment*. New York: Harry N. Abrams, 1966.

Bowra, C. M., and the editors of Time-Life Books. *Classical Greece*. New York: Time, 1965.

Braun-Ronsdorf, Margarete. *The Wheel of Fashion*. London: Thames & Hudson, 1964.

Butler, Ewan. *The Horizon Concise History of Scandinavia*. New York: American Heritage, 1973.

Carco, Francis. *Vertes*. New York: Atheneum, 1946.

Casson, Lionel, and the editors of Time-Life Books. *Ancient Egypt*. New York: Time, 1965.

Chase, Edna Woolman, and Ilka Chase. *Always in Vogue*. Garden City, N.Y.: Doubleday, 1954.

Chastel, André. *The Flowering of the Italian Renaissance*. Translated by Jonathan Griffin. New York: Odyssey Press, 1965.

Clark, Kenneth. *Civilisation: A Personal View*. New York and Evanston: Harper & Row, 1969.

*Columbia-Viking Desk Encyclopedia*. Edited by William Bridgwater. New York: Viking Press, 1953.

Contini, Mila. *Fashion: From Ancient Egypt to the Present Day*. Edited by James Laver. New York: Odyssey Press, 1965.

Corson, Richard. *Fashions in Hair: The First Five Thousand Years*. London: Peter Owen, 1965.

Coughlan, Robert, and the editors of Time-Life Books. *The World of Michelangelo*. New York: Time, 1966.

Craven, Thomas. *The Story of Painting: From Cave Pictures to Modern Art*. New York: Simon & Schuster, 1943.

Crawford, Morris De Camp. *The Philosophy of Dress*. New York: Bonwit-Teller, 1925.

———. *The Ways of Fashion*. New York: G. P. Putnam, 1941.

Cronin, Vincent. *The Horizon Concise History of Italy*. New York: American Heritage, 1972.

Cross, Milton. *Encyclopedia of the Great Composers and Their Music*, vol. II. New York: Doubleday, 1962.

Cunnington, Cecil Willett. *Why Women Wear Clothes*. London: Faber & Faber, 1941.

———, and Phillis Cunnington. *The History of Underclothing*. London: Michael Joseph, 1957.

D'Assailly, Gisele. *Ages of Elegance*. Paris: Hachette, 1968.

Davenport, Millia. *The Book of Costume*. New York: Crown, 1966.

Davidson, Marshall B. *The Horizon Concise History of France*. New York: American Heritage, 1971.

Dobkin, Alexander. *Principles of Figure Drawing*. New York: World, 1966.

Doten, Hazel, and Counstance Boulard. *Fashion Drawing, How to Do It*. New York: Harper Brothers, 1953.

Dubouchet, engr. Sigmund Freudenberger. *Estampes de Freudenberg pour le Monumen du Costume*. Paris: L. Conquet, 1885.

Eimerl, Sarel, and the editors of Time-Life Books. *The World of Giotto*. New York: Time, 1967.

Eliot, Alexander. *The Horizon Concise History of Greece*. New York: American Heritage, 1972.

Fogarty, Anne. *Wife Dressing*. New York: Julian Messner, 1959.

**Foote, Timothy, and the editors of Time-Life Books.** *The World of Bruegel*. New York: Time, 1968.

**Frankenstein, Alfred, and the editors of Time-Life Books.** *The World of Copley*. New York: Time, 1970.

**Fraser, Antonia.** *Dolls*. New York: Putnam, 1963.

————. *A History of Toys*. London: Spring Books, 1972.

**Fremantle, Anne, and the editors of Time-Life Books.** *Age of Faith*. New York: Time, 1965.

**Frost, Rosamund, and Aimée Crane.** *Contemporary Art, the March of Art from Cézanne until Now*. New York: Crown, 1942.

*Funk & Wagnalls New Encyclopedia*, vols. 7, 9, and 21. Edited by Joseph Laffin Morse. New York: Funk & Wagnalls, 1972.

**Galvel, Wencealea.** *Costtumbres Sateras Observacioneis*. N.d.

**Gardner, Helen.** *Art through the Ages*. 3d ed. New York: Harcourt, Brace & World, 1948.

**Garland, Madge.** *The Changing Face of Beauty: Four Thousand Years of Beautiful Homes*. New York: M. Barrows, 1959.

**Grunwald, Henry A., and the editors of Time-Life Books.** *The Age of Elegance*. New York: Time, 1968.

**Hadas, Moses, and the editors of Time-Life Books.** *Imperial Rome*. New York: Time, 1965.

**Hale, John R., and the editors of Time-Life Books.** *Age of Exploration*. New York: Time, 1966.

**Hawes, Elizabeth.** *Fashion Is Spinach*. New York: Random House, 1938.

**Head, Edith.** *The Dress Doctor*. Boston: Little, Brown, 1959.

**Hill, Margaret Hamilton, and Peter A. Buchnell.** *The Evolution of Fashion*. London: B. T. Batsford, 1967.

*Horizon Quarterly*. New York: American Heritage, Spring, 1967.

**Huer, Phillip.** *Great Masters in Art*. New York: Crown, 1960.

**Janson, H. W.** *History of Art*. New York: Harry N. Abrams, 1969.

**Jarnow, Jeannette A., ed.** *Inside the Fashion Business*. New York: John Wiley, 1965.

**Kaufmann, Edgar, Jr.** *What Is Modern Design?* New York: Museum of Modern Art, 1950.

**Kelly, Francis M., and Randolph Schwabe.** *Historic Costume, 1490–1790*. London: B. T. Batsford, 1925.

**Köhler, Carl.** *A History of Costume*. Edited by Emma von Sichart. New York: Dover, 1963.

**Koningsberger, Hans, and the editors of Time-Life Books.** *The World of Vermeer*. New York: Time, 1967.

**Kramer, Samuel Noah, and the editors of Time-Life Books.** *Cradle of Civilization*. New York: Time, 1973.

**Kybalová, Ludmila; Olga Herbenová; and Milena Lamarová.** *The Pictorial Encyclopedia of Fashion*. 2d ed. Translated by Claudia Rosoux. Feldham, England: Hamlyn, 1968.

**Labovitch, Mark.** *Clothes through the Ages*. London: Quality Press, 1944.

**Laver, James.** *The Concise History of Costume and Fashion*. New York: Charles Scribner, 1969.

————. *Costumes in Antiquity*. New York: Potter, 1964.

**Leepa, Allen.** *The Challenge of Modern Art*. New York: Beechhurst Press, 1957.

**Leloir, Maurice.** *Dictionnaire du Costume*. Paris: Librairie Grund, 1951.

**Lester, Katherine, and Bess Oerke.** *Accessories of Dress*. Peoria, Ill.: Charles A. Bannett, 1940.

**Levin, Phyllis Lee.** *The Wheels of Fashion*. Garden City, N.Y.: Doubleday, 1965.

**Levy, Emile, ed.** *M. Paul Cerau*. Paris: Librairie Centrale des Beaux Arts, 1882–1887.

**Lewison, Sam Adolph.** *Painters and Personality, a Collector's View of Modern Art*. New York: Harper Brothers, 1948.

**Leymarie, Jean.** *The Drawings of Degas*. New York: Continental Book Center, 1948.

**London, Adelaide Bolton.** *Historic Costume through the Ages*. Philadelphia: H. C. Perleberg, 1936.

**Lucas, E. V.** *The Wanderer in Florence*. New York: Macmillan, 1912.

**Marshall, Francis.** *Fashion Drawing*. London and New York: Studio, 1948.

**McClellan, Elisabeth.** *History of American Costume 1607–1807*. New York: Tudor, 1937.

**McJimsey, Harriet T.** *Art in Clothing Selection*. New York: Harper & Row, 1963.

**Mercer, Charles.** *Alexander the Great*. New York: American Heritage, 1962.

**Monro, Isabel Stevenson, and Dorothy Elizabeth Cook.** *The Costume Index*. New York: H. H. Wilson, 1937.

**Moore, Nonnie.** *Prêt-à-Porter*. New York: Condé Nast, 1974.

**Morse, Harriet Klamroth.** *Elizabethan Pageantry: A Pictorial Survey of Costume and Its Commentators from c. 1560–1620*. London: Studio, 1934.

**Payne, Blanche.** *History of Costume*. New York: Harper & Row, 1965.

**Picken, Mary Brooks.** *The Language of Fashion*. New York: Funk & Wagnalls, 1929.

**Planché, James Robinson.** *A Cyclopaedia of Costume or Dictionary of Dress*. London: Chatto & Windus, 1876–1879.

**Pope-Hennessy, John.** *The Portrait in the Renaissance*. New York: Pantheon Books, 1966.

**Praz, Mario.** *An Illustrated History of Furnishing from the Renaissance to the 20th Century*. Translated by William Weaver. New York: George Braziller, 1964.

**Prideaux, Tom, and the editors of Time-Life Books.** *The World of Delacroix*. New York: Time, 1966.

**Rand, Paul.** *Thoughts on Design*. New York: Wittenborn, Schultz, 1951.

**Rashco, Bernard.** *The Rag Race*. New York: Funk & Wagnalls, 1963.

**Richardson, Herbert.** *Costume in History*. London: Royal Society of Arts, 1934.

**Rosenberg, Adolph.** *The Design and Development of Costume from Prehistoric Times up to the Twentieth Century*. London: W. & G. Foyle, 1925.

**Rudofsky, Bernard.** *The Unfashionable Human Body*. Garden City, N.Y.: Anchor-Doubleday, 1973.

**Ruhemann, H., and E. M. Kemp.** *The Artist at Work*. London: Penguin Books, 1951.

**Russell, Francis, and the editors of Time-Life Books.** *The World of Dürer*. New York: Time, 1967.

**San Diego Union Newspaper.** *Answers to Juniors*. San Diego, Calif.: Copley Press, January 10, 1974.

**Schneider, Pierre, and the editors of Time-Life Books.** *The World of Watteau*. New York: Time, 1967.

**Sherrard, Philip, and the editors of Time-Life Books.** *Byzantium*. New York: Time, 1966.

**Simon, Edith, and the editors of Time-Life Books.** *The Reformation*. New York: Time, 1966.

**Simon, Howard.** *500 Years of Art and Illustration, from Albrecht Dürer to Rockwell*. New York: Garden City, 1948.

**Simons, Gerald, and the editors of Time-Life Books.** *Barbarian Europe*. New York: Time, 1968.

**Sooy, Louise Pickney.** *Syllabus on Costume*. N.d.

**Stites, Raymond Somers.** *The Arts and Man*. London and New York: McGraw-Hill, 1940.

**Tenner, Edmond.** *Tableau de Paris*. Paris: Lechevalier (Editions Paul), 1853.

**Toynbee, Arnold.** *A Study of History*. Oxford, England: Oxford University Press, 1970.

**Viking Press and *Vogue*,** compilers. *The World in Vogue*. New York: Viking Press, 1963.

**Vreeland, Diana.** *The 10s, The 20s, The 30s: Inventive Clothes 1909–1939*. New York: Metropolitan Museum of Art, 1974.

**Wallace, Robert, and the editors of Time-Life Books.** *The World of Leonardo*. New York: Time, 1966.

———. *The World of Rembrandt*. New York: Time, 1968.

**Wallis, Canon Residentiary John E. W.** *Litchfield Cathedral*. London: Pitkin Pictorials, 1970.

**Wedgwood, C. V., and the editors of Time-Life Books.** *The World of Rubens*. New York: Time, 1967.

**West, Willis Mason.** *Modern History*. Boston and Chicago: Allyn & Bacon, 1907.

**Wheeler, Monroe.** *Modern Drawing*. New York: Museum of Modern Art, 1946.

**Wilcox, R. Turner.** *The Mode in Costume*. London and New York: Charles Scribner, 1958.

**Williams, Jay, and the editors of Time-Life Books.** *The World of Titian*. New York: Time, 1968.

**Woodham-Smith, Cecil.** *Queen Victoria*. New York: Alfred A. Knopf, 1972.

**Worth, Jean Philippe.** *A Century of Fashion*. Translated by Ruth Scott Miller. Boston: Little, Brown, 1928.

## IN-PRINT PERIODICALS

*Elle*. 133 Champs Elysées, Paris, France.

*Femina*. Published by Societé d'Etudes et des Publications Economiques, 13 rue St. George, Paris, France (currently published as *Réalités*).

*Harper's Bazaar*. Published by Hearst Magazines, 717 Fifth Avenue, New York 10022.

*Horizon, A Magazine of the Arts*. Published by American Heritage, 554 Fifth Avenue, New York 10017.

*Time*. Published by Time, Time-Life Building, Rockefeller Center, New York 10020.

*Town and Country*. Published by Hearst Magazines, 717 Fifth Avenue, New York 10022.

*Vogue*. Published by Condé Nast, 420 Lexington Avenue, New York 10017.

*Women's Wear Daily*. Published by Fairchild, 7 East Twelfth Street, New York 10003.

## OUT-OF-PRINT PERIODICALS

*Allgemeine Modenzeitung*

*Arbiter*

*Ars Suteria*

*Belle Assembles*

*Cahiers Bleus*

*Der Bazar*

*Flair*

*Frank Leslie's Ladies Gazette*

*Galerie des Modes et Costumes Français*

*Gazette de Bon Ton*

*Gazette de la Famille*

*Godey's Lady's Book*

*Journal des Dames*

*Journal des Dames et des Modes*

*La Femme Chic*

*La Mode*

*La Mode Illustrée*

*Les Modes Parisiennes*

*Peterson's Magazine*

*Vanity Fair*

# Glossary and Pronunciation

**à bourrelets** /ah-boor-rŭh-lā'/ [French]: barrel form of panier, eighteenth century (ch. 12)

**à coupole** /ah-koo-pawl'/ [French]: dome-shaped panier, eighteenth century (ch. 12)

**adrienne** /ah-drē-ĕn'/ [French]: sack-style gown, early eighteenth century (ch. 12)

**à gondoles** /ah-goN-dohl'/ [French]: paniers wide at hips but flat in front and back, eighteenth century (ch. 12)

**agrafa** /ah-grahf'-ă/ [French]: fourteenth-century brooch (ch. 9)

**à grandes assiettes** /ah-grähNd-zah-sīĕt'/ [French]: peplum form on doublets, sixteenth century (ch. 10)

**aiguillettes** /ĕ-gē-yĕt'/ [French]: metal-tipped tapes or ribbons (points), seventeenth century (ch. 11)

**ailes de pigeon** /ĕl-dŭh-pē-zhoN'/ [French]: male wig style, eighteenth century (ch. 12)

**à la circassienne** /ah-lah-sĕr-kah-syĕn'/ [French]: variant of Polonaise gown, eighteenth century (ch. 12)

**à la créole** /ah-lah-krā-awl'/ [French]: one-piece dress style, late eighteenth century (ch. 12)

**à la française** /ah-lah-frahN-sĕz'/ [French]: snug jacket; ceremonial gown, eighteenth century (ch. 12)

**à la girafe** /ah-lah-zhē-rahf'/ [French]: hairstyle, mid-nineteenth century (ch. 14)

**à la grecque** /ah-lah-grĕk'/ [French]: one-piece sheath dress, late eighteenth century (ch. 13)

**à la jardinière** /ah-lah-zhar-dē-nyĕr'/ [French]: dress-sleeve style, early nineteenth century (ch. 14)

**à la lionne** /ah-lah-lē-ō-nā'/ [French]: female trouser suit, early nineteenth century (ch. 14)

**à la malakoff** /ah-lah-mah-lah-kawf'/ [French]: stiff jacket, nineteenth century (ch. 14)

**à l'anglaise** /ah-lahN-glĕz'/ [French]: dress form, late eighteenth century (ch. 12)

**à l'antique** /ah-lahN-tĕk'/ [French]: dress style, early nineteenth century (ch. 13)

**à la piémontaise** /ah-lah-pĕeh-moN-tĕz'/ [French]: sack dress, mid-eighteenth century (ch. 12)

**à la romaine** /ah-lah-raw-mĕn'/ [French]: chemise style, late eighteenth-early nineteenth centuries (ch. 13)

**à la suisse** /ah-lah-swĕs'/ [French]: tricorn style, late eighteenth century (ch. 12)

**à la sultane** /ah-lah-sul-tahn'/ [French]: gown open in front to reveal contrasting underskirt, late eighteenth century (ch. 12)

**à la turque** /ah-lah-teŭrk'/ [French]: gown style, late eighteenth century (ch. 12)

**à la vestale** /ah-lah-vĕs-tahl'/ [French]: chemise style, late eighteenth-early nineteenth centuries (ch. 13)

**à la victoire** /ah-lah-vēk-twahr'/ [French]: hairstyle celebrating military victory, eighteenth century (ch. 12)

**à l'espagnole** /ah-lĕs-pahn-yawl'/ [French]: nineteenth-century toque head covering; complex sleeve, late eighteenth century (chs. 13, 14)

**Alexandrina paile** /ah-lĕx-ahn-drē'-nah pī-lā/ [Italian]: silk brocade from Egypt (ch. 9)

**à l'imbécile** /ah-lēhM-bā-sĕl'/ [French]: sleeve form, early nineteenth century (ch. 14)

**à l'invisible** /ah-laN-vē-zēbl'/ [French]: hat form, early nineteenth century (ch. 13)

**amice** /ah-mēs'/ [French]: hood, early Renaissance (ch. 9)

**amictus** /ah-mĭk'-tŭs/ [Latin]: wrap or shawl (female), Rome (ch. 6)

**amulet** /ah-myeū-lā'/ [French]: jewelry charm (ch. 7)

**Andriana** /ahn-drē-ah'-nah/ [Italian]: early eighteenth-century drama (ch. 12)

**andrienne** /ahN-drē-ĕn'/ [French]: sack gown named for a drama of the period, early eighteenth century (ch. 12)

**à parer** /ah-pah-rā'/ [French]: circular cape, thirteenth-fifteenth centuries (ch. 9)

**apotygma** /ah-pō-tĭg'-mah/ [Greek]: free-hanging over-fold of female chiton, Greece (ch. 4)

**Art Nouveau** /ar-noo-vō'/ [French]: art form based on natural and floral forms, early twentieth century (ch. 15)

**à six garnements** /ah sēs gar-nuh-mahN'/ [French]: six garments; "layered look," early Renaissance (ch. 9)

**asterin** /ahs-tŭ-raN'/ [French]: purple silk fabric (ch. 9)

**aumusse** /ō-meūs'/ [French]: hood or hooded shoulder cape, Dark Ages (ch. 9)

**balandran** /bah-lahN-drahN'/ [French]: floor-length hooded cape, Dark Ages (ch. 9)

**balayeuse** /bah-lah-yuz'/ [French]: ruffle trim around hem of princess underskirt, late nineteenth century (ch. 15)

**Balenciaga** /bah-lĕn-se-ah'-gah/ [Italian]: Italian fashion designer (ch. 16)

**Balmain, Pierre** /pē-ār bahl-maN'/ [French]: French fashion designer (ch. 17)

**balzo** /bahl'-zō/ [Italian]: high, dome-shaped hat, Renaissance (ch. 10)

**bandeau** /bahN-dō'/ [French]: belt, nineteenth century (ch. 14)

**bandier** /bahN-dyā'/ [French]: belt, Renaissance (ch. 10)

**bardocucullus** /bahr-dō-kŭh-kŭl-lŭs/ [Latin]: floor-length hooded cape, Rome (ch. 6)

**barrette** /bahr-rĕt′/ [French]: hat, early Renaissance (ch. 9)

**Bartelli, Pietro** /bahr-tĕl′-lē/ [Italian]: artist and fashion illustrator, Italian Renaissance (ch. 10)

**basquine** /bas-kēn′/ [French]: jacket (female), mid-nineteenth century (ch. 14)

**battantes** /bah-tahNt′/ [French]: gown style with a soft silhouette, seventeenth century (ch. 11)

**bauta** /bō-tah′/ [French]: white half mask, early eighteenth century (ch. 12)

**bavaroise** /bah-vah-rwahz′/ [French]: trouser closure, seventeenth century (ch. 11)

**bayadere** /bah-yah-dĕr′/ [French]: narrow, striped-silk scarf, late eighteenth century (ch. 13)

**bazazinkoff** /bah-zah-zaN-kawf′/ [French]: fabric, nineteenth century (ch. 14)

**Belle Assemblée** /bĕl ah-sahN-blā′/ [French]: English fashion periodical, nineteenth century (ch. 13)

**Bellini, Jacopo** /yah-kō′-po bĕl-lē′-nē/ [Italian]: artist and costume designer, Italian Renaissance (ch. 10)

**Bernard, Augusta** / bĕr-nar′ ō-geūs-ta/ [French]: fashion designer of 1920s and 1930s (ch. 18)

**Bertin, Rose** /rawz bĕr-taN′/ [French]: designer to Marie Antoinette, eighteenth century (ch. 12)

**Biedermeier** /bē′-der-my-er/ [German]: male fashion look of the Romantic period, nineteenth century (ch. 14)

**birrhus** /bĭr′-rŭs/ [Latin]: cape made of red fabric, Rome (ch. 6)

**blanchet** /blahN-shā′/ [French]: long, fur-lined indoor coat, fifteenth century (ch. 10)

**bliaud** /blē-ō′/ [French]: simple sleeved garment (male/female), eleventh-thirteenth centuries (ch. 9)

**bliaus** /blē-ows′/ [French]: simple tunic, Dark Ages (ch. 9)

**bliaut** /blē-owt/ [Greek]: simple tunic, Dark Ages (ch. 9)

**boa** /bō′-ah/ [French]: feathered scarf, late nineteenth-early twentieth centuries (ch. 15)

**bonnette** /bawn-nĕt′/ [French]: hat form, early Renaissance (ch. 9)

**Borea, Vera** /vē′-rah bō′-rē-ah/: fashion designer (ch. 16)

**bottes à relever** /bawt′-zah rŭhl-vā′/ [French]: bedroom slippers, Renaissance (ch. 10)

**Bouché** /boo-shā′/ [French]: twentieth-century fashion illustrator (ch. 17)

**Boucher, François** /frăhN-swăh′ boo-shā′/ [French]: French author and Museum of Fashion curator

**boulevard** /boo-lŭh-var′/ [French]: trouser detail, Renaissance (ch. 10)

**bourrelet** /boo-rŭh-lā′/ [French]: roll of felt tied around the waist as a skirt support, Renaissance (ch. 10)

**bout-en** /boo-ahN′/ [French]: bag wig (male), eighteenth century (ch. 12)

**braccae** /brahk′-kī/ [Latin]: trouser form (male), Rome (ch. 6)

**braguette** /bră-gĕt′/ [French]: codpiece, Renaissance (ch. 10)

**braies** /brā′-ēs/ [Latin]: pants form (male), Rome (ch. 6)

**brassard** /brahs-sar′/ [French]: elbow-to-wrist half sleeve, Renaissance (ch. 10)

**braye** /brī/ [French]: trouser closure (male), sixteenth-seventeenth centuries (ch. 10)

**bretelles** /brĕ-tĕl′/ [French]: heavy fabric suspenders, eighteenth century (ch. 12)

**brodequins** /braw-dŭh-kaN′/ [French]: heavy shoes, Dark Ages (ch. 7)

**Broderie anglaise** /braw-dŭh-rē ahN-glĕz′/ [French]: lace used for trimming, nineteenth century (ch. 14)

**Bruyère** /breū-yĕr′/ [French]: twentieth-century millinery designer (ch. 17)

**bucksain** /bŭk′-sān/ [English]: short jacket (male), nineteenth century (ch. 14)

**burnous** /bur-noos′/ [French]: full knee-length coat with an attached hood, nineteenth century (ch. 14)

**busc, busque** /beūsk′/ [French]: wedge of whalebone used as a figure control, Renaissance (ch. 10)

**caban** /kah-baN′/ [French]: double-breasted coat, Renaissance (ch. 10)

**cacei** /kah′-kē-ī/ [Latin]: shoe form, Rome (ch. 6)

**Cacharel, Jean** /kah-shah-rĕl′/ [French]: French designer of separates (ch. 18)

**cachefolies** /kah-shŭh-faw-lē′/ [French]: false switch worn to recreate ancient Greek coiffure (female), early nineteenth century (ch. 13)

**cadenette** /kah-dĕ-nĕt′/ [French]: lock of hair tied with a ribbon (male), seventeenth century (ch. 11)

**cainsie** /kaN-sīah/ [Byzantine]: sleeved tunic-style undergarment (female), Dark Ages (ch. 9)

**calamint** /kah-lah-maN′/ [French]: ingredient in medieval deodorant (ch. 9)

**caleche** /kah-lĕhsh′/ [French]: folding hat or hood form (female), eighteenth century (ch. 12)

**caliga** /kah′-lĭ-gă/ [Latin]: shoe form, Rome (ch. 6)

**Callot Soeurs** /kah-lō′ sur′/ [French]: French couture house (1895-1935) (ch. 15)

**calotte** /kah-lawt′/ [French]: medieval skull cap, Dark Ages (ch. 9)

**calyptra** /kah-lĭp′-trah/ [Latin]: arched-polygon headdress of Byzantine emperor (ch. 8)

**camelle** /kah-mĕl′/ [French]: chemise dress, late eighteenth-early nineteenth centuries (ch. 13)

**camisia** /kah-mĭ′-sĭ-ah/ [Latin]: medieval undershirt, Dark Ages (ch. 7)

**campagus** / kahm-pah′-gŭs/ [Latin]: slipper (male), Rome (ch. 6)

**canegou** /kah-nĕ-goo′/ [French]: nineteenth-century fabric (ch. 14)

**canezou** /kah-nĕ-zoo'/ [French]: shoulder cape (female), early nineteenth century (ch. 13)

**canon** /kah-nōN'/ [French]: upper leg covering (male), High Renaissance (ch. 10)

**capaud** /kah-pō'/ [French]: bag wig (male), eighteenth century (ch. 12)

**capotes** /kah'-pōt/ [French]: redingote-style coat (female), nineteenth century (ch. 13)

**caracalla** /kah-rah-kahl'-lah/ [Latin]: hooded woolen cloak, Rome (ch. 6)

**caraco** /kah-rah-kō'/ [French]: short, fitted jacket (female), eighteenth century (ch. 12)

**carcaille** /car-cah'-ē-yuh/ [Spanish]: high, standing collar (male), Renaissance (ch. 10)

**carbatina** /kar-bah-tē'-nah/ [Latin]: shoe form, Rome (ch. 6)

**Cardin, Pierre** /kar-daN'/ [French]: French fashion designer (ch. 17)

**carmagnole** /kahr-mahn-yawl'/ [French]: double-breasted coat-jacket, late eighteenth century (ch. 13)

**Carven** /kahr-vahN'/ [French]: French fashion designer (ch. 17)

**casaque** /kah-sahk'/ [French]: wrap of straight cut, Renaissance (ch. 10)

**casaquin** /kah-sah-kaN'/ [French]: hip-length jacket with fitted front and loose back (female), eighteenth century (ch. 12)

**casimir** /kah-sē-mēr'/ [French]: very snug, knee-length breeches (male), eighteenth century (ch. 13)

**casque** /kahsk'/ [French]: puff-crowned bonnet with bill visor, eighteenth century (ch. 13)

**Castillo** /kah-stēl'-yō/ [Spanish]: fashion designer (ch. 17)

**casula** /kah-soo'-lah/ [Latin]: simple cape, Rome (ch. 6)

**cauls** /kawlz'/ [French]: fine wire hairnets for reticulated coif, fourteenth-fifteenth centuries (ch. 9)

**causia** /kow'-sē-ah/ [Latin]: low-crowned hat with ear flaps, Rome (ch. 6)

**cendal** /sahN-dahl'/ [French]: Byzantine taffeta (ch. 9)

**chainse** /shaNz'/ [Byzantine]: tunic-style undergarment (female), Dark Ages (ch. 9)

**chamarre** /chah-mah'-rrā/ [Italian]: fur-lined silk wrap (male), High Renaissance (ch. 10)

**chape** /shawp'/ medieval cape (ch. 9)

**chapeau-bras** /shah-pō-brah'/ [French]: hat form (male), eighteenth century (ch. 12)

**chapeau paré** /shah-pō pah-rā'/ [French]: hat form (female), late nineteenth century (ch. 15)

**chaperon** /shaw-pĕ-rōN'/ [French]: complex head covering, early Renaissance (ch. 9)

**charmeus** /shar-meūs'/ [French]: jacket with dolman sleeves (female), early twentieth century (ch. 15)

**chasuble** /shah'-zuh-bĕl/ [Latin]: oblong or circular cape, early Renaissance (ch. 9)

**chausses** /shōs/ [French]: hose (male), early Renaissance (ch. 9)

**chausses à plain fond** /shōs ah-plaN'-fōN'/ [French]: full-bottom hose (male), Renaissance (ch. 10)

**chausses à queue** /shōs' ah kuh'/ [French]: waist-to-toe leg covering (male), Renaissance (ch. 10)

**chemise** /shŭh-mēz'/ [French]: simple straight gown, late eighteenth-early nineteenth centuries; undergarment, Dark Ages to Renaissance

**chemisette** /shŭh-mē-zĕt'/ [French]: undergarment, early nineteenth century (ch. 14)

**Chéruit, Madeleine** /shā-rwē'/ [French]: French couturiere, 1920s (ch. 16)

**chérusque** /shĕ-reūsk'/ [French]: collarette neckline trim, late eighteenth-early nineteenth centuries (ch. 13)

**chérusse** /shĕ-reūs'/ [French]: see *chérusque* (ch. 13)

**cheveaux à la conseillère** /shŭh-vō' ah lah kōN-sā-yěr'/ [French]: towering coiffure, eighteenth century (ch. 12)

**chic** /shēk/ [French]: currently fashionable (ch. 18)

**chien couchants** /shēĕN' koo-shahN'/ [French]: inverted-pyramid pompadour hairstyle, eighteenth century (ch. 12)

**chiton** /kī'-tŏn/ [Greek]: main body covering worn by Greeks and Etruscans, 1200-150 B.C. (chs. 3,4)

**chlamydon** /klahm'-ĭ-dŏn/ [Etruscan]: wound festival garment (male), Etruria (ch. 5)

**chlamys** /klah'-mĭs/ [Greek]: simple calf-length wrap pinned on right shoulder, Greece (ch. 4)

**chloene** /klō-ē'-nē/ [Greek]: short off-the-shoulder cape, Greece (ch. 4)

**chopine** /shō-pēn'/ [French]: pedestal-sole footwear, early Renaissance (ch. 9)

**cingulum** /kĭn-goo'-lŭm/ [Latin]: band worn beneath the breasts (female), or on the hips (male) to hold in the tunic, Rome (ch. 6)

**clavi** /klah'-wē/ [Latin]: vertical purple bands trimming a tunic, Rome (ch. 6)

**clicula** /klik'-yoo-lah/ [Latin]: light wrap or circular cape, Rome (ch. 6)

**cloche** /klawsh'/ [French]: close-fitting hat, 1920s (ch. 16)

**coiffure** /kwahf-feūr'/ [French]: hairstyle

**coiffure à la flore** /kwahf-feūr' ah lah flawr'/ [French]: flower-trimmed female coiffure, eighteenth century (ch. 12)

**cole** /cōl/ [French]: fur-lined skullcap with ear tabs, Dark Ages (ch. 9)

**collarette** /kawl-lă-rĕt'/ [French]: small collar, nineteenth century (ch. 14)

**collet** /kaw-lā/ [French]: heavily embroidered cape that was attached to doublet, seventeenth century (ch. 11)

**colletti Jatto di balena** /kawl-let-tē yaht′-tō dē bah-lē′-nah/ [Italian]: collar form, early nineteenth century (ch. 14)

**colletti Russi** /kawl-let-tē roo′-se/ [Italian]: collar and necktie style, nineteenth century (ch. 14)

**colobium** /kō-lō′-bē-ŭm/ [Latin]: simple sleeveless fur vest, Dark Ages (ch. 7)

**compères** /koN-pĕr′/ [French]: two-piece false front simulating a waist coat and attached to the bodice, eighteenth century (ch. 12)

**Cordia** /kawr′-dē-ah/ [Italian]: frock style for a young girl, 1919 (ch. 16)

**cordonnet** /kawr-dŭhn-nā′/ [French]: triple-thread embroidery (ch. 12)

**corp piqué** /kawr pēk′/ [French]: firmly boned bodice lined with heavy linen, seventeenth century (ch. 11)

**corsage** /kawr-sahzh′/ [French]: two-piece bodice of intricate design, early nineteenth century (ch. 13)

**corset à la Ninon** /kawr-sā-tah lah nē-nōN′/ [French]: simple undergarment, early nineteenth century (ch. 13)

**cotehardie** /kōt-ar-dē′/ [French]: sleeved outer garment (male), Dark Ages (ch. 9)

**cotte** /kawt′/ [French]: jacket with sleeves (male), Dark Ages (ch. 9)

**cotteron** /kawt-tuh-rōN′/ [French]: smocklike garment, Dark Ages (ch. 9)

**coureur** /koo-rur′/ [French]: short jacket (female), late eighteenth century (ch. 13)

**Courrèges, André** /ahN-drā′ koo-rĕzh′/ [French]: French fashion designer, 1960s (ch. 17)

**crackow** /krǎ′-kow/ [English]: pointed-toed shoes (male); also called "devil's fingers," late twelfth-early thirteen centuries (ch. 9)

**cravat** /krah-vaht′/ [French]: neckwear accessory, late seventeenth century (ch. 11)

**Creed** /krēd′/ [French]: fashion designer (ch. 16)

**Cremona** /crā-mō′-nah/ [Italian]: lace-trimmed ribbon neckpiece (male) made of muslin, early eighteenth century (ch. 12)

**crepida** /krĕp′-ĭ-dah/ [Greek]: boot with heavy leather sole, Greece (ch. 4)

**criardes** /krē-ahrd′/ [French]: stiffly starched petticoats, eighteenth century (ch. 12)

**crinolette** /krē-naw-lĕt/ [French]: skirt support, mid-nineteenth century (ch. 15)

**crispine** /krēs-pēn′/ [French]: headband used in reticulated coif, thirteenth-fourteenth centuries (ch. 9)

**crotali** /krō-tah′-lē/ [Latin]: double-pendant earring, Rome (ch. 6)

**cucullus** /kŭh-kŭl-lŭs/ [Latin]: short cape, frequently with an attached hood, Rome (ch. 6)

**cuerpo baxo** /cwĕr′-pō bǎ-sō/ [Spanish]: balloon-shape sleeve style, Renaissance (ch. 10)

**culanta** /keū-lahN-tah′/ [French]: band-and-tape hooped skirt, eighteenth century (ch. 12)

**cul de paris** / keūl dŭh pah-rē′/ [French]: skirt support, mid-nineteenth century (ch. 14)

**culottes** /keū-lawt′/ [French]: divided skirt, twentieth century (ch. 18)

**culottes à la bavaroise** /keū-lawt′-zah lah bah-vah-rwahz′/ [French]: breeches (male), eighteenth century (ch. 12)

**cyclas** /sī′-klahs/: floor-length surcoat that featured deep armholes (female), twelfth-fourteenth centuries (ch. 9)

**dalmatic** /dahl-mah′-tĭk/ [Latin]: floor-length tunic (male), Rome (ch. 7)

**décolletage** /dē-kawl-tahzh′/ [French]: lowcut, revealing neckline

**de la Falaise, Maxime** /mahk-sēm′ duh lah fah-lĕz′/ (French): American designer of sportswear (ch. 18)

**de la Renta, Oscar** /aws-kar′ dē la ren-tah′/ [Spanish]: American fashion designer (ch. 18)

**demiceint** /dŭh-mē-saN′/ [French]: belt made of hinged metal plaques, worn low on the hips (female), Renaissance (ch. 10)

**demi-converti** /dē-mē-kōn-vĕr′-tē/ [Italian]: male overcoat, late eighteenth-early nineteenth centuries (ch. 13)

**de Monnier, Elisa** /ā-lē-sah dŭh maw-nēā′/ [French]: founded the first tailoring school in Paris in 1852 (ch. 14)

**de Montijo, Eugénie** /ū-zhĕh-nē′ duh mon-tē′-hō/ [French]: wife of Napoleon III; introduced bleached-blonde hair (ch. 14)

**deplos** /dĕp′-lōs/ [Greek]: female variation of himation, Greece (ch. 4)

**deshabillée** /dē-shah-bē-yā′/ [French]: loose-fitting house dress or boudoir gown, seventeenth century (ch. 11)

**Dessès, Jean** /dĕ-sĕs′/ [French]: French couturier, 1930s-1960s (ch. 17)

**Dior, Christian** /dē-or/ [French]: French couturier, 1940s and 1950s (ch. 17)

**diphtera** /dĭf′-tĕr-ă/ [Greek]: brief cape, Crete, 2000-1000 B.C. (ch. 3)

**diplax** /dĭp′-lăx/ [Greek]: off-the-shoulder cape pinned on right side, Greece (ch. 4)

**Directoire** /dē-rĕc-twahr′/ [French]: period of French history, 1795-1799 (ch. 13)

**Doucet, Jacques** /zhahk doo-sā′/ [French]: French couturier (ch. 15)

**Duchesse de Berry** /deū-shĕs′ dŭh bĕr-rē′/ [French]: fashion trend-setter of the early eighteenth century (ch. 12)

**Durst** /deūrst′/ [French]: fashion photographer of the early twentieth century (ch. 17)

**ecrouellique** /ā-kroo-ĕh-lēk′/ [French]: woman's cravat, late eighteenth century (ch. 13)

**effrontée** /ĕf-froNt-ā′/ [French]: a style of Fontanges cap, seventeenth century (ch. 11)

**Élice** /e-lēs′/ [French]: young girl's dress style, 1919 (ch. 16)

**empire** /ahN′-pēr′/ [French]: garment with a raised waistline and shallow bodice (ch. 16)

**en bourse** /ahN-boors′/ [French]: breeches without padding, late sixteenth-early seventeenth centuries (ch. 11)

**en chemise** /ahN-shŭh-mēz′/ [French]: in the chemise style, late eighteenth century (ch. 12)

**escarcelle** /ĕs-kar-sĕl′/ [French]: bag or pouch suspended from a belt (male/female), Renaissance (ch. 10)

**escarpins** /ĕs-kahr-paN′/ [French]: lowcut pumps with slender toes and slight heels (female), early nineteenth century (ch. 13)

**escoffion** /ĕs-kōf-fēōN′/ [French]: double-horned hennin, Gothic period (ch. 9)

**espadrilles** /ĕs-pah-drē′-yah/ [French]: boot with straps laced through eyelets, Rome (ch. 6)

**exomis** /ĕx-ō-mĭs/ [Greek]: simple body covering, shoulder-to-calf length, Greece, Etruria, Rome (chs. 4,5,6)

**exteriodum (tunica)** /ĕx-tē-rē-ō′-dūm/ [Latin]: full outer tunic (male), Rome (ch. 6)

**falbala** /fahl-bah-lah′/ [French]: pleated or gathered ruffles, eighteenth century (ch. 12)

**farthingale** /far′-thĭn-gāl/ [English]: skirt support (female), Renaissance (ch. 10)

**Fath, Jacques** /zhahk′ fahth′/ [French]: French couturier (ch. 17)

**feminalia** /fē-mĭ-nah′-lē-ah/ [Latin]: trouser form (male), Rome (ch. 6)

**femoralia** /fē-mō-rah′-lē-ah/ [Latin]: trouser form (male), Rome (ch. 6)

**fernails** /fer-nī′/ [French]: brooch, Dark Ages (ch. 9)

**ferreruolo** /fĕr-rā-roo′-lō/ [Italian]: long cape with a velvet collar, sixteenth century (ch. 10)

**ferronnière** /fer-ron-nēā′-rā/ [Italian]: jewel on a fine gold chain worn across the forehead, High Renaissance and early nineteenth century (ch. 14)

**fêtes galantes** /fĕt gah-lahnt′/ [French]: group of paintings by Watteau, eighteenth century (ch. 12)

**fibula** /fĭb′-yoo-lă/ [Latin]: pin used by Greeks, Etruscans, and Romans (chs. 4,5,6)

**fichu** /fē-sheū′/ [French]: neckerchief (female), eighteenth century (ch. 12)

**fillet** / fē-lā′/ [French]: crownlike coif trim, Dark Ages (ch. 9)

**flammeum** /flahm′-mē-ŭm/ [Latin]: flame-colored ceremonial wedding veil (female), Rome (ch. 6)

**fourreau** /four-rō′/ [French]: sheath gown, late eighteenth century (ch. 12)

**frac** /frahk′/ [French]: waistcoat (male), eighteenth century (ch. 12)

**frac habillé** /frahk ah-bē-yā′/ [French]: formal suit coat trimmed with buttons and braid (male), eighteenth century (ch. 12)

**friponnes** /frē-pawn′/ [French]: gown style, seventeenth century (ch. 11)

**fustian** /feū-stēahN′/ [French]: medieval corduroy or velveteen fabric (ch. 9)

**futera** /foo-tā′-rah/ [Italian]: cape style, sixteenth century (ch. 10)

**gabiana (toga)** /gah-bĭ-ah′-nah/ [Latin]: toga worn by cavalrymen, Rome (ch. 6)

**galarus** /gah-lah′-rŭs/ [Latin]: close-fitting cap, Rome (ch. 6)

**galler** /gahl-lā′/ [French]: see *collet* (ch. 11)

**Galerie des Modes** /gahl-lĕ-rē′ dā mawd′/ [French]: fashion periodical, eighteenth century (ch. 13)

**Galeries du Commerce et de l'Industrie** /gah-lĕ-rē dū kaw-mers′ ā dŭh laN-deū-strē′/ [French]: group of small Parisian shops, 1838-41 (ch. 14)

**gallia braccata** /gahl′-ē-ah brahk-kah′-tah/ [Latin]: French pants; trouser form, Dark Ages (ch. 7)

**gallia narbonenis** /gahl′-ē-ah nar-bō-nĕ-nĭs/ [Latin]: deprecatory name for trouser form, Dark Ages (ch. 7)

**gallica** /gahl′-lĭ-kă/ [Latin]: knee-high closed boot (male), Rome (ch. 6)

**gambeson** /gahN-bŭh-zōN′/ [French]: quilted, padded jacket (male), Gothic period (ch. 9)

**gamboisée** /gahN-bwah-zā′/ [French]: see *gambeson* (ch. 9)

**gamurra** /gah-moo′-rrah/ [Italian]: wrap combination of surcoat and houppelande (female), sixteenth century (ch. 10)

**garde-corps** /gard-kōr′/ [French]: tippet-trimmed outer garment (male/female), Gothic period (ch. 9)

**garnache** /gar-nahsh′/ [French]: surcoat-style lightweight outer garment, Gothic period (ch. 9)

**gaulle** /gōl′/ [French]: simple chemise gown, late eighteenth century (ch. 13)

**gauzier** /gō-zēā′/ [French]: folding hood made of transparent fabric, eighteenth century (ch. 12)

**gens de robe longue** /zhahN dŭh rawb lōNg/ [French]: long academic robes (male), Gothic period (ch. 9)

**gilet** /zhē-lā/ [French]: vest (male), eighteenth century (ch. 12)

**giornea** /jor-nē′-ah/ [Italian]: two-panel ceremonial garment, sixteenth century (ch. 10)

**gipon** /zhē-pōN/ [French]: underdoublet (male), Gothic period (ch. 9)

**Givenchy, Hubert de** /gah-vĕn′-chē/ [Italian]: French couturier (ch. 17)

**Godey, Louis Antoine** /gō'-dē/ founder of *Lady's Book*, nineteenth-century fashion magazine (ch. 14)

**gonelle** /gō-něl/ [French]: long tuniclike garment (male/female), Dark Ages (ch. 7)

**gorget** /gor-zhā'/ [French]: neck-concealing veil (female), Gothic period and early Renaissance (chs. 9 and 10)

**gorgerette** /gor-zhuh-rět'/ [French]: see *gorget* (chs. 9 and 10)

**gorgias** /gor-zhē-ahs'/ [French]: see *gorget* (ch. 10)

**gourgandine** / goor-gahN-dēn'/ [French]: outer bodice stiffened with staves, seventeenth century (ch. 11)

**granatza** /grah-nah'-tsah/ [Latin]: long-sleeved, floor-length gown (male/female), Byzantium (ch. 8)

**grègues** /grā-gŭh'/ [French]: male trouser form, seventeenth century (ch. 11)

**guepes** /gāp'/ [French]: a style of Fontanges cap, seventeenth century (ch. 11)

**gueredon** /gĕ-rŭh-dōN'/ [French]: funnel form of panier, eighteenth century (ch. 12)

**guigne-galants** /gēn-yŭh-gah-lahN'/ [French]: a style of Fontanges cap, seventeenth century (ch. 11)

**guimp** /gaNp'/ [French]: head veil (female), Dark Ages (ch. 7)

**guirlande** /gēr-lahNd'/ [French]: a string of decorative beads worn around the head (female), Dark Ages (ch. 9)

**gules** /gūl'/ [French]: fur trims, Gothic period (ch. 9)

**gunna** /gū'-nah/ [Breton]: simple gown (female), Dark Ages (ch. 7)

**habit** /ah-bēt'/ [French]: general term for several garments worn at once; term referring to clothes with a particular purpose

**haik** /hīk'/ [Egyptian]: simple transparent tunic, Egypt (ch. 2)

**haincelin** /aN-sŭh-laN'/ [French]: short houppelande (male), Renaissance (ch. 10)

**haute couturier** /ō koo-teŭ-rē-ā'/ [French]: high-style designer (ch. 1)

**hennin** /ěn-năN'/ [French]: tall, horned headdress (female), Gothic period (ch. 9)

**hérigaute** /ě-rē-gōt'/ [French]: decorative outer garment (male), Gothic period and Renaissance (ch. 9)

**himation** /hǐ-mā'-shǔn/ [Greek]: rectangular outer wrap draped about figure (male/female), Greece (ch. 4)

**hongreline** /ahN-grě-lēn'/ [French]: overcoat with two collars (male), early eighteenth century (ch. 12)

**hoqueton** /aw-kŭh-tōN'/ [French]: short, padded tunic (male), early Renaissance (ch. 9)

**hosen** /hō'-zen/ [German]: hose, Gothic period (ch. 9)

**houppelande** /oo-pŭh-lahNd'/ [French]: full, floor-length overdress with organ-pipe pleats and wide, conical sleeves, Gothic period and early Renaissance (ch. 9)

**huque** /eūk'/ [French]: short decorative outer wrap (male), Renaissance (ch. 10)

**hurluberlu** /eūr-leū-běr-leū'/ [French]: hairstyle of short curls covering the entire head (female), seventeenth century (ch. 11)

**hurlupée** /eūr-leū-pā'/ [French]: see *hurluberlu* (ch. 11)

**Incroyable** /aN-krwah-yahbl'/ [French]: outlandishly dressed activist of French Revolution (ch. 13)

**Indienne** /aN-děēn'/ [French]: chemise dress, late eighteenth century (ch. 13)

**indumenta** /ǐn-du-měn'-tah/ [Latin]: undergarments (male), Rome (ch. 6)

**innocentes** /ēn-nō-sahN'/ [French]: gown style, seventeenth century (ch. 11)

**insita** /ǐn'-sǐt-ah/ [Latin]: pleated gusset of talaris (female), Rome (ch. 6)

**intima (tunica)** /ǐn'-tǐ-mah/ [Latin]: undergarment (female), Rome (ch. 6)

**jabot** /zhah-bō'/ [French]: a fall of lace covering the shirt front (male), eighteenth century (ch. 12)

**jaque** /zhahk/ [French]: heavily padded, loose doublet (male), Renaissance (ch. 10)

**jeune fille** /zhŭn fē'/ [French]: young girl (ch. 16)

**Jodelle** /zhaw-děl'/ [French]: fashion designer (ch. 16)

**journade** /zhoor-nahd'/ [French]: ceremonial wrap made with two ankle-length panels, mid-fifteenth to mid-sixteenth century (ch. 10)

**jubon** /zheū-bōN'/ [French]: long-sleeved underbodice or camisole, Renaissance (ch. 10)

**juive** /zhwēv'/ [French]: tunic dress with short puffed sleeves, nineteenth century (ch. 13)

**Julienne** /zheū-lē-ěn'/ [French]: fashion designer (ch. 18)

**jupe** /zheūp'/ [French]: sleeveless, padded jacket (male/female), Gothic to Baroque periods (chs. 9-11)

**justaucorps** /zheūs-tō-kor'/ [French]: fitted outer doublet (male), thirteenth-nineteenth centuries (ch. 9)

**juste** /zheūst'/ [French]: tight-fitting vestlike jacket (male), eighteenth century (ch. 12)

**kalasiris** /kah-lah-sī'-rǐs/ [Greek]: simple tunic, or pleated and draped garment, Mesopotamia and Egypt (ch. 1)

**kaunakes** /kah-nah'-kēs/ [Greek]: earliest known body covering—animal-pelt skirt, Sumeria (ch. 1)

**kepos** /kěp'-ōs/ [Greek]: hairstyle with curls over forehead (male), Greece (ch. 4)

**kirtle** /kur'-tl/ [Breton]: simple gown or underdress with side laces (female), Dark Ages (ch. 7)

**klaft** /klahft/ [Egyptian]: kerchieflike head covering of upper class, Egypt (ch. 2)

**kolpos** /kōl-pōs/ [Greek]: blouse section of chiton, Greece (ch. 4)

**laena** /lī'-nah/ [Latin]: decorative circular cape (male), Rome (ch. 6)

**lamé** /lah-mā'/ [French]: metallic-appearing fabric (ch. 16)

**lappet** /lăp'-pět/ [English]: cheek-hugging, gabled-headdress veil, Renaissance (ch. 10)

**Lanvin, Jeanne** /zhahn lahN-vaN′/ [French]: French couturiere (ch. 15)

**Lelong, Lucien** /lŭh-lōN′/ [French]: French couturier (ch. 16)

**Lepape** /lŭh-pahp′/ [French]: fashion illustrator, early twentieth century (ch. 17)

**levantine** /lŭh-vahN-tēn′/ [French]: gown style, late eighteenth century (ch. 12)

**lévite** /lŭh-vēt′/ [French]: gown style, late eighteenth century (ch. 12)

**liripipe** /ler′-ĭ-pīp/ [English]: hood with a long peak and shoulder cape, Gothic period (ch. 9)

**lodier** /lō-dēr/ [German]; /law-dyā′/ [French]: short male trousers, Renaissance (ch. 10)

**loros** /lō′-rōs/ [Greek]: narrow, jeweled scarf worn by royalty, Byzantium (ch. 8)

**lügner** /lewg′-nĕr/ [German]: supported neckerchief (female), late eighteenth century (ch. 12)

**Magazine des Modes** /mah-gah-zēn′ dā mawd′/ [French]: French fashion periodical, eighteenth century (ch. 13)

**Mainbocher** /măN-baw-shā′/ [French]: fashion designer (ch. 16)

**mameluck** /mah-mŭh-look′/ [French]: double- or triple-puffed sleeve, Renaissance; twentieth centuries (ch. 13)

**mamillare** /mah-mĭ-lah′-rē/ [Latin]: bust band (female), Rome (ch. 6)

**mancheron** /mahN-shuh-rōN′/ [French]: tight, elbow-length sleeve (male/female), Renaissance (ch. 10)

**manches pertuisées** /mahNsh pĕr-twē-sā′/ [French]: sleeves slit from shoulder to wrist, Renaissance (ch. 10)

**maniakis** /mah-nē-ah′-kĭs/ [Greek]: circular jeweled collar worn by royalty (male/female), Byzantium (ch. 8)

**manicata (tunica)** /mah-nĭ-kah′-tah/ [Latin]: tunic with long sleeves, Rome (ch. 6)

**manteau** /mahN-tō′/ [French]: two-part formal gown, seventeenth century (ch. 11)

**mantelet à coqueluchon** /mahN-tŭh-lā′-tah kawk-leū-shoN′/ [French]: cape form (female), eighteenth century (ch. 12)

**manteline** /mahN-tĕ-lēn′/ [French]: see *giornea* (ch. 10)

**mantilla** /mahn-tē′-yah/ [Spanish]: short cape with detachable hood (female), seventeenth century (ch. 11)

**Marionette** /mah-rē-ō-nĕt′/ [French]: frock style, mid-nineteenth century (ch. 14)

**marlotte** /mahr-lawt′/ [French]: French gown style (female), Renaissance (ch. 10)

**Marquise de Pompadour** /mahr-kēz′ dŭh poN′-pah-dūr′/ [French]: mistress to Louis XV and eighteenth-century fashion arbiter (ch. 12)

**mathilde** /mah-tĭl′-duh/ [German]: short cape style (female), nineteenth century (ch. 14)

**menteur** /mahN-tur′/ [French]: sarcastic term for supported neckerchief, eighteenth century (ch. 12)

**Merveilleuse** /mĕr-vā-yuz′/ [French]: bizarrely dressed female activist of French Revolution (ch. 13)

**minette** /mē-nĕt′/ [French]: young girl's frock style, 1919 (ch. 16)

**mode à l'anglaise** /mawd-dah lahN-glēz′/ [French]: in the English fashion

**Molyneux** /maw-lē-nur′/ [French]: French and English couturier (ch. 16)

**moreta** /maw-rē-tah/ [Italian]: round black mask, eighteenth century (ch. 12)

**mouchoir** /moo-shwar′/ [French]: bouffant neckerchief, eighteenth and twentieth centuries (chs. 12,16)

**moustache** /moos-tash′/ [French]: one lock of hair brushed forward, seventeenth century (ch. 11)

**nankeen** /nahN-kēn′/: cotton trouser fabric, early nineteenth century (ch. 14)

**Narducci, Leo** /nar-doo′-chē/ [Italian]: American fashion designer (ch. 18)

**nebula** /nĕb′-ŭl-lah/ [Latin]: pleated, semicircular head cover similar to a face-framing ruff (female), Gothic (ch. 9)

**negligée** /nĕ-glē-zhā′/ [French]: loose-fitting gown, seventeenth century (ch. 11)

**negligée à la patriot** /nĕ-glē-zhā′ ah lah pah-trēō′/ [French]: red, white, and blue skirt, shirt, and jacket (female), French Revolution (ch. 13)

**Nemes headdress** /nĕ′-mĕs/ [Egyptian]: klaft variation worn by royalty, Egypt (ch. 2)

**nouvelle vogue** /noo-vĕl′-vōg′/ [French]: new fashion (ch. 17)

**olicula** /ō-lĭk′-yoo-lah/ [Latin]: shoulder shawl (female), Rome (ch. 6)

**Orcel, Gilbert** /zhēl-bĕr′ awr-sĕl′/ [French]: fashion designer (ch. 17)

**paenula** /pī-noo′-lah/ [Latin]: voluminous poncho cape, Rome and Dark Ages (ch. 6)

**pagne** /pahg′-nē/ [Latin]: brief shorts (female), Rome (ch. 6)

**paison** /pī′-sŏn/ [Breton]: loose waist-to-ankle trousers (male), Dark Ages (ch. 7)

**Palais Bonne-Nouvelle** /pah-lā′ bŭhn noo-vĕl′/ [French]: nineteenth-century Parisian department store (ch. 14)

**palatine** /pah-lah-tēn′/ [French]: light-weight scarf wrap (female), late eighteenth century (ch. 14)

**paletot** /pah-lŭh-tō′/ [French]: cape (male), Renaissance; intricately trimmed, hip-length jacket (female), early nineteenth century (chs. 10,14)

**palissade** /pah-lēs-sahd′/ [French]: a style of Fontanges cap, seventeenth century (ch. 11)

**pallium** /pahl′-lē-ŭm/ [Latin]: circular wrap with attached hood, Greece (ch. 4)

**palmata (tunica)** /pahl-mah′-tah/ [Latin]: tunic worn by army generals, Rome (ch. 6)

**paludamentum** /pah-loo-dah-mĕn′-tŭm/ [Latin]: large cape made of coarse wool (male), Rome (ch. 6)

**panier** /pa-nēā′/ [French]: skirt support (female), eighteenth century (ch. 12)

**pantalets** /pahN-tah-lā′/ [French]: waist-to-ankle underpants (female), early nineteenth century (ch. 13)

**pantoffle** /pahN-tawfl′/ [French]: heeled scuffs worn in inclement weather, seventeenth century (ch. 11)

**Paquin** /pah-kaN′/ [French]: French couturiere (ch. 15)

**paragaudion** /pah-rah-gō-dĭ-ōN′/ [French]: tuniclike garment trimmed at neckline, shoulders, and hem (male), Byzantium (chs. 7,8)

**parament** /pah-rah-mahN′/ [French]: embroidered neckline trim, Renaissance (ch. 10)

**pardessus** /par-dŭh-seū′/ [French]: full, black formal cape (male), early nineteenth century (ch. 14)

**parisien** /pah-rē-zēan′/ [French]: tiered, ruffled crinoline hoop skirt, mid-nineteenth century (ch. 14)

**parterres galantus** /pahr-tĕr gah-lahN-teūs′/ [French]: elaborate hairstyle (female), eighteenth century (ch. 12)

**partlet** /part′-lĕt/ [English]: linen or silk underwaist (female), Renaissance (ch. 10)

**patent medicis** /pah-tahN′ mĕh-dē-sē′/ [French]: hoop skirt, flat in front and full on the sides and back (female), mid-nineteenth century (ch. 14)

**pattens** /pah-tahN′/ [French]: rain shoe (male/female), Gothic period (ch. 9)

**pelerine** /pĕ-lŭh-rēn′/ [French]: floor-length circular cape (female), eighteenth century (ch. 12)

**pelicon** /pĕ-lē-kōN′/ [French]: fur-lined, quilted under-doublet (male), Gothic period (ch. 9)

**pelisse** /pĕ-lēs′/ [French]: floor-length cape (female), eighteenth-nineteenth centuries (chs. 12,14)

**pellotes** /pĕl-lawt′/ [French]: see *cyclas* (ch. 9)

**peplos** /pĕp′-lōs/ [Greek]: bound overfold of chiton, or a simple, decorative free-hanging wrap, Greece (ch. 4)

**perizoma** /pĕr-ĭ-zō′-mah/ [Etruscan]: tight-fitting trunks, Etruria (ch. 5)

**peruke** /pĕ-reūk′/ [English]: elaborately curled wig (male), seventeenth century (ch. 11)

**Pesellino** /pĕ-sĕl-lē′-nō/ [Italian]: artist and costume designer, Renaissance (ch. 10)

**petasus** /pĕ-tah′-sŭs/ [Latin]: wide-brimmed felt hat, Greece (ch. 4)

**phaecassium** /fī-kăs′-sē-ŭm/ [Latin]: soft leather boots laced with silk straps (female), Rome (ch. 6)

**phallustache** /fahl′-lŭs-tahsh/ [Cretan]: skirt form with a variety of arrangements (male), Crete (ch. 3)

**pharos** /fah′-ros/ [French]: slender scarf, Greece (ch. 4)

**Phrygian cap** /frĭ′-jun kap/ [Greek]: hood with a rounded point projecting forward, Greece (ch. 4)

**piccolomoni** /pēk-kō-lō′-mō-nē/ [French]: quilted-velvet house robe (female), nineteenth century (ch. 14)

**picta (toga)** /pĭk′-tah/ [Latin]: purple toga worn by a victorious army officer, Rome (ch. 6)

**pièce d'estomac** /pēĕs dĕs-taw-mahk′/ [French]: stomacher (female), eighteenth century (ch. 12)

**pierrot** /pyĕr-rō′/ [French]: short jacket with a peplum in back (female), eighteenth century (ch. 12)

**Piguet, Robert** /pē-gā′/ [French]: French dressmaker, 1930s (ch. 17)

**pileus** /pĭ′-lē-ŭs/ [Latin]: tall-crowned skull cap, Greece (ch. 4)

**pistachio** /pĭs-tah′-shēō/ [Italian]: see *crackow* (ch. 9)

**plastron** /plahs-trōN′/ [French]: front panel of cyclas (female), Gothic period (ch. 9)

**Poiret, Paul** /pawh-rā′/ [French]: French couturier, early twentieth century (ch. 15)

**Pollaiuolo** /pawl-lahē-uō-lo/ [Italian]: artist and costume designer, Renaissance (ch. 10)

**Polonaise** /paw-law-nĕz′/ [French]: gown with a skirt divided into three swags held up by drawstrings, eighteenth century (ch. 12)

**porc-épic** /pawr-kā-pēk′/ [French]: hair cut short and standing up like bristles (female), late eighteenth century (ch. 13)

**postiche** /paws-tēsh′/ [French]: false beard, Egypt (ch. 2)

**poulaine** /poo-lĕn′/ [French]: see *crackow* (ch. 9)

**pourpoint** /poor-pawN′/ [French]: doublet style, Renaissance and Baroque period (chs. 10,11)

**praetexta (toga)** /prī-tĕx′-tah/ [Latin]: toga with purple or red band (male, boys, girls), Rome (ch. 6)

**Prêt-à-Porter** /prĕ-tah pawr-tā′/ [French]: French fashion report (ch. 18)

**prétintailles** /prĕ-tăN-tī′/ [French]: motifs appliquéd to gown front, seventeenth century (ch. 11)

**procardium** /prō-car′-dē-ŭm/ [Latin]: bust-to-ankle-length wrapped garment with one or two shoulder straps, Egypt (ch. 2)

**pschent** /psh′-ent/ [Egyptian]: royal crown, Egypt (ch. 2)

**pulla** /pool′-lah/ [Latin]: shaped toga (female), Rome (ch. 6)

**queue** /kuh′/ [French]: wig style with the back hair tied with a bow (male), eighteenth century (ch. 12)

**Raimbaut, Mme.** /raN-bō′/ [French]: partner of French couturier Leroy, late eighteenth and early nineteenth centuries (ch. 13)

**Ramilie** /rah-mē-lē′/ [French]: wig (male), eighteenth century (ch. 12)

**rebalzo** /rā-bahl′-zō/ [Italian]: see *balzo* (ch. 10)

**Reboux, Caroline** /kah-raw-lēn′ rŭh-boo′/ [French]: French designer of millinery, late nineteenth-early twentieth centuries (chs. 15, 16)

**rebras** /rŭh-brah′/ [French]: matching cuffs or revers, Renaissance (ch. 11)

**regate** /rā-gah′-tā/ [Italian]: cravat (male), nineteenth century (ch. 14)

**repoussé** /rŭh-poo-sā′/ [French]: enameling technique (ch. 11)

**retonné** /rŭh-tŭhn-nā′/ [French]: light-weight overcoat (male), eighteenth century (ch. 12)

**Révillon** /rā-vē-yōN′/ [French]: French designer in furs (ch. 15)

**rhinegrave** /rīn′-grăf/ [German]: petticoat breeches (male), seventeenth century (ch. 11)

**rhino** /rī-nō/ : simple cape form made of unshaped animal fur or skin, 3000-600 B.C. (ch. 1)

**Ricci, Nina** /nī′-nah rē′-chē/ [Italian]: French couturiere (ch. 17)

**ricinium** /rī-kĭ′-nē-ŭm/ [Latin]: square head veil (female), Rome (ch. 6)

**robe en calecon** /rawb′ ahN kah-luh-soN′/ [French]: snug-fitting gown with narrow skirt, early nineteenth century (ch. 13)

**robe de chambre** /rawb dŭh shahm-brŭh′/ [French]: loose-fitting at-home gown (female), seventeenth century (ch. 11)

**robe retroussée dans les poches** /rawb rŭh-troo-sā′ daN lā pōsh′/ [French]: gown with slit skirt turned up into pockets (female), eighteenth century (ch. 12)

**robe ronde** /rawb roNd′/ [French]: decorative gown (female), eighteenth century (ch. 12)

**Rochas, Marcel** /mar-sĕl′ rō′-kahs/: fashion designer (ch. 16)

**rochet** /raw-shā′/ [French]: short bolero jacket (female), seventeenth century (ch. 11)

**ropa** /rō′-pah/ [Spanish]: gown style (female), Renaissance (ch. 10)

**ropillas** /rrō-pēl-yahs/ [Spanish]: padded shoulder roll (male/female), Renaissance (ch. 10)

**roquelaure** /raw-kŭh-lohr′/ [French]: heavy overcoat (male), eighteenth century (ch. 12)

**Rouff** /roof/ [French]: French couturiere (ch. 16)

**Rykiel, Sonia** /sōn-yah rī-kĕl′/ [French]: French ready-to-wear designer (ch. 18)

**saccoz** /sahk′-kōs/ [Greek]: long, stiff imperial robe, Byzantium (ch. 8)

**sacque** /sahk/ [French]: loose gown (female), eighteenth century (ch. 12)

**sagum** /sah′-goom/ [Latin]: wrapped outer garment worn by soldiers or travelers (male), Rome (ch. 6)

**Saint-Laurent, Yves** /ēv saN-lō-rahN′/ [French]: French fashion designer (ch. 17)

**sakkos** /sahk′-kōs/ [Greek]: pointed cap with tassel trim (male), Greece (ch. 4)

**sansculotte** /sahN-skeū-lawt′/ [French]: baggy trousers that were worn by the working class, late eighteenth century (ch. 13)

**sapparum** /sahp-par′-rŭm/ [Latin]: loose-fitting short jacket (female), Rome (ch. 6)

**saya** /sah′-yah/ [Spanish]: three-piece costume (female), Renaissance (ch. 10)

**sayon** /sah-yōN/ [French]: simple, sleeved garment worn by peasants, Dark Ages (ch. 9)

**Scheling, André** /ahN′-drā shĕ′-ling/ [French/German]: fashion designer, nineteenth century (ch. 13)

**Schiaparelli, Elsa** /skă-pah-rĕl′-lē/ [Italian]: French couturiere (ch. 16)

**semigigot** /sĕh-mē-zhē-gō′/ [French]: small leg-of-mutton sleeves (female), nineteenth century (ch. 15)

**shendot** /shĕn-dŏt/ [Egyptian]: kilt decoration, Egypt (ch. 2)

**shenti** /shĕn′-tē/ [Egyptian]: wrapped skirt with one over-the-shoulder strap, prehistory and Egypt (ch. 2)

**siglaton** /sē-glah-tōN′/ [French]: fabric from the Cyclades, Dark Ages (ch. 9)

**simarra** /sē-mah′-rrah/ [Italian]: Italian gown style (female), Renaissance (ch. 10)

**singlet** /saN-glā/ [English]: sleeveless undertunic (male), Dark Ages (ch. 7)

**skiradion** /skĭ-rah′-dē-ŏn/ [Greek]: oval tiara worn by empress, Byzantium (ch. 8)

**snood** /snood′/ [English]: net used to support an elaborate coiffure, Greece (ch. 4)

**solea** /sō′-lē-ah/ [Latin]: slipper (female), Rome (ch. 6)

**sordida (toga)** /sor-dē′-dah/ [Latin]: peasant toga (male), Rome (ch. 6)

**sorquenie** /sor-kŭh-nē′/ [French]: snug, hip-length blouse (female), Dark Ages and Gothic period (ch. 9)

**steinkirk** /stīn′-kĭrk/ [German]: necktie or cravat, late seventeenth century (ch. 11)

**stemma** /stĕm′-mah/ [Byzantine]: fabric crown worn by emperors, Byzantium (ch. 8)

**stephanos** /stĕ-fah′-nōs/ [Greek]: crown worn by dignitaries, Byzantium (ch. 8)

**stephone** /stĕ′-fō-nē/ [Latin]: diadem-shaped cloth hair decoration (female), Rome (ch. 6)

**stokolmic** /staw-kawl-mēk′/ [French]: nineteenth-century fabric (ch. 14)

**strophion** /strō′-fē-ŭn/ [Greek]: figure-controlling girdle (female), Greece (ch. 4)

**strophium** /strō′-fē-ŭm/ [Latin]: bust band (female), Rome (ch. 6)

**subligaculum** /sŭb-lĭ-gah′-koo-klŭm/ [Latin]: undergarment (male), Rome (ch. 6)

**succincta** /sŭk-sĭnk′-tah/ [Latin]: girdle encircling the hips (female), Rome (ch. 6)

**sultana** /seūl-tah′-nah/ [French]: puffed hairstyle (female), seventeenth century (ch. 11)

**surtout** /seūr-too′/ [French]: heavy broadcloth overcoat (male), eighteenth century (ch. 12)

**synthesis** /sĭn′-thē-sĭs/ [Latin]: toga-tunic combination (male), Rome (ch. 6)

**tabarrino** /tah-bahr-rē′-nō/ [Italian]: knee-length cape (male), eighteenth century (ch. 12)

**tablier** /tah-blē-ā′/ [French]: overdress with an apron skirt, eighteenth century (ch. 12)

**tablion** /tah-blĭoN′/ [French]: embroidered decoration on the chlamys of dignitaries, Byzantium (ch. 8)

**talaris** /tah-lah′-rĭs/ [Latin]: stola with gusset train (female), Rome (ch. 6)

**tasseau** /tah-sō′/ [French]: skirt pin-hook (female), Dark Ages (ch. 9)

**tatez-y** /tah-tā-zē′/ [French]: (lit., touch here), low neckline trim (female), eighteenth century (ch. 12)

**tebenna** /tĕ-bĕn′-nah/ [Etruscan]: semicircular cloak—forerunner of Roman toga (male), Etruria (ch. 5)

**Theseid** /thĕs′-ē-ĭd/ [Greek]: hairstyle with bangs in front and long hair in back (male), Greece (ch. 4)

**tholia** /thō-lē-ah/ [Greek]: conical brimmed hat of straw (female), Greece (ch. 4)

**thorakion** /thō-rah′-kĭon/ [Greek]: shieldlike ornament of heavy fabric, Byzantium (ch. 8)

**tibialia** /tĭ-bē-ah′-lē-ah/ [Latin]: leg windings (male), Dark Ages (ch. 7)

**tippet** /tĭp′-pĕt/ [English]: free-hanging sleeve trim (male/female), Gothic period (ch. 9)

**toga** /tō′-gah/ [Latin]: oval-shaped wrapped garment (male), Rome (ch. 6)

**toile de Jouy** /twahl-dŭh-zhwē′/ [French]: printed fabric, eighteenth century (ch. 12)

**tonneau** /tŭh-nō′/ [French]: below-the-hip, back-draped silhouette (female), early twentieth century (ch. 16)

**toque** /tawk′/ [French]: off-the-face hat (female), late nineteenth-early twentieth centuries (ch. 14)

**toupet** /too-pā′/ [French]: wig (male), eighteenth century (ch. 12)

**touret** /too-rā′/ [French]: close-fitting cap that fastened under the chin (female), thirteenth century (ch. 9)

**touret de col** /too-rā dŭh kawl′/ [French]: see *gorget* (ch. 10)

**trabea** /trā′-bē-ah/ [Greek]: see *tebenna* (ch. 5)

**tribon** /trī′-bŏn/ [Greek]: heavy-duty circular wrap tied or pinned at throat, Greece (ch. 4)

**trompeuse** /troN-puz′/ [French]: supported neckerchief (female), eighteenth century (ch. 12)

**truffles** /troo′-fl/ [French]: hairstyle covered with a caul (female), Gothic period (ch. 9)

**tunique** /teū-nēk′/ [French]: slim, simple undergarment, Dark Ages (ch. 9)

**tutulus** /too-too′-lŭs/ : tall hat with a cone-shaped crown and a narrow, upturned brim (female), Etruria (ch. 5)

**vaquero** /vah-kwā′-ro/ [Spanish]: bodice of the three-piece saya costume (female), Renaissance (ch. 10)

**Vecellio, Cesare** /chā′-zah-rā va-chĕl′-ēō/ [Italian]: sixteenth-century artist and fashion illustrator (ch. 10)

**verdingale** /vur-den-gah′-lā/ [Spanish]: Spanish farthingale (female), High Renaissance (ch. 10)

**vergette à la chinoise** /vĕr-zhĕt-tah lah shē-nwahz′/ [French]: Chinese-brush wig style (male), eighteenth century (ch. 12)

**Verot** /vŭh-rō′/ [French]: designer of millinery, nineteenth century (ch. 15)

**veste** /vest′/ [French]: sleeveless vest (male), seventeenth century (ch. 11)

**veston** /vĕs-tōn′/ [French]: sleeved vest (male), eighteenth century (ch. 12)

**Vionnet, Madeleine** /vē-ŭn-nā′/ [French]: French couturiere, late nineteenth-early twentieth centuries (chs. 15,16)

**virilis (toga)** /wĭ-rī′-lĭs/ [Latin]: toga worn by all freemen (male), Rome (ch. 6)

**visite** /vē-zēt′/ [French]: little decorative cape (female), mid-nineteenth century (ch. 14)

**vitrea (toga)** /wĭt′-rē-ah/ [Latin]: decorative toga worn by wealthy men, Rome (ch. 6)

**vlieger** /flē′-gĕr/ [Dutch]: Dutch gown style (female), Renaissance (ch. 10)

**volant** /vaw-laN′/ [French]: ruffle used extensively on Cretan tiered skirts (female), Crete (ch. 3)

**Vramant** /vrah-mahN′/ [French]: fashion designer (ch. 17)

**Watteau** /wah-tō′/ [French]: eighteenth-century painter, sometimes credited with designing the Watteau gown (ch. 12)

**wimple** /wĭm′-pl/ [English]: head veil (female), Dark Ages (ch. 9)

**witchoura** /vē-choo-rah′/ [French]: fur overcoat (female), early nineteenth century (ch. 13)

**witzchoura** /witz-choo′-rah/ [Polish]: fur-lined overcoat (female), early nineteenth century (ch. 13)

# Index

Italicized page numbers refer to illustrations.